PSYCHOLOGY
IN ACTION   *BASIC READINGS*

Michael Argyle

PSYCHOLOGY IN ACTION

BASIC READINGS

Second Edition

EDITED BY **Fred McKinney**

Professor of Psychology—University of Missouri • Columbia

THE MACMILLAN COMPANY • **New York**
COLLIER-MACMILLAN PUBLISHERS • London

TO MARGERY

The Macmillan Company
866 Third Avenue, New York, New York 10022
Collier-Macmillan Canada, Ltd., Toronto, Ontario

Library of Congress catalog card number: 72–86797

Printing: 1 2 3 4 5 6 7 8   Year: 3 4 5 6 7 8 9

PREFACE

Every instructor of the introductory course in psychology knows that many of the students in the class are interested in the application of psychological fact and method to their milieu—the student world of preparing for and choosing jobs, questions about marriage, activity in politics, attitudes toward war, and involvement in sports. But frequently those interests are evaded by instructors who hope to entice the abler student into more intensive and direct contact with psychological theory and methodology. How to bridge the gap between these purposes?

I have undertaken, in assembling these selections, to provide demonstration and proof that the psychologists' endeavors in the applied fields relate very closely to the concerns of most students. My assumption has been that students will acquire from textbooks their basic psychological knowledge; they will inform themselves about the application of this basic knowledge through such articles as these. The selections in this book show how the psychologist uses essential fact and methodology to deal realistically with a remarkable and rich variety of problems common to the interests of both the student and the instructor.

The origins of these selections are varied; they have been culled from professional journals as well as from popular publications. Their subjects are the same as those in the traditional survey of beginning contemporary psychology. Complex passages that might be irrelevant to students at that level have been excised or footnoted.

Multiple suggestions for use of the book for brief reports or discussions, as well as a list of concepts covered to aid in a review of some of the basic ideas presented, are included. References to other research and writing that appear in the selected papers have been retained, for the most part, to increase the potential utility of the volume. These references appear in alphabetical order at the back of the book.

Although I suspect that some of my views of psychology are readily apparent, I have not attempted primarily to support my favorite ideas, to solve or simplify any complexities of the subject, or to illustrate any single theoretical bias. I have departed from the prevailing practice for readings of this sort by favoring readability and brevity in my selections, many of which are excerpts from books, lending a broader perspective to the collection.

Various important characteristics of each article should be apparent to the reader, for they are the germ and, I hope, the fruit of this volume. Beyond serving the function assigned to it, each article does put forth strength, clarity, and individuality. Each was chosen for its potential to evoke thought and discussion. A central criterion was, of course, representation of the wide range of the interests, assumptions, and methodology of recognized contributors to psychology and to its sister behavioral sources. Gathered from among many hundreds, these source articles do, it seems to me, faithfully represent various applications of basic psychological processes. They can add a significant dimension to the student's understanding of the beginning course and appreciation of the work of the psychologist.

In this second edition, I have had to omit certain articles because of limitations of space and the need to add articles of more timely significance. These newer articles include studies on the student activist, the rehabilitation of the sexually inadequate, the psychological basis for the movements to change the status of women, black identity and its relationship to social conditions, the controversy over the use of drugs (particularly marihuana), discussion of the fast-growing sensitivity groups, and a sample of research studies in an important new area—imitation (modeling) and self-concept. The older articles are retained because of their continuing relevancy to students and contemporary thought.

I am indebted to many of my colleagues for assistance in the selection and processing of these writings as well as to those who permitted the use of their works. Dr. Melvin Marx assisted me in reaching the objective of the volume. Dr. Robert Daniel contributed advice from his experience in editing the introductory readings. Dr. Wayne Anderson examined the selections and reacted to them. Dr. M. Mike Nawas helped with the choice of the title of the book. Many students at the University of Missouri–Columbia assisted me in the details of preparing the manuscript, particularly Dan Dana, who assumed many of the tasks necessary to assemble a text of readings.

I am deeply grateful to the users of the first edition for their suggestions concerning which articles to reprint and which new ones to add. As always, my wife, Margery Mulkern McKinney, contributed daily and valuable editorial assistance.

FRED McKINNEY
University of Missouri–Columbia

TO THE STUDENT

I have collected these articles with you foremost in mind. They are in response to your questions, your observed interests, and your searches for understanding of yourself and the world of today and tomorrow. May you and your instructors find in these selections a view of the broad activity of the modern psychologist. May they, in addition, stimulate thought about contemporary and future realistic problems with which you and your contemporaries must cope.

The modern psychologist is empirically oriented. He bases his generalizations on responsible observations of human behavior and experience. I have, therefore, included studies from the laboratory and field studies that I hope will attract you to further exploration. The studies in this collection are, however, largely concerned with practical problems.

The range of issues include development of individual selfhood and emotional balance, personal learning and training, leadership, management and decision making, communication, religion, creativeness, research on sexual behavior and peace, as well as the less rational phases of man—dreams, hypnosis, neurotic self-defeating activity, psychoses, homosexuality, and alcoholism. As a source book, it is planned with more attention to subjective matters and human experience than your text can give to them and has a more humanistic emphasis—more difficult phenomena to study. Even though these studies arouse more interest, they are given relatively less space in most academic texts. Though they may not be in the mainstream of psychological investigation, they are receiving more attention than previously. Because this book is primarily a supplement to a basic text, it is appropriate to include these phenomena.

You will note also that the selections are relatively brief. I have included not only writings by well-known psychologists but also selections by engaging writers that have appeared in the current magazines and less technical journals. You may want to continue to read such readily accessible articles and think about them in the leisure time that our industrial society is making increasingly available to you. Not all selections are as simply and delightfully written as those of professional writers, but most of the selections should have meaning for *you*, today's student, in your understanding of how the psychologist and his colleagues in related fields think and work. Several of the selections describe experiments in detail. These illustrate how experiments are conducted and how theory develops into practice.

Following each article are questions and comments about the implications of the selection. Surely you will raise other questions. You may want to discuss the implications of the selections with fellow students and instructors in and out of class. I trust that the contents and format of the book will help to reverse today's unfortunate tendency for knowledge to be imparted to students while they sit passively in large lecture sections. I am suggesting that your instructors may find it convenient for you to divide into small groups on certain days to discuss these articles and their implications. To indicate important points for these discussions, I have italicized some words and phrases in the texts. For further suggestions on how the group discussion and other class procedures might produce more reaction on your part to ideas and findings, see "Use of the Selections" at the back of the book.

Last, I have hoped that you might, sometime during the course, raise questions about this book, such as: What, in general, are the different authors saying? What are the trends in man's behavior and experience? *What is man, essentially?* How does the psychologist go about studying and understanding him, and how is this knowledge used? Are there some unifying trends within this diversity? What are they?

And now I bid you enjoyable and enriching reading and discussion.

FRED McKINNEY

CONTENTS

IV. GROWTH AND MATURITY

V. TRAINING AND EDUCATION

VI. CAREERS AND LEADERSHIP

VII. PERSONNEL ISSUES

VIII. HUMAN RELATIONS, INDUSTRY, AND LAW

IX. ABNORMALITY AND MENTAL HEALTH

X. COUNSELING AND PSYCHOTHERAPY

XI.   RELIGION, DREAMS, HYPNOSIS, ESP

CHAPTER *1*

PERSONAL LIFE

1 MAN'S SEARCH FOR MEANING

Viktor E. Frankl

The following excerpt is a good note on which to begin these selections. Man is a restless, striving, purposeful creature, and in his self-conscious moments he attempts to find meanings for his life. These strivings and purposes are of central interest to a growing number of psychologists who direct their studies toward careful scientific analyses of behavior and toward man as a personality, an individual.

A recent trend in the thinking of some writers in psychology and related fields has been called the *existential movement*. It is not a systematized school of thought. The writers who reflect this viewpoint differ in many particulars, but they have in common a certain way of viewing man.

Very briefly, the existentially oriented psychologist emphasizes the total dynamic, self-conscious individual who is striving in the real world to find meanings for his life; coming to grips with his conflicts and anxieties; making concrete choices in everyday life; and thereby enhancing his own values and making his life more worth living.

The following excerpt gives you a glimpse of the existential posture. It shows how a man, if he assumes this stance, views life—his own and others'—and the values that give meaning to those lives. Other selections in this book will deal with an approach to understanding man that is antithetical to this one—more atomistic, analytical, and abstract.

Gordon W. Allport was impressed with the existential movement in behavioral science. He wrote the introduction to the small volume *Man's Search for Meaning*, written by a psychiatrist who first called his book "From Death-Camp to Existentialism." First we read Allport's reaction to Frankl's experiences in a concentration camp and his system of psychotherapy. Then we dip into a part of this gripping book to observe how Frankl helped his fellow prisoners during "a very low mood." Finally, we look into some of Frankl's basic concepts of logotherapy, his means of assisting a person to find meaning in his life.

Preface (by Gordon W. Allport)

D<small>R.</small> FRANKL, author-psychiatrist, sometimes asks his patients who suffer from a multitude of torments great and small, "Why do you not commit suicide?" From their answers he can often find the guideline for his psychotherapy: in one life there is love for one's children to tie to; in another life, a talent to be used; in a third, perhaps only lingering memories worth preserving. To weave these slender threads of a broken life into a firm pattern of meaning and responsibility is the object and challenge of *logotherapy*, which is Dr. Frankl's own version of modern *existential analysis*.

In this book, Dr. Frankl explains the experience which led to the discovery of logotherapy. As a long-time prisoner in bestial concentration camps he found himself stripped to naked existence. His father, mother, brother, and his wife died in camps or were sent to the gas ovens, so that, excepting for his sister, his entire family perished in these camps. How could he—every possession lost, every value destroyed, suffering from hunger, cold and brutality, hourly expecting extermination—how could he find life worth preserving? A psychiatrist who personally has faced such extremity is a psychiatrist worth listening to. He, if anyone, should be able to view our human condition wisely and with compassion. Dr. Frankl's words have a profoundly honest ring, for they rest on experiences too deep for deception. What he has to say gains in prestige because of his present position on the Medical Faculty of the University of Vienna and because of the renown of the logotherapy clinics that today are springing up in many lands, patterned on his own famous Neurological Poliklinik in Vienna.

One cannot help but compare Viktor Frankl's approach to theory and therapy with the work of his predecessor, Sigmund Freud. Both physicians concern themselves primarily with the nature and cure of neuroses. Freud finds the root of these distressing disorders in the anxiety caused by conflicting and unconscious motives. Frankl distinguishes several forms of neurosis, and traces some of them (the noögenic neuroses) to the failure of the sufferer to *find meaning and a sense of responsibility in his existence.** Freud stresses frustration in the sexual life; Frankl, frustration in the *will-to-meaning*. In Europe today there is a marked turning away from Freud and a widespread embracing of existential analysis, which takes several related forms—the school of logotherapy being one. It is characteristic of Frankl's tolerant outlook that he does not repudiate Freud, but builds gladly on his contributions; nor does he quarrel with other forms of existential therapy, but welcomes kinship with them.

The present narrative, brief though it is, is artfully constructed and gripping. On two occasions I have read it through at a single sitting, unable to break away from its spell. Somewhere beyond the midpoint of the story Dr. Frankl introduces his own philosophy of logotherapy. He introduces it so gently into the continuing narrative that only after finishing the book does the reader realize that here is an essay of profound depth, and not just one more brutal tale of concentration camps.

---

* Editor's italics.

From this autobiographical fragment the reader learns much. He learns what a human being does when he suddenly realizes he has "nothing to lose except his so ridiculously naked life." Frankl's description of the mixed flow of emotion and apathy is arresting. First to the rescue comes a cold detached curiosity concerning one's fate. Swiftly, too, come strategies to preserve the remnants of one's life, though the chances of surviving are slight. Hunger, humiliation, fear, and deep anger at injustice are rendered tolerable by closely guarded images of beloved persons, by religion, by a grim sense of humor, and even by glimpses of the healing beauties of nature—a tree or a sunset.

But these moments of comfort do not establish the will to live unless they help the prisoner make *larger sense out of his apparently senseless suffering*.* It is here that we encounter the central theme of existentialism: *to live is to suffer, to survive is to find meaning in the suffering*.* If there is a purpose in life at all, there must be a purpose in suffering and in dying. But no man can tell another what this purpose is. Each must find out for himself, and must accept the responsibility that his answer prescribes. If he succeeds, he will continue to grow in spite of all indignities. Frankl is fond of quoting Nietzsche, "He who has a *why* to live can bear with almost any *how*."

In the concentration camp, every circumstance conspires to make the prisoner lose his hold. All the familiar goals in life are snatched away. What alone remains is "the last of human freedoms"—the ability to "choose one's attitude in a given set of circumstances." This ultimate freedom, recognized by the ancient Stoics as well as by modern existentialists, takes on vivid significance in Frankl's story. The prisoners were only average men, but some, at least, by choosing to be "worthy of their suffering" proved man's capacity to rise above his outward fate.

As a psychotherapist, the author, of course, wants to know how men can be helped to achieve this distinctively human capacity. How can one awaken in a patient the feeling that he is responsible to life for something, however grim his circumstances may be? Frankl gives us a moving account of one collective therapeutic session he held with his fellow prisoners.

EXPERIENCES IN A CONCENTRATION CAMP

I remember an incident when there was occasion for psychotherapeutic work on the inmates of a whole hut, due to an intensification of their receptiveness because of a certain external situation.

It had been a bad day. On parade, an announcement had been made about the many actions that would, from then on, be regarded as sabotage

* Editor's italics.

and therefore punishable by immediate death by hanging. Among these were crimes such as cutting small strips from our old blankets (in order to improvise ankle supports) and very minor "thefts." A few days previously a semistarved prisoner had broken into the potato store to steal a few pounds of potatoes. The theft had been discovered and some prisoners had recognized the "burglar." When the camp authorities heard about it they ordered that the guilty man be given up to them or the whole camp would starve for a day. Naturally the 2,500 men preferred to fast.

On the evening of this day of fasting, we lay in our earthen huts—in a very low mood. Very little was said and every word sounded irritable. Then, to make matters even worse, the light went out. Tempers reached their lowest ebb. But our senior block warden was a wise man. He improvised a little talk about all that was on our minds at that moment. He talked about the many comrades who had died in the last few days, either of sickness or of suicide. But he also mentioned what may have been the real reason for their deaths: giving up hope. He maintained that there should be some way of preventing possible future victims from reaching this extreme state. And it was to me that the warden pointed to give this advice.

God knows, I was not in the mood to give psychological explanations or to preach any sermons—to offer my comrades a kind of medical care of their souls. I was cold and hungry, irritable and tired, but I had to make the effort and use this unique opportunity. Encouragement was now more necessary than ever.

So I began by mentioning the most trivial of comforts first. I said that even in this Europe in the sixth winter of the Second World War, our situation was not the most terrible we could think of. I said that each of us had to ask himself what irreplaceable losses he had suffered up to then. I speculated that for most of them these losses had really been few. Whoever was still alive had reason for hope. Health, family, happiness, professional abilities, fortune, position in society—all these were things that could be achieved again or restored. After all, we still had all our bones intact. Whatever we had gone through could still be an asset to us in the future. And I quoted from Nietzsche: "*Was mich nicht umbringt, macht mich stärker.*" (That which does not kill me, makes me stronger.)

Then I spoke about the future. I said that to the impartial the future must seem hopeless. I agreed that each of us could guess for himself how small were his chances of survival. I told them that although there was still no typhus epidemic in the camp, I estimated my own chances at about one in twenty. But I also told them that, in spite of this, I had no intention of losing hope and giving up. For no man knew what the future would bring, much less the next hour. Even if we could not expect any sensational military events in the next few days, who knew better than we, with our experience of camps, how great chances sometimes opened up, quite suddenly, at least for the individual. For instance, one might be attached unexpectedly to a special group with exceptionally good working conditions—for this was the kind of thing which constituted the "luck" of the prisoner.

But I did not only talk of the future and the veil which was drawn over it. I also mentioned the past; all its joys, and how its light shone even in the present darkness. Again I quoted a poet—to avoid sounding like a preacher myself—who had written, "*Was Du erlebt, kann keine Macht der Welt Dir rauben.*" (What you have experienced, no power on earth can take from you.) Not only our experiences, but all we have done, whatever great thoughts we may have had, and all we have suffered, all this is not lost, though it is past; we have brought it into being. Having been is also a kind of being, and perhaps the surest kind.

Then I spoke of the many opportunities of giving life a meaning. I told my comrades (who lay motionless, although occasionally a sigh could be heard) that human life, under any circumstances, never ceases to have a meaning, and that this infinite meaning of life includes suffering and dying, privation and death. I asked the poor creatures who listened to me attentively in the darkness of the hut to face up to the seriousness of our position. They must not lose hope but should keep their courage in the certainty that the hopelessness of our struggle did not detract from its dignity and its meaning. I said that someone looks down on each of us in difficult hours —a friend, a wife, somebody alive or dead, or a God—and he would not expect us to disappoint him. He would hope to find us suffering proudly —not miserably—knowing how to die.

And finally I spoke of our sacrifice, which had meaning in every case. It was in the nature of this sacrifice that it should appear to be pointless in the normal world, the world of material success. But in reality our sacrifice did have a meaning. Those of us who had any religious faith, I said frankly, could understand without difficulty. I told them of a comrade who on his arrival in camp had tried to make a pact with Heaven that his suffering and death should save the human being he loved from a painful end. For this man, suffering and death were meaningful; his was a sacrifice of the deepest significance. He did not want to die for nothing. None of us wanted that.

The purpose of my words was to find a full meaning in our life, then and there, in that hut and in that practically hopeless situation. I saw that my efforts had been successful. When the electric bulb flared up again, I saw the miserable figures of my friends limping toward me to thank me with tears in their eyes. But I have to confess here that only too rarely had I the inner strength to make contact with my companions in suffering and that I must have missed many opportunities for doing so.

The Essence of Existence

This emphasis on responsibleness is reflected in the categorical imperative of logotherapy, which is: "So live as if you were living already for the second time and as if you had acted the first time as wrongly as you are about to act now!" It seems to me that there is nothing that would stimulate a man's sense of responsibleness more than this maxim, which invites him to imagine first that the present is past and, second, that the past may yet be changed and amended. Such a precept confronts him with life's *finiteness* as well as the *finality* of what he makes out of both his life and himself.

Logotherapy tries to make the patient fully aware of his own responsibleness; therefore it must leave to him the option for what, to what, or to whom he understands himself to be responsible. That is why a logotherapist is the least tempted of all psychotherapists to impose value judgments on the patient, for he will never permit the patient to pass on to the doctor the responsibility of judging.

It is, therefore, up to the patient to decide whether he should interpret his life task as being responsible to society or to his own conscience. The majority, however, consider themselves accountable before God; they represent those who do not interpret their own lives merely in terms of a task assigned to them but also in terms of the taskmaster who has assigned it to them.

Logotherapy is neither teaching nor preaching. It is as far removed from logical reasoning as it is from moral exhortation. To put it figuratively, the role played by a logotherapist is rather that of an eye specialist than that of a painter. A painter tries to convey to us a picture of the world as he sees it; an ophthalmologist tries to enable us to see the world as it really is. The logotherapist's role consists in widening and broadening the visual field of the patient so that the whole spectrum of meaning and values becomes conscious and visible to him. Logotherapy does not need to impose any judgments on the patient, for, actually, truth imposes itself and needs no intervention.

By declaring that man is a responsible creature and must actualize the potential meaning of his life, I wish to stress that the true meaning of life is to be found in the world rather than within man or his own *psyche,* as though it were a closed system. By the same token, the real aim of human existence cannot be found in what is called self-actualization.* Human existence is essentially self-transcendence rather than self-actualization. Self-actualization is not a possible aim at all, for the simple reason that the more a man would strive for it, the more he would miss it. For only to the extent to which man commits himself to the fulfillment of his life's meaning, to this extent he also actualizes himself. In other words, self-actualization cannot be attained if it is made an end in itself, but only as a side effect of self-transcendence.

The world must not be regarded as a mere expression of one's self. Nor must the world be considered as a mere instrument, or as a means to the

---

* *Self-actualization*: refers to the need to become what one is capable of becoming.—Ed.

end of one's self-actualization. In both cases, the world view, or the *Weltanschauung,* turns into a *Weltentwertung,* i.e., a depreciation of the world.

Thus far we have shown that the meaning of life always changes, but that it never ceases to be. According to logotherapy, we can discover this meaning in life in three different ways: (1) by doing a deed; (2) by experiencing a value; and (3) by suffering. The first, the way of achievement or accomplishment, is quite obvious. The second and third need further elaboration.

The second way of finding a meaning in life is by experiencing something, such as a work of nature or culture; and also by experiencing someone, i.e., by love.

The Meaning of Love

Love is the only way to grasp another human being in the innermost core of his personality. No one can become fully aware of the very essence of another human being unless he loves him. By the spiritual act of love he is enabled to see the essential traits and features in the beloved person; and even more, he sees that which is potential in him, that which is not yet actualized but yet ought to be actualized. Furthermore, by his love, the loving person enables the beloved person to actualize these potentialities. By making him aware of what he can be and of what he should become, he makes these potentialities come true.

In logotherapy, love is not interpreted as a mere epiphenomenon [1] of sexual drives and instincts in the sense of a so-called sublimation. Love is as primary a phenomenon as sex. Normally, sex is a mode of expression for love. Sex is justified, even sanctified, as soon as, but only as long as, it is a vehicle of love. Thus love is not understood as a mere side effect of sex but sex as a way of expressing the experience of that ultimate togetherness that is called love.

A third way to find a meaning in life is by suffering.

IMPLICATIONS

How do you express purpose and meaning in your life? One approach to finding the meaning of life is to ask oneself this question: "What would I be willing to die for?" What is your answer?

Which of these suggestions seems most feasible in finding greater life meaning: (1) doing a deed; (2) experiencing a value (including experiencing someone); (3) suffering?

---

[1] A phenomenon that occurs as the result of a primary phenomenon.

Another approach we shall leave until later: How does Frankl's kind of directive therapy differ from the other attempts to help emotionally disturbed persons (which we discuss under counseling and psychotherapy in chapter X)?

REFERENCES

You can find further discussion of the existential movement in psychology in May (1961) and Maslow (1962). Allport has written a book, *Becoming* (1955), that may interest you.

2   LAUGHTER: ITS FUNCTIONS

Brian Foss

It has been said that he who laughs, lasts! Laughter, as a form of human behavior, has long interested writers—Sophocles wrote about it some time around 450 B.C. Today, anyone who can make others laugh is appreciated; moreover, he is handsomely rewarded if he makes jest his vocation. In fact, the nationally known comedians earn some of the highest personal incomes.

The comments on laughter made by the ancients vary in their evaluation of this form of behavior. In Ecclesiastes we read, "A fool lifteth up his voice with laughter, and a wise man doth scarcely smile a little." Contrast this with Martial, who wrote in his epigrams, about 86 A.D., "If you are wise, laugh." Literature is sprinkled with references to laughter. We find it in folk sayings, in proverbs, in Shakespeare's plays, and in the writings of philosophers.

Now a modern psychologist appears on the scene to write from the studies, placing laughter in a more biological context. Laughter has not yet been systematically subjected to experiment, but using the available knowledge, our contributor, Brian Foss of the University of London, wrote an interesting popular essay, pointing out that in fifty years we may have controlled experiments to give us more hard facts. What are the functions of laughter in a psychological context?

Reprinted from Brian Foss, "The Functions of Laughter," *New Scientist*, Vol. 11, No. 242 (London: New Scientist, 1961), pp. 20–22, by permission of the publisher and the author.

Laughter has many biological functions—for example, as an expression of joy in social situations, as an aggressive weapon in competitive situations, as a relief of tension. In convulsive laughter it appears that energy radiates from a "laughing center" in the brain to other parts of the nervous system.

Darwin thought that laughter was of no great biological use. He considered that laughing and crying were the results of a single mechanism working in opposite directions. In one direction the mechanism produced crying, which Darwin thought to be defensive and useful, and which justified the existence of the mechanism; but the laughter which resulted from its working in the opposite direction was thought to be a by-product of little biological importance. New ways of thinking, largely inspired by Darwin, suggest that he was wrong. Laughing has many important functions and many causes.

An American, P.T. Young, has made a list of occasions for laughter as recorded by American undergraduates. The records were made at the end of the day and are therefore of the more memorable occasions. The following are examples:

A pillow fight in the dormitory
A girl friend tore her dress
I fell during skating
A dog came in during a lecture
A mispronounced word in rhetoric class
Being teased about my corpulence
Lizzie trying to do a fairy dance
My opponents in a bridge game bidding four spades when I held two
   aces and the king, jack and five of spades
An article by a priest on the sex life of H.G. Wells

The most commonly recalled occasions were ordinary conversations, jokes, puns, and wisecracks; then came humorous situations, incidents, actions, or antics of people. In 98 per cent of cases, laughter occurred in a social setting. In fact, it is very rare for a person to laugh if he knows he is entirely out of earshot. This applies even to laughing while reading, and it suggests that one of the more important functions of laughter is communication. The varieties of facial expression and noise produced by one person in laughter can constitute a language. There is no reason why the laugher need be aware of what he is communicating; nor need the listener and viewer be aware that he is interpreting (and sometimes misinterpreting) the signals and often acting on them. Some of this language can be easily classified, and fits with a biological view of behavior. The following are some of the easier examples.

1. The laugh that means "I'm happy." The expectation is that it will be answered by a similar laugh, or at least a smile, the absence of which can be very chilling.

2. The laugh, produced in a group of people, which means "I'm *persona grata* with this group. I'm in." This laugh makes for group cohesion, but it is also used as a ploy in gamesmanship. It is very "one up" to be seen in a group laughing heartily with the VIP of the party.

3. The laugh which is used to get attention. This is often obvious, especially in its gauche form (when it clearly derives from example 1), but it can be subtle. There is an allied laugh which means "I'm listening (still)."

4. A common use of spoken language is as a prod to force someone into reacting. Many conventional phrases (or just "hullo!") are used in this way. One function seems to be to sound the other person's attitude—for instance, to find out if "he's on my side." Laughs and smiles are used a great deal like this, often between complete strangers.

5. A rather unpleasant laugh is the "I'm all right, Jack" laugh. It is one example of competitive behavior, a jockeying for position, which is very obvious in children, and which is analogous to "dominance fighting" in animals.

If we look at these examples biologically, three basic principles can be seen.

1. Laughing may occur as an expression of joy. It appears in babies at about twenty weeks of age, and it may be instinctive. This laugh tends to make bystanders behave pleasantly to the child, and the child will therefore tend to repeat it. In psychological jargon, the laugh is reinforced and the probability of its occurrence increases as a result.

2. Laughing makes for group cohesion through homogeneity of feeling within the group. It is likely that this increases the viability of groups. Animal ethologists have pointed out that, in social animals, evolution has often favored characteristics which are important for homogeneous action of the group as a whole. For instance, many birds display their tail feathers at the approach of danger and this results in the whole flock taking to flight. Such "social releasers" increase the survival chances of the group. Also, when they involve movements or sounds, many members of the group may start producing them. There is a contagion analogous to that found when laughter spreads in a group of people. Nevertheless it seems far-fetched to suppose that this contagious laughter exists because it increases the probability of human survival. A child's first laughs are reinforced *only* in a social situation, so that when he grows up he will be *conditioned* to laughing in social situations.

3. Laughing can be used as a weapon in competitive situations. Competition is so common in the animal kingdom that one might expect any means of human communication to be used competitively. Animals achieve domi-

nance by actual fighting, but also by less destructive methods such as threatening displays, loud noises, and birdsong. Such behavior has two main functions: the selecting and keeping of a mate and the defense of territories. The biological value of dominance fighting could be that the rearing of young is carried out more efficiently as a result; but it also has the effect that the more dominant animals are the more likely to propagate, and they are usually the largest and strongest. Hence the species benefits in the long run. Hierarchies emerge as the result of such fighting, and they are very clear in the monkey and ape groups, where there is usually a single male overlord. Human societies also have their hierarchies, but they are established through more subtle means than fighting, threatening or shouting (except perhaps in some juvenile gangs). Nevertheless there is a strong element of aggression in the methods used by man to achieve status, and this is true of laughing when it is used in this particular way.

There remain several kinds of laughter in which it is difficult to see a biological function. For example—laughing after a period of tension; laughing at jokes, antics, etc.; laughing at deformities and stuttering (frowned on, but common in children); laughing caused by tickling. Animal behavior can again throw light on the first of these.

When two herring gulls meet at the boundary of their territories, the tendencies to fight and to flee may be in balance, and the result is a conflict between these opposing tendencies. On these occasions gulls often indulge in what appears to be quite irrelevant behavior: they peck at bits of grass, twig, etc., and throw them sideways. This looks like part of their nest-building behavior appearing out of context and is known as "displacement activity." The ethologists have suggested that this is a "sparking over" of energy in the nervous system as a result of the blocking of the usual outlets. This sort of thing can be seen at a reflex level in humans when overstimulation occurs. For instance, a person coming into bright sunlight may sneeze; or if the semicircular canals of the inner ear are overstimulated through bodily motion, there may be a "sparking over" of energy to the nearby center in the brain which initiates vomiting, and travel sickness is the result.

Everyday observations suggest that laughter may result from a similar mechanism. Subjectively it feels as if tension builds up and is relieved by laughing. This can happen after the natural response to a situation has been inhibited (usually so that behavior will conform to what the group expects of one). If people have been frightened but have suppressed their overt reactions of fear, they will laugh readily when an opportunity occurs. Many jokes and comic situations rely on the building up of tension in a similar way.

Crying is the natural reaction of a small child who has fallen down. (Crying in some form is the instinctive reaction of many diverse animals in situations where it is necessary to attract the parent.) As the child gets older the attitude of parents and other children is that this is a "cry baby" reaction, and the child learns to suppress the crying, and gradually comes to relieve the pent-up tension by laughing instead. (Perhaps this transition is "easy" for the nervous system, since the two conditions have much in common, especially the diaphragm movements and the tears.) There are many situations in which society exerts pressure on the child to inhibit unpleasant emotional responses, and in most cases laughing may occur as a substitute. This is true for reactions to anything sudden and startling, to sinister objects, and for occasions when aggression or fleeing would be natural responses.

In adults, this transition period is long forgotten, but the substitute responses remain. We laugh, especially in company, at the mildly shocking, startling, sinister, frightening, aggression-provoking. Indeed, occasions for mirth can be found in any situations in which society has enforced an inhibition of primitive responses. This seems the most plausible explanation for the existence of sex and lavatory jokes, many of which overdetermine the laughter in that they involve a building up of tension, and unexpectedness of *dénouement*, and a use of socially disapproved subjects.

One of the puzzling things is that people laugh not only when mishaps occur to themselves but to others. One explanation of this is that the laugher "identifies" himself with the victim. But there is another possibility. Laughter is used a great deal as a weapon against people who do not conform to one's own group. Teen-agers laugh at "oldies"; old people laugh at the antics of jive; laymen laugh at the jargon of scientists. Christopher Fry's heroine, accused by the majority group of being a witch, sought a world of more reasonable people—"I have come to have the protection of your laughter." Laughter functions to withstand outside onslaughts on a group, and to preserve its mores. If a child fails to conform to his gang, he will be laughed at. If he fails to conform to that other gang, the adult world of his own society, he will also be laughed at. But once he has become a conformist, he will suppress his nonconformist behavior and replace it by laughter at those who are still outside. The American undergraduate who laughed at "a mispronounced word in rhetoric class" was showing that he was now a conformist, and that such mishaps no longer happened to him.

Is laughing at deformity and stuttering also of this kind? Possibly it may be even more primitive. It is well known that many animals will destroy or drive out a member of their species that is injured or deformed or otherwise unusual. This behavior seems to be instinctive. It suggests that human laughing at deformity might also have an instinctive basis (and hence not be susceptible to analysis by introspection).

It is often said that tickling is a social phenomenon—that one cannot tickle oneself. In fact, many people can tickle themselves, but they cannot so easily make themselves laugh by doing this. The laughter again seems to depend on a social situation. Tickling would normally be the result of a small live object on the skin, a potentially noxious body, and the natural response is avoidance. Horses are well endowed with an ability to twitch a small area of skin to ward off insects. We cannot do this and have to take grosser avoiding action. When tickling is done by another human being, avoidance is usually made difficult, and tension builds up so that intense body movements, and perhaps laughter, may follow. This response to such a small stimulus seems excessive, and some psychologists would have it that tickling originally has a quasi-sexual significance, the natural responses to which have become inhibited. Hence the great release of energy would result from the displacing of instinctive urges. It is certainly puzzling that a baby will smile, laugh, and gurgle when being tickled, in a way that seems completely devoid of the underlying displeasure of the adult's response.

Why is it that laughter has come to have so many functions? It may be because it is one of the more efficient ways of communicating. It is the most accurately recognized of all facial expressions. This is contrary to the general rule that the more primitive emotional expressions are the easiest to recognize, since laughing is generally judged to be a late development in evolution (though probably not as recent as smiling). Also contrary to the general rule is that anger is one of the most difficult to recognize. The most important clue in discriminating facial expressions is the conformation of the mouth, and the human face has evolved in such a way that it can express laughing and smiling in an exaggerated form, largely because of hairlessness and the mobility of the lips. In anger, the corners of the lips are raised so as to show the canine teeth, but this has become rather ineffective in man because of his small canines. Also a laugh can be heard as well as seen, and both sound and appearance can be modulated in a variety of ways, so making it possible to convey a wealth of information.

What happens in the brain during laughing? It was explained that travel sickness is thought to be due to a spread of excitation to the "vomiting center," a locus in the brain which, when stimulated, results in vomiting. Is there a similar center for laughing? The neurologist Sir Henry Head thought that there might be one in the thalamus, since lesions in this area often result in pathological laughter—laughter with no obvious cause and no appropriate feeling; but it is now known that lesions in many parts of the nervous system may have this result. However, it is true that electrical stimulation of part of the thalamus will produce laughing responses, at least in the chimpanzee.

Laughing in excess is usually accompanied by many other responses— gross body movements, foot stamping, hand clapping, and even convulsions. It is as though there were a building up of energy which radiates to the parts of the nervous system which control these movements. Professor D.O. Hebb, of McGill University, believes that the irradiation occurs in certain networks in the nervous system, which have come to be called "arousal systems," since they have the functions of increasing both sensations and movements, usually in a gross fashion, but sometimes favoring certain patterns of movement. Hebb suggests that one of these patterns might be the excessive movements seen in hearty laughter.

Any account of laughter cannot easily be put to the test. It would require experiments in which humans were submitted to exactly controlled conditions from birth onward—a quite impracticable and unethical requirement. In these circumstances it is impossible to be certain of any one explanation. It is necessary to argue largely by analogy, trying to produce an account which is not incompatible with scientific beliefs of the moment. An account in fifty years' time is likely to be very different.

IMPLICATIONS

What meanings of laughter that are mentioned in the selection have you noticed in your experience? Does laughter have any other meanings to you? What hypothesis might be advanced about the personality organization of the individual who rarely laughs? How do you evaluate now the humorous remark, "I am laughing to keep from crying"? What are some reasons why people do not laugh at a remark that is intended to be funny?

REFERENCES

The author refers to a study of laughter by Young (1937). See also Leuba (1941).

3   A SENSE OF HUMOR

Gordon W. Allport

Rare is the individual who will confess that he lacks a sense of humor, yet relatively little has been written about this trait, even by psychologists who are interested in all aspects of human behavior. A sense of humor is closely akin to the capacity to laugh, but it is more subtle, more valuable, and is associated with greater maturity.

This trait seems to be held universally in high esteem. Recently, humor has come to the fore in psychological writings as the more humanistic psychologists have pointed to the neglect of the study of such human experiences and behavior as spontaneity, humor, naturalness, and courage. Moreover, some empirical studies of creativity have shown the creative individual to have a sense of humor more generally than the noncreative.

The topic has interested the psychologist Gordon W. Allport in his attempt to answer the question: What is a mature personality? Here is Allport's brief discussion of the nature of a sense of humor and some suggestions as to where we might find it.

Humor

Perhaps the most striking correlate of insight is the sense of humor. In one unpublished study where subjects rated one another on a large number of traits, the correlation between ratings on insight and humor turned out to be .88. Such a high coefficient means either that personalities with marked insight are also high in humor, or else that the raters were not able to distinguish between the two qualities. In either case the result is important.

The personality of Socrates shows the close association of the two traits. Legend tells how at a performance of Aristophanes' *Clouds* he stood up in order that the amused audience might better compare his face with the mask that was intended to ridicule him. Possessed of good insight, he was able to view the caricature in a detached way, and to aid the jest by laughing at himself.

What, then, is a sense of humor? The novelist Meredith says it is the ability to laugh at the things one loves (including, of course, oneself and all that pertains to oneself), and still to love them. The real humorist perceives behind some solemn event—himself, for instance—the contrast between pretension and performance.

The sense of humor must be distinguished sharply from the cruder sense of the comic. The latter is a common possession of almost all people, children as well as adults. What is ordinarily considered funny—on the stage, in comic strips, on TV—consists usually of absurdities, horse play, or puns. For the most part it consists in the degradation of some imagined opponent. The aggressive impulse is only slightly disguised. Aristotle, Hobbes, and many others have been in this "sudden glory" of one's own ego the secret of all laughter. Related to aggressive wit (which derides the other fellow) is laughter at the risqué which seems due to the release of suppressions. Aggression and sex are at the basis of much that we call comic.

A young child has a keen sense of the comic, but seldom if ever laughs at himself. Even during adolescence the youth is more likely to view his failings with acute suffering than with laughter. There is evidence that people who are less intelligent, who have low aesthetic and theoretical values, prefer the comic and lack a sense of humor based on the real relationships in life. Landis & Ross (1933).

The reason why insight and humor march hand in hand is probably because at bottom they are a single phenomenon—the phenomenon of self-objectification. The man who has the most complete sense of proportion concerning his own qualities and cherished values is able to perceive their incongruities and absurdities in certain settings.

As with insight, almost everyone claims to have a rare sense of humor. The same students who evaluated their own insight in comparison with that of other people were asked to estimate their sense of humor. Ninety-four per cent replied that it was as good as or better than the average.

Stephen Leacock has observed the same conceit. In *My Discovery of England,* he writes: "A peculiar interest always attaches to humor. There is no quality of the human mind about which its possessor is more sensitive than the sense of humor. A man will freely confess that he has no ear for music, or no taste for fiction, or even no interest in religion. But I have yet to see the man who announces that he has no sense of humor. In point of fact, every man is apt to think himself possessed of an exceptional gift in this direction. . . ."

It is only fair to state that up to now psychologists have had very little success in measuring either insight or the sense of humor. We are dealing here with the subtler reaches of personality—a territory which we hope psychologists will explore with more success in the future than in the past.

IMPLICATIONS

What are the specific questions you think Allport answered in his discussion? Do you know persons with a sense of humor who also possess superior intelligence and aesthetic and theoretical values? How do you explain the finding that people who are more creative tend to have a better sense of humor?

Guilford takes a slightly different view than Allport. He takes note of findings by Andrews (1943)—who factorially analyzed humor into these forms: (1) derisive humor, (2) immoral humor, (3) insight humor, (4) pun humor, (5) risqué humor, and (6) incongruity humor—and suggests that when a person perceives another as having a sense of humor, he means that that person is strong in the form that he himself appreciates. This is a cautious scientific approach, and it raises a question about the existence of a unitary sense of humor. Reread the Allport excerpt and decide which of these views seem hypothetically most tenable until your further research helps you to answer this question more completely.

REFERENCES

For a discussion of humor in terms of factors, see Guilford (1959). Maslow (1950) offers a study of *self-actualizing persons* who seem to reach their potential in a balanced manner. A citation of the relationship between creativity and sense of humor can be found in Berelson and Steiner (1964). See also Andrews (1943). Some interesting laboratory studies on humor have appeared. (See Gollop & Levine, 1967; Shurcliff, 1968.)

4

EGO STRENGTH AND THE POWER TO RALLY FROM SETBACK

Frank Barron

Why is it that some individuals seem to be able to withstand crises better than others? The term *will power* was frequently used, long before systematic investigations were conducted on voluntary behavior. Usually, when this term was used, the speaker or writer inferred that those who lacked this capacity were morally weak and that the development of will power was itself a completely voluntary matter. Thus, if one failed to have will power, it was one's own fault. Since then, this capacity to make realistic decisions and sustain them has been examined in many clinical situations. The term *ego* has come into being; *ego functions* is probably a better substitute phrase. This concept refers to those processes concerned with decision-making, planning, and psychological defense.

Barron attempts to explore the idea of ego strength, a condition that varies with individuals and that explains to a large extent why some individuals can withstand trouble and misfortunes and even use such experiences for personal growth while others cannot. He has done this in a scientific manner, using terms in a well-explored inventory, the Minnesota Multiphasic Personality Inventory. Examples of the relevant items are given in this selection. Barron thus has been able to assess ego strength by comparing self-evaluating statements of those individuals who recover more readily from *emotional disturbance* with statements of those who do not.

Everyone alive has troubles and problems, and as we learned from our studies of especially "sound" individuals, the most important consideration in determining personal effectiveness is not the amount of trouble or misfortune (within limits) a person encounters, but *how he responds* to the vicissitudes and challenges of life. This capacity to meet problems without being dismayed and overwhelmed, to endure suffering and face great loss without foundering, is an aspect of psychological strength and vitality that deserves special study.

In what follows, we shall first describe the development and cross-validation of a scale originally designed to predict the response of psychoneurotic patients to psychotherapy. Consideration of the scale content and its correlates, however, has suggested that a somewhat broader psychological interpretation being placed upon it, making it useful as an assessment device in any situation where some estimate of adaptability and personal resourcefulness is wanted. It appears to measure the various aspects of effective personal functioning that are usually subsumed under the term "ego strength."

The scale consists of 68 items from the Minnesota Multiphasic Personality Inventory, selected from a total MMPI pool of 550 items on the basis of significant correlation with rated improvement in our 33 psychoneurotic patients who had been treated for six months in a clinic. The test responses of the patients were obtained before psychotherapy began, so that the scale, so far as logic of construction is concerned, is designed to predict whether or not after about six months of therapy the patient will have improved.

The sample of 33 patients . . . was divided into two groups: 17 patients who were judged to have clearly improved, and 16 patients who were judged to be unimproved. And although the sample was small, the cases were intensively studied, and the two skilled judges who had thoroughly acquainted themselves with the course of the therapy (although not themselves involved in it otherwise) were in considerable agreement (r of .91 *) in their independent ratings of degree of improvement. While one would not ordinarily base scale development on a sample of this size, it was reasoned here that a small number of well-studied cases who were classified with high reliability, and, as collateral evidence indicated, with high accuracy as well, would serve better than the practical alternative, which was to get a large sample in which the therapist's rating of outcome was accepted uncritically.

When the Improved and Unimproved groups were scored on this 68-item

---

* These are standard measures of reliability or significance.

scale, the mean of the Improved group proved to be 52.7, that of the Unimproved group 29.1, a difference which is significant well beyond the .01 level (t of 10.3 *). The odd-even reliability of the scale in a clinic population of 126 patients is .76. Test-retest reliability after three months in a sample of 30 cases is .72.

The 68 items of the scale are presented below,† arranged in groups according to the kinds of psychological homogeneities that, in the judgment of the writer, are involved in the item content.

Physical functioning and physiological stability. 153. During the past few years I have been well most of the time (T). 51. I am in just as good physical health as most of my friends (T).

Psychasthenia and seclusiveness. 384. I feel unable to tell anyone all about myself (F). 489. I feel sympathetic toward people who tend to hang on to their griefs and troubles (F).

Attitudes toward religion. 95. I go to church almost every week (T). 488. I pray several times every week (F).

Moral posture. 410. I would certainly enjoy beating a crook at his own game (T). 181. When I get bored, I like to stir up some excitement (T).

Sense of reality. 33. I have had very peculiar and strange experiences (F). 349. I have strange and peculiar thoughts (F).

Personal adequacy, ability to cope. 389. My plans have frequently seemed so full of difficulties that I have had to give them up (F). 82. I am easily downed in an argument (F).

Phobias, infantile anxieties. 367. I am not afraid of fire (T). 525. I am made nervous by certain animals (F).

Miscellaneous. 221. I like science (T). 513. I think Lincoln was greater than Washington (T).

The pretherapy *characteristics of patients who improve in therapy, as compared with those who do not improve,‡* might be summarized as follows:

Improved: (a) good physical functioning; (b) spontaneity, ability to share emotional experiences; (c) conventional church membership, but nonfundamentalist and undogmatic in religious beliefs; (d) permissive morality; (e) good contact with reality; (f) feelings of personal adequacy and vitality; (g) physical courage and lack of fear.

Unimproved: (a) many and chronic physical ailments; (b) broodiness, inhibition, a strong need for emotional seclusion, worrisomeness; (c) intense religious experiences, belief in prayer, miracles, the Bible; (d) repressive and punitive

* These are standard measures of reliability or significance.
† Included here are only two sample items in each group. T or F indicates the favorable answer.
‡ Editor's italics.

morality; (e) dissociation and ego alienation; (f) confusion, submissiveness, chronic fatigue; (g) phobias and infantile anxieties.

. . . At this point, however, it may be useful to give a very brief résumé of the determinants and marks of ego strength as the term is here being used, drawing both upon these statistical findings and upon general observation of normal psychological functioning.

Ego strength is, first of all, a function simply of intelligence. Since comprehension of experience depends mostly on the degree of organization in the central nervous system, the scope of the ego will vary with the quality of the brain.

Scope does not depend solely upon cognition, however. Psychodynamics enter chiefly in relation to the mechanism of repression. Repression operates in the service of homeostasis, and so serves an economic function that is indispensable in maintaining the organism in an integral form in its environment. However, repression may be so extensive as to become a false economy; when broad areas of experience are lost to consciousness through repression, the ego may be said to be less strong (*i.e.*, less able to adapt) as a consequence. To state the matter positively, ego strength requires a flexible repression mechanism, so that the person may be said to be optimally open to experience, though capable of excluding phenomena that cannot be assimilated to the structure of the self.

Physiological stability and regularity of physical functioning is the biological matrix in which the ego thrives, or attains maximum strength. Generally speaking, the ego is at its strongest in the years of physical maturity, granting good bodily health. Ego strength is increasing as the organism grows toward maturity, levels off in the "prime of life," and declines thereafter with increasing age.

The crucial years in determining ego strength are the first five years of life. Severe ego dysfunction in those years is virtually irreversible. In the normal course of development, a regular sequence of ego crises and ego achievements may be discerned. The first achievement of the ego in relation to experience is the attainment of a stable and facile distinction between inner and outer sources of stimulation. This is the indispensable basis of the "sense of reality"; an inability to make this distinction is the primary mark of functional psychosis, in which introjection and projection no longer operate under the control of the ego. Paranoias and psychotic depressions and excitements are the diagnostic syndromes consequent upon such ego failure. A strong ego, on the other hand, consistently recognizes the independent and autonomous existence of objects other than itself, and also is able to take a reflective attitude toward its own existence and the laws of its being. Building upon this basic distinction of inner and outer sources of experience, the ego gradually attains mastery of bodily functions involving intake and output, which includes experiencing the erotic component in such functions. Such later character traits as the ability to get and to give good things, to hold on to what one wants and to let go when necessary, to be able to rise to the occasion, to make things go, to build and to conserve, to understand and to predict, all have their beginnings in the early years when the most important of ego crises occur. The later achievements of the normal ego involve primarily the synthesis of these earlier acquisitions of mastery; the most important outcomes have to do with personal identity in work and in love, and finally with the individual's participation in community experience, which would include some understanding of man in relation to nature, and of nature itself.

IMPLICATIONS

Try to state in your own words what you understand ego strength to be. What are the specific indices of a strong versus a weak ego as described in this selection? Reread the items that separate individuals who improve in therapy from those who do not. Can you also, in terms of these items, formulate some personal suggestions for more hygienic attitudes and habits? Try it. Would you venture to formulate some child-rearing advice that may help to develop healthier attitudes? To what extent does this selection give you some insight into yourself and those you know best? Why do you think current thinkers like Barron have achieved greater clarity in their thinking about stability by defining it as ego function than the earlier writers who discussed the matter in terms of will power?

REFERENCES

Is making an effective personal adjustment a matter of following rules? As previously implied, it is not. When individuals who are judged to be stable, mature, and in reasonable control of their own lives are compared with persons of low emotional stability, the differences seem to be in terms of developmental background. Factors such as stable family setting, the presence of both parents who are respected, establishment of independence from the family, and, later, enduring heterosexual relations are important. The importance of these factors has emerged in carefully designed studies of stable and unstable persons.

These studies reveal that the *psychological climate* in which the individual lives is important—a healthy one fosters the potentialities for personal growth and encourages development of those attitudes and traits characteristic of stable people. These characteristics are (1) capacity to deal with one's environment and an effective organization of effort toward goals, (2) a correct perception of oneself and the world, and (3) a unity of personality, an integrity that allows one to live satisfactorily with oneself and one's fellows (see Jahoda, 1958).

The emphasis is not only on understanding the forces of one's physical equipment and environment but on using one's individuality for responsible social growth. (See White, 1952; Shoben, 1957; McKinney, 1960; Symonds, 1951.) Those in the existential movement in psychological thinking emphasize particularly the achievement of a personally meaningful and responsible existence. (See Maslow, 1962; Frankl, 1963.)

5 SELF-UNDERSTANDING IN THE PREDICTION OF BEHAVIOR

Carl R. Rogers, Bill L. Kell, and Helen McNeil

Have you ever considered the many factors that influence your behavior? Some of these major factors are heredity, physical condition, mental capacity and aptitudes, family environment, cultural background, social experience, educational experience, and self-insight. Which of these factors would you speculate have been most important in the development of what you are today? How essential is self-insight in the control of one's behavior? Self-insight includes the individual's understanding and acceptance of himself and of the real situations in which he finds himself.

Rogers and his associates show us in this study how these complex and sometimes elusive factors are rated and evaluated. They state in specific terms how *extremely poor adjustment* differs from *excellent adjustment*, and how the individual with poor self-understanding and self-acceptance differs from the individual who has achieved these qualities.

A NUMBER of years ago, a study in prediction of the behavior and adjustment of delinquent adolescents was made by Kell (1942) under the supervision of the senior author. The major finding of the study was so striking and so unexpected that the completed research was laid aside until it might be confirmed or disproved by additional work.

Later, Miss McNeil (1944) repeated the identical method of study on a new group of cases with results which confirmed, though less strikingly, the same findings. It now appears appropriate to present these two studies in somewhat condensed form, together with some of the implications which they seem to have for clinical practice and personality research.

The Hypothesis

The hypothesis was the same in both studies. It was that given sufficient information concerning the factors which presumably enter into the determination of an individual's behavior, it should be possible to make ratings of these factors which would predict with some degree of accuracy the individual's later adjustment. More specifically, given information regarding an *individual's heredity, physical condition, mental status, family environment, cultural background, social experience, educational experience, and self-insight,** it should be possible to rate these factors as to their favorableness for normal development, and on the basis of these ratings predict future adjustment. If behavior is caused by factors such as those listed, then an evaluation of such factors should provide a basis for estimating the type of behavioral adjustment which is likely to ensue.

The Plan of the Studies

The plan of both studies was identical and contained the following general elements.

1. To select a group of delinquent children for whom there was an adequate amount of diagnostic information, and follow-up reports of adjustment covering a period of approximately two years following the initial study.

2. To make ratings of the various factors which might determine behavior, by means of the so-called "Component Factor Method" (described below), these ratings to be entirely on the basis of information available at the time of the initial study, without any reference to the follow-up data.

3. To make independent ratings of the adjustment of the individual two years after the diagnostic study, these ratings to be made without reference to the information obtained in the diagnostic evaluation.

4. To analyze the material for possible correlations between each component factor and later adjustment, also for correlations between all the factors taken together and later adjustment. To consider whether the behavior of these delinquents might have been in any way predicted by this method, from the information available at the time of the initial study.

* Editor's italics.

The way in which these steps were carried out is presented in some detail in the sections which follow.

The Selection of the Groups

The cases which were used in this study were obtained from the files of the Bureau of Juvenile Research, Columbus, Ohio, and it was due to the wholehearted cooperation of this organization that the research was possible. The procedure was as follows. Mr. Kell went over a few cases to see whether the information contained in the case histories and in the follow-up files was adequate for the type of analysis which he wished to make. It appeared that in many cases the information was adequate for his purposes. None of these preliminary cases was used in the research. He then took 155 cases which had been studied by the BJR after June 1937, and on which there was reported to be follow-up information two to three years after the diagnostic study. Cases were selected at random except that there was some perusal of the follow-up reports to make sure that both failures and successes in adjustment were being included. This was the only contact with the follow-up reports prior to the specific study of the follow-up material reported later.

When the Component-Factor ratings were made on these 155 cases, it was found that the information was inadequate in 71 cases, and these were dropped. In making the ratings on follow-up adjustment, information was found to be inadequate in 9 additional cases, thus bringing the total number included in the research to 75. It does not appear that lack of information in the case record would be a selective factor related to the problems being studied in this research.

In the study made by Miss McNeil, 141 cases were initially selected, the criteria being similar, with the added item that they should all be new cases which had not been utilized in the Kell study. She found it necessary to drop out 65 cases because of inadequate information, thus leaving 76 individuals in her group. Thus in the two studies taken together, there are 151 individuals on whom the reported findings are based.

Certain general facts about the two groups are listed in Table 1.

In an analysis made by Miss McNeil's group, it was found that the behavior difficulties were those that we have come to regard as typical of a juvenile delinquent group—stealing, truancy from school and home, incorrigible behavior, untruthfulness, and sex misdemeanors heading the list of complaints. There were 27 of the group who had previously been in court. Broken and discordant homes were the rule, and more than half of the group had had some foster home or institutional experience away from their own home. In general it may be said that the adolescents included in the study appear to be typical of individuals coming to a juvenile court or behavior clinic.

Table 1
Characteristics of the Groups Included in the Kell and McNeil Studies

Characteristic	Kell's Group	McNeil's Group
Average age at time of diagnostic study	15–2	14–6
Range in age	8–9 to 17–11	7–9 to 18–1
Number of boys	57	59
Number of girls	18	17
Whites	65	66
Negroes	10	10
Average I.Q.	94	90
Range in I.Q.	45 to 136	41 to 140
From rural homes	unknown	9
From urban homes	unknown	67

The Rating of Component Factors

When the groups had been selected, the next step was to rate those factors in the child's background and experience which might presumably be related to future behavior and adjustment. For this purpose the component factor method of case analysis, devised by Rogers and the staff of the Rochester Guidance Center, and described in an earlier publication (Rogers, 1939) was used. Since the findings are in terms of the categories used in this device, some description of it is given here, though for a full account of its development or its use in other research (Kell, 1942; Bennett & Rogers, 1941b), the reader is referred elsewhere.

The rationale behind this method of rating and analysis, and a brief description of the method, is given by Rogers in the following statement:

Behavior problems are due to the fact that a child of certain hereditary equipment is dealt with in a certain manner by members of his family environment and at the same time affected by certain broader cultural and social influences. If any one of these elements is altered, the behavior picture is also altered. To understand behavior we must view it as the complex result of all these component factors. Thus in the method under consideration, the forces which have operated in the child's experience are grouped under eight factors, defined so far as possible in terms which will have general understanding. Each of these factors . . . is rated in the case of the individual child on a seven-point scale, ranging from influences which are destructive to the child's welfare, to conditions and forces ideal for the child's adjustment. This rating scale is made more objective by means of sample ratings, with experimentally determined values, set up as guideposts ·(Rogers, 1939).

The eight factors which are to be rated on the basis of material in the case history are defined in specific terms. For each factor there are also a series of illustrative ratings, taken from cases, and showing the average scale value which was given to the material by six clinician judges. The definitions to be kept in mind by the rater are stated below as given in the original description by Rogers, and as used by Kell and McNeil in these studies. In the interests of brevity the illustrative ratings have been omitted, except for the family factor, the factor of social experience, and the factor of self-insight. These are included to show the type of guide which was available to the rater.

Rating on Hereditary Factor

Consider the child's strain of inheritance, as evidenced by parents, relatives, siblings; hereditary predisposition to disease; feeble-mindedness, epilepsy, or psychoses in the ancestry; evidence of neuroses or physical or emotional instability in the ancestry; marked social inadequacy in the ancestry as shown by chronic alcoholism, repeated jail terms. On the constructive side consider freedom from disease and taints and marked social adequacy.

Rating on Physical Factors

Consider the child's inherited physical and neurological constitution; his physical development, size, and weight in relation to norm; physical defects, inferiorities, or abnormalities; glandular dysfunction; physical instability, nervousness, hyperactivity; disease history, with special attention to long periods of illness, or diseases such as tuberculosis, epilepsy, encephalitis, venereal disease, chorea; defects of the special senses. On the constructive side consider freedom from illness or defects, superior physique.

Rating on Mentality Factor

Consider the child's mental capacities as shown by his development, intelligence test ratings, school achievement, vocational achievement. Consider special abilities and disabilities which have a bearing on his mental functioning. Consider the quality of his intelligence, alertness, persistence, ability to concentrate.

Rating on Family Influences

Consider the family circle within which the child has developed—the attitudes which have surrounded him. Consider the emotional atmosphere within the home—marital discord or harmony, sibling rivalries, attitudes of domination, oversolicitude, rejection, or normal parental love. Frictions or conflicts in regard to illegitimacy or other family irregularity. The child's reaction to the home is also to be considered—reactions toward parents and siblings, toward family standards and discipline. Degree of community of interests with other members of the family.

Rating on Economic and Cultural Influences

Consider the family income, status of father's occupation, social standing in the community, degree of comfort and educative influences within the home; consider the community type—whether delinquency area, residential area, rural area; consider the community standards of behavior and culture; the school, libraries, and recreational resources available.

Rating on the Social Factor

Consider range and extent of child's social experience; isolation or group contacts; the type of companions available; the social skills the child has achieved considered in relation to his age; experience in group membership and leadership; organizing ability and social initiative; status in the schoolroom group; friendships with own and opposite sex, considered in relation to age; social relationships with adults; social adjustment to the neighborhood and community; general social maturity or lack of it.

Rating on Education, Training, and Supervision

Consider the education, training, and supervision the child has had outside the home. Ordinarily this will mean primarily his school experience. Consider such things as the type of school which the child has attended; the changes of school; the continuity and consistency of school experience; consistency of discipline, both in school and between home and school; the degree of healthy stimulation, the extent to which tasks have been adapted to ability; the insight shown by teachers and school authorities; the behavior ideals actually inculcated; the cooperation and similarity of viewpoint between home and school.

Rating on Self-Insight

Consider in relation to the norm for his age, the degree to which the child has or lacks understanding of his own situation and problems; consider such things as defensiveness; inability to admit faults, or tendency to depreciate self and exaggerate faults. Consider not only intellectual understanding of problem but emotional acceptance of the reality situation. Consider child's planfulness and willingness to take responsibility for self; ability to be objectively self-critical. Consider stability of attitudes—whether erratic and changeable or cautious and settled.

In view of some of the findings to be presented later, it should be pointed out that in the development of this instrument, the factor of self-insight was added rather apologetically at the end of the list. Says Rogers, in introducing a discussion of this factor, "The seven factors which have been described would seem to be the basic elements which, coming together in complex fashion, determine the behavior of the individual. For the young child an evaluation of these factors should be sufficient to gain an understanding of the child's reactions. With the older child, however, the attitudes which he holds toward himself and his behavior are decidedly significant and worthy of evaluation. That these attitudes are formed by the interaction of the other factors in the child's experience is undoubtedly true, but they also operate as an important influence to shape his future behavior" (Rogers, 1939).

Using this component factor instrument as described, Kell and McNeil rated each of the eight factors for each of the subjects in their groups. The material on which the ratings were based was the initial diagnostic study of the child made while he was at the Bureau of Juvenile Research. This material included written case histories, psychometric examinations, interviews with the child by a psychologist or psychiatrist, or both, report of physical examination, and other similar information. The only materials which were not used in making the rating judgments were the over-all diagnostic report compiled by the Bureau, and the follow-up information. The former was excluded because it was felt the ratings should be made on the basis of the material itself, rather than on someone's interpretation of that material. The follow-up information was of course excluded because it was to be rated independently.

No measure of the reliability of the ratings in the present studies was made, but it has been shown by Rogers that the degree of reliability in the clinical use of these rating scales may be expressed by the statement that in rating specific items, the standard deviation of clinician's judgments ranges from .3 to .6 of a scale step, with heredity and mentality showing the highest reliability, and family and self-insight factors the lowest. When six clinicians rated five cases (rather than specific items from cases) on every factor, the reliability was somewhat lower, 66 per cent of the judgments being in agreement within two scale steps on the seven-point scale (Rogers, 1939).

The Rating of Later Adjustment

In order to provide an objective measure of the individual's later adjustment, with which the initial ratings might be correlated, Kell devised a scale for rating the behavior of the individual during the two- or three-year period following the diagnostic study. This too was a seven-point scale, ranging from extremely poor adjustment to excellent adjustment. The typical characteristics which were set up for the different points on the scale are as follows:

Rating Scale of Follow-Up Adjustment

−3 Extremely poor adjustment. Individual in difficulties constantly. A confirmed delinquent or criminal. If institutionalized, makes an unsatisfactory adjustment there—fights continuously against regulations, disliked by other inmates, etc. If in own home, continually disrupts the family, a constant behavior problem at home and in school. Insane or extremely neurotic. Finds few, if any, normal satisfactions. No satisfactory adjustment in any situation.

−2 Poor adjustment. Continues in some delinquent or criminal activities, but does not seem hopeless. In court a number of times. Gains most satisfactions in an antisocial manner. If institutionalized, makes a partial adjustment to the institution's routine and regulations. If in own home, continues as a behavior problem most of the time, in conflict with school and may drop out. Cannot hold a job or function satisfactorily at one. May adjust satisfactorily in a few situations. Seems quite neurotic. Cannot adjust in foster home.

−1 Near average adjustment. Continues in a few delinquent activities. May be in court once or twice. If institutionalized, makes a satisfactory adjustment and shows evidence of adjusting outside the institution. If in own home, continues as a problem, but not as a severe one. Continues as a school problem, but makes some progress. May be able to hold a job, but does not function too well at it. May exhibit some neurotic symptoms which have a slight effect on total adjustment. May have to be placed in several foster homes, but finally makes a fairly satisfactory adjustment. Adjusts in some situations and not in others.

 0 Average adjustment. In few, if any, delinquencies. May be in court once for minor delinquencies and then released. Neurotic tendencies mild and have little effect on total adjustment. Makes a satisfactory adjustment in the home—may have a few minor family difficulties. Makes average progress in school in relation to ability. Makes satisfactory adjustment in foster home. Is able to hold a job, but is not exceptional at it. Adjusts in most situations.

+1 Above average adjustment. Never in court again. Delinquent tendencies, if any, must be so mild that he is never in any serious difficulty. No evident neurotic symptoms. Very little aggressive, antisocial behavior. Makes a good adjustment to the family situation if returned home. Makes good progress in school. Does quite well on a job. Makes a good foster-home adjustment. Adjusts in nearly all situations.

+2 Very good adjustment. Seems to make the best of nearly every situation. No evidence of any delinquent tendencies. No antisocial behavior. Makes a good school adjustment. Does very well on a job. Never any evident conflict with family if returned home. Makes a very satisfactory foster-home adjustment.

+3 Excellent adjustment. Makes the best of every situation. Never any question of stability or antisocial trends. Seems to make best possible adjustment to family. Excellent adjustment in school, college indicated, etc. Makes excellent progress on a job. Foster-home adjustment the best possible (Kell, 1942).

Using this rating scale, Kell and McNeil turned to the follow-up report of the cases in their respective groups, and, without reference to the diagnostic study, evaluated the two to three years of behavior which were described in the follow-up material. This material was made up of reports from probation officers, social workers, and institution officials.

To illustrate the range of later adjustments which were found in the group, and the use of the rating scale on adjustments, Kell's notes abstracting the follow-up reports on three cases, and the ratings assigned to these cases, are given below:

−3 Ran away from foster home. Committed to Boys' Industrial School for stealing. Later released. Practiced sex perversion. Committed to Massillon State Hospital—ran away from there. Very poor present adjustment. Continuing sex perversion.

 0 Girl made a fair adjustment in first foster home. Did not get along well in second and third foster homes. Later made a good adjustment in a fourth foster home. Now married. Apparently is doing well.

+2 Boy has graduated from high school with good marks. Now employed as a blueprint reader at $40.00 per week. Adjustment very good. Says, "BJR is the best thing that ever happened to me" (Kell, 1942).

A word is in order in regard to the experiences of these children during the follow-up period. It is fortunate for the purposes of this study (though not for the children) that very little in the way of intensive casework or psychotherapy was utilized in the treatment of these delinquents. We say that this is fortunate for the study, because obviously the aim of all treatment is to defeat the statistical probabilities involved in prediction. That is, the caseworker or therapist in working with a person is endeavoring to alter the behavior which would objectively be predicted for this individual, and thus is hoping to make the prediction an erroneous one. The only type of treatment recommendations which were apt to be carried out in the group under study were the recommendations that the child be placed on probation, or placed in a foster home or institution. There is no way of measuring or indicating the amount of treatment effort invested in these children. It may be said, however, that the amount was relatively small, and that if one grants any efficacy to treatment effort then in so far as this study is concerned, it would only act to reduce the accuracy of behavioral prediction. In other words, whatever predictive accuracy is achieved by the method used, it is safe to say that it would have been greater had no treatment of any kind been attempted.

Findings

We are now ready to consider the analysis of the data collected. It should be clear that for each child in the two groups we have a rating on each of eight factors as to the extent to which those factors are likely to produce normal or well-adjusted behavior. These ratings were made on the basis of information available at the time the child came to the BJR. We have also independent ratings of the child's adjustment during the two-year period following the initial study. The major aspect of the analysis consists in the correlation of these predictive judgments with the evaluations of actual behavior.

The first finding of significance is that all the predictive factors which were rated showed a positive correlation with later adjustment. That is, the child with good heredity, or good health, or favorable family environment, etc., is more likely to display normal and well-adjusted behavior during the two-year period following the study than is the child who is less favored in any of these respects. This would tend to support the general hypothesis that behavior is the result of multiple causation, and that the factors which were selected for study are at least some of the effective elements which seem to determine adjustment or maladjustment.

But the unexpected finding which gives quite a different meaning to this material is the predictive importance of the individual's understanding of himself. As will be seen from Table 2, the correlation between self-insight and later adjustment was .84, an unusually high relationship for material of this sort. It was this surprising finding which lead the investigators first to check the data for possible errors and finally to lay it aside until it could be thoroughly rechecked on a new group. In the McNeil study, all the correlations are consistently lower, a puzzling fact which we have been unable to explain, but self-insight again comes out as the best predictor of behavior, correlating .41 with outcome.

Table 2

Correlation of Ratings on Component Factors with Ratings of Later Adjustment

	Correlations with adjustment	
Factor	Kell study N = 75	McNeil study N = 76
Self-insight	.84**	.41**
Social experience	.55**	.36**
Mentality	.39**	.15
Hereditary	.37**	.23*
Family environment	.36**	.14
Economic and cultural	.28*	.07
Physical	.25*	.13
Education and training	.11	.20
Total averaged ratings	.66**	.27*

* These correlations are significant at the 5-per-cent level of confidence.
** These correlations are significant at the 1-per-cent level of confidence.

In both studies the factor which was second in predictive significance was the social experience and social adequacy of the child. The respective correlations were .55 and .36, both statistically significant. The relationship between the other factors and adjustment was positive, but lower than these two, with the McNeil study finding lower significance for the factors of mentality and economic-cultural influence, and somewhat higher weight for education and training, when her results are compared with those of Kell.

As would be expected, when the various ratings on the separate factors were averaged, they correlated positively with outcome, r's of .66 and .27 respectively being obtained in the two studies. This represents a questionable method of prediction, where the factors obviously have different weightings.

The material from Table 2 may be summarized by stating that in predicting the behavior of a problem adolescent, the *extent to which he faces and accepts himself, and has a realistic view of himself and reality,** provides, of the factors studied, the best estimate of his future adjustment. The second best predictor would be the *satisfactoriness of his social contacts, the adequacy of his social relationships.** These two are outstandingly better bases of prediction than any of the other factors studied, but positive correlation with later adjustments is found in ratings of the hereditary stock from which the individual has sprung; his mentality and mental functioning; the emotional climate of his family environment; his physical condition and health; and finally the economic, cultural, and educational influences to which he has been exposed. These factors would be of predictive significance roughly in the order named.

Further Analysis Related to Self-Insight

Since the factor which had most doubtfully been included in the Component Factor method proved to correlate most highly with outcome, special attention will be given to its analysis.

In the first place, the reader may wish to know the type of material upon which the ratings were based. Here are some of the summarized notes from the two investigators' records, indicating the material relating to self-insight which was found in the cases, and the rating based upon it.

—3 Refuses to discuss his delinquencies; will not or cannot discuss problems arising out of family conflicts; denies his share of responsibility even when confronted with the facts (McNeil, 1944).

—2 Quite frank and open in discussing her misbehavior, but stories are unreliable. Is proud of her misbehavior—does not feel responsible. Does not recognize that family situation is the cause of much of her trouble (Kell, 1942).

—1 Cautious, fairly truthful, correcting statements on own initiative. Feels some responsibility, realizing he is too easily influenced. Makes no complaints about the family but appears to understand somewhat its poor influence (McNeil, 1944).

+1 Understands his home situation fairly well, not clear about his relationship to it. Recognizes source of difficulties, but needs help in managing them.

* Editor's italics.

Admits his delinquencies truthfully with something similar to "They were not to blame. I was on the wrong track" (McNeil, 1944).

+2 Freely admits her delinquencies, recognizing and accepting the basis of parental antagonism and rejection. Planful and cooperative. Responsible when placed on her own. Tells facts frankly, recognizes and understands mother's instability and her own need for personal responsibility. Responsive and cooperative in behavior and in making future plans (McNeil, 1944).

These examples may be sufficient to indicate the rather crude character of the material available for making this as well as the other ratings. If such significant correlations are achieved on the basis of general case material, the possibility is at least suggested that more refined ways of investigating the degree of self-understanding might give even more significant results.

Since both self-insight and the social factor gave high correlations with outcome, it was thought wise to investigate the degree of relationship between these two factors. In the Kell group, the correlation between the ratings on self-insight and the ratings on the social factor was .66, in the McNeil group, .63. This is a high degree of interrelationship which does not seem to be explainable on the basis of similarity of definitions of the two factors, or similarity of the material being rated. For example, the notes from three cases as to the social factor, with their respective ratings, are as follows:

−3 Does not get along well with sibs or school companions. Quarrelsome. Mistreats other children, and cruel to small children and animals. Not successful in trial social adjustment opportunities.

 0 Somewhat of a leader among the older delinquent boys. Has a passable manner, likes sports, likes to impress the girls.

+2 Plays on a team. Friends are not delinquents. Good mixer, liked by others in the neighborhood and school. Has a good stamp collection. Has three very close friends (McNeil, 1944).

There would seem to be no obvious reason why ratings based on this type of data should correlate closely with ratings made on self-insight. It would seem that the relationship may be of a more underlying nature.

In another attempt to analyze the meaning of the high correlation of the self-insight factor with later adjustment, this correlation was separately computed for boys and girls, and for Negroes and whites. The differences were not striking, and some of the groups were small, but in both studies the correlation was higher for the girls than for the boys, and for the Negroes than for the whites.

Another line of investigation gave special consideration to those children who remained in their own homes during the follow-up period. It had been a surprise to the investigators that family environment had not correlated highly with outcome, and that self-understanding had correlated so highly. As the material was examined, it appeared possible that the fact that a sizable number of children from the poorest homes had been removed from their own families as a result of the diagnostic study might have influenced these results. Consequently both Kell and McNeil selected from their groups those children who had been returned to their own homes during the follow-up period. They also endeavored to determine whether the factor of self-insight was less operative when the home conditions were very unfavorable, by selecting out those with family factors rated -2 or -3, who had been returned to these very unfavorable homes.

Table 3
The Correlation of Self-Insight with Adjustment Among Children Returned to Their Own Homes

	Kell's study		McNeil's study	
Group	N	r	N	r
Children whose family environment was rated -2 or -3	28	.76*	28	.31
Children whose family environment was rated -1 or 0	15	.78*	12	.49
All children returned to their own homes	43	.79*	47	.43*

* Significant at the 1-per-cent level of confidence.

The results are shown in Table 3. It will be seen that the correlation between insight and later adjustment is relatively unchanged, even when the child comes from, and returns to, a very unfavorable home situation. It is still true that a much better prediction of adjustment can be based upon a consideration of the degree of self-understanding, than upon any analysis of the home environment. McNeil further checked this by correlating the family environment factor with later adjustment in the group of 47 children returned to their own homes. This r was .20. It is higher than the similar correlation for the group as a whole (.14 in her study), but much lower than the correlation of .43 between self-insight and later adjustment.

When the child is removed from his own home and placed in a foster home, the operation of self-insight as a predictor is enhanced. There were 10 children in Kell's group thus placed and 15 in McNeil's. The correlations between self-insight and later adjustment for these two small groups were .98 (!) and .54 respectively. Both of these correlations are significant, the first at the 1-per-cent level and the second at the 5-per-cent level, in spite of the small numbers involved.

Limitations of the Findings

Since some of the findings of these studies appear to have considerable significance if they are confirmed by other research, it should be mentioned that they were uncovered in investigations which have certain flaws and limitations. Those limitations which are evident to the investigators will be briefly stated.

It is unfortunate that there is no study of the reliability of the Component-Factor ratings in these two studies. Knowledge of the degree of reliability present in a previous study does not entirely compensate for this. There is no study of the reliability of the ratings on final adjustment.

A more serious flaw is the fact that the same judge rated both the initial factors and the final adjustment, even though these ratings were made independently and some time apart. The investigator made some 600 ratings of individual factors in the 75 cases; then, without reference to these or to the material upon which they were based, made the ratings on the follow-up material. It would certainly be preferable to have another judge make these judgments. It may be said, however, that if there was any unconscious bias operating in this situation, it could not account for the surprising showing of the self-insight factor, since whatever bias existed was in the direction of supposing that the emotional climate of the family was probably the most influential factor in the determination of behavior.

Another limitation of the studies as a whole is the fact that the rating scales for the eight factors and also for the later adjustment are crude instruments lacking in the degree of refinement which would be desirable in objective research. The information in the case folders was also often lacking in the specificity which would be desirable.

These limitations are real, yet their operation would for the most part tend to reduce correlations. There would seem to be nothing in the design or conduct of the study which would explain the degree of relationship which was found between self-insight and adjustment.

There is one other element in the studies which deserves critical consideration, and that is the sharp difference in the correlations found by the two investigators. It appears from an examination of the data that it is not due to any difference in the range of the ratings, or to any statistical artifact which can be discovered. Whether it is due to a difference in clinical discrimination in making the ratings, or to some other cause, is unknown. As long as it is unexplained, it would appear that it might cover some unrecognized source of error.

Summary of the Findings

To recapitulate the findings of the two investigations:

1. The ratings of the eight factors specified in the component-factor method all showed a positive correlation with ratings of the individual's later adjustment, in the group of 151 cases studied.

2. The size of these correlations as found in the two studies differed sharply in amount, but there was a high degree of correspondence in the relative significance of the factors.

3. The rating of the *individual's understanding and acceptance of himself and the reality situation* * was, in both studies, the best predictor of what his future adjustment would be.

4. In both studies the factor which was second in predictive capacity was the *social experience and social adequacy* * of the individual.

5. In decreasing order, these factors were also found to have some capacity for prediction of future behavior: the heredity of the individual; his intellectual functioning; the emotional atmosphere which the child has experienced in the family; the economic and cultural conditions which have surrounded him; the quality and consistency of his educational environment.

6. A high degree of relationship was found between the rating on self-insight and the rating on social experience. This correlation does not appear to be explained on the basis of simple overlapping of materials rated, but may involve some deeper relationship between the two factors.

7. In the group of children who came from, and remained in, highly undesirable atmospheres, it was still true that the degree of *self-understanding** was the best predictor of adjustment, much better than an evaluation of the home influence itself.

8. In children who are removed from highly undesirable home atmosphere and placed in foster homes, the degree of *self-understanding* * is a decidedly accurate predictor of future adjustment or maladjustment.

Implications of the Findings

Only gradually, as the clinical experience of the authors has pointed in the same direction as the results of this research, has the full significance of the foregoing findings been recognized and appreciated. Only as work in psychotherapy has driven home the importance of the individual's concept of himself and his relation to reality, and the close relationship between these perceptions and his behavior, have the findings of this research been understood. (See reference 6 for an expression of this line of thought.) It is another experience to illustrate that objective facts have little meaning until they fit, in some recognizable way, into our frame of reference.

If the present studies are confirmed in their central findings by further research, then there are three broad implications which deserve consideration. The *first is the socially hopeful character of the findings.* * Studies in prediction based upon correlating isolated background facts with later adjustment seem uniformly depressing because they add up to the total conclusion that the more adverse the factors operating in the individual's

---

* Editor's italics.

life, the more hopeless he becomes from any social point of view. The present studies do not flatly contradict this conclusion. It is true that a poor heredity and the presence of destructive organic factors, and a culturally deprived background, all predispose, to some degree, toward a less adequate adjustment. But the significant fact is that the element which above all others should be the most subject to natural change or planned alteration, the individual's acceptance of himself and of reality, is also the most important determiner of his future behavior. Rather than feeling that a person is inevitably doomed by unalterable forces which have shaped him, this study suggests that the most potent influence in his future behavior is one which is certainly alterable to some degree without any change in his physical or social heredity or in his present environment. The most powerful determinant would appear to lie in the attitudes of the person himself.

A *second implication* * which should be mentioned is that the results of these studies would point toward a *drastic revision of the methods of dealing with or treating individuals who exhibit delinquent or problem behavior.** In the groups which were studied, and in other similar groups, practically all of the investment of money and effort is directed toward altering factors which appear to be only to a small degree determinative of behavior. Vast amounts are expended on foster homes and children's institutions in order to alter the child's whole environment, considerable amounts on probationary supervision which is little more than a checking up on the youngster, considerable sums on the alleviation of physical deficiencies, but practically nothing on any direct approach to the problem of revising the child's attitudes toward himself. Likewise only a small fraction of the total treatment effort goes to changing the child's social adjustment, which appears to be second only to self-insight in its significance.

If treatment effort was to be expended in most efficient form, in the light of the results of this study, then effective psychotherapy, either individual or group, aimed at *helping the child achieve a more realistic acceptance of his impulses and abilities, and a realistic appraisal of his situation,** would be the major investment. Social experiences might need to be provided concurrently, or the psychotherapy might assist him in developing more constructively the social relationships which he has. In any event, it would not be the quantity of social contact, but the degree to which the individual built mature give-and-take relationships with others, which would be regarded as important. A distinctly lesser amount of effort might be expended in endeavoring to improve the family relationships and the economic status. Some effort to enrich the cultural stimulation of the child might also be justified. The primary aim throughout would

* Editor's italics.

be to provide the opportunities for emotional release, insightful acceptance of self, and positive reorientation of self, which every successful psychotherapy entails. Such opportunities might be offered through the clinic, through the classroom with a specially trained teacher, through special school counseling services, or through group therapy carried on in conjunction with a recreational group. The whole focus of effort would be almost the reverse of the accepted procedures at the present time.

The final implication carried by the results of this study is that if the individual's view of himself and reality is so important—the degree of his defensiveness, the degree of acceptance of himself, his realistic appraisal of reality, his degree of independence and planfulness, his ability to be objectively self-critical—then a great deal of research is needed in this area. Studies are needed to discover how healthy perceptions of this sort occur, and the circumstances which cause the individual to become defensive and lacking in insight. We need much deeper research into the way in which the individual views himself, and the fashion in which his internal view of experience influences his behavior. Finally we need penetrating investigations of the ways in which such views of experience may be altered in the direction of realism and self-acceptance. Such research would move us forward a great distance in our knowledge of how to deal with those with behavior disorders.

IMPLICATIONS

How would you now go about evaluating a child in respect to such factors as heredity, physique, mentality, family influences, and so on? What are the implications of the major findings that self-understanding and acceptance of oneself and reality are of vital importance in predicting later adjustment? Why do you think these factors are apparently so important? You may want to come back to a discussion of these findings after you have read the selections in Chapter XI on counseling and psychotherapy. Do these findings recommend one kind of therapy over another?

REFERENCES

Consult the Bibliography for references cited in the article.

6 MODERN APPROACH TO VALUES: MATURITY

Carl R. Rogers

"What am I to believe? People who are important in my life differ in what they think is right and wrong, and what I have held as right all my life is challenged daily—by others' behavior and attitudes, by the movies, by my reading—what can I believe is right?" In our revolutionary era, many people are searching for values to guide their lives; they are at a loss to know in what direction they should search for standards.

Turning from the personal to the social, all of our major institutions inculcate, reinforce, and reprimand in terms of values. Law, religion, and education deal with rights and wrongs and, theoretically, in a democracy these institutions are modifiable by the people.

What is the process by which a mature individual reaches his personal values? Rogers explores this process, with an emphasis on values in the mature person.

THERE IS a great deal of concern today with the problem of values. Youth, in almost every country, is deeply uncertain of its value orientation; the values associated with various religions have lost much of their influence; sophisticated individuals in every culture seem unsure and troubled as to the goals they hold in esteem. The reasons are not far to seek. The world culture, in all its aspects, seems increasingly scientific and relativistic, and the rigid, absolute views on values which come to us from the past appear anachronistic. Even more important perhaps, is the fact that the modern individual is assailed from every angle by divergent and contradictory value claims. It is no longer possible, as it was in the not too distant historical past, to settle comfortably into the value system of one's forebears or one's community and live out one's life without ever examining the nature and the assumptions of that system.

In this situation it is not surprising that value orientations from the past appear to be in a state of disintegration or collapse. Men question whether there are, or can be, any universal values. It is often felt that we may have lost, in our modern world, all possibility of any general or cross-cultural basis for values. One natural result of this uncertainty and confusion is that there is an increasing concern about, interest in, and a searching for, a sound or meaningful value approach which can hold its own in today's world. I share this general concern. I have also experienced the more specific value issues which arise in my own field, psychotherapy. The client's feelings and convictions about values frequently change during therapy. How can he or we know whether they have changed in a sound direction? Or does he simply, as some claim, take over the value system of his therapist? Is psychotherapy simply a device whereby the unacknowledged and unexamined values of the therapist are unknowingly transmitted to an unsuspecting client? Or should this transmission of values be the therapist's openly held purpose? Should he become the modern priest, upholding and imparting a value system suitable for today? And what would such a value system be? There has been much discussion of such issues, ranging from thoughtful and empirically based presentations such as that of D.D. Glad, to more polemic statements. As is so often true, the general problem faced by the culture is painfully and specifically evident in the cultural microcosm which is called the therapeutic relationship.

I should like to attempt a modest approach to this whole problem. I have observed changes in the approach to values as the individual grows from infancy to adulthood. I observe further changes when, if he is fortunate, he continues to grow toward true psychological maturity. Many of these observations grow out of my experience as a therapist, where I have had the rich opportunity of seeing the ways in which individuals move toward a richer life. From these observations I believe I see some directional threads emerging which might offer a new concept of the valuing process, more tenable in the modern world. I have made a beginning by presenting some of these ideas partially in previous writings; I would like now to voice them more clearly and more fully.

I would stress that my vantage point for making these observations is not that of the scholar or philosopher: I am speaking from my experience of the functioning human being, as I have lived with him in the intimate experience of therapy, and in other situations of growth, change, and development.

Some Definitions

Before I present some of these observations, perhaps I should try to clarify what I mean by values. There are many definitions which have been used, but I have found helpful some distinctions made by Charles Morris. He points out that value is a term we employ in different ways. We use it to refer to the tendency of any living beings to show preference, in their actions, for one kind of object or objective rather than another. This preferential behavior he calls "operative values." It need not involve any cognitive or conceptual thinking. It is simply the value choice which is indicated behaviorally when the organism selects one object, rejects another.

When the earthworm, placed in a simple Y maze, chooses the smooth arm of the Y, instead of the path which is paved with sandpaper, he is indicating an operative value.

A second use of the term might be called "conceived values." This is the preference of the individual for a symbolized object. Usually in such a preference there is anticipation or foresight of the outcome of behavior directed toward such a symbolized object. A choice such as "Honesty is the best policy" is such a conceived value.

A final use of the term might be called "objective value." People use the word in this way when they wish to speak of what is objectively preferable, whether or not it is in fact sensed or conceived of as desirable. What I have to say involves this last definition scarcely at all. I will be concerned with operative values and conceptualized values.

The Infant's Way of Valuing

Let me first speak about the infant. The living human being has, at the outset, a clear approach to values. He prefers some things and experiences, and rejects others. We can infer from studying his behavior that he prefers those experiences which maintain, enhance, or actualize his organism, and rejects those which do not serve this end. Watch him for a bit:

Hunger is negatively valued. His expression of this often comes through loud and clear.

Food· is positively valued. But when he is satisfied, food is negatively valued, and the same milk he responded to so eagerly is now spit out, or the breast which seemed so satisfying is now rejected as he turns his head away from the nipple with an amusing facial expression of disgust and revulsion.

He values security, and the holding and caressing which seem to communicate security.

He values new experience for its own sake, and we observe this in his obvious pleasure in discovering his toes, in his searching movements, in his endless curiosity.

He shows a clear negative valuing of pain, bitter tastes, sudden loud sounds.

All of this is commonplace, but let us look at these facts in terms of what they tell us about the infant's approach to values. It is first of all a flexible, changing, valuing *process*, not a fixed system. He likes food and dislikes the same food. He values security and rest, and rejects it for new experience. What is going on seems best described as an organismic valuing process, in which each element, each moment of what he is experiencing is somehow weighed, and selected or rejected, depending on whether, at this moment, it tends to actualize the organism or not. This complicated weighing of experience is clearly an organismic, not a conscious or symbolic function. These are operative, not conceived values. But this process can none the less deal with complex value problems. I would remind you of the experiment in which young infants had spread in front of them a score or more of dishes of natural (that is, unflavored) foods. Over a period of time they clearly tended to value the foods which enhanced their own survival, growth, and development. If for a time a child gorged himself on starches, this would soon be balanced by a protein "binge." If at times he chose a diet deficient in some vitamin, he would later seek out foods rich in this very vitamin. He was utilizing the wisdom of the body in his value choices, or perhaps more accurately, the physiological wisdom of his body guided his behavioral movements, resulting in what we might think of as objectively sound value choices.

Another aspect of the infant's approach to value is that the source or locus of the evaluating process is clearly within himself. Unlike many of us, he *knows* what he likes and dislikes, and the origin of these value choices lies strictly within himself. He is the center of the valuing process, the evidence for his choices being supplied by his own senses. He is not at this point influenced by what his parents think he should prefer, or by what the church says, or by the opinion of the latest "expert" in the field, or by the persuasive talents of an advertising firm. It is from within his own experiencing that his organism is saying in non-verbal terms, "This is good for me." "That is bad for me." "I like this." "I strongly dislike that." He would laugh at our concern over values, if he could understand it. How could anyone fail to know what he liked and disliked, what was good for him and what was not?

The Change in the Valuing Process

What happens to this highly efficient, soundly based valuing process? By what sequence of events do we exchange it for the more rigid, uncertain, inefficient approach to values which characterizes most of us as adults? Let me try to state briefly one of the major ways in which I think this happens.

The infant needs love, wants it, tends to behave in ways which will bring a repetition of this wanted experience. But this brings complications. He pulls baby sister's hair, and finds it satisfying to hear her wails and protests. He then hears that he is "a naughty, bad boy," and this may be reinforced by a slap on the hand. He is cut off from affection. As this experience is repeated, and many, many others like it, he gradually learns that what "feels good" is often "bad" in the eyes of others. Then the next step occurs, in which he comes to take the same attitude toward himself which these others have taken. Now, as he pulls his sister's hair, he solemnly intones, "Bad, bad boy." He is introjecting the value judgment of another, taking it as his own. He has deserted the wisdom of his organism, giving up the locus of evaluation, and is trying to behave in terms of values set by another, in order to hold love.

Or take another example at an older level. A boy senses, though perhaps not consciously, that he is more loved and prized by his parents when he thinks of being a doctor than when he thinks of being an artist. Gradually he introjects the values attached to being a doctor. He comes to want, above all, to be a doctor. Then in college he is baffled by the fact that he repeatedly fails in chemistry, which is absolutely necessary to becoming a physician, in spite of the fact that the guidance counselor assures him he has the ability to pass the course. Only in counseling interviews does he begin to realize how completely he has lost touch with his organismic reactions, how out of touch he is with his own valuing process.

Let me give another instance from a class of mine, a group of prospective teachers. I asked them at the beginning of the course, "Please list for me the two or three values which you would most wish to pass on to the children with whom you will work." They turned in many value goals, but I was surprised by some of the items. Several listed such things as "to speak correctly," "to use good English, not to use words like ain't." Others mentioned neatness—"to do things according to instructions"; one explained her hope that "When I tell them to write their names in the upper right-hand corner with the date under it, I want them to do it *that way*, not in some other form."

I confess I was somewhat appalled that for some of these girls the most important values to be passed on to pupils were to avoid bad grammar, or meticulously to follow teacher's instructions. I felt baffled. Certainly these behaviors had not been *experienced* as the most satisfying and meaningful elements in their own lives. The listing of such values could only be accounted for by the fact that these behaviors had gained approval—and thus had been introjected as deeply important.

Perhaps these several illustrations will indicate that in an attempt to gain or hold love, approval, esteem, the individual relinquishes the locus of evaluation which was his in infancy, and places it in others. He learns to have a basic *dis*trust for his own experiencing as a guide to his behavior. He learns from others a large number of conceived values, and adopts them as his own, even though they may be widely discrepant from what he is experiencing. Because these concepts are not based on his own valuing, they tend to be fixed and rigid, rather than fluid and changing.

Some Introjected Patterns

It is in this fashion, I believe, that most of us accumulate the introjected value patterns by which we live. In this fantastically complex culture of today, the patterns we introject as desirable or undesirable come from a variety of sources and are often highly contradictory in their meanings. Let me list a few of the introjections which are commonly held.

Sexual desires and behaviors are mostly bad. The sources of this construct are many—parents, church, teachers.

Disobedience is bad. Here parents and teachers combine with the military to emphasize this concept. To obey is good. To obey without question is even better.

Making money is the highest good. The sources of this conceived value are too numerous to mention.

Learning an accumulation of scholarly facts is highly desirable.

Browsing and aimless exploratory reading for fun is undesirable. The source of these last two concepts is apt to be in school, the educational system.

Abstract art or "pop" art, or "op" art is good. Here the people we regard as sophisticated are the originators of the value.

Communism is utterly bad. Here the government is a major source.

To love thy neighbor is the highest good. This concept comes from the church, perhaps from the parents.

Cooperation and teamwork are preferable to acting alone. Here companions are an important source.

Cheating is clever and desirable. The peer group again is the origin.

Coca-colas, chewing gum, electric refrigerators, and automobiles are all utterly desirable. This conception comes not only from advertisements, but is reinforced by people all over the world. From Jamaica to Japan, from Copenhagen to Kowloon, the "coca-cola culture" has come to be regarded as the acme of desirability.

This is a small and diversified sample of the myriads of conceived values which individuals often introject, and hold as their own, without ever having considered their inner organismic reactions to these patterns and objects.

Common Characteristics of Adult Valuing

I believe it will be clear from the foregoing that the usual adult—I feel I am speaking for most of us—has an approach to values which has these characteristics:

The majority of his values are introjected from other individuals or groups significant to him, but are regarded by him as his own.

The source or locus of evaluation on most matters lies outside of himself.

The criterion by which his values are set is the degree to which they will cause him to be loved or accepted.

These conceived preferences are either not related at all, or not clearly related, to his own process of experiencing.

Often there is a wide and unrecognized discrepancy between the evidence supplied by his own experience, and these conceived values.

Because these conceptions are not open to testing in experience, he must hold them in a rigid and unchanging fashion. The alternative would be a collapse of his values. Hence his values are "right"—like the law of the Medes and the Persians, which changeth not.

Because they are untestable, there is no ready way of solving contradictions. If he has taken in from the community the conception that money is the summum bonum and from the church the conception that love of one's neighbor is the highest value, he has no way of discovering which has more value for *him*. Hence a common aspect of modern life is living with absolutely contradictory values. We calmly discuss the possibility of dropping a hydrogen bomb on Russia, but then find tears in our eyes when we see headlines about the suffering of one small child.

Because he has relinquished the locus of evaluation to others, and has lost touch with his own valuing process, he feels profoundly insecure and easily threatened in his values. If some of these conceptions were destroyed, what would take their place? This threatening possibility makes him hold his value conceptions more rigidly or more confusedly, or both.

The Fundamental Discrepancy

I believe that this picture of the individual, with values mostly introjected, held as fixed concepts, rarely examined or tested, is the picture of most of us. By taking over the conceptions of others as our own, we lose contact with the potential wisdom of our own functioning, and lose confidence in ourselves. Since these value constructs are often sharply at variance with what is going on in our own experienceing, we have in a very basic way divorced ourselves from ourselves, and this accounts for much of modern strain and insecurity. This fundamental discrepancy between the individual's concepts and what he is actually experiencing, between the intellectual structure of his values and the valuing process going on unrecognized within him—this is a part of the fundamental estrangement of modern man from himself. This is a major problem for the therapist.

Restoring Contact with Experience

Some individuals are fortunate in going beyond the picture I have just given, developing further in the direction of psychological maturity. We see this happen in psychotherapy where we endeavor to provide a climate favorable to the growth of the person. We also see it happen in life, whenever life provides a therapeutic climate for the individual. Let me concentrate on this further maturing of a value approach as I have seen it in therapy.

In the first place let me say somewhat parenthetically that the therapeutic relationship is *not* devoid of values. Quite the contrary. When it is most effective, it seems to me, it is marked by one primary value: namely, that this person, this client, has worth. He as a person is valued in his separateness and uniqueness. It is when he senses and realizes that he is prized as a person that he can slowly begin to value the different aspects of himsef. Most importantly, he can begin, with much difficulty at first, to sense and to feel what is going on within him, what he is feeling, what he is experiencing, how he is reacting. He uses his experiencing as a direct referent to which he can turn in forming accurate conceptualizations and as a guide to his behavior. E.T. Gendlin has elaborated the way in which this occurs. As his experiencing becomes more and more open to him, as he is able to live more freely in the process of his feelings, then significant changes begin to occur in his approach to values. It begins to assume many of the characteristics it had in infancy.

Introjected Values in Relation to Experiencing

Perhaps I can indicate this by reviewing a few of the brief examples of introjected values which I have given, and suggesting what happens to them as the individual comes closer to what is going on within him.

The individual in therapy looks back and realizes, "But I *enjoyed* pulling my sister's hair—and that doesn't make me a bad person."

The student failing chemistry realizes, as he gets close to his own experiencing—"I don't value being a doctor, even though my parents do; I don't like chemistry; I don't like taking steps toward being a doctor; and I am not a failure for having these feelings."

The adult recognizes that sexual desires and behavior may be richly satisfying and permanently enriching in their consequences, or shallow and temporary and less than satisfying. He goes by his own experiencing, which does not always coincide with the social norms.

He considers art from a new value approach. He says, "This picture moves me deeply, means a great deal to me. It also happens to be an abstraction, but that is not the basis for my valuing it."

He recognizes freely that this communist book or person has attitudes and goals which he shares as well as ideas and values which he does not share.

He realizes that at times he experiences cooperation as meaningful and valuable to him, and that at other times he wishes to be alone and act alone.

Valuing in the Mature Person

The valuing process which seems to develop in this more mature person is in some ways very much like that in the infant, and in some ways quite different. It is fluid, flexible, based on this particular moment, and the degree to which this moment is experienced as enhancing and actualizing. Values are not held rigidly, but are continually changing. The painting which last year seemed meaningful now appears uninteresting, the way of working with individuals which was formerly experienced as good now seems inadequate, the belief which then seemed true is now experienced as only partly true, or perhaps false.

Another characteristic of the way this person values experience is that it is highly differentiated, or as the semanticists would say, extensional. As the members of my class of prospective teachers learned, general principles are not as useful as sensitively discriminating reactions. One says, "With this little boy, I just felt I should be very firm, and he seemed to welcome that, and I felt good that I had been. But I'm not that way at all with the other children most of the time." She was relying on her experiencing of the relationship with each child to guide her behavior. I have already indicated, in going through the examples, how much more differentiated are the individual's reactions to what were previously rather solid monolithic introjected values.

In another way the mature individual's approach is like that of the infant. The locus of evaluation is again established firmly within the person. It is his own experience which provides the value information or feedback. This does not mean that he is not open to all the evidence he can obtain from other sources. But it means that this is taken for what it is—outside evidence—and is not as significant as his own reactions. Thus he may be told by a friend that a new book is very disappointing. He reads two unfavorable reviews of the book. Thus his tentative hypothesis is that he will not value the book. Yet if he reads the book his valuing will be based upon the reactions it stirs in him, not on what he has been told by others.

There is also involved in this valuing process a letting oneself down into the immediacy of what one is experiencing, endeavoring to sense and to clarify all its complex meanings. I think of a client who, toward the close of therapy, when puzzled about an issue, would put his head in his hands and say, "Now what *is* it that I'm feeling? I want to get next to it. I want to learn what it is." Then he would wait, quietly and patiently, trying to listen to himself, until he could discern the exact flavor of the feelings he was experiencing. He, like others, was trying to get close to himself.

In getting close to what is going on within himself, the process is much more complex than it is in the infant. In the mature person, it has much more scope and sweep, for there is involved in the present moment of experiencing the memory traces of all the relevant learnings from the past.

This moment has not only its immediate sensory impact, but it has meaning growing out of similar experiences in the past. It has both the new and the old in it. So when I experience a painting or a person, my experiencing contains within it the learnings I have accumulated from past meetings with paintings or persons, as well as the new impact of this particular encounter. Likewise the moment of experience contains, for the mature adult, hypotheses about consequences. "I feel now that I would enjoy a third drink, but past learnings indicate that I may regret it in the morning." "It is not pleasant to express forthrightly my negative feelings to this person, but past experience indicates that in a continuing relationship it will be helpful in the long run." Past and future are both in this moment and enter into the valuing.

I find that in the person I am speaking of (and here again we see a similarity to the infant) the criterion of the valuing process is the degree to which the object of the experience actualizes the individual himself. Does it make him a richer, more complete, more fully developed person? This may sound as though it were a selfish or unsocial criterion, but it does not prove to be so, since deep and helpful relationships with others are experienced as actualizing.

Like the infant, too, the psychologically mature adult trusts and uses the wisdom of his organism, with the difference that he is able to do so knowingly. He realizes that if he can trust all of himself, his feelings and his intuitions may be wiser than his mind, that as a total person he can be more sensitive and accurate than his thoughts alone. Hence he is not afraid to say—"I feel that this experience (or this thing, or this direction) is good. Later I will probably know *why* I feel it is good." He trusts the totality of himself.

It should be evident from what I have been saying that this valuing process in the mature individual is not an easy or simple thing. The process is complex, the choices often very perplexing and difficult, and there is no guarantee that the choice which is made will in fact prove to be self-actualizing. But because whatever evidence exists is available to the individual, and because he is open to his experiencing, errors are correctable. If a chosen course of action is not self-enhancing this will be sensed and he can make an adjustment or revision. He thrives on a maximum feedback interchange, and thus, like the gyroscopic compass on a ship, can continually correct his course toward becoming more of himself.

Some Propositions Regarding the Valuing Process

Let me sharpen the meaning of what I have been saying by stating three propositions which contain the essential elements of this viewpoint. While it may not be possible to devise empirical tests of each proposition in its entirety, yet each is to some degree capable of being tested through the methods of science. I would also state that though the following propositions are stated firmly in order to give them clarity, I am actually advancing them as decidedly tentative hypotheses.

1. *There is an organismic base for an organized valuing process within the human individual.*

It is hypothesized that this base is something the human being shares with the rest of the animate world. It is part of the functioning life process of any healthy organism. It is the capacity for receiving feedback information which enables the organism continually to adjust its behavior and reactions so as to achieve the maximum possible self-enhancement.

2. *This valuing process in the human being is effective in achieving self-enhancement to the degree that the individual is open to the experiencing which is going on within himself.*

I have tried to give two examples of individuals who are close to their own experiencing: the tiny infant who has not yet learned to deny in his awareness the processes going on within; and the psychologically mature person who has relearned the advantages of this open state.

3. *One way of assisting the individual to move toward openness to experience is through a relationship in which he is prized as a separate person, in which the experiencing going on within him is empathically understood and valued, and in which he is given the freedom to experience his own feelings and those of others without being threatened in doing so.*

This proposition obviously grows out of therapeutic experience. It is a brief statement of the essential qualities in the therapeutic relationship. There are already some empirical studies, of which the one by Barrett-Lennard is a good example, which gives support to such a statement.

Propositions Regarding the Outcomes of the Valuing Process

I come now to the nub of any theory of values or valuing. What are its consequences? I should like to move into this new ground by stating bluntly two propositions as to the qualities of behavior which emerge from this valuing process. I shall then give some of the evidence from my own experience as a therapist in support of these propositions.

4. *In persons who are moving toward greater openness to their experiencing, there is an organismic commonality of value directions.*

5. *These common value directions are of such kinds as to enhance the development of the individual himself, of others in his community, and to make for the survival and evolution of his species.*

It has been a striking fact of my experience that in therapy, where individuals are valued, where there is greater freedom to feel and to be, certain value directions seem to emerge. These are not chaotic directions but instead have a surprising commonality. This commonality is not dependent on the personality of the therapist, for I have seen these trends emerge in the clients of therapists sharply different in personality. This commonality does not seem to be due to the influences of any one culture, for I have found evidence of these directions in cultures as divergent as those of the United States, Holland, France, and Japan. I like to think that this commonality of value directions is due to the fact that we all belong to the same species—that just as a human infant tends, individually, to select a diet similar to that selected by other human infants, so a client in therapy tends, individually, to choose value directions similar to those chosen by other clients. As a species there may be certain elements of experience which tend to make for inner development and which would be chosen by all individuals if they were genuinely free to choose.

Let me indicate a few of these value directions as I see them in my clients as they move in the direction of personal growth and maturity.

They tend to move away from façades. Pretense, defensiveness, putting up a front, tend to be negatively valued.

They tend to move away from "oughts." The compelling feeling of "I ought to do or be thus and so" as negatively valued. The client moves away from being what he "ought to be," no matter who has set that imperative.

They tend to move away from meeting the expectations of others. Pleasing others, as a goal in itself, is negatively valued.

Being real is positively valued. The client tends to move toward being himself, being his real feelings, being what he is. This seems to be a very deep preference.

Self-direction is positively valued. The client discovers an increasing pride and confidence in making his own choices, guiding his own life.

One's self, one's own feelings come to be positively valued. From a point where he looks upon himself with contempt and despair, the client comes to value himself and his reactions as being of worth.

Being a process is positively valued. From desiring some fixed goal, clients come to prefer the excitement of being a process of potentialities being born.

Perhaps more than all else, the client comes to value an openness to all of his inner and outer experience. To be open to and sensitive to his own *inner* reactions and feelings, the reactions and feelings of others, and the realities of the objective world—this is a direction which he clearly prefers. This openness becomes the client's most valued resource.

Sensitivity to others and acceptance of others is positively valued. The client comes to appreciate others for what they are, just as he has come to appreciate himself for what he is.

Finally, deep relationships are positively valued. To achieve a close, intimate, real, fully communicative relationship with another person seems to meet a deep need in every individual, and is very highly valued.

These then are some of the preferred directions which I have observed in individuals moving toward personality maturity. Though I am sure that the list I have given is inadequate and perhaps to some degree inaccurate, it holds for me exciting possibilities. Let me try to explain why.

I find it significant that when individuals are prized as persons, the values they select do not run the full gamut of possibilities. I do not find, in such a climate of freedom, that one person comes to value fraud and murder and thievery, while another values a life of self-sacrifice, and another values only money. Instead there seems to be a deep and underlying thread of commonality. I dare to believe that when the human being is inwardly free to choose whatever he deeply values, he tends to value those objects, experiences and goals which make for his own survival, growth, and development, and for the survival and development of others. I hypothesize that it is characteristic of the human organism to prefer such actualizing and socialized goals when he is exposed to a growth-promoting climate.

A corollary of what I have been saying is that in *any* culture, given a climate of respect and freedom in which he is valued as a person, the mature individual would tend to choose and prefer these same value directions. This is a highly significant hypothesis which could be tested. It means that though the individual of whom I am speaking would not have a consistent or even a stable system of conceived values, the valuing process within him would lead to emerging value directions which would be constant across cultures and across time.

Another implication I see is that individuals who exhibit the fluid valuing process I have tried to describe, whose value directions are generally those I have listed, would be highly effective in the ongoing process of human evolution. If the human species is to survive at all on this globe, the human being must become more readily adaptive to new problems and situations, must be able to select that which is valuable for development and survival out of new and complex situations, must be accurate in his appreciation of reality if he is to make such selections. The psychologically mature person as I have described him has, I believe, the qualities which would cause him to value those experiences which would make for the survival and enhancement of the human race. He would be a worthy participant and guide in the process of human evolution.

Finally, it appears that we have returned to the issue of universality of values, but by a different route. Instead of universal values "out there," or a universal value system imposed by some group—philosophers, rulers, or priests—we have the possibility of universal human value directions emerging from the experiencing of the human organism. Evidence from therapy indicates that both personal and social values emerge as natural, and experienced, when the individual is close to his own organismic valuing process. The suggestion is that though modern man no longer trusts religion or science or philosophy nor any system of beliefs to *give* him his values, he may find an organismic valuing base within himself which, if he can learn again to be in touch with it, will prove to be an organized, adaptive and social approach to the perplexing value issues which face all of us.

Summary

I have tried to present some observations, growing out of experience in psychotherapy, which are relevant to man's search for some satisfying basis for his approach to values.

I have described the human infant as he enters directly into an evaluating transaction with his world, appreciating or rejecting his experiences as they have meaning for his own actualization, utilizing all the wisdom of his tiny but complex organism.

I have said that we seem to lose this capacity for direct evaluation, and come to behave in those ways and to act in terms of those values which will bring us social approval, affection, esteem. To buy love we relinquish the valuing process. Because the center of our lives now lies in others, we are fearful and insecure, and must cling rigidly to the values we have introjected.

But if life or therapy gives us favorable conditions for continuing our psychological growth, we move on in something of a spiral, developing an approach to values which partakes of the infant's directness and fluidity but goes far beyond him in its richness. In our transactions with experience we are again the locus or source of valuing, we prefer those experiences which in the long run are enhancing, we utilize all the richness of our cognitive learning and functioning, but at the same time we trust the wisdom of our organism.

I have pointed out that these observations lead to certain basic statements. Man has within him an organismic basis for valuing. To the extent that he can be freely in touch with this valuing process in himself, he will behave in ways which are self-enhancing. We even know some of the conditions which enable him to be in touch with his own experiencing process.

In therapy, such openness to experience leads to emerging value directions which appear to be common across individuals and perhaps even across cultures. Stated in older terms, individuals who are thus in touch with their experiencing come to value such directions as sincerity, independence, self-direction, self-knowledge, social responsivity, social responsibility, and loving interpersonal relationships.

I have concluded that a new kind of emergent universality of value directions becomes possible when individuals move in the direction of psychological maturity, or more accurately, move in the direction of becoming open to their experiencing. Such a value base appears to make for the enhancement of self and others, and to promote a positive evolutionary process.

IMPLICATIONS

To what extent are the differences between various groups—the blue-collar worker, the intellectual, the devout Catholic, the liberal Jew, the Southerner who supports segregation, and the New York integrationist—a matter of values? How does the valuing process differ in two contrasting groups? What would you expect the conventional, conservative, authoritative person to say about Rogers' concept of values in the mature person? What suggestions can you give to a person to convince him that the evaluating process is within himself?

REFERENCES

The topic of values has increasingly held interest for psychologists. Some of the established authors have for some time included a section on values in their major works. Gardner Murphy (1947), Gordon Allport (1961, 1968), and Ross Stagner (1961) are a few of such authors. Recently, Kelley (1971) reviews the psychological contributions to moral values and Feshbach (1971) discusses the morality of violence and aggression. Both include an impressive list of references on the subject.

CHAPTER 11

RESEARCH ON SEX

7

SEXUAL BEHAVIOR:
REVIEWS OF THE KINSEY REPORTS

Abraham Stone

In early 1948, there appeared a thick volume filled with statistical tables and with what seemed, to some curious purchasers, rather dull technical writing. The book, *Sexual Behavior in the Human Male,* rapidly became the second-least-read best seller.

One reviewer of the book said that it contained more dynamite than any other scientific document since Darwin's *Origin of Species.* Another reviewer, a distinguished psychologist, observed that "no one has ever obtained so much information from so many persons regarding the most secret phases of their sexual histories." The author's name, Kinsey, became widely known. More lines were written about the book than it contained. It elicited comment from practically all professional groups, and it was responsibly praised and criticized. Now, a quarter century later, sex attitudes and, possibly, sex behavior in the Western world have undoubtedly been influenced by its publication.

It would be difficult to present the total findings reported in *Sexual Behavior in the Human Male* and in its companion volume, *Sexual Behavior in the Human Female,* by quoting brief selections or the books' summaries. Moreover, the critical reactions and evaluations of the reports are as important as the findings. Kinsey, as a scientist, was frankly interested in the relationship of various classifiable factors to *orgasm*—a somewhat restricted biological problem. However, the orgasm is the climax of a sexual experience, and it has wide ramifications in Western culture. It involves individual *self and social attitudes,* various ambivalent feelings, guilt, and the many responses motivated by these experiences. To introduce Kinsey's revolutionary books, we are giving three reviews published soon after the volumes appeared by writers with different backgrounds who were writing for different audiences.

ABOUT . . . THE HUMAN MALE

Reviewers of books like those by Alfred Kinsey and his co-workers, with so many reported findings, will differ in what impresses them. We see here the emphases of two reviewers of the book, published in two different magazines.

From a review by Abraham Stone, *Saturday Review* (New York: Saturday Review, 1948), pp. 17–18. Copyright 1948 The Saturday Review Associates, Inc. Reprinted by permission of the publisher and Charles Korn, Executor of Dr. Stone's Estate.

Our first selection, a review by a physician and marriage counselor, lists the implications related to (1) the influence of early conditioning, (2) age in relationship to frequency of sexual activity, (3) difference in sex behavior among different social levels, (4) intensity of drive and the age at which the individual becomes adolescent, (5) the moral and medical problems of premarital relations, and (6) the frequency of homosexual relationships.

K INSEY HAS DONE for the present generation what Havelock Ellis did for the previous one. Ellis, with few valid statistical data but with deep insight and understanding, depicted the various manifestations of human sex behavior and opened man's mind to an appreciation of the varieties of human sex patterns. Kinsey and his co-workers, on the basis of a unique collection of sex histories obtained through personal interviews of some 5,000 men, have given us in the present volume a factual and provocative study of male sex behavior which will enrich human knowledge and which is bound to influence markedly man's thinking and attitudes.

The main theme of the Kinsey book is a study of the frequency of male sex experiences, and of the types of "sexual outlets" which lead to orgasm. These two manifestations are analyzed in great, often in minute, detail in accordance with several biological and social factors. They are correlated with the age of the individual, the age at which he becomes adolescent, his educational background, the occupational class to which he belongs, his rural or urban background, and the nature and strength of his religious affiliations.

The emphasis of the study is perhaps too exclusively upon the physical and mechanistic aspects of sex activity. Little attention is given to the psychological and emotional overtones of sex satisfaction—to affection and tenderness and human sentiment as influences in sex behavior. The word "love," for instance, is hardly mentioned and does not even appear in the index. But this is only the first volume and the subsequent ones will perhaps deal more fully with the more subtle aspects of human sex conduct.

At the beginning of the volume, Kinsey states that "each person who reads the report will want to make interpretations in accordance with his understanding of moral values and social significance; but that is not part of the scientific method, and indeed scientists have no special capacities for making such evaluations. Nevertheless, throughout the report, directly or indirectly, bluntly or subtly, in many ways, Kinsey does make interpretations and evaluations" of his findings. He does not, it is true, pass judgment on any form of sexual activity, but he does point out the social implications, and creates an "attitude" in his approach to these problems. . . .

The statistical data collected by Kinsey and his co-workers on the sexual behavior of the American male will be the source of a vast amount of comment, discussion, and debate. Some of the findings have been fairly well known before and will not cause much surprise to the informed reader. There are other data in the report, however, that had hitherto not been recognized that are of tremendous social significance. Many of them have a direct and immediate bearing upon the problems of sex education, marriage, and family living.

What are some of the implications of the Kinsey report?

1. Of basic importance is Kinsey's *emphasis on early conditioning* * as of paramount importance in determining the sex pattern of the individual. The attitudes engendered in childhood may determine a boy's sex pattern for life. This fact may have long been recognized by psychiatrists and child educators, but Kinsey reinforces this knowledge with impressive statistical data. This knowledge will have to filter down to the general public so that parents may re-evaluate their thinking, their attitudes, and their approach in child rearing and development.

2. Also of importance is the question of *age in relation to the frequency of sexual activity.** A fact which had hitherto perhaps not been recognized is that maximum sexual activity occurs in the teens. Boys between sixteen and seventeen have more frequent sexual arousals leading to orgasms than they will have at any other period in their lives. With an increasing lag between the ages at which boys biologically mature and economic security is reached, there is a period of several years in the life of every boy when his sexual drive is apparently at its highest and for which no socially sanctioned outlet has yet been provided. The boy seeks his outlet in various fashions, in masturbation, in petting, in hetero- or homosexual relations— but all of these outlets still have the stamp of social disapproval and are therefore a source of much anxiety and conflict to the individual. What can be and should be done to alleviate the physical and psychological harm thus induced is a problem which the educator, social scientist, religious teacher, and physician will have to face frankly and squarely in the future.

3. The striking *differences in sex behavior among different social levels* * as revealed in the Kinsey report opens a new field for social thinking and social education. Throughout his life, the boy who is destined to have only a grade-school education will differ materially in the degree of his sex behavior and the source of outlets he will seek for his sexual satisfaction from the boy who will go to high school and to college. The psychiatrist and physician, the jurist and the minister who deal with sex problems and sex delinquencies will henceforth have to be much more aware of the educational and occupational background of those who come to them for counsel or before them for judgment.

4. The intensity of a boy's sexual drive is, according to the report, determined to a considerable degree by the *age at which he becomes adoles-*

---

* Editor's italics.

*cent.** The earlier adolescence begins, the more sexually active the boy will be not only during his youth but even in later life. There may be some question about the accuracy of this particular inquiry so far as it depended upon men trying to reconstruct from memory the date of the onset of their adolescence, but if the data are accurate, they show that frequent sexual activity in youth does not impair the sexual capacities at a later age. This is contrary to some statements found in literature on sex behavior and should help to allay many fears and anxieties of young people who have believed that their energies are being "used up" in frequent sexual arousal and orgasm.

As the age at which a boy becomes adolescent depends to a considerable degree upon his constitutional characteristics and the level of his general metabolic processes, it would seem that the degree of a man's sexual capacity is genetically determined. How he will exercise his sexual functions, however, the outlets he will seek for his sexual needs, whether he will resort to masturbation, premarital relations, or other sexual experience—this, according to the Kinsey findings, will be determined by his social culture and other environmental influences.

5. The problem of *premarital relations* * confronts us with two aspects for consideration—the moral and the medical. From the latter point of view, the dangers inherent in promiscuous sex relations before marriage are the spread of venereal disease and the occurrence of unwanted pregnancies. The data show that at college level contraceptives are almost universally used and the incidence of both venereal disease and pregnancies is low. On the other hand, among the grade-school population contraceptives are rarely used, with a consequent high frequency of venereal infections and premarital pregnancies.

6. On the basis of the Kinsey report, the *frequency of homosexual relations* * is high. Kinsey's studies indicate that "at least 37 per cent of the male population has some homosexual experience between the beginning of adolescence and old age." It should be made very clear, however, that unless carefully read and interpreted the 37 per-cent figure may be misleading. It applies to men who have had any kind of homosexual experience in their lives, and in some instances this may have been but a single experience. It would be like assuming that anyone who had ever stolen a penny from his mother's pocketbook should be classed as a thief. Aside from this, however, the figures still show that 10 per cent of men between the ages of sixteen and sixty-five are homosexuals for at least three years and 4 per cent are exclusively homosexuals throughout their lives. This is very much higher than previously reported figures on the incidence of homosexuality in our culture.

How valid are the statistical data presented? . . . A word of caution,

* Editor's italics.

however, is essential. The Kinsey data should not be regarded as final authority on questions of male sex behavior. Kinsey's findings will have to be more adequately supported by physical and psychological studies. . . .

But whether the statistics in this first study are representative of the entire American population or not is really hardly of basic importance. The fact remains that Kinsey has successfully broken through an almost impenetrable wall of taboos, prohibitions, and inhibitions and has explored many "untrodden paths" of human sex behavior. These areas he has clearly marked and charted for those who have sight to read and the will to understand. His report will have immeasurable influence upon the sex mores of our time and our civilization.

MORE ABOUT . . . THE HUMAN MALE
James R. Newman

The second selection, part of a review by James R. Newman, emphasizes the relationship of *social level* to American patterns of sex behavior. Here we get some suggestions as to the interrelationship between the *organic drive factors*, influenced by age and individual constitution, and the *social climate* of a subculture, operating through the family and the neighborhood. This review also discusses Kinsey's findings and the present sex laws. Finally, it includes Newman's discussion of Kinsey's methods of collecting the data.

Class and Sex

No GENERAL STATEMENT about the behavior of the American white male, as a class, is particularly revealing or useful. "There is no American pattern of sexual behavior, but scores of patterns, each of which is confined to a particular segment of our society."

For the purposes of this study, correlations and statistical breakdowns have been made for a number of factors; social level in particular has been measured by three "criteria": (1) educational level attained at termination of formal education; (2) occupational class; (3) occupational class of the person's parents.

The educational levels divide into three categories of duration: 0–8 years; 9–12 years; 13–plus years. Occupational class is broken into nine categories, ranging from laborers, skilled and unskilled, through professional men to the extremely wealthy. (Kinsey says his spectrum runs from "ne'er-do-wells

From "The Proper Study of Mankind," *The New Republic,* February 9, 1948. Reprinted by permission of *The New Republic,* © 1948, Harrison-Blaine of New Jersey, Inc.

to the Social Register," which may involve occasional circularity.) While the terms "upper" and "lower" social level are sometimes ambiguously used, I take it, in general, that "upper level" refers to persons with educational attainments of 13–plus (*i.e.*, at least one year of college), *or* to those in occupational class 7 (professional) or higher.

Kinsey shows no rosy embarrassment in the presence of the terms "upper class" and "lower class." "Social levels are hierarchies which are not supposed to exist in a democratic society, and many people would, therefore, deny their existence." But the fact is that "most persons do not in actuality move freely with those who belong to other levels"; social stratifications are real, and the various groups differ markedly in social custom and in many other areas of practice and belief. A gentleman jockey may, to be sure, not be a gentleman, but there are criteria, even beyond the economic, to distinguish him from a hard-working pickpocket.

The justification for differentiating by social level is strikingly demonstrated by the differences in sexual mores among the several groups. Differences in style of clothing, food habits, table manners, social courtesies, vocabulary, and so on are widely recognized, but Kinsey's findings of marked differences in sexual behavior comes, I think, as a surprise and is, in any case, a major contribution to a fresh appraisal of social problems related to sex.

In total sexual outlet, boys who will stop their education somewhere in grade school will average 20 to 30 per cent higher frequencies (number of orgasms per week) than boys who will ultimately go to college. Presumably these differences cannot be ascribed to formal schooling—since the same grade school holds both groups; thus either social or biologic factors, or both, may be responsible for these differing patterns of behavior.

Remark now one of Kinsey's most startling conclusions. The sexual behavior already discernible in grade school (and certainly fixed by age 16) in terms of both incidence (percentage of any particular group having experience with a particular outlet) and frequency of outlet is that which is usually adhered to with remarkable tenacity *for the balance of the person's life.* "The social-level picture for total outlet among married males is quite the same as for single males. The married males who have the highest total outlet are those who went into high school and not beyond. . . . What is true of populations in their teens usually holds true for those same populations at later ages, throughout the life span."

In the occupational classification the highest total outlet is among semi-skilled laborers, and the next highest in the professional group. It is important here, as will appear immediately, to distinguish between total outlet and frequencies of particular outlets.

The highest incidence and the highest frequencies of masturbation among all single males, at all age levels, are on the college level. In the grade-school group of married males, only 1 to 3 per cent of total outlet comes from masturbation; among the married college group, the outlet from this source begins at 8.5 per cent during early years of marriage and rises to as much as 18 per cent in the later years.

It is in the attitudes on masturbation, premarital and extramarital intercourse, and prostitution that one may see the "most marked of all distinctions between social levels, and this is true whether the calculations are made by educational levels or by occupational classes."

Generally speaking, persons on the lower levels look upon masturbation as "unnatural" (and unnecessary), are less interested in kissing or petting, and find their highest outlet at almost all ages, single or married, in heterosexual intercourse, which they regard as a "natural, inevitable, and desirable thing" whether practiced with wives, companions, or prostitutes. "So nearly universal is premarital intercourse among grade-school groups that in two or three lower-level communities in which we have worked, we have been unable to find a solitary male who had not had sexual relations with girls by the time he was 16 or 17 years of age. In such a community, the occasional boy who has not had intercourse by that age is either physically incapacitated, mentally deficient, homosexual, or earmarked for moving out of his community and going to college."

The silhouette of upper-level behavior is in striking contrast as regards all these factors. The college male, as a result of social restraints, often chooses masturbation and petting as a substitute for intercourse with either companions or prostitutes. In the case of premarital intercourse, for example, the incidence figures are: grade-school level, 97 per cent; high-school level, 84 per cent; college level, 67 per cent. If frequencies are considered, the discrepancy is even more arresting, there being between seven and eight times as much premarital intercourse on the lower as on the higher levels. Again, 74 per cent of grade-school males, unmarried by 25, patronize prostitutes; the corresponding figure for college-bred males in the same class is 28 per cent.

A curious anomaly arises regarding marital intercourse. The college male, having adhered to the mores of his group before marriage, continues to conform afterward by finding 85 per cent of his total outlet in marital intercourse. The percentages for high-school and grade-school males are, corresponding to their mores, somewhat lower. But after a few years, the statistical curves of the lower- and upper-level married groups change direction and cross. By the time the college male is in his fifties, only 62 per cent of his total sexual outlet is in marital intercourse, while grade-school males of the same age find 88 per cent of their outlet in marriage.

"Some persons may interpret the data to mean that the lower level starts out by trying promiscuity and, as a result of that trial, finally decides that strict monogamy is a better policy; but it would be equally correct to say that the upper level starts out by trying monogamy and ultimately decides that variety is worth having."

The explanations, Kinsey admits, are not "quite correct," yet they undoubtedly embody elements of truth. To the extent that upper-level males diminishingly select marital intercourse as an outlet (for other than biologic reasons, such as age) they tend to revert to the premarital outlets of their class, notably masturbation. Kinsey offers the further explanation that the "coital adjustments of this group in marriage are frequently poor, particularly because of the low degree of erotic responsiveness which exists among many of the college-bred females."

For single males, homosexual relations occur most often among those who go to high school, but not beyond; least often in the group that goes to college. For both groups, however, the figures are amazingly high.

The accumulative incidence figure (total percentage of those who have had at least some homosexual contact resulting in orgasm) for single males of the high-school group is 32 per cent in the early adolescent years, 54 per cent of those not married by 30. The college-level percentages are 17 per cent by age 30 (all classes), although the number who ultimately have homosexual experience is 40 per cent of those not married by age 30. Ultimately, also 45 per cent of the grade-school group is involved.

Since many of the men in the army, navy, merchant marine, and similar organizations belong to the high-school educational level, the official announcement that less than one per cent of all American males applying for or inducted into war service were homosexual is not altogether convincing. On the other hand, one may not with wholly unimpaired sanity contemplate the judgment of those psychoanalysts who, as reported by Kinsey, estimate that no less (and, one may hope, no more) than 100 per cent of all males are homosexual.

Obviously, the difficulty of obtaining reliable data on this taboo-cursed activity is, as Kinsey repeatedly emphasizes, extreme. In general, the higher the social level the greater the urge to conceal the practice of "perversion." In regard to masturbation, however, what is "perverse" for a lower-level group may be accepted as a "lesser evil" and therefore scientifically rationalized by a higher-level group. As an example of the variations of cover-up, there is Kinsey's classic history of the army colonel who denied that he had ever had homosexual experience "unless it happened at night when he did not know anything about it." The only other person, according to Kinsey, who gave a similar explanation was a four-year-old boy.

Contrary to the fastidious pretensions of his level, the upper-level male responds much more readily than does his low-level counterpart to a variety of erotic stimuli, many of which would be classed as "vulgar." These would include pictures, burlesque shows, obscene stories, the sight of animals in coitus, love stories in moving pictures, and so on. There is no ready explanation for the difference—it is pointless to assert vaguely that the upper-level male has more imagination—although Kinsey suggests that since the lower-level male "comes nearer having as much coitus as he wants," he may well

"look on such things as the use of pictures or literature to augment mastur-
batory fantasies as the strangest sort of perversion."

American attitudes on nudity are in a sense derived from the British,
who, as Kinsey remarks, are the "most completely clothed people in the
world." Group mores again account for a much higher acceptance of nudity
at upper than at lower social levels. The act of undressing is so often looked
upon, at the lower levels, as an affront to decency, even when executed in
solitude, that many persons at this level "acquire a considerable knack of
removing daytime clothing and of putting on night clothing, without ever
exposing any part of the body." It goes almost without saying that the
attitude toward nudity bears closely on many features of sexual practice.

What are the restraints on premarital intercourse at the various levels?
One of Kinsey's excellent tables provides considerable enlightenment. At
the upper level, more than 60 per cent are inhibited by moral considerations; the same suasion operates among only 20 to 25 per cent of those who
have had, at most, only a high-school education. More than 20 per cent of
college-bred males fear public opinion on their coital activities; at the lower
levels the percentage is about 13 per cent. Fear of veneral disease, on the
other hand, impresses 29 per cent of grade-school males, 25 per cent of
high-school males and 24 per cent of the college males. Lack of opportunity
keeps 35 per cent of lower-level males from this outlet, but operates in the
case of 51 per cent of the upper level.

The item in the table, "Lack of interest in having more," is accompanied
by percentages quite consistent with other data, indicating that at the lower
levels the outlet of heterosexual intercourse is adopted much more frequently than at upper levels. Nineteen per cent of college men show this
apathy, but more than 40 per cent of grade- and high-school men assert
they are affected by indifference. The desire of the male "to marry a virgin"
is strong at all levels, but slightly higher among college males. This of
course cannot really be considered a restraint on intercourse, since there is
the widespread distinction between "the kind of a girl one marries" and
"the other kind."

Even in a practice so old and, as one might have judged, so uniform and
so limited in variability of technique as kissing, there are great differences
of practice depending on social level. What Kinsey calls the "deep kiss,"
which is apparently "a regular concomitant of coital activity among many
of the vertebrates, and particularly among the mammals," is regularly experienced by nine out of ten males of the upper level. Its sanitary implications
exercise no deterring influence on the better educated, even though the
same group would for hygienic reasons disdain use of a common drinking
glass. On the lower level, though a single drinking cup over the sink or in
the water pail is often wholly acceptable, deep kissing is usually thought to
be "dirty, filthy, and a source of disease." The arguments, at both levels,
"have nothing to do with the real issues. They are rationalizations of mores

which place taboos upon mouth contacts for reasons which only the student of custom can explain. Once again, it is the upper level which first reverted, through a considerable sophistication, to behavior which is biologically natural and basic."

This oral phase of sex play deserves particular attention for the light it may throw on the sometimes glib psychoanalytical generalizations respecting oral and anal eroticism.

"Most persons will be surprised to learn that positions in intercourse are as much a product of human cultures as languages and clothing, and that the common English-American position is rare in some other cultures. . . . The origin of our present custom is involved in early and later church history, and needs clarification before it can be presented with any authority. . . . What has been taken to be a question of biologic normality proves, once again, to be a matter of cultural development." Kinsey has abundant data to show that upper- and lower-level practices are widely divergent so far as coital positions are concerned.

The rationalizations of group behavior present a formidable obstacle to the improvement of understanding and forbearance in social attitudes and social action. It is difficult to make headway against deep-rooted customs at every level. Morality and sexual morality are approximately equivalent terms on the upper level; clean, fine, upright, honorable, etc., there "refer primarily to abstinence from socio-sexual relations"; masturbation, if not approved, is at least more readily condoned, and in any case is infinitely to be preferred to premarital intercourse; in the rare instances where unsanctioned coitus may be "forgiven," "love" is involved. At the lower levels, in all sexual behavior, even where moral issues play a part, by and large it is recognized that "nature will triumph over morals."

In studying social implications, assuming one credits Kinsey's findings, the world must be recognized as it is and not as one would want it to be. The sexual advice given by physicians, clinical psychologists, nurses, psychiatrists, marriage counselors, and others with similar responsibility is valuable, informed and enlightened only if it takes into serious account the sex attitudes and practices of the group from which each person stems. The bias of the upper levels is no less a bias because it comes from the upper levels or because it has the prestige and authority of church, state, and learning behind it. Both church and state have been known to err, and the theorems of the science of sex are not as persuasive as the theorem of Pythagoras.

Marriage counseling [writes Kinsey in a brilliant paragraph], as set up today, is based upon concepts of marriage, goals, and ideals which may appear right to the educational level from which the marriage counselors come, and from which most of the counselors' clients also come, but which mean something else in the communities from which a lower-level client may come. The sexual techniques which marriage counsels and marriage manuals recommend are designed to foster the sort of intellectual eroticism which the upper level esteems, and most of which would be anathema to a large portion of the population, and an outrage to their mores. Many marriage counselors would like to impose their own upper-level patterns on their clients, without regard to the complications which may develop when an individual is educated into something that puts him at discord with the mores of the society in which he was raised and in which he may still be living.

Sex and the Law

Our sex laws are a "codification of the sexual mores of the better educated portion of the population." Kinsey finds that the police often evince a better understanding of the vagaries of "delinquents" than do the college-bred judges. Only rarely will an arrest be made for violation of the laws against nonmarital intercourse, an illegal activity which the policeman most likely once practiced or is still practicing without any heavy sense of wrongdoing. "There are policemen who frankly state that they consider it one of their functions to keep the judge from knowing things that he simply does not understand."

While there are judges, from all levels, who have some understanding of the dimensions of the problem, most of them, like ourselves, do not. Considering the hideous taboos involved, the strict legal penalties, the periodic outbursts of the press to round up sex "fiends," and the small number of actual arrests, it would startle most of those (including judges) who assume the law is being enforced to learn that 85 per cent of the total male population has premarital intercourse, 59 per cent has experience in mouth-genital contacts, nearly 70 per cent has relations with prostitutes, between 35 and 40 per cent has extramarital intercourse, 37 per cent has homosexual experience, and 17 per cent of farm boys have animal intercourse—altogether a grand total of 95 per cent of the entire male population involved in illicit activities. The call for a "clean-up of the sex offenders in a community . . . is, in fine, a proposal that 5 per cent of the population should support the other 95 per cent in penal institutions."

The Detective Work

Kinsey's entire work rests on the validity of his statistical data. If these are badly astray, his findings and conclusions are equally astray. Fully cognizant of this dependency, he has described his methods of investigation, including his interviewing technique, in some detail, setting forth the drawbacks and advantages of each step in the process with admirable candor.

If, then, there are misgivings with respect to his report, he deserves candor in return.

Specialists undoubtedly have grounds for complaint and criticism as well as much to be grateful for. There are not a few, as Kinsey has foreseen, who are sharpening their knives and heating the cauldron in anticipation of the feast at which Kinsey will be the main dish. But even from the standpoint of the general reader, there are understandable doubts as to the accuracy of many of Kinsey's results.

Each person interviewed was asked between 300 and 570 questions. These were asked at a rapid-fire rate in order (a) to cover the necessary ground in a feasible time, (b) to provide a "check" on fabrications. According to Kinsey, this staccato tempo is an effective check "as detectives and other law-enforcement officials well know."

This sounds to me a bit of precious nonsense bearing no relation, except by opposites, to sound scientific method. It may indeed have been necessary to ask that many questions, and to ask them rapidly in order to cover the ground, but there is no use pretending that the method was intrinsically desirable. Above all, Kinsey, who has dispelled so many vulgar errors, must realize by now that the phrase "as everybody well knows" is merely another way of saying "there is no shred of evidence to prove."

The answers given by the subjects were subsequently cross-checked, examined for internal consistency, correlated with findings of other studies, subjected to statistical tests, and in a number of cases there were "retakes." Other steps included a comparison of answers between spouses and a detailed comparison of the separate results obtained by each of the three principal interviewers.

Reservations

No one who has examined these correlations will doubt the impartiality and competence of the investigators; it remains that this is not the same thing as giving unqualified credence to the results of their work. Kinsey himself reminds us of this point repeatedly. Especially the data on total outlet and frequencies of particular sexual outlets must be scrutinized with the greatest care, periodically re-examined and correlated with fresh data. The age factor will in part determine what is and is not remembered, and at certain ages persons may exhibit peculiar attributes for recalling experiences which could not be recalled at another age.

Group attitudes may well have significant influence on the power of recall, although Kinsey, who deliberately omits any but brief references to psychological factors, scarcely examines the point. Surely the capacity for recalling, let alone uttering, descriptions of events involving sex behavior strongly disapproved by one's own group must differ from that of recalling events only mildly disapproved or fully accepted. If an individual, despite the attitude of his group, admits to an action strongly disapproved, the probability is high that he is speaking the truth. But what of the opposite case?

On balance, one should expect incidence, and perhaps frequency data, on such outlets as homosexuality and animal contacts to be low. Some males will boast, others will cover up; some of Kinsey's subjects were ready to talk to him (or to one of his associates) "in a few minutes" after being introduced, revealing their innermost intimacies at a headlong pace; others were extremely reluctant, and had to be coaxed, wined, dined, and socially stimulated before they would spout. The interviewing of children raised unusual obstacles, but the indefatigable interviewers were not to be discouraged. Kinsey's description of the interviewer "tussling" with a four-year-old boy while asking him whether he kissed neighborhood females of the same age, makes a memorable tableau in the history of science.

There are also some curious passages about the importance of looking people "square in the eye," a technique which will be regarded as an innovation in scientific method. At one point, in discussing the validity of his data, Kinsey claims no more than that the individual record is at least "not wholly specious." Elsewhere, in answer to the inquiry how an interviewer knows whether people are telling the truth, he asserts almost contemptuously, "As well ask a horse trader how he knows when to close a bargain"—a dangerous analogy.

Final Estimate

I must fall back on a trite phrase. None of the deficiencies to which I have alluded detracts seriously, in my opinion, from the great, solid virtues of the Kinsey report or fatally undermines the organic soundness of its foundations. It may well be, as Kinsey himself re-emphasizes throughout, that few portions of the data are free of uncertainties, and that some of the statistics, while the best hitherto available, should be regarded with the most cautious skepticism. Yet the report as a whole in its major composites and correlations, in its silhouettes of group patterns and trends, constitutes a chart to which the social scientist must accord the most careful attention. To reject it on the ground that it is statistically unreliable would require, by parity of reasoning, the flat rejection of most of the social and medical sciences, since their statistical bricks have at least as much straw.

ABOUT . . .

THE HUMAN FEMALE: 5,940 WOMEN

Staff of Time *Magazine*

The findings of the Kinsey team of investigators are just as startling for the female as for the male. The book, *Sexual Behavior in the Human Female,* corrects some commonly held notions about the sexual attitudes and behavior of women. Are the differences in sexual behavior found to exist between men and women the same as those perpetuated in the folklore? Certain relationship between *age and sex outlet* was found in the study of males. Does this exact relationship hold in the case of the female? How do women *differ* from men in what arouses and satisfies them sexually? These are a few of the questions answered by the study and reviewed in this magazine article, which was published shortly after the book appeared.

The Key Findings

From what he has learned, within these limitations, Kinsey is convinced that a sexual revolution has taken place in the United States in the last thirty years, with women's behavior changed even more sharply than men's. His key findings about U.S. women:

They are by no means as frigid as they have been made out, and their sex lives often become more satisfactory with age.

Almost exactly 50 per cent have sexual intercourse before marriage (compared to 83 per cent of U.S. men, as reported in Kinsey's first volume).

About 26 per cent have extramarital relations (compared to 50 per cent of the males).

Ancient and modern myths which have pictured women as practicing fantastic secret perversions have little basis in fact. These aberrations are far commoner among the men, and the myths represent "the male's wishful thinking, a projection of his own desire . . ."

The Big Change

The Gibson Girl of half a century ago, whaleboned into an hourglass shape, almost never heard the word "sex." It was a relatively new scientific term, to be distinguished from "love," which was too idealized, and "lust," which was too blunt.

Probably the Gibson Girl never heard of "petting" either, but if she was a late model (born in the 1890's and therefore included in Kinsey's sample), the chances are four out of five that she indulged in it under another name. Says Kinsey: "Many consider petting an invention of modern

American youth—the by-product of an effete and morally degenerate . . . culture. It is taken by some to reflect the sort of moral bankruptcy which must lead to the collapse of any civilization. Older generations did, however, engage in flirting, flirtage, courting, bundling, spooning, mugging, smooching, larking, sparking . . ." But the late Gibson Girls rarely went further. If their testimony to Kinsey held back nothing, only one out of seven unmarried women born in the nineties had sexual intercourse by age 25, though the proportion jumped to two out of five by age 40.

Once married, there was a four-to-one chance that the girl who had been raised under Queen Victoria's long shadow would remain faithful to her husband, no matter how often he might be unfaithful to her. The double standard was still secure.

Then came the big change.

It happened, according to Kinsey's figures, around the end of World War I. The causes were various. Kinsey cites the writings of Havelock Ellis, one of the first scientists to combine psychology and biology, and Sigmund Freud, who put the spotlight on sex as a cause of human behavior. Of more immediate effect on the United States was the draft army, which threw together men from all walks of life and exposed 2,000,000 of them, overseas, to standards more sophisticated than their own. When they came home, they found U.S. women largely emancipated and close to winning the vote. There were other causes to which Kinsey pays little or no heed. One was Prohibition, which helped destroy respect for law and, indirectly, for all authority (and which also taught women to drink). Another was the widespread breakdown of formal religion. Perhaps at the root of all the causes was the inevitable reaction against the prim Victorian era, which itself was not nearly so safe and sound as it appeared. For beneath its placid surface, a social and intellectual revolution had long been rumbling, which enshrined science and progress as twin gods and established a view of man as a creature governed more by "environment" than by preordained morality.

By the mid-1920's, the new century seemed to be talking (and worrying) more about sex than previous ages. "Frankness" became a respectable pose for cocktail parties, parent-teachers' meetings, and literature. The novelists —Hemingway, D.H. Lawrence, and later Erskine Caldwell and Faulkner— were blatantly detailed, and behind them stood the anthropologists and psychoanalysts with their case histories. But the generation still had no Kinsey. It was left to him to clothe the subject in the sober, convincing, guaranteed-to-be-scientific garb of statistics.

Frigidity

When the Gibson Girls' daughters arrived on the scene, cloche-hatted flappers, short-skirted and prattling about repressions, this is what happened to the sex lives of U.S. women, according to Kinsey:

The number of women who went in for petting jumped to 91 per cent among those born in the first decade of the century, and to 99 per cent among their kid sisters and their daughters. The proportion of those who would carry petting, as Kinsey puts it, "to the point of orgasm" rose from one fourth to more than half.

Among women born in the early 1900's, intercourse before marriage was twice as frequent as among those born in the nineties. More than one out of three lost their virginity by age 25, and three out of five, if they were still unmarried at 40.

These more daring women of the restless generation enjoyed marriage more. Kinsey takes sharp issue with psychiatrists and a few gynecologists who have estimated that anywhere from one third to two thirds of U.S. women are frigid. Even during the first year of marriage, when the most drastic adjustments have to be made, three wives out of four reach complete fulfillment at least once. Between the ages of 21 and 40 they attain it from 84 per cent to 90 per cent of the time. In sum, says Kinsey, about three quarters of all sexual relations within marriage end in a satisfactory climax for the wife. However, he reports no case of a woman who attained climax 100 per cent of the time.

Most women born before 1900 had enjoyed no such fulfillment. Many of them, according to Kinsey, did not know that it was possible for a woman to have an orgasm, and if they did know, they thought it was "not nice." Now, says Kinsey, who puts great stock in quantitative analysis: "To have frigidity so reduced in the course of four decades is . . . a considerable achievement which may be credited, in part, to the franker attitudes and the freer discussion of sex which we have had in the U.S. during the past twenty years and to the increasing scientific and clinical understanding . . ."

Fidelity

Among Kinsey's sample of women who had premarital intercourse, one third had relations with from two to five men, more than half with only one man—and 46 per cent only with the fiancé in the year or so before marriage. Are these women sorry? No. Whether they had later married or not, about three fourths said they had no regrets, and 12 to 13 per cent had only "minor" qualms. Among those who avoided intercourse before marriage, nine out of ten said they had done so primarily for moral reasons.

There have been other changes. A full third of the women born before 1900 told Kinsey that they wore night clothes during sexual intercourse. Now, more and more U.S. couples are having intercourse without covers or clothes (all but 8 per cent of today's newlyweds), and sleep "in the raw."

Most societies, remarks Kinsey in an anthropological aside, have a double standard about marital fidelity. A few, though they take a dim view of a woman who strays openly, covertly condone her actions if she is discreet and her husband does not become particularly disturbed. That, suggests Kinsey, is "the direction toward which American attitudes may be moving."

Among the 2,480 married women in his sample, one fourth eventually had relations outside marriage by age 40. The rate rose from 6 per cent in the late teens and 9 per cent in the twenties, to 26 per cent in the thirties and early forties. Women with different family and social backgrounds behave about the same, but the infidelity rate goes up with education: 31 per cent among those who have been to college, against 24 per cent of high-school graduates.

As for what Kinsey calls "other sexual outlets": 62 per cent of the women in his sample had masturbated at some time in their lives, but the activity was, for most, not continuous. (At some time, 92 per cent of men masturbate, and for most the activity is more continuous than for women). Homosexual relationships are far less frequent among women than among men. The activity is virtually confined to unmarried women or those no longer married; a fifth of all Kinsey's subjects had had some such experience by age 40; one fourth of the unmarried, only 3 per cent while married. (Among unmarried men, half; of the married, 4.6 per cent.)

But unlike homosexual males, many of whom change partners frequently, half of these women had had only one partner, and one fifth had had only two.

Age and Sex

Many who profess not to be shocked by Kinsey's findings dispute them on the coldly factual basis that Kinsey has only his subjects' word that they are telling the truth. To this, Kinsey can only reply that he does the best he can to insure accuracy by a kind of cross-reference questioning, so that a subject who has lied at the beginning of the interview will expose himself near the end. Beyond this, he has re-interviewed hundreds of subjects after lapses of two to ten years and they have told substantially the same story; this rules out carefree, offhand lying. However, Kinsey has found that males who have not gone beyond grade school are less reliable informants than the more highly educated, and probably they have exaggerated their juvenile conquests. Similarly, he concedes, women are likely to cover up, so that some of their indiscretions before or after marriage might not show up in his figures.

More important to Kinsey than mere tables of incidence are the underlying biological, physiological and psychological factors which determine sexual behavior. Kinsey believes that he has found out a lot about what men and women must know and do if they are to make a success of marriage.

The answers go back to puberty, and the popular fallacy that girls mature faster than boys. Kinsey notes that girls reach puberty a year earlier than boys, but this is only the beginning of adolescence and is no index to sexual maturity. Boys reach maturity (the height of their physical power for sexual activity) by their late teens, and are already on the downgrade in their early twenties. But the curve of a girl's growing need for sex (or the breaking down of her inhibitions) rises only slowly in her teens, keeps on rising slowly until she is 29 or 30. Even then there is no sharp peak: the curve levels off, leaving a smooth plateau until age 50 or 60. But the man's curve keeps on dropping, *i.e.*, his need for sexual activity generally declines while the woman's stays fairly high. This, says Kinsey, is one of the difficulties he has found in many marriages. It is heightened by the fact that in the early peak years of a man's activity, he resents his wife's seeming coldness. When her coldness has passed, so has his interest—"especially [if she] has previoulsy objected to the frequency of his requests."

What Every Woman Wants

Another common fallacy, says Kinsey, is the idea that the female is slower to respond sexually than the male. Not proved, he says. "Females appear to be capable of responding to the point of orgasm as quickly as males, and there are some females who respond more rapidly than any male." But there is a difference in responsiveness which may explain the common fallacy. It lies in women's psychology.

They are not as easily stimulated to sexual response as are men. Most of them get no reaction from seeing the male form in the nude, from "beef-cake" pictures of undraped athletes, or from erotic stories. What every woman wants, Kinsey has gathered from long hours of listening, is "a considerable amount of generalized emotional stimulation before there is any specific sexual contact." This is an ancient truth, known to scientists in the field and every successful husband, now confirmed by Kinsey's massive statistics.

IMPLICATIONS

You have read three reviews of the on-going studies by Kinsey and his co-workers on American sexual behavior. What comments impressed you most? What remarks in the reviews motivate you to read the original volumes for further facts and discussion?

To what extent can the findings about the sexual behavior of thousands of individuals, representing various backgrounds and personal organizations, have significance for a *single individual?* We really know nothing about the personality of the interviewed individual, of his thoughts, emotions, and the state of his physical or mental health.

74

We are not told of his reactions to these sexual experiences or what motivational insecurities may have led to them. Some reviewers of these volumes, including the psychiatrist Karl Menninger, have reminded us that Kinsey has forced human sexual behavior into a zoological frame of reference and thereby neglected human psychology. It has been pointed out that the orgasm of a loving husband in the arms of his wife differs from that of a desperate homosexual trying to prove his masculinity. Why do you think Kinsey has regarded sex primarily as a biological reaction? What effect does this have on the interpretation of his findings?

Will these volumes, as the contents become known, reduce the widespread *guilt* felt from unconventional sex episodes? And how is guilt-lifting compatible with rational ethics and morality? Doubtless, sex is a strong biological urge in the years of youth, but so are the taboos and social consequences of impulsive sexual union. Would a case study of the individual and the conditions that led up to his behavior and his entanglements, the guilt or scandal that resulted, give us a more realistic picture of the *total person* in his attempt to make an adjustment to his urges as well as to his self-respect and integrity?

REFERENCES

Consult the Bibliography for reference to a thorough review by the veteran psychologist Terman (1948), an evaluation by the psychiatrist Menninger (1953), and the original volumes of Kinsey, Pomeroy, and Martin (1948), and Kinsey, Pomeroy, Martin, and Gebhard (1953). Since then, Gebhard and others (1965) have published a book on sex offenders.

SEXUAL INADEQUACY: MASTERS AND JOHNSON EXPLAINED

Nat Lehrman

Several paperback books written for popular consumption have described the pioneering work on sexual behavior by Masters and Johnson (see references at the end of this section). The following excerpt is from such a book, authorized by Masters and Johnson. It presents a description of the patients and the treatment of dysfunctions, using a journalistic style.

> *This chapter represents a short, explanatory tour through the key concepts in Masters and Johnson's clinical report on the psychology of sex and the treatment of sexual problems in marriage. Intended as a supplement rather than as a substitute for a reading of the text, it should help the reader put the subtle and complex concepts of the work into perspective. Anyone truly wishing to appreciate the momentously new and important theories of* Human Sexual Inadequacy *should take the time to make an extended visit with that book.*

The Patients

FIFTY PERCENT of all marriages in this country are beset with some form of sexual inadequacy, ranging from serious problems (e.g., impotence, frigidity, premature ejaculation) to lesser complaints such as unequal levels of sexual response. This is the opinion of William H. Masters and Virginia E. Johnson, director and associate director of the Reproductive Biology Research Foundation, a clinic whose aim is to improve the quality of some of these marriages, and ultimately to train other therapists to treat the rest.

And make no mistake about it—the foundation treats *marriages*, not only the sexual component thereof. A sexual distress does not develop in a vacuum; rather, it reflects the accumulation of the partners' backgrounds and personalities combined with their marital interaction. If a male is impotent, or a wife nonorgasmic, the other partner cannot claim to be "uninvolved": More than any other kind of intercourse, the sexual kind represents a mutual feedback situation. In fact, in many cases of sexual distress, the partner will have a complementary sexual difficulty: 44 percent of all couples who came to the foundation for treatment suffered from such dual dysfunctions.

The total number of patients treated by the foundation during the period 1959–1969 (11 years, during which records were kept for analysis in *Human Sexual Inadequacy*) was 790. As just mentioned, some of these represent both sides of a marriage (of 510 couples, 223 had dual sexual distresses, making a total of 446 patients in this category whose treatment was statistically recorded); others represent just the suffering half (287— the ratio here was 60 male distresses to 40 female). There were 54 unmarried males and three single women.

What are the patients like? Mostly American, some Canadian; about 12 percent living right in St. Louis, where the therapy is administered. Socially, the patients are described as middle class and above, with 72.7 percent having had some higher education.

In this period of concern for the underprivileged, the question occurs: Why so many people with financial and educational privileges? Don't "hard hats" ever suffer from soft penises? At first glance, one might attribute the high-income distribution to the ample fee charged by the foundation, plus the cost of travel and living in a St. Louis hotel for two weeks. The charge is $2500 per unit (the "unit" is the focus of treatment—it might be a single-person unit or a marital unit). But the cost doesn't explain everything, because no fee was charged patients during the period 1959–1964, while the program was being stabilized, and since then only 50 percent of the patients have paid a full fee. Twenty-five percent were treated free, and the remaining 25 percent were charged cost ($1250) or less.

Another possible explanation for the dearth of lower-stratum patients is that the psychiatrists and other counselors who refer patients to the St. Louis clinic do not deal with this kind of client. Still another explanation arises from the fact that the double sexual standard is stronger among people of low education than among the middle class. This would account for women in the lower group not *expecting* to have orgasms and for men fearing to report impotence to an outsider because of the tremendous loss of *machismo* it represents. Moreover, among such men, premature ejaculation is probably not considered a dysfunction, but rather the normal mode of operation.

A final explanation is that members of the lower stratum either do not experience or do not recognize as such the problems suffered by better-educated, higher-income men and women. Masters and Johnson, while mentioning all these possibilities, state that they do not yet have the data even to speculate on any of them.

Whatever stratum they represent, all the patients must be screened by a "referral authority." This means they must have undergone treatment—or at least an interview—by a physician, clergyman, psychiatrist, psychologist, social worker or marriage counselor. In many cases, the two-week rapid-treatment program at the foundation is an integral part of a larger regimen of therapy administered elsewhere. For example, an individual diagnosed as neurotic may be undergoing a five-year course in psychoanalysis back home. There is no reason why he cannot interrupt it temporarily for a rapid-treatment reversal of his sexual-dysfunction symptoms; in fact, this may help speed his general recovery. On the other hand, Masters and Johnson point out that sexual dysfunction is not *always* a symptom of a psychiatric problem; it is often caused by little more than pervasive ignorance, both of sexual physiology and of human relations.

Some exceptions to the foundation screening rules: They will not accept acute psychotics, and they will accept physicians and clinical psychologists who refer themselves (there were 89 couples in the program in which either the husband or wife or both had had medical training).

The Treatment

The rapid therapy administered at the Reproductive Biology Research Foundation takes a total of two weeks and consists of a combination of interviewing and physical-therapy sessions that are practiced by the distressed couple in the privacy of their hotel or rented apartment. The ultimate purpose of the therapy is to restore sex to its natural context, so that it functions, as it should, like breathing—spontaneously and without conscious effort. Sex, of course, is unique among physiological functions in that it can be delayed and denied indefinitely. This quality can be a great advantage in a busy, complex society, because it allows us to defer our sexual impulses when they are untimely or inappropriate. But somewhere along the road to building our society, we confused the healthy, civilized control of sexuality with almost total repression of it. Those who suffer most acutely from this confusion are the patients at the foundation. They have to be helped—by word and deed—to breach the formidable barriers their life experiences have erected against their natural desires.

The first step in this direction consists of history taking with the emphasis on relating the patients' sexual past to their basic personality structure and to the context of the rest of their lives—in other words, their sexual value system. The couple is informed up front that the interviews will be taped and that they will not be asked to perform as subjects for laboratory experiments. The format of the first day's history is male therapist with male patient, female with female.

On the second day, the therapist-and-patient teams are switched, and the interviews are structured on material obtained the preceding day.

The third day includes medical examinations and a roundtable discussion among the husband, wife and therapists. The foursome format emphasizes that it is the marital relationship not its members that is being treated. During the roundtable, one of the most important concepts in sexual dysfunction—*the spectator role*—is explained in detail. Using the example of erective inadequacy, the therapists explain how the impotent male suffers from being overaware of his (and his partner's) responses. Instead of becoming immersed in the natural sensory feelings that accompany the growth of an erection, he tries self-consciously, by the numbers, to will the raising of his penis with his mind, literally setting his intelligence apart from his senses, so that it is a "spectator" observing an action unrelated to it. The bedroom spectator can no more influence the stiffening of his penis than a football grandstander can cheer a pigskin across the line. The erection must occur naturally, like breathing, or it will not occur at all.

The wife in this situation often becomes a spectator, too. Leaving her own sensory responses, she places her mind outside the arena and observes her progress and her partner's progress—or lack of it. Frequently she herself becomes so absorbed in the spectator role that she's unable to respond when the opportunity is provided.

By the end of the third day, the patients have given clues to the therapists about their individual sexual value systems—what turns them on and what turns them off—and they have heard authoritatively suggested forms of sexual interaction that might have been unfamiliar—or even forbidden—to them. From then on, the aim of the therapy will be to help the patients lose the negative values of the SVS, retain the positive ones and add new experiences and values that are appropriate to their ongoing relationship.

Implicit in the Masters and Johnson therapy is the evidence that people with sexual dysfunctions have been negatively conditioned to sex during their formative years. The therapists attempt to decondition the inhibiting values and recondition new, positive values (see Chapter 7 for a description of the relatively new science of behavior therapy). Negative-type values, usually learned early in life when comparatively few experiences are required to make an enduring mark, were explained individually in earlier sections of this chapter. Just to recapitulate with a single example, the little girl's hand is slapped when she touches her genitals; she may become conditioned to a "no-no" reaction when her genitals are touched at any time in later life—even by herself or her husband, because the person who slapped her hand did not attempt to distinguish for the child when it is appropriate or inappropriate to touch.

Masters and Johnson attempt not only to decondition these negative values, but they try to recondition new ones that will be remembered with positive connotations when the patients resume their normal lives. The therapists assume that the only *psychological* constant in human sexual response is the memory of pleasurable sensate reactions. It is these memories that, when combined with the input of a new experience, serve to facilitate the signals from the brain to the genitals that result in uninhibited sexual response.

The therapists attempt to initiate this relearning process by starting with the senses. Since they are central to sexual response, an effort is made to bring the patient back into contact with them (bearing in mind, as just explained, that he has become a "spectator" to his sensory reactions because he has lost the ability to *feel* them). The core of "sensate focus," as Masters and Johnson term it, is the sense of touch, because most individuals have been conditioned to associate touch with the communication of such positive emotions as comfort, solace, reassurance, devotion, love and physical need. By refocusing the patient's awareness of his sense of touch, the therapists begin to decondition his physical restraint. The other senses—smell, sight, hearing—are not approached directly, but they come into play and serve as a reinforcement of the touching experience.

The exercises to accomplish this are not introduced until the third day. The couple is instructed to retire to their private quarters at a time when they feel a minimum of stress and tension, when they're rested and don't fear interruption. They take all their clothes off. One of the partners is arbitrarily designated the "giver of pleasure," the other is delegated to "get pleasure." Assuming the giver is the male, he uses his fingers and hands to touch, massage, fondle his partner's body—but not her genitals or her breasts. The "getting" partner simply tries to relax and become enveloped in sensory pleasure. If the giver has some notion of what his partner likes, he pays special attention to it; if he doesn't, a gentle trial-and-error method is used. The only taboos, besides avoidance of the genitalia, are that both partners eschew discomfort, distraction, irritation and any sense of compulsion to verbally communicate their pleasure. This may be the first opportunity, the authors explain, for the couple to have a sensory experience without pushing for orgasm, "without need to explain their sensate preferences, without the demand for personal reassurance, or without a sense of need to rush to 'return the favor.' "

After a while, the partners change assignments and soon begin to lose the initial sense of artificiality. It is at this point that the therapist's role as catalyst begins to diminish and the patients begin to be on their own.

A fascinating discovery serendipitously developed out of the touch therapy. In response to complaints by patients that dry and rough hands distracted from the pleasures of touching and feeling, Masters and Johnson commissioned the creation of a special lotion, which at the same time was used to test fragrance preferences among the patients and to enhance the touching by reducing skin friction. The fragrance tests were abandoned as inconclusive for the present study, but the therapists were unwittingly provided with a useful tool as a result of their lotion experiments. One of the hang-ups experienced by many sexually inhibited individuals is a feeling of discomfort with the sexual fluids—the woman's vaginal lubrication, the man's seminal fluid. Touching each other with the lotions, many of the patients gradually became accustomed to the feel of liquid during a sexual encounter and consequently lost this inhibition.

The exercises designed to enhance "sensate focus" are continued through the fourth day of therapy, after which permission is given for the couple to include the genitals and female breasts in their touch sessions. A lesson in sexual anatomy, with specific reference to the husband understanding the female genitalia, is given, and permission is also given for the partners to verbally express enjoyment during their training periods. However, the couple should never be made to feel that this is a necessary part of the "pleasuring" process, because the inhibited type of individual who needs this kind of therapy is frequently distracted by verbalization during sexual activity.

With the termination of the fourth day of therapy—all four days approximately the same for any kind of sexual distress—attention is thereafter directed to the individual's or couple's specific dysfunction.

(A footnote should be added here about "replacement partners and partner surrogates." Obviously, there are individuals suffering from sexual distress who are not married. But since the foundation's techniques are based on interaction between partners, how can they treat an unmarried client? There are two answers. Thirteen men and three women brought partners of their choice to whom they were not married. These were called *replacement partners*. And 41 men were provided with female partners [*not* prostitutes] who volunteered their help to the foundation. These women were called *partner surrogates*. See Chapter 2 for a discussion of this by Dr. Masters and Mrs. Johnson, 1966.)

IMPLICATIONS

In terms of the kinds of therapy discussed in Articles 43, 44, and 46, how can you describe the methods of Masters and Johnson? To what extent do they use reconditioning therapy? Are there other forms of therapy involved? What can you say, in terms of the description of subjects, about the kinds of subjects who are amenable and those who probably are not amenable to this type of treatment?

REFERENCES

Masters and Johnson have published extensively. Their publications are listed in the starred (*) paperbacks below. A major publication is Masters, W.H. and Johnson, V.E., *Human Sexual Response* (Little, Brown and Co., Boston, 1966). * Robbins, John and June, *An Analysis of Human Sexual Inadequacy* (New York, The New American Library, 1970). * Brecher, Ruth, and Edward, *An Analysis of Human Sexual Response* (New York, The New American Library, 1966). Belliveau, F., and Richter, L., *Understanding Human Sexual Inadequacy* (New York, Bantam Books, Inc., 1970).

9 HOMOSEXUALITY—WHY?

Graham B. Blaine, Jr. and Charles C. McArthur

Homosexuality is a personal and social problem as well as a psychological phenomenon. There are strong attitudes about it among the general public. The individual himself experiences conscious fears and vague anxieties, and the lack of understanding by those around him adds immensely to the problem. Often he feels he leads a double life.

An important issue, from the psychological standpoint, is the influence of constitutional or genetic predispositions as well as the complex environment surrounding development—especially interactions with parents. Such factors include *fear of the opposite sex, dependence and self-centeredness encouraged by the boy's mother, lack of interest or hostility on the part of the father,* and *feelings of inadequacy and self-contempt.*

Only recently has the topic of homosexuality been discussed openly in popular media. It is not unusual for a baffling and frightening problem to remain in the "unspeakable" category; many diseases considered incurable and not amenable to scientific study some years ago went through a period in which the public referred to them only in whispers. It is not surprising, therefore, that considerable confusion and ignorance surrounds homosexuality, although the efforts of the Gay Liberation movement to inform the public and to achieve social status for its members will dispel much of the ignorance and negative attitudes that they have hitherto encountered.

Blaine, a psychiatrist, and McArthur, a psychologist, constantly see college students in the university health services at Harvard University. Their article introduces us to the subject of homosexuality and briefly gives the known hypotheses concerning the development, nature, and possible outcome of homosexuality in the college student.

ACCORDING TO KINSEY, over 27 per cent of the young men in America between the ages of seventeen and twenty-five, who have reached the college level in education, have had at least one homosexual experience. This represents a significantly smaller number than those of the same age in the total population who have had a similar experience (36.3 per cent) and seems to be generally consistent with what our experience would lead us to believe to be the prevalence of homosexuality at Harvard.

Making a statistical survey of the prevalence of homosexuality, however, is complicated by the vagueness of the concept. Kinsey, in his work, defined a homosexual experience as a relationship between people of the same sex which leads to orgasm. While this would seem to be a relatively sharp distinction, it does not really tell us very much about the amount of homosexuality which is actually present in a community. Many students have strong homosexual inclinations which they are able to keep so completely under control that they do not engage in any homosexual acts. Other students engage in one homosexual act more or less experimentally, and this one isolated experience serves to solidify their feelings against homosexuality and enables them to put it out of their minds for the rest of their lives. These two types of students obviously distort any kind of statistical analysis of the total situation. The former is often preoccupied so much with thoughts about homosexuality that he should be classified in the homosexual category, while the latter is so briefly concerned with the subject that he does not deserve to be included, and yet, because of his one experience, he would be labeled in Kinsey's statistics as homosexual.

We are a long way from a real understanding of homosexuality. We do not have any clear-cut conclusions to offer about the origin or the causes of this type of deviation. Most psychiatrists and psychoanalysts today seem to feel that a combination of constitutional and environmental factors is involved. There seems to be fairly complete acceptance of the fact that everyone has some degree of homosexuality in his make-up and that there is a variation in amount from one person to another. This variation extends from the rare experiencing of a homosexual dream or a homosexual yearning all the way to the living of a homosexual life with heterosexual desire nonexistent. Although we feel that some people are born with a stronger homosexual instinct than others, we also believe that certain factors in the growth and development of an individual are responsible for the reinforcement or the repression of these instincts.

These factors are, for the most part, concerned with parental characteristics and attitudes. Parents who dress and treat a child of one sex as though he had been born another, even during the earliest stages of the child's development, can have an effect on the sexual orientation of the child during later years. This relatively uncommon treatment of a child is not the only environmental factor, however, which is important. In order for a boy to develop into an independently functioning, normally aggressive man, he must be able to identify to a considerable extent with his father, and this can be accomplished only if he is able to enjoy a relationship with his father in which there is a substantial degree of warmth and closeness. If this cannot be achieved during childhood, it often is sought during adolescence, and it is at this time that substitutes for a cold and rejecting father are sought out. Since adolescence is also a time when sexual impulses are most strongly felt, it is not surprising that the seeking out of a close relationship at this age should be contaminated by some sexual needfulness. It is thought that much of the temporary and sporadic quality of the relationship between homosexuals is due to the fact that each is seeking the gratification of impossible needs—the need of a child for a father—and because of this each homosexual partner in turn is bound to be a disappointment.

The mother, too, plays an important role and can influence her son's future sexual orientation adversely in two strikingly different ways. If she is an overly aggressive, frightening kind of woman who depreciates and humiliates the father, she contributes to the growing boy's picture of all womankind as frightening and dangerous. He then often will feel safer with those of his own sex and grow up preferring their company to that of girls who are associated in his own mind with the dominating and destructive qualities of his mother's personality. On the other hand, we have seen many cases where an overly feminine, seductive type of mother seems to have contributed to the development of homosexual inclinations in her son later in life. This seems to be due in large part to the fact that any introduction of sexuality into the mother-son relationship is felt as threatening and dangerous by the son because of his instinctual feelings of revulsion toward incest. Heterosexual relationships then are associated later in life with these same feelings of disgust in such a way that the burgeoning sexual desires of the adolescent are channeled away from the opposite sex and toward individuals of the same sex instead.

Because adolescence is the time when the first strong outwardly directed sexual impulses are experienced, there is a good deal of confusion in the minds of college boys as to what sort of outlet is most healthy and appropriate. Sexual feeling is at its strongest at this period also, so that whatever degree of homosexuality one may have inherently or as a result of environmental influences is felt more powerfully and urgently during these years. Many students feel and do things at this time which they never repeat again during their adult life. Many students believe, and some physicians agree with them, that this is a time when young men pass through a critical period of choice—a time when their actions and behavior may determine in the period of a few weeks or months their sexual orientation for the entire remaining period of their lives. It is our opinion that this is not a voluntary choice but something which has been predetermined many years before and, for the most part, remains uninfluenced by the ordinary occurrences and encounters during college years. We often see students who feel strongly tempted to experiment with a homosexual experience but fear that doing so will bring about the release of powerful forces within them over which they would then have no control. Their feeling is that they are constantly walking on the brink of the pit of homosexuality and that one misstep will plunge them in forever. Often, however, after they have achieved a more enlightened view of homosexuality, they are able to experiment; and after profiting from the experience by learning more about the details of homosexuality and their own disinclination to pursue it, they can proceed to develop a fulfilling heterosexual life for themselves.

Another manifestation of this fear that homosexuality is lurking deep within and waiting to pounce is the kind of acute panic reaction often seen in students who have suddenly experienced a homosexual dream or a transitory homosexual yearning for a classmate. These students often appear at the clinic in states of extreme anxiety and tension, stating that they have never before been aware of any kind of homosexual feeling and, quite the contrary, have been extremely interested in girls and have had many satisfying heterosexual experiences. They are at a loss to explain the sudden appearance of these obviously homosexual feelings in themselves and are filled with disgust and terror. They are almost always quickly relieved of this anxiety when it is explained to them that there are elements of homosexuality in everyone, and that while they are more than offset by stronger heterosexual elements in most of us, occasionally the homosexual constituent comes into consciousness undiluted and causes a homosexual dream or impulse to flash across the mind.

Many boys come to the service each year for help with the resolution of problems which do not appear, at first, to be associated with homosexuality. Sometimes these center around difficulty in accepting a mode of behavior which may be protecting the individual against the expression of homosexual wishes. This behavior sometimes is not accepted as being appropriate and yet when it is understood that it serves as a replacement for much less socially accepted activities, it can be tolerated by the student without causing him concern.

A student in the Divinity School came to the psychiatric clinic because he was worried about the fact that he preferred to take boy scouts on camping trips to going out on dates with girls. He was disappointed in himself because of this, feeling that it singled him out as different from others. It also made him feel discouraged about the possibility of eventually getting married. In the course of a few interviews, he was able to see that he had never felt any sexual desire for girls, in fact, had no real interest in them at all as individuals, although the general concept of being married appealed to him. He was naturally a very conservative individual and considered that getting married was one of those things which every normal person does. He recalled having had a number of very close emotional relationships with contemporaries during college and told of some homosexual fantasies which he remembered having had at that time. His need for unusually close emotional relationships with men, as well as his fantasies, had been absent since he had been in the Divinity School and taken so much interest in the boy scouts and other youth activities. As a result of therapy he came to understand that while he had no sexual interest in the work he was doing with boys, still it was somehow satisfying to him. By associating with members of the male sex in a helpful and altruistic manner, he was utilizing a defense mechanism in an effective way and by means of it, he was gaining a gratification through companionship with boys which satisfied him to such an extent that his homosexual fantasies were entirely eliminated. This understanding about what was going on within him relieved this student of his anxiety completely. . . .

There are some students for whom the relative strength of heterosexual and homosexual impulse is so close to being equal that they feel continually pulled in both directions. For them, there does not seem to be any possible, complete commitment either to men or to women and they feel constantly disloyal to one or the other. Such students often profit from a series of interviews over a fairly long period of time which are directed toward the achievement of insight into the causes of the conflicting impulses as well as toward the ways in which the student himself can help to resolve specific conflicts when they arise. . . .

Students of college level who have homosexual inclinations behave almost without exception in a discreet and inoffensive manner. They do not attempt to seduce other students; nor do they blatantly proclaim their difference from the average student. They do not constitute a menace and they often come from the most creative and academically productive contingent. The psychiatrist can often allay the fears of administrative officers in this respect.

IMPLICATIONS

Despite the lack of clarity as to whether there are predisposing genetic factors conducive to the development of homosexual tendencies, there seem to be implications in the opinions and studies quoted for healthier psychological climates and relationships within the family. What are they? What mother-son and father-son relationships may prevent homosexual tendencies?

Why is there less discussion of homosexuality in women? Are the same interpersonal relationships between girl and parents factors in encouraging girls to become homosexual? Is there anything the heterosexual person can do to help reduce the personal and social problem of individual homosexuals?

To what extent do you feel that articles devoted to the subject will bring about a more tolerant attitude toward the nonpredatory homosexual who lives quietly and possibly creatively and whose private life is lived within a society of those of similar inclination?

REFERENCES

Another concise discussion of homosexuality as a character disorder will be found in Stern (1965). Cory (1960) is an intimate account of the homosexual and the society in which he lives.

Homosexuality is essentially an individual problem to which some adjust better than others, and it rarely occurs in a personality vacuum. The individual's "ego strength," discussed in Selection 5, is relevant, as is the social milieu in which he lives. Those who are encouraged to make adjustments in a society that accepts their obvious differences and rewards them for their personal contributions seem to make better adjustments. McKinney (1965) presents a case covering approximately twenty years of a homosexual's life.

A modern summary discussion of homosexuality is available on pp. 481–495 of Coleman (1972). Also, see Martin Hoffman's *The Gay World: Male Homosexuality and Social Creation of Evil*. Basic Books. Written by a psychiatrist who treats homosexuals.

CHAPTER *III*

CURRENT ISSUES

10

THE STUDENT ACTIVIST

Leah V. Honea

It is quite appropriate that a student should review the literature on student activism. Mrs. Honea was a graduate student in psychology in 1970 and wrote this paper to meet a class requirement. The paper deals with the background and personality of the student activist. It touches also on the *alienated* and *constructivist* student.

IF POSTERITY REMEMBERS the decade of the sixties for nothing else, it will never forget the upheaval across the campuses of our nations, the dissent, the mass protest, the unrest, the movements for social reform of student political activism. Historians will note the three necessary ingredients contributing to these happenings: (1) the historical setting or cultural climate (our unpopular war in Vietnam, racial problems, and poverty); (2) the physical setting or place (usually the college campus); and (3) individuals (the students with the predispositions for committing themselves to causes and taking stands on issues).

This paper will be concerned with ingredient number (3), the individuals who become involved in current uprisings. Its purpose will be to present a compilation of the research on the background and personality of the student activists and to give some speculations on the causes of these individuals in our society.

Family Background and Parental Attitudes

The general public has often stereotyped the activist student as a recruit from the ranks of the underprivileged and a rebel against a society which has done him personal injustice. But, from all recent research (Craise and Trent, 1967), (Flacks, 1967a), (Bay, 1967), this is definitely *not* the case. The activists are a select group. They come from well-to-do upper-middle-class families in which both parents are highly educated. Most often the father is a doctor, college faculty member, lawyer, or other high status professional, and many times the mother as well has a career (Flacks, 1967a). Obviously, the children of these parents have not been attracted to radicalism because they have been deprived—economically or otherwise.

Another much perpetuated theme that crumbles under authenic research is that these young protestors are rebelling against the traditional established societal values of their parents. Though these students are actively

---

Reprinted by permission of the author.

questioning the values of our society (Block and Haam, 1967), their dominant values are much in line with those of their parents (Fishman and
Solomon). Their parents, however, characteristically hold liberal values,
often not typical of their positions and social status (Flacks, 1967b). Parents of activists as compared to the parents of non-activist students were
found to be significantly more characterized by the following values:

Humanitarianism, or concern for individual development and self-expression and "authentic" behavior, and, also, a real concern for, and a strong
awareness of, the social conditions of others.

Romanticism, or interest in the arts, desire for experience combined with
a love of wandering and a need for a free social environment.

Intellectualism, or concern for ideas and realization of one's intellectual
capacities, appreciation of creativity, knowledge and intellectual activity.
And, there was one value researched that characterizes the non-activist
parents, but did not characterize the parents of activists:

Moralism and Self-control, or opposition to impulsive behavior, concern
with keeping tight controls on emotion, adherence to conventional authority, and conventional morality (Flacks, 1967a).

Thus it is evident that the parents of the activists have the more liberal
values, and it is the parents of the non-activists that hold the conventional,
strictly traditional views.

Child-rearing Practices

Since it has been shown that activist parents have liberal ideas, place
high value on self-expressive and spontaneous behavior, appreciation of
creative actions, and, that they scorn emphasis on self-control and strict
moralism, it is not surprising that their mode of child rearing tends to be
permissive. The politically active students see their parents as permissive
and the parents themselves agree with this concept of their children. These
parents with strongly humanistic values raised their children in an environment relatively free of constraints and favorable to experimentation, expres-
siveness, and autonomous behavior. And, this group of parents with their
interest in aesthetic and intellectual capacities were greatly concerned with
the self-development of their children (Flacks, 1967b).

An equalitarian or democratic environment seems to be another outstanding theme in the families of the activist students. Kenneth Keniston, in his
article "The Sources of Student Dissent," has projected the most likely
family environment of these students:

Given what we know about the general characteristics of the families of
protest-prone students, it also seems probable that the dominant ethos of their
families is unusually equalitarian, permissive, "democratic," and highly indi-
viduated. More specifically, we might expect that these will be families where
children talk back to their parents at the dinner table, where free dialogue and

discussions of feelings is encouraged, where "rational" solutions are sought to every day family problems and conflicts. We would also expect that such families would place a high premium on self-expression and intellectual independence, encouraging their children to make up their own minds and to stand firm against group pressures (1967, p. 120).

Other important attitudes taught in the home are an intrinsic value of knowledge and experience rather than achievement and the "capacity for nurturant identification," or empathy and sympathy with the oppressed and the poor (Keniston, 1967a).

Personality

Personality characteristics of the political students as concluded in several research studies are not unduly surprising when considered in light of their typical backgrounds as reviewed above. Student activists are humanitarian, romantic, intellectual, and "anti" moralistic and self-controlling, much like their parents, but to an even greater degree (Solomon and Fishman, 1964).

Studies show that these youth are also exceptionally high in autonomy, flexibility, and liberalism when contrasted with a more representative sample of the general college population (Somers, 1965; Watts and Wittaker, 1965).

Since most of the personality research of the activist students has been done by contrasting to another "type" of group of students, often the "apolitical" students, the "alienated" students, or the "constructivist" students, it is important and instructive to note the personality differences between them and the activist student.

Christian Bay, in his review of the political vs. the apolitical student, shows the activist as one who *less* frequently than the apolitical student has deeply "repressed anxieties" about his own worth and is less characterized by milder ego deficiencies, such as worry about popularity or career prospects. Bay theorizes that the protest-prone individual is psychologically more healthy, that his views are generally more rationally and independently motivated than his more neurotic and authoritarian-oriented conservative counterpart. He theorized further by comparing the activist to the idealized rebel in the philosophy of Albert Camus who believed that to be fully human you must be revolted by and must rebel against oppression and injustice (Bay, 1967).

Kenneth Keniston, in his book *The Uncommitted*, distinguishes the *alienated* student from the active dissenters. The alienated (whom most would consider the typical "Hippie") are characterized by a great deal of feelings of estrangement from family and the American society in general. They are diametrically opposite the activist students in that they show an extreme *lack* of commitment to people or causes. They did not have the elite and liberal family background of the protesters and, in contrast to them, are rejecting their parents' values. Although they tend to be artistic and talented, they are more likely to be disturbed psychologically and to withdraw into privatism and subjective experience. The alienated student's protest is in nonconformity of dress, behavior, and ideology, but he makes no attempts to change society; he just "drops out" of it (1965b).

The *constructivist* student, like the activist, is much concerned with social reform and also works hard to achieve it. He prefers, however, to use the existing framework and institution to achieve it. The constructivists are the typical Peace Corps and Vista volunteers, workers in mental health, and other individuals in full-time service commitments (Block, Haam, and Smith, 1967). Not unexpectedly, the constructivist and activist personalities show striking similarities in humanitarianism, intellectualism, romanticism, and especially in their rejection of conventional careers, although both groups are usually of the socially advantaged and could easily attain lucrative careers. The one difference in the groups is that political values are likely to be articulated mainly by the activists.

An additional important characteristic of the activist students that has not been brought out in the above discussion of contrasting groups of students is their academic excellence. Somers (1965) found—and several other studies give supportive evidence—that there is a strong relationship between academic achievement and activism, whereas mediocre grades are associated more with the conservatives in the student population. The Selven and Hagstorm (1967) study of the Berkeley population also found a clear relationship between very high grades and libertarians in the senior and graduate divisions, although their data were inconclusive for freshman students. Keniston, in summarizing the many studies in this area from the last three years, says:

> A large and still growing number of studies, conducted under different auspices at different times and about different students, presents a remarkably consistent picture of the protest prone individual. . . . [list of studies] For one, student protestors are usually outstanding students; the higher the student's grade average, the more likely he will become involved in any given political demonstration (1967a, p. 117).

What Produces the Student Activist?

The most probable "cause" of the activist individual has already been implied in this paper—the liberal and humanitarian parents, the equalitarian family structure, the permissive and stimulating home environment in which the children grow up. A recent issue of *Newsweek* magazine carries an article which considers the probability that the permissive child-rearing practices advocated by the famed American authority on child care, Dr. Benjamin Spock, are the "causes" of current student activism; the article asks "Is Dr. Spock to Blame?" (*Newsweek*, Sept. 1968). A cursory reading of the pediatrician's perennial best-seller, *Baby and Child Care*, makes evident that his post-Freudian, freedom- and love-oriented, and relaxed philosophy of child-rearing very much parallels the attitudes found in the parents of the student activists (Spock, 1946, 1st printing). However, it is more probable that both the attitude of these parents and Dr. Spock's suggestions are merely reflections of society's general move away from its past Victorian morality (*Newsweek*, Sept. 1968).

Richard Flacks, who has done so much work on the background and the current personality of the protesters, believes that the catalyst for explosion of dissent is the clash between the youth's democratic, nonauthoritarian upbringing and the college or university, which expects them to submit to its authority, respect its established "status" distinctions, and to participate in its highly competitive status races. It is at school that these students first became aware that society at large expects them to be centrally motivated around values and goals they cannot accept. They are pressured to pursue status goals which to them can only mean hypocrisy and sacrifice of personal integrity (Flacks, 1967b).

To this hypothesis, Sampson adds another factor which tends to increase the chances of the clash of students against established values. This factor is the admission policies and the academic standards of the different campuses which causes a concentration of the protest-prone individuals on the same campuses. This is not to say that certain colleges directly recruit activists, but rather, that their high admission standards, along with their reputations for academic excellence, result in a relatively large proportion of their students being characteristically upper-middle class and very intellectually oriented, which is indicative of an activist person. Also, the recent innovations on most compuses like honors colleges and seminar classes for the top students and abolition of on-campus housing rules have further concentrated these students. Close personal contacts among individuals with similar views serves to strengthen their ideals and commitment to various reform movements.

Various other reasons have been brought forth as causes of these individuals' high degree of protest and outspokenness. Bay (1967) explains it as a result of their great desire and capacity for experience, for challenge, and for awareness of reality. Keniston attributes their reform commitments to their mature morality and sensitivity to world events (1967a). Sampson describes it as part of their "intellectual anti-intellectualism," their vigorous opposition to the rationalization and trends of dehumanization in the world of increasing technology and urbanization (1967).

A good summary of all the studies in this paper is the provocative hypothesis presented in Povl Toussieng's article, "Hangloose Identity, or Living Death, The Agonizing Choice of Growing up Today." He believes protest and dissent among youth reflects their disappointment and dissatisfaction with the false values they are expected to adopt in order to live successfully in their society. They have been reared to be too honest and stubborn to accept false compromise. Toussieng mentions in contrast to the active protesters Keniston's "uncommitted or alienated," or those youth who resolve their conflict with society by withdrawing from it. Also as a contrast, he tells of the so-called "ideal kids" who have surrendered to the pressure and allowed themselves to be fitted into false identity with established, but outdated values; these are the "living dead." Then, to present his view of the activist youth, Toussieng states:

> Between the uncommitted and the living dead there is a large group of youngsters who engage in vigorously independent behavior. Many of these young people are considered delinquent by adult society because they are caught breaking some law. . . .
> A closer look at these "bad" youngsters will reveal that their behavior represents a refusal to choose "living death." These youngsters are stubbornly, clumsily, dangerously, and often vainly searching, and what they seek is a workable ego identity that will lead to adult maturity in the style of the second half of the 20th century.

IMPLICATIONS

See Peterson's reference below, and you can determine what aspect of student life you and your acquaintances emphasize. Those who have been in touch with college students for a few years may be able to judge the tendency of various groups to increase or decrease on your campus.

REFERENCES

Peterson (1968) has considered the entire range of students in higher education and adds other kinds of students to the student groups discussed above. They are vocationalist and professionalist (acquiring skills), collegiates (playboys and extracurricular participants), academics (oriented toward scholarship), intellectuals (oriented toward ideas). See also references cited in the article.

11 PSYCHOLOGY OF WOMEN

Judith M. Bardwick

This selection is the summary of a chapter in a book written by a woman psychologist who has reviewed the available data on women's psychology. Mrs. Bardwick began the review of this literature early in her graduate studies and has led seminars on the subject since then. Her attitude is objective; her goal is to integrate biological and psychological data. To understand some of the literature on the women's liberation movement, one must understand the complex and varying subjective experiences of being a man or a woman in our culture.

Mrs. Bardwick's book is, however, more than a review of the studies of women. The author discusses the crises of development, the independent sense of self, the criteria of self-evaluation, the degree of ambivalence toward one's sex role, and the personal cultural demands in different decades of development.

MANY OF THE THEMES that have been developed in this book can be described in terms of a series of crises that are the process of growing up. A crisis is an unsettled time, a period of stress, in which anxiety about one's esteem, abilities, or identity increases. These *normal developmental crises* *—periods of stress which occur to most or all members of a culture—are also opportunities for growth in psychological health and maturity when they are resolved. At times, males and females may experience similar crises but, overall, the nature and the timing of their sex-linked crises will tend to differ. The development of one's identity is inextricably linked with the development of one's masculinity and femininity, and the crises experienced will be interwoven with the tasks of one's sex-role—its challenges, gratifications and frustrations.

We have suggested that the behavior of infants seems largely an unfolding of personal qualities some of which may be sex-linked, having origins partly in endocrine and central-nervous-system differences. The importance of these qualities and differences is that they enable children to cope more or less well with the tasks appropriate to their ages. Girls seem initially better equipped than boys to perceive cues from people, to appraise responses accurately, to respond verbally—in short, to be "good." The internal

* Editor's italics.

qualities of the boy, his greater size, activity level, impulsiveness, genital sexuality, and externalized aggression in conjunction with the norms of socialization, especially the expectations of parents, result in an earlier stress—on boys who are more likely to be "bad."

I believe that sex is simply a verbal label to a young child. Sex is one of the few attributes which children do not earn, and which does not change as they succeed or fail, as they are good or bad. As a result, in the beginning, one's sex is one of the attributes that children are not anxious about. This changes when masculinity or femininity are defined by qualities that children develop or have to learn, and anxiety about one's "sex identity" begins. Because the cultural criteria for masculinity involve giving up dependency behaviors which are normal to young children of both sexes and because the boy's impulsive aggressive and sexual responses are likely to lead him into trouble, socialization for masculinity and being "good" makes sex identity a crisis and a task much earlier for boys; that is, the range of acceptable behaviors narrows earlier for boys than for girls. While dependent behaviors are perceived as sissyish and motoric aggression is perceived as destructive, the boy is pushed to conform to criteria of goodness and masculinity that force him to adopt styles of behavior that are significantly different from those tendencies he starts with. Compared with boys, until adolescence girls continue to be rewarded by significant adults just as they were rewarded in early childhood, and their natural responses are acceptable or even desirable. Dependence is acceptable, as is independence. Verbal girls use acceptable forms of aggression that do not threaten the authority of adults and, similarly, they do not invoke rejection from adults because of obvious sexual behaviors. We are suggesting that the general tendencies of girls are not likely to lead them into serious confrontations with adults, and simultaneously, that the range of acceptable behaviors, from tomboy to lady, is much wider for girls than for boys. Because girls are more rewarded by adults they have less need to look within themselves for rewards or esteem, and they continue to depend upon others for feelings of esteem. Compared with boys, there is *a delay in the girl's development of an independent sense of self.**

Thus, at about the age of 2 to 2½ boys begin to be pressured to give up their babyish characteristics, notably their dependency and passivity. Simultaneously, they are punished for acting out impulsive, aggressive, and sexual behaviors. At the age of 5 boys typically experience castration fears and know the anxiety that comes from Oedipal wishes. In contrast, I do not believe that young girls typically experience important feelings of rejection, castration, Oedipal jealousies and rages, or genital sexuality.

The differential stresses upon the sexes continue with their entrance into school. The beginning of school is more likely to be a crisis for the boy because he is not as adept as the girl at verbal and cognitive skills and

_____

* Editor's italics.

because the school demands inhibition of muscular impulsivity and aggression. Compared with girls, the boys are immature, less able to cope with the demands of this institution. For boys the early years of school may be perceived as a feminine world, negative and threatening, a place where girls do better, a place where one's masculinity is threatened. The verbally adept girl—neither impulsive nor motorically aggressive, skillfully cued into accurately perceiving the responses of others, modifying her behavior with ease in order to be liked—conforms to expectations and is rewarded with affection and cognitive success. Compared with boys, girls know few crises in the early years of childhood, but of the few the most important are concerned with efforts to secure esteem from others. In many ways we can describe the development of a girl's self-esteem and identity in terms of her interpersonal successes and failures. Does she succeed in interpersonal relationships and evolve a capacity to interact as a confident and autonomous human being? Or does she fail to develop an independent sense of self and thus remain vulnerable in her need to be liked, esteemed, loved by others?

In school, both sexes learn *criteria of self-evaluation* * that are related to mastering tasks. For some years the nature of the tasks—comprehension, memorization, verbal fluency—favor girls. Girls are also likely to be rewarded by their female teachers for their likability and good behavior at a time when one of the important sources of self-esteem is becoming linked to achievement in academics. While the preadolescent boy is becoming involved in needs to lead, to assert himself, to sublimate aggression, girls are occupied with the establishment of peer friendships. To the extent that girls are able to feel assured about the esteem in which they are held by their parents and their teachers, they can turn to peers for new sources of esteem. Dyadic and triadic friendships are characteristic for girls in the preadolescent years of latency, and rejection by friends is cyclic, predictable, and personal. The academically able girl is simultaneously evolving some personal concept of esteem that is based upon objective criteria of achievement at the same time that she is dependent on others and is aware that achievement results in approval from others. My feeling is that compared with boys, girls are not significantly stressed nor pressured until puberty and there is a critical delay in the establishment of an independent concept of the self and internalized criteria of self-esteem.

During latency and on into puberty the boy is unambivalently and increasingly preoccupied with defining himself as masculine. He is rewarded for developing qualities of masculinity and his anxieties are linked to the possibility of failure rather than to negative feelings about becoming a man. Despite stresses, unambivalently, boys value men and want to be men. In strong contrast, prepuberty and especially puberty are likely to be very ambivalent periods in the life of the girl. While the boy may experience

* Editor's italics.

puberty as a genital-sexual and vocational crisis, the girl must come to terms with *ambivalence inherent in the value of being female.** Thus girls may simultaneously enjoy and dislike their femininity, their rewarded qualities of passivity and dependency, their sexual bodies and reproductive functions, and their future traditional role. Despite the lack of stress, girls may not want to become women.

What are the most important crises normal to the adolescent girl? The physical changes of puberty are frightening in their link with blood and pain, and in the future link with pregnancy and childbirth. Simultaneously, these body changes are an assurance of normality and become the cues by which adults and peers perceive that she is no longer a child and is a potential sexual object. Success in affiliative relationships, notably heterosexual relationships, evolves as a more and more important source of esteem (or rejection), and the need to be chosen and loved renders the girl vulnerable to rejection and susceptible to ambivalently experienced sex play. Not experiencing high levels of genital arousal, fearful of pregnancy, aware of internalized moral standards, she is simultaneously responsible for seduction and inhibition. (We can see this conflict most clearly in the unusually lovely adolescent girl who fears that she is esteemed only as a sex object and, frankly, is.) At the same time girls are receiving cues that achievement in school is the preparation for adult professions, and while it is desirable to do well it is preferable not to do "too well." The awareness of competition and its relationship to aggression, and the fear of peer (and parental) rejection for outstanding academics, makes success in school both a source of esteem and a source of fear. Simultaneously the physical and emotional variability that derive from the menstrual cycle, the emphasis on the competitive-cosmetic body, and unresolved repressed fears about the reproductive body render a girl ambivalent about her body, while her body is critically important in terms of her self-esteem and future role responsibilities. Thus we can sometimes see in adolescent girls the beginning of psychosomatic symptoms, especially in the reproductive system.

When we observe girls in high school and in college, we find they have typically evolved different goals from boys and their perceived crises are notably linked to the interpersonal. The concept of the feminine self has become defined by the girls in terms of relationships with men, with the assumption that the primary role tasks will be the nurturant and supportive tasks characteristic of the traditional role. Other sources of esteem derive from peers, parents, and teachers—all of whom support this concept. Intimacy issues, the *capacity to establish and sustain meaningful, important, nondestructive intimate relationships become the major goal* * and the most important crisis during adolescence and the college years.

By adolescence one's sex-role has become an important part of the search for identity for both males and females. The male role is traditionally

* Editor's italics.

defined largely vocationally, but the specifics of the role are open to choice; there is the explicit assumption that no matter what else girls do, they will assume the traditional responsibilities and they will have failed in the task of achieving femininity if they do not succeed in the traditional tasks. Women have a choice between working and not working and men do not. But women do not have the psychological freedom of not marrying while men (to some extent) do.

But internalizing this normative female goal may itself be a crisis. Girls who are in college today do not make the assumption that marriage and motherhood mean giving up their professional aspirations—although it may work out that way. The essence of the conflict is not at the behavioral level; it is internal and psychological. We reward achievement, successful competitiveness, leadership, innovativeness, productivity—and girls know that. To the extent that a girl does not have these qualities or to the extent that she masks them, she really does see herself, her abilities, her potential, her role, as second rate. But simultaneously she does value the traditional qualities and roles and these are part of her own internal criteria of normal achieved femininity. Femininity, when it is defined by the traditional role behaviors and attributes, continues to be an identity that is evaluated by other people and is conceived of in terms of others' responses. Thus, perhaps even more than they did as children, women are motivated to search for esteem that comes from others' evaluations.

When adolescent and college-age girls withdraw from competitive achievement because of fears of failure and because of fears of success, they ensure that their self-esteem will continue to depend upon reflected appraisals and this makes them perceptually attuned to others, empathic but vulnerable. On the other hand, a good, strong affiliative commitment is also their route to feelings of esteem, a sense of self, achieved femininity.

The 1969 Handbook of Women Workers, released by the Women's Bureau of the Labor Department, reports that by the end of 1969 there were 31.4 million women workers. This statistic obviously reveals that very large numbers of American women are fulfilling work responsibilities in addition to their traditional ones. But while they work, few are attempting professional-level careers. (Another recent statistic, compiled by the National Register of Scientific and Technical Personnel, reported that in 1968 only 9 percent of American scientists were women.) One reason for American women's lack of professional participation is the critical salience of affiliative motivations which makes the establishment of marriage the most critical task for girls during their late adolescence and through their twenties. This contrasts strongly with the vocational-achievement goals more typical of boys.

Marriage is the resolution of one identity crisis and the beginning of another. While men are also invested in the development of healthy intimacy, of a strong marriage, they are simultaneously invested in their vocational commitment. The order of priorities is reversed for women; they are overwhelmingly invested in the creation and maintenance of the relationship with far less involvement in professions. *Marriage* * is an enormous commitment, an unmasking of self, a relationship where rejection is searing. Because of their investment in the relationship, because of their history of assessing themselves by others' responses, and because they really do perceive reality in interpersonal terms, they overwhelmingly define and evaluate identity and femininity within the context of this relationship. And it is very difficult. Girls assume the female role-responsibilities without preparation—happy, excited, frightened, and apprehensive. While girls perceive that they are normal, selected, and lovable, they also perceive that they are no longer becoming intellectual, professional, independent. While the establishment of a stable marriage is the most frequent route to self-esteem for the majority of women, in the short run the critical question is whether her husband will support and love her. Simultaneously a source of esteem and identity, marriage also increases needs for reassurance of love.

I believe that, more than any of the preceding developmental tasks, the birth of the first child is ultimately the greatest crisis. A child is a real threat to the marriage partners, not just because of time, fatigue, and money problems, or the incurring of new responsibilities and the loss of some real freedoms, but because of the psychological investment in the child. Parents identify with the child and there is normally a change in the hierarchy of values such that the infant's welfare becomes the first concern; and the infant makes enormous demands. I am impressed by the swift identification of the parents with their child, their delight in the child's achievements and triumphs, and their extraordinary pain when the child is injured. Overall, both parents relate to the child but probably the mother's investment is greater. The birth of the first child means that the wife-mother shifts her psychological needs for emotional gratification from the interpersonal relationship with the husband to the interpersonal but nonetheless more objective relationship with the child. Creating a child is a real achievement and its value does not depend on others' responses.

I think that descriptions of the rewards of early *maternity* * miss the essence of the experience. These are extremely difficult emotions to describe and those who have been there will understand and the rest will think me sentimental. Having a child means that you have created a human being. The words are banal but the emotions experienced are, I think, the most profound one ever knows (with the possible exception of the loss that accompanies death). When laymen talk about motives for conceiving they say things like, "That's what it's all about." The referrent is to life. Observations of my peers, my professionally involved friends, reveal that during the infancy and early years of their children's lives these professionally ambitious and successful women experience the same change in priorities, the same enormous investment in the child. My hunch, and it is no more than

* Editor's italics.

that, is that there is a phylogenetic inheritance that makes maternity the most fulfilling role for women, at least when children are young. Pregnancy and early maternity may be "peak" experiences, the emotion felt toward the child, largely joy.

For most women maternity looms as a critical life task because the internalized values of the culture have defined it as the most important task and symbol of normality and maturity, because it gives them a feeling of having achieved adult status and of having joined the community of adult women, because it is a criterion for self-esteem, and because it is one route to identity and a lifetime of defined behaviors. Ideally, children are conceived in love and are perceived as a commitment to the marriage. Though the reality is often different, this stereotype is widespread.

But maternity is also an ambivalent role. In addition to real curtailments on one's style of life, on freedom and the ability to be spontaneous, child-rearing is a role that we are invested in and one gauges success by the success of the children. Living for children means living through children, potentially crippling the children and failing in the task. While evaluative pressures from society to be a good parent have increased enormously (pathologically?) since World War II, publicized criteria for parental behavior have become too idealistic. It is common to find guilt and anxiety because of presumed parental inadequacy. We also have a tendency to deny the unpleasantness of child-rearing and the psychological cost to the parent.

For the woman who has evolved a self-percept which includes being involved with the outer world, the new small, self-contained, and withdrawn world with young children may be threatening to her self-esteem. She may ask what she has become, who she is, what has she done with her potential. Motherhood is not only a *source of esteem and role definition*,* it can also be a *threat* * to esteem and self-definition. Frequently, mothers are now, in the small nuclear family, dependent upon the husband for some feeling of participation in the real world. This leads to demands for a feeling of participation or an increase in the need to feel important to the husband that he typically cannot fulfill. This is the potential beginning of the wife's romanticism about the world of work—romanticized because she cannot or does not participate in it. Other women will be threatened because their image of themselves was as sophisticated, achievement-oriented, able, outer-directed, independent women. They can become unhappy simply because they are content with the baby within their home.

The particular importance of parenthood for women is that it is simultaneously the gratification of some of their most important needs, an extraordinary source of self-esteem, and a further commitment to the very important marital relationship. It is success within the traditional role and the fulfillment of femininity. It is a most important source of confidence that can enhance those directions begun with the successful establishment

* Editor's italics.

of an important intimate relationship. At the same time, while maternity gratifies affiliative motives, the time-consuming, energy-draining, emotionally invested responsibility of the child-rearing role usually precludes the development of occupational-professional skills. This situation can be satisfactory if achievement-vocational motives are not strong, or while there is a natural redirection of investment from the outside world to the child and to the self, so long as achievement is perceived within traditional nurturing responsibilities. But this total investment in mothering is psychologically dangerous for that part of the population of women who are invested in professional achieving, who perceive traditional activities as second rate, who view themselves as less than perfect parents, who are aware that children become independent and leave home for school, or who are aware that their husbands are increasingly preoccupied with their achievements and there is a psychological separation between man and wife which will become more important when the children are grown. Women can redirect their search for affiliative rewards from their husband to their children, but this maintains their vulnerability—their self-esteem still is based on appreciation from other people.

When role definitions for women are no longer clear or restricted, then freedom of choice can be costly to individual women who are no longer certain of the cultural norms of their own normality. Educated women frequently leave their professions when their children are young and then suffer anxiety because they feel that they are losing their professional-intellectual abilities, because they have ceased developing their potentials, because they feel that their daily housework is repetitive and unimportant. On the other hand, the woman who elects to participate simultaneously in the traditional mothering role and in her professional capacity often feels guilty because her working evokes obvious, surface changes in the family. I mean very simply that she is busy and does not undertake the leadership of the PTA or become a girl-scout leader or take part in other activities that her children and the community perceive as her normal responsibilities. On another level, the dually committed mother can feel anxious about whether she is injuring her children because she is not solely preoccupied with them, whether she is placing stress on her husband, whether her independence, her achievement-oriented self-concept, her professional success, are evidence of her lack of femininity. This is especially likely to be true if she is uncertain about her femininity, if she achieves as well as her husband, or if her profession is atypical for women.

The *breakup of a marriage* * always seems to be a devastating experience to both partners. This seems to be true even when divorce is clearly better than continuing the marriage. Divorce is a personal failure; if there are children there is usually much guilt; there is an economic crisis; and there is the resurgence of the threat of dating with its potential of new rejections.

* Editor's italics.

Divorce evokes tragic feelings of aloneness. Divorce is also the failure of "affiliation achievement," characteristically a woman's most important source of esteem. Divorce is likely to rearouse basic questions of identity because marriage has become one's reference point, the major definition of self. For the woman who never really confronted questions of her own identity, who went from the role-identity of daughter to that of wife, divorce may be the first time, in her aloneness and failure, that she confronts the issue of her values, her needs, her goals. The delay in the evolution of a sense of identity in women, which seems characteristic for women in this culture, makes it plausible and common for identity to be defined by interpersonal roles, notably those of daughter and then of wife and mother. Failure within these relationships or the feeling that the relationships are no longer rewarding enough is most likely to lead to low feelings of esteem and a search for new relationships where critically important rewards will again be forthcoming—or it may lead to giving up and withdrawing from the painful fears of new relationships.

In some ways the years of the thirties can often be perceived as dependent upon the important decisions, commitments, and responsibilities that were made during the twenties. The woman in her thirties is likely to feel that she is going on the momentum of previous decisions and that alternatives, role freedoms, are closing in. There can be conflict if she perceives the reality of her responsibilities and feels that she is the sum of her obligations. Simultaneously, in the decade of the thirties she frequently finds that the time-consuming routine demands of the previous decade have declined and the possibility for new commitments, of expansion, are increasing. The change in responsibilities invites new psychological evaluations, a development that continues into the forties. While on the one hand there are new freedoms, on the other hand there can be a fear of freedom as one realizes the restrictions one has evolved as a consequence of previous commitments. What then, are the consequences of having acted only within one traditional role for so long? Characteristically, women can be afraid because they lack the skills, the confidence, the self-concept that could enable them to participate in the competitive, impersonal, outer-directed, achievement-oriented world of work. Twenty years out of school. Twenty years out of the office. Free of old time-consuming responsibilities, motivated to achieve, to be creative, to find fulfillment, it is an act of courage when these women return to school or profession.

Involved here is not simply a question of filling time, but a question of what it means to *grow older*.* The realization that half of one's life is likely to be over, that one's physical desirability is declining, may force a very new appraisal of values and life patterns. For many the thirties and the forties may be a time when one feels it is imperative to gratify one's needs now because otherwise one may never do so. Statistics tell us that some percent-

* Editor's italics.

age of women resolve this identity question and take advantage of new freedoms by entering into professions, jobs, volunteer activities, or school. For others, there is the real possibility of participation in love affairs, possible divorce, and remarriage.

If the 30- to 40-year-old woman has a good marriage, it is likely to be about fifteen years old. If it is a good relationship, both partners have evolved a marvelous feeling of basic trust—a kind of trust that does not evolve with anyone else. But the marriage has tended to evolve into routines of living and relating, tied up with the realities of coping or the minutiae of tasks. Characteristically, while they may love, they don't feel acutely loving. The crisis of the thirties may become the need to recapture the passions remembered from adolescence and the twenties. Contributing to this development may be the mother's identification with her adolescent children and her envy of their passions. Participation in a love affair can be an attempt to reaffirm one's general lovability, one's sexual desirability, and one's youthfulness. It is simultaneously an attempt to recapture a feeling of being alive, of being aware of feelings. That is, participating in this new relationship, which has the potential for happiness and love, and grief and rejection, is also an attempt to recreate excitements that decline within any routinized experience.

If being loved is the major route not only for self-esteem but for feeling that one exists, then self-esteem is jeopardized when the other participants in these important relationships are invested in themselves, in their tasks, in their accomplishments. In a routinized relationship one can be taken for granted. Similarly, sex within a routinized relationship is not only likely to have become routinized itself, it is also likely to lack that quality of communicating love because the relationship takes that for granted.

In brief, it might be said:

> I love and I am alive.
> I am alive and therefore I love.
> I am lovable; I can love; I am a woman.
> I am not yet middle-aged.

I might add that I think similar motives impel men. Probably more men than women engage in affairs earlier in the marriage because sexuality for men is less likely to be tied to crises in life-stages. That is, sexual motives for men are more closely linked to sex *qua* sex and questions of masculinity and potency, while sex for women is more fused with issues of love, femininity, and identity. This is a matter of degree rather than a significant difference in kind. It is also plausible to hypothesize that investment in new sex-love affairs may occur characteristically later for men than for women because men may be invested professionally during their thirties and because threats to their self-esteem that emerge from changes in their bodies may be more critical in their forties. The establishment of a new heterosexual relationship may, in sum, be a major route for both sexes to reaffirm worth, lovability, and identity.

When parents are *in their forties* * most children are grown and leave home, marry, and establish their own nuclear families. This not only invokes questions about one's identity, it can also cause a separation trauma similar to the mourning process. Some women become widows, and for others the specter of a lonely and empty future becomes perceived as a threatening possibility. Both parents, but especially mothers, are forced to ascertain who they are when they are no longer parents, before they are grandparents. Women experience menopause with its physical symptoms and the psychological implications of the loss of fertility, youth, and, for some, femininity. For some women, new goals and new capacities for self-realization may emerge at this time. For others the loss of identity as mother or wife is the loss of self. For both men and women, the loss of important sources of self-esteem and criteria of identity have to be replaced and new tasks evolved in order to experience a feeling of growing, living, being.

In some ways the data in this book raise questions about the extent of *human variability*.* Endocrine data from animal studies, observations of infants, the longitudinal studies of human beings, and the implications of the endocrine-related effects in adult woman all lend support to the idea that there are differences between the sexes that have, as one origin, differences in the endocrine systems and possible differences in the central nervous system. The existence of these differences implies that there are modal differences in response potentials between the sexes and it further implies that there are likely to be other differences of which we are not yet aware. To the extent that there are physical contributions to the psychological development of human beings, there is likely to be a limit upon changes in the characteristic distribution of traits that can be wrought by different socialization practices. Neither the extent of the physical contribution nor the variability that socialization can effect are presently known. Thus far in history the overwhelming majority of cultures have socialized their children in such a way that original differences between the sexes are maximized. Simultaneously it is obvious that cultures have needed the products resulting from activity directed outward, of achievements resulting in things, and have rewarded those who possess these qualities and increase these contributions. De facto this means that both the personality qualities and the activities that are characteristically and traditionally male have been held in the highest esteem. The derivative of this has been that both the qualities and the activities characteristic of females have been denigrated.

If the self-esteem of women is to be enhanced, either the socialization of girls will alter so that they will be more likely to have "masculine" qualities of independence, activity, and assertiveness, or the values of cultures will

* Editor's italics.

change so that "feminine" humanistic goals—the enhancement of empathy, nurturance and sensitivity—will become esteemed. Or both.

From a psychologist's point of view, many of the problems besetting women can be understood as *internal phenomena* *—motives, anxieties, guilts, fears, low self-esteem. But many of these negative feelings result from *society's preference* * for and reward of occupational achievement and its inhibition of women through legislation, hiring practices, differential pay and prestige, the lack of child-care facilities, and so on. This inevitably leads to anger, especially among aware and educated women. Although I do not expect really radical changes in occupational and familial role-responsibilities (assuming we will not have a major crisis that would make women's professional contributions essential to the economy), large numbers of dissatisfied or angry women can exert pressure simply because of their numbers. It would seem that while revolution is not probable, compromise is inevitable. The extreme proponents of women's liberation movements are a small part of the population, but their extreme position establishes a new frame of reference for the rest of the population. Changes in role allocation that seemed extreme five years ago do not seem so extreme today.

It seems obvious that a society cannot educate large segments of its population to want to and to be able to participate in the larger culture and then effectively prohibit their participation without discontent. The formalization of adult sex-roles not only enhances differences between the sexes, it also goes, in stereotyped form, beyond what is necessary or desirable. I don't believe that one is a human being independent of one's masculinity or femininity but it is equally wrong to ascribe characteristics and limit goals solely in terms of sex. While the sexes appear to have characteristic qualities which are more or less functional in different activities, traditional role divisions have been far too restrictive for both sexes.

I hope that this generation of women will be better able to understand the origins for their motives, the sources of their anxieties, the reasons for their conflicts, and the time perspective of their lives. Then they may be better able to approach nurturance with more confidence, with self-esteem, with the capacity to empathize, protect and enhance—as the result of choice, as a means of realizing more of their potential. And similarly, they may attempt nontraditional achievements, from choice, relieved of anxiety about femininity or normality.

Women have role freedoms that men do not have and restrictions that men do not experience. I do not see that any one pattern of life-style will enable women as a group to achieve happiness. Some women will need to achieve within the occupational-professional sphere; others may feel fulfilled when they transfer their highly developed, active, interpersonal skills of relating, empathy, and nurturance to people outside of their nuclear family relationships. As with work, those typically voluntary activities are likely to

* Editor's italics.

be a source of self-esteem proportionate to one's investment in the task.

As is too often true, happiness is often an elusive goal that exists in some hoped-for future and is the property only of a role one is prevented from participating in. In reality there are no unambivalent roles. But to the extent that members of society feel that their capacities have been severely limited, feelings of resentment, emptiness, and futility pervade.

This generation of college students may be rejecting the traditional middle-class assumption that only occupational achieving is the route to success and self-esteem. Many of my students seem to perceive that their mothers' sole investment in child-rearing was futile—equalled only by the emptiness of their fathers' preoccupation with work. This is an affluent generation which takes money and economic security for granted. Perhaps this sociologic development is limited to the affluent members of a society and will persist as long as affluence does.

But I am equally impressed with the large numbers of 30- to 40-year-old professional men who seem to have achieved success in their occupational goals and who now, in an era of employment opportunities, are changing professions in search of new goals. It is possible that the contemporary women's revolution may be reflecting a larger sociological change wherein everyone is asking himself why he is doing what he is doing. New goals seem to be developing, and they seem to be personal, interpersonal, and humanistic: happiness, creativity, fulfillment, expansion, and personal growth. In order to achieve these goals one needs a fusion of what have been "masculine" and "feminine" qualities. It is not impossible that the women's revolution is the forerunner of a larger revolution in which men and women will experience both role freedom and the responsibility that always accompanies freedom.

IMPLICATIONS

What does this contribution tell you about the development of women, especially the discussion of concepts, such as: criteria of self-evaluation, nondestructive intimate relations, identity crises, esteem, role definition? To what extent are other articles in this volume related to this one? Consider Selections 7, 12, 16, 18, 20, and 28.

REFERENCES

Of the references in the Bibliography, Kinsey et al. (1953) is most relevant to this subject. The original volume from which this summary chapter was taken has an excellent classified bibliography. See reference at beginning of article.

12 BLACK IDENTITY AND PERSONALITY

M. L. Goldschmid

Here we have a social-psychological review of the studies on social awareness and identification, role models for blacks, alienation, and the lack of knowledge about real personality differences between black and white Americans. These studies are a beginning of an objective basis for discussing the problems of the black and white Americans and their relationships.

> *I am an invisible man. . . . It is sometimes advantageous to be unseen, although it is most often rather wearing on the nerves.*
>
> *Then too, you're constantly being bumped against by those of poor vision. Or again, you often doubt if you really exist. . . . It's when you feel like that, out of resentment, you begin to bump people back. And, let me confess, you feel that way most of the time.*
>
> RALPH ELLISON, *Invisible Man*

Introduction

A SENSE OF IDENTITY is a feeling of self or individuality, which is acquired through stages of development as a person interacts and compares himself with others—his family, his peer group, and the larger society. For a positive personal identity to emerge, an individual must receive at least some measure of reinforcement for and *acceptance of his unique characteristics* * and behavior and perceive continuity in his actions and relationships.

Both the formation and stability of individual *identity appear threatened* * by the swiftly changing values and standards of contemporary American society (Stein, Vidich, & White, 1960). Yesterday's "facts" are undermined by today's technological advances. Mass media and rapid means of transportation have expanded our consciousness and "shrunk" the world, forcing us to participate in the fate of distant lands and peoples. Modern

* Editor's italics.

man's great mobility often prevents him from sinking roots. Increasing awareness of the relativity and transitory nature of many of our customs and traditions has resulted in the large-scale rejection of rigidly held standards and morals. Increasing human interdependency and the anonymity fostered by bureaucratic structures have contributed to the creation of the "other-directed" personality and to feelings of powerlessness. Existential psychologists (for example, May, 1967), psychoanalysts (for example, Erikson, 1959; Wheelis, 1958), sociologists (for example, Reisman, 1950; Seeman, 1966), theologians (for example, Tillich, 1952) and others who have addressed themselves to issues attendant upon man's search for identity have suggested that such problems represent modern man's greatest challenge.

Although anxiety and insecurity may accompany the white man's attempts to find and define himself, the black man's struggle for identity is even more arduous. No matter how hard a black individual may try to conform to the dominant culture, the color of his skin prevents him from becoming fully acceptable to large segments of the white population and, often, to himself. Baldwin (1962) asserts that "Negroes in this country . . . are taught really to despise themselves from the moment their eyes open on the world. The world is white and they're black" (p. 65). Thus, while the white person's skin color has relatively little bearing upon his emerging self-concept, *black skin in a white society is a crucial factor in identity development* * (Dreger & Miller, 1960).

An important element of identity is an individual's group membership. As Erikson (1950) has stated, "The growing child must at every step derive a vitalizing sense of reality from the awareness that his individual way of mastering experiences . . . is a successful variant of group identity" (p. 208). Black identity obviously has a multitude of dimensions, but here we shall concentrate on specific aspects of the *interplay between individual and group identity*,* such as racial awareness and identification, the modeling process, and feelings about the larger community.

Racial Awareness and Identification

Ever since the Clarks' classical study (Clark & Clark, 1947), researchers have tried to identify the earliest signs of racial awareness and racial preference. A study by Morland [2],† included in this chapter, was directed at determining North-South differences in racial self-identification between black and white nursery school children. His findings were consistent with his own previous ones and with those of other studies. White children preferred and identified with members of their own race, whereas black children tended to prefer and identify with members of the other race. Thus, it appears that American society encourages *all children to develop a bias in*

* Editor's italics.
† Bracketed and chapter numbers refer to chapters in Goldschmid's book.

*favor of whites regardless of geographical region.** The accentuation of this bias in the South is presumed by Morland to be a result of the segregated southern system, which places even more importance on being white than does the less segregated North. In a similar study, Gregor and McPherson (1966a) assessed racial attitudes of black and white children in segregated elementary schools of the deep South. They suggested that since their black subjects projected a more positive self-image than that reported in studies conducted with northern subjects segregation may well enhance a more "viable self-system." This conclusion is questionable in view of studies reported by Dreger and Miller (in press) and Morland's findings, based on more socioeconomically comparable samples, that only 22 percent of the black children in the South as compared with 46 percent in the North preferred their own race. The results of another study (Gregor & McPherson, 1966b), however, support Gregor and McPherson's line of argument. They found that rural Bantu children in South Africa, who had little contact with whites, showed fewer signs of identity confusion than their urban peers, who were more exposed to biracial interactions. As did black children in the United States, a large majority of Bantus preferred and identified with whites, however. In view of the conflicting results more research is required to determine the influence of relatively segregated or integrated environments upon a black child's emerging self-concept. Richardson and Royce (1968), studying bases for prejudicial discrimination among slightly older American children, found evidence among white children that physical handicaps represent a more powerful stimulus to discrimination than skin color.

Morland (1963) has documented that racial bias develops early. He found that a majority of three-year-olds of both races preferred and identified with whites, even before they were able to make correct racial self-identifications.

How can these consistent and early preferences for whites be explained? The most obvious explanation is that they reflect the inferior status of black people in society. Discriminatory cues are all-pervasive in our environment, through mass media, housing, allocation of funds, and employment practices, so that direct parental communication of prejudicial beliefs might even be unnecessary for a young child to learn to assign less desirable status to black persons. Moreover, generations of slavery and discrimination have inculcated negative self-images in many black parents, who in turn pass them on to their children. Epstein and Komorita's [3] study, which is included herein, addresses itself to the role parental ethnocentrism and punitiveness play in the development of prejudice in black fifth graders. Their findings suggest that strong self-rejection may be the result of an early incorporation of white prejudices. Black children's negative feelings about their own race were associated with their perception of their parents' self-

* Editor's italics.

rejecting attitudes, suggesting that a black child's negative self-concept is in part learned at home. Other parental and personality factors in the child's developing self-concept will be considered in the next chapters.

The *blacks' low self-esteem* * and the inferior position assigned to them by whites may also be related to the traditional meaning of color codes, which are frequently applied to designate racial groups. Williams [4] investigated the meaning of color names used in isolation and as adjectives in the description of people. He found that favorable ratings were assigned to "white," followed by successively more negative evaluations of "yellow," "red," "brown," and "black," by both white and black college students. As would be expected, blacks disagreed with whites, however, with respect to racial concepts. They rate Negro, for example, as good, Caucasian as relatively bad, and a brown person as "more good" than a white or black person. The white subjects' evaluations of colors, on the other hand, were consistent with their most favorable attitudes toward Caucasians, but were less favorable toward American Indians and Orientals, and least favorable toward Asiatic Indians and Negroes.

Many black leaders have recognized that their children need an early positive identification with being black. Increased efforts have taken place to reverse a negative self-image by instilling in very young children a feeling of pride in being "black and beautiful." Indeed, the change in names from "colored" to "American Negro" to "Negro American" to "Black American" or "Afro-American" must be seen as a commitment by black people to articulate a new self-image of which they can be proud (Browne, 1967). The data in Williams [4] and Caldwell, Richardson, Waage, and Dean (1969) suggest how difficult this struggle will be. The negative connotations of black in this culture ("black magic," "blacklisted," "black lies," and associations of black with evil, darkness, and so forth) and the more positive values ascribed to white ("white lie," "whitewash," associations of white with purity, goodness, light, and so forth) appear to be deeply entrenched in the greater proportion of black and white American society as well as in many other cultures. The gap between the two races is further expressed by Williams' finding that "each racial group saw its own racial designation of the other racial group as most similar to enemy and foreigner." (A study by Renninger and Williams [23] which deals with the development of racial concepts in young *white* children is included in Chapter 6.)

Measures of self-concept have been related to such variables as personality characteristics, intelligence, and achievement (for example, Bledsoe, 1964; Boyd, 1952; Combs, 1952; Dreger & Miller, in press; Gibby & Gabler, 1967; Henton & Johnson, 1964; Kardiner & Ovesey, 1951; Keller, 1963; McDonald & Gynther, 1965; Roen, 1960), but, in general, neither definite associations have emerged, nor have the cause-and-effect relationships

---

* Editor's italics.

among different variables been clarified. Coleman et al. (1966) and McGhee and Crandall (1968), on the other hand, have found that black children, who lack a sense of control over their own fate, have lower scores on achievement tests.

Relationships that may exist among dimensions of *self-concept and achievement* * should not be thought of as unidirectional. Not only does a secure self-image enhance adjustment and achievement, but as Erikson (1950) has stated, "Ego identity gains real strength only from the whole-hearted and consistent recognition of real accomplishment, i.e., of achievement that has meaning in the culture" (p. 208). Thus, a vicious circle appears in which many Afro-Americans are ensnared. Centuries of white racism and discrimination have inflicted deep wounds upon the black man's sense of identity and worth, the consequences of which serve to impede his performance in almost all areas of endeavour. Poor performance lowers his self-esteem and appears to provide further evidence for white superiority.

Few rigorous research studies (especially of a longitudinal nature) are available to illuminate the development of the black man's identity. Social scientists (for example, Clark, 1965; Derbyshire & Brody, 1964a; Erikson, 1964, 1966; Pettigrew, 1964a; Proshansky & Newton, 1968; Rainwater, 1966) have begun to address themselves to this problem, however, and some black authors (for example, Baldwin, 1963; Brown, 1965; Cleaver, 1968; Malcolm X, 1965) have given us moving personal accounts of their own lives and feelings.

Role Models

Conflicting pressures are exerted on the growing black individual during his first identification with his subculture, whether this occurs in a middle-class or slum environment. Black leaders represent a variety of role models; their philosophies have ranged from passive submission and patience (often with religious overtones), to passive resistance, to a search for political and economic opportunities, to militant nonviolence, and finally to violent revolt. Thus, attempts to establish cohesiveness and group identity have been frustrated (Lomax, 1960; Comer, 1967). Comer has traced the historical roots of this fragmentation in the black community. (For other historical analyses see also Bronz, 1964; Fishel & Quarles, 1967; Killian, 1968; Killian & Grigg, 1964; Wish, 1964.) Comer points out that a most vicious form of slavery was practiced in America. All elements of African heritage and kinship were systematically destroyed. In addition, rivalries among slaves themselves made it impossible for them to organize effectively. Immediately after the brief reconstruction period following the Civil War, racial antagonism was at its peak and severe segregation laws were introduced and strictly enforced. There followed almost a century of discrimination and

* Editor's italics.

112   M. L. Goldschmid

deprivation, which prevented black people from gaining political and economic power and forging a cohesive group identity. Consequently black people, although American in every way, remain among the *least assimilated minorities in this country.**

Derbyshire and Brody, in a series of studies (Brody, 1961, 1963; Derbyshire, 1966; Derbyshire & Brody, 1964a, 1964b, 1964c; and Derbyshire, Brody, & Schleifer, 1963) involving a variety of samples, have found indications of identity confusion in black Americans "stemming from culture conflict, caste restrictions, and minority status, mediated in part through the family structure" (Derbyshire & Brody, 1964b, p. 202).

In addition to black leaders, whites have served as role models for those large segments of the black community that perceive in their adoption of middle-class values and behaviors an escape from the stranglehold of the ghetto life and a promise that they can achieve security and respect. Maliver's study [5] raised the identification-with-the-aggressor hypothesis among black college students; that is, to what extent can black self-rejection be interpreted as reflecting identification with white aggressor attitudes toward black Americans? His hypothesis was only partially supported by his results. Students who accepted anti-Negro statements demonstrated a negative view of their fathers and a generalized fear of rejection. Rejection of anti-Negro statements, on the other hand, was associated with a positive view of the father and active involvement in the civil rights movement. Bayton, Austin, and Burke (1965) were also interested in the identification-with-the-aggressor theory. Their subjects, also black college students, assigned more positive values to whites on 6 of the 10 personality traits rated, suggesting that they perceived whites to be better adjusted than blacks. The judgments were influenced, however, by the trait being rated, the sex of the person assessed, and the sex of the rater. The authors state that their results reflect a tendency to both idealize the aggressor and incorporate negative views toward the minority group.

As the black child grows up and as pressures to interact with the white community increase, he may be confronted with a new set of values, that which characterizes the dominant middle-class society. Avenues for individual advancement, such as education, employment, and housing, are for most black Americans linked to *white expectations and behavioral norms.** It is not surprising, then, as we have seen in the studies reported above, that many black people incorporate negative views of their own subculture and identify with white middle-class standards. This may be particularly true of upwardly mobile Negroes, the "black bourgeoisie," as Frazier (1957) has labeled them. The next paper included in this chapter, by Parker and Kleiner [6] reports the results of intensive interviews with 1,500 black urban adults to assess the relationship between mental illness and the discrepancy between aspiration and achievement. Their findings support Frazier's thesis

* Editor's italics.

that the black bourgeoisie internalizes the aspirations and standards of the white middle and upper classes. High black status position was associated with acceptance of white attitudes, low preference for blue collar work, a desire for living among whites, weak involvement in racial aspects of a situation, and weak identification with the black community.

Alienation

To many white persons the most "acceptable" blacks are those who become "super-middle-class." This preference exacerbates the split between these blacks and those who remain segregated and impoverished. As each group has grown in number, the distance between poor blacks and those "who have made it" has increased in recent years (Moynihan, 1966). Although the black rural southerner's status has hardly improved, more black people in the North have obtained an adequate education and employment than ever before. On the other hand, living conditions in northern ghettos, which have multiplied as a function of steady emigration of poor southern blacks and high birth rates, have deteriorated. In the process, large segments of the poor black population have become *alienated not only from whites, but also from their more successful fellow blacks.** Members of the black bourgeoisie who are not fully accepted by their ghetto brothers nor by the white bourgeoisie, feel alienated too, although perhaps to a lesser degree than less-educated, lower-class blacks (Middleton, 1963).

Derbyshire and Brody (1964a) discuss the black American's marginality in terms of Merton's (1957) reference group theory. Merton suggests that an individual tends to orient his values according to the normative reference group, which may consist of his membership group (for example, the black community in the case of the black person) or one to which he aspires (for example, the white middle class). Despite the fact that social advancement, in terms of educational, occupational, and financial success, is a principal feature of American culture, racial discrimination and segregation have made the black man's ascent on these dimensions very difficult relative to that of whites. Gerson (1966), for example, has found that black adolescents report that they use and depend on mass media (television, movies, books, and magazines) to a much greater extent than do whites for both norm acquisition and norm reinforcement. Gerson suggests that these results indicate that "many Negro adolescents are using mass media to learn how to behave like whites, i.e., behave in a socially acceptable way" (p. 40).

Although mass media may thus help some black people learn behavior that is rewarded in the larger society, it has also served to alienate many others who find little content that is not expressly geared to white audiences. Television could play a crucial role in presenting black heroes and

* Editor's italics.

black actors portraying real flesh-and-blood characters with whom black children could identify, but it obviously does not. Television programs and commercials, furthermore, feed the rage and despair of the black masses by exposing them daily to a way of life they cannot attain and which they are led to believe the typical white person enjoys. Unfortunately, there is little research evidence available that deals with the role mass media play in the identification and modeling process, despite their crucial importance in the black man's quest for identity.

By giving more black actors meaningful and substantial roles, television could also make headway toward modifying white racism; it is not only the black audience that needs a depiction of the normal black family. It is equally important for the huge majority of whites who lack interracial contact and who have formed their negative stereotypes of the Negro on the basis of old myths and crime and riot reports. The black man's accomplishments as well as his everyday life are excluded from mass media presentations, just as they are from most public-school textbooks (Dreger & Miller, in press). More and more black people are claiming their rights; they no longer want to be ignored. Chapter 7 will further examine the relationship between the black man's drive to find pride and the new militancy and black rebellion.

A final and perhaps more promising aspect of black identity is introduced by the last study included in the chapter. Bullough [7] studied alienation in two groups of well-educated black families, one living in a segregated, the other in an integrated neighborhood. She found that her integrated subjects showed fewer feelings of alienation; they expressed less powerlessness and normlessness. They also were more inclined to orient themselves toward the mainstream of society rather than toward the more limited segregated institutions of the black subculture. Bullough argues for a circular interpretation of ghetto alienation—that it not only results from ghetto living, but also keeps ghetto dwellers locked in their segregated community.

Battle and Rotter (1963) found that lower-class black children demonstrated a significantly stronger belief in external control or reinforcement than did middle-class black and white children. Works (1962) found that improvement in self-concept was more pronounced in black tenants in integrated housing than in black couples in segregated housing. Haggstrom's (1963) results suggested that black couples living in desegregated housing had significantly higher self-esteem and less hostility toward whites than matched couples living in segregated housing.

These results *strengthen the demands* * of "traditional" civil rights leaders *for complete integration* * and promise a more viable identity for those individuals who are able to escape from the constraints of a segregated environment. They also suggest that expecting to control one's own destiny is a result of perceiving that rewards of a particular culture are available.

* Editor's italics.

Personality

Personality may be viewed as a mediator between environmental stimuli and subsequent behavior. Objective personality assessment can be helpful both in describing individual differences along a variety of measurable dimensions (hostility, flexibility, tolerance, and so forth) and in predicting the likelihood of specific behaviors (for example, a person's behavior under stress). Such measures are often difficult to find, owing to validity and reliability considerations as well as conditions of assessment.

When measures of personality are applied to black individuals, problems are further compounded. In comparing black and white subjects on a personality test, for example, should we rely on norms that are typically standardized on white middle-class samples? Will comparisons among black individuals based on white norms be meaningful? The arguments for or against a particular procedure are complex, but generally speaking, those procedures (and norms) are most appropriate which most accurately predict the specific behaviors in which we are interested.

An entire issue of the *Journal of Social Issues* was devoted to the topic of Negro personality (Pettigrew & Thompson, 1964). Pettigrew (1964b) addresses himself to the question of why we know so little about personality features of black Americans. He answers by pointing to the lack of a social-psychological theory, focus on narrow problems, and methodological difficulties that characterize previous research efforts. These problems have already been referred to in Chapter 1 and will not be further elaborated here. Pettigrew (1964a, b) and Megargee (1966) have provided reviews of personality studies including Negro-white comparisons; a recent example is included in the last paper in this chapter. Harrison and Kass [8] express surprise that so few significant and consistent differences between the two races have been found. In their study, they analyzed the Minnesota Multiphasic Personality Inventories (MMPI) of approximately 800 Negro and white pregnant women who visited an urban prenatal clinic serving the lowest socioeconomic classes exclusively. They found only minimal racial differences on conventionally scored MMPI scales. An item analysis, however, revealed striking differences between the two groups, close to half the 550 items being statistically significant. A subsequent factor analysis of the most significant items yielded 20 factors that provided even sharper distinction between the two races. The black group appeared to be relatively more anxious in their thoughts, but less anxious in social situations, less inclined to act out destructive impulses and relatively more introverted, romantic, and religious. Harrison and Kass contend that racial differences (of the order they found) may have been masked in previous studies, which have relied exclusively on scale scores rather than on item responses. Their contention was substantiated by an internal analysis, which revealed that about half the race-significant items in each scale were scored in the direction of the black group, the other in the white direction.

Cameron (1967) was interested in personality differences among black Americans, rather than in differences between whites and blacks. He employed Edwards Personal Preference Schedule (EPPS) and the Perceived Parental Attitude Inventory (PPAI), using over 800 black male and female college students, to investigate regional differences in emotional dependency. He found that the incidence of high dependency was higher among southern blacks (over 40 percent) than among northern blacks (over 22 percent) and border state students (25 percent). He suggested that these results may be "a manifestation of the effects of an oppressive culture and/or a particular child-rearing pattern" (p. 119). He pointed out that in contrast to popular opinion and studies with whites, he did not find sex differences in the incidence of overdependent behavior. As expected, however, overdependent subjects in his sample perceived their parents' discipline to be more physical and restrictive and to demand greater accomplishments than independent subjects. Comparing his results with those obtained from white subjects, Cameron suggests that his own and previous studies point to a much higher degree of emotional dependency among blacks than whites. If this is the case, it may well be a result of black Americans being forced to or choosing to act deferentially and submissively in order to get ahead or merely survive in a white-dominated society.

It is *difficult to say at this point what major personality differences, if any, exist between black and white Americans.** It does not appear as though we have advanced much beyond Pettigrew's evaluation in 1964. The question of why so little is known about racial differences in personality remains, although Harrison and Kass' methodological argument offers one provocative answer.†

IMPLICATIONS

Again, here is a discussion of important psychological concepts, such as identity, self-esteem, self-concept, expectations, and alienation. These concepts apply to other minorities as well. What minority problems do you perceive other than those mentioned in this article?

REFERENCES

The references cited within this article constitute an excellent bibliography to this subject. There is also a book edited by Wilcox (1971) with contributions of black American psychologists on the consequences of being black in America.

* Editor's italics.
† A chapter in Goldschmid's book.

13 PSYCHOLOGICAL ALTERNATIVES TO WAR

Morton Deutsch

One of the most serious problems we face as a civilization is the possibility of a nuclear war. Why, at this stage of our cultural progress, should war be a possibility? What do psychologists and other behavioral scientists know about present-day man and his social milieu that may enable us to understand his potentialities for war or peace?

In the following selection, Deutsch first raises the question of the inevitability of war. He points out the human misunderstandings that lead to war and presents some psychological alternatives. He cites as an example of an important achievement in complex human understanding that between management and union. Deutsch employs such interesting psychological concepts as the *pressure for self-consistency,* which leads to oversimplified views; the *mote-beam mechanism,* which fosters misunderstanding in human relations; and *distorted perception.* He treats a complex problem simply, and illustrates abstract ideas carefully.

I SHALL assume the truth of the following propositions:

1. A large-scale nuclear war would achieve a result that no sane man could desire.

2. When a small war occurs, there is a risk that it may turn into a large war; this risk would be considerably enhanced by the use of nuclear weapons. In the course of many small wars, the probability of a great war would become almost a certainty.

3. The knowledge and capacity to make nuclear and other weapons of mass destruction cannot be destroyed; they will exist as long as mankind exists.

4. Any war in which a nuclear power is faced with the possibility of major defeat or a despairing outcome is likely to turn into a large-scale nuclear war even if nuclear disarmament had previously occurred.

5. A hostile peace will not long endure. From these propositions it follows that, if mankind is to avoid utter disaster, we must see to it that irrational men are not in a position to initiate nuclear war, we must find alternatives to war for resolving international conflicts and we must develop the conditions which will lead conflicting nations to select one or another of these alternatives rather than resort to war.

Reprinted from Morton Deutsch, "Psychological Alternatives to War," *Journal of Social Issues,* Vol. 17, No. 2 (Washington, D.C.: The Society for the Psychological Study of Social Issues, 1962), pp. 97–119, by permission of the publisher and the author.

My discussion in this paper centers primarily on the question of: How do we take the hostility out of the hostile peace? This question proliferates into other, related questions: How do we prevent the misperceptions and misunderstandings in international relations which foster and perpetuate hostility? How do we move from a delicately balanced peace of mutual terror to a sturdy peace of mutual trust? How do we move in the direction of a world community in which law, institutions, obligations, and simple human decencies will enable mankind to enjoy a more amiable life? These are the central questions which must be answered if the world is to avoid disaster. The world will never again be in a position where it cannot destroy itself.

It is well for me to emphasize that opposition to war as a means of conflict resolution does *not* connote an opposition to controversy among nations. Controversy is as desirable as it is inevitable. It prevents stagnation, it is the medium through which problems can be aired and solutions arrived at; it is the heart of social change. Our objective is not to create a world in which controversy is suppressed but rather a world in which controversy is civilized; in which it is lively rather than deadly.

I do not pretend to have answers to the difficult questions I have raised. I raise them because I have something relevant to say and because I believe it is important to confront the fundamental questions. Too often we are distracted from them by short-run urgencies. You may well ask what can a psychologist say that is relevant? A wide reading, however, of acknowledged authorities in the study of war and international relations has convinced me that the dominant conceptions of international relations are psychological in nature. Such psychological concepts as "perception," "intention," "value," "hostility," "confidence," "trust," and "suspicion" recur repeatedly in discussions of war and peace.[1]

I wish to make it clear that what I have to say in this paper is *not* based upon well-established, scientifically verified, psychological knowledge. As psychologists, we have only meager, fragmentary knowledge of how to prevent or overcome distortions in social perceptions, of how to move from a situation of mutual suspicion to a situation of mutual trust, of how to establish cooperative relationships despite intense competitive orientations, of how to prevent bargaining deadlocks. I take it for granted that we need more and better research before we may claim to speak authoritatively on these matters. However, my intent here is not to outline the research which is needed but rather to discuss these urgent matters as wisely as I can. In

---

[1] Perhaps there has been too much psychologizing about these matters; there are, after all, critical differences between persons and nations. Not the least of these is the fact that in a deadly quarrel between people it is the quarrelers who are most apt to be killed while, in a deadly quarrel among nations, the decision-makers are rarely the ones who have the highest probability of dying. Be that as it may, I shall assume that there is some merit in viewing nations, like persons, as behaving units in an environment and to conceive of international relations in terms somewhat analogous to those of interpersonal relations.

so doing, I shall necessarily go beyond the facts to draw upon the insights and orientations which I have developed in a research career devoted to the understanding of the conditions affecting cooperation and in a psycho-analytic practice devoted to helping people overcome their self-defeating attitudes and their interpersonal distortions. The proposals which I make in this paper flow from these personal insights and orientations. They are, I believe, consistent with the meager knowledge that we have; but it is ap-parent that much more research-grounded knowledge is necessary if we are ever to get beyond the stage of "informed hunches." Although my "in-formed hunches" are offered with personal conviction, I hope that you will understand that my research continues and that I do not plan to leave these hunches untested.

Is War Inevitable?

Is it possible that war in inevitable, that the psychological nature of man is such that war is an indispensable outlet for his destructive urges? True, there have been wars throughout human history and men have found out-lets for psychological drives of all kinds in war—sadistic, masochistic, crea-tive, heroic, altruistic, adventurous, etc. Yet, as Jerome Frank . . . has pointed out, the historical prevalence of a behavior pattern is not proof of its inevitability. Human sacrifice in religious rites, slavery, sorcery, certain forms of child labor, etc., have largely disappeared in modern, industrialized nations although such practices have existed throughout human history.

William James, in his classic paper, "The Moral Equivalent of War" (1911), recognized that war and the military spirit produced certain virtues which are necessary to the survival of any society. However, he went on to point out that militarism and war is not the only means for achieving the virtues of self-discipline and social cohesiveness, that it is possible to find alternative means for achieving the same psychological ends. (It is of inter-est to note that James's suggestion for a moral equivalent to war was a "Peace Corps" of youth enlisted in an army against Nature.) The view that alternative means for satisfying psychological motives can always be found is, of course, a basic concept in modern psychology. Egon Brunswick (1952) went so far as to elevate "vicarious functioning" (i.e., the equivalence and mutual intersubstitutability of different behaviors in relation to goal achieve-ment) to the defining criterion of the subject matter of psychology.

Man's make-up may always contain the psychological characteristics which have found an outlet in militarism and war. There is no reason, how-ever, to doubt that these characteristics can find satisfactory outlets in peaceful pursuits. Aggressiveness, adventurousness, idealism, and bravery will take a peaceful or destructive outlet depending upon the social, cultural, and political conditioning of the individual and upon the behavioral possi-bilities which exist within his social environment. Some may assert that war provides a more natural, spontaneous, or direct outlet for hostility and aggressiveness than any peaceful alternatives. Such an assertion is based upon a fundamental misconception of war: war is a highly complex, organized social activity in which personal outlets for aggression and hostility are primarily vicarious, symbolic, indirect, and infrequent for most of the participants. This is especially true for the highly mechanized warfare of modern times which largely eliminates the direct physical contact between the aggressor and his victim.[2] Moreover, it is evident that no matter what his psychological make-up an individual, *per se*, cannot make war. War-making requires the existence of complex social institutions necessary to organize and maintain a "war machine." This is not to say that a war machine cannot be activated by the decision of strategically placed individuals. Obviously, one of the great dangers of our era is that a small group of men have the power to create a nuclear holocaust. Even a strategically placed individual can only activate a war machine if it exists; the mass of people, not being strategically placed, cannot directly activate a war no matter what their psychological predispositions are. It is relevant to note here that research by T. Abel[3] indicates that warlike attitudes in the populace tend to follow rather than precede the outbreak of war.

The impersonal character of modern war, as Erich Fromm (1960) has pointed out, makes it difficult for an individual to comprehend fully the meaning of his actions as he kills. It is easier for most people to kill faceless symbols of human beings at a distance, than to kill people with one's bare hands. Thus, if the airmen of our Strategic Air Command were suddenly ordered to fly to the Soviet Union or China (or if Soviet airmen were ordered to fly to the United States) to drop nuclear weapons, most of them would comply. They would, I assume, be distressed by the thought, but they would comply. Would they comply if the killings were personal —if they had to burn, mutilate, or suffocate the victims one by one? The psychological danger of modern impersonal war is not that it is a good outlet for aggression but rather, to the contrary, that it does not permit the button-pusher to appreciate fully the destructive nature of his actions. Were he to do so, his destructive actions might be inhibited rather than encouraged.

Misperceptions Which Lead to War

Neither war nor peace is psychologically inevitable. Exaggeration of the inevitability of war contributes to a self-fulfilling prophecy: it makes war

[2] War is vastly overrated as an outlet for direct aggressiveness; it does not compare with the directness of reckless automobile driving, a boxing match, or a football game. War is defined to be such a good outlet *only* because of our cultural conditioning: the military toys children are given to play with, the identification of heroism and bravery with war in so many novels, TV dramas, and films that we all are exposed to; the definition of patriotism in military terms in so many of our public ceremonials and holidays, etc.
[3] T. Abel is cited in Jessie Bernard (1957).

more likely. Exaggeration of the inevitability of peace does not stimulate the intense effort necessary to create the conditions for a durable peace: a stable peace has to be invented and constructed. There is nothing inevitable about it.

A fundamental theorem of the psychological and social sciences is that man's behavior is determined by the world he perceives. Perception is not, however, always veridical to the world which is being perceived. There are a number of reasons why perceptions may be distorted. I would like to consider with you five common causes of misperception, to illustrate the operation of each in international relations, and to indicate how these misperceptions can be counteracted or prevented.

1. *The perception of any act is determined both by our perception of the act itself and by our perception of the context in which the act occurs.* Thus, the statement "You did that extremely well" will be perceived rather differently if a captain is saying it to a private than if a private is saying it to a captain. A common source of distorted social perception results from misconceptions or false perceptions of context. The contexts of social acts are often not immediately given in perception and often they are not obvious. When the context is not obvious, we tend to assume a familiar context—*i.e.,* the context which is most likely in terms of our own experience. Since both the present situations and past experiences of the actor and the perceiver may be rather different, it is not surprising that they will supply different contexts and interpret the same act quite differently. Misunderstandings of this sort, of course, are very likely when the actor and the perceiver come from rather different cultural backgrounds and they are not fully aware of these differences. The stock conversation of returning tourists consists of amusing or embarrassing anecdotes based upon misunderstandings of this sort.

Urie Bronfenbrenner's first-hand observations (1961) lead him to conclude that the Soviets and Americans have a similar view of one another; each says more or less the same things about the other. For example, each states: "*They* are the aggressors"; "*their* government exploits and deludes the people"; "the mass of *their* people is not really sympathetic to the regime"; "*they* cannot be trusted"; "*their* policy verges on madness"; etc.

It is my contention that mutual distortions such as those described above arise, in part, because of an inadequate understanding of the other's context. Take, for instance, the Soviet Union's reluctance to conclude any disarmament agreement which contains adequate provisions for international inspection and control. We view this as a device to prevent an agreement or to subvert any agreement on disarmament which might be worked out. However, as Joseph Nogee has pointed out in his monograph on "The Diplomacy of Disarmament" (1960, p. 275): "Under present circumstances, any international control group reflecting the realities of political power would inevitably include a majority of non-Communist nations. Decisions involving actual and potential interests vital to the USSR would have to be made continuously by a control board, the majority of whose members would represent social and economic systems the USSR considers inherently hostile. Any conflicts would ultimately have to be resolved by representatives of governments, and it is assumed that on all major decisions the capitalist nations would vote as a bloc. . . . Thus, for the Soviet Union, representation on a control board along the lines proposed by the West would be inherently inequitable. . . ."

I may assert that one can subjectively test the creditability of the Soviet position by imagining our own reactions if the Soviet bloc could consistently outvote us at the UN or on an international disarmament control board. Under such conditions, in the present world situation, would we conclude an agreement which did not give us the security of a veto? I doubt it. Similarly, one can test the creditability of the American position by imagining that the Soviet Union had experienced a Pearl Harbor in a recent war and that it had no open access to information concerning the military preparations of the United States. Under such circumstances, in the present world situation, would it be less concerned about inspection and control than we are? I doubt it. . . .

How can we prevent and overcome distortions and misunderstandings of this sort? Obviously, more communication, a great increase in interchanges of scholars, artists, politicians, tourists, and the like might be helpful. However, I think we should take cognizance of the findings of the vast body of research on intergroup contact: casual contact of limited duration is more likely to support deeply rooted distortions than remove them. To have any important effect, contact must be prolonged, functional, and intimate.

I suggest that the most important principle to follow in international communication on issues where there is controversy is one suggested by Anatol Rapoport. . . . He advocates that each side be required to state the position of the other side to the other side's complete satisfaction before either side advocates its own position. Certainly the procedure would not eliminate all conflict, but it would eliminate those conflicts based upon misunderstanding. It forces one to place the other's action in a context which is acceptable to the other and, as a consequence, prevents one from arbitrarily rejecting the other's position as unreasonable or badly motivated. This is the strategy followed by the good psychotherapist.* By communicating to the patient his full understanding of the patient's behavior and by demonstrating the appropriateness of the patient's assumptions to the patient's behavior and past experiences, he creates the conditions under which the current validity of the patient's assumptions can be examined. The attempt to challenge or change the patient's be-

* See Selection 43.—Ed.

havior without mutual understanding of its assumptions usually produces only a defensive adherence to the challenged behavior.

2. *Our perceptions of the external world are often determined indirectly by the information we receive from others rather than by our direct experiences.* Human communication, like perception itself, is always selective. The perception of an event is usually less detailed, more abstract, and less complex than the event which is perceived; the communication about an event is also likely to be less detailed and less complex than its perception. The more human links there are in the communication of information about any event, the more simplified and distorted will be the representation of the event. Distortion in communication tends to take characteristic form: on the one hand, there is a tendency to accentuate the unusual, bizarre, controversial, deviant, violent, and unexpected; on the other hand, there is a tendency for communicators who are communicating to their superiors to communicate only that information which fits in with the preconceptions of their superiors.

If we examine our sources of information about international affairs, we see that they are particularly vulnerable to distorting influences. There are only a small number of American reporters in any country; they do not necessarily work independently of one another. They are under subtle pressure to report items which will catch the reader's interest and conform to their publisher's viewpoint. In a period of hostility between nations, these conditions are not conducive to getting a clear understanding of how events are perceived by the other side or a clear understanding of the other's frame of reference.

I suggest that we should recognize the dangers inherent in not perceiving the other side's point of view regularly. Recognizing these dangers, shouldn't we offer to make arrangements with the Soviet Union whereby we would each be enabled to present our own point of view over the other's radio and TV and in their leading newspapers? Suppose the Soviet leaders are afraid to participate on a reciprocating basis, should we make the offer anyway? My answer is in the form of a question: Do we have anything to lose by understanding their viewpoint as well as we can; wouldn't "truth squads" adequately protect us from deliberate attempts to mislead us?

3. *Our perceptions of the world are often very much influenced by the need to conform to and agree with the perceptions of other people.* Thus, in some communities it would be difficult for an individual to survive if he perceived Negroes as his social equals or if he perceived Communist China as having legitimate grievances against the United States. If he acted upon his perceptions, he would be ostracized socially; if he conformed to the perceptions of other people without changing his own perceptions, so that they were similar to those prevalent in his community, he might feel little self-respect.

It is my impression that most social and political scientists, most specialists in international relations, most intellectuals who have thought about it, and many of our political leaders personally favor the admission of Communist China into the UN and favor our taking the initiative in attempting to normalize our relations with Communist China. Yet, conformity pressures keep silent most of us who favor such a change in policy. The strength of these conformity pressures in the United States on this issue is so great that it is difficult to think of Communist China or to talk about it in any terms except those which connote absolute, incorrigible evil. I believe this is an extremely dangerous situation, because without a fundamental change in United States–Chinese relations the world may be blown up shortly after China has acquired a stockpile of hydrogen bombs; this may take less than a decade.

How can we break through the veil of conformity and its distorting influences? Asch's (1956) insightful studies of conformity pressures point the way. His studies reveal that when the monolithic social front of conformity is broken by even one dissenter, other potential dissenters feel freer to break with the majority. The lesson is clear: those who dissent must express their opinions so that they are heard by others. If they do so, they may find more agreement than they anticipate.

4. *A considerable body of psychological research* [4] *indicates that an individual attempts to perceive his environment in such a way that it is consistent with his self-perception.* If an individual feels afraid, he tends to perceive his world as frightening; if he feels hostile, he is likely to see it as frustrating or unjust; if he feels weak and vulnerable, he is apt to see it as exploitative and powerful; if he is torn by self-doubt and self-conflict, he will tend to see it as at odds with him. Not only does an individual tend to see the external world in such a way as to justify his feelings and beliefs but also so as to justify his behavior. If an individual is a heavy smoker, he is apt to perceive cigarette smoking as less injurious to health than a nonsmoker; if he drives a car and injures a pedestrian, he is likely to blame the pedestrian; if he invests in something (e.g., a munitions industry), he will attempt to justify and protect his investment. Moreover, there is much evidence that an individual tends to perceive the different parts of his world as consistent with one another. Thus, if somebody likes you, you expect him to dislike someone who dislikes you. If somebody disagrees with you, you are likely to expect him to agree with someone who disagrees with you.

The danger of the pressure for consistency is that it often leads to an oversimplified black-white view of the world. Take, for instance, the notions that since the interests of the United States and the Soviet Union are opposed in some respects, we must be opposed to or suspicious of anything that the Communists favor and must regard any nation that desires

[4] Much of this research is summarized in various articles in Katz (1960).

friendly relations with the Soviet Union as opposed to the United States. If the Soviet Union is against colonialism in Africa, must we be for it? If nations in Latin America wish to establish friendly, commercial relations with the Communist nations, must we feel threatened? If Canada helps Communist China by exporting food to it, must we suspect its loyalty to us? Are nations which are not for us necessarily for the Communists? The notions expressed in affirmative answers to these questions are consistent with the view that the conflict between the United States and the Soviet Union can only be ended by total defeat for one or the other. But is it not possible that the conflict can be resolved so that both sides are better off than they are now? Recognition of this latter possibility may suggest that what benefits the Soviet Union does not necessarily harm us, and that nations with amicable relations with both the United States and the Soviet Union may be an important asset in resolving the cold war before it turns into a hot one.

The pressure for self-consistency often leads to rigid, inflexible positions because it may be difficult to change a position that one has committed oneself to publicly without fear of loss of face. To some extent, I believe this is our situation vis-à-vis the admission of Communist China to the United Nations and with regard to our policies toward Cuba. We are frozen into positions which are unresponsive to changing circumstances because a change in our positions would seem to us to be admission of mistaken judgment which could lead to a loss of face.

What can we do to avoid the "consistency of little minds" and the rigidities of false pride? These dangers to accurate perception are most likely when an individual feels under threat, when his self-esteem is at stake. I think in such circumstances it is prudent to seek the advice and counsel of trusted friends who are not so emotionally involved in the issues. Thus, I think it would be wise to consult with such nations as Brazil, France, and Great Britain on our policy toward Cuba and Communist China precisely because they do not have as deep an involvement with these countries as we do. Similarly, consultation with more or less neutral nations such as India, Sweden, Austria, and Nigeria might prevent us from developing an oversimplified view of the nature of our relations with the Soviet Union.

5. Ichheiser (1949) has described a mechanism, similar to that of projection, which leads to misunderstandings in human relations: the *mote-beam mechanism*. It consists in perceiving certain characteristics in others which we do not perceive in ourselves. Thus, the characteristics are perceived as though they were peculiar traits of the others and, hence, the differences between the others and ourselves are accentuated. Since the traits we are unable or unwilling to recognize in others are usually traits we consider to be undesirable, the mote-beam mechanism results in a view of the other as peculiarly shameful or evil. Thus, although many of us who

live here in the North easily recognize the shameful racial discrimination and segregation in the South, we avoid a clear awareness of the pervasive racial discrimination in our own communities.

Similarly, in international relations it is easy to recognize the lack of political liberties in the Soviet Union, their domination of the nations in Eastern Europe, their obstructiveness in the United Nations, etc., but it is difficult for us to recognize similar defects in the United States: e.g., the disenfranchisement of most Negro voters in many states, our domination of Latin America, our unfair treatment of the American Indian, our stubbornness in the UN in pretending that the representative from Taiwan is the representative of Mainland China. Since the mote-beam mechanism, obviously, works on both sides, there is a tendency for each side to view the other as peculiarly immoral and for the views to mirror one another.

What can be done to make the mote-beam mechanism ineffective? The proposals I have made to counteract the effects of the other type of perceptual distortions are all relevant here. In addition, I would suggest that the mote-beam mechanism breeds on a moral-evaluative approach to behavior, on a readiness to condemn defects rather than to understand the circumstances which produced them. Psychoanalytic work suggests that the capacity to understand rather than to condemn is largely determined by the individual's sense of self-esteem, by his ability to cope with the external problem confronting him, and by his sense of resoluteness in overcoming his own defects. By analogy, I would suggest that we in the United States will have less need to overlook our own shortcomings or to be fascinated with the defects of others to the extent that we have a thriving society which is resolutely overcoming its own problems of racial prejudice, economic stagnation, and lack of dedication to common public purposes.

While distortions in perception are very common for the reasons I have outlined above, it is also true that, in many instances, everyday experience provides a corrective to the distortions. When reality is sufficiently compelling and when the contact with reality occurs with sufficient frequency, the distortions will be challenged and may yield. However, there are circumstances which tend to perpetuate and rigidify distortions. Let me briefly describe three major reasons for the perpetuation of distortions:

1. A *major psychological investment has been made in the distortion.* As a consequence, the individual may anticipate that giving up the investment will require drastic personal reorganization which might result in personal instability and the loss of social face and might precipitate unknown dangers. Anyone who has done psychoanalytic therapy with neurotic patients knows that no matter how costly and painful it is, a distorted but familiar mode of adjustment is hard to give up until the patient has sufficient self-confidence or confidence in his analyst to venture into unfamiliar terrain.

With regard to international relations, I think we have to consider that a disarmed world, a world without external tensions to justify internal political policies, a world without violence as a means of bringing about changes in the status quo would be an unfamiliar world: a world in which some would feel that their vested interests might be destroyed. For example, I am sure that many military men, scientists, industrialists, workers, and investors fear a disarmed world because they anticipate that their skills and knowledge will become obsolete, or they will lose social status, or they will lose financially. These fears have to be dealt with constructively or else they may produce defensive adherence to the views which justify a hostile, armed world. I suggest that we must carefully plan to anticipate the psychological difficulties in the transition to a peaceful, disarmed world. As a basic strategy to overcome some of these difficulties, I would recommend that we consider a policy of *overcompensating* those who might be adversely affected by the change: we want to change the nature of their psychological investment from an investment in military pursuits to one in peaceful pursuits.

2. *Certain distorted perceptions perpetuate themselves because they lead the individual to avoid contact or meaningful communication with the object or person being perceived.* This is especially true when the distortions lead to aversion or hostility toward the object being perceived. For example, for reasons which go back to my childhood and about which I am not clear, I have a strong aversion to coffee, becoming nauseated at the thought of drinking it. As a consequence, I avoid coffee and my aversion is perpetuated. Newcomb (1947) has described a similar process of *autistic hostility* in interpersonal relations in which a hostile impulse may give rise to barriers to communication behind which a persistent attitude is protected. Similarly, in international relations, hostile attitudes between the United States and Communist China produce barriers to communication which eliminate the possibility of a change in attitudes. Here, the best antidote would seem to be communication which followed the rules of procedure suggested by Anatol Rapoport.

3. Merton, in his classic paper on *The Self-fulfilling Prophecy* (1957), has pointed out that distortions are often perpetuated because they may evoke new behavior which makes the originally *false* conception come true. The specious validity of the self-fulfilling prophecy perpetuates a reign of error. The prophet will cite the actual course of events as proof that he was right from the very beginning. The dynamics of the self-fulfilling prophecy help to explain individual pathology—e.g., the anxious student who, afraid he might fail, worries so much that he cannot study, with the consequence that he does fail. It also contributes to our understanding of social pathology—e.g., how prejudice and discrimination against the Negro keeps him in a position which seems to justify the prejudice and discrimination. So, too, in international relations. If the representatives of East and West believe that war is likely and either side attempts to increase

its military security vis-à-vis the other, the other side's response will justify the initial move. The dynamics of an arms race has the inherent quality of a "folie à deux," wherein the self-fulfilling prophecies mutually reinforce one another.

Psychological Alternatives to War

In the preceding section, I have attempted to indicate some of the sources of misperception in international relations and some of the conditions which tend to perpetuate the distortions or make them come true. Our present international situation suggests that the distortions have come true. The East and the West are in an arms race and in the throes of an ideological conflict in which each side, in reality, threatens and feels threatened by the other. How can we reverse this hostile spiral which is likely to result in mutual annihilation?

As I present some specific proposal, I will indicate the psychological assumptions underlying them: assumptions which come from theoretical and experimental research I have been doing on interpersonal trust and suspicion and interpersonal bargaining (Deutsch, 1949, 1958, 1960a, 1960b, 1961; Deutsch & Krauss, 1960).

1. *There are social situations which do not allow the possibility of "rational" behavior so long as the conditions for mutual trust do not exist.* Let me illustrate with a two-person game that I have used in my experimental work on trust and suspicion. In this game, each player has to choose between pressing a red button and a green button: if both players press the red button each loses $1.00; if both players press the green button, each wins $1.00; if Player A presses the green button and Player B presses the red button, A loses $2.00 and B gains $2.00; and if Player B presses the green button and Player A presses the red button, B loses $2.00 and A gains $2.00. A superficial rational calculation of self-interest would lead each player to press his red button since he either wins as much as he can or loses as little as he can this way. But, if both players consider only their self-interest and press their red buttons, each of them will lose. Players oriented toward defeating the other player or toward their self-interest only, when matched with similarly oriented players, do in fact choose the red button and do end up losing consistently.

I believe our current international situation is in some respects similar to the game I have described. A characteristic symptom of such "non-rational situations" is that any attempt on the part of any individual or nation to increase its own welfare or security (without regard to the security or welfare of the others) is self-defeating. In such situations the only way that an individual or nation can avoid being trapped in a mutually reinforcing, self-defeating cycle is to attempt to change the situation so that a basis of mutual trust can develop.

Comprehension of the basic nature of the situation we are in suggests that *mutual security* rather than national security should be our objective. The basic military axiom for both the East and West should be that *military actions should only be taken which increase the military security of both sides; military actions which give a military superiority to one side or the other should be avoided.* The military forces of both sides should be viewed as having the *common* primary aim of preventing either side (one's own or the other) from starting a deliberate or accidental war. Awareness of this common aim could be implemented by regular meetings of military leaders from East and West; the establishment of a continuing joint technical group of experts to work together to formulate disarmament and inspection plans; the establishment of mixed military units on each other's territory (see Kelman . . .), etc. The key point we must recognize is that if military inferiority is dangerous, so is military "superiority"; it is dangerous for either side to feel *tempted* or *frightened* into military action.

2. *Our research indicates that mutual trust is most likely to occur when people are positively oriented to each other's welfare—i.e., when each has a stake in the other's doing well rather than poorly.* Unfortunately, the East and West, at present, appear to have a greater stake in each other's defects and difficulties than in each other's welfare. Thus, the Communists gloat over our racial problems and our unemployment and we do likewise over their agricultural failures and their lack of political liberties.

We should, I believe, do everything possible to reverse this unfortunate state of affairs. First of all, we might start by accepting each other's existence as *legitimate* and by rejecting the view that the existence of the other, *per se*, is a threat to our own existence. As Talcott Parsons . . . has pointed out, there is considerable merit in viewing the ideological battle between East and West in the world community as somewhat akin to our own two-party system at the national level. An ideological conflict presupposes a common frame of reference in terms of which the ideological differences make sense. The ideologies of East and West do share many values in common: technological advance, economic development, universal education, encouragement of science, cultural progress, health advances, peace, national autonomy, etc. We must accept the possibility that one side or the other will obtain an advantage on particular issues when there is a conflict about the procedures for attaining these objectives. But this is not catastrophic unless each side views the conflict as an all-or-none conflict of survival.

To establish a basis for mutual trust we, of course, have to go beyond the recognition of each other's legitimacy to a relationship which promotes cooperative bonds. This would be facilitated by recognition of the profound human similarities which link all mankind together. The human situation no longer makes it feasible to view the world in terms of "we" or "they";

in the modern era, our destinies are linked objectively; the realistic attitude is "we" *and* "they." More specifically, I think our situation would be improved rather than worsened if the people in the various Communist nations had a high standard of living, were well educated, and were reaping the fruits of the scientific revolution. Similarly, I think we would be better off rather than worse off if the political leaders of the Communist nations felt they were able to provide their citizenry with sufficient current gratifications and signs of progress to have their support; and if they were sufficiently confident of their own society not to fear intensive contacts with different points of view.

The implication of the above calls for a fundamental reorientation of our foreign policy toward the Communist nations. We must initiate coopera-tive trade policies, cooperative research programs, cooperative cultural exchanges, cooperative loan programs, cooperative agricultural programs, etc., and we must not be concerned if, at first, they appear to benefit more than we. We are, after all, more affluent than the Communist nations. Our objective should be simply to promote the values of economic well-being, educational attainment, scientific and industrial development which we share in common and which we believe are necessary to a stable, peaceful world. Let me emphasize here that I think this is especially important to do in our relations with Communist China. (It amazes me constantly that so little public attention is given to the extraordinary dangers involved in allowing our current relations with Communist China to continue in their present form.) The Communist nations (especially China) are likely to be suspicious of our motives, may even rebuff our initial attempts to establish cooperative relationships, and will undoubtedly not feel grateful for any assistance they may receive. These reactions are all to be expected because of the present context of international relations. Our policy of cooperation must be a *sustained* policy of *massive reconciliation* which does not reciprocate hostility and which always leaves open the possibility of mutual cooperation despite prior rebuff. In my view, we must sustain a cooperative initiative until it succeeds; in the long run, the alternative to mutual cooperation is mutual doom.

My rationale here is very simple. We have no realistic alternative but to coexist with the Soviet Union and Communist China. Coexistence among nations will be considerably less dangerous if we each recognize that poverty, illiteracy, economic difficulties, internal strain and crisis in a nation are likely to produce reckless, belligerent international policies rather than peaceful ones. After all, the delinquents and criminals in our local communities rarely come from those segments of our populace that are successfully dealing with their own internal problems or that are well integrated into and accepted by the broader community.

3. *To induce a cooperative orientation in another and to develop adher-ence to a set of rules or social norms for regulating interaction and for*

resolving disputes, it is necessary: (a) to demonstrate that one's own orientation to the other is cooperative; (b) to articulate fair rules which do not systematically disadvantage the other; (c) to demonstrate one's adherence to these rules; (d) to demonstrate to the other that he has more to gain (or less to lose) in the short and long run by adherence to the rules than by violation of them; and (e) to recognize that misunderstandings and disputes about compliance will inevitably occur and hence are not necessarily tokens of bad faith.

The importance of a cooperative orientation to the development of mutual trust has been discussed above; it is reiterated here to emphasize the significance of a cooperative orientation in the development of any workable system of rules to regulate international relations. In discussion and negotiations concerning arms control and disarmament, there has been much emphasis on developing rules and procedures for inspection and control which do not rely upon cooperative orientations; surveillance of the other's actions is to replace trust in the other's intent. I think it is reasonable to assert that no social order can exist for long without a minimum basis in mutual trust; surveillance cannot do the trick by itself. This is not to deny the necessity of surveillance to buttress trust, to enable one's trustworthiness to be confirmed and one's suspicions to be rejected. However, I would question the view which seems to characterize our approach to arms control negotiations: namely, the less trust, the more surveillance. A more reasonable view might state that when there is little trust the only kinds of agreements which are feasible are ones which allow for simple, uncomplicated but highly reliable techniques of surveillance. Lack of trust between equals, paradoxically, calls for but also limits surveillance when the negotiations are not part of an effective community.

How can the formulation of fair rules be facilitated? A suggestion by Bertrand Russell . . . is pertinent here. He proposes the formation of a conciliation committee composed of the best minds from the East and West, with some of the leading thinkers from neutral nations also included. Such a committee, meeting together in quiet, unpublicized deliberation, might be given the responsibility of formulating rules which would be acceptable to both sides. The hope is that, with sufficient time, intelligent men of good will whose perspectives reach beyond the cold war may be able to formulate rules that are fair to all mankind.

Fair rules for certain matters, of course, do already exist. Some of these rules are written in the Charter of the United Nations, some in the decisions of the International Court of Justice at the Hague, some in the legal traditions which have governed various aspects of international relations through the centuries (e.g., the international postal system, international trade, "freedom of the seas," ambassadorial rights). As Arthur Larson . . . has pointed out, there is much need for legal research to make the existing body of international rules accessible and up-to-date and establish a legal machinery which is also accessible and adapted to settling the kinds of disputes that today's world produces. In addition, there is a need to induce acceptance of the body of law and legal machinery by the persons affected.

4. *Mutual trust can occur even under circumstances where the parties involved are unconcerned with each other's welfare providing their relations to an outside, third party are such that this trust in him can substitute for their trust in one another.* This indirect or mediated trust is, of course, a most common form of trust in interpersonal relations. Since we exist in a community in which various types of third parties—the law, the police, public opinion, mutual friends, etc.—can be mobilized to buttress an agreement, we can afford to be trusting even with a stranger in most circumstances. Unfortunately, in a bipolar world community, which does not contain powerful "third parties," it is difficult to substitute mediated trust for direct trust.

There are two policy implications of this fact which I would like to stress. The first is the importance of encouraging the development of several strong, neutral groups of nations and the development of a strong, neutral United Nations that might mediate in conflicts between East and West. We have, of course, to be aware of the dangers of a *tertius gaudens*, in which a third party would attempt to play East and West off against one another to its own advantage. However, what I am suggesting is not a third bloc but rather a group of diverse, independent nations with criss-crossing interests that have the common objective of developing and maintaining an orderly world. In a neutral United Nations, with a large group of independent voters, we would sometimes find ourselves on the losing side. But can we afford a United Nations in which the other side has little chance of ever winning a dispute with us?

The second implication follows from the realization that strong, responsible, independent nations and a strong, neutral United Nations do not yet exist and will take time to develop. Where no strong external community exists, it is important to recognize that bargaining—i.e., the attempt to find a mutually satisfactory agreement in circumstances where there is a conflict of interest—cannot afford to be guided by a Machiavellian or "outwitting the other" attitude. Where no external community exists to compel agreement, the critical problem in bargaining is to establish sufficient community between the bargainers that a mutually satisfactory agreement becomes possible: the question of who obtains the minor advantages or disadvantages in a negotiation is trivial in comparison to the question of whether an agreement can be reached which leaves both parties better off than a lack of agreement. I stress this point because some political scientists and economists, misled by the fact that bargaining within a strong community can often fruitfully be conducted with a Machiavellian attitude, unwittingly assume that the same would be true where no real community exists.

In concluding this section, let me quote from a monograph on the *Causes of Industrial Peace* (National Planning Association, 1953, p. 92) which lists the conditions that have led to peaceful settlement of disputes under collective bargaining:

1. There is full acceptance by management of the collective bargaining process and of unionism as an institution. The company considers a strong union an asset to management.

2. The union fully accepts private ownership and operation of the industry; it recognizes that the welfare of its members depends upon the successful operation of the business.

3. The union is strong, responsible, and democratic.

4. The company stays out of the union's internal affairs; it does not seek to alienate the workers' allegiance to their union.

5. Mutual trust and confidence exist between the parties. There have been no serious ideological incompatibilities.

6. Neither party to bargaining has adopted a legalistic approach to the solution of problems in the relationship.

7. Negotiations are "problem-centered"—more time is spent on day-to-day problems than on defining abstract principles.

8. There is widespread union-management consultation and highly developed information-sharing.

9. Grievances are settled promptly, in the local plant whenever possible. There is flexibility and informality within the procedure.

This is in accord with our discussion of the basic conditions for world peace: namely, the necessity of developing attitudes which consciously stress mutual acceptance, mutual welfare, mutual strength, mutual interest, and mutual trust and the necessity of developing approaches to disputes which consistently emphasize full communication, willingness to negotiate, and the specific issues in dispute rather than the ideological frame of reference of the parties in dispute.

IMPLICATIONS

This substantial selection on a crucial current problem deserves careful reading, a search for understanding, and detailed discussion. Which of Deutsch's ideas do you heartily endorse? Of which are you skeptical? Consider the psychological assumptions underlying his proposals and react to them.

You and your peers may find it interesting and profitable to use the content of this selection for a debate among several students who react differently to it.

Deutsch mentions a game experiment that may be duplicated by several members of your group. You can, by playing this experimental game, demonstrate the self-defeating nature of extreme self-interest.

REFERENCES

Consult the Bibliography for references cited in the article.

Many other outstanding members of the profession have been concerned with the psychological aspects of national and international affairs, as shown in Murphy (1953), Osgood (1961), Nielson (1962), Russell (1960), Janis and Katz (1959), Katz (1961), and Jacobson and Schachter (1954).

14   MARIHUANA RECONSIDERED

James L. Goddard

The use of drugs, especially by young people, has aroused great interest in the scientific facts about drugs and their use. Marihuana, particularly because of its widespread social use by young people, is a center of much controversy. This selection is a review, by a former commissioner of the Federal Food and Drug Administration, of a book on marihuana written by Lester Grinspoon, a psychiatrist in the Harvard University Medical School. The review deals with the general misinformation about marihuana and the severe penalties for possession of the drug. He contrasts the public attitude toward alcohol and tobacco (both known as health hazards) and toward marihuana.

Pot use "leads to violence and crime . . . opens the mind and enhances creativity . . . smoking is the first step in the use of such drugs as cocaine, morphine and heroin . . . is an aphrodisiac . . . has a causal relationship to psychosis . . . is an extremely safe drug when compared to secobarbital and alcohol."

Each of these partial quotations from Lester Grinspoon's recent book

From a review by James L. Goddard, *New York Times Book Review*, June 27, 1971. © 1971 by The New York Times Company. Reprinted by permission of the publisher and the author.

"Marihuana Reconsidered" can become the departure point for an evening-long discussion with one's friends, reaffirming for the cognoscenti the suspicion that demonologists are in our midst. Having tilted on numerous occasions with those whose minds have been captured by the "demonology" of marijuana I am particularly sensitive to how deeply we as a society have been committed to a position that is based on superstition and un-documented hearsay. For three generations misinformation about this drug has been embedded into our literature, our minds, our ethos and, increasingly, our laws.

How well this misinformation has been planted and carefully nurtured is attested to by our continued inability to use the available scientific evidence to modify Federal statutes which are not only unrealistic but Draconian in nature. This societal "blindspot" has created a dilemma. One facet of the dilemma is the Alice-in-Wonderland relationship we have fashioned between marijuana and alcohol.

On the one hand we find that possession of alcohol, a central nervous system depressant which has produced physical dependence in an esti-mated 6,000,000 Americans and psychological dependence in perhaps five times that number, is not only free of penalty but its use is even en-couraged by our society to such a degree that nonusers of the drug are regarded by most as being somewhat peculiar. On the other hand mere possession of *marijuana, a mild "hallucinogen" incapable of producing physical dependence and whose ability to create psychological dependence is judged to be less than that of alcohol and tobacco,** is considered a heinous crime punishable upon conviction by imprisonment for varying periods up to 99 years.

Grinspoon, a Harvard Medical School psychiatrist, analyzes this and other aspects of the marijuana problem and concludes that, "we must consider the enormous harm, both obvious and subtle, short range and long-term, inflicted on the people, particularly the young, who constitute or will soon constitute the formative and critical members of our society by the present punitive, repressive approach to the use of marijuana. And we must consider the damage inflicted on legal and other institutions when young people react to what they see as a confirmation of their view that those institutions are hypocritical and inequitable. Indeed the *greatest potential for social harm lies in the scarring of so many young people and the reactive, institutional damages that are direct products of present marijuana laws.** If we are to avoid having this harm reach the proportion of a national disaster within the next decade, we must move to make the social use of marijuana legal."

Before reaching this conclusion Grinspoon covers, in an unusually well documented fashion, the biology, chemistry, pharmacology and toxicity

* Editor's italics.

of marijuana; the potential medical uses which merit further study; the psychological effects of using the drug; and the social and legal implications of usage both with regard to the individual and society. For the serious student who seeks original sources a 42-page section of notes has been provided.

That there will be criticisms of the conclusions and the manner in which they were reached goes without question, for the issues involved are so emotionally laden that reason will be cast aside and specious arguments introduced. There will be critics who will find fault on the grounds that the potential dangers have been minimized and that we know too little to legalize usage at this point in time. Others will argue that undue bias was involved in the exclusion of reports which document the problems associated with usage of *cannabis sativa* (marijuana).

As to the first criticism the author in anticipation states, "it is quite true that among the hundreds and hundreds of papers dealing with cannabis, there is relatively little methodologically sound research. Yet out of this vast collection of largely unsystematic recordings comes *the strong impression that no amount of research is likely to prove that cannabis is as dangerous as alcohol and tobacco.*" * On this point I would agree that research may not be able to demonstrate equivalent dangers, but I would hasten to point out *if usage were at the same level and over as prolonged a period of time we might find that lung cancer, or emphysema or other disorders would occur as often as with tobacco.** This does not invalidate Grinspoon's conclusions but rather suggests that if the use of marijuana were to be made legal it should be made available in dosage forms that are potentially less dangerous.

On the second point concerning the bias in selection of material, having personally reviewed the English portion of the world literature in preparation for Congressional hearings, I can only express my admiration for the manner in which Grinspoon has extracted, analyzed and synthesized the most relevant literature to present the reader with a coherent, logical case. He inevitably leads to the conclusion that, as a society, we were systematically coerced into making the same mistake in 1937 with marijuana that was made earlier with alcohol by the passage of the Volstead Act.

It is difficult to understand why this "error" was made by many of the same legislators who just a few years earlier had in repealing the Volstead Act recognized the wisdom of Spinoza's admonition: "He who seeks to regulate everything by law is more likely to arouse vices than reform them." Difficult, at any rate, unless one speculates that the liquor lobby played a critical, albeit subtle role in the "legal onslaught" which occurred during the early and mid-thirties and culminated in the passage of the Federal Marijuana Tax Act of 1937.

* Editor's italics.

Knowing something of the inner workings of Federal regulatory agencies, this speculation, which Grinspoon notes in his especially interesting first chapter, "The History of Marihuana in the United States," is not an implausible one and on several occasions in the past the press has pointedly ignored my suggestion that the archives be searched for evidence to support the thesis that alcohol was "protected" against the burgeoning menace of the "killer drug, marijuana" during the post-repeal era of the 1930's. Such a finding would, however, have little effect today other than to strengthen the suspicions held by many of the young generation concerning the Establishment and its illogical positions on drugs in society.

Why and how such positions could occur is dealt with by the author in his all too brief discussion of the "possible" causes of our attitudes to marijuana, LSD and amphetamines. Grinspoon believes that a displacement phenomenon operates within our society: ". . . people may unconsciously transfer affect from its real object to substitute objects." Thus our concern about nuclear holocausts, environmental pollution, social instability, crowding and population may be displaced by attaching affect to substitute issues, such as drugs. If true, this provides partial explanation for the unwillingness of Congress to listen to knowledgeable witnesses who have counseled against repressive legislation and subsequent Congressional reluctance to take cognizance of evidence clearly indicating the need for change.

One group opposing the passage of the 1937 Act outlawing marijuana was The American Medical Association. The opposition was based on concern that the act would not accomplish its objectives, would be unnecessarily expensive for the physicians to comply with and that the drug should continue to be available for restudy by modern means—such studies they believed could show "other advantages to be obtained from its medicinal use." Their concern with the ineffectiveness of the act has proven to be well founded. Less well appreciated is the fact that research was for all practical purposes completely stifled for over 30 years. Fortunately that situation has now been remedied, and we are now well into the efforts to derive therapeutically useful substances from the very complex constituents which make up the marijuana plant.

Grinspoon's evaluation is that new products may be developed from either naturally occurring marijuana or one of the synthetic forms which have: (1) analgesic properties in combination with mood elevating abilities; (2) the effect of lowering blood pressure through different mechanisms than today's drugs; and (3) have antidepressant and antianxiety effects again different in their mechanism of action than today's drugs. Emergence of a new drug in any one of these three classes would be a substantial contribution, particularly if the drug possessed greater margins of safety or fewer side effects than drugs presently being used.

The development of a new drug, no matter how valuable, would of course not change the major issue for the 20 million or so users in our society today. They will continue to press for legalization of marijuana in the face of opposition from the majority of the citizenry, who although ill-informed and overactive, feel that to take this step "would be to invite national tragedy."

As for myself, I would favor legalization only if I were confident that a control system could be devised to preclude widespread usage by adolescents. They are not well equipped to handle a drug which provides a pleasant escape from reality, promotes inattention and would distract them from their main task—growing up. But hopefully many Americans will read Lester Grinspoon's "Marihuana Reconsidered" and utilize the information so well presented in reaching their own decision on "pot," to legalize or not.

IMPLICATIONS

It will be interesting to compare the evaluation of the effects of marihuana suggested by the reviewer and the action in 1972 by the President's Commission on Drugs. The reviewer suggests that there are some defense mechanisms operating in the illogical position taken by the Establishment on marihuana. What, in your thinking, is the possible conflict and anxiety in the behavior of those who are acting so defensively?

REFERENCES

Discussions of other drugs are found in Blum et al. (1969), E. Goode (1969), and Jarvik (1967).

CHAPTER IV

GROWTH AND MATURITY

15 THE NATURE OF LOVE

Harry F. Harlow

How have psychologists explained the development of love, which has long held, as Harlow points out, a vast interest and fascination for human beings? Is the expression of love learned? Is it a *secondary drive* or a *basic motive*? Can its bases and development be discovered by carefully controlled experiments? How does a psychologist manipulate the stimulus and response variables to discover the nature of love? Let us see Harry Harlow's discoveries from his studies of neonatal and infant monkeys, which he presents in a scientific but delightful manner.

L OVE IS a wondrous state, deep, tender, and rewarding. Because of its intimate and personal nature it is regarded by some as an improper topic for experimental research. But, whatever our personal feelings may be, our assigned mission as psychologists is to analyze all facets of human and animal behavior into their component variables. So far as love or affection is concerned, psychologists have failed in this mission. The little we know about love does not transcend simple observation, and the little we write about it has been written better by poets and novelists. But of greater concern is the fact that psychologists tend to give progressively less attention to a motive which pervades our entire lives. Psychologists, at least psychologists who write textbooks, not only show no interest in the origin and development of love or affection, but they seem to be unaware of its very existence.

*The apparent repression of love** by modern psychologists stands in sharp contrast with the attitude taken by many famous and normal people. The word "love" has the highest reference frequency of any word cited in Bartlett's book of *Familiar Quotations*. It would appear that this emotion has long had a vast interest and fascination for human beings, regardless of the attitude taken by psychologists; but the quotations cited, even by famous and normal people, have a mundane redundancy. These authors and authorities have stolen love from the child and infant and made it the exclusive property of the adolescent and adult.

Thoughtful men, and probably all women, have speculated on the nature of love. From the developmental point of view, the general plan is quite

* Editor's italics.

From Harry F. Harlow, "The Nature of Love," *American Psychologist*, Vol. 13, 1958, 673–685. Copyright 1958 by the American Psychological Association, and reproduced by permission of the publisher and the author.

clear: the initial love responses of the human being are those made by the infant to the mother or some mother surrogate. From this intimate attachment of the child to the mother, multiple learned and generalized affectional responses are formed.

Unfortunately, beyond these simple facts we know little about the fundamental variables underlying the formation of affectional responses and little about the mechanisms through which the love of the infant for the mother develops into the multifaceted response patterns characterizing love or affection in the adult. Because of the dearth of experimentation, theories about the fundamental nature of affection have evolved at the level of observation, intuition, and discerning guesswork, whether these have been proposed by psychologists, sociologists, anthropologists, physicians, or psychoanalysts.

*The position commonly held by psychologists** and sociologists is quite clear: the basic motives are, for the most part, the primary drives—particularly hunger, thirst, elimination, pain, and sex—and all other motives, including love or affection, are derived or secondary drives. The mother is associated with the reduction of the primary drives—particularly hunger, thirst, and pain—and through learning, affection or love is derived.

It is entirely reasonable to believe that the mother through association with food may become a secondary-reinforcing agent, but this is an inadequate mechanism to account for the persistence of the infant-maternal ties. There is a spate of researches on the formation of secondary reinforcers to hunger and thirst reduction. There can be no question that almost any external stimulus can become a secondary reinforcer if properly associated with tissue-need reduction, but the fact remains that this redundant literature demonstrates unequivocally that such derived drives suffer relatively rapid experimental extinction. Contrariwise human affection does not extinguish when the mother ceases to have intimate association with the drives in question. Instead, the affectional ties to the mother show a lifelong, unrelenting persistence and, even more surprising, widely expanding generality.

Oddly enough, one of the few psychologists who took a position counter to modern psychological dogma was John B. Watson, who believed that love was an innate emotion elicited by cutaneous stimulation of the erogenous zones. But experimental psychologists, with their peculiar propensity to discover facts that are not true, brushed this theory aside by demonstrating that the human neonate had no differentiable emotions, and they established a fundamental psychological law that prophets are without honor in their own profession.

*The psychoanalysts** have concerned themselves with the problem of the nature of the development of love in the neonate and infant, using ill and

---

* Editor's italics.

aging human beings as subjects. They have discovered the overwhelming importance of the breast and related this to the oral erotic tendencies developed at an age preceding their subjects' memories. Their theories range from a belief that the infant has an innate need to achieve and suckle at the breast to beliefs not unlike commonly accepted psychological theories. There are exceptions, as seen in the recent writings of John Bowlby, who attributes importance not only to food and thirst satisfaction, but also to "primary object-clinging," a need for intimate physical contact, which is initially associated with the mother.

As far as I know, there exists no *direct experimental analysis** of the relative importance of the stimulus variables determining the affectional or love responses in the neonatal and infant primate. Unfortunately, the human neonate is a limited experimental subject for such researches because of his inadequate motor capabilities. By the time the human infant's motor responses can be precisely measured, the antecedent determining conditions cannot be defined, having been lost in a jumble and jungle of confounded variables.

Many of these difficulties can be resolved by the use of the neonatal and infant macaque monkey as the subject for the analysis of basic affectional variables. It is possible to make precise measurements in this primate beginning at two to ten days of age, depending upon the maturational status of the individual animal at birth. The macaque infant differs from the human infant in that the monkey is more mature at birth and grows more rapidly; but the basic responses relating to affection, including nursing, contact, clinging, and even visual and auditory exploration, exhibit no fundamental differences in the two species. Even the development of perception, fear, frustration, and learning capability follows very similar sequences in rhesus monkeys and human children.

*Three years' experimentation** before we started our studies on affection gave us experience with the neonatal monkey. We had separated more than sixty of these animals from their mothers six to twelve hours after birth and suckled them on tiny bottles. The infant mortality was only a small fraction of what would have obtained had we let the monkey mothers raise their infants. Our bottle-fed babies were healthier and heavier than monkey-mother-reared infants. We know that we are better monkey mothers than are real monkey mothers thanks to synthetic diets, vitamins, iron extracts, penicillin, chloromycetin, 5 per cent glucose, and constant, tender, loving care.

During the course of these studies, we noticed that the laboratory-raised babies showed strong attachment to the cloth pads (folded gauze diapers) which were used to cover the hardware-cloth floors of their cages. The infants clung to these pads and engaged in violent temper tantrums when

* Editor's italics.

the pads were removed and replaced for sanitary reasons. Such contact need or responsiveness had been reported previously by Gertrude van Wagenen for the monkey and by Thomas McCulloch and George Haslerud for the chimpanzee and is reminiscent of the devotion often exhibited by human infants to their pillows, blankets, and soft, cuddly stuffed toys. . . . The baby, human or monkey, if it is to survive, must clutch at more than a straw.

We had also discovered during some allied observational studies that a baby monkey raised on a bare wire-mesh cage floor survives with difficulty, if at all, during the first five days of life. If a wire-mesh cone is introduced, the baby does better; and, if the cone is covered with terry cloth, husky, healthy, happy babies evolve. It takes more than a baby and a box to make a normal monkey. We were impressed by the possibility that, above and beyond the bubbling fountain of breast or bottle, contact comfort might be a very important variable in the development of the infant's affection for the mother.

At this point we decided to study the development of affectional responses of neonatal and infant monkeys to an artificial, inanimate mother, and so we built a surrogate mother which we hoped and believed would be a good surrogate mother. In devising this surrogate mother, we were dependent neither upon the capriciousness of evolutionary processes nor upon mutations produced by chance radioactive fallout. Instead, we designed the mother surrogate in terms of modern human-engineering principles. We produced a perfectly proportioned, streamlined body stripped of unnecessary bulges and appendices. Redundancy in the surrogate mother's system was avoided by reducing the number of breasts from two to one and placing this unibreast in an upper-thoracic, sagittal position, thus maximizing the natural and known perceptual-motor capabilities of the infant operator. The surrogate was made from a block of wood, covered with sponge rubber, and sheathed in tan cotton terry cloth. A light bulb behind her radiated heat. The result was a mother, soft, warm, and tender, a mother with infinite patience, a mother available twenty-four hours a day, a mother that never scolded her infant and never struck or bit her baby in anger. Furthermore, we designed a mother-machine with maximal maintenance efficiency since failure of any system or function could be resolved by the simple substitution of black boxes and new component parts. It is our opinion that we engineered a very superior monkey mother, although this position is not held universally by the monkey fathers.

Before beginning our initial experiment we also designed and constructed *a second mother surrogate,** a surrogate in which we deliberately built less than the maximal capability for contact comfort. This surrogate mother is illustrated in Figure 1. She is made of wire mesh, a substance entirely adequate to provide postural support and nursing capability, and she is

* Editor's italics.

Figure 1. Wire and cloth mother surrogates.

warmed by radiant heat. Her body differs in no essential way from that of the cloth mother surrogate other than in the quality of the contact comfort which she can supply.

In our initial experiment, the dual mother-surrogate condition, a cloth mother and a wire mother were placed in different cubicles attached to the infant's living cage as shown in Figure 1. For four newborn monkeys the cloth mother lactated and the wire mother did not; and, for the other four, this condition was reversed. In either condition the infant received all its milk through the mother surrogate as soon as it was able to maintain itself in this way, a capability achieved within two or three days except in the case of very immature infants. Supplementary feedings were given until the milk intake from the mother surrogate was adequate. Thus, the experiment was designed as a test of the relative importance of the variables of contact comfort and nursing comfort. During the first 14 days of life, the monkey's cage floor was covered with a heating pad wrapped in a folded gauze diaper, and thereafter the cage floor was bare. The infants were always free to leave the heating pad or cage floor to contact either mother, and the time spent on the surrogate mothers was automatically recorded. Figure 2 shows the total time spent on the cloth and wire mothers under the two conditions

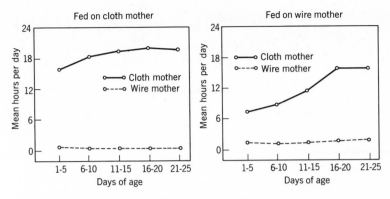

Figure 2. Time spent on cloth and wire mother surrogates.

of feeding. These data make it obvious that contact comfort is a variable of overwhelming importance in the development of affectional responses, whereas lactation is a variable of negligible importance. With age and opportunity to learn, subjects with the lactating wire mother showed decreasing responsiveness to her and increasing responsiveness to the nonlactating cloth mother, a finding completely contrary to any interpretation of derived drive in which the mother form becomes conditioned to hunger-thirst reduction. The persistence of these differential responses throughout 165 consecutive days of testing is evident in Figure 3.

One control group of neonatal monkeys was raised on a single wire mother, and a second control group was raised on a single cloth mother. There were no differences between these two groups in amount of milk ingested or in weight gain. The only difference between the groups lay in the composition of the feces, the softer stools of the wire-mother infants suggesting psychosomatic involvement. The wire mother is biologically adequate but psychologically inept.

We were not surprised to discover that contact comfort was an important basic affectional or love variable, but we did not expect it to overshadow so completely the variable of nursing; indeed, the disparity is so great as to suggest that the primary function of nursing as an affectional variable is that of insuring frequent and intimate body contact of the infant with the mother. Certainly, man cannot live by milk alone. Love is an emotion that does not need to be bottle- or spoon-fed, and we may be sure that there is nothing to be gained by giving lip service to love.

A charming lady once heard me describe these experiments; and when I subsequently talked to her, her face brightened with sudden insight: "Now I know what's wrong with me," she said, "I'm just a wire mother." Perhaps she was lucky. She might have been a wire wife.

We believe that contact comfort has long served the animal kingdom as

* Editor's italics.

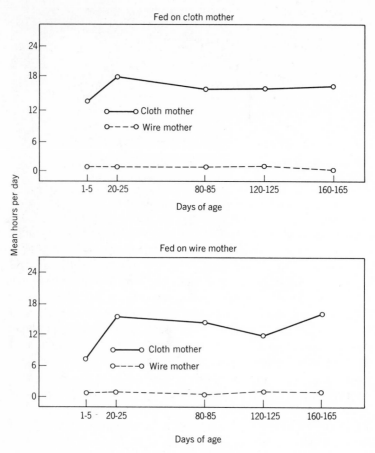

Figure 3. Long-term contact time on cloth and wire mother surrogates.

a motivating agent for affectional responses. Since at the present time we have no experimental data to substantiate this position, we supply information which must be accepted, if at all, on the basis of face validity. . . .

One function of the real mother, human or subhuman, and presumably of a mother surrogate, is to provide a haven of safety for the infant in times of fear and danger. The frightened or ailing child clings to its mother, not its father; and this selective responsiveness in times of distress, disturbance, or danger may be used as a measure of the strength of affectional bonds. We have tested this kind of differential responsiveness by presenting to the infants in their cages, in the presence of the two mothers, various fear-producing stimuli such as the moving toy bear. A typical response to a fear stimulus is shown in Figure 4, and the data on differential responsiveness are presented in Figure 5. It is apparent that the cloth mother is highly preferred over the wire one, and this differential selectivity is enhanced by age and experience. In this situation, the variable of nursing appears to be

Figure 4. Typical response to cloth mother surrogate in fear test.

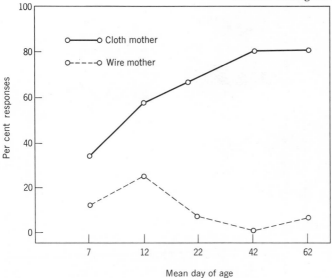

Mean day of age

Figure 5. Differential responsiveness in fear tests.

of absolutely no importance: the infant consistently seeks the soft mother surrogate regardless of nursing condition.

Similarly, the mother or mother surrogate provides its young with a source of security, and this role or function is seen with special clarity when mother and child are in a strange situation. At the present time we have completed tests for this relationship on four of our eight baby monkeys assigned to the dual mother-surrogate condition by introducing them for three minutes into the strange environment of a room measuring six feet by six feet by six feet (also called the "open-field test") and containing multiple stimuli known to elicit curiosity-manipulatory responses in baby monkeys. The subjects were placed in this situation twice a week for eight weeks with no mother surrogate present during alternate sessions and the cloth mother present during the others. A cloth diaper was always available as one of the stimuli throughout all sessions. After one or two adaptation sessions, the infants always rushed to the mother surrogate when she was present and clutched her, rubbed their bodies against her, and frequently manipulated her body and face. After a few additional sessions, the infants began to use the mother surrogate as a source of security, a base of operations. They would explore and manipulate a stimulus and then return to the mother before adventuring again into the strange new world. The behavior of these infants was quite different when the mother was absent from the room. Frequently they would freeze in a crouched position, as is illustrated in Figure 6. Emotionality indices such as vocalization, crouching, rocking, and sucking increased sharply. Total emotionality score was cut in half when the mother was present. In the absence of the mother, some

Figure 6. Response in the open-field test in the absence of the mother surrogate.

of the experimental monkeys would rush to the center of the room where the mother was customarily placed and then run rapidly from object to object, screaming and crying all the while. Continuous, frantic clutching of their bodies was very common, even when not in the crouching position. These monkeys frequently contacted and clutched the cloth diaper, but this action never pacified them. The same behavior occurred in the presence of the wire mother. No difference between the cloth-mother-fed and wire-mother-fed infants was demonstrated under either condition. . . .

We have already described the *group of four control infants that had never lived in the presence of any mother surrogate and had demonstrated no sign of affection or security in the presence of the cloth mothers** introduced in test sessions. When these infants reached the age of 250 days, cubicles containing both a cloth mother and a wire mother were attached to their cages. There was no lactation in these mothers, for the monkeys were on a solid-food diet. The initial reaction of the monkeys to the alterations was one of extreme disturbance. All the infants screamed violently and made repeated attempts to escape the cage whenever the door was opened. They kept a maximum distance from the mother surrogates and exhibited a considerable amount of rocking and crouching behavior, indicative of emotionality. Our first thought was that the critical period for the development of maternally directed affection had passed and that these macaque children were doomed to live as affectional orphans. Fortunately, these behaviors continued for only 12 to 48 hours and then gradually ebbed, changing from indifference to active contact on, and exploration of, the surrogates. The home-cage behavior of these control monkeys slowly became similar to that of the animals raised with the mother surrogates from birth. Their manipulation and play on the cloth mother became progressively more vigorous to the point of actual mutilation, particularly during the morning after the cloth mother had been given her daily change of terry covering. The control subjects were now actively running to the cloth mother when frightened and had to be coaxed from her to be taken from the cage for formal testing.

Objective evidence of these changing behaviors * is given in Figure 7, which plots the amount of time these infants spent on the mother surrogates. Within 10 days, mean contact time is approximately nine hours and this measure remains relatively constant throughout the next 30 days. Consistent with the results on the subjects reared from birth with dual mothers, these late-adopted infants spent less than one and one half hours per day in contact with the wire mothers, and this activity level was relatively constant throughout the test sessions. Although the maximum time that the control monkeys spent on the cloth mother was only about half that spent by the original dual mother-surrogate group, we cannot be

* Editor's italics.

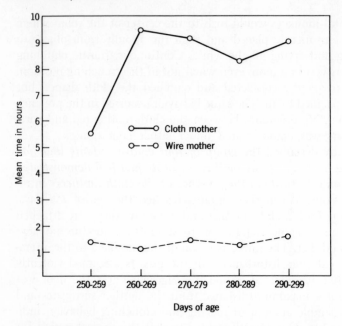

Figure 7. Differential time spent on cloth and wire mother surrogates by monkeys started at 250 days of age.

sure that this discrepancy is a function of differential early experience. The control monkeys were about three months older when the mothers were attached to their cages than the experimental animals had been when their mothers were removed and the retention tests begun. Thus, we do not know what the amount of contact would be for a 250-day-old animal raised from birth with surrogate mothers. Nevertheless, the magnitude of the differences and the fact that the contact-time curves for the mothered-from-birth infants had remained constant for almost 150 days suggest that early experience with the mother is a variable of measurable importance. . . .

That the control monkeys develop affection or love for the cloth mother when she is introduced into the cage at 250 days of age cannot be questioned. There is every reason to believe, however, that this interval of delay depresses the intensity of the affectional response below that of the infant monkeys that were surrogate-mothered from birth onward. In interpreting these data, it is well to remember that the control monkeys had had continuous opportunity to observe and hear other monkeys housed in adjacent cages and that they had had limited opportunity to view and contact surrogate mothers in the test situations, even though they did not exploit the opportunities.

During the last two years, we have observed the behavior of two infants raised by their own mothers. Love for the real mother and love for the surrogate mother appear to be very similar. The baby macaque spends many hours a day clinging to its real mother. If away from the mother when frightened, it rushes to her and in her presence shows comfort and composure. As far as we can observe, the infant monkey's affection for the real mother is strong, but no stronger than that of the experimental monkey for the surrogate cloth mother, and the security that the infant gains from the presence of the real mother is no greater than the security it gains from a cloth surrogate. . . . But, whether the mother is real or a cloth surrogate, there does develop a deep and abiding bond between mother and child. In one case it may be the call of the wild and in the other the McCall of civilization, but in both cases there is "togetherness."

In spite of the importance of contact comfort, there is reason to believe that other variables of measurable importance will be discovered. Postural support may be such a variable, and it has been suggested that, when we build arms into the mother surrogate, 10 is the minimal number required to provide adequate child care. Rocking motion may be such a variable, and we are comparing rocking and stationary mother surrogates and inclined planes. The differential responsiveness to cloth mother and cloth-covered inclined plane suggests that clinging as well as contact is an affectional variable of importance. Sounds, particularly natural, maternal sounds, may operate as either unlearned or learned affectional variables. Visual responsiveness may be such a variable, and it is possible that some semblance of visual imprinting may develop in the neonatal monkey. There are indications that this becomes a variable of importance during the course of infancy through some maturational process. . . .

Since we can measure neonatal and infant affectional responses to mother surrogates, and since we know they are strong and persisting, we are in a position to assess the effects of feeding and contactual schedules; consistency and inconsistency in the mother surrogates; and early, intermediate, and late maternal deprivation. Again, we have here a family of problems of fundamental interest and theoretical importance.

If the researches completed and proposed make a contribution, I shall be grateful; but I have also given full thought to possible practical applications. The socioeconomic demands of the present and the threatened socioeconomic demands of the future have led the American woman to displace, or threaten to displace, the American man in science and industry. If this process continues, the problem of proper child-rearing practices faces us with startling clarity. It is cheering in view of this trend to realize that the American male is physically endowed with all the really essential equipment to compete with the American female on equal terms in one essential activity: the rearing of infants. We now know that women in the working classes are not needed in the home because of their primary mammalian capabilities; and it is possible that in the foreseeable future neonatal nursing will not be regarded as a necessity, but as a luxury—to use Veblen's term

—a form of conspicuous consumption limited perhaps to the upper classes. But whatever course history may take, it is comforting to know that we are now in contact with the nature of love.

IMPLICATIONS

What do you think are the implications of this study for early child care? Read the paragraph under "References," which mentions other studies that show the effect of inadequate mothering. What are the next studies that you think need to be conducted in his area?

REFERENCES

Harlow and his associates have continued experiments on affectional responses. The monkeys that were raised with cloth-surrogate mothers showed inadequate sex behavior later and became poor mothers when they were finally impregnated and then bore young. In addition, the researchers found that monkeys that had been separated from their mothers and raised in wire cages that permitted them to see, hear, and call to other infants but not to touch them became mute, stared fixedly into space, and appeared indifferent to people and other monkeys. Some clutched their head in their hands and rocked back and forth, others went into violent rages, tearing at their own legs with such fury that some required medical attention. These monkeys, obviously abnormal, also failed to show normal sex behavior. Monkeys that have never known a real mother "become mothers—helpless, hopeless, heartless mothers, devoid, or almost devoid, of any maternal feelings." (See Harlow, 1962.)

H. F. Harlow and M. K. Harlow (1966) have also studied affectional relationship between age mates. They found monkeys that had been raised with cloth surrogate mothers were slow in forming play patterns with their peers, but by the end of a year they were interacting effectively.

16 GROWTH AND CRISES OF THE HEALTHY PERSONALITY

Erik H. Erikson

Erik Erikson has made one of the most significant contemporary contributions to the process of personality development in our culture. He begins by accepting Jahoda's criteria of a healthy personality: (1) active mastery of environment, (2) unity of personality, and (3) correct perception of the world and himself. He then describes the significant crises that the individual faces at various stages of development. The early stages are (1) basic trust, (2) autonomy, and (3) initiative, from which the child develops hope, self-control, and direction and purpose, respectively. Other traits to be developed later are (4) industry and competence (from 6 years of age to onset of puberty), (5) personal identity (at adolescence), (6) intimacy (early adulthood), (7) generativity (young and middle adulthood), and (8) integrity (later adulthood).

I WILL start out from Freud's far-reaching discovery that neurotic conflict is not very different in content from the conflicts which every child must live through in his childhood, and that every adult carries these conflicts with him in the recesses of his personality. I shall take account of this fact by stating for each childhood stage what these critical psychological conflicts are. For man, to remain psychologically alive, must resolve these conflicts unceasingly, even as his body must unceasingly combat the encroachment of physical decomposition. However, since I cannot accept the conclusion that just to be alive, or not to be sick, means to be healthy, I must have recourse to a few concepts which are not part of the official terminology of my field. Being interested also in cultural anthropology, I shall try to describe those elements of a really healthy personality which—so it seems to me—are most noticeably absent or defective in neurotic patients and which are most obviously present in the kind of man that educational and cultural systems seem to be striving, each in its own way, to create, to support, and to maintain.

I shall present human growth from the point of view of the conflicts, inner and outer, which the healthy personality weathers, emerging and re-emerging with an increased sense of inner unity, with an increase of good judgment, and an increase in the capacity to do well, according to the standards of those who are significant to him. The use of the words "to do

Reprinted from Erik H. Erikson, "Identity and the Life Cycle," *Psychological Issues*, Vol. 1, No. 1, by permission of International Universities Press, Inc. and the author. Copyright 1959 by International Universities Press, Inc.

well," of course, points up the whole question of cultural relativity. For example, those who are significant to a man may think he is doing well when he "does some good"; or when he "does well" in the sense of acquiring possessions; or when he is doing well in the sense of learning new skills or new ways of understanding or mastering reality; or when he is not much more than just getting along.

Formulations of what constitutes a healthy personality in an adult are presented in other parts of the Fact-finding Committee's work. If I may take up only one, namely, Marie Jahoda's (1950) definition, according to which a healthy personality *actively masters his environment*, shows a certain *unity of personality*, and is able to *perceive the world and himself correctly*, it is clear that all of these criteria are relative to the child's cognitive and social development. In fact, we may say that childhood is defined by their initial absence and by their gradual development in many complicated steps. I consider it my task to approach this question from the genetic point of view: How does a healthy personality grow or, as it were, accrue from the successive stages of increasing capacity to master life's outer and inner dangers—with some vital enthusiasm to spare?

On Health and Growth

Whenever we try to understand growth, it is well to remember the *epigenetic principle* which is derived from the growth of organisms *in utero*. Somewhat generalized, this principle states that anything that grows has a *ground plan*, and that out of this ground plan the *parts* arise, each part having its *time* of special ascendancy, until all parts have arisen to form a *functioning whole*. At birth the baby leaves the chemical exchange of the womb for the social exchange system of his society, where his gradually increasing capacities meet the opportunities and limitations of his culture. How the maturing organism continues to unfold, not by developing new organs, but by a prescribed sequence of locomotor, sensory, and social capacities, is described in the child-development literature. Psychoanalysis has given us an understanding of the more idiosyncratic experiences and especially the inner conflicts, which constitute the manner in which an individual becomes a distinct personality. But here, too, it is important to realize that in the sequence of his most personal experiences the healthy child, given a reasonable amount of guidance, can be trusted to obey inner laws of development, laws which create a *succession of potentialities for significant interaction* with those who tend him. While such interaction varies from culture to culture, it must remain within the *proper rate and the proper sequence* which govern the *growth of a personality* as well as that of an organism. Personality can be said to develop according to steps predetermined in the human organism's readiness to be driven toward, to be aware of, and to interact with, a widening social radius, beginning with the dim image of a mother and ending with mankind, or at any rate that segment of mankind which "counts" in the particular individual's life.

It is for this reason that, in the presentation of stages in the development of the personality, we employ an *epigenetic diagram* analogous to one previously employed for an analysis of Freud's psychosexual stages.[1] It is, in fact, the purpose of this presentation to bridge the theory of infantile sexuality (without repeating it here in detail), and our knowledge of the child's physical and social growth within his family and the social structure. An epigenetic diagram looks like this (see Diagram A).

	Component 1	Component 2	Component 3
Stage I	I_1	I_2	I_3
Stage II	II_1	II_2	II_3
Stage III	III_1	III_2	III_3

DIAGRAM A

The double-lined squares signify both a sequence of stages (I to III) and a gradual development of component parts; in other words the diagram formalizes a *progression through time of a differentiation of parts*. This indicates (1) that each item of the healthy personality to be discussed is *systematically related to all others*, and that they all depend on the *proper development in the proper sequence of each item;* and (2) that each item *exists in some form before "its" decisive and critical time* normally arrives.

If I say, for example, that a *sense of basic trust* is the first component of mental health to develop in life, a *sense of autonomous will* the second, and a *sense of initiative* the third, the purpose of the diagram may become clearer (see Diagram B).

	Component 1	Component 2	Component 3
First Stage (about first year)	BASIC TRUST	Earlier form of AUTONOMY	Earlier form of INITIATIVE
Second Stage (about second and third years)	Later form of BASIC TRUST	AUTONOMY	Earlier form of INITIATIVE
Third Stage (about fourth and fifth years)	Later form of BASIC TRUST	Later form of AUTONOMY	INITIATIVE

DIAGRAM B

[1] See Part I of the author's *Childhood and Society* (1950).

This diagrammatic statement, in turn, is meant to express a number of fundamental relations that exist among the three components, as well as a few fundamental facts for each.

Each comes to its ascendance, meets its crisis, and finds its lasting solution (in ways to be described here) *toward the end of the stages* mentioned. All of them exist in the beginning in some form, although we do not make a point of this fact, and we shall not confuse things by calling these components different names at earlier or later stages. A baby may show something like "autonomy" from the beginning, for example, in the particular way in which he angrily tries to wriggle his hand free when tightly held. However, under normal conditions, it is not until the second year that he begins to experience the whole *critical alternative between being an autonomous creature and being a dependent one*; and it is not until then that he is ready for a *decisive encounter* with his environment, an environment which, in turn, feels called upon to convey to him its *particular ideas and concepts of autonomy and coercion* in ways decisively contributing to the character, the efficiency, and the health of his personality in his culture.

It is this *encounter*, together with the resulting crisis, which is to be described for each stage. Each stage becomes a *crisis* because incipient growth and awareness in a significant part function goes together with a shift in instinctual energy and yet causes specific vulnerability in that part. One of the most difficult questions to decide, therefore, is whether or not a child at a given stage is weak or strong. Perhaps it would be best to say that he is always vulnerable in some respects and completely oblivious and insensitive in others, but that at the same time he is unbelievably persistent in the same respects in which he is vulnerable. It must be added that the smallest baby's weakness gives him power; out of his very dependence and weakness he makes signs to which his environment (if it is guided well by a responsiveness based both on instinctive and traditional patterns) is peculiarly sensitive. A baby's presence exerts a consistent and persistent domination over the outer and inner lives of every member of a household. Because these members must reorient themselves to accommodate his presence, they must also grow as individuals and as a group. It is as true to say that babies control and bring up their families as it is to say the converse. A family can bring up a baby only by being brought up by him. His growth consists of a series of challenges to them to serve his newly developing potentialities for social interaction.

Each successive step, then, is a potential crisis because of a radical *change in perspective*. There is, at the beginning of life, the most radical change of all: from intrauterine to extrauterine life. But in postnatal existence, too, such radical adjustments of perspective as lying relaxed, sitting firmly, and running fast must all be accomplished in their own good time. With them, the interpersonal perspective, too, changes rapidly and often radically, as is testified by the proximity in time of such opposites as "not letting mother out of sight" and "wanting to be independent." Thus, *different capacities use different opportunities* to become full-grown components of the ever-new configuration that is the growing personality.

IMPLICATIONS

The importance of Erikson's system of development is indicated by the number of articles in this volume that use his concepts. The article on women (11) discusses women's identity from a developmental viewpoint and in terms of the crises met at several stages in development. The article on black identity (12) takes a similar stance. Finally, the article on competence (19) empirically shows the importance of the acquisition of valued skills at a certain stage of development.

REFERENCES

For more detailed discussion, see Erikson (1963).

17 THE CHILD'S INNER LIFE: INTERPRETATION OF PROJECTIVE DEVICES

Charlotte Buhler, Faith Smitter, Sybil Richardson, and Franklyn Bradshaw

What are some of the methods used by the psychologist to explore the inner life of the child? The clinical psychologist uses the child's responses to ambiguous pictures and figures as well as the child's own drawings to learn something of his needs and anxieties. These inner concerns influence the child's behavior even though he is not clearly aware of them. The techniques are known as *projective methods*.

A highly respected psychologist and her associates have reproduced children's drawings, which we include in this excerpt. The authors show us how the drawings have been used to obtain further understanding of the motivation and adjustment of the youngster.

You will notice that these drawings are interpreted with caution and

From *Childhood Problems and the Teacher* by Charlotte Buhler, Faith Smitter, Sybil Richardson, and Franklyn Bradshaw. Copyright, 1952, by Holt, Rinehart and Winston, Inc. Reprinted by permission of Holt, Rinehart and Winston, Inc. and the senior author.

responsibility and are supplementary to other data obtained on the child, his history, and observations of his behavior in important every-day situations. The qualified clinical psychologist advances hypotheses about the underlying motivation of his client, to be substantiated or negated by the bulk of the observations made. In doing this, he exemplifies the scientific attitude.

THE MAIN OBJECTION to projective techniques has been the difficulty of reliable interpretation of an individual's projections. Because of this difficulty there is danger of abusing projective methods.

People with empathy, intuition, and imagination often feel that they can interpret another's feelings and motives. Although they succeed often, their interpretations are far from reliable. Children's drawings, for instance, seem to offer an almost irresistible invitation to interpretation. For the alert and interested teacher, the temptation to think of the child who uses gay colors as gay, and to find clues to the child's personality in certain contents, is very great. But this should be done only with extreme caution unless the teacher has had clinical training. In order to interpret projective self-expression, the examiner must recognize that there are unique personal features in self-expression which exist only in this individual's "private world." Such features are understood only if one knows something about the individual's history. To the experienced worker, the detection of these unique features becomes an important clue to the discovery of emotionally traumatic experiences.

An interesting example is the little three-year-old girl who evidently had some problem in connection with the use of her hands. She went around the room touching things so that they fell down, but she never used her hands directly. She touched objects by pushing her doll's head toward the toys.

Later this same child built a stable for a toy cow and built it almost like a hand with blocks protruding like fingers. But there were six, not five blocks.

This child had been born with the anomaly of six fingers on one hand. Although operated on as a baby, she no doubt had heard about it and had also raised questions regarding the scar on her hand.

Another interesting example is the forty-one-year-old man who saw injured birds in the Rorschach ink blots in seven places in which most people saw quite different things. After the test, when the examiner asked whether he had any particular experience with birds, the subject was astonished by the question—he had not been conscious of seeing so many birds. Then he began to think and suddenly exclaimed that indeed as a boy of seven he had accidentally stepped on a little bird and crushed it. The incident bothered him for many years, after which he forgot it completely.

In addition to such unique experiences, projective techniques also show general human trends. These recurring content or form characteristics of projective productions have been submitted to standardizing procedures and can be interpreted generally as will be shown in the following.

Samples of Projective Material

Drawings and Paintings

For the teacher, drawings and paintings, including finger paintings, are so much a part of her experience and interest that a sampling of this important material is given here.

A good example is *Vigdis* whose drawings (Figure 1) were reproduced with a short explanation of her problem. . . .

She is quite *conscious* of the fact that she loves her teacher more than her grandparents; she wants her teacher to love her and to take her away from her grandparents into her own new home; Vigdis hopes to be welcome to the new husband also. She wants to be their child. She is *unconscious* of the fact that her drawings make a plea to the teacher to take her into her married life and into her new home as her child.

She gives a *direct* picture of herself with her grandparents and herself with the new couple. By the symbol of hand-holding she also *indirectly* expresses being close to the teacher and the husband but not to the grandparents.

In five-year-old *Tommy's* picture (Figure 2), there is an equally complex pattern of his conscious longing for the mother to be home, his unconscious fear and loneliness, his direct picture of the children at the windows, and his symbolic multiplication of many faces expressing the urgency he feels.

The deeper a child's problem, the more unconscious and unrealistic becomes the symbolism that expresses his disturbance. When *Frick* . . . ties the house he draws to a tree, he forgets reality in which houses are never tied to trees. He just expresses his fear and his wish concerning his home's stability.

The relationship between *Leigh's* apple tree (Figure 3) and himself was even deeper. When Leigh came to therapy . . . he was deeply disturbed by his soiling. The "ugly brown leaves" of the tree as well as the "dirty balls" of sand were semiconscious references to the soiling which shamed him. The leaves had to be burned; the balls to be buried. But the tree also had nice green leaves, and the tree must not burn. This was an unconscious reference to himself, to his good potentialities, and his wish that not Leigh but his shameful deeds be abolished.

This symbolic self-expression is deep because Leigh is not aware that his drawings and his sand formations relate to himself, or that he tells the therapist his problem by means of these products.

The therapist may or may not explain this symbolism to the child. Psychoanalysts formerly considered these interpretations to be essential. At

Figure 1. Vigdis, by the symbol of hand holding, indirectly expresses being close to the teacher and the husband but not to the grandparents. The house is the teacher's new home with all three of them looking out the window.

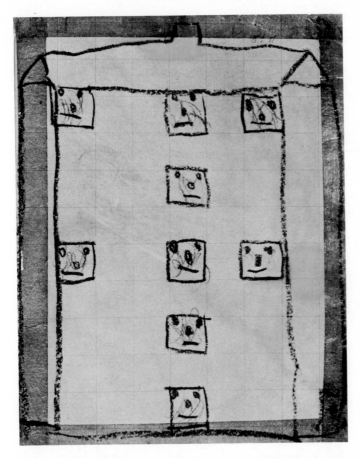

Figure 2. Tommy suggests longing for his mother to be home. The many faces in the windows express the urgency of his fear and loneliness.

present the prevailing tendency is to refrain from many interpretations, especially with younger children, and to achieve a certain amount of insight without making the child conscious of the way in which he revealed himself.

Leigh's apple tree is an *individual symbol* which refers to his private world. Leigh has been much interested in the burning of old leaves in his parents' back yard where grows this apple tree which he loves and climbs and which he identified with his home and himself. Other symbols are much more general and repetitious.

In spontaneous drawings of young children, the *house* appears most frequently. There seems to be a strong feeling about the protection that his home gives to the child. The strong identification of family and house is shown in one of the drawings that Wolff collected. At his instruction to

Figure 3. Leigh's apple trees—the "ugly brown leaves" and "dirty balls" of sand 'were semiconscious references to the soiling that shamed him.

"draw your family," a number of children drew the family beside their house.

In their drawings, many children surround their houses with fences, whether or not their own houses and yards have fences. The *fence* is another of the most frequently used symbols—to fence out potential aggressors or to imprison "bad" people.

Charlie, age eleven, makes a self-protective fence (Figure 4). So does nine-year-old *Henry* (Figure 5). *Henk*, an eight-year-old boy with severe anxieties caused by a very strict and punitive father, at first expresses his feelings that his house is a prison by painting barred windows. Then (Figure 6), probably becoming fearful that someone will guess how he feels, he covers the windows with paint, but expresses his feeling about lack of freedom everywhere by enclosing every object in his world—the trees, the flowers, even the sun and garden. There is only one hope, the boat with which to escape outside.

The most unhappy feeling seems expressed in *Hallie's* drawing (Figure 7). The whole world is only fence and sky. It is empty of people, of things, of anything to have fun with—an empty prison.

Figure 4. Charles makes a self-protective fence.

The depth of feelings of imprisonment and the need for self-protection cannot be decided by looking at the drawings. The interpreter has to know more about the child, his background and history, his symptoms, and his ability or inability to project his feelings appropriately.

In remedial release work, children will quite frequently draw jails or witches. This need not always mean deep feelings of deprivation and hatred. Sometimes these drawings may express only acute anger and acute unhappiness. It is helpful, whenever possible, to have the child's comments on his drawings. . . .

To the child, the *human figure* is as important as the *house*. The Goodenough "Draw-a-Man" test, originally devised for the purpose of testing intelligence, finds increasing application as a projective technique, because the attributes given to the human figure are often more expressive of the child's emotional responses than they are of his intellectual responses.

Children's self-portraits are also of great interest, revealing as they do children's attitudes toward their personalities and their moods. A frequent self-portrait is of the "lonely" child (Figure 8), done with unusually painstaking care.

Many of the examples we have used here show that *contents* as well as *formal* characteristics can be used for projection. This is as true of drawings as of other projective techniques, for example, the Rorschach and World tests. Protective fences, rigid schemation, confused disarrangements, over- or underemphasis of items, repetitions, worry over or disregard of detail—

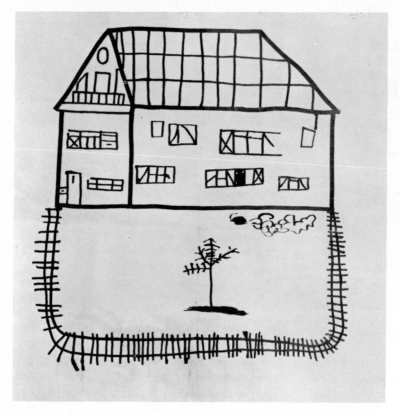

Figure 5. Henry shows great detail in his self-protective fence.

all are formal charactertistics produced by an individual similarly in all these techniques. . . .

An unconscious formal symptom of importance is the child's worry over much detail and his overconscientious efforts to produce the most careful detail. This is almost always a sign of excessive worry and of an emotionally disturbing perfectionism.

. . . *Paulinke's* flower garden (Figure 9), which is a happy content but, even so, not a release from worry, *Dagny's* detailed work on the girl in the snow (Figure 8), and *Henry's* detail on the garden fence (Figure 5) all belong in the same category.

A frequent content symbol used by little five- and six-year-old girls is the lonely child, as Dagny, age five, paints herself in the snow (Figure 8). "I want to stand all by myself," said another little girl who made such a drawing. Older lonely children paint "lonely" landscapes without people, sometimes without a sign of life, as *Ingrid* does in her second picture, "Road in

Figure 6. Henk paints barred windows and then covers them to disguise his feelings; the boat is a hope to escape outside.

Figure 7. Hallie draws the whole world as fence and sky—empty of people and anything to have fun with.

Figure 8. Dagny's self-portrait of a lonely child done with unusual painstaking care.

Figure 9. Paulinke's flower garden—a happy content but not a release from worry.

166

Figure 10. Ingrid's lonely landscape, "Road in the Sun."

Figure 11. Jerry's lonely landscape, "The Desert."

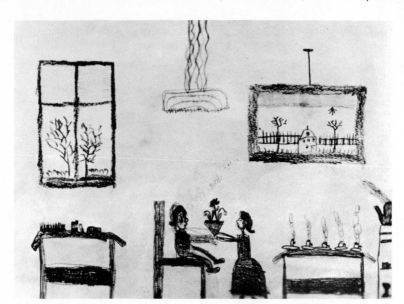

Figure 12. Irma's "Happy Birthday."

Figure 13. Douglas represents intellectual and artistic interests in his "The Battle of Hastings."

the Sun" (Figure 10), or *Jerry* does in "The Desert" (Figure 11). Older children also sometimes express their distrust of people by choosing animals, particularly horses, as their friends.

It would be wrong to assume that all children's paintings refer to emotionally disturbing events. Six-year-old *Irma's* "Happy Birthday" (Figure 12) and ten-year-old Paulinke's "Flower Garden" (Figure 9) project happy feelings, and drawings such as "The Battle of Hastings" (Figure 13) by Douglas, age nine, represent intellectual and artistic interests.

IMPLICATIONS

Which of the authors' interpretations of the drawings was clearest to you? If certain interpretations impressed you more than others, try to explain why. Did any ideas other than those stated by the authors occur to you as you observed the drawings? What differences do you note between those drawings that indicate emotional disturbance and those that do not? What cautions do you think psychologists should use in interpreting drawings?

REFERENCES

For further discussion of clinical application of projective drawings see Hammer (1958), Machover (1962) for personality projection in the drawing of a human figure, Allen (1958) for a review of drawing tests. Murstein (1965) and Rabin (1968) have chapters on drawings as projective devices as well as discussions of other projective techniques. See Axline (1947) for a treatment of children's play and drawings as an avenue for therapy.

18

PERSONALITY:
ITS BIOLOGICAL FOUNDATIONS

Roger J. Williams

Psychologists have been impressed by the pervasiveness of *learning* in human behavior. Almost every human act is and can be, with planning, greatly modified through learning. This fact led some early behavioristic psychologists to assume that, with planning, a child could be molded into almost any kind of personality the parent or teacher desired. Much has been accomplished by *conditioning* and regimentation, but, as any experienced parent will attest, not all children can be taught the lessons that are carefully planned for them, and contrariwise, children learn and develop as the result of basic talents and equipment rather than of external pressures.

Learning is important in human behavior; however, what is learned is not only a matter of environmental stimuli but also of inner motivations. Individuals differ greatly in physical and chemical structure, and the individual constitution determines, in relationship with the environment, what development will take place. Different people are different kinds of hosts to the environment they meet; some invite certain influences and repel others.

Roger J. Williams' selection shows the wide variation in biological equipment in the human being. At present there is not enough research on the complex *interrelationship between biological conditions and environmental influences* that together shape development in specific ways. However, the wide variation in anatomy and physiology presented in this selection can certainly be hypothesized to be related to the numerous individual differences found in personality, particularly as physiological function interacts with environment to motivate certain learned acts and not others.

Pavlov (1941) found as a result of extensive study of many dogs that they often exhibited innate tendencies to react very differently to the same stimulus. He recognized in his dogs four basic types (1) excitable, (2) inhibitory, (3) equilibrated, and (4) active, as well as intermediate types. He recognized enormous differences in dogs with respect to their conditionability, and was by no means inclined to focus his attention solely upon the behavior of "*the* dog." Scott and others have in more recent times found ample justification for Pavlov's concern over the fundamental differences between dogs of different breeds and between individual

Reprinted from Roger J. Williams, "The Biological Approach to the Study of Personality" (Conference on Personality Development, May 5, 1960), by permission of the author and the Elizabeth McCormick Memorial Fund (The Chicago Community Trust).

dogs within each breed. These differences, which can be studied under controlled conditions in dogs vastly easier than in human beings, are *not* the result of training.

It is beyond dispute, of course, that dogs, cats, rats, and monkeys, for example, show species differences with respect to their patterns of conditionability. Stimuli which are highly effective for one species, may be of negligible importance for another. If hereditary factors make for interspecies differences, it is entirely reasonable to suppose that intraspecies differences would exist for the same reason. . . .

It seems indefensible to assume that people are built in separate compartments, one anatomical, one physiological, one biochemical, one psychological, and that these compartments are unrelated or only distantly related to each other. Each human being possesses and exhibits unity. Certainly, anatomy is basic to physiology and biochemistry, and it may logically be presumed that it is also basic to psychology.

Let us look therefore in the *field of anatomy* * for facts which are pertinent to our problem.

Anatomists, partly for reasons of simplicity, have been prone in centuries past to concentrate on a single picture of the human body. Obvious concessions are made, when necessary, in considering the male and the female of the species, and always anatomists have been aware that within these two groups there are variations and anomalies. Only within the past decade (Anson, 1951), however, has comprehensive information been published which indicates how great these interindividual variations are and how widespread they are in the general population.

It makes no difference where we look, whether at the skeletal system, the *digestive tract,** the muscular system, the circulatory system, the respiratory system, the endocrine system, the nervous system, or even at the microscopic anatomy of the blood, we find tremendous morphological variations within the so-called normal range.

For example, normal stomachs vary greatly in shape, and about sixfold in size. Transverse colons vary widely in the positions at which they cross over in the abdomen, pelvic colon patterns vary widely. Arising from the aortic arch are two, three, four, and sometimes five and six branch arteries; the aorta itself varies greatly in size, and hearts differ morphologically and physiologically so that their pumping capacities in healthy young men vary widely. The size of arteries and the branching patterns are such that in each individual the various tissues and organs are supplied with blood unequally well, resulting in a distinctive pattern of blood supply for each.

Morphological differences in the *respiratory systems* * of normal people are basic to the fact that each person exhibits a distinctive breathing pattern

* Editor's italics.

as shown in the spirograms of different individuals made under comparable conditions.

Each *endocrine gland* * is subject to wide variation among "normal" individuals. Thyroid glands vary in weight about sixfold (Grollman, 1947), and the protein-bound iodine of the blood which measures the hormonal output varies to about the same degree (Williams, 1956). Parathyroid glands also vary about sixfold in total weight in so-called "normal" individuals, and the number of lobes vary from 2 to 12 (Grollman, 1947). The most prevalent number of lobes is 4, but some anatomists estimate that not over 50 per cent of the population have this number. The number of islets of Langerhans, which are responsible for insulin production, vary over a tenfold range in diabetes-free individuals (Pincus and Thimann, 1948). The thickness of the adrenal cortex where the critical adrenal hormones arise, is said to vary from 0.5 mm to 5 mm (tenfold) (Goldzieher, 1939).

The morphology of the pituitary glands which produce about eight different hormones is so variable, when different healthy individuals are compared, as to allow for severalfold differences in the production of the individual hormones (Rasmussen, 1924, 1928). The male sex glands vary in weight from 10 to 45 grams (Grollman, 1947) in so-called "normal" males and much more than this if those with "subnormal" sex development are included. The female sex glands vary in weight over a fivefold range and the number of primordial ova present at the birth of "normal" female infants varies over a thirteenfold range (Grollman, 1947). It is evident that all individuals possess distinctive endocrine systems and that the individual hormonal activities may vary over a severalfold range in individuals who have no recognized hormonal difficulty.

The *nervous system* * is, of course, particularly interesting in connection with the personality problem, and the question arises whether substantial variations exist. The classification of the various kinds of sensory nerve endings, for example, is by no means complete nor satisfactory, and the precise functioning of many of the recognized types is unknown. Investigations involving "cold spots," "warm spots," and "pain spots" on the skin indicate that each individual exhibits a distinctive pattern of each. In a relatively recent study of pain spots in twenty-one healthy young adults, a high degree of variation was observed (Tindall and Kunkle, 1957). When subjected to carefully controlled test conditions, the right hand of one young man "A" showed 7 per cent of the area tested to be "highly sensitive," while in another, "B," the right hand showed 100 per cent "highly sensitive" areas. On A's hand, 49 per cent of the area registered "no pain" under standard pain producing test conditions. On B's hand, however, there was no area which registered "no pain."

It is evident that there is room for wide variations with respect to the

* Editor's italics.

numbers and distributions of sensory nerve endings in different individuals. That such differences exist is indicated by the extreme diversity in the reactions of individuals to many stimuli such as those involving seeing, hearing, and tasting. An entire lecture could easily be devoted to this subject alone.

The branching of the trunk nerves is as distinctive as that of the blood vessels. Anson (1951), for example, shows eight patterns of the branching of the facial nerve, each type representing, on the basis of examination of one hundred facial halves, from 5 to 22 per cent of the specimens. About 15 per cent of people do not have a direct pyramidal nerve tract in the spinal column; an unknown percentage have three splanchnic nerves as compared with the usual two; recurrent laryngeal nerves may be wholly unbranched or may have as many as six brances (Rustad, 1954); the termination of the spinal cord varies in different individuals over a range of three full vertebrae.

Variations in *brain anatomy* * have received little attention. Thirteen years ago, however, Lashley (1947) in a review wrote: "The brain is extremely variable in every character that has been subjected to measurement. Its diversities of structure within the species are of the same general character as are the differences between related species or even between orders of animals. . . . Even the limited evidence at hand, however, shows that individuals start life with brains differing enormously in structure; unlike in number, size, and arrangement of neurons as well as in grosser features."

Unfortunately, partly due to the complexity of the problem, there is no information whatever available as to how these enormous anatomical differences are related to the equally striking personality differences which are commonplace. Recently there has been published, primarily for the use of surgeons, an extensive study of differences in brain anatomy (Schattenbrand and Bailey, 1959). Up to the present in our discussion, we have paid attention only to certain facts of biology—those in the field of anatomy. Before we consider other areas—physiology, biochemistry, and psychology —it seems appropriate to note whether we have made any progress in uncovering facts that have important implications for personality development.

Consider the fact (I do regard it a fact and not a theory) that every individual person is endowed with a distinctive gastrointestinal tract, a distinctive circulatory system, a distinctive respiratory system, a distinctive endocrine system, a distinctive nervous system, and a morphologically distinctive brain; furthermore that the differences involved in this distinctiveness are never trifling and often are enormous. Can it be that this fact is inconsequential in relation to the problem of personality differences?

I am willing to take the position that this fact is of the *utmost* impor-

* Editor's italics.

tance. The material in the area of anatomy alone is sufficient to convince anyone who comes upon the problem with an open mind that here is an obvious frontier which should yield many insights. Those who have accepted the Freudian idea that personality disorders arise from infantile conditioning will surely be led to see that, *in addition*, the distinctive bodily equipment of each individual infant is potentially important.

The failure of psychologists—and of biologists too—to deal seriously with innate individual differences in connection with many problems probably has deep roots.

McGill (1957) has said "Experimental psychologists . . . ignore individual differences almost as an item of faith." The same statement holds, in the main, for physiological psychologists, physiologists, and biochemists. Anatomists have adopted in the past (and some do even at present) the same attitude. Generally speaking, individual differences are flies in the ointment which need to be removed and disregarded. Every subject becomes vastly simpler and more "scientific" when this is done.

If one is pursuing knowledge about personality, however, neglect of innate individual differences is fatal. All of biology and all of psychology have suffered, in my opinion, from at least a mild case of "universalitis," an overruling desire to generalize immediately—oftentimes long before sufficient facts are gathered to give the generalization validity. This desire to generalize is of itself laudable, but the willingness to do so without an adequate background of information is unscientific and has devastating effects in the area of personality study.

The most treacherous type of premature generalization is the one that is not stated, but is merely accepted as obvious or axiomatic. Such a generalization is hidden, for example, in the famous line of Alexander Pope, "The proper study of mankind is man." This common saying *assumes* the existence of a meaningful prototype, *man*, a universalized human being— an object of our primary concern. From the standpoint of the serious realistic study of personality, I object to this implied generalization. If we were to alter Pope's line to read "The proper study of mankind is men," we would have detracted from its poetic excellence, but we would have added immeasurably to its validity in the area of personality study.

"Universalitis"is probably born of fundamental egotism. If one can make sweeping generalizations, they are self-gratifying, they can be readily passed on to disciples, the atmosphere seems to clear, life becomes simple, and we approach being gods. It is more pleasant often to retain one's conceit than it is to be realistically humble and admit ignorance. "Universalitis" is thus a sign of immaturity. When personality study has grown up it will recognize realistically the tremendous diversity in personalities, the classification of which is extremely difficult and must be based upon far more data than we now have.

With these ideas as additional background for our thinking let us consider some of the other aspects of biology. *Physiologically and biochemically* * distinctiveness in gastrointestinal tracts is just as marked as is the distinctiveness in anatomy. The gastric juices of 5,000 individuals free from gastric disease were found to contain from 0 to 4300 units of pepsin (Osterberg, *et al.*, 1936). The range of hydrochloric acid in a smaller study of normal individuals was from 0.0 to 66.0 millequivalents per liter (Bernstein, 1952). No one can deny the probability that large variations also exist in the digestive juices which cannot be so readily investigated. Some "normal" hearts beat more than twice as fast as other (Heath, *et al.*, 1945), some have pumping capacities at least three times as large as others (King, *et al.*, 1952), and the blood of each individual is distinctive. The discovery of the existence of "blood groups" was just the beginning of our knowledge of the individuality of the blood. Enzyme levels in the blood, which are a reflection of fundamental biochemical differences, vary from one well individual to another over substantial ranges, sometimes tenfold or even thirtyfold or more (Williams, 1956).

Our *neuromuscular systems* * are far from assembly-line products as can easily be demonstrated by a study of motor skills and by a large number of physiological tests. Our senses are by no means identical as has been made clear by taste tests for PTC and many other substances (Williams, 1956), by tests involving sense of smell (verbenas [Blakeslee, 1932], hydrocyanic acid [Kirk and Stenhouse, 1953]), sense of sight (peripheral vision, foveal size, flicker fusion, and related phenomena, eighteen types of color "blindness"), sense of balance, pitch discriminations and hearing acuities at different frequencies, etc., etc. From the tremendous variation in the action of specific drugs and chemicals on different individuals, we gain further evidence of fundamental differences in physiology and biochemistry (Williams, 1956).

Thurstone's pioneering work on primary mental abilities called attention to the fact that human minds have different facets, and that some individuals may be relatively well endowed with respect to arithmetical facility, for example, while being relatively deficient in word familiarity or spatial imagery. Others may be strong in the area of word familiarity but weak in rote memory or arithmetic. Guilford has more recently suggested that there are at least forty facets to human minds, involving a group of memory factors, four groups of thinking factors, the latter involving abilities relating to discovering, evaluating and generating ideas (Guilford, 1955). All of this leaves room for a multitude of mental patterns (patterns of conditionability) which it seems reasonable to suppose must be related to the enormous variation in the anatomy of human brains. People, even when confronted with the same facts, do not think alike, and this appears to have a sound anatomical as well as psychological basis.

* Editor's italics.

Those social anthropologists and other social scientists, who regard culture as the one factor which determines what an individual will be like, often say or imply that adult members of a society bear a very great resemblance to each other because of the similarities of their upbringing. In view of this common implication, it may be well to ask whether inborn differentness and distinctiveness fades out as a result of the adjustment of the individuals to the culture to which they are exposed. . . .

At the risk of being naive, it appears that the whole story we have been unfolding hangs together. Individual infants are endowed with far-reaching anatomical distinctiveness; each has a distinctive endocrine system, a highly distinctive nervous system, a highly distinctive brain. The same distinctiveness carries over into the sensory and biochemical realms, and into their individual psychologies. It is not surprising, therefore, that each individual upon reaching adulthood exhibits a distinctive pattern of likes and dislikes not only with respect to trivialities but also with respect to what may be regarded the most important things in life.

That culture has a profound influence on our lives no one should deny. The serious question arises, however, as to the relative position that different factors occupy in producing distinctive personalities. To me it seems probable that one's distinctive endocrine system and one's distinctive brain morphology are more important factors than the toilet training one receives as an infant.

We cannot state as a demonstrated fact that differences in brain morphology or in endocrine systems have much to do with personality differences. On the other hand, we have no rigorous scientific proof that toilet training has any substantial effect on personality development. We can only surmise. In one sense, personality study is in its very early infancy.

Another pertinent question—simple but important—awaits a clear answer: Are patterns of *brain morphology inherited?* * On the basis of what is known about the inheritance of other morphological features, including fingerprints and the branching of blood vessels on the chest, etc., it may be *inferred* that specific morphological features in the brain are handed down by inheritance, but we do not have definitive proof.

A fact which makes the study of the inheritance of such morphological features difficult is that expressed by geneticists David and Snyder (1951) ". . . it has become more and more widely recognized that single-gene differences which produce readily distinguishable discontinuities in phenotype variation are completely nonrepresentative of the bulk of genetic variability in any species." Multiple-gene effects are extremely common and in many cases, because of the complexity of the inheritance process, it is impossible to trace them in families or to know when and where such effects may be expected to arise. This complication is not the only one

* Editor's italics.

which exists; there is also the possibility (and certainty in some species) of maternal influence (cytoplasmic) which does not follow the rules of gene-centered genetics, and can thus throw one's calculations off (Williams, 1960).

The complications of broad genetic study are so great that closely inbred animals which, according to the simpler concepts of genetics, should be nearly identical in body make-up, are often relatively far from it. Even within relatively closely inbred groups of animals each has a distinctive pattern of organ weights, a distinctive excretion pattern, and at the same time a distinctive pattern of behavioral responses. . . .

Consideration of the available facts leads me to suppose, in the absence of completely definitive information, that differences in brain morphology, in endocrine patterns, in digestive, circulatory, muscular and nervous systems, etc., have important roots in heredity. It is difficult to see how such differences as exist could arise independent of heredity. The exact mechanisms whereby all these differences are inherited will probably be obscure many decades hence.

The recognition of hereditary factors does not by any means exclude from consideration the dynamic aspects of personality development. Potentialities and conditionabilities are inherited, not fixed characteristics. The widespread idea that personalities are developed from early childhood is fully in accord with an appreciation of the hereditary factors. Conditioning still takes place, but the recognition of innate biological differences calls attention to distinct make-up that each newborn baby possesses. Conditioning does not take place starting with assembly-line babies, each one, according to Watson, possessing exactly the same potentialities to develop into a "doctor, lawyer, artist, merchant, chief, and yes, even beggarman and thief.". . .

To tackle in one giant undertaking the problem of understanding, characterizing, and cataloguing all personalities from the biological or any other point of view seems hopeless. A strategy which seems far from hopeless, however, involves studying *one at a time* various personality characteristics to ascertain what biological roots they may have. The personality characteristics to be chosen for investigation should, obviously, be as definite as possible. They might include not only matters of temperament or emotion but also the ability to perform specified types of mental processes, or they might include personality problems of numerous types.

Studying even one particular personality characteristic to ascertain its biological roots is a large undertaking and might involve making scores, possibly hundreds, of measurements on every individual subjected to study. If one has some rational basis for selecting wisely the measurements to be made, the number of desirable measurements might be reduced. This fact would constitute an argument for selecting as the "personality problem" to be investigated, one for which the type of biological roots *might be* successfully guessed in advance. Such might include hyper- or hyposexuality, homosexuality, obesity, depressions, alcoholism, insomnia, accident proneness, etc. When one after another of personality disorders have been studied from this standpoint, it seems very likely that the whole picture will begin to clear and that the study of specific personality characteristics and problems will become successively easier the farther it progresses. What I am considering is obviously a relatively long-range proposal. . . .

Time will not permit a discussion of the numerous ways in which my own discipline, *biochemistry*,* impinges on personality problems (Williams, 1956). The effects of various chemicals on personality behavior, the correlations between brain metabolism and behavior, the effects of various hormones on personality characteristics are all well recognized. What is not so well recognized is that each individual's body chemistry is distinctive and different, and that complex biochemical roots of personality characteristics are likely to be found when we look for them with due care and thoroughness.

Before I close this discussion, I want to stress a most important environmental factor which is capable of contributing enormously to healthy personality development.

The monumental work of Beadle and Tatum (1941) demonstrated for the first time the vital connection between genes and enzymes, and in effect, between heredity and biochemistry. Their work made clear the inevitable basis for individual body chemistry. As a direct consequence of this finding, it becomes inevitable that the nutritional needs of genetically distinctive individuals are quantitatively not the same. Carrying the idea still further, it becomes inescapable that the brain cells of individual people do not have quantitatively identical nutritional needs.

It has been amply demonstrated that malnutrition of various kinds can induce personality disorders. This was observed in the starvation studies of Keys and associates (1952), in thiamin deficiency studies (Wilder, 1952), in amino acid deficiency studies † and perhaps most notably in pellagra where unequivocal insanity may result from niacin deficiency and can be abolished promptly by administration of the missing vitamin. It has also been shown repeatedly that inadequacy of prenatal nutrition can cause all sorts of developmental difficulties and abnormalities in the growing fetus.

One of the most obvious environmental measures that can be taken to insure favorable personality development is to see, for example, that the nervous system of each distinctive individual, with his distinctive needs, receives prenatally and postnatally the best possible nourishment. Nourishment of brain cells like the nourishment of other cells throughout the body can be maintained at many levels of excellence, and, of course, achieving the best is no small order.

* Editor's italics.
† W. C. Rose, personal communication.

Serious attention to nutrition which must involve the utilization of substantial manpower and a great deal of human ingenuity and persistence can, I believe, make tremendous contributions to our knowledge of personality states and personality disorders, and to the alleviation and prevention of personality difficulties.

In *conclusion* * I would emphasize that the biological approach to personality, outstandingly important as I believe it to be, is not a substitute for all other valid approaches. Whatever we may know or may be able to accomplish by other approaches, if valid, is not lost. Consideration of the biological approach expands our horizon and gives us a much broader view. In my opinion, the insight we may gain from this approach will be most valuable and productive. I should reiterate also what I have said before, that personality study is in its early infancy.

IMPLICATIONS

In what anatomical and physiological areas shown to yield wide individual differences would you expect the greatest influence on behavior? In your own experience, have you thought that certain physical factors might have influenced your development? Have you also suspected that certain physiological and biochemical processes have caused you —more than other children with whom you grew up—to tend to move toward or away from certain environmental situations?

REFERENCES

Consult the Bibliography for references cited in the article.

Other reviews of the biological bases of adjustment and personality are in Lazarus (1969) and Sechrest and Wallace (1967).

* Editor's italics.

19 COMPETENCE AND PERSONALITY CHANGE

Gerald P. Koocher

What events operate to give persons a feeling of self-esteem? Here is a study that demonstrates one valued skill, usually acquired in pre-puberty and puberty, that adds to one's self-esteem.

This study was designed to show that increasing competence in one's environment leads to enhancement of self-esteem. Using pretest and posttest measures of the discrepancy between the ideal self and self-concept of 65 boys between 7 and 15 years old at a YMCA summer camp, it was found that success in learning to swim reduced the discrepancy significantly ($p < .05$). Subjects who did not learn to swim, and controls who could already swim and were matched to experimental subjects in age and socioeconomic status, did not experience significant changes in the ideal-self—self-concept discrepancies in either direction.

THE SELF-CONCEPT has been a topic of study and conjecture since antiquity. Its development and functioning are central concerns of theorists and clinicians throughout psychology, and indeed, the last 2 decades have seen a resurgence of interest in personality theories pertaining to the self-concept. The present study was designed to investigate personality changes which may occur as a result of an individual's increasing competence in his environment. At various points, efficacy in dealing with one's environment has been thought to play a central role in determining the self-concept, but few investigators have attempted to experimentally examine the links which may be forged between development of competence in a specific area and its personality correlates. Using the self-concept paradigm, personality change was explored in the context of learning to swim.

The primary function of the present study was to test the general hypothesis that newly developed competence in a specific area, swimming in this case, would create changes in the self-concept of the individual concerned. It was also predicted that these changes would occur in a positive direction.

From Gerald P. Koocher, "Swimming, Competence, and Personality Change," *Journal of Personality and Social Psychology*, Vol. 18, 1971, 275–278. Copyright 1971 by the American Psychological Association, and reproduced by permission of the publisher and the author.

These predictions might be made on the basis of theoretical constructs such as Allport's (1961) adequacy, Adler's (Kelly & Ansbacher, 1956) superiority, Woodworth's (1958) mastery, and White's (1959) effectance. There is, however, little research to provide empirical support for these theories that is not drawn from limited case studies or broad generalizations.

The selection of learning to swim as a specific case of competence development was not accidental. Aside from the almost universal recognition of swimming as a valuable skill, no great proficiency is necessary in order for a person to feel that he has succeeded in this area. Even momentary self-propulsion and unsupported control in the water can represent a quite significant mastery for many children. Simply daring to challenge the water in an attempt to gain control of oneself in the medium may carry powerful implications. In this learning situation the child needs no outside approval to tell him when he has succeeded.

In view of the preceding arguments and theoretical considerations, certain hypotheses were posited as follows: First, the self-ideal minus self-concept discrepancy decreases when the subject learns to swim. The amount of this decrease should be significantly greater than any changes which occur in the self-ideal minus self-concept discrepancy of a similar control subject over the same period of time. Second, the discrepancy reduction anticipated should result from a change of the self-concept in the direction of the self-ideal.

Method

Subjects

Sixty-five boys aged 7 to 15 years who were attending the summer program at a YMCA resident camp qualified as subjects. They had a mean age of 10.3 years and a mean socioeconomic level of 3.0 on the Index of Social Position developed by Hollingshead and Redlich (1958, p. 394), which ranges from a high-status position of 1 to a low position of 5.

Measures

The instrument used as a measure of self-concept, self-ideal, and self-acceptance was a modification of the Index of Adjustment and Values (IAV) developed by Bills, Vance, and McLean (1951). The original IAV consists of 49 adjectives which the subject must mark in checklist fashion as descriptive of himself, his satisfaction with himself, and his ideal self in three columns, respectively. The present study used a form modified for use with school-age children (Bills, 1961), consisting of 35 adjectives, each of which was to be marked as describing the self "Most of the time," "About half the time," or "Hardly ever." In the second column, the subject expressed his feelings about the self as described in column 1 as, "Like it," "Neither like nor dislike it," or "Dislike it." Finally, in the third column, the subject described his ideal self on the same basis as the self. The IAV in this form was found to be easily within the capabilities of nearly all potential subjects.

Several studies have shown the IAV to have good reliability and validity. The most complete summary of these may be found in Wylie (1961, pp. 70–75). In her comprehensive critique of research on the self-concept, Wylie expressed skepticism regarding the construct validity of all instruments. She added, however, that Bills's work with the IAV "presents the most pertinent and convincing evidence on the question [p. 107]."

Procedure

All boys who had never attended this particular camp before took the IAV in groups upon arrival. The tests were administered by volunteer students not connected with the camp situation. The volunteers were given a set of guidelines for eliminating potential subjects from the study or assisting them if necessary. Subjects were disqualified if they could not complete the inventory without requesting definitions for more than three items, if their parents insisted on "helping" them, or if they appeared to rush through the IAV in a haphazard manner. On the other hand, many subjects could not pronounce some of the words properly, but recognized the word when it was spoken. In this case the subjects could have the words read aloud to them. Of 72 boys tested, 7 were eliminated from the study on the basis of these criteria, leaving the total N at the end of the study at 65.

The day after their arrival, all campers took a swimming test as part of the camp routine. The basic criterion for differentiating swimmers from nonswimmers was the ability of the boy to swim 25 yards unassisted. This judgment was made by members of the camp aquatic staff who were unfamiliar with the variables of the study or results of prior testing. All boys were encouraged to at least attempt the task, and were provided with assurance of assistance by at least two staff members who would accompany them each foot of the way. As a result campers were classified as P (passed the test), R (refused to attempt the test), or F (attempted, but failed). A sharp dichotomy was noted between those who attempted the task and those who refused. Although no one was forced to take the test, those who refused were unwilling to even venture an estimate as to what part of the distance they might be able to swim. All those who were rated as R or F were immediately qualified as subjects. A group of those who passed the test were selected as controls and approximately matched to the other subjects in age and socioeconomic status.

Since the basic period of camp operation was 2 weeks, a cutoff of 12 days was set. At the end of this period, the IAV was readministered to all subjects. Since the retest group contained boys of many ages and levels of swimming ability, there was no observable suspicion as to the purpose of the inventory.

It should be noted that an intensive learn-to-swim program was conducted by the camp aquatic staff during each 12-day period. All campers were encouraged to participate, and all subjects did attend swim instruction at least once.

Results

For purposes of analysis the subjects were divided into three data groups: those who learned to swim during the 12-day period (Group A); those who had failed or refused originally and did not learn to swim during the observation period (Group B); and the control group, consisting of boys who passed the initial swimming test and spent the next 12 days improving their swimming skills (Group C). The total number of subjects was 65, divided as follows: Group A = 19, Group B = 16, and Group C = 30.

The discrepancy between the ideal self and the perceived self, as calculated by the column 1 score subtracted from the column 3 score on the IAV, was significantly lower in the Group A posttest, than in the pretest. The t of 2.17 is significant at the .05 level and in the direction predicted. These data are presented in Table 1. The discrepancies of Groups B and C

Table 1
Intergroup Differences

Group	Status	n	M socioeconomic status	M age in years	M Self-ideal– self-concept discrepancy pretest	M Self-ideal– self-concept discrepancy posttest	t
A	Passed	0					
	Failed	16	3.26	9.82	8.26	3.37	2.17*
	Refused	3					
B	Passed	0					
	Failed	6	3.25	10.25	8.88	10.75	<1
	Refused	10					
C	Passed	30	2.53	10.80	7.83	6.30	<1
	Failed	0					
	Refused	0					

* $p < .05$.

did not change significantly between the pretest and posttest in either direction. In addition, the pretest and posttest scores were not significantly different from each other between the three groups per se. This is taken to show that those who learned to swim in the program did experience a decrease in self-ideal–self-concept discrepancy of significant proportions as a result of increases in self-concept. Subjects for whom swimming was already an area of competence, or who had failed to learn to swim (Groups B and C), maintained essentially the same self-ideal–self-concept discrepancy as they had from the outset.

Table 2 compares the net change (pretest to posttest) in the two experimental groups. This analysis yielded a t of 2.57, significant at the 0.2 level in the predicted direction. This comparison lends additional strength to the above results.

Table 2
Net Change in Experimental Groups

Group	n	M change pretest to posttest	df	s^2
A	19	4.89	18	93
B	16	−1.88	15	−30

Note.—$t = 2.57, p < .02$.

It should be noted that the subjects did not differ significantly in age or socioeconomic status. All members of Group C passed the initial swim test by definition. Of those who eventually learned to swim (Group A), only 16% had refused to attempt the test, while 84% tried but failed. Of those who did not learn to swim (Group B), 62% had initially refused the swimming test. These data are summarized in Table 3, and show a chi-square of 6.24, which is significant at the .02 level.

Table 3
Failed versus Refused Comparison

Status	Learned to swim	Did not learn
Failed test	16	6
Refused test	3	10

Note.—$\chi^2 = 6.24, p < .02$ (with Yates correction for continuity).

An item analysis was executed for all IAV pretest and posttest adjectives in order to determine which, if any, of these single items were significant discriminators between the three groups. Seventy 3×2 contingency tables were constructed, representing each of the 35 test items twice, once each for pretest and posttest conditions. Each item could have one of three possible self-ideal minus self-concept discrepancy scores. There might be no discrepancy, or a net difference of 1 or 2 points. Since few items showed any 2-point discrepancies, the contingency tables divide the item responses into discrepant or nondiscrepant columns, which were then divided into rows representing the three subject groups. Using a chi-square $(df = 2)$, 12 items were found to be significant predictors of one or more groups in the pretest, posttest, or both test conditions. These data are presented in Table 4.

Table 4
Results of Item Analysis

Test item	Pretest p	Posttest p	High discrepancy group on this item
1. Agreeable	ns	.05	B
2. Alert	.05	ns	A
8. Cooperative	ns	.05	B
9. Dependable	ns	.05	B
11. Friendly	.05	.05	pre = A & B post = B
16. Helpful	ns	.05	B
18. Kind	ns	.01	B
19. Loyal	ns	.05	B
21. Obedient	ns	.05	B
23. Polite	ns	.05	B
32. Trustworthy	.05	.001	pre = B post = B
33. Understanding	ns	.05	B

Note.—The 23 items not listed were not significant for either the pretest or posttest conditions.
Levels of chi-square, $df = 2$.

Discussion

The data support the hypotheses, indicating that the development of competence in an area heretofore marked by failure or avoidance results (at least in the case of swimming) in enhancement of the self-concept. These findings represent some behavioral support of White's (1959) theoretical approach to the study of the self-concept, which emphasizes the role played by gaining competence or the "experience of efficacy" in building self-esteem. Although well reasoned and illustrated with case studies, White's position lacks empirical support which the present study helps provide.

Diggory (1966) has suggested that people will tend to withdraw from situations in which they perceive their probability of success as low. The present findings are consistent with this view to the extent that boys who refused to take the swimming test (low estimate of probable success) were unlikely to learn to swim (possibly due to avoidance), as shown in Table 3.

Finally, it is important to note that the increased self-esteem attained in learning to swim, while significant, specific to the camp context, does not exert a generalized or long-lasting effect. This conclusion follows from the fact that the self-concepts of youngsters who already knew how to swim (i.e., had achieved that competence earlier) did not differ from those who could not swim at the beginning of camp. Coopersmith's (1967) conclusions also suggest that this should be the case. He found that external indicators of prestige do not have a pervasive effect or cross-situational transfer. When the child leaves camp and his new-found competence is less frequently demonstrated or praised, the gains specifically attributable to it may tend to fade. The self-concept changes found in the present case may be viewed as reflecting a somewhat momentary "aura" about mastery of swimming in the context of the camp experience.

IMPLICATIONS

Recall your own competencies and their role in developing areas of self-esteem and confidence. What does this study suggest about the nature of self-confidence and how it is developed in a given area of endeavor?

REFERENCES

See White (1959) on the issue of the development of competence from early childhood on. Allport (1961) has an excellent chapter on the development of selfhood. Coopersmith's (1967) experiments show the nature of parents of children who develop high self-esteem.

20 HAPPINESS IN MARRIAGE: PSYCHOLOGICAL FACTORS

Lewis M. Terman

Why are some individuals happier in marriage than others? This is an important question, since, in the United States, at least every fourth marriage ends in divorce. American students are sometimes appalled when their Asian contemporaries on the campus seem satisfied with the vital role their parents play in choosing a spouse for them. The Asian students might point out that their marital customs have certain advantages in that their spouses are chosen by mature people, whereas Western choices of marital partners are usually made by immature persons. Moreover, they may argue that the comparative status of marriage in the two different parts of the world, in terms of overt conflict in the families and divorce rates, does not reflect credit on the American freedom of choice. Of course, many issues are involved here besides the manner in which a spouse is chosen, but the article does raise questions about *readiness* and *compatibility* in marriage.

This selection is a classic; it is one of the early studies of marriage, conducted by a distinguished pioneer in American psychology, Lewis M. Terman.

An EXAMINATION of recent contributions to the literature on marriage reveals a great diversity of opinion about the factors most responsible for marital success or failure. On practically every aspect of the problem the pronouncements by leading authors are highly contradictory. The explanation of this situation lies partly in the bias of authors, partly in their willingness to generalize from inadequate data, and partly in the use of faulty techniques in the collection of information.

A study was accordingly planned which would investigate for a larger number of subjects the relationship between happiness scores and a great variety of possible factors, including not only personality factors but also background factors and factors having to do with sexual adjustments in the marriage. By the use of an improved technique for assuring anonymity of response, data were secured on these three sets of variables from 792 married couples who filled out the information schedules in the presence of a field assistant. The group studied represents a reasonably good sampling of the urban and semiurban married population of California at the middle and upper-middle cultural levels, though the sampling appears to be somewhat biased in the direction of superior marital happiness.

The Measure of Happiness Used

The marital-happiness score which was computed for each subject was based upon information regarding communality of interests, average amount of agreement or disagreement between spouses in ten different fields, customary methods of settling disagreements, regret of marriage, choice of spouse if life were to be lived over, contemplation of separation or divorce, subjective estimates of happiness, direct admission of unhappiness, and a complaint score based upon domestic grievances checked in a long list presented. Graded weights were assigned the various possible responses to these items on the basis of intercorrelations, and the total happiness score of a given subject was the sum of the weights corresponding to his individual responses. The resulting numeral score is a serviceable index of the degree of satisfaction that a subject has found in his marriage even though it cannot be regarded as a precise quantitative measure of such satisfaction.

The happiness scores ranged from practically zero to a maximum of 87 points, with a mean of 68.40 for husbands and 69.25 for wives. The respective standard deviations of the distributions were 17.35 and 18.75. The distributions for husbands and wives agreed closely throughout and were markedly skewed in the direction of high happiness. The scores of husbands and wives correlated to the extent of approximately .60, showing that the happiness of one spouse is to a surprising degree independent of the happiness of the other. This finding is new and perhaps rather significant. Its newness is probably explained by the fact that no previous investigation based upon a large group of subjects had secured its data by methods which prevented collaboration between husband and wife in filling out the information schedules. It is significant in the suggestion it carries that the degree of satisfaction which one finds in a marriage depends partly upon one's own characteristic attitudes and temperament and so need not closely parallel the happiness of one's marital partner.

Personality Correlates of Marital Happiness

The information schedule that was filled out by the subjects contained 233 personality test items dealing with interests, attitudes, likes and dislikes, habitual response patterns, and specific opinions as to what contitutes the ideal marriage. Of these, approximately 140 were found to show an appreciable degree of correlation with the happiness scores of either husbands or wives. The various possible responses to the valid items were then assigned score weights roughly in proportion to the extent to which they differentiated between subjects of high and low happiness scores. This made it possible to compute for each subject a "personality" score, which was merely the sum of the weights corresponding to the responses the subject had given. The personality score may be thought of as in some degree an index of the subject's temperamental predisposition to find happiness rather than unhappiness in the marital relationship. This index correlates approximately .46 with the marital-happiness scores of each spouse. Evidently the attitudes and emotional response patterns tapped by the personality items are by no means negligible as determiners of marital happiness.

By noting and classifying the individual items that differentiate between subjects of high and low happiness, it has been possible to piece together descriptive composite pictures of the happy and unhappy temperaments. For example, it is especially characteristic of unhappy subjects to be touchy or grouchy; to lose their tempers easily; to fight to get their own way; to be critical of others; to be careless of others' feelings; to chafe under discipline or to rebel against orders; to show any dislike that they may happen to feel; to be easily affected by praise or blame; to lack self-confidence; to be dominating in their relations with the opposite sex; to be little interested in old people, children, teaching, charity, or uplift activities; to be unconventional in their attitudes toward religion, drinking, and sexual ethics; to be bothered by useless thoughts; to be often in a state of excitement; and to alternate between happiness and sadness without apparent cause.

The above characterizations hold for the unhappy of both sexes. In many respects, however, the differences between the happy and unhappy follow a different pattern for husbands and wives.

The qualities of personality that predispose a person to happiness or unhappiness in his relations with others are of course far from being the sole cause of success or failure in marriage. Their importance, however, is so obvious from our data that the problem calls for further investigation, preferably by a combination of the statistical and clinical approaches.

Background Correlates of Happiness

Background factors which in these marriages were totally uncorrelated with happiness scores, or for which the correlation was so small as to have almost no practical significance, include family income, occupation, presence or absence of children, amount of religious training, birth order, number of opposite-sex siblings, adolescent popularity, and spouse differences in age and schooling. Nearly all of the factors in this list have been regarded by one writer or another as highly important, especially presence or absence of children in the home and differences between husband and wife in age and schooling.

It is doubtlessly true that the presence of children often prevents the breaking up of a marriage, but the evidence indicates that it has little effect on the general level of marital happiness. Childless women past middle age do show a slight tendency to be less happy than the average, but childless men of this age tend to have happiness scores above the average. If there are individual marriages that are made more happy by the presence of children, these appear to be offset by other marriages that are made less happy.

From the vantage point of our data it appears that much nonsense has been written about the risks entailed by marrying on inadequate income or by marrying out of one's age or educational class. The correlation of income with happiness scores is zero. The happiest wives in our group are those who are from four to ten years older than their husbands; the happiest husbands are those who are twelve or more years older than their wives. Moreover, the spouses of these subjects rate as happy as the average for the entire population of subjects.

As for religious training, if this was ever a factor in marital happiness, it appears no longer to exert such an influence.

We may designate as of slight importance the factors that show a barely significant relationship to the happiness of one or both of the spouses. This list includes age at marriage, absolute amount of schooling, rated adequacy of sex instruction, sources of sex information, age of learning the origin of babies, number of siblings, circumstances of first meeting between the spouses, length of premarital acquaintance, length of engagement, attractiveness of opposite-sex parent, resemblance of subject's spouse to subject's opposite-sex parent, amount of adolescent "petting," and wife's experience of sex shock or her age at first menstruation. No factor in this list is sufficiently related to marital happiness to warrant a prediction weight of more than one point [1] for either husbands or wives. There has been a vast amount of exaggeration about the risks to marital happiness of early marriage, brief premarital acquaintance, inadequate sex instruction, adolescent "petting," and a history of sex shock on the part of the wife.

Expressed desire to be of the opposite sex tends to be associated with unhappiness in wives but not in husbands. A premarital attitude of disgust toward sex is unfavorable to happiness, and more so in men than in women. Frequent or severe punishment in childhood is reliably associated with unhappiness in both husbands and wives. The items mentioned in this paragraph carry a maximum prediction weight of two points for at least one of the spouses.

Next are five items carrying a maximum weight of three points for one spouse and two points for the other. They are: estimates on husbands and wives of their relative mental ability, parental attitudes toward the subject's early sex curiosity, amount of conflict with father, and amount of attachment to both father and mother.

As to relative mental ability, the most favorable situation is equality or near equality. Marked mental superiority of husband makes for happiness in the wife but for unhappiness in the husband; marked inferiority of husband makes the wife unhappy but does not greatly affect the husband.

---

[1] The "prediction weights," ranging from one to five points, were based on the reliability of the differences between characteristics of two extreme groups (high and low happiness) of husbands and wives taken separately.

Subjects whose parents rebuffed or punished them because of their early sex curiosity are definitely less happy than the average, this effect being somewhat more marked in husbands than in wives.

Strong attachment to either parent is markedly favorable to happiness, especially in the case of husbands. Conflict with the father is unfavorable to happiness, especially in the case of wives.

We come now to the four most important of the background items: happiness of parents, childhood happiness, conflict with mother, and type of home discipline. All of these carry a maximum weight of four or five points.

Happiness of parents rates highest, with a maximum weight of five points for husbands and four for wives. This item is more predictive of success or failure in marriage than a composite of half a dozen items such as income, age at marriage, religious training, amount of adolescent "petting," or spouse difference in age or schooling.

Hardly less important is the rated happiness of respondent's childhood, with a maximum weight of four points for each spouse. Carrying the same weights is absence of conflict with mother. It appears that a record of conflict with mother constitutes a significantly greater threat to marital happiness than a record of conflict with father.

Childhood discipline that is firm, not harsh, is much more favorable to happiness than discipline that is lax, irregular, or excessively strict.

The ten background circumstances most predictive of marital happiness are (1) superior happiness of parents, (2) childhood happiness, (3) lack of conflict with mother, (4) home discipline that was firm, not harsh, (5) strong attachment to mother, (6) strong attachment to father, (7) lack of conflict with father, (8) parental frankness about matters of sex, (9) infrequency and mildness of childhood punishment, (10) premarital attitude toward sex that was free from disgust or aversion.

The subject who "passes" on all ten of these items is a distinctly better-than-average marital risk. Any one of the ten appears from the data of this study to be more important than virginity at marriage.

Sex Factors in Marital Happiness

Our study shows clearly that certain of the sex factors contribute materially to marital happiness or unhappiness. It shows no less clearly that others which have long been emphasized by sexologists as important are practically uncorrelated with happiness scores. The data, in fact, indicate that all of the sex factors combined are far from being the one major determinant of success in marriage.

Among the items yielding little or no correlation with happiness are both reported and preferred frequency of intercourse, estimated duration of intercourse, husband's ability to control ejaculation, methods of contraception used, distrust of contraceptives, fear of pregnancy, degree of pain experienced by wife at the first intercourse, wife's history of sex shock, rhythm in wife's sexual desire, ability of wife to experience multiple orgasms, and failure of the husband to be as dominant as the wife would like him to be in initiating or demanding intercourse.

The sex techniques that many writers regard as the primary key to happy marriage may be worth cultivating for their immediate sensual returns, but they exert no appreciable effect upon happiness scores. Their absence or imperfection is evidently not a major source of conflict or a major cause of separation, divorce, or regret of marriage. What is even more surprising, it appears that such techniques have no very marked effect on the wife's ability to experience the orgasm.

On the other hand, the wife's happiness score (though not her husband's) is reliably correlated with the amount of pleasure that she experienced at her first intercourse, and the husband's happiness is reliably correlated (negatively) with the wife's tendency to prudishness or excessive modesty.

Five of the six items that correlate quite markedly with the happiness scores are: number of sexual complaints checked, rated degree of satisfaction from intercourse with spouse, frequency with which intercourse is refused, reaction of the spouse who is refused, and frequency of desire for extramarital intercourse. The correlations, however, probably do not mean that the factors in question are to any great extent actual determiners of happiness or unhappiness. It is more likely that they are primarily symptoms. The discontented spouse rationalizes his (or her) unhappiness by finding fault with the sexual partner and at the same time develops longings for extramarital relationships.

Among the sex factors investigated are two that not only correlate markedly with happiness scores but are in all probability genuine determiners of them: viz., the wife's orgasm adequacy and husband-wife difference in strength of sex drive.

Two measures were available on relative strength of sex drive. One of these was the ratio (computed for each subject) between actual and preferred number of copulations per month; the other was based on husband's and wife's ratings of their relative passionateness. The two measures agree in showing that equality or near equality in sex drive is an important factor in happiness. As the disparity in drive increases to the point where one spouse is in a more or less chronic state of sex hunger and the other in a state of satiety, the happiness scores of both drop off significantly.

First in importance among the sex factors is the wife's orgasm adequacy, which correlates about .30 both with her own and with her husband's happiness score. It is of special interest that orgasm inadequacy of the wife affects her husband's happiness almost as unfavorably as her own. Between wives of the "never" group and wives of the "always" group, there is a difference of 16.3 points in mean happiness, and a difference of 13.0 points in the mean happiness scores of their husbands. Nevertheless, one finds every grade of happiness both in the "never" group and the "always" group.

Adequacy of the wife in this respect favors happiness but does not guarantee it, while on the other hand a considerable minority among the inadequates have happiness scores above the general average.

The Relative Importance of Sexual and
Psychological Compatibility

Our data do not confirm the view so often heard that the key to happiness in marriage is nearly always to be found in sexual compatibility. They indicate, instead, that the influence of the sexual factors is at most no greater than that of the combined personality and background factors, and that it is probably less. The problem is complicated by the fact that the testimony of husband and wife regarding their sexual compatibility is influenced by their psychological compatibility. Couples who are psychologically well-mated are likely to show a surprising tolerance for the things that are not satisfactory in their sexual relationships. The psychologically ill-mated show no such tolerance but instead are prone to exaggeration in their reports on sexual maladjustments. The two sexual factors of genuine importance are wife's orgasm adequacy and relative strength of sex drive in the two spouses.

IMPLICATIONS

Most of us have an opportunity to observe the state of marriage because we are reared in families and live in neighborhoods of married people. From your experience, choose the marriages you know best and estimate whether the partners would have a high, low, or average happiness probability in terms of the items mentioned in the article. Now note the factors that you would surmise contributed most to happiness and unhappiness in these marriages. What features in your life would tend to produce happiness or unhappiness in your own?

To what extent may we expect Terman's findings to hold for some economic groups other than the middle class? To what extent do you see factors that are discussed here operating in the young marriages you know?

REFERENCES

Other publications in this general area deserve mention: see Burgess and Cottrell (1939). Burgess and Wallin (1953) and Kelly (1939) are two studies on personality-background factors before and after marriage.

These investigations indicate that some people are better marital risks than others.

An area of professional psychology shared with other behavioral descriptives has developed, known as *marriage counseling*. Specialists in this area are qualified to assist the individual when he is having interpersonal difficulties in marriage. (See Kimber, 1961.) Communication between spouses is recognized as one of the difficulties in marriage. Spouses play games (Berne, 1964). The message sent by a spouse may not be received accurately by the other (Selections 46 and 35). Aronson's (1972) gain-loss theory of personal attraction suggests answers to why someone outside the family, who is rewarding to us, may have more impact than a member of the family who has been rewarding to us over a period of years.

V

TRAINING
AND EDUCATION

21 CONTROLLING BEHAVIOR: PREMACK PRINCIPLE

L. E. Homme, P. C. deBaca, J. V. Devine, R. Steinhorst, E. J. Ricket

Parents, teachers, supervisors, and others have the responsibility of controlling the behavior of people in their charge. Each of us has the responsibility of controlling our own behavior—completing assignments, doing necessary but dull or distasteful tasks, and so on. Reinforcement (strengthening the response that precedes an event) has been used quite effectively in establishing desired behavior. The Premack principle holds that a well-established behavior can be used to reinforce one that is less well established. For example, a student who has difficulty starting to study and prefers to talk with a friend who lives down the hall can plan his schedule so the rap session always follows an hour or two of study. By this plan he uses the rap session (a well-established behavior) to reinforce the study period (the less well established one).

One corollary of the Premack principle is that we can often find out what reinforcer is appropriate for a given person simply by observing his behavior. The solution to the riddle of "How can we motivate the behavior of someone we hardly know?" is charmingly illustrated by the following article, which is reprinted in its entirety.

PREMACK'S PRINCIPLE (Premack, 1959) can be stated: if behavior B is of higher probability than behavior A, then behavior A can be made more probable by making behavior B contingent upon it.

In a preliminary exploration of nursery school procedures, three 3-yr-old subjects (Ss) were available three hours a day, five days a week, for about one month. On the first day, in the absence of any aversive control, verbal instructions usually had little effect on the Ss' behavior. When they were instructed to sit in their chairs, Ss would often continue what they were doing—running around the room, screaming, pushing chairs, or quietly working jigsaw puzzles. Taking Premack seriously, such behaviors were labeled as high probability behaviors and used in combination with the

From L.E. Homme, P.C. deBaca, J.V. Devine, R. Steinhorst, E.J. Rickert, "Use of the Premack Principle in Controlling the Behavior of Nursery School Children," *Journal for the Experimental Analysis of Behavior,* Vol. 6, p. 544. Copyright 1963 by the Society for the Experimental Analysis of Behavior. Reprinted by permission of the publisher and the senior author.

signals for them as reinforcers. These high probability behaviors were then made contingent on desired behaviors. For example, sitting quietly in a chair and looking at the blackboard would be intermittently followed by the sound of the bell, with the instruction: "Run and scream." The Ss would then leap to their feet and run around the room screaming. At another signal they would stop. At this time they would get another signal and an instruction to engage in some other behavior which, on a quasi-random schedule, might be one of high or low probability. At a later stage, Ss earned tokens for low probability behaviors which could later be used to "buy" the opportunity for high probability activities.

With this kind of procedure, control was virtually perfect after a few days. For example, when Ss were requested to "sit and look at the blackboard" (an activity which in the past had intermittently been interrupted by the signal for some higher probability behavior), they were under such good control that an observer, new on the scene, almost certainly would have assumed extensive aversive control was being used.

An examination of high probability behaviors quickly showed that many, if not most of them, were behaviors which ordinarily would be suppressed through punishment. Extrapolating from this we were able to predict the reinforcing properties of some behaviors which had never been emitted. For example, throwing a plastic cup across the room and kicking a waste basket had never been observed but proved to be highly reinforcing activities after they had once been evoked by instructions. (Some unpredicted behaviors proved to be highly reinforcing, e.g., pushing the experimenter around the room in his caster-equipped chair.)

In summary, even in this preliminary, unsystematic application, the Premack hypothesis proved to be an exceptionally practical principle for controlling the behavior of nursery school Ss.

IMPLICATIONS

You might find it interesting to cooperate with a friend or roommate and each list the other's observed well-established activities or sources of reinforcement. These then may be used as potential reinforcers to follow activities that are not well established.

REFERENCES

See original articles by Premack (1965). The concept of reinforcement is associated with the work of B. F. Skinner (1938), author of Selection 23.

22

IMITATION, MODELING, AND SELF-REWARD

Mark H. Thelen, Jerry L. Fryrear, and David L. Rennie

In our development from early childhood we have much to learn. If all details of personality and social behavior had to be learned by direct experience, human development would be a slow process indeed. Fortunately, much of our complex social behavior occurs as a result of vicarious learning, by observation of what other people do in a situation.

Imitation has long been recognized as an important factor in the development of personality and social behavior. What is new is the use of an experimental method of testing the extent and the factors involved in imitative behavior.

Research has flourished in the field, as reported by Bandura (1969) and has confirmed that subjects can acquire intricate response patterns by observing other people. Furthermore, behavior can be changed by observing the different behavior of other persons: Various emotional responses can be changed, fears can be extinguished, and inhibitions can be induced in this way. Self-regulating behavior, too, can be learned by watching and imitating others.

The experiment described below involved delinquent boys and a model (the person imitated). The subject responded in the manner in which the model responded, and this behavior was retained over a period of time. It shows that a modeled response can be retained over a period of time.

The authors attempted to determine if subjects would imitate a model three months after observing the model, when they had not been previously tested for imitation. Black and white delinquent adolescent males were assigned, respectively, to one of three groups. Within each race, one group saw a video-tape of a white adult male reward himself liberally for his predetermined performance at a pursuit rotor task. Another group saw the same model reward himself stringently. The third group did not see a model. Three months later, each subject was given an opportunity to reward himself for a pursuit rotor performance that was ostensibly equal to that of the model. The results showed that the liberal and stringent self-reward behaviors of the model were imi-

tated after the 3-month delay. There were no differences in imitation between the black subjects and white subjects, nor was there any correlation between imitation and assessed racial attitudes.

D ESPITE THE RECENT voluminous work on imitation, scant attention has been given to the appraisal of observational learning retained over prolonged periods of time. Bandura and his associates found that the vicarious acquisition of self-imposed delay of reward (Bandura & Mischel, 1965) and the vicarious extinction of dog fears (Bandura & Menlove, 1968) were in evidence one month after the observation of a model. Hicks (1965) reported that one of four experimental groups performed significantly more imitative aggression than a no-model control group six months after exposure to an aggressive model. And Thelen (1970) found evidence of imitative self-blame responses in elementary school children seven months after an initial test for imitation.

None of the above studies has demonstrated the retention of *modeled* behavior. Each of the studies gave the Ss* an opportunity to perform the modeled behavior either during or immediately after the modeling sessions. Hence it is impossible to determine whether the follow-up tests for imitation measured delayed imitation of the models' behavior or the retention of the Ss' own behavior. Perhaps the Ss simply remembered what they had done before.

The main purpose of the present study was to investigate the delayed imitation of modeled standards of self-reward when the S was denied an opportunity to perform the modeled behavior prior to a test for imitation given three months after the modeling session. The present study also provided for a more rigorous test of the imitation of standards of self-reward than previous studies (e.g., Bandura & Kupers, 1964) because some of the Ss were provided with normative information which was not congruent with the standards of self-reward exhibited by the model.

A secondary purpose of the present study was to examine whether there were differences between black and white Ss in the retention of self-reward standards of a white model. Research concerning racial differences in imitation has yielded equivocal results. Breyer and May (1968) found no differences between black and white children in their imitation of the irrelevant behavior of male and female models in a two-choice discrimination task. Thelen and Soltz (1969) found that white kindergarten children imitated the aggressive behavior of a verbally praised white model more than Head Start children most of whom were black, but found no differences between the racial groups who observed a non-praised white model. While Thelen (1971) found differences in imitation associated with model race,

* Ss = symbol for subjects in the experiment.

black and white Ss imitated about equally. In a prototype of the present study (Thelen & Fryrear, 1971a,b), a test for immediate imitation of the same standards of self-reward reported here failed to demonstrate S racial differences in imitation.

In order to help explain any racial differences in imitation, evaluative ratings toward black people and white people were obtained from all Ss. Although Thelen and Fryrear (1971a,b) failed to find a relationship between the racial attitudes of black or white males or females and their immediate imitation of a black or white model, evaluative ratings were obtained in the present study to allow an analysis of the relationship between attitudes and delayed imitation.

Method

Subjects

Seventy-two 15-, 16-, and 17-year-old males, who had been committed by the court to the Missouri state institution for delinquents, served as Ss. Half of the Ss were black and half were white. Within each racial group, the Ss were randomly assigned (12 in each condition) to a Liberal or Stringent White Model Condition, or to a No-Model Control Condition. During the 3-month interim between the Ss' observation of the model and subsequent performance at the imitation task, 15 Ss left the institution and were unavailable for testing. This attrition resulted in a final sample composed of 8 black and 10 white Ss who saw a stringent model, 8 black and 7 white Ss who saw a liberal model, and 12 black and 12 white Ss who saw no model. The mean educational achievement scores of the black Ss and white Ss were 5.84 and 6.71 respectively. Although these means are significantly different ($t = 2.06$; $p < .05$), there is no relationship between the Ss' educational achievement and their delayed imitation scores ($r = .006$).

Attitude Measure

The Ss' attitudes toward White People and Black People were assessed with a semantic differential. Five evaluative scales (fair–unfair, valuable–worthless, pleasant–unpleasant, clean–dirty, and good–bad) were scored and the sum used as a measure of attitude. Osgood, Suci, and Tannenbaum (1957) reported that ratings of the Negro on these five scales correlated .82 and .81 with the Thurstone (1931) scales, which were designed to assess attitudes toward Negroes.

The concepts to be rated, White People and Black People, were included in a 6-page booklet with four other unscored concepts (Men, Chinese People, Women, and Myself) and counterbalanced within each group. Each concept was printed at the top of a semantic differential which contained the evaluative scales randomly interspersed among four additional unscored scales.

Model Tapes

Two TV tapes were constructed which depicted a 27-year-old white male performing a pursuit rotor task. The model was seated on one side of a small table, facing the camera, and the experimenter sat on the other side, with his profile to the camera. On the table was the pursuit rotor, a chronometer that was attached to the pursuit rotor, a timer that automatically started and stopped the rotor, and a large glass ash tray filled with poker chips. An enlarged target area was painted on the pursuit rotor so that it was impossible to tell when the stylus was actually on the part of the target which moved the chronometer. The two tapes were identical except that the model was stringent with self-rewards on one tape and liberal on the other. As the tape began, the experimenter gave the following instructions to the model:

Experimenter: "This is a test of arm coordination and how well people think you do."

Model: "This looks like fun! I'm going to like this!"

Experimenter: "As this target goes around and around, your job is to keep the end of this pointer as near to the center of the bullseye as you can. The target will go around several times, stop for a few seconds, then go around again several times. After the second time, I will give you your score from this counter (pointed to chronometer). Most people get a score anywhere from 1 second to 9 seconds. Now each of these chips here is worth one nickel (experimenter held chips up). Every time I give you your score, *you* decide if you did well enough for a chip. Do you have any questions?"

Model: "How do you hold this?" (Held up stylus)

Experimenter: "Just hold the wooden handle so that the metal part is free to move up and down . . . that's right."

After these instructions to the model, six trials were performed (two efforts of 15 seconds each per trial at 60 RPM). After each trial the experimenter gave the following predetermined scores: 6, 7, 8, 7, 8, and 9 seconds.

On the liberal model tape, the model took a chip after each trial, with appropriate verbalizations. For example, after being given a score of 7 on the second trial, the model took a chip and said, "7 seconds! That's a fairly good score. 7 seconds is good for a chip."

On the stringent model tape, the model took a chip for a score of 8 or 9 but declined to reward himself for a score of 6 or 7. On the rewarded trials, the model took a chip and made a comment similar to those on the liberal tape. On the non-rewarded trials, the model refused to take a chip, and said, for example, "7 seconds! Still not very good. I won't take a chip for 7 seconds."

The tapes were presented to the Ss by means of a G.E. Model 4TD1B2 audio-video tape recorder and Model 4TH3183 monitor that resembled an ordinary portable television set.

Procedure

Liberal and Stringent Model Groups

The Ss were brought individually to the testing room where the experimenter first administered the semantic differential to assess the S's attitude toward the different racial groups. Then the experimenter drew the S's attention to the pursuit rotor and explained that it was used to test arm coordination and how well people think they do. The S was told that the easiest way to explain the testing procedure would be to show him a demonstration on the television. The S then watched one of the model tapes. Following the tape, the experimenter informed the S that he was behind schedule and would not have time to give him the test for arm coordination. The experimenter told the S that he would be back at the institution in about three months and that S could take the test at that time.

Three months later (± seven days) each S was brought back to the experimental room where the experimenter reintroduced himself and reminded S of the initial session when he had seen the television demonstration. Instructions similar to those given the model on the tape were then given to the S. The experimenter drew the S's attention to normative information, which was directly in front of the S, and indicated that most people get a score on the pursuit rotor anywhere from 1 second, which is a low score, to 9 seconds, which is a high score. The normative information before the S depicted the scores 1 through 9 with the word "low" written under the number 1, the word "average" under numbers 4 and 5, and the word "high" under number 9.

The S was further advised that each of the chips in the nearby container was worth one nickel and could be cashed in for candy, potato chips, cigarettes, and pop immediately after the test. The S was told that each time he was given his score, he should decide if he did well enough to take a chip. He was then given a practice round to assure that he understood how the pursuit rotor would operate. He was reminded that most people get a score between 1 and 9 seconds, and was again referred to the normative chart that was kept in front of him throughout the experiment.

The S then performed six trials and was given the following predetermined scores (the chronometer could not be read by S) in the following order: 6, 7, 8, 8, 7, and 9. Thus all the scores given to the S and the model were higher than the average score of 4 or 5 that was presented as normative information. The scores given to the Ss were identical to those given to the model, but in a different order. After the first trial, the S was reminded that each time he was given his score, he was to decide if he did well enough for a chip. None of the Ss appeared suspicious that the scores given to the model and to them were predetermined.

No Model Control Groups: The Ss who did not see a tape were brought to the experimental room for the first time during the testing period for the experimental Ss. They took the semantic differential just as the other Ss had three months earlier, and instructions concerning the pursuit rotor were then given corresponding to the instructions given the experimental Ss following the model tape. The remainder of the procedure was the same for all Ss.

Results

Delayed Imitation of Self-Reward Standards

Overall Analysis The reader is reminded that Ss in the Liberal Model condition observed a model reward himself on all six trials, whereas Ss in the Stringent Model condition observed a model reward himself for scores of 8 or 9, but not for scores of 6 or 7. The liberal and stringent models thus behaved similarly after scores of 8 or 9, and differently after scores of 6 or 7. Therefore, the trials after which scores of 6 or 7 were given to the Ss (trials 1, 2, and 5) can be considered "critical" trials. Unless stated otherwise, the overall analyses reported were performed on the number of chips taken by Ss on these critical trials so that the Liberal and Stringent Model conditions could be compared directly.

An unequal-n analysis of variance indicated that there were systematic treatment effects due to the liberal-stringent self-reward variable ($F = 3.61$, $p < .05$, error mean square $= 0.96$). Neither the subject race variable, nor the treatment $\times$ subject race interaction was significant ($p > .20$).

Because the analysis of variance showed no significant effects due to the race of the Ss, the black and white Ss within each model condition were then pooled, resulting in a Stringent Model group ($n = 18$, $X = 1.89$), a Liberal Model group ($n = 15$, $X = 2.67$), and a No-Model Control group $n = 24$, $X = 2.29$). A Duncan's Multiple Range Test showed a significant difference between the Liberal and Stringent groups ($p < .05$). Neither pooled experimental group was significantly different from the pooled Control group.

In order to study the data in more detail, additional analyses were carried out within and between the Liberal, Stringent, and Control groups.

Liberal Condition As stated above, the Ss exposed to a liberal model did not differ significantly from the No-Model Control group when trials with scores of 6 or 7 were used to assess delayed imitation. But because the liberal model rewarded himself on all six trials, it is appropriate to use a second and more comprehensive criterion for self-reward among the liberal model Ss—the number of self-rewards over all six trials. Using the latter criterion, the pooled Liberal Model group yielded a mean imitation score of 5.60, which is significantly different from the mean score of 4.79 for the pooled No-Model group ($t = 1.94$, $p < .05$, one-tailed test).

Stringent Condition As a follow-up analysis, a Duncan's Multiple Range Test was used to compare all the groups on the three critical trials. The Stringent Model black Ss showed more delayed imitation than the black No-Model Control Ss ($p < .05$). There was a similar trend among the white Ss (Stringent Model greater than No-Model Control) but the difference did not reach significance.

Comparison of the critical trials alone precludes a determination of whether the Stringent Model Ss had imitated a response to specific scores or had merely become generally more stringent no matter what their score. If the Stringent Model Ss imitated a response to particular scores, there should be no difference between the Liberal Model groups and Stringent Model groups on the non-critical trials (trials 3, 4, and 6) because the two models exhibited identical self-reward behavior on those trials. A t-test of the self-reward scores for the non-critical trials revealed that there were no significant differences between the Liberal and Stringent Ss ($t = .43$, $p > .50$).

Actual Time on Target

It is possible that the Ss' actual time on target interacted with the different model conditions to influence the self-reward scores. If such were the case, the liberal model Ss should differ from the stringent model Ss with respect to their actual time on target. Using actual time on target for all six trials and pooling for S race, the liberal model Ss were on target almost exactly the same amount of time as the stringent model Ss ($X = 33.8$ and $X = 33.6$ respectively; $t = .03$). It appears that the Ss' performance on the pursuit rotor was not affected by the different experimental conditions nor were there pursuit rotor performance differences which might account for the differences in self-reward behavior.

Racial Attitudes and Imitation

The white Ss and black Ss did not differ significantly in their ratings of White People ($t = .21$, $p > .50$). Within each racial group, Pearson Product-Moment Correlation coefficients were calculated between imitation scores and the evaluative semantic differential ratings of White People, and between imitation scores and the difference in ratings of White People and Black People. No significant correlations were found. These data were further analyzed by pooling the liberal and stringent model Ss and determining the upper and lower one-third on the measure of attitudes toward White People. The two groups did not differ in imitation on the critical trials ($t(20) = .42$). According to the measurements of imitation and racial attitudes used in the present study, there does not seem to be a relationship between racial attitudes toward White People and imitation of a white model by black or white Ss.

Discussion

The present study clearly demonstrated the delayed imitation of modeled self-reward standards. Researchers concerned with imitation have shown that imitative learning can be retained over various periods of time (e.g., Bandura & Menlove, 1968; Bandura & Mischel, 1965; Hicks, 1965; and Thelen, 1970), but the studies reported in the literature have all been designed so that there was an opportunity for the observers to practice the modeled behavior prior to a test for retention of the modeled responses. Therefore, these studies did not permit for a determination of whether the Ss retained the model's behavior, or whether the Ss retained their own behavior, behavior that had been performed either during or immediately after the modeling session. The present study is the first study known to the authors that demonstrated delayed imitation under conditions wherein the Ss had not been tested for imitation prior to the retention measure. The demonsration of the retention of modeled behavior thus went one step beyond previous research.

The imitation by the Stringent Model Ss is particularly noteworthy because they faced several barriers against imitation. First, the stringent model consistently performed above the norm provided to the Ss yet did not reward himself every time. Second, the norm was present during testing, whereas the model had demonstrated his standards of self-reward three months earlier. Third, the Stringent Model Ss had to learn a separate criteria of rewards and non-rewards while the Liberal Model Ss had merely to learn to reward themselves on all trials. Finally, the Control group's relatively high mean number of rewarded trials $(X = 4.79)$ suggests a tendency toward self-reward that had to be overcome by the stringent model's influence.

The tendency toward high self-reward behavior among the No-Model Ss may have been a function of the experimental design. In order to achieve a balanced design, the Control Ss were exposed to the same performance norm given to the experimental Ss. As a consequence, all of the performance scores received by the Control Ss were above the norm, which may have prompted them to reward themselves more often than would have been the case if they had not been provided with such a norm. This feature of the design may have diminished the magnitude of the liberal model effect because the number of self-rewards of the Control Ss approached the reward ceiling of the Liberal Model Ss. It may have been this ceiling effect which led to the significant difference in self-reward behavior between Liberal Model Ss and Control Ss for six trials but not for just the three critical trials. The former criterion allowed more room for subject variability.

There were no differences between black and white Ss in the delayed imitation of either the liberal or the stringent model. These findings are consistent with research on the immediate spontaneous imitation of aggressive behavior under conditions of no vicarious reinforcement (Thelen & Soltz, 1969; Thelen, 1971), the immediate imitation of motor behavior in a two-choice discrimination task (Breyer & May, 1968), and the immediate imitation of patterns of self-reward (Thelen & Fryrear, 1971a,b).

It was hoped that the attitude measure would help explain any differential imitation by the black and white Ss but, since there were no differences between the racial groups in imitation, the attitude data were not germane to between-group comparisons. Within each group there were individual differences in both imitation and racial attitudes, but analyses revealed no significant correlations between these two variables. Hence the present study has provided no reason to believe that there is an association between evaluative attitudes as measured on the semantic differential and delayed imitation of a white model's self-reward standards. This finding is consistent with results obtained by Thelen and Fryrear (1971a,b) on the immediate imitation of self-reward standards.

Overall, the demonstration that adolescent boys retained the standards of a model and incorporated them into their own behavior three months after exposure to the model has two important implications. Since the model was a televised stranger who played no role in the lives of the Ss beyond a 7-min demonstration, the findings of the study suggest that even an incidental model can have more than an immediate influence over an observer's subsequent behavior. This finding underscores the growing body of evidence which points to the pervasive influence of mass media models.

A second implication is that, even in a population of juvenile delinquents with limited school achievement and borderline intelligence (mean IQ = 87), standards can be systematically modeled with the distinct possibility that the standards will be incorporated, retained, and acted upon.

IMPLICATIONS

Can you see modeling (imitative) behavior among college students? Observe which behavior seems to be modeled more readily. To what extent can ideas be models, and what is the behavioral vehicle? Who seem to be the most effective models for college students?

REFERENCES

See Bandura (1969) and the other references cited in the article by name and date.

23 TEACHING MACHINES

B. F. Skinner

Most of today's students have heard of or have used teaching machines. Some students have used them knowingly—the machines in the language laboratories; other students have used them, unaware that their learning aid, a programed workbook, is in fact a teaching machine.

Industry, which long ago learned to appreciate machines, has found the teaching machine; so has the military establishment, which has included the teaching machine in training programs.

Why are the teaching machine and *programed learning* valuable? Basically, what do they consist of? What are the learning principles involved in constructing an efficient teaching machine? Skinner, an outstanding experimentalist and systematist in the psychology of learning, has worked with the teaching machine and in this selection answers some of these questions.

THERE ARE more people in the world than ever before, and a far greater part of them want an education. The demand cannot be met simply by building more schools and training more teachers. Education must become more efficient. To this end, curricula must be revised and simplified, and textbooks and classroom techniques improved. In any other field, a demand for increased production would have led at once to the invention of labor-saving capital equipment. Education has reached this stage very late, possibly through a misconception of its task. Thanks to the advent of television, however, the so-called audio-visual aids are being re-examined. Film projectors, television sets, phonographs, and tape recorders are finding their way into American schools and colleges.

Audio-visual aids supplement and may even supplant lectures, demonstrations, and textbooks. In doing so they serve one function of the teacher: they present material to the student and, when successful, make it so clear and interesting that the student learns. There is another function to which they contribute little or nothing. It is best seen in the productive interchange between teacher and student in the small classroom or tutorial situation. Much of that interchange has already been sacrificed in American education in order to teach large numbers of students. There is a real danger that it will be wholly obscured if use of equipment designed simply to *present* material becomes widespread. The student is becoming more and more a mere passive receiver of instruction. . . .

From B.F. Skinner, "Teaching Machines," *Science*, Vol. 128, October 24, 1958, 969–977. Copyright 1958 by the American Association for the Advancement of Science. Reprinted by permission of the publisher and the author.

If our current knowledge of the acquisition and maintenance of verbal behavior is to be applied to education, some sort of teaching machine is needed. Contingencies of reinforcement which change the behavior of lower organisms often cannot be arranged by hand; rather elaborate apparatus is needed. The human organism requires even more subtle instrumentation. An appropriate teaching machine will have several important features. The student must *compose* his response rather than select it from a set of alternatives, as in a multiple-choice self-rater. One reason for this is that we want him to recall rather than recognize—to make a response as well as see that it is right. Another reason is that effective multiple-choice material must contain plausible wrong responses, which are out of place in the delicate process of "shaping" behavior because they strengthen unwanted forms. Although it is much easier to build a machine to score multiple-choice answers than to evaluate a composed response, the technical advantage is outweighed by these and other considerations.

A second requirement of a minimal teaching machine also distinguishes it from earlier versions. In acquiring complex behavior, the student must pass through a carefully designed sequence of steps, often of considerable length. Each step must be so small that it can always be taken, yet in taking it the student moves somewhat closer to fully competent behavior. The machine must make sure that these steps are taken in a carefully prescribed order.

Several machines with the required characteristics have been built and tested. Sets of separate presentations or "frames" of visual material are stored on disks, cards, or tapes. One frame is presented at a time, adjacent frames being out of sight. In one type of machine, the student composes a response by moving printed figures or letters (Skinner, 1954). His setting is compared by the machine with a coded response. If the two correspond, the machine automatically presents the next frame. If they do not, the response is cleared, and another must be composed. The student cannot proceed to a second step until the first has been taken. A machine of this kind is being tested in teaching spelling, arithmetic, and other subjects in the lower grades.

For more advanced students—from junior high school, say, through college—a machine which senses an arrangement of letters or figures is unnecessarily rigid in specifying form of response. Fortunately, such students may be asked to compare their responses with printed material revealed by the machine. In the machine shown in Figure 1, material is printed in thirty radial frames on a 12-inch disk. The student inserts the disk and closes the machine. He cannot proceed until the machine has been locked, and, once he has begun, the machine cannot be unlocked. All but a corner of one frame is visible through a window. The student writes his response on a paper strip exposed through a second opening. By lifting a lever on the front of the machine, he moves what he has written

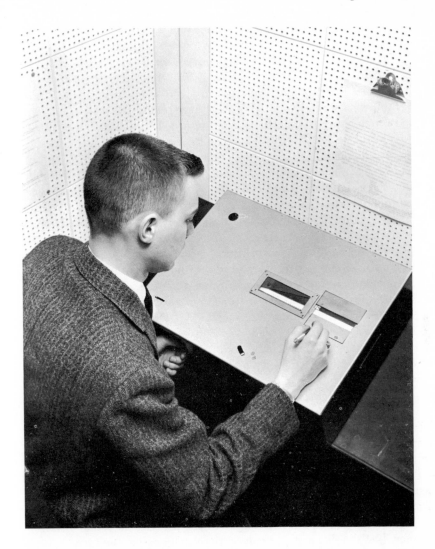

Figure 1. Student at work on a teaching machine. One frame of material is partly visible in the left-hand window. The student writes his response on a strip of paper exposed at the right. He then lifts a lever with his left hand, advancing his written response under a transparent cover and uncovering the correct response in the upper corner of the frame. If he is right, he moves the lever to the right, punching a hole alongside the response he has called right and altering the machine so that that frame will not appear again when he goes through the series a second time. A new frame appears when the lever is returned to its starting position.

under a transparent cover and uncovers the correct response in the remaining corner of the frame. If the two responses correspond, he moves the lever horizontally. This movement punches a hole in the paper opposite his response, recording the fact that he called it correct, and alters the machine so that the frame will not appear again when the student works around the disk a second time. Whether the response was correct or not, a second frame appears when the lever is returned to its starting position. The student proceeds in this way until he has responded to all frames. He then works around the disk a second time, but only those frames appear to which he has not correctly responded. When the disk revolves without stopping, the assignment is finished. (The student is asked to repeat each frame until a correct response is made to allow for the fact that, in telling him that a response is wrong, such a machine tells him what is right.)

The machine itself, of course, does not teach. It simply brings the student into contact with the person who composed the material it presents. It is a labor-saving device because it can bring one programmer into contact with an indefinite number of students. This may suggest mass production, but the effect upon each student is surprisingly like that of a private tutor. The comparison holds in several respects. (1) There is a constant interchange between program and students. Unlike lectures, textbooks, and the usual audio-visual aids, the machine induces sustained activity. The student is always alert and busy. (2) Like a good tutor, the machine insists that a given point be thoroughly understood, either frame by frame or set by set, before the student moves on. Lectures, textbooks, and their mechanized equivalents, on the other hand, proceed without making sure that the student understands and easily leave him behind. (3) Like a good tutor the machine presents just that material for which the student is ready. It asks him to take only that step which he is at the moment best equipped and most likely to take. (4) Like a skillful tutor the machine helps the student to come up with the right answer. It does this in part through the orderly construction of the program and in part with techniques of hinting, prompting, suggesting, and so on, derived from an analysis of verbal behavior (Skinner, 1957). (5) Lastly, of course, the machine, like the private tutor, reinforces the student for every correct response, using this immediate feedback not only to shape his behavior most efficiently but to maintain it in strength in a manner which the layman would describe as "holding the student's interest."

Programing Material

The success of such a machine depends on the material used in it. The task of programing a given subject is at first sight rather formidable. Many helpful techniques can be derived from a general analysis of the relevant behavioral processes, verbal and nonverbal. Specific forms of behavior are to be evoked and, through differential reinforcement, brought under the control of specific stimuli.

This is not the place for a systematic review of available techniques, or of the kind of research which may be expected to discover others. However, the machines themselves cannot be adequately described without giving a few examples of programs. We may begin with a set of frames (see Table 1) designed to teach a third- or fourth-grade pupil to spell the word *manufacture*. The six frames are presented in the order shown, and the pupil moves sliders to expose letters in the open squares.

Table 1

A set of frames designed to teach a third- or fourth-grade pupil to spell the word "manufacture."

1. Manufacture means to make or build. Chair factories manufacture chairs. Copy the word here:

   □□□□□□□□□□□

2. Part of the word is like part of the word <u>factory</u>. Both parts come from an old word meaning <u>make</u> or <u>build</u>.

   m a n u □ □ □ □ u r e

3. Part of the word is like part of the word <u>manual</u>. Both parts come from an old word for <u>hand</u>. Many things used to be made by hand.

   □ □ □ □ f a c t u r e

4. The same letter goes in both spaces:

   m □ n u f □ c t u r e

5. The same letter goes in both spaces:

   m a n □ f a c t □ r e

6. Chair factories □□□□□□□□□□ chairs.

The word to be learned appears in boldface in frame 1, with an example and a simple definition. The pupil's first task is simply to copy it. When he does so correctly, frame 2 appears. He must now copy selectively: he must identify "fact" as the common part of "manufacture" and "factory." This helps him to spell the word and also to acquire a separable "atomic" verbal operant (Skinner, 1957). In frame 3 another root must be copied selectively from "manual." In frame 4 the pupil must for the first time insert letters without copying. Since he is asked to insert the same letter in two places, a wrong response will be doubly conspicuous, and the chance of failure is thereby minimized. The same principle governs frame 5. In frame 6 the pupil spells the word to complete the sentence used as an example in frame 1. Even a poor student is likely to do this correctly because he has just composed or completed the word five times, has made two important root-responses, and has learned that two letters occur in the word twice. He has probably learned to spell the word without having made a mistake.

Teaching spelling is mainly a process of shaping complex forms of behavior. In other subjects—for example, arithmetic—responses must be brought under the control of appropriate stimuli. Unfortunately the material which has been prepared for teaching arithmetic [1] does not lend itself to excerpting. The numbers 0 through 9 are generated in relation to objects, quantities, and scales. The operations of addition, subtraction, multiplication, and division are thoroughly developed before the number 10 is reached. In the course of this the pupil composes equations and expressions in a great variety of alternative forms. He completes not only $5 + 4 = \square$, but $\square + 4 = 9$, $5 \square 4 = 9$, and so on, aided in most cases by illustrative materials. No appeal is made to rote memorizing, even in the later acquisition of the tables. The student is expected to arrive at $9 \times 7 = 63$, not by memorizing it as he would memorize a line of poetry, but by putting into practice such principles as that nine times a number is the same as ten times the number minus the number (both of these being "obvious" or already well learned), that the digits in a multiple of nine add to nine, that in composing successive multiples of nine one counts backward (nine, eighteen, twenty-seven, thirty-six, and so on), that nine times a single digit is a number beginning with one less than the digit (nine times six is fifty something), and possibly even that the product of two numbers separated by only one number is equal to the square of the separating number minus one (the square of eight already being familiar from a special series of frames concerned with squares).

Programs of this sort run to great length. At least five or six frames per word, four grades of spelling may require 20,000 or 25,000 frames, and three or four grades of arithmetic, as many again. If these figures seem large, it is only because we are thinking of the normal contact between teacher and pupil. Admittedly, a teacher cannot supervise 10,000 or 15,000 responses made by each pupil per year. But the pupil's time is not so limited. In any case, surprisingly little time is needed. Fifteen minutes per day on a machine should suffice for each of these programs, the machines being free for other students for the rest of each day. (It is probably because traditional methods are so inefficient that we have been led to suppose that education requires such a prodigious part of a young person's day.)

A simple technique used in programing material at the high-school or college level, by means of the machine shown in Figure 1, is exemplified in teaching a student to recite a poem. The first line is presented with several unimportant letters omitted. The student must read the line "meaning-

[1] This material was prepared with the assistance of Susan R. Meyer.

fully" and supply the missing letters. The second, third, and fourth frames present succeeding lines in the same way. In the fifth frame the first line reappears with other letters also missing. Since the student has recently read the line, he can complete it correctly. He does the same for the second, third, and fourth lines. Subsequent frames are increasingly incomplete, and eventually—say, after 20 or 24 frames—the student reproduces all four lines without external help, and quite possibly without having made a wrong response. The technique is similar to that used in teaching spelling: responses are first controlled by a text, but this is slowly reduced (colloquially, "vanished") until the responses can be emitted without a text, each member in a series of responses being now under the "intraverbal" control of other members.

"Vanishing" can be used in teaching other types of verbal behavior. When a student describes the geography of part of the world or the anatomy of part of the body, or names plants and animals from specimens or pictures, verbal responses are controlled by nonverbal stimuli. In setting up such behavior, the student is first asked to report features of a fully labeled map, picture, or object, and the labels are then vanished. In teaching a map, for example, the machine asks the student to describe spatial relations among cities, countries, rivers, and so on, as shown on a fully labeled map. He is then asked to do the same with a map in which the names are incomplete or, possibly, lacking. Eventually he is asked to report the same relations with no map at all. If the material has been well programed, he can do so correctly. Instruction is sometimes concerned not so much with imparting a new repertoire of verbal responses as with getting the student to describe something accurately in any available terms. The machine can "make sure the student understands" a graph, diagram, chart, or picture by asking him to identify and explain its features—correcting him, of course, whenever he is wrong.

In addition to charts, maps, graphs, models, and so on, the student may have access to auditory material. In learning to take dictation in a foreign language, for example, he selects a short passage on an indexing phonograph according to instructions given by the machine. He listens to the passage as often as necessary and then transcribes it. The machine then reveals the correct text. The student may listen to the passage again to discover the sources of any error. The indexing phonograph may also be used with the machine to teach other language skills, as well as telegraphic code, music, speech, parts of literary and dramatic appreciation, and other subjects.

A typical program combines many of these functions. The set of frames shown in Table 2 is designed to induce the student of high-school physics to talk intelligently, and to some extent technically, about the emission of light from an incandescent source. In using the machine the student will write a word or phrase to complete a given item and then uncover the corresponding word or phrase shown here in the column at the right. The reader who wishes to get the "feel" of the material should cover the right-hand column with a card, uncovering each line only after he has completed the corresponding item.

Several programing techniques are exemplified by the set of frames in Table 2. Technical terms are introduced slowly. For example, the familiar term "fine wire" in frame 2 is followed by a definition of the technical term "filament" in frame 4; "filament" is then asked for in the presence of the non-scientific synonym in frame 5 and without the synonym in frame 9. In the same way "glow," "give off light," and "send out light" in early frames are followed by a definition of "emit" with a synonym in frame 7. Various inflected forms of "emit" then follow, and "emit" itself is asked for with a synonym in frame 16. It is asked for without a synonym but in a helpful phrase in frame 30, and "emitted" and "emission" are asked for without help in frames 33 and 34. The relation between temperature and amount and color of light is developed in several frames before a formal statement using the word "temperature" is asked for in frame 12. "Incandescent" is defined and used in frame 13, is used again in frame 14, and is asked for in frame 15, the student receiving a thematic prompt from the recurring phrase "incandescent source of light." A formal prompt is supplied by "candle." In frame 25 the new response "energy" is easily evoked by the words "form of . . ." because the expression "form of energy" is used earlier in the frame. "Energy" appears again in the next two frames and is finally asked for, without aid, in frame 28. Frames 30 through 35 discuss the limiting temperatures of incandescent objects, while reviewing several kinds of sources. The figure 800 is used in three frames. Two intervening frames then permit some time to pass before the response "800" is asked for.

Table 2
Part of a Program in High-School Physics. The Machine Presents One Item at a Time. The Student Completes the Item and Then Uncovers the Corresponding Word or Phrase Shown at the Right.

Sentence to be completed	Word to be supplied
1. The important parts of a flashlight are the battery and the bulb. When we "turn on" a flashlight, we close a switch which connects the battery with the _____.	bulb
2. When we turn on a flashlight, an electric current flows through the fine wire in the _____ and causes it to grow hot.	bulb
3. When the hot wire glows brightly, we say that it gives off or sends out heat and _____.	light

Table 2 (continued)

Sentence to be completed	Word to be supplied
4. The fine wire in the bulb is called a filament. The bulb "lights up" when the filament is heated by the passage of a(n) _____ current.	electric
5. When a weak battery produces little current, the fine wire, or _____, does not get very hot.	filament
6. A filament which is *less* hot sends out or gives off _____ light.	less
7. "Emit" means "send out." The amount of light sent out, or "emitted," by a filament depends on how _____ the filament is.	hot
8. The higher the temperature of the filament the _____ the light emitted by it.	brighter, stronger
9. If a flashlight battery is weak, the _____ in the bulb may still glow, but with only a dull red color.	filament
10. The light from a very hot filament is colored yellow or white. The light from a filament which is not very hot is colored _____.	red
11. A blacksmith or other metal worker sometimes makes sure that a bar of iron is heated to a "cherry red" before hammering it into shape. He uses the _____ of the light emitted by the bar to tell how hot it is.	color
12. Both the color and the amount of light depend on the _____ of the emitting filament or bar.	temperature
13. An object which emits light because it is hot is called "incandescent." A flashlight bulb is an incandescent source of _____.	light
14. A neon tube emits light but remains cool. It is, therefore, not an incandescent _____ of light.	source
15. A candle flame is hot. It is a (n) _____ source of light.	incandescent
16. The hot wick of a candle gives off small pieces or particles of carbon which burn in the flame. Before or while burning, the hot particles send out, or _____, light.	emit
17. A long candlewick produces a flame in which oxygen does not reach all the carbon particles. Without oxygen the particles cannot burn. Particles which do not burn rise above the flame as _____.	smoke
18. We can show that there are particles of carbon in a candle flame, even when it is not smoking, by holding a piece of metal in the flame. The metal cools some of the particles before they burn, and the unburned carbon _____ collect on the metal as soot.	particles
19. The particles of carbon in soot or smoke no longer emit light because they are _____ than when they were in the flame.	cooler, colder

Table 2 (continued)

Sentence to be completed	Word to be supplied
20. The reddish part of candle flame has the same color as the filament in a flashlight with a weak battery. We might guess that the yellow or white parts of a candle flame are _____ than the reddish part.	hotter
21. "Putting out" an incandescent electric light means turning off the current so that the filament grows too _____ to emit light.	cold, cool
22. Setting fire to the wick of an oil lamp is called _____ the lamp.	lighting
23. The sun is our principal _____ of light, as well as of heat.	source
24. The sun is not only very bright but very hot. It is a powerful _____ source of light.	incandescent
25. Light is a form of energy. In "emitting light" an object changes, or "converts," one form of _____ into another.	energy
26. The electrical energy supplied by the battery in a flashlight is converted to _____ and _____.	heat, light; light, heat
27. If we leave a flashlight on, all the energy stored in the battery will finally be changed or _____ into heat and light.	converted
28. The light from a candle flame comes from the _____ released by chemical changes as the candle burns.	energy
29. A nearly "dead" battery may make a flashlight bulb warm to the touch, but the filament may still not be enough to emit light—in other words, the filament will not be _____ at that temperature.	incandescent
30. Objects, such as a filament, carbon particles, or iron bars, become incandescent when heated to about 800 degrees Celsius. At that temperature they begin to _____ _____.	emit light
31. When raised to any temperature above 800 degrees Celsius, an object such as an iron bar will emit light. Although the bar may melt or vaporize, its particles will be _____ no matter how hot they get.	incandescent
32. About 800 degrees Celsius is the lower limit of the temperature at which particles emit light. There is no upper limit of the _____ at which emission of light occurs.	temperature
33. Sunlight is _____ by very hot gases near the surface of the sun.	emitted
34. Complex changes similar to an atomic explosion generate the great heat which explains the _____ of light by the sun.	emission
35. Below about _____ degrees Celsius an object is not an incandescent source of light.	800

Unwanted responses are eliminated with special techniques. If, for example, the second sentence in frame 24 were simply "it is a(n) _____ source of light," the two "very's" would frequently lead the student to fill the blank with "strong" or a synonym thereof. This is prevented by inserting the word "powerful" to make a synonym redundant. Similarly, in frame 3 the words "heat and" pre-empt the response "heat," which would otherwise correctly fill the blank.

The net effect of such material is more than the acquisition of facts and terms. Beginning with a largely unverbalized acquaintance with flashlights, candles, and so on, the student is induced to talk about familiar events, together with a few new facts, with a fairly technical vocabulary. He applies the same terms to facts which he may never before have seen to be similar. The emission of light from an incandescent source takes shape as a topic or field of inquiry. An understanding of the subject emerges which is often quite surprising in view of the fragmentation required in item building.

It is not easy to construct such a program. Where a confusing or elliptical passage in a textbook is forgivable because it can be clarified by the teacher, machine material must be self-contained and wholly adequate. There are other reasons why textbooks, lecture outlines, and film scripts are of little help in preparing a program. They are usually not logical or developmental arrangements of material but stratagems which the authors have found successful under existing classroom conditions. The examples they give are more often chosen to hold the student's interest than to clarify terms and principles. In composing material for the machine, the programmer may go directly to the point.

A first step is to define the field. A second is to collect technical terms, facts, laws, principles, and cases. These must then be arranged in a plausible developmental order—linear if possible, branching if necessary. A mechanical arrangement, such as a card filing system, helps. The material is distributed among the frames of a program to achieve an arbitrary density. In the final composition of an item, techniques for strengthening asked-for responses and for transferring control from one variable to another are chosen from a list according to a given schedule in order to prevent the establishment of irrelevant verbal tendencies appropriate to a single technique. When one set of frames has been composed, its terms and facts are seeded mechanically among succeeding sets, where they will again be referred to in composing later items to make sure that the earlier repertoire remains active. Thus, the technical terms, facts, and examples in Table 2 have been distributed for re-use in succeeding sets on reflection, absorption, and transmission, where they are incorporated into items dealing mainly with other matters. Sets of frames for explicit review can, of course, be constructed. Further research will presumably discover other, possibly more effective, techniques. Meanwhile, it must be admitted that a considerable measure of art is needed in composing a successful program.

Whether good programing is to remain an art or to become a scientific technology, it is reassuring to know that there is a final authority—the student. An unexpected advantage of machine instruction has proved to be the feedback to the *programmer*. In the elementary school machine, provision is made for discovering which frames commonly yield wrong responses, and in the high-school and college machine the paper strips bearing written answers are available for analysis. A trial run of the first version of a program quickly reveals frames which need to be altered, or sequences which need to be lengthened. One or two revisions in the light of a few dozen responses work a great improvement. No comparable feedback is available to the lecturer, textbook writer, or maker of films. Although one text or film may seem to be better than another, it is usually impossible to say, for example, that a given sentence on a given page or a particular sequence in a film is causing trouble.

Difficult as programing is, it has its compensations. It is a salutary thing to try to guarantee a right response at every step in the presentation of a subject matter. The programmer will usually find that he has been accustomed to leave much to the student—that he has frequently omitted essential steps and neglected to invoke relevant points. The responses made to his material may reveal surprising ambiguities. Unless he is lucky, he may find that he still has something to learn about his subject. He will almost certainly find that he needs to learn a great deal more about the behavioral changes he is trying to induce in the student. This effect of the machine in confronting the programmer with the full scope of his task may in itself produce a considerable improvement in education.

Conclusion

An analysis of education within the framework of a science of behavior has broad implications. Our schools, in particular our "progressive" schools, are often held responsible for many current problems, including juvenile delinquency and the threat of a more powerful foreign technology. One remedy frequently suggested is a return to older techniques, especially to a greater "discipline" in schools. Presumably this to be obtained with some form of punishment, to be administered either with certain classical instruments of physical injury—the dried bullock's tail of the Greek teacher or the cane of the English schoolmaster—or as disapproval or failure, the frequency of which is to be increased by "raising standards." This is probably not a feasible solution. Not only education but Western culture as a whole is moving away from aversive practices. We cannot prepare young people for one kind of life in institutions organized on quite different principles. The discipline of the birch rod may facilitate learning, but we must remember that it also breeds followers of dictators and revolutionists.

In the light of our present knowledge, a school system must be called a failure if it cannot induce students to learn except by threatening them for not learning. That this has always been the standard pattern simply emphasizes the importance of modern techniques. John Dewey was speaking for his culture and his time when he attacked aversive educational practices and appealed to teachers to turn to positive and humane methods. What he threw out should have been thrown out. Unfortunately he had too little to put in its place. Progressive education has been a temporizing measure which can now be effectively supplemented. Aversive practices cannot only be replaced, they can be replaced with far more powerful techniques. The possibilities should be thoroughly explored if we are to build an educational system which will meet the present demand without sacrificing democratic principles.

IMPLICATIONS

Have you ever used a teaching machine or a programmed workbook? What is your impression of it? What did you like or dislike about it? What are the learning principles employed in the use of the teaching machine? What implications does it hold for traditional teaching? What advantages has traditional teaching over it? If you have not used a teaching machine or programmed workbook, you may be better able to evaluate the process by working the programmed material in Table 2.

Some research has been conducted with a computer-assisted instructor, which is a more complex teaching machine that uses a computer to keep track of the student's progress. It is also programmed to present what the student should do next, in terms of his previous responses.

REFERENCES

For further discussion of the use of computer-assisted instruction, see Atkinson and Wilson (1969) and Suppes and Morningstar (1969).

24

HUMAN RELATIONS: A TECHNIQUE FOR TRAINING SUPERVISORS

Norman R. F. Maier and Lester F. Zerfoss

Today in the United States, there is a general interest in understanding and influencing human relations. To influence the interactions between individuals in crucial everyday situations, however, we need more than understanding. People are interested in developing the *skills* involved in supervising men and conducting meetings in which conflict over ideas is inevitable. This article, written by psychologists with considerable experience in group relations, suggests one of the realistic methods of training individuals in human-relations skills through multiple role-playing.

It is suggested that you use this role-playing problem in your class. If this suggestion is followed, a decision should be made as to which students are to play certain roles before reading the part of the article entitled "Setting up the role-playing procedure."

HUMAN-RELATIONS SKILLS are difficult to learn merely through reading or by hearing lectures. To be effective, training in the skills must be accompanied by attitude and feeling changes. A supervisor who does not respect his employees will have difficulty in practicing effective methods because his approaches will not hide his basic attitude. It is because skills and attitudes are so interdependent in personnel work that training methods must incorporate both.

One of the important approaches in the improvement of supervisors is that of increasing their employees' participation in the solving of some of the day-to-day job problems. Many employees are distrustful of changes in the job, and there frequently is a feeling that the supervisor plays favorites and discriminates against others. Techniques of selling employees on changes that affect them, and the usual procedures designed to develop fair practices, usually fail to solve these attitudinal problems (Coch and French, 1948; Lewin, 1947). It is exactly in these areas that employee participation seems to be most valuable and for which the group decision method (Bradford and Lippitt, 1945; Lewin, 1947; Lewin, et al., 1939; Maier, 1948) (in which the supervisor shares his problem with his group) has been developed.

However, there is great deal of resistance on the part of supervisors to

Reprinted from Norman R.F. Maier and Lester F. Zerfoss, "MRP: A Technique for Training Large Groups of Supervisors and Its Potential Use in Social Research," *Human Relations,* Vol. 5 (Ann Arbor: The University of Michigan, Research Center for Group Dynamics, 1952), pp. 177–186, by permission of the publisher and the senior author.

sharing work problems with their groups because they feel they are giving up something in the process (Maier, 1949). In order to overcome this resistance, new types of training methods are needed. These new methods require that the supervisors learn through participation because they, like rank and file employees, also shy away from changes that affect them.

Discussion meetings (Coch and French, 1948; Maier, 1948, 1949) and role-playing procedures (Bavelas, 1947; Bradford and Lippitt, 1945; Lippitt, et al., 1947) are two of the best participation training methods. However, their nature is such as to limit their uses to training in small groups. In training large groups, it has been necessary to confine one's procedures to lectures, visual aids, movies, and demonstrations. None of these approaches permits active participation and practice. An audience-participation technique, recently developed by Donald Phillips (1948), has received a high degree of acceptance in industry. It is one of the first methods to permit small group discussions within the general framework of an audience situation. The procedure, often referred to as "Phillips 66," accomplishes general participation by dividing the audience into committees of six, each of which holds a discussion for six minutes on some specific question previously put to them. The major limitation of the Phillips 66 method is that the subject matter to be used for discussion is limited in scope, and it can only be adapted to certain types of situations.

Recently, we have tested a procedure at The Detroit Edison Company which combines the role-playing approach with Phillips 66, and which may be described as Multiple Role Playing (MRP). This method permits role-playing to be carried out in such a manner that all members of a large audience can participate. The purpose of the technique is to give each member of an audience a first-hand experience in the group decision method. It permits the training of supervisors in skills of leading discussions and at the same time gives them an experience of the way things appear to employees, by finding themselves placed in the employee's position. Training supervisors to use group decision requires that they develop: (1) confidence in the way employees behave when given an opportunity to solve job problems, and (2) skill in putting a problem to the group. The MRP method serves in both of these capacities. The experiences obtained in these group discussions give the participants an opportunity to discover that the way employees behave depends greatly upon the kind of situation the supervisor creates. Thus, both the attitude of the supervisor and his skill in leading the discussion directly determine the outcome of the conference. Participants who function as employees see the errors that the supervisor makes and discover how their own reactions are influenced by the situation he creates. Participants who serve as supervisors can discover how conflicts in groups become resolved and find ways to help the process along. All can experience some of the emotional loadings that attach themselves to matters of prestige and fair play. The few participants who function as observers can discover how lifelike a role-playing process might become, and they can observe how the discussion process leads to attitude changes. As an observer, a person can have a disinterested attitude and objectively evaluate the process.

In repeating this method, different persons can function as observers, supervisors, and employees and thus gain a variety of experiences from these exchanges in function.

In order to make the group decision experience a success with untrained leaders, it is important that the problem be so structured that the leader is likely to do a good job and that the group will readily participate in the discussion. To accomplish good discussion leadership, the problem used for our demonstration was one for which the supervisor is unlikely to have a ready-made solution. In having no preferred solution himself, he is inclined to act permissively, and thus encourage free and frank discussion instead of imposing or selling his own views. To produce a lively discussion, the problem that is used must be one which creates a conflict in attitudes. In order to solve the problem, these attitudes have to become reconciled.

The work situation described in this article is based on an actual case in industry and raises the type of problem that a crew can solve more satisfactorily than a supervisor. As such, it readily lends itself to a group decision rather than an autocratic decision which is imposed on the crew by the supervisor. In the real-life situation, the foreman had a new truck to distribute. He realized that his decision would not meet with approval since each man would feel he had a claim. He therefore put the problem to the crew. The crew solved the problem in such a way that there was a general exchange of trucks so that each man got a different truck, and at the same time the poorest truck was discarded. Everyone was satisfied with the solution.

In setting up this problem for role-playing, we have given each participant a personal attitude so that a typical set of lifelike conflicts would be created. This is the usual procedure in role-playing. The deviation from the usual procedure is that the same roles are simultaneously played by many groups, each without the guidance of a trainer. This absence of specific guidance during the role-playing process makes standardization more essential and requires the use of clear-cut problems. However, we find that these limitations are not serious.

Setting Up the Role-Playing Procedure

1. The first step in the procedure is for the trainer or the person in charge of the meeting to request the audience to divide itself into groups of six, with three persons in one row turning around to meet with three persons directly behind them. Assistants can be an aid to help persons in odd seats join others in making up these groups. By arranging the seating

rows in multiples of three, the task of organizing the groups is simplified. (In our situation, the seats themselves could be turned around and thus made for more comfort.)

Since the number of persons required in a group is six, there may be a remainder of from one to five persons. Each of those extra persons is asked to join one of the discussion groups and serve as an observer.

2. When the audience has been divided into groups, the trainer announces that each group will receive a set of instructions. The persons who pass out the material will hand these instructions to one member of each group. This member will play the part of Walt Marshall, the foreman of a crew of repairmen. The other five members of the group will be repairmen who report to Walt Marshall. The foreman is to keep this material until instructed further. In the meantime, he may look over the top page, labeled "Walt Marshall—Foreman of the Repair Crew."

3. The trainer then asks the crew members of all groups to give their attention while he reads them their instructions.

General Instructions for Crew:

You are repairmen for a large company and drive to various locations in the city to do your work. Each of you drives a small truck, and you take pride in keeping it looking good. You have a possessive feeling about your trucks and like to keep them in good running order. Naturally, you like to have new trucks, too, because a new truck gives you a feeling of pride.

Here are some facts about the trucks and the men in the crew who report to Walt Marshall, the supervisor of repairs:

George—17 years with the company, has a two-year-old Ford truck.
Bill—11 years with the company, has a five-year-old Dodge truck.
John—10 years with the company has a four-year-old Ford truck.
Charlie—5 years with the company, has a three-year-old Ford truck.
Hank—3 years with the company, has a five-year-old Chevrolet truck.

Most of you do all of your driving in the city, but John and Charlie cover the jobs in the suburbs.

In acting your part in role-playing, accept the facts as given as well as assume the attitude supplied in your specific role. From this point on let your feelings develop in accordance with the events that transpire in the role-playing process. When facts or events arise which are not covered by the roles, make up things which are consistent with the way it might be in a real-life situation.

The names of the five men, years of service, age, and make of truck should then be placed on an easel chart or blackboard so that ready reference to them can be made.

4. The foreman is then asked to pass out the material he has been given, which consists of six sets of instructions, one for each person in the group. He should keep the top set for himself and pass out one set of instructions, beginning on his left, to each of his five crewmen. The sequence of the instructions should be George, Bill, John, Charlie, and Hank so that the seating order corresponds to the order of seniority as listed on the easel.

The content of the specific instructions for each member of the group is as follows:

Walt Marshall—Foreman of Repair Crew

You are the foreman of a crew of repairmen, each of whom drives a small service truck to and from his various jobs. Every so often you get a new truck to exchange for an old one, and you have the problem of deciding to which of your men you should give the new truck. Often there are hard feelings because each man seems to feel he is entitled to the new truck; so you have a tough time being fair. As a matter of fact, it usually turns out that whatever you decide, most of the men consider wrong. You now have to face the issue again because a new truck has just been allocated to you for distribution. The new truck is a Chevrolet.

Here are some brief facts about your situation:

George—17 years with the company, has a two-year-old Ford truck.

Bill—11 years with the company, has a five-year-old Dodge truck.

John—10 years with the company, has a four-year-old Ford truck.

Charlie—5 years with the company, has a three-year-old Ford truck.

Hank—3 years with the company, has a five-year-old Chevrolet truck.

All of the men do city driving, making fairly short trips, except for John and Charlie who cover the suburbs.

In order to handle this problem you have decided to put the decision up to the men themselves. You will tell them about the new truck and will put the problem in terms of what would be the most fair way to distribute the truck. Avoid taking a position yourself because you want to do what the men think is most fair.

George: When a new Chevrolet truck becomes available, you think you should get it because you have most seniority and don't like your present truck. Your own car is a Chevrolet, and you prefer a Chevrolet truck such as you drove before you got the Ford.

Bill: You feel you deserve a new truck. Your present truck is old, and since the senior man has a fairly new truck, you should get the next one. You have taken excellent care of your present Dodge and have kept it looking like new. A man deserves to be rewarded if he treats a company truck like his own.

John: You have to do more driving than most of the other men because you work in the suburbs. You have a fairly old truck and feel you should have a new one because you do so much driving.

Charlie: The heater in your present truck is inadequate. Since Hank backed into the door of your truck, it has never been repaired to fit right. The door lets in too much cold air, and you attribute your frequent colds to this. You want a warm truck since you have a good deal of driving to do. As long as it has good tires, brakes, and is comfortable you don't care about its make.

Hank: You have the poorest truck in the crew. It is five years old, and before you got it, it had been in a bad wreck. It has never been good, and you've put up with it for three years. It's about time you got a good truck to drive, and you feel the next one should be yours. You have a good accident record. The only accident you had was when you sprung the door of Charlie's truck when he opened it as you backed out of the garage. You hope the new truck is a Ford since you prefer to drive one.

Members are asked to study their roles until they have a feeling for them. It is perhaps necessary to caution them not to show their roles to each other, but to put them aside when they have finished with them.

5. When everyone is ready, the trainer gives the signal for the foreman to take the responsibility of starting their meetings. Each foreman should assume that he has called his men together and that he is seated with them to discuss a problem.

6. Less than half an hour is adequate for most groups to solve the problem. (If the leader and his assistants observe the groups, they can pretty well judge when most of the groups have reached a solution.) Before interrupting the discussion, it is desirable to announce from the floor that three more minutes will be allowed the groups to settle on some arrangement.

7. At the end of the three-minute period, the members are asked to break off their discussions and join in the analysis of the results.

Analyzing the Results

The extent of the analysis need not be confined to the points discussed below, but the analysis should cover the following points:

1. Determination of the number of groups arriving at a solution. (In obtaining this figure, only the foreman should vote.)

2. Determination of the number of men who are satisfied with the solution. (In this case, only the repairmen of crews which reached a solution should raise their hands.) This figure is important because it indicates the degree of satisfaction obtained from the procedure. The chairman may ask how this degree of acceptance compares with what would have been obtained if the foreman had supplied the solution.

3. Determination of number of crews which discarded Hank's truck. (In this case only the foremen should raise their hands.) The proportion of the number of times that Hank's truck was discarded to the number of groups becomes a measure of the quality of the solution. The fear that men might fail to discard the poorest truck would constitute one of the reasons why a foreman might hesitate to put such a problem to them. If the proportion of crews discarding the poorest truck is very large, it indicates that the danger of not having the poorest truck discarded is more imagined than real.

4. Determination of the number of crews in which the new truck went to various members of the crew. (In this case only the foreman should vote on the five alternatives.) This analysis brings out the variety of solutions obtained and shows that the same problem with the same roles produces different solutions. Under such circumstances it becomes clear that a company could not work out a policy that would be satisfying to all crews.

This analysis might also be followed by questions such as, "In how many cases did George use his seniority and make a strong demand for the new truck?" "How often did he get it when he was that kind of a George?" "How often did George get the new truck when he did not throw his seniority around?" Such questions frequently reveal that George is more likely to get the new truck when he is a reasonable person and is considerate of men with less service than when he is demanding.

5. Determination of the number of crews in which
   (a) All men obtained a different truck.
   (b) Four men obtained a different truck.
   (c) Three men obtained a different truck.
   (d) Two men obtained a different truck.
   (e) No exchange in old trucks were made and only the man receiving the new truck benefited.

(Only the foreman should vote on these alternatives.) This analysis gives an idea of the extent to which all men were given consideration. If time is taken to analyze these data, it might be found that the foreman's conduct of the meeting determined the number of men who benefited by the addition of a new truck to the crew.

Following the analysis of the crews, the persons serving as observers should be asked to give their evaluations of the discussion meetings they observed. Their report may include: (a) the way the foreman put the problem, (b) the extent to which he hampered the discussion, (c) the extent to which he imposed his own ideas, and (d) evaluation of things he did which helped things along. These reports not only involve the observers in the procedure, but add supplementary material on the different approaches various foremen may have used.

Some Sample Results

We have tested the case in three audiences. In one of these, 17 groups were formed and in 14 of these, all persons were satisfied with the solution they had reached. A total of 5 individuals out of 102 were dissatisfied with the solutions of their groups. In the second group tested, 6 groups were used and 2 persons (in two different groups) out of 42 were dissatisfied. In the third audience, 19 out of 21 groups had time to reach a decision and only one person in each of two groups was dissatisfied. If we combine our groups, we find that 42 out of 44 groups reached a decision and only 9 out of 220 repairmen (4.1 per cent) were dissatisfied.

In each of three tests of the method, all persons participating readily agreed that anything approaching the degree of satisfaction shown could not have been obtained if supervisors had supplied the solution.

In 41 out of the 42 groups, Hank's truck (the poorest one) was eliminated. This result clearly shows that the group decisions were in accordance with the interests of good management. Thus the fear that group decisions might lead to poor-quality decisions was not supported.

The new truck went to George, the senior man, in 20 of the 42 groups. In 16 cases out of 28, he got it when he did not insist on it because of his seniority, and in 4 cases out of 10, he got it by defending his rank. Thus George gained most when he acted least in his own selfish interests.

A great variety of solutions developed in these groups. The new truck went to each of the individuals in one group or another; the frequency being in the order of George, John, Hank, Bill, and Charlie. In most instances there was a general exchange of trucks. All men got a different truck in 4 groups; 4 men got a different truck in 10 groups; 3 men in 16 groups; 2 in 8 groups; and only 1 got a different truck (the new one) in 4 groups.

From descriptions of the discussion process, there seemed to be a trend in which the general exchange of trucks was greatest when the leader was permissive. The first part of the discussion develops a conflict of interests, and if the leader is permissive at this stage, the idea of exchanging trucks develops. Many men who played the part of the supervisor were surprised at this development because most of them went into the discussion with the idea of getting the new truck assigned to some particular individual and getting the rest of the group to agree on who was most needy. It is this emphasis on the leader's part which prevents the general exchange which usually develops out of the free discussion. Thus the idea that all can profit when the crew gets a new truck emerges as a new idea, and it is a group product.

General Evaluation

The technique of MRP has some distinct advantages over ordinary role-playing. When many groups of persons engage in role-playing at the same time, the process is facilitated since all of them enter into it without the embarrassment that comes from feeling that they are being observed. Thus groups which have never experienced role-playing quickly get the spirit of the procedure and go into the process in a natural and interested manner. The feeling that the situation is unreal and artificial, which non-participants frequently report, is eliminated because all become involved. Because this method reduces self-consciousness, it is particularly helpful for initiating role-playing techniques in supervisory training.

A second value that emerges is the fact that real-live data are obtained from the subsequent analysis. A single role-playing case raises questions which have to do with the fact that a certain individual determined the outcome and so the result may not be typical. In being able to draw upon various groups, one is able to make comparisons and generalizations which could not be made without a rich background of experience. The idea that solutions are tailored to fit a particular group of personalities is clearly brought home by the fact that solutions vary even when the problem and the roles are identical.

Thus we find that in the process of attempting to induce into a large group some of the benefits of small group discussion and role-playing, we not only succeeded in achieving some of these advantages, but captured some entirely new ones.

The MRP method can be used for all types of role-playing which are so effective for attitude change and the development of skills. One must, however, structure the roles so as to conform to the purpose of the training and the experience of the participants. Thus, if one wishes to emphasize (a) leadership skills in putting a problem to a group, (b) discussion-leading skills, (c) sensitivity to the feelings of others, (d) ways for dealing with hostile persons, (e) skills to upgrade the quality of decisions, and (f) methods to cause a group to feel responsible for reaching decisions acceptable to all, one must design role-playing situations which will highlight these performance areas.

Uses of MRP in Social Research

MRP also can be used as a tool to evaluate various kinds of leadership approaches, as well as to measure the effect of different kinds of participants on the outcome of a discussion. For example, the leaders of half of the groups may receive instructions which differ from those supplied by the other half. These differences may be as follows:

(a) Encourage disagreement in your group vs. discourage disagreement in your group;

(b) Suggest possible solutions to your group vs. be careful not to suggest any solutions yourself;

(c) Try to sell a particular solution that seems fair to you vs. be careful not to show any preference for any solution suggested; and,

(d) Have your group explore a variety of solutions before selling on any one idea vs. hurry the group along so that leisurely exploration of many ideas is discouraged.

The effect of different kinds of participants can be tested by making the roles slightly different for two sets of groups. For example, (a) George can be asked to insist on getting the truck in one set and asked to help out Hank's case in the other; (b) one set of groups might be so instructed that they form two cliques, whereas the other set of groups are not so instructed; and (c) one set of groups may have one member who is asked to play the part of a conciliatory individual, whereas in the other set of groups the same individual may be requested to play the part of a belligerent person.

By comparing the outcomes of two sets of groups with similarly instructed leaders and the differences obtained with differently instructed leaders working with similarly instructed groups, one can demonstrate the importance of the injected differences.

The use of the observer can also be expanded by having one or two such persons in each group. (The purpose of two observers is to see to what extent different persons vary in what they see in the same situation. With experience these differences rapidly decline.)

The observers' reports are of particular value in pointing up how each person's remarks has an effect on the behavior of others. Their comments would tend to sensitize participants to important details in the discussion process, and the reports of skilled observers would become a valuable training aid to participants. The use of observers would be of special value in the training of individuals who meet repeatedly in conferences.

IMPLICATIONS

Do you understand the Phillips 66 method well enough to use it in student groups? What application of it can you see in the college situation? What are its advantages over lectures, movies, and demonstrations? When is multiple role-playing more appropriate?

You and other members of your class might use the method suggested in this article for a role-playing situation. This will give you some experience in human relations and furnish you with examples of what happens when a decision has to be made as a result of human give and take. Read the article up to the section headed "Analyzing the Results"; then, together with six fellow students (each reading only materials on his role), set up the role-playing situation. After your group has reached some decision, the observer, who is taking notes on the behavior of the group, can report to the class what has happened. The experiences of the different groups then can be compared, including the participant's approach to the problem. You will then be in a position to analyze your results and to compare them with those reported in the article.

REFERENCES

Consult the Bibliography for references cited in the article.

25 BIO-FEEDBACK TRAINING

Barnard Law Collier

This pioneering area of psychophysiological research has implications for physical and mental health. The early applications of the technique have been so successful that visceral learning through bio-feedback has been suggested as a possible alternative for drugs. More research must be done before widespread clinical application is possible, but investigators anticipate the successful use of bio-feedback techniques in the clinical rehabilitation of the anxious person. The relationship of bio-feedback to yoga and Zen are pointed out in this article.

INSIDE A DARKENED CHAMBER in the laboratory of Dr. Lester Fehmi sits Ralph Press, a nineteen-year-old mathematics student at the State University of New York in Stony Brook, Long Island. Relaxed in an armchair with his eyes closed, Ralph is undergoing his eleventh session of bio-feedback training to help him learn to control his brain waves.

Four silver electrodes are pasted to Ralph's scalp, their orange lead wires plugged into an electroencephalograph that is tracing his brain-wave activity on thick ribbons of EEG paper in the next room. The silence in the soundproofed chamber is broken only by the long and short beepings of a rather high-pitched tone: the key to Ralph's bio-feedback training.

Dr. Fehmi, a professor of psychology at Stony Brook, has told Ralph that he can learn to increase his brain's output of an eight-to-fourteen-cycle-per-second brain sine wave called alpha. Alpha waves are one of four known brain waves. They are generated, billions of them, by the tiny electrical pulses that surge through the brain as it does its complex chores. High production of alpha waves is often associated with the objective state of peak mental and physical performance, a relaxed yet extremely sensitive alertness.

Dr. Fehmi and George Sintchak, the Stony Brook psychology department's chief electronic engineer, have rigged the EEG machine and a computer so that each time Ralph's brain generates a burst of alpha activity the occurrence is recorded, timed, and almost instantly made known to Ralph by means of the beeping tone. *The tone is Ralph's bio-feedback.** It is an audible signal that lets Ralph be consciously aware of a

---

* Editor's italics.

From Barnard Law Collier, "Brain Power: The Case for Bio-Feedback Training," *Saturday Review*, April 10, 1971. Copyright © 1971 by Saturday Review, Inc. Reprinted by permission of the publisher and the author.

visceral function, in this case *the production of his alpha brain waves,* which his mind ordinarily blocks out, ignores, or is unable to perceive without external assistance. When Ralph's brain generates only snippets of alpha radiation, the tone comes in staccato little blips. As he produces more and more alpha, the tone stays on longer and longer. Ralph, of course, wants to succeed by producing as much alpha as he can.

For nearly an hour, *Ralph shows minute-by-minute improvement in his ability to keep the tone on.** A computer read-out verifies that he is maintaining the tone for a cumulative average of twenty-eight seconds out of each minute. "He's one of our super-subjects," Dr. Fehmi remarks. "He's not the best, but he's getting pretty good."

Ralph's alpha waves are of high amplitude, very rhythmic and regular. This is what they look like as they are traced by the jiggling pens of the EEG machine:

"OK, Ralph," Dr. Fehmi says quietly over the intercom, "I want you to turn the tone off and keep it off."

The tone that Ralph has learned to sustain for upwards of three seconds now goes beep, beep, *blip;* within seconds, it has died away except for tiny random beeps. This is what it looks like on the EEG tracing as Ralph begins to stop his alpha waves:

"Now turn the tone back on," Dr. Fehmi says.

A pause of a second or so and the tone beeps back to life and stays on for seconds at a time. Then on, off, on, off. The tests continue until it is clear that Ralph is in personal command of his brain's alpha-wave activity as evidenced by the EEG machine's record.

A steady flow of new scientific findings indicates that, with the aid of the teaching technique called bio-feedback training, man can learn to

* Editor's italics.

control willfully his body and his state of consciousness to a degree that traditionally has been dismissed in Western cultures as mere trickery or condemned as somehow wicked or blasphemous.

Projects in hospitals and research laboratories around the world are convincingly demonstrating that it may be possible to learn personal mastery over the functions of our visceral organs—the heart, liver, kidneys, intestines, glands, and blood vessels—in the same specific way that we learn to manipulate our fingers to play Chopin or our legs to kick a field goal. There is also highly intriguing research going on in laboratories like Dr. Fehmi's to demonstrate that with bio-feedback training we can learn self-control over the electrical activity of our brain. These studies indicate that man may possess the ability to will himself into whatever state of consciousness seems most appropriate to his environment, to accomplishing a task at hand, or to some special pursuit.

The implications of bio-feedback training are proving terribly *easy to overstate,** given the limited amount of solid experimental evidence that presently exists. People seem peculiarly ready nowadays to lunge at the adventurous prospect of employing new methods and modern technology to explore and conquer one's own brain and body instead of, say, the moon or Southeast Asia. The propensity for *exaggeration about progress in this area frightens prudent scientists.** Already they are encountering the con artists, the charlatans, and the quacks who are taking people's money by glibly mouthing the jargon associated with bio-feedback research and similar studies of the mind's control over internal organs. This caveat is offered early because it is difficult to keep one's imagination reined in unless one is warned that much of the data accumulated so far are limited to experiments with rats, monkeys, rabbits, or other lab animals. And the remarkable results with animals may not travel well from the laboratory to humans. Nevertheless, research teams are reporting an ever increasing number of cases in which human subjects have unquestionably gained conscious control over visceral organs once thought beyond the mastery of the mind.

In Baltimore, for example, Dr. Bernard T. Engel, a psychologist, and Dr. Eugene Bleecker, a cardiovascular specialist, have conducted bio-feedback training sessions with eight patients suffering from premature ventricular contractions, a dangerous irregularity of the heartbeat involving the heart's main pumping chamber. With significant success, these patients have learned to speed, slow, and narrowly regulate their heart by force of mental discipline alone.

At the Gerontology Research Center of the National Institute of Child Health and Human Development, Dr. Engel and Dr. Bleecker use a visual form of bio-feedback training to help patients *control their heart.** In a

---

* Editor's italics.

typical experiment, the patient lies quietly on a hospital bed in a small, windowless laboratory near Dr. Engel's office. The electrodes of an electro-cardiograph are attached to his chest and pulse points, and the EKG machine is hooked up with a specially programed computer. On the bed table in front of the patient sits a small metal box fitted with a red, a yellow, and a green light in the same pattern as a regular traffic signal. The display is hooked into the computer, which almost instantly analyzes the EKG readings and provides bio-feedback information to the patient by means of the flashing colored lights.

The first phase of the training is speeding the heart rate. The patient may be told that when the yellow light goes on he will know that his heart is beating faster; the green light flashing on means it is slowing down. A small meter next to the light box indicates to the patient what percentage of the time he is succeeding in keeping the yellow light lit. The goal for the heart patient, of course, is to gain control over the lights and his heart-beat in the same way Ralph Press controlled the beeping tone and his alpha-wave production: by sheer mental effort, and without any muscular exertion—which amounts to cheating.

After a patient learns to speed his heart, he is then taught to slow it down with the red light and later to keep it beating within narrow normal limits, with the three lights acting as too fast, too slow, and normal signals. Some of Dr. Engel's patients have achieved a 20 per cent speeding or slow-ing of their hearts—about sixteen beats a minute from an eighty-beat-per-minute base. This self-willed rate change in one direction or the other tends to even out the irregular beats. Why? Researchers are not quite sure, but it works.

But what happens when the patient goes home, away from Dr. Engel's bio-feedback light box? The final stage of the five-phase training program is the stepped withdrawal of the bio-feedback light signals. The patient, *after extensive training,* finds he can deliberately alter his heartbeats in the desired direction without artificial feedback.* One of Dr. Engel's patients could still remember how to control his rate after two years. That Dr. Engel's patients retain what they have learned without the aid of an electronic device to provide feedback is what excites many researchers who feel that we may be capable of discovering unknown mechanisms, or "feedback loops," within ourselves that will allow us, after some basic training, to monitor our viscera and their functions at will throughout life.

In Boston and New York City, scientists are trying to see how people with hypertension can effectively *lower their abnormally high blood pres-sure* * by thinking it down. Under the direction of Dr. Neal E. Miller, a professor of physiological psychology at Rockefeller University in New York and a pioneer in the brain sciences, experiments are now proceeding

---

* Editor's italics.

to discover if human subjects can learn to control the contractions of their intestinal tract. Laboratory rats have learned to control these contractions with notable success. If humans can do as well, it could mean relief from much suffering for people with spastic colons and similar gastrointestinal ailments usually associated with stress and psychosomatic illness.

Dr. Miller was in the forefront of what seemed, just a decade or so ago, a vain and somewhat foolhardy challenge to the bedrock idea that the viscera and the autonomic nervous system that controls them operate entirely independently of an animal's deliberate control. Dr. Miller has traced back to Plato the dogma that the organs controlled by the autonomic nervous system function at a kind of cave-mannish level, learning only in classical Pavlovian fashion to react to such stimuli as sour lemons and growling bears. On the other hand, the somatic, or cerebrospinal, nervous system, which transmits nerve signals from the brain to the spinal cord and directly to the skeletal muscles, can learn by the sophisticated trial-and-error instrumental process. Perhaps the Greeks considered it an act of hubris to believe that they, not the gods, exercised command of their heart, brain, and guts. Dr. Engel, who also has studied the accumulated prejudices against the viscera, can recite a chain of erroneous proofs put forth until only a few years ago by scientists who, with a kind of religious fervor, had shunned anatomical facts and new information in order to steadfastly support Plato.

At the root of the research reports on bio-feedback training is what Dr. Miller describes as "an almost complete change in our way of thinking about our viscera and their ability to learn. *We are now able to regard the activities of our internal organs as behavior in the same sense that the movements of our hands and fingers* * are behavior. This is the basic stem of it all, but just where this rather radical new orientation will lead, we can't be sure yet."

Some indications that we can possibly control our viscera have been around for centuries without anyone's grasping their import. Dr. Miller points out that actors and actresses can control their tear glands, which are visceral organs, to make themselves cry on cue. It is possible that some classical conditioning is involved: The actor recalls something sad and the sadness makes him cry. But many actors and actresses say they can cry without any recalling, that all they have to do is think "cry" and the tears flow.

Magicians and mystics and meditators* have often gained mental control over visceral organs to a significant degree. Harry Houdini is said to have been able to swallow and regurgitate a key that would unlock him from some otherwise unopenable box. If he did this, it would mean he had

---

* Editor's italics.

gained mastery over the muscles of his esophagus and stomach, part of the viscera.

A few yogis, it would seem, can control their metabolism to some extent. But whether or not they "cheat" by using skeletal muscles instead of only their mind to perform their tricks is unknown. Scientists have found that some yogis who can "stop" their hearts so that no pulse or sound of beating can be detected are actually performing what is called the Valsalva maneuver. By taking a deep breath, closing their windpipe, and breathing hard to increase the pressure inside their chest and around their heart, they collapse the veins to the heart and clamp off the return of blood. This arrests heart sounds and the pulse, but an EKG shows that the heart is still beating and usually quite fast. "We must re-examine a lot of phenomena we may have dismissed as fakery before," Dr. Miller says.

The belief in a "superior" somatic nervous system and an "inferior" autonomic nervous system was so strong that, according to Dr. Miller, "for more than a dozen years I had extreme difficulty getting students or even paid assistants to conduct experiments on the control of internal organs." But Dr. Miller persisted, and his research has led many other scientists to abandon the old dogma. He has shown that the internal organs in animals and to a significant extent in man, as well, are capable of learning by trial and error—and with a startling degree of specificity and discrimination. In one experiment, which Dr. Miller particularly enjoys mentioning, he and his research colleague, Dr. Leo V. DiCara, tuned their instrumental conditioning process down so fine that a rat learned to blush one ear and blanch the other. In almost all of his animal experiments, Dr. Miller paralyzes the rats and other lab animals with curare, a powerful drug used by South American Indians to tip their poison darts. The curare interferes with all the nerve impulses that keep the skeletal muscles working—including respiration. The paralyzing of the skeletal muscles ensures that the animals do not "cheat" by somehow using their skeletal muscles to affect their visceral responses. (It is thus far a frustration for Dr. Miller and others that non-curarized animals are slower to learn viscerally than the curarized ones.)

The difference between the way the body learns by classical conditioning and by instrumental conditioning is crucial to understanding how biofeedback training works. *Classical conditioning,** or learning, always demands a stimulus that elicits an innate response. For example, the first time you ever saw a lemon, nothing much happened with your saliva glands, which are visceral organs. But after you first tasted its sour juice, your saliva glands automatically secreted lots of saliva to dilute and wash away the puckering citric acid. You cannot control the response of your saliva glands to the lemon juice, and after you have tasted several lemons

* Editor's italics.

your mouth will start watering at the very sight of one. You have been classically conditioned to salivate at the sight of lemons. The same thing works for other such stimuli: a mad dog, for example. The sight of one will boost your heart rate, increase your adrenaline flow, and generally activate other innate fear responses.

The process of *instrumental learning* * is much less limited since it requires no specific stimulus to provoke a response. If you want to sink a twelve-foot golf putt, for instance, there is nothing anyone can offer you, not a lemon or $5,000, that will get your body to hole the ball out with Pavlovian sureness. But by the process of trial and error, or instrumental conditioning, you can learn to coordinate your muscles and other responses. You stroke the ball toward the hole and it glides by. You try again and again. Each time you get closer. You are not aware of precisely what you are doing to improve; you cannot say which muscles are contracting or relaxing and in what order. But you get closer nonetheless, and each near success is a reward that is likely to keep you trying. At last you are in control of your muscles, your responses, and the golf ball. It plunks into the hole. This trial-and-error process is called instrumental learning.

Now imagine that you are trying to make the same putt blindfolded. Very difficult, if not impossible. Why? Because something essential is missing from the learning process: *feedback.* * In this case, the feedback is the sight of the ball getting closer to the cup. Of course, you could learn to make the putt blindfolded if you substituted for the feedback of your visual perception the voice (feedback) of your caddy. He might, at the simplest level, say "yes" when your direction was right and say nothing or "no" when it wasn't. He might offer more guidance: "A little more to the right" or "A little to the left and harder." You would still be badly handicapped by the imprecision of your caddy's secondhand information, but eventually you would sink one and then perhaps quite a few.

Our mind is in some ways like the blindfolded golfer where the viscera are concerned. Scientists are trying to find new ways to remove the blindfold, which is enormously difficult indeed, or to substitute the guidance of the caddy-type feedback for sensory information about visceral organs that the mind for some reason dismisses or never perceives. Dr. Fehmi's beeping tone and the mini-volt currents of pleasurable brain stimulation that lab rats get are simple reward bio-feedback signals; Dr. Engel's colored lights represent more guidance. All are examples of bio-feedback used to instrumentally condition internal organs by letting the mind know, within predetermined limits, what those organs are up to.

One path of bio-feedback research has branched slightly away from the strictly therapeutic approach and is investigating the ability of human beings to exert purposeful control over their visceral functions, especially

* Editor's italics.

their *brain functions*,* with the goal of making the essentially healthy person better able to cope with his world. At the United States Navy Medical Neuropsychiatric Research Unit in San Diego, California, Dr. Ardie Lubin and Dr. David Hord, both psychologists, are studying the relationship between the output of alpha waves and sleep. What they want to determine is whether or not a person deprived of sleep can be returned to a state of effectiveness and acceptable decision-making capacity by willing himself into an alpha state for a certain length of time. Some preliminary tests have shown that alpha states may be recuperative.

At the Langley Porter Neuropsychiatric Institute, part of the University of California Medical Center in San Francisco, a research group headed by Dr. Joe Kamiya is exploring the possibility that brain-wave control may have important effects on health, creativity, and such mental functions as perception and memory. Dr. Kamiya is regarded by most psychologists as the pioneer in the field of brain-wave control. Dr. Kamiya and his research team have found that subjects who do best at mastering their alpha-wave output are those who have had some training in meditation, as in Zen. At Stony Brook, Dr. Fehmi has noted that musicians, athletes, and artists are especially adept at control over their brain waves. Conversely, he has found that subjects who come into his chamber and slouch in their armchair in the spaced-out way associated with drug trips produce precious little alpha.

It is frustrating to researchers that the subjects who are most proficient in gaining brain-wave control are often strangely tongue-tied when it comes to telling just how they do it. Some say they relax and wipe everything from their mind. Others concentrate on some infinite point like a mystical third eye in the middle of their forehead. Some are unable to verbalize the experience at all.

"The best way I can describe the *feeling of alpha*," * says Dr. Fehmi, "is a relaxed but alert and sensitive 'into-it-ness.' " Dr. Edgar E. Coons, a physiological psychologist at New York University and a musician, has been trained to produce alpha waves in Dr. Fehmi's lab; he says the alpha state "makes me feel as if I'm floating about half an inch above my seat." A talented young musician named David Rosenboom, who recently presented a bio-feedback brain-wave concert at Automation House in New York (brain-wave activity was fed into a computer and an ARP synthesizer; the result was a weird but not unpleasing effect), is the reigning champion brain-wave producer for Dr. Fehmi. When his alpha is really going strong in all parts of his brain, Rosenboom says he is plugged in to a "great energy source." Another musician named LaMonte Young, who keeps a forty-cycle "home" tone going in his Manhattan studio at all times, explained that he had no trouble generating alpha the first time he ever tried it, because his mind "is tuned to frequencies and intervals."

* Editor's italics.

At the University of Colorado Medical School, Dr. Hans Stoyva has had notable success in teaching his patients how to relax specific muscles that tense up and cause certain kinds of *tension headaches.** The easing of pain has been swift and dramatic.

Dr. Martin Orme, director of experimental psychiatry at the University of Pennsylvania Medical School in Philadelphia, is studying the alpha-wave phenomenon with an eye toward finding out what exactly an alpha state does to or for an individual and how it might be beneficial to him. "It's not enough to know you can contemplate your navel," Dr. Orme says. "You then have to ask, 'What happens?'" Experiments conducted with subjects who have been trained to produce a reliably high alpha-wave output show, according to Dr. Orme, that *critical thinking* * tends to interfere with alpha waves, but that alpha-wave production does not mean blunted intellectual capacity. What alpha production seems to do best for the alpha producer is relax him, insulate him from stressful critical thought, and rehabilitate his autonomic nervous system to some degree.

"What this may mean," Dr. Orme says, "is that alpha might be used to bring down the level of a person's *anxiety* * to a point where he can function at his best. We all need a certain amount of anxiety to function. It is well accepted that we function best as anxiety rises to a certain point on a bell-shaped curve, and past that point we do increasingly worse as anxiety increases. If alpha can be used to knock down anxiety to the point on the curve where we work most effectively, it can be a most important development." However, Dr. Orme is quick to point out that "this is three levels or more from where we are now, but it is something to consider."

Another prospect for visceral learning is its use as a possible *alternative to drugs.** If, for example, a high alpha output can cause deep relaxation, or a specific focusing of bio-feedback training can loosen up a taut muscle, this could well substitute for the billions of tranquilizers consumed to achieve essentially the same effect. The advantage over drugs might be considerable. For instance, while a tranquilizer acts in a general way on the whole body or an entire bodily system (perhaps with unwanted side effects), bio-feedback training might be specific enough to do the job required and let the rest of the body function undisturbed.

"There is also," says Dr. Orme, "the general question of personal control and how we might be able to bring our emotions under control. We want to know, of course, to what extent an individual can gain control with precision and reliability over the things he fears. A good part of fear is the fear of fear. If you know you are going to be hurt, you will hurt more with exactly the same degree of hurting stimulus. If we can break into some of the feedback loops that are part of the fear cycle, we may be able to control unpleasant and unproductive anxiety."

* Editor's italics.

To Dr. Orme, the goal is clear. "We may be able to become actual masters of our destiny. As a psychiatrist, my purpose is to enable man to decide his own fate instead of his juices deciding for him."

At Rockefeller University, Dr. DiCara, a burly ex-football player, is attempting to unravel some of the whys and hows of visceral learning. In one recent experiment, he and Dr. Eric Stone found that rats trained to increase their heart rate had significantly more of a powerful group of chemicals called *catecholamines* * in their brains and hearts than rats who learned to *lower* their heart rates. In humans, catecholamines are associated with hypertension and coronary artery disease. The possibility of learning to slow the heart rate to achieve beneficial effects on hypertension and heart ailments is intriguing; however, a major obstacle still to be overcome is the inability at present to measure catecholamines in the human brain.

An equally intriguing possibility has been raised by an experiment conducted by Dr. DiCara and Dr. Jay M. Weiss. Rats that had learned to slow their heart rates subsequently showed excellent *ability to learn* * to move back and forth in a shuttle box to avoid an electric shock. Rats trained to speed their hearts learned very poorly and exhibited signs of extreme fearfulness by leaping into the air, squealing, and turning toward their tails with each pulse of shock instead of getting away from it. In contrast, the slow heart-rate rats took each shock in stride, with only "mild jerks," and slowly walked out of the electrified side of the box.

"It is crystal-clear," says Dr. Miller, with whom Dr. DiCara has worked as co-experimenter on many projects, "that heart rate training affects rats' learning. What is further indicated is that the training also affects their emotionality. We cannot jump from the laboratory to the clinic, but we may indeed find that in human subjects trained to lower their heart rates there could be an increased capacity to *adapt to stressful situations* * and a corresponding decrease in emotionality."

The field of bio-feedback training and visceral learning is still only crudely charted. New research teams are forming to explore further; the mechanical and electronic spin-offs of the space age are providing the new tools and infinitely more sensitive measuring devices that are required for progress. But most of all there seems to be a new attitude.

"We have brought four to five thousand years of cultural myths into the laboratory to be investigated," says Dr. Miller, who, in just a few years, has seen the pendulum of interest swing from "great resistance to great readiness." Although he is understandably reluctant to speculate on what the future holds, he is nonetheless confident that the new knowledge about our internal organs will stimulate much more research into the astonishing ability of human beings to learn.

* Editor's italics.

IMPLICATIONS

You will note the caution about overgeneralization concerning the application of bio-feedback possibilities. There is a limited amount of solid experimental information, although it is rapidly accumulating. What are the possible dangers in the unwary use of this method?

The author mentions *meditation,* as found among Eastern mystics. There has been experimentation on the physiological processes during meditation. The work by Wallace and Benson (1972) finds the physiological processes to be opposite of those in strong emotion—a decrease in most of the physiological processes that are found in emotional states.

REFERENCES

Those interested in greater understanding of bio-feedback research and its implications may consult the following three source books: Barber, DiCara, Kamiya, Miller, Shapiro, and Stoyva. These references are in an original readings book (1970) and two yearly supplements (1970, 1971).

26

SEEING IN THE DARK

Edwin G. Boring and Marion Van de Water

Among the students in the introductory course in psychology there are some who regard the topic of sensation as dull and of little practical use. However, many of the findings from the psychological laboratory that at first glance seem technical and of little significance can be related to real-life situations with value.

During World War II, *Psychology of the Fighting Man* was compiled for the man in uniform. Approximately one third of its useful advice pertained to the psychology of sensation and perception. The following selection is a chapter from that book. Facts about vision in the dark, technically known as *rod vision,* are presented simply and interestingly and are followed by practical rules for seeing in the dark.

Reprinted from Edwin G. Boring and Marion Van de Water, "Seeing in the Dark," *Psychology of the Fighting Man* (Washington, D.C.: Division of Behavioral Sciences National Academy of Sciences–National Research Council), pp. 60–75, by permission of the publisher and Mrs. Edwin G. Boring.

MODERN WAR is often war at night. That means that men must learn to see in the dark and to use their eyes in new and unfamiliar ways.

So the fighting man needs to know how to make the best use of his eyes at night—whether his job puts him in an airplane or a tank, on a ship, driving a truck, or just getting about on his own feet.

You can't make a man into an owl or a cat, but you can let him have rules and aids that will give him just enough edge on the enemy so that he can get in the first shot.

Everyone knows that when you go into a dark room from a bright one it is hard to see until your eyes have become used to the gloom. At a movie it takes a minute or two to see the vacant seat. It may take a couple of minutes more before you can recognize a friend. During these minutes your eyes are steadily becoming more sensitive to the faint light.

There are two ways in which your eyes adjust for seeing in the dark. They can open up to let in more light, and they can shift over to a more sensitive set of light detectors. They do both.

It's the pupil of the eye that opens up in the dark to let more light in—and closes down in bright light to a pinhead opening so as to keep out too much light. The pupil works like the diaphragm in a camera, which you open wide for taking pictures in dim light.

But the important change is this shift to the more sensitive set of detectors.

The retinas of your eyes (Fig. 1) have two batteries of light detectors called *cones* and *rods*. The nerve fibers run from them to the brain. The cones do the seeing in bright light, the rods at night. In twilight and bright moonlight both are working together.

The cones—there are millions of them in each eye—are packed together most closely in the very center of the retina, the part that does the most accurate seeing in daylight. That's why in daylight you always have to look directly at something in order to see it best. The cones also see colors.

The rods—and there are millions of them, too—are color-blind. That is why "all cats look gray at night." Cats really do—and so do trees and flowers, provided the night is dark enough. But a red or green signal light is seen as colored at night because it is bright enough to get the cones working.

The rods are packed most closely together at the outside edges of your retinas, and there aren't any rods at all in the very center. The part of your eye that is most sensitive in daylight is actually blind at night. So don't look directly at a thing to see it in the dark. Look alongside of it. That faint object out there in the dark, it caught your attention because it moved a little. What is it? It disappears when you look at it closely, but it's there again when you look to one side. Keep looking to one side or the other and you may be able to tell whether it's a man, or simply a bush that moved in the wind.

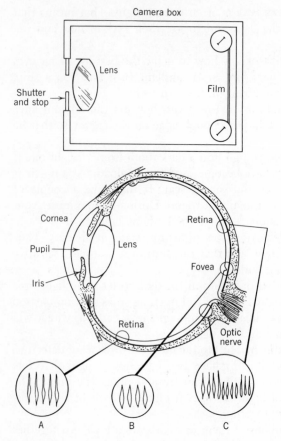

Figure 1. The eye and the camera in this much simplified diagram show the principal parts of a camera and the corresponding parts of the eye. The three circles beneath the eye are enlargements of the spots at which rods and cones appear on the retina. (A) Only rods present; (B) only cones present; and (C) rods and cones together.

Both the rods and the cones are differently sensitive to different colors of light. The cones are most sensitive to yellow light. That's why yellows in daylight are brighter than reds, greens, and blues. The rods are most sensitive to yellow-green light, but they differ most from the cones in seeing blue light. To blue light they are one thousand times as sensitive as the cones. So don't use blue lights in blackouts. The enemy's eyes, like your own, can see blues easily in the dark. Use red lights instead, for the rods see pure red light as black. But don't use intense ordinary red light, because that is not pure and will affect the rods.

Night-eyes lack the sharp vision for detail that your day-eyes have. You can't read, or study an instrument dial, or examine a map, a road sign, or your watch, by using your rods. For that you must put your cones to work by having more light, of course, shielding it carefully from the enemy if he is not to know where you are.

But night-eyes are extraordinarily sensitive to faint light. An ordinary candle flame or a lighted match could be seen ten miles away if the night were completely black, if there were no haze at all in the air. Even with haze and starlight, a match can be seen for many miles. So don't strike matches in a blackout or when the enemy may be watching.

It takes time—half an hour or more—for the rods to get completely into action after you have been in the light. When you first go from a brightly lighted room into a blacked-out night, you are at first completely blind. Neither the cones nor the rods work.

Then three things happen. First the pupils of your eyes dilate, letting more light into your eyes. That helps a little.

Next the cones get more sensitive. They divide up the blacks into blacks, dark grays and light grays. That takes about five minutes.

More slowly the rods get adjusted. You begin to see shapes and outlines in the gloom where there were not even vague bulking shadows when you first came in. This is due to a slow chemical change, which is rapid at first but not fully completed for half an hour.

The soldier who at a command or an alert signal leaves a lighted room to run on duty without having prepared his eyes is completely at the mercy of the enemy as far as his vision is concerned. By the time he gains the use of his night-eyes, the emergency may be all over.

And even when your eyes are adapted to the dark, flashing on a light, though only for a short time, may ruin your night vision for another half hour. You can lose by a few minutes of light all you gained by a half hour in the dark. The brighter the light and the longer you look at it, the more you lose.

Getting Ready to See in the Dark

Complete darkness is the best preparation for night fighting. Protect your eyes from light before you start and while you are out. If you can't stay in darkness, keep the lights around you as low as possible and never look straight at them. And if you have to look at a lighted object, be quick about it. Looking at an instrument dial lighted only by radium paint can cut down the distance at which you can see a friendly or an enemy plane by 50 per cent. So don't look at the dial any longer than you must.

Experienced gun pointers and spotters know that they must not watch the flashes of their own guns as they fire. The flash of a six-inch gun can dull the eyes for more than a minute. Under continuous fire at dawn or dusk it is impossible to aim some rapid-fire guns accurately at a target when the gunners let themselves watch the flash. At night the effect is even greater. Luckily the flashes of rifles and small-caliber guns have much less effect on the eyes.

There are several ways in which you can become adapted to the dark even though you must work in fairly bright light. Each way is suitable only for certain kinds of jobs.

Ship pilots and bridge officers have long known a clever but simple trick. When they have to work their way among dark islands with the beacons unlit, or to move in company with other blacked-out ships, these men often have to go back and forth from a lookout post to a lighted bridge or chart-room.

When they go into the light, they cover one eye and use the other.

Then, when they come out into the night, they uncover this eye and use it.

To cover the eye, an ordinary black eye patch is sometimes used. This trick should not be used, however, to prepare for night duty except in an emergency. Experienced men know they must stay out of the light for fifteen minutes to half an hour before they go on night duty. With the patch over but one eye, only that eye becomes prepared, and two eyes are always better than one.

A better way to get the eyes dark-adapted is to work in deep *red light*. Remember that pure red has almost no effect on the rod cells of your night-eyes. So, if deep red light is available, you can read or work—if you have to— and still be dark-adapting your night-eyes so that you will be ready for nearly instant action in the dark. If you can't get bulbs of deep red, you may get by with a red cellophane covering for a light or an instrument. But the red cellophane is pretty poor because it lets through some orange and some white light that tend to desensitize your rods. Even the red bulb is not perfect and it ought not to be any brighter than is absolutely necessary.

The very best arrangement is tight-fitting *goggles* with red filters in them. They can be made so that only red light gets through, so that the rods are not affected at all. Put them on half an hour before your night duty begins. And take them off, of course, when you are outside in the dark or you will be quite blind.

The trouble with the use of red light and the goggles is that they keep you from distinguishing colors properly. Red lines on a white chart dis-appear in red light. Red and white signal lights look alike. All red objects become white or gray or some other color. Be careful about color if you have red goggles on.

It isn't enough to get your night-eyes working at full capacity by staying in the dark or using red light, red goggles, or patches. You have to learn to use night-eyes after you get them.

First try an experiment to show you how your eyes work in the dark. You must have a room that can be completely blacked out into which you can let just a little light, shutting the light out gradually. If the windows are dark, you can close the door slowly.

Take a sheet of typewriter paper. Cut it in two. Then cut one half in two, then one of these quarters in two, and keep on until you have a piece not more than a quarter of an inch across. You now have almost a dozen pieces of white paper ranging in size from a tiny scrap up to a piece about 8 by 5 inches. Lay them out on a black table or other dark surface.

Now shut the door and let your eyes get used to the dark. Wait ten minutes at the least—half an hour if you can spare the time.

Now open the door a crack until you can just see the smallest piece. The bigger pieces will be brighter than the smaller. The biggest piece will almost glow. The more light a piece reflects, the brighter it appears.

Now watch the big piece. You are seeing it with your cones. Gradually it will fade out until you cannot see it at all. That is the cones getting fatigued.

Now pay attention to the other pieces while trying to keep your eyes fixed on the place where the big piece disappeared. They are still visible—to the rods. In fact, viewed this way, out of the corner of your eye, they seem to glow as though phosphorescent.

If you look directly at one though, it disappears—because there are no rods in the center of the retina. Move your eyes away, however, and the little piece that disappeared pops back again into view. You can make them come and go. A piece is there when you don't look at it, gone when you fix your eyes on the spot where it was.

That's one alarming thing about being in a strange area in the dark. The object that might possibly be a sniper isn't there when you look at it, comes back when it thinks you aren't noticing.

You may not in the dark be able to spot an airplane if you look directly at it. Yet you can pick it up again out of the corner of your eye if you will look away. It disappears again if you look straight at it. The same thing is true if you try to see a distant ship, an unlighted car or tank, or even a faint star.

Always remember, therefore, that you must look a little to one side in order to see best on a very dark night. Learn to pay attention to things which are just a little off the center of your field of vision. Learn to keep from looking directly at any object in the dark. As you feel your eyes drawn almost irresistibly toward what you want to see, just let them slide on over to the other side of it and look again with the tail of your eye. It takes practice to learn to do this without fail, but it is worth the trouble to learn the trick.

And don't keep looking steadily to the same side of the object, because then it will disappear too. Use first one side and then the other.

Try this out.

When you are in a darkened room or outdoors on a dark night, hold up your finger and look steadily at it. It will disappear. Look a little to one side and make it appear again. Keep staring and it will go again. Then look to the other side of it and let it come back.

This means that in searching the sea or sky for a dark object, you must look first at one area and then at another. When you think you have spotted something, look first to one side of it and then to the other—then above it, below it.

But don't ever try sweeping your eyes over the sky or horizon. You can't see well when the eyes are moving. Scan the sky, don't sweep it. Look here, then there, then at the next place.

Night-eyes are slow in responding except to bright objects and moving objects. You may have to look several times before you can be sure you have spotted something. But don't stare. Keep looking again and again, always just alongside of the dark, still object.

Small objects are much harder to see at night than in daytime. The average airplane becomes too small to be seen beyond 1000 feet on a clear starry night. But the plane is smaller when seen on edge from ahead, behind, or at the side. Then you may not spot it more than 400 or 500 feet away. So, if you are pursuing a plane, try to keep above or below it until you are close in.

The same thing should be done in chasing a boat. Keep off to one side when far away, if you can, so that the boat will be seen more nearly broadside on.

Night glasses are useful because they magnify an object without much loss of light. Binoculars magnify too, but they cut down the light so much that a very faint object disappears. The night glasses do not give so clear a view as the binoculars, but your night-eyes cannot see sharp outlines anyhow.

Darkness may make things look smaller. A tree in the dark in winter looks smaller because you cannot see the twigs and the ends of the branches at all. A plane at night seems to get larger when a searchlight falls upon it, because the light brings out so many details that could not be seen before.

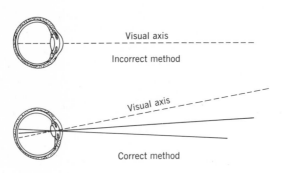

Figure 2. Technique for visual accuracy at night. Practice the use of the "corners of the eyes." Night targets are better seen by not looking directly at them. This is because the edges of the retina are more sensitive to dim light than is the very center of the retina.

The best you can do at night is to see dark fuzzy silhouettes of objects. That makes it hard to recognize objects, but you can learn recognition.

Even in daytime, *recognition* is largely a matter of jumping to conclusions from slight hints. You can recognize a friend long before you can see the color of his eyes, even before you can tell whether he has his nose on this morning. His general shape or his style of walk may be enough.

At night the clues are still fewer, and so it pays to study the silhouettes of ships and planes, to study them at all possible angles and positions. Then you may learn to tell one plane from another, one ship from another, even though you never do know just what clues you are using.

A lookout or scout at night can't afford to wait to be sure just what he has seen before reporting it or taking cover. Follow your hunches. Trust vague impressions. Those are the best rules for night seeing. The cautious man who waits to be sure may not live that long.

Sometimes you may be able to detect a moving airplane in the sky by its motion alone, or by what you don't see, more than by what you do see. If a star blinks out and then on again, something may have passed between you and it.

Contrast

Contrast helps vision. If the thing observed is much lighter or darker than its background, it is much more easily seen. Even at night the sky is so much lighter than the ground or the water that the chances of seeing an airplane from below against the sky are ever so much better than of seeing it from above against the ground—especially if it is painted dark on top to match the ground. A ship is easily seen against a dimly lighted sky. It is very clear against a coast not properly dimmed out. It may be invisible against the dark sea, or to an airplane flying over it.

But, if the white underside of a plane is illuminated by moonlight reflected from clouds beneath the plane, then the plane as seen from below may almost match the moonlit haze of the sky and disappear. That's in moonlight. You can't get the shaded underside of a plane light enough in daylight to match the daytime sky.

But contrast helps vision only when outlines are clear. For this reason the windshields of night fighters must be kept clear and free of scratches or fog. These scatter the light, make contours fuzzy, and reduce contrast. Careless night fighters have been known to tolerate enough dirt on their windshields to double the time it takes them to see a plane moving along nearby. And sailors on ships sometimes let the salt from the spray pile up in blotches on the glass. That is courting death.

For the same reason, it is important to keep down the light on your own side of the windshield. It produces glare, spoils outlines, reduces contrast, makes faint objects invisible. That is why you push up close to the window when you try to look out at night. By coming up close, you shade part of the glass and reduce the glare. If there has to be any light on your side of the glass, screen it from the glass.

Good Food and Good Health

There has been a great deal of talk about the effect of shortages of vitamins A and C on ability to see at night. These are the vitamins in fresh vegetables, cheese, and fruit. People who don't get enough of these vitamins do become poor in night vision, but the regular army and navy rations supply plenty of them. Occasionally, when ships are on long trips or when fighting lasts until fresh foods are all gone, a shortage of vitamins may occur. Then medical officers supply men who are likely to be on night duty with vitamin capsules. Extra vitamins don't improve night vision when your diet and your night vision are already normal.

Night vision is affected by fatigue. Anything that reduces your physical well-being has a greater effect on night vision than on day vision. Hangovers, slight illnesses, or excessive fatigue may double or even triple the amount of light needed to see a faint object in the dark.

So the night fighter must train for his job as a boxer trains for the big match. The boxer who is not at the peak of training is likely to be knocked out. The night fighter whose eyes are not at the peak of efficiency is likely to be killed.

Rules for Seeing in the Dark

1. *Protect your eyes from light* before you go on night duty and while you are out.

2. *Stay in the dark* beforehand, or use *red light* or red goggles. The goggles are best, when you can get them.

3. *Never look directly at any light,* nor at any illuminated object except in red light. If you must break this rule, be quick with your looking.

4. *Use the corners of your eyes* when you are out on duty. Keep looking alongside of what you think is there, until you have made up your mind about it.

5. *Keep your eyes moving.* Look and move, look and move. Don't sweep them over large regions, and don't stare continuously at one spot.

6. *Keep your windshield spotless,* free of dirt, salt, fog, and scratches.

7. *Keep down the light on your own side of the windshield,* and screen it from the windshield.

8. *Keep yourself wide awake and on the alert.* Don't break training. Use good sense about eating, drinking, and smoking. Keep rested, if you can.

9. *Practice recognition.* Learn by experience to recognize from slight clues the objects you need to recognize.

10. *Practice all the rules* for seeing at night until they become second nature to you. And use every possible device to aid you.

It is the night fighter with the best eyes who wins his part of the war.

IMPLICATIONS

Do the suggestions at the end of the article have any value in civilian life as, for example, for safety in night-driving? Almost all of the topics in discussion of sensation and perception in introductory psychology can be converted into practical information concerning the use of your senses in work or play situations. In fact, in the book from which this excerpt is taken, there are chapters on sight as a weapon, colors as camouflage, hearing as a tool in warfare, smell as a sentry, the sense of position, and the sense of direction. You may find it interesting to see how many practical suggestions on sensation you can derive from your textbook material, and how these suggestions may be as simply stated as those given in the article.

REFERENCES

For other examples of applied psychology, based in part on the psychology of sensation and perception, see Anastasi (1964), especially the chapters on working environment and equipment design.

CHAPTER VI

CAREERS AND
LEADERSHIP

27

A CAREER IN PSYCHOLOGY

C. Alan Boneau, Stuart E. Golann, and Margaret M. Johnson

Here are answers to questions undergraduates ask as they discover that psychology is an area they may enter vocationally: What do psychologists do? What is the future of psychology and for psychologists? How long is the preparation? What universities offer graduate programs?

What Is Psychology?

Major Facets

PSYCHOLOGY IS at one time a scholarly discipline, a scientific field, and a professional activity. Its overall focus is on the study of both animal and human behavior and related mental and physiological processes.

As a scholarly discipline, psychology represents a major field of study in academic settings, with emphasis on the communication and explanation of principles and theories of behavior.

As a science, it is a focus of research through which investigators collect, quantify, analyze, and interpret data describing animal and human behavior, thus shedding light on the causes and dynamics of behavior patterns.

As a profession, psychology involves the practical application of knowledge, skills, and techniques for the solution or prevention of individual or social problems; the professional role also provides an opportunity for the psychologist to develop further his understanding of human behavior and thus to contribute to the science of psychology.

Subject-Matter Areas

Like any field, psychology is organized into subject-matter areas, each with its own methods of study and focus of concerns:

Experimental psychology refers to a method by which a number of behavioral processes are studied, particularly learning, perception, motivation, emotion, language, and thinking. The term is used in relation to subject-matter areas of psychology in which experimental methods are emphasized. *Mathematical psychology*, a branch of experimental psychology, is concerned with the development, application, and evaluation of mathematical descriptions and explanations of psychological processes.

Comparative psychology focuses on comparisons of the behavior of different organisms; its scope encompasses the study of evolutionary and genetic determinants of behavior, thus giving it a close identity with the biological sciences.

Physiological psychology probes the relationship between behavior and the biological and physiological processes of the body—for example, between emotion and the function of the brain and nervous system.

Social psychology, concerned with human interaction in the social environment, examines such phenomena as attitude development and change, social pressures, leadership, and mass movements; group dynamics, with its increasingly broad and important social applications, is another emphasis of the area.

Developmental psychology focuses on the development of the organism from its prenatal origins through old age. The important subarea of *child psychology* studies how, for example, the infant's growing repertoire of behavior and feeling is related to biological growth patterns of the body or how the processes of social learning and socialization contribute to an infant's development into a socialized person.

Psychology of personality is concerned with the processes by which a person becomes a unique individual; many of the best known theoretical statements about human behavior—for example, those of Sigmund Freud—are part of its substance. *Psychopathology*, or abnormal psychology, is an important branch of this area; it is concerned with those factors that contribute to deviant and maladjusted behavior and the processes or techniques by which such behavior may be modified; the exceptional, creative, and highly effective personality is a subject of interest along with the disordered personality.

Psychometrics deals with the development and application of procedures—for example, psychological tests—for measuring the many psychological variables which underlie and affect human behavior; the area emerged from observations of differences in behavior among individuals and has developed into a highly technical area relevant to all subject-matter areas.

Educational psychology encompasses the study of such phenomena as individual differences, learning, motivation, group behavior, and personality, all in the context of education; its principal focus is on the interaction of the child with his educational environment, but it also includes the selection and training of teachers.

What Do Psychologists Do?

Because psychology tends to be confused with psychiatry, a medical specialty, many people erroneously assume that psychologists concern themselves primarily with psychopathology and deviant behavior. Although some psychologists do, of course, deal with abnormal persons and phenomena, the concerns of psychology are considerably more diverse.

Psychology began in the classroom as a philosophical approach to understanding behavior and in the laboratory as a scientific approach toward the same goal. Its association with both the classroom and the laboratory has changed dramatically, however, over the last 50 years. Many psychologists now work in various social, institutional, and industrial settings such as schools, community agencies, mental health clinics, and private industries. Indeed, psychologists today rarely are exclusively scholars, scientists, or professionals; most combine these roles. Thus, a psychologist may be primarily a teacher, but he may also conduct research and provide services as part of his regular activities.

Specialty Areas

Whereas basic subject-matter areas define the substance of psychology, its specialty areas reflect how psychologists work with that substance. Each specialty is built on a base of knowledge in one or more of the subject-matter areas. Psychologists who function primarily as scientists or scholars will usually concentrate their research or study on a single subject-matter area such as experimental psychology, or on an even more circumscribed topic such as human learning. On the other hand, psychologists who function primarily as professionals outside academic or research settings are usually knowledgeable in a cluster of relevant subject-matter areas which they apply in their work.

Following are sketches of those specialty areas in which psychologists apply various combinations of subject matter to specific kinds of problems in unique settings.

Clinical Psychology

Psychologist in Community Mental Health Clinic   Peter Newman, PhD, clinical psychologist . . . Conducts individual and group psychotherapy . . . Meets in 50-minute sessions with several adults . . . Is Cotherapist with two graduate students from a local university in group therapy sessions, one with adolescent boys, the other with three sets of parents . . . Confers with other psychologists and with psychiatrists and social workers on planning and evaluation of community programs . . . Maintains contact with representatives of school, correctional and welfare systems. Collaborates with a psychiatrist in providing consultation to a prison system . . . Is a member of community committees evaluating preschool enrichment programs and studying riot prevention.

The clinical psychologist specializes in the assessment and therapeutic treatment of persons suffering emotional or adjustment problems. Typical, he is knowledgeable in the psychology of personality, psychopathology, and psychometrics, and he is also trained in the application of diagnostic and psychotherapeutic techniques; other skills and techniques may be acquired as he assumes new responsibilities—for example, mental health consultation with community agencies.

Like most psychologists, the clinician is also trained in the skills and methods of scientific inquiry. Thus, in addition to or instead of his applied professional activities, he may conduct research—for example, to determine the characteristics of a psychotherapist which are related to patient improvement or the conditions under which young children develop a sense of responsibility.

Counseling Psychology

Psychologist in University Counseling Center   Robert Franklin, PhD, counseling psychologist . . . Interviews and tests students to assess ability, motivation, and interests . . . Works intensively with students who are having serious difficulty adjusting to college or are experiencing emotional problems which hamper their college work . . . Conducts group meetings in reading and study skills . . . Supervises three interns enrolled in the university's doctoral programs in counseling psychology . . . Teaches undergraduate courses in child psychology, psychology of personality, and tests and measurements . . . Is faculty adviser to a group of student volunteers in mental hospitals.

In contrast to clinical psychologists, who deal with maladaptive behavior, counseling psychologists place greater emphasis on facilitating normal development and on helping people cope with important problems of everyday living—for example, the choice of a career or the improvement of interpersonal relationships. Many counseling psychologists help persons by measuring their abilities, interests, and temperament; this service is especially important in *rehabilitation psychology*, a specialty in which human disability is often a consideration. The subject-matter areas typically utilized by counseling and rehabilitation psychologists are developmental psychology, psychopathology, psychology of personality, educational psychology, and psychometrics.

Like the clinician, the counseling psychologist may also use his scientific training—for example, in standardizing tests of vocational interests. In another role, he may consult with business executives on the selection of personnel for various jobs or on the development of programs to maximize job satisfaction and performance.

School Psychology

Psychologist in Public School System   Frank Wright, PhD, school psychologist . . . Employed by an urban school system of 6 high schools, 14 junior high schools, and 45 elementary schools . . . Supervises two psychologists who administer and interpret individual tests and conduct a standardized testing program for entire system . . . Plans and conducts frequent workshops for teachers on such skills and techniques as effective classroom management, diagnosis of learning problems, and role playing . . . Acts as consultant to system-wide committee planning preschool programs for inner-city children . . . Currently experimenting with computer-assisted instruction in 1 elementary school and advising two graduate students on related thesis research.

Psychologists working in this specialty area are concerned with increasing the effectiveness of educational institutions to facilitate the intellectual, social, and emotional development of children. They may function in various roles within the school system—for example, as research specialists in the development of programs to implement and evaluate special educational projects; as leaders of inservice training programs for teachers and as their consultants regarding specific teaching or classroom behavior problems; or as clinicians treating the interrelated psychological and educational problems of children. Many school psychologists also have responsibility for administering and interpreting the results of standardized tests.

Industrial Psychology

Psychologist in Industrial Plant   Judith Simmons, PhD, industrial psychologist . . . Consults on selection and placement of employees and training of employment interviewers and personnel specialists . . . Is conducting a study to evaluate new interview techniques . . . Confers with department heads, union representatives, and foremen on criteria for performance evaluation . . . Advises management on questions of employee morale . . . Supervises applied research program to reduce accidents and worker fatigue . . . Is developing a special training program for workers from disadvantaged backgrounds.

The industrial psychologist focuses his scientific research on and applies his professional skills to problems that people encounter at work. He may function in several capacities within an organization: He may study the way work is organized, making changes to improve productivity, the quality of services, and consumer satisfaction; he may consult with management in the development of employee training programs to maximize employee potential; or he may use scientific techniques to measure employee morale, analyzing the data in terms of their implications for job definitions, training programs, and the organization of work. *Personnel psychology* focuses more specifically on the selection and assignment of personnel to enhance job satisfaction and productivity. Both industrial and personnel psychologists work with the subject matter of experimental, developmental, and social psychology, and psychometrics.

Engineering Psychology

The engineering psychologist is concerned with the development and improvement of man–machine systems. He advises on the design of equipment intended to maximize human performance—for example, the control systems of spacecraft. His expertise finds applications in such fields as communications, transportation, and commercial and industrial production. Knowledge of sensory processes, perception, motor skills, and psychometrics is essential to the work of the engineering psychologist.

Consumer Psychology

This specialty area involves the study of psychological factors that determine an individual's behavior as a consumer of goods and services. The consumer psychologist is interested in learning, for example, why people buy certain kinds of toothpaste or automobiles or what strategies might be used to help an individual reduce his rate of consumption. He attempts also to improve the acceptability and safety of products offered to the consumer and to enhance the consumer's capacity for decision making, such as in the selection of newly available public health services.

An Overview

Psychologist in a University   Alan Stuart, PhD, social psychologist . . . Employed by a large state university as an associate professor of psychology . . . Teaches two courses each semester, from repertoire that includes psychology, introduction to social psychology, group dynamics and specialized topics of social psychology . . . Chairs departmental committees on undergraduate curriculum and graduate examinations . . . Sits on university committee on institutional goals . . . Is conducting research program on group reactions to the introduction of deviant members and supervising related thesis research of two master's degree students . . . Is member of dissertation committees of several doctoral candidates . . . Is consulting editor for the *Journal of Personality and Social Psychology*.

Figure 1 describes the proportions of psychologists engaged in various specialty areas, and Figure 2 reveals the percentages employed by various institutions and agencies. Clinical psychologists are shown to constitute the largest specialty area, while the largest number of psychologists are employed by academic institutions. This apparent contradiction is explained by the fact that, for the large majority of psychologists, the primary identification is with a college or university. It is in this environment that the three roles—scientist, scholar, and professional—may be combined most conveniently. Here, a psychologist in any of the specialties normally has access to the institution's research facilities, to its counseling centers, and to a variety of other facilities. Here, too, a psychologist, whatever his specialty, may teach undergraduate students the general principles and methods of psychology, or he may guide the studies of graduate students in his own or a related specialty area.

Because of their knowledge of a particular subject matter, psychologists are frequently called upon to solve practical problems. For example, social psychologists may act as consultants to community action projects, or experimental psychologists may help in the designing of teaching devices.

One Career May Equal Many

The work that an individual psychologist actually does is determined by a number of factors: the subject-matter emphasis of his training, his level of education, the setting in which he works, and the specific day-to-day demands confronting him. In addition, the psychologist is free to follow his own inclinations. He may choose among the rigors and excitement of science, the challenge of understanding and helping individuals, the rewards of promoting social change, the demands of teaching, or the satisfaction of enhancing an institution's effectiveness.

The psychologist's level of education is often a major factor in shaping his career. Because most doctoral level psychologists have been exposed to a large and diversified body of knowledge and techniques in psychology,

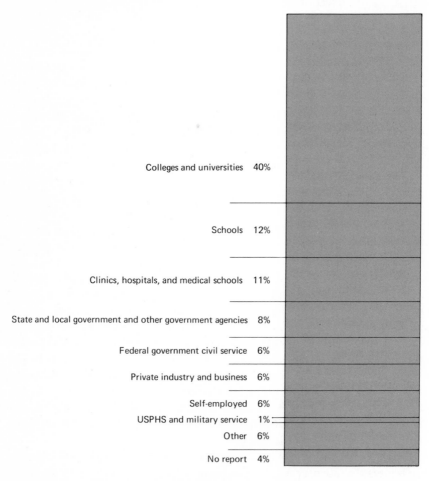

Colleges and universities   40%

Schools   12%

Clinics, hospitals, and medical schools   11%

State and local government and other government agencies   8%

Federal government civil service   6%

Private industry and business   6%

Self-employed   6%

USPHS and military service   1%

Other   6%

No report   4%

Figure 1. Subfields of psychology. (Figures taken from 1968 National Register of Scientific and Technical Personnel.)

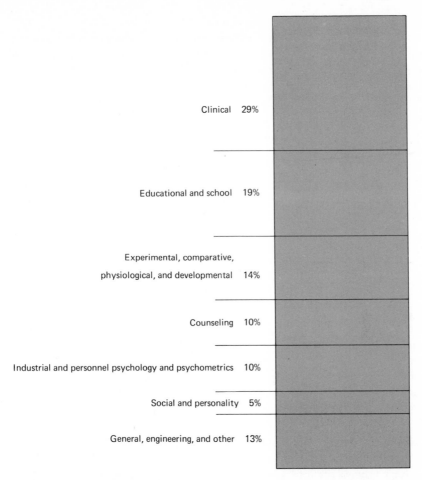

Clinical   29%

Educational and school   19%

Experimental, comparative,
physiological, and developmental   14%

Counseling   10%

Industrial and personnel psychology and psychometrics   10%

Social and personality   5%

General, engineering, and other   13%

Figure 2. Employers of psychologists. (Figures taken from 1968 National Register of Scientific and Technical Personnel.)

those who hold the doctoral degree enjoy the widest range of work choices and the most responsible positions. A clinical psychologist with a doctoral degree may thus be qualified to function in a school setting, or a rehabilitation setting, or even an industrial setting where, among other responsibilities, he might deal with the adjustment problems of executives. In contrast the psychologist with master's level training usually finds a more limited range of opportunities open to him, partly because of the position qualifications prescribed by potential employers and partly because he must limit his responsibilities only to those for which his background has prepared him.

Traditionally, a bachelor's level education has not been considered sufficient for a career in psychology. Bachelor's degree programs have not covered in depth either the subject matter or scientific method of psychology, nor have they provided professional training for dispensing psychological services. However, several recent developments have emphasized the importance of reexamining psychological training and the uses of manpower. These include the rapid growth in the number of programs designed to meet the educational and mental health needs of society, the concomitant need for more manpower to provide the psychological services involved in these programs, and changing conceptions of the psychologist's role. An outgrowth of these developments may be more numerous and more diversified careers in psychology than presently exist and more opportunities at different levels of training. The new programs in community colleges for training mental health technicians suggest at least one of many possibilities for diversification in psychological careers.

Looking Ahead

With the continuing impetus provided by social change and development, psychology will make important advances in the 1970s. Three examples are illustrative.

In the field of education, psychology has only begun to realize its potential contribution. The schools are natural laboratories for research-minded psychologists who study such processes as learning, motivation, and thinking. The schools are also natural work settings for psychologists with professional knowledge, skills, and techniques that can be utilized in planning for educational change and reform. Psychologists will play important roles in the 1970s as they grapple with such basic educational issues as measurable effects of student protest, design of optimum curricula, and effective methods for teaching children and training teachers.

In the field of health, the programs of Medicare and Medicaid may evolve in the 1970s into a national health care program, challenging psychology and other health-related professions to respond adequately to public needs. In the field of mental health, a recently initiated federal program of community-based mental health centers has made psychological services accessible and economical for many thousands of citizens. This program and the growing emphasis on preventive mental health are creating new demands on psychology and other mental health fields in terms of manpower and diversification of services. Already, a new specialty area, community psychology, has emerged from clinical and social psychology to cope with this and other broad challenges posed by social change.

How Do You Become a Psychologist?

Education

In a time of change and progress—as the decade ahead promises to be —educational requirements for a career in any field will be changing to keep pace with the demands of new jobs and new demands on established jobs. Thus, at any given time, the best source of information about educational requirements for careers in psychology, will be the institutions that offer training programs for such careers. What follows is general guidance only.

Preparation for a career in psychology at the master's or doctoral level begins with enrollment in a graduate program for advanced study in psychology. Receipt of the master's degree will generally involve completion of one or two years of course work beyond the bachelor's degree and the completion of additional requirements such as practical experience in an applied setting and/or a thesis based on a research project. Doctoral training requires a minimum of three years beyond the bachelor's degree and ordinarily consumes four or more years. Earning the doctorate demands a high level of academic achievement and may require a research project that makes an original contribution to the field of psychology. Doctoral students in many professional specialties may complete an internship either prior to or immediately after receiving their degrees; such internships normally involve at least an additional year of formal training.

Admission to graduate programs is highly competitive. Since graduate work in psychology requires close supervision, enrollment is limited in order to insure high quality in the preparation of students. Even with such constraints, there are approximately 2,000 doctoral and 5,000 master's degree recipients emerging from psychology graduate programs each year, with many of the latter going on to earn the doctorate. Approximately 25,000 bachelor's degrees are awarded to psychology majors each year.

Specific information about opportunities for graduate study in psychology and possible financial support is contained in an annual publication of the American Psychological Association, *Graduate Study in Psychology*, available from the Educational Affairs Office of the APA at a cost of $.50.

A career choice should, of course, be based on a thorough exploration of various alternatives so that one's interests, abilities, and values are most suitably matched with one's lifework. There are various other careers in which psychological knowledge, techniques, and skills are applied, but which differ substantially from psychology itself. Among these are psychiatry, psychiatric nursing, social work, work as a mental health technician, and certain aspects of student personnel work such as guidance counseling.

Accreditation and Certification

To insure that psychologists who perform public service functions are adequately trained, the American Psychological Association evaluates doctoral programs in clinical and counseling psychology and accredits those programs that meet minimum standards. Following is a list of universities with APA-approved doctoral programs in clinical and counseling psychology for 1969–70. (For a more current listing, write to the Educational Affairs Office of the APA.)

List of Universities with APA-Approved Doctoral Programs in Clinical and Counseling Psychology for 1969–70

Clinical Psychology

Adelphi University
Alabama, University of
Arizona State University
Arizona, University of
Arkansas, University of
Boston University
California, University of (Berkeley)
California, University of
 (Los Angeles)
Case Western Reserve University
Catholic University of America
Chicago, University of, Committee on
 Human Development
Chicago, University of, Department
 of Psychology
Cincinnati, University of
Clark University
Colorado, University of
Connecticut, University of
Denver, University of
Duke University
Florida State University
Florida, University of
Fordham University
George Peabody College for Teachers
Georgia, University of
Harvard University, Department
 of Social Relations
Houston, University of
Illinois, University of
Indiana University
Iowa, University of
Kansas, University of
Louisiana State University
Loyola University (Chicago)
Maryland, University of
Massachusetts, University of
Miami, University of
Michigan State University
Michigan, University of
Minnesota, University of
Missouri, University of
Nebraska, University of
New York, State University of
 (Buffalo)
New York University, Graduate
 School of Arts and Sciences
North Carolina, University of

Clinical Psychology

Northwestern University
Ohio State University
Oklahoma, University of
Oregon, University of
Pennsylvania State University
Pennsylvania, University of
Pittsburgh, University of
Purdue University
Rochester, University of
Rutgers—The State University
Southern California, University of
Southern Illinois University
St. Louis University
Syracuse University
Teachers College,
 Columbia University
Temple University
Tennessee, University of
Texas, University of
Utah, University of
Vanderbilt University
Washington State University
Washington, University of
Washington University (St. Louis)
Wayne State University
West Virginia University
Wisconsin, University of
Yale University
Yeshiva University

Counseling Psychology

Boston University
Catholic University of America
Florida, University of
George Peabody College for Teachers
Illinois, University of
Iowa, University of
Maryland, University of
Michigan, University of
Minnesota, University of,
 Department of Psychology,
 College of Liberal Arts
Minnesota, University of,
 Department of Educational
 Psychology, College of Education

Counseling Psychology

Missouri, University of, Department of
Psychology and Counseling and
Personnel Services
Nebraska, University of, Department of
Educational Psychology
and Measurements
New York, State University of
(Buffalo)
Ohio State University
Oregon, University of,
School of Education
Purdue University
Southern Illinois University
Teachers College,
Columbia University
Temple University
Texas Technological College
Texas, University of, Departments of
Education and of Psychology

Counseling Psychology

Utah, University of, Departments of
Educational Psychology
and of Psychology

Newly Approved Programs

All newly approved university programs
are listed on a provisional status for two
years.

Clinical Psychology

Emory University—Approved 1968
Kent State University—Approved 1969
McGill University, Montreal,
Canada—Approved 1968
New York, City University of
(City College)— Approved 1969
Ohio University—Approved 1968

Although the APA presently accredits only doctoral programs in the two specialties noted previously, plans are under way to broaden the accrediting authority to apply to all professional programs in psychology offered by universities and colleges.

In most states, the use of the title "psychologist" by those who have a private practice is restricted to persons with adequate training as defined by law. Standards set by the profession itself and by most state laws define a qualified professional psychologist as one with a doctoral degree in psychology and at least one year and preferably two years of supervised experience in the practice of psychology. Many psychologists work in institutional settings that are governed by state or federal regulations, and, almost universally, these regulations require at least a master's degree for a position as a psychologist.

The American Board of Professional Psychology offers diplomate status to individual practitioners of clinical, counseling, industrial, and school psychology who meet certain standards of excellence.

IMPLICATIONS

This article does not deal with those students (about 25,000 with bachelor degrees who are majoring in psychology) who do not plan to continue their study in a graduate program in psychology. Possibly, some of these undergraduate majors will go into vocations that use psychological knowledge and techniques, for example, personnel work, social work, education, rehabilitation of the handicapped, mental health, criminology, or advertising. Ordinarily, they will have learned some statistical, evaluative, or experimental skills that, if further perfected, can be used in a related area of endeavor.

REFERENCES

Note references to other publications by the American Psychological Association, mentioned on page 261. The journal, *American Psychologist,* published monthly by the association, will hold interest for some undergraduates in psychology. This journal contains articles and news about activities in the profession as a whole.

28   WHO IS THE CREATIVE PERSON?

P.E. Vernon

Is the individual who obtains a high score on an intelligence test and receives good school grades always the most creative person? If not, how can we locate the child or youth who has great promise of being a creative individual and who will in the future make original contributions to the arts, sciences, and technology?

What do we know at present about the personality, the motivations, hobbies, and upbringing of individuals who show creativity? Can we detect them by widely administering to groups tests of creative *abilities?* If not by ability tests alone, what aspects of personality should we seek to assess in order to locate creative persons?

Does the American educational system favor the development of creativity, or does it encourage conformist mentality? To what extent are creatively oriented children interesting to their teachers and peers?

We lack conclusive answers to all these questions, but we have data on many of them. Also, there are available reports of attempts to investigate the distinctions between those who show originality in their personal productions and those who do not. Here is an article by P.E. Vernon, who discusses briefly some of the independent investigations in different places and presents a summary of many of the findings. He concludes with his own evaluations of some of the psy-

Reprinted from P.E. Vernon, "Creativity and Intelligence," *Educational Research,* Vol. 6, No. 3 (Slough, Bucks, England: National Foundation for Educational Research), pp. 163–169, by permission of the publisher and the author.

chological means of investigating creativity as well as with a helpful list of references on these researches.

Introduction

CREATIVITY IS the latest fashion in American educational psychology. In broad outline, such writers as Getzels and Jackson (1962), Torrance (1962), and Calvin Taylor (1962), hold that not only our current intelligence and attainment tests but also the whole educational system tend to favor the conformist mentality, the pupil or student who is good at amassing facts, accepting what his teachers and lecturers tell him, and thinking and writing along conventional lines; that truly creative ability is relatively independent of whatever is measured by intelligence tests or by school grades, and that we are therefore discouraging the production of creative individuals who will make future original contributions to the arts, sciences, and technologies.

The Work of Calvin Taylor

Calvin Taylor (1962) is the energetic organizer of a number of research conferences on creativity at the University of Utah. He has carried out various studies himself, or brought together the work of others, all tending to show that creative adults are not necessarily superior to less creative workers in scholastic achievement or in whatever is measured by intelligence tests. For example, industrial or air force scientists were assessed by their superiors for the productivity and originality of their work, and there was generally little relation to their previous educational achievement. Admittedly, they were pretty homogeneous, high-level groups, otherwise they could not have got their present jobs. But Taylor estimates—it is not quite clear on what evidence—that over the whole range of ability, the correlation of creativity with intelligence or other tests would not exceed .2 to .4. In another study the IQ's were available for air force recruits who submitted original suggestions in suggestion boxes, and the distribution of these was said to be no different from the distribution for recruits in general. Obviously, it is doubtful how far this can be regarded as a manifestation of creative talent. One of the main difficulties, Taylor admits, is that—with such groups as scientists—there is little consistency between different criteria. For example, number of publications, assessed worth of publications, ratings by superiors or peers on various aspects of creativeness tend to give quite low correlations with one another. It is not surprising that few if any ability tests give consistently worthwhile correlations with these somewhat conflicting criteria. There seems to be more promise in biographical inventory data. Here again the picture is far from clear, but more creative persons tend to claim more creative hobbies in their youth, to be rather solitary, independent people, nonconformists, with strong drives and motivation for distant goals.

Terman's Studies

Terman's (1947) follow-up of high IQ children should also be mentioned. This group showed enormously greater productivity in the arts and sciences than would any group of average ability, though, at the same time, rather few reached the highest flights of creative talent, or could be called geniuses. This suggests that intelligence is of some relevance, and I would be inclined to give more weight to this evidence than to that of Taylor both because the IQ was tested in childhood, not concurrently, and because a good individual test—the Stanford-Binet—was used, rather than a conventional printed multiple-choice group test. Terman, in his survey with Cox (1926) of admitted geniuses from history, found quite a wide range of intelligence as estimated from recorded childhood achievements; but very few outstanding men in the arts and sciences fell below IQ 120. While rejecting the popular theory of the insanity of genius, Terman agreed that character and motivational factors were probably more important than purely intellectual ones—given a requisite (and high) level of general ability to begin with.

MacKinnon's Researches at the Californian Institute

Anne Roe's (1952) studies of small groups of eminent scientists also throw some light on their personality make-up, their tendency to be lone wolves with an overriding sense of the worth of their own ideas. But the outstanding researches in this area are those of MacKinnon and his colleagues at the Californian Institute for Personality and Ability Research. They have taken immense trouble to collect large and representative groups of men who are accepted by their professions as among the most creative architects, scientists, engineers, writers, and inventors, to bring them—along with control groups of more pedestrian people in the same line—to the Institute for a few days and subject them to an intensive battery of personality and ability measures. The most accessible summary of MacKinnon's (1962) results is published in the Proceedings of the 1961, Copenhagen, International Applied Psychology Congress—the volume on personality studies. He, too, tends to find all his subjects above average on ability tests and academic achievement—writers on verbal tests, scientists and engineers on nonverbal and spatial tests—though there was no strong differentiation between the more and the less creative; and he suggests that IQ is relatively unimportant beyond a certain minimum, probably around 120. About the only ability test that gave good differentiation was the Barron-Welsh Art test, where the creative individuals showed a greater liking for complex, asymmetrical as against conventional, abstract line drawings.

Some mean scores quoted in this table:

Artists	39
Highly creative architects	37
Writers	31½
Research scientists	30½
Architects generally	26
Low-creative scientists	19
Normal sample	18

Similarly on a word-association test, they tend to give unusual, but not highly unusual, associations.

Three tests in the personality area have consistently shown good differentiation—the Allport-Vernon-Lindzey Study of Values, where the creatives are characteristically high in artistic and theoretical, low in religious, economic and social values; secondly, the Strong Vocational Interest Blank, where they favor occupations like psychologist, architect, author as against banker, farmer, carpenter, salesman; and thirdly, the Myers-Briggs inventory, which tries to assess a person's Jungian type. Creatives are far more given to intuition- than to sensation-type thinking, and are more often introverted than extraverted. The Strong Blank also indicates a strong streak of femininity; creatives show a much greater willingness to accept and express their own feelings than is usual in the American male.

The Personality of Creative Individuals *

By interviews and questionnaires, a good deal was found about their personalities and upbringing which cannot be more than summarized briefly here. Though not emotionally unstable in the ordinary sense, they had often had *unhappy childhoods* † and school days and were *rebellious against school and college teachers*; † and, as previously suggested, they were characterized by a sense of *egoistic resoluteness, a belief in the value of their own work, and strong motivation to achieve by independent thought and action. Their parents tended to encourage this autonomy and self-responsibility.* * Of course, there is no single pattern, but this picture seems sufficiently general to justify the conclusion that *creative persons are distinguished more by interests, attitudes, and drives than by abilities,* * and that, though schooling may contribute little but basic knowledge and skills, the truly creative individual survives poor teaching and even thrives on rebelling against it.

* Editor's heading.
† Editor's italics.

Guilford and the Factorial Approach

We may now turn to the entirely different approach of the factor analyst and mental tester, whose aim is to measure creativeness and to show that it is a factor distinct from g * or other accepted factors. J.P. Guilford (1955, 1956), at the University of Southern California, has carried out over the past twenty years an elaborate series of studies of high-grade adults, and claims to have isolated some sixty or more factors in the domains of cognition, memory, reasoning, planning, judgment and evaluation. In particular, he distinguishes, in the realm of thinking, what he calls convergent and divergent abilities—convergent when there is one right answer, predetermined by the tester, as happens in all multiple-choice tests, and divergent when the testee is encouraged to give as many different responses of his own as possible. The ordinary tests of fluency or speed and richness of association are examples of the latter, and factorists have distinguished several types of fluency, the chief ones being word fluency—for example, writing as many words ending in "–tion" as possible, regardless of meaning; and ideational fluency—writing as many names of animals, birds, or flowers, or as many descriptions of a parcel as possible, or giving inkblot associations, and so on.

Guilford claims at least three other factors in this area, originality, spontaneous flexibility, and adaptive flexibility. Originality is defined by tests involving unusual and clever responses. For example, the familiar consequences test—What would happen if everybody in the world suddenly doubled in size? Or writing down impossibilities; or making up anagrams from the letters contained in a long word. These can be scored for rarity or rated for cleverness. Spontaneous flexibility is freedom from inertia in giving a diversity of ideas. For example: Write down as many unusual uses as possible for a brick—say, murdering somebody, or using it as a paper weight; this is scored for the number of changes of category or type of response. Adaptive flexibility is measured by tricky problem tests where the solution involves ingenuity or thinking along unconventional lines.

Now one would certainly agree with Guilford that high-level intellectual abilities are much richer and more varied than what is measured by standard vocabulary, analogies, classification, reasoning, and similar tests. But psychometrists other than Guilford's own followers have not generally confirmed the enormous number of distinct factors that he claims. Almost certainly there is much overlapping, and a good deal of what is common to them could probably more simply be attributed to g, or to such well-established group factors as verbal and spatial abilities, ideational fluency, and inductive reasoning. In a research at the London Institute of Education, Dr. Sultan (1962) tried out examples of most of Guilford's best creativity

---

* The letter g refers to a theoretical common *general* factor underlying all intellectual activities.—Ed.

tests on second- and third-year English grammar-school pupils, along with reference tests of familiar factors. In his battery of forty variables, the factors with most variance were first the spatial, which covered also all the flexibility-of-closure and adaptive-flexibility tests; secondly, ideational fluency, which covered a large proportion of originality- and spontaneous-flexibility tests. Only one small factor appeared that could be named originality, and this was much better measured by a questionnaire test of creative vs. noncreative leisure-time interests and by teachers' art grades and Rorschach inkblots original responses than by Guilford's tests. Admittedly, these negative results could be attributed to Sultan's using much younger students, with less mature intellects than Guilford's, though in fact their scores were mostly fairly close to those of Guilford's adults. Or it may be that the English grammar school is apt to dampen creative talents, and that different results might be obtained at a more "progressive" type of school. But the conclusion I would draw is that factor analysis by itself cannot provide the answer. It is always possible to break down broader group factors into additional narrower ones by developing more and more detailed tests; but this does not prove that the additional factors correspond to important mental faculties. Just because a set of tests looks as though it involves creativity and gives lowish correlations with g, v, or k * tests does not mean that it measures what we recognize as creativity in daily life, unless we can show that they actually differentiate between adults or children known on other grounds to be creative and noncreative, and that they are consistently more valid for this purpose than g or other tests.

Now there is some validatory evidence of this type, but even Taylor admits that Guilford's tests are of doubtful practical value, and MacKinnon obtained entirely negative results on applying them to his creative groups. However, an interesting study by Barron (1955) did indicate some overlap with personality and attitude characteristics similar to those found among true creatives. Men who scored highly on originality, flexibility, or ideational fluency tests were apt to be more self-sufficient, radical, introverted, and nonconformist than low scorers.

Getzels and Jackson's Research

This brings us to Getzels and Jackson's (1962) much publicized research, which was on very similar lines to Guilford's, but was carried out with younger high-school pupils. The main study consisted of a comparison of 26 pupils who were in the top 20 per cent of a battery of creativity tests, ingeniously adapted from Guilford's tests, but who were not outstanding in IQ, with another 28 who were in the top 20 per cent for IQ but not outstanding on creativity tests. The two groups were found to be about

---

* The v and k refer to broad group factors, *verbal* and *practical*, respectively, underlying intellectual activities.—Ed.

equally good in school attainment, and this appears to contradict the claim that creative individuals do not do as well in the conventional school system as conformists. But, as both groups happened to be very superior in IQ, the high-IQ group averaging 150, the high-creativity lower-IQ group averaging 127, the finding probably has no general significance. The high creatives did, however, do somewhat *better on tests of humor and wit,** and in breaking away from the stimulus in tests of free expression. They were *less conventional in their attitudes and aspirations.** On the whole, they *came from business classes rather than from professional-class families;* * professional parents would understandably be more apt to favor conformity to the school's intellectual ideals. Perhaps the most interesting finding was that the high-IQ group was rated superior on desirable personality traits by teachers, and that the sociometric status tended to be greater than that of the high-creativity group. This suggests a real possibility that, in Britain, some of the potentially most creative eighteen-year-olds may fail to get university places because they tend to be unpopular with their heads and are less good mixers. Conceivably this could also happen at 11+.

A General Discussion and Some Criticisms

Now this seems to be rather weak evidence on which to base such far-reaching conclusions as Getzels does. The populations were too small and far too atypical of the normal range of ability to tell us anything worthwhile about the relative value of new and old tests. Moreover, the old tests consisted of various group intelligence tests which had been applied at various times in previous years so the scales were weighted against them. The correlations between IQ and creativity tests were around 0.3; or to put it in a more tendentious way as Getzels and Taylor do—had the pupils been selected by IQ, 70 per cent of those with high creativity would have been missed. Obviously, the correlation would have been very much higher with (a) a more representative range of ability, (b) a more up-to-date and reliable battery of g and v tests. Burt (1962) points out, moreover, that the correlations among the separate creativity tests were much about the same level as their correlations with the intelligence tests; in other words, there was even less evidence for a factor of creativity distinct from g and v than there was in Guilford's investigations.[1] Had a well-balanced set of intelligence tests like the Stanford-Binet been used, which includes divergent

* Editor's italics.
[1] E.P. Torrance has carried out several further researches on children and students in which creativity tests likewise appeared to give very low correlations with standard intelligence tests. However, R.L. Thorndike, after examining Getzels', Guilford's, and Torrance's evidence, concludes that divergent thinking tests still involve a fair amount of g, and that, though a broad domain of creative thinking over and above g can be distinguished, it is relatively "nebulous and loosely formed."

as well as convergent thinking items, it might well have covered all that is measured by the creativity tests. Indeed, Burt suggests that the creativity tests might be quite useful as component items in a new general intelligence scale.

Nevertheless, he agrees, as I do, that with a more adequately designed research, in which better g and v as well as creativity tests were applied to a more typical population, it might be possible to distinguish one or more small divergent-thinking group factors, though it is noteworthy that Sultan obtained very little beyond ideational fluency at second-year-grammar-school level; hence, it is even more doubtful whether at 11+ tests of a more creative nature than the typical battery of verbal intelligence, English, and arithmetic would cover any fresh ground.

Another point which American workers have failed to consider is the long-term reliability or predictive value of divergent-thinking tests. The situation is likely to be quite similar to that with Thurstone's Primary Mental Abilities tests. We know that it is fairly easy to measure verbal, spatial, inductive, and other factors as partially distinguishable from g at age thirteen or earlier. But it has been shown that such factor scores are far from stable; for example, the correlation between induction at thirteen and induction at sixteen is scarcely any higher than that between verbal ability at thirteen and induction at sixteen. I would suspect, then, that one might get at least as good, if not better, predictions of performance on adult creativity tests from a reliable all-round measure of g and v at thirteen or at 11+ than one could from Getzels' tests.

However, the most serious flaw is, of course, that Getzels, Guilford, and others provide no real evidence for the assumption that their tests are valid tests of creativity in general. They give us a few findings about the current characteristics of the high scorers, but no follow-up data. True, it is interesting and suggestive that these high scorers appear to show some of the personality characteristics and attitudes which are consonant with the characteristics of the truly creative individuals studied by MacKinnon and Roe, but the jump from creativity tests in the secondary school, or at 11+, to true creativity at the university or later is far too great. Nor would one be justified in trying to diagnose and select the potentially most creative at eleven or eighteen on personality grounds, since there are lots of rebels, delinquents, beatniks, introverts, CND's, idealists, and so forth with very much the same personality pattern who never create anything worthwhile. Leisure-time interests such as scientific hobbies and research, poetry writing and artistic talents, I would suggest, do begin to show themselves fairly definitely by sixteen, or even by twelve or ten, though these are obviously both difficult to evaluate and pretty unstable; they may or may not be diagnostic of future creative capacities. Burt makes the good point that we may be *barking up the wrong tree in thinking of, or trying to measure, creativity in general; it may be something highly specific to a particular field of interest.** Nevertheless, Terman's gifted pupils and his historical geniuses did appear to be characterized by great versatility; most of them might well have made their mark in a number of different fields.

Conclusions

I would not, of course, for a moment disparage further research in this country into possible diagnostic tests of the Getzels-Guilford type, although I have given, what seem to me, good reasons for doubting their reliability and validity. Incidentally, they are also exceedingly troublesome to score; it would be almost impossible to use them on any large scale in the same way as convergent tests like Moray House and National Foundation tests. The crucial difficulty in such research is, of course, to get a criterion without long-term follow-up over ten or twenty years. Assessments of creative talent by schools and even by universities are known to be far too heavily biased in favor of conventional academic attainment, though I would have thought that by 22 or so, good college tutors could give fairly useful judgments. But I would suggest that there is an even stronger case for research into the home and leisure and educational backgrounds of creative individuals. I strongly suspect that some schools do much more to stimulate and foster, or else to inhibit, creative talent than others. The fact that grammar-school work is so closely geared to G.C.E. may well be a highly adverse factor; though we have a slight advantage over the American high school in that our examinations are creative-response type instead of mostly multiple-choice; so that pupils who are lucky in being marked by examiners who welcome a spark of originality may stand more chance. I would suspect also that the influence of an inspiring teacher at school or university may be tremendously important. These then are the kind of topics which could, I believe, be more fruitfully investigated than the will-o'-the-wisp of selecting or not selecting potentially creative persons by creativity tests.

IMPLICATIONS

Were there certain findings in this article that were surprising, perhaps even mildly shocking? To what extent do the statements support the popular view of the creative child? What are the implications for the education of the creative individual?

What has been your experience with the creative person? To what extent do you see creativity in yourself or in some persons whom you know well? What are the *problems* of the individual with creative proclivities?

* Editor's italics.

REFERENCES

Consult the Bibliography for references cited in the article. See also Golann (1963), MacKinnon (1965), McNemar (1964), and Thorndike (1962). For a good selective annotated bibliography on creativity, see Hall (1971).

29

THE BUSINESS EXECUTIVE

William E. Henry

What has been discovered about the psychodynamics of a successful business executive as compared with an unsuccessful one? What do the executives have in common? Is intellectual aptitude the major factor, or is it skill in social relationships? What are the psychodynamics in the role the successful executive plays? What are the costs of being a successful executive? Why do some business executives choose not to pay this price? Here is how Henry's research answers these questions. A brief description of the techniques used to obtain the data is given in footnote 1 of the selection.

THE BUSINESS EXECUTIVE is a central figure in the economic and social life of the United States. His direction of business enterprise and his participation in informal social groupings give him a place of significance in community life. In both its economic and social aspects, the role of the business executive is a highly visible one sociologically. It has clearly definable limits and characteristics known to the general public. These characteristics indicate the function of the business executive in the social structure, define the behavior expected of the individual executive, and serve as a guide to the selection of the novice.

Social pressure, plus the constant demands of the business organization of which he is a part, direct the behavior of the executive into the mold appropriate to the defined role. "Success" is the name applied to the wholehearted adoption of this role. It assumes that the individual behaves in the manner dictated by the society, and society rewards the individual with "success" if his behavior conforms to the role. It punishes him with "failure" should he deviate from it.

Reprinted from William E. Henry, "The Business Executive—the Psychodynamics of a Social Role," *The American Journal of Sociology,* Vol. 54, pp. 286–291, by permission of the author and The University of Chicago Press. © Copyright 1949 by the University of Chicago.

The participation in this role, however, is not a thing apart from the personality of the individual participant. It is not a game that the person is playing, it is the way of behaving and thinking that he knows best, that he finds rewarding, and in which he believes.

Thus the role as socially defined has its counterpart in the personality structure of the individuals who participate in it. To some extent the personality structure is reshaped to be in harmony with the social role. The extent to which such reshaping of the adult personality is possible, however, seems limited. An initial selection process occurs in order to reduce the amount of time involved in teaching the appropriate behavior. Those persons whose personality structure is most readily adaptable to this particular role tend to be selected to take this role. Whereas those whose personality is not already partially akin to this role are rejected.

This paper describes the personality communalities of a group of successful business executives. The research upon which it is based was undertaken to explore the general importance of personality structure in the selection of executive personnel. Many aptitude tests have been employed in the industry to decrease the risk involved in the hiring of untried personnel and to assist in their placement. These tests have been far less effective in the selection of high-level executive personnel than in the selection of clerical and other nonadministrating persons. Many business executives have found persons of unquestioned high intelligence often turn out to be ineffective when placed in positions of increased responsibility. The reasons for their failure lie in their social relationships. No really effective means has yet been found to clarify and predict this area of executive functioning. It is to this problem that our research [1] was directed.

From the research it became clear that the "successful" [2] business executives studied had many personality characteristics in common. It was equally clear that an absence of these characteristics was coincident with "failure" [2] within the organization. This personality constellation might be

---

[1] The research . . . involved the study of over 100 business executives in various types of business houses. The techniques employed were the Thematic Apperception Test, a short undirected interview, and a projective analysis of a number of traditional personality tests. The validity of our analyses, which were done "blind," rested upon the coincidence of identical conclusions from separately analyzed instruments, upon surveys of past job performance, and the anecdotal summary of present job behavior by the executive's superiors and associates. The writer wishes to express his thanks to these executives, to Dr. Burleigh Gardner of Social Research, Inc., under whose auspices the study was made, and to Carson McGuire, Robert F. Peck, Norman Martin and Harriett Bruce Moore of the University of Chicago for their assistance in the collection and analysis of data and clarification of conclusions.

[2] Success and failure as here used refer to the combined societal and business definition. All of our "successful" executives have a history of continuous promotion, are thought to be still "promotable" within the organization, are now in positions of major administrative responsibility, and are earning salaries within the upper ranges of current business salaries. Men in lower-level supervisory positions, men who are considered "failures" in executive positions, and men in clerical and laboring jobs show clear devia-

thought of as the minimal requirement for "success" within our present business system and as the psychodynamic motivation of persons in this occupation. Individual uniqueness in personality was clearly present but despite these unique aspects, each executive had in common this personality pattern.

Achievement Desires

All show high drive and achievement desire. They conceive of themselves as hard working and achieving people who must accomplish in order to be happy. The areas in which they do their work are clearly different, but each feels this drive for accomplishment. This should be distinguished from a type of pseudo-achievement drive in which the glory of the end product alone is stressed. The person with this latter type of drive, seldom found in the successful executives, looks to the future in terms of glory it provides him and the projects that he will have completed—as opposed to the achievement drive of the successful executive, which looks more to the sheer accomplishment of the work itself. The successful business leader gets much satisfaction from doing rather than merely from contemplating the completed product. To some extent this is the difference between the dreamer and the doer. It is not that the successful executives do not have an over-all goal in mind, nor that they do not derive satisfaction from the contemplation of future ease, nor that they do not gain pleasure from prestige. Far more real to them, however, is the continual stimulation that derives from the pleasure of immediate accomplishment.

Mobility Drive

All the successful executives have strong mobility drives. They feel the necessity to move continually upward and to accumulate the rewards of increased accomplishment. For some the sense of successful mobility comes through the achievement of competence on the job. These men struggle for increased responsibility and derive a strong feeling of satisfaction from the completion of a task. Finished work and newly gained competence provide them with their sense of continued mobility.

A second group rely more upon the social prestige of increased status in

---

tions from this pattern. This suggests, of course, that this pattern is specific for the successful business executive and that it serves to differentiate him from other groupings in industry. The majority of these executives come from distributive (rather than manufacturing) businesses of moderately loose organizational structure where cooperation and teamwork are valued and where relative independence of action is stressed within the framework of a clearly defined over-all company policy. In organizations in which far greater rigidity of structure is present or where outstanding independence of action is required, it is possible that there will be significant variations from the personality pattern presented here.

their home communities or within the organizational hierarchy. To them the real objective is increased status. Competence in work is of value and at times crucial. But the satisfactions of the second group come from the social reputation, not from the personal feeling that necessary work has been well done. Both types of mobility drive are highly motivating. The zeal and energy put into the job is equal in both instances. The distinction appears in the kinds of work which the men find interesting. For the first group, the primary factor is the nature of the work itself—is it challenging, is it necessary, is it interesting? For the second group, the crucial factor is its relation to their goals of status mobility—is it a step in the direction of increased prestige, is it appropriate to my present problem, what would other people think of me if I did it?

The Idea of Authority

The successful executive posits authority as a controlling but helpful relationship to superiors. He looks to his superiors as persons of more advanced training and experience whom he can consult on special problems and who issue to him certain guiding directives. He does not see the authority figures in his environment as destructive or prohibiting forces.

Those executives who view authority as a prohibiting and destructive force have difficulty relating themselves to superiors and resent their authority over them. They are either unable to work smoothly with their superiors, or indirectly and unconsciously do things to obstruct the work of their bosses or to assert their independence unnecessarily.

It is of interest that the dominant crystallization of attitudes about authority of these men is toward superior and toward subordinates, rather than toward Self. This implies that most crucial in their concept of authority is the view of being a part of a wider and more final authority system. In contrast, a few executives of the "Self-made," driving type characteristic of the past of business enterprise maintain a specific concept of authority with regard to Self. They are the men who most always forge their own frontiers, who are unable to operate within anyone else's framework, to whom cooperation and teamwork are foreign concepts. To these men, the ultimate authority is in themselves and their image does not include the surrounding area of shared or delegated power.

Organization and Its Implications

While executives who are successful vary considerably in their intelligence-test ratings, all of them have a high degree of ability to organize unstructured situations and to see the implications of their organization. This implies that they have the ability to take several seemingly isolated events or facts and to see relationships that exist between them. Further, they are interested in looking into the future and are concerned with predicting the outcome of their decisions and actions.

This ability to organize often results in a forced organization, however. Even though some situations arise with which they feel unfamiliar and are unable to cope, they still force an organization upon it. Thus they bring it into the sphere of familiarity. This tendency operates partially as a mold, as a pattern into which new or unfamiliar experiences are fit. This means, of course, that there is a strong tendency to rely upon techniques that they know will work and to resist situations which do not readily fit this mold.

Decisiveness

Decisiveness is a further trait of this group. This does not imply the popular idea of the executive making quick and final decisions in rapid-fire succession, although this seems to be true of some of the executives. More crucial, however, is an ability to come to a decision among several alternative courses of action—whether it be done on the spot or whether after detailed consideration. Very seldom does this ability break down. While less competent and well-organized individuals may become flustered and operate inefficiently in certain spots, most of these men force their way to a conclusion. Nothing is too difficult for them to tackle at least and try to solve. When poorly directed and not modified by proper judgment, this attitude may be more of a handicap than a help. That is to say, this trait remains in operation and results in decision-making action regardless of the reasonableness of the decision or its reality in terms of related facts. The breakdown of this trait (usually found only in cases where some more profound personality change has also occurred) is one of the most disastrous for the executive. As soon as this trait shows disturbance, the executive's superiors become apprehensive about him. This suggests an interesting relationship to the total executive constellation. Whenever a junior executive loses this quality of decisiveness, he seems to pass out of the socially defined role. It is almost as though the role demanded conviction and certainty as an integral aspect of it. The weakening of other aspects of the ideal executive constellation can be readily reintegrated into the total constellation. The questioning of the individual's certainty and decisiveness, however, results in a weakening of the entire constellation and tends to be punished by superiors.

Strong Self-Structure

One way of differentiating between people is in the relative strength or weakness of their notions of self-identity, their self-structure. Some persons lack definiteness and are easily influenced by outside pressures. Some, such as these executives, are firm and well defined in their sense of self-identity. They know what they are and what they want and have well-developed techniques for getting what they want. The things they want and the techniques for getting them are of course quite different for each individual, but this strength and firmness is a common and necessary characteristic. It is, of course, true that too great firmness of sense of self-identity leads to rigidity and to inflexibility. And while some of these executives could genuinely be accused of this, in general they maintain considerable flexibility and adaptability *within the framework of their desires and within the often rather narrow possibilities of their own business organization.*

Activity and Aggression

The executive is essentially an active, striving, aggressive person. His underlying personality motivations are active and aggressive—although he is not necessarily aggressive and hostile overtly in his dealings with other people. This activity and aggressiveness are always well channelized into work or struggles for status and prestige. This implies a constant need to keep moving to do something, to be active. This does not mean that they are always in bodily movement and moving physically from place to place (though this is often true), but rather that they are mentally and emotionally alert and active.

This constant motivator unfortunately cannot be shut off. It may be part of the reason why so many executives find themselves unable to take vacations leisurely or to stop worrying about already solved problems.

Apprehension and the Fear of Failure

If one is continually active and always trying to solve problems and arrive at decisions, any inability to do so successfully may well result in feelings of frustration. This seems to be true of the executives. In spite of their firmness of character and their drive to activity, they also harbor a rather pervasive feeling that they may not really succeed and be able to do the things they want. It is not implied that this sense of frustration comes only from their immediate business experience. It seems far more likely to be a feeling of long standing within the executives and to be only accentuated and reinforced by their present business experience.

This sense of the perpetually unattained is an integral part of this constellation and is part of its dilemma. It means that there is always some place to go, but no defined point at which to stop. It emphasizes the "self-propelled" nature of the dynamics of this role and highlights the inherent need to always keep moving and to see another goal always ahead. This also suggests that cessation of mobility and of struggling for new achievements will be accompanied by an inversion of this constant energy. The person whose mobility is blocked, either by his own limitations or by those of the social system, finds this energy diverted into other channels. Psychosomatic symptoms, the enlargement of interpersonal dissatisfactions, and the development of rationalized compulsive and/or paranoidlike defenses may reflect the redirection of this potent energy demand.

Strong Reality Orientation

The successful executives are strongly oriented to immediate realities and their implications. They are directly interested in the practical and the immediate and the direct. This is, of course, generally good for the immediate business situation, though an overdeveloped sense of reality may have secondary complications. If a man's sense of reality is too highly developed, he ceases to be a man of vision. For a man of vision must get above reality to plan and even dream about future possibilities. In addition, a too strong reality sense that does not find the realities in tune with the individual's ambitions may well leave a further sense of frustration and unpleasantness of reality. This happens to many executives who find progress and promotion too slow for their drives. The result is often a restlessness rather than activity, a fidgetiness rather than a well-channelized aggression, and a lack of ease that may well disrupt many of their usual interpersonal relations.

The Nature of Their Interpersonal Relations

In general, the mobile and successful executive looks to his superiors with a feeling of personal attachment and tends to identify with them. His superior represents for him a symbol of his own achievement and activity desires and he tends to identify himself with these traits in those who have achieved more. He is very responsive to his superiors—the nature of this responsiveness of course depending on his other feelings, his idea of authority, and the extent to which his sense of frustration is present.

On the other hand, he looks to his subordinates in a detached and impersonal way, seeing them as "doers of work" rather than as people. He treats them impersonally, with no real feeling of being akin to them or having deep interest in them as persons. It is almost as though he viewed his subordinates as representatives of things he has left behind, both factually and emotionally. Still uncertain of his next forward step, he cannot afford to become personally identified or emotionally involved with the past he has left behind. The only direction of his emotional energy that is real to him is upward and toward the symbols of that upward interest, his superiors.

This does not mean that he is cold and treats all subordinates casually.

In fact, he tends to be generally sympathetic with many of them. This element of sympathy with subordinates is most apparent when the subordinate shows personality traits that are most like those of the superior. Thus the superior is able to take pride in certain successful young persons without at the same time feeling an equal interest in all subordinates.

The Attitude Toward His Own Parents

In a sense the successful executive is a "man who has left home." He feels and acts as though he were on his own, as though his emotional ties and obligations to his parents were severed. It seems to be most crucial that he has not retained resentment of his parents, but has rather simply broken their emotional hold on him and been left psychologically free to make his own decisions. We have found those who have not broken this tie to be either too dependent upon their superiors in the work situation, or to be resentful of their supervision (depending, of course, upon whether they have retained their dependency parental ties or rather they are still actively fighting against them).

In general, we find the relationship to the mother to have been the most clearly broken tie. The tie to the father remains positive in the sense that he views the father as a helpful but not restraining figure. Those men who still feel a strong emotional tie to the mother have systematically had difficulty in the business situation. The residual emotional tie seems contradictory to the necessary attitude of activity, progress, and channelized aggression. The tie to the father, however, must remain positive—as the emotional counterpart of the admired and more successful male figure. Without this image, struggle for success seems difficult.

The Nature of Dependency Feelings and Concentration upon Self

A special problem in differentiating the type of generally successful executive is the nature of his dependency feelings. It was pointed out above that the dependency upon the mother-image must be eliminated. For those executives who work within the framework of a large organization where cooperation and group-and-company loyalty are necessities, there must remain feelings of dependency upon the father-image and a need to operate within an established framework. This does not mean that the activity-aggression need cannot operate or that the individual is not decisive and self-directional. It means only that he is so within the framework of an already established set of over-all goals. For most executives, this over-all framework provides a needed guidance and allows them to concentrate upon their achievement and work demands with only minimal concern for policy making of the entire organization. For those executives who prefer complete independence and who are unable to work within a framework established by somebody else, the element of narcissism is much higher and their feelings of loyalty are only to themselves rather than to a father-image or its impersonal counterpart in company policy. These feelings differentiate the executives who can cooperate with others and who can promote the over-all policy of a company from those who must be the whole show themselves. Clearly, there are situations in which the person of high concentration upon self and low dependency-loyalty feelings is of great value. But he should be distinguished in advance and placed only in such situations where these traits are of value.

The successful executive represents a crystallization of many of the attitudes and values generally accepted by middle-class American society. The value of accumulation and achievement, of self-directedness and independent thought and their rewards in prestige and status and property are found in this group. But they also pay the price of holding these values and by profiting from them. Uncertainty, constant activity, the continual fear of losing ground, the inability to be introspectively leisurely, the ever present fear of failure, and the artificial limitations put upon their emotionalized interpersonal relations—these are some of the costs of this role.

IMPLICATIONS

Have you known both types of executives mentioned in this article—those who have the psychodynamics that lead directly to success and those whose characteristics do not lead to continual promotion and increased responsibility but to life satisfaction from other sources? How might an individual who is effective in working for a legislative or welfare-centered program, such as the Peace Corps, differ in personality pattern from the business executive? For example, would he have as strong a reality orientation, or have the same tie with his father, or represent as well middle-class America? Using the article as reference, you may choose several from among your friends and define their personality structure according to your own judgment. (Do not use this procedure to derogate any of your associates.) To what extent do you see the twelve aspects of a common personality pattern mentioned in this selection as being compatible with each other? Remember, too, that success as an executive is only *one* kind of success in our complex society.

REFERENCES

Fleishman (1967) has published a group of articles on leadership and supervision in industry that includes a fairly large number of references.

Bass (1965) has a chapter on supervisory behavior and another on psychological aspects of executive decision making. Likert (1961) discusses the executive use of employees in *decision making.*

Maier (1965) summarizes the studies on supervisory and executive leadership. See Selection 24 for one of the techniques he uses for training.

30

BUDDY RATINGS: POPULARITY CONTEST OR LEADERSHIP CRITERIA?

Robert J. Wherry and Douglas H. Fryer

Buddy rating, used in military service, is a term for ratings by peers or co-workers who, by associating with a ratee during much of the day, have an opportunity to observe him in realistic situations.

The following study describes the use of buddy ratings. The score is based on the number of fellow students who place the ratee among the five who possess the most desirable personality traits and the number who place him among the five who possess the least desirable traits. How do these buddy ratings, when analyzed, compare with supervisory ratings? Do they furnish a measure of effective performance in a complex social situation, other than the assessment of aptitude? How is a given procedure such as this tested for *reliability* or consistency and for *validity* or efficiency?

In Brief [1]

THE NEED for criteria against which to test predictors of leadership potential led some of the armed forces personnel research organizations to turn to "buddies," "peers" or co-workers for ratings in preference to evaluation by superiors. Industrial personnel research is also turning to this technique. There has been some criticism that "buddy ratings" are not criteria of leadership, but rather mere popularity contests. This criticism deserves investigation. This study conducted on two officer candidate classes investigates the interrelationship of a dozen different

---

[1] This study is based upon data collected in connection with Project No. 4071, Personnel Research Section, Adjutant General's Office, Department of the Army. The opinions expressed are those of the authors and do not necessarily express the official views of the Department of the Army.

Reprinted from Robert J. Wherry and Douglas H. Fryer, "Buddy Ratings: Popularity Contest or Leadership Criteria?" *Personnel Psychology,* Vol. 2 (Cleveland: Personnel Psychology, 1949), pp. 147–159, by permission of the publisher.

criteria secured from several sources. These included ratings at various times throughout the six-month course by fellow students and by superiors as well as various course grades. Intensive statistical analysis of the results seem to justify the continued use of buddy ratings as leadership criteria. The buddy nominations (variable 1) measured as early as the first month of training the same factors which they measured three months later. Moreover, what they measured in the first month is the same as that rated by superiors, rating after four months' observation. The ratings by superiors measured something quite different in the first and fourth months. It was not until the fourth month that superiors' ratings reflected the leadership factor which fellow students identified in their first-month ratings.

The Search for Criteria

One problem is common to all groups engaged in personnel research. It is that of developing criteria of performance, efficiency, or behavior against which to test personnel devices, procedures, and methods. This problem is equally present in civilian and military research. In many situations, the only feasible measure consists of a rating of performance. But who can best do the rating—superiors, of whom there are at most one or two who know each worker; or co-worker, from whom a number of independent judgments can be secured?

When the war created an urgent need for research in almost every aspect of personnel, the workers in the field were faced with the need for developing criteria for numerous jobs. In many instances, selection programs were developed for training courses, and academic success could be used as a criterion for predictors in the aptitude areas. But most of the jobs for which selection was desired encompassed a great deal more than these aptitudes. Leadership, personality, and interest factors were at least as important as academic success. To secure criteria against which to test predictors in these areas, research workers were forced to fall back on ratings.

Well aware of the weaknesses of conventional rating methods, the personnel technicians sought to minimize them. To overcome the unreliability of individual ratings, they looked for situations in which a number of independent raters could be used. Even though a single rating may be unreliable, the average of a number of such ratings may provide a stable measure relatively free of bias and the idiosyncrasies of every single rater.

They recognized the fact that in any group it was easier to identify and rank the individuals who were extremely good and those who were extremely poor in the job than to rank the middle group. With only one or two raters for each man, this method identifies only extreme groups. However, with a sizable number of raters, it was possible to have each rater nominate the best four or five and the poorest four or five members of the group. Subtracting the number of "poor" from the number of "good" mentions and dividing the remainder by the number of possible mentions yielded a continuum usable for criterion purposes.

There was seldom if ever a situation in which the number of supervisors familiar with the efficiency of the worker was adequate to permit multiple nominations. For most jobs, on the other hand, there was a substantial number of co-workers in a position to observe the man's work if only they could, and would, evaluate it properly. The next natural step was to have the nominating of best and poorest workers done by the workers themselves. Many jobs lent themselves very well to this procedure. Groups in which the members worked close together, so that each worker knew the others, seemed so suited.

There were other aspects of peer or co-worker ratings that recommended this procedure to the personnel research worker. There are often aspects of a position which the co-worker is in a better position to evaluate than is the supervisor: *e.g.*, aspects of personality often carefully concealed from higher-ups.

Under the stimulus of this set of circumstances, evaluation by peers— "buddy ratings," if you will—increased in frequency in armed forces personnel research.

Like all criteria, they suffer from the need to accept them at face value. Standards against which to test them—criteria of criteria—do not usually exist. If there is available a yardstick against which to test a criterion, it would itself become the primary measure and the need for the criterion would at once vanish.

Thus, when the critics of buddy ratings objected and said they were no more than popularity contests, there was little evidence on which to refute the criticism. True, the critics offered no data in support of their contentions. Yet the burden of the proof rests with the advocates rather than with the critics of the procedure.

A Rare Opportunity

Usually the personnel research worker considers himself fortunate to be in a position to secure a single adequate criterion. In developing devices for the selection of enlisted men to attend Army Officer Candidate Schools, the staff of the Personnel Research Section found that it was in a position to collect *performance measures* * from a variety of sources. Further, it was possible to identify the situations in which several different kinds of raters were able to observe trainees. Finally, it was possible to observe a newly formed group that worked at a common task and whose members were in close association with each other.

* Editor's italics.

The Groups We Studied

The studies were conducted at the Signal Corps Officer Candidate School at Fort Monmouth, N.J. The data were gathered in the summer of 1945. Two classes were studied. There were 82 officer candidates in the first class and 52 in the second.

The Variables

In addition to scores on a high-level intelligence test (Officer Candidate Test) and academic grades, *nine sets of ratings* * were collected by different methods, from different raters, and at different times. The ratings were collected from the first class (82 students) at the end of one, two, and four months in the school. In the case of the second class, ratings were collected only at the end of the first month of training. Table 1 describes the several criterion and predictor variables. . . .

Table 1 *
The Criterion Variables Studied

No.	*Nature of Criterion*
1.	*Anonymous Nominations by Students by Section:* Each student nominated 5 men in his section "who possess the personality traits least desirable in an Army officer." Score in this and other nominating criteria was: "most" mentions minus "least" mentions divided by possible mentions.
3.	*Average Leadership Ratings by Students by Section:* Every student rated each of the other students in his section for 10 leadership qualities on a school form. Each rating form was first averaged for the 10 ratings, and then all forms for a given student were in turn averaged.
5.	*Leadership Ranking by Senior Tactical Officer by Class:* The Senior Tactical Officer ranked the students in each class according to leadership. Position in the ranking was the student's score.
10.	*Average Academic Grades by Academic Instructors:* Based upon an average of daily and monthly objective examinations.

* Table 1 has been modified to describe samples of the criteria of conditions of each rating.—Ed.

In addition to the variables described in Table 1,† data were also available on the following:

* Editor's italics.
† Condensed.

Retention Beyond Two Months. Officer candidates were discharged at any time during the training period for academic inaptitude, disciplinary reasons, or failure to show promise of having the personality characteristics thought necessary in an officer. For purposes of study, each class was divided into two parts, those who were released prior to the end of the second month of work and those who were retained beyond that time.

Graduation. Failure (for any reason) to graduate from OCS and receive a commission represented a waste of time, money, and manpower. To determine the relationship between the various other variables and this personnel action, the classes were divided on the basis of whether or not each individual successfully completed the course.

Officer Candidate Test. This is a high-level pencil-and-paper test of general intelligence which had been administered to all applicants for OCS prior to their admission to the school.

Recommendation Blank. This is a standard form sent to civilian acquaintances of the applicant. The names are supplied by the candidate. It is primarily a checklist and rating form which is objectively scored.

OCS Interview. Prior to being selected to attend OCS, each candidate is interviewed by a board of officers. A standardized interview is employed and the members of the board rate the candidate on several traits observable in the interview and thought relevant to officer success. The forms are objectively scored.

Previous Performance. Ratings by noncommissioned officers under whom they had previously served were available for the officer candidates studied.

The Analysis

Four separate factorial analyses were computed. Three of the analyses were for the three sets of ratings collected in the first, second, and fourth month for class one. The fourth analysis was done for the variables collected on the second class at the end of the first month of training. Four factors were identified by the analyses. The first three of these were common to all four analyses. The fourth was present only for the ratings collected from the first class in its fourth month.

Factor I. *Academic Standing.* Highest loadings for this factor are for academic grades (10),* leadership ratings by academic instructors (9), and for the Officer Candidate Test of Intelligence (11). Moderate to small, but always significant, loadings appear also on the Anonymous Nominations by Students (1) and for Average Leadership Ratings by Students (3), indicating that sectional standing among "buddies" was determined in part by the observed performance in the classroom. Student nominations by class (2) and all ratings by tactical officers (4, 5, 6, 7, 8) who were unacquainted with classroom performance showed insignificant loadings (with a slightly negative trend) on this factor. The factor is therefore identified as *Academic Standing.*

Factor II. *Leadership.* High loadings on this factor occur for all student

* These are the numbers of the criteria in the original Table I condensed.—Ed.

nominations and ratings by class or section (1, 2, 3) for all periods for both classes. While loadings are only moderate for early periods for ratings or ranking by tactical officers (4, 5), the loadings become equally high for ratings, rankings, and nominations by the tactical officers (4, 5, 6, 7, 8) after 4 months' acquaintanceship. Ratings by academic instructors (9) were low but significant, while those for grades (10) and the OCT (11) were not significant. The fact that both students and officers agree on this factor serves to identify it as *the leadership* factor which both were attempting to rate.

Factor III. *Tactical Standing.* This factor has loadings on all, and only on ratings, ranking, and nominations by tactical officers (4, 5, 6, 7, and 8). Loadings are about equally high for all periods. The lowest significant loading occurs on the officer efficiency report (8), where the nature of the forced-choice items in part controls the ratings. This factor is therefore identified as *standing in tactical performance.*

Factor IV. *Group Difference Correction.* This factor has moderate loadings on only the anonymous nominations *by class* of students (2) and tactical officers (7). The only other loading is a barely significant one for leadership ratings by junior tactical officers by class (4). This factor appears to be a *corrective element* based upon unequal range of leadership ability within the various sections.

Reliability

To be at all useful, a criterion must naturally be reliable, *i.e.,* those who are rated high on the measure at one time should continue to be so rated after an elapse of time. This study permitted the comparison of a number of rating techniques on the first class after the passage of one month and again three months after the original ratings had been made. Table 2 shows these reliabilities. While student nominations and student leadership ratings were about equal in stability after the passage of one month, both were more reliable than ratings assigned by either the junior or senior tactical officers.

Table 2
Repeat Reliability of Selected Criteria

Criterion	After 1 Month	After 4 Months
1. (Buddy Nominations)	.75	.58
3. (Buddy Ratings)	.76	.17
4. (Superiors' Ratings)	.42	.19
5. (Superiors' Ratings)	.58	.28

All of the reliability coefficients over a three-month period are smaller than over a one-month interval. The reliability of student nominations, however, remains at a level that may be considered useful. The reliability of the other three variables is such as to make doubtful their usefulness as criteria. In the case of the student's rating (as distinguished from nomination) and both junior and senior tactical officer ratings, it is clear that what they measure in the fourth month is something quite different than what they measure in the first month.

Predictability

To the extent that criteria are collected for the purpose of using them as a basis for the testing and weighting of selection instruments, it is essential that they be predictable. The entire philosophy of personnel selection rests on the assumption that, to a degree at least, it is possible to predict in advance of selection which applicants for a job will be more and which less successful. If the measure of success criterion cannot be predicted even by itself, it is neither feasible nor worthwhile to predict it by any battery of personnel instruments.

Table 3 compares the predictability of the nominating technique with that of academic grades for a number of possible selection instruments. Comparisons are presented for both class one and class two. The Officer Candidate Test is the only selection instrument for which academic grade is more predictable than buddy nominations. This is gratifying, since the test was included to predict academic success. The other predictors were included to afford measures of the nonacademic aspects of leadership.

Table 3

Predictability of Criterion 1 (Buddy Ratings) and Criterion 10 (Academic Grades) by Various Kinds of Predictors After One Month (Higher Coefficient in Each Comparison Is Underlined)

	Buddy Ratings (Var. 1)		Academic Grades (Var. 10)	
	(1) Class (2)		(1) Class (2)	
Aptitude:				
Officer Candidate Test	.23	.29	.56	.80
Personality:				
Biographical Information Blank'	.38	.43	.17	.34
Recommendation Blank	.41	.36	.12	.14
Interview	.18	.13	.05	−.04
Previous Performance:				
Ratings by Noncommissioned Officers	.19	.33	−.15	.15

Relation to Personnel Actions

Personnel who fail the training course for a position (in this case those who do not graduate from Officer Candidate School) represent a waste of time and money. There is obviously no point in hiring employees who will never be put on the job for which they were employed or of sending men who will never become officers to Officer Candidate School. From this point of view, a desirable criterion should be fairly well related to retention in the school and to its successful completion. Table 4 compares buddy nominations and academic grades with respect to their relationship to these personnel actions. Both criteria are equal in their relationship to separation and nongraduation. Thus it would appear that each is measuring an important aspect of success. Since the two criteria have low correlation, it is also clear that each is measuring a different aspect. In this situation, use of only one (and academic success is frequently used alone in such situations) would be doing only half the job. Obviously, ultimate success at Officer Candidate School depends as much on what buddy nominations measure as it does on what academic grades measure.

Table 4

Correspondence of Criterion 1 (AN-S-S) and Criterion 10 (AAG-AI) to Retention (for at Least 2 Months) and to Graduation

	Buddy Ratings (AN-S-S)	Academic Grades (AAG-AI)
Retention		
(at least 2 months)	.70	.71
Graduation	.49	.50

What Does It All Add Up To?

The analysis of criteria has necessarily been predicated on what amounts to an examination of the internal relationships among the various ratings and other measures of success. The study has looked into the comparative predictability of buddy ratings and such other criteria as academic grades, attrition, and graduation. Moreover, the various available criterion measures have been shown to differ widely in their reliability.

From the analyses presented above, we may make the following tentative conclusions about the use of buddy nominations as criteria:

1. *From the factor analyses:*
   (a) Buddy ratings appear to be the purest measure of "leadership." Tactical officers are also able to rate this trait, but their ratings are quite heavily weighted by tactical standing. Academic instructor's ratings are practically useless for the evaluation of this trait.
   (b) Co-workers are able, at the end of one month, to evaluate leader-

ship to a degree equaled by instructors (tactical, not academic) only after four months of observation.

(c) Nominations (variable 1) which are more reliable than graphic ratings (variable 3) are equally good measures of leadership. They have the added advantage of being easier to secure.

(d) Nominations by class appear to be better measures of the leadership factor than any other variable. This would appear to indicate the advisability of predicting buddy ratings on the widest base upon which the acquaintanceship of the members of the group permits.

2. *From the reliability comparisons.* While both nominations and graphic ratings by co-workers show quite satisfactory reliability after one month, the reliability of nominations after four months is outstandingly higher than that of any of the other variables upon which the test was made. This is probably further evidence of the fact that the nominating technique has the property of early identification of the members of the group who constitute the two extremes of the leadership distribution.

3. *Predictability.* Except for prediction by the aptitude test, nominations were better predicted by all of the proposed selection devices than was the more commonly used academic grade criterion.

4. *Agreement with personnel action.* If ability to remain in the school at least two months is considered desirable, it may seem that nominations by buddies are as highly correlated as are academic grades, with this overall measure of success. Similarly, buddy ratings contribute as much as academic grades to the overall criterion of graduation.

IMPLICATIONS

We have here the application of psychological methodology to a complex workaday situation—a military training program. Observe how the psychologists have, without intrusion, found various criteria of merit in the performance of the trainees. In addition to nominations and ratings, such records as retention in training, graduation, test scores, scored recommendation blanks, and previous performance ratings were utilized and described. The authors arrived at these central variables: (1) academic standing, (2) leadership, and (3) tactical standing. Which ratings contributed most to each of these factors? To what extent can this sort of complex analysis apply to a situation in a large business enterprise? Do you have a situation in mind in which buddy ratings might contribute significantly to the evaluation of individuals?

REFERENCES

The nomination technique, utilizing peer ratings, has proved to be a promising technique for industry for a number of reasons: the number of ratees is large; the individual peer has had opportunity to observe the typical behavior of his colleagues; the opinions of group members influence an individual's actions. See Chapter IV in Anastasi (1964) for a discussion of the use of nomination and related techniques in *personal appraisal*. Weitz (1958) describes the use of peer ratings in predicting supervisory success.

31   SENSITIVITY TRAINING

Max Birnbaum

Most students have heard of or may have participated in groups called by various names—sensitivity groups, T-groups, encounter groups, and marathon labs. These groups differ in their purpose, their membership, and their leaders. This article, although pivoting on the implications for education, gives some information about the purposes and activities in various sensitivity groups. It also raises some questions about the effects of the groups on the participants.

DURING THE 1960s, public education discovered the emotions. Cognitive learning and skill training, the traditional components of education, no longer satisfied the needs of a generation that had experienced the civil rights revolt, the widening generation gap, and the increasing confusion of teachers, administrators, and school board members about ends and means in education. The result was a growing interest in various approaches to affective learning that assigns to the emotional factor in education a role as important as—or, perhaps, more important than—the traditional substantive content and skills. Among these approaches the most enthusiastically embraced has been the so-called sensitivity training.

The term is used loosely to include a wide range of laboratory training approaches in human relations, group dynamics, organizational development (or, as I prefer, applied human relations training), as well as a number of *verbal and non-verbal experiences that seek to increase awareness*

Reprinted from Max Birnbaum, "Sense and Nonsense About Sensitivity Training," *Saturday Review*. Copyright 1969 Saturday Review, Inc. Reprinted by permission of the publisher and the author.

*and release human potential.** It is an unfortunate term because of its vagueness, but it appears that its very impreciseness and beguiling simplicity are the qualities that have helped it gain wide currency.

By whatever name it is known, however, human relations training is capable, if properly employed, of producing substantial educational change. It holds tremendous potential for improving education by dealing with its affective components, reducing the unnecessary friction between generations, and creating a revolution in instruction by helping teachers to learn how to use the classroom group for learning purposes.

The pity is that this promising innovation may be killed before its unique properties have a fair chance to demonstrate their worth. The opposition to its serious exploration is strong and is apt to grow. But it is not those who oppose sensitivity training because it smacks of therapy, which to a very small degree it does, nor even the members of the renascent John Birch Society, who would equate it with brainwashing, who pose the major challenge. Rather, the most serious threat to sensitivity training comes first from its enthusiastic but frequently unsophisticated school supporters, and second from a host of newly hatched trainers, long on enthusiasm or entrepreneurial expertise, but short on professional experience, skill, and wisdom.

What is needed today is a clearer sense of *how sensitivity training developed, the varied forms it may take, and the results that can be anticipated** in any given situation. Unfortunately, not all of the "experts" agree on the many issues raised by this kind of training, and there will be those who disagree strongly with many of the judgments presented here. But clearer definition of the issues, wider discussion, and more careful analysis of results should help schoolmen toward more effective use of training for fundamental improvement in the schools.

Contrary to the impression given by some recent popular writing on the subject, it was neither the author of *Joy* nor the devoted creators of Esalen who were responsible for the development of human relations training. Rather, it was Leland Bradford, then director of the Adult Education Division of the National Education Association, together with his old friends and collaborators Ronald Lippitt, now of the University of Michigan, and Kenneth Benne, now of the Boston University Human Relations Center, who were primarily responsible. Drawing on the work of the great social psychologist Kurt Lewin, they established the first training center more than two decades ago at Bethel, Maine, and founded the National Training Laboratories (NTL). And it was Bradford's tough and dogged fight against strong opposition within education that finally won sanction and support for human relations training, first from industry, then from the social and behavioral scientists, and finally from the education hierarchy

* Editor's italics.

itself. Now, as he is about to retire as director of NTL, Lee Bradford has the satisfaction of seeing human relations training widely embraced by the education world.

As the field developed, the *T-group* (*Training group*) * became the heart of any laboratory or workshop that is devoted to the study of group dynamics or human relations. The traditional T-group consists of a small group of people—ideally ten to sixteen—who meet in a residential setting (the laboratory) for approximately two weeks. Although only one part of this educational experience (theory, interpretation, and skill development are also included), the T-group is, because of its intense emotional impact, by far the most significant aspect of any human relations lab. The objectives of the T-group are to *help individual participants become aware of why both they and others behave as they do in groups* *—or, in the jargon of the professional, become aware of the underlying behavior dynamics of the group. This is accomplished, with the help of a trainer, by creating an atmosphere in which the motivations for typical human behavior, of which individuals are often unaware, are brought to the surface in an exaggerated form. Once they are made clear and explicit, they can be discussed and analyzed. Thus, the individual participant can observe both his own behavior and that of others in the group, discover sources of different kinds of behavior, and identify the effect they have upon the functioning of the group. The effort to stimulate exaggerated behavior in order to get at the motivation behind it more explicitly is an uncomfortable experience for many people, but the feeling is usually transitory. The emotional component of the experience makes it appear to verge on therapy, but there is a significant difference between therapy that is focused on the problems of emotionally disturbed people and training that aims at the improvement of human relations skills of normal people.

In the early years of the movement, the T-group emphasis was primarily on the sociology of groups rather than on their psychology—that is, on the roles and functions of leadership and membership, rather than on the individual personality and personal development. (Bradford, Benne, and Lippitt came from adult education, philosophy, and social psychology.) The trend toward a psychological emphasis appeared in the early 1950s when the movement began to attract a larger number of people trained in clinical psychology or psychiatry. And it was at that point the T-group emerged as a new social invention that bears some rough resemblance to a combination of seminar and therapy group, but it actually is neither.

Recognition of the power of the T-group, as well as its limitations, has led to wide experimentation with other applications. Laboratory sessions of varying length and widely differing objectives have been developed,

* Editor's italics.

ranging from a single day or weekend to two or three weeks, and having as their purpose varying kinds of individual and organizational change. Much of the confusion in the field stems from the lack of clearly defined purposes, and guidelines that indicate the kind of training session most effective in achieving a particular objective. Most specifically, confusion results from the failure to differentiate between those training experiences that are designed to improve an individual's capacity to work effectively as a manager or member of a group for educational or re-educational purposes, and those that are designed to stimulate the individual's personal growth and so are clearly in a domain that might be labeled para-therapy, in the sense that it is parallel to therapy, rather than therapy itself. Therefore, it is necessary to look at the varying kinds of training that are becoming popular today to see what purposes each is best designed to serve.

Organizational development is a general term that includes a variety of approaches that combine affective and intellectual components in the use of small groups as a medium for consultation, problem solving, and re-education of individuals in both public and private organizations. It developed primarily out of the earlier, sociologically oriented focus of the T-group that emphasized organizational change rather than personal development. My experience with school systems and other organizations with a process that I term applied human relations training probably falls within this definition. . . .

Encounter groups, confrontation sessions, and marathon labs are usually short term—most often twenty-four-hour or weekend—experiences where the emphasis is on the direct exposure of beliefs and feelings that usually are not put on public display by individuals. The term "encounter group" derives from the phrase "basic encounter group" that Carl Rogers, the noted exponent of non-directive counseling, coined to differentiate a new kind of experience from the traditional T-group. Trainers in these sessions usually encourage participants to *explore in some depth their own feelings and motivations,** as well as those of other group members. The objective is to stimulate an exchange that is inhibited by a minimum of reserve and defensiveness in order to *achieve a maximum of openness and honesty.** Marathons differ from encounter groups primarily in the unremitting intensity of the experience that seeks to achieve a significant break-through in normal defenses and so attain what many practitioners believe is a new level of open behavior. Confrontation sessions are usually contrived racial encounters in which militant blacks literally "confront" members of the white community (teachers, police, industrial management, etc.) with their angry reaction to white racism, discrimination, and prejudice. The theoretical basis for this type of experience is that the social conditions requiring this form of learning demand a maximum dose of aggression and

* Editor's italics.

hostility in order to convince the targets—the whites—of the seriousness of the personal situation. (Because most confrontation sessions of this kind are not part of a plan for organizational change, they usually end as para-therapeutic experiences rather than training.)

Non-verbal exercises have invaded the training field with a vengeance in recent years. The techniques employed are numerous and range from simple exercises with a minimum of body contact to physically intimate and emotionally revealing designs of the kind most often associated with Esalen and its derivatives. (It should be noted that the explorations of Esalen, on the West Coast, are making major contributions to the field of therapy, but it is less clear how the techniques developed there can contribute to education.) Non-verbal techniques derive their theoretical justification from theories of personality that stress the possibility of achieving greater honesty and authenticity through bodily expression that can become uninhibited more quickly than can verbal communication. Thus, participants can reach deeper levels of consciousness more quickly.

Each of these varied approaches to sensitivity training is designed to serve specific purposes. Undoubtedly each can be immensely beneficial to certain individuals—and provide little help, or have negative results, for others. What must be made clear is the purpose to be achieved, and the kind of training best designed to serve that purpose.

Clearly, organizational development—or applied human relations training—that is focused on organizational change, problems of human relations, and morale within an organization belong in the training area. These experiences may bring to participants great personal insights and lead to new ways of relating to family and friends, but these are *accidental* consequences of the experience that is directed toward increasing individual effectiveness as a member of the organization. Marathons, personal growth labs, encounter groups, and non-verbal exercises belong in the para-therapeutic area. These are frankly concerned primarily with individual growth and development, the achievement of authenticity, or "therapy for normals." In some cases, labs of this kind assume that there will be an organizational payoff from the experience, but others do not. The original T-group, from which all the forms of sensitivity training developed, can serve either purpose. It can provide the basis for a lab devoted primarily to personal growth, or one that rigorously relates all personal learning to an organizational context. But experience teaches that, unless a lab is consciously dedicated to the latter, the high degree of personal involvement inevitably pulls the focus toward individual growth.

When lab organizers are unable or unwilling to differentiate between various kinds of training, the results can be disastrous. There are many tales, some maliciously embellished, but many all too true, of school systems and communities where bad situations have been made worse by the unintelligent application of inappropriate forms of sensitivity training. Some examples of such misuse of training may help to clarify the point.

The T-group that aims at personal growth, for instance, is an experience that has tremendous validity for school people as long as it takes place in a setting away from home where the individual can be relatively anonymous —a summer laboratory or workshop, for example. But trouble comes when it is applied uncritically within a school system where the participants are co-workers. The result in this case is either impossible resistance, or, even worse, the revelation of intimate personal information that is so highly charged that it makes continuing work relationships very difficult, if not impossible.

Similarly, encounter groups or confrontation sessions between blacks and whites in the same school or community may lead to problems. In the past, such sessions have sometimes had useful shock value in revealing quickly the crucial problems that are polarizing the races today. Under skillful management, with careful control over degrees of resistance and levels of anxiety, and a systematic effort to relate the encounter experience to specific educational issues so that it can lead to follow-up plans for action and change, such training labs can be quite useful. Unfortunately, it appears that too often difficulty arises as a result of routine application of what are basically gimmicks to an involved and highly charged area.

In one large city school system an encounter group recently included teachers, most of whom were white, and students, most of whom were black, from the same school. The result was the opposite of what was sought—increased physical and verbal hostility of students to the teachers in the school. Carefully managed, however, the encounter between teachers and students, away from the school setting, has enormous possibilities for re-educating both teachers and students for a needed revolution in their relationships. But even at its most effective, the encounter session is a *shocking and bruising experience*.* And because of the failure to follow through with concrete plans for specific action, it too often remains a memorable experience, but not one that produces change.

Non-verbal exercises also are susceptible to both effective and inappropriate use. In one recent case at a conference of foundation executives, a trainer was employed to lead the group in several non-verbal exercises designed to stimulate greater openness and trust—two attributes much to be desired in any conference. The result, however, was unexpected. The initially surprised and then outraged participants displayed an enormous amount of openness—all of it hostile—toward both the trainer and the conference sponsors. The simple exercises that may be effective in settings where people are clearly experimenting with behavior are often *completely inappropriate in another context. . . .**

---

* Editor's italics.

There are, however, cases where non-verbal experiences are very much to the point. In police-community relations training sessions, simple physical contact exercises—a hand shake or, in special circumstances, a hug or touching another person's face—can be helpful. Where ghetto residents have never felt a policeman as a human being, such contact can be a wholesome revelation. For the white police, the personal experience that the black on the skin will not rub off has been equally salutary.

Two kinds of sensitivity training are particularly susceptible today to exploitation by the enthusiastic amateur or the enterprising entrepreneur: the area of non-verbal experience, and the confrontation session. Each requires a minimum of experience and knowledge to stimulate an initial response among participants, but in each case a maximum of expert knowledge and sophistication is required to extract a positive educational outcome. The most damning judgment that can be made about the non-verbal field is that a small bag of easily learned exercises, plus several 33⅓ rpm records, makes anyone a trainer. As for confrontation sessions, it is not difficult to evoke profound guilt feelings among participants by employing the tactics of staged aggression, but it *requires great skill and understanding to follow through to a positive learning experience.**

Despite all the possible pitfalls, however, it is necessary today to recognize the affective aspect of the educational process, and to train both teachers and administrators for mastery of the area. Too many of today's teaching-learning problems—in the suburbs as well as the inner city—are in the emotional rather than the cognitive or the skill areas. Change is imperative. But changing individual behavior and organizational structure are extraordinarily difficult and thorny objectives. . . . The longer one works in the field of planned change, the more difficult the task appears. . . .

Finally, appropriate human relations training should begin to equip teachers with a new teaching technology that is based on a learning group of peers, in contrast to the traditional classroom with the teacher as an authority figure and the students as a group of charges. The capacity to be a group process teacher is undoubtedly the most difficult of all goals for human relations training. But the ability to make a classroom into a learning group where peers share in the teaching-learning transaction holds the greatest promise for overcoming the all too familiar pattern—in the suburbs as well as the inner city—of sullen and disaffected children mobilizing to impede the educational process. The objective of making use of the emotional factor in teacher training, school reorganization, and classroom learning is an extraordinarily difficult one, but the revolution in education that this will achieve makes it imperative that school systems begin now.

* Editor's italics.

IMPLICATIONS

As you read this article, did you envision yourself in such a group? To what extent do you feel you could be open and honest about feelings that you have difficulty admitting to yourself? Also, how would you react to others in the group who openly referred to your defenses and façade? Your answers raise questions about the effectiveness of the leader in properly screening the members of the group and in assuring you that the knowledge you gain about yourself and your social relations can be effectively used.

REFERENCES

Two articles that raise evaluative questions about the groups and that cite criticisms and the means to meet them are Cashdan (1970) and Greening (1964). Cashdan's article contains bibliographies for those who want to investigate this subject further. Two recent discussions of sensitivity training groups will be found in E. Aronson (1972) and L.N. Solomon and Betty Berzon, *New Perspectives on Encounter Groups,* San Francisco: Jossey-Bass, 1972.

CHAPTER *VII*

PERSONNEL ISSUES

32

THE GULLIBILITY OF PERSONNEL MANAGERS

Ross Stagner

For a long time, charlatans or psychological quacks have operated successfully, using untested and sometimes invalid personality-test devices and selling them to otherwise shrewd businessmen. Why are they successful? In his clever but bold study, Stagner gives us some insight into the reasons for their success.

Contrasted to the nostrums sold by the quacks are the selection-and-appraisal devices, bolstered by statistical tests, that are employed by well-trained and reputable psychologists. These instruments are accompanied by indication of *reliability* (consistency of measurement) and frank *validity* data (showing the extent to which the instrument measures that which it is proposed to measure). These more scientific devices are often more difficult to use and to understand. In terms of high-level predictability, they promise much less than fraudulent devices; but they are always considerably superior to chance or non-critical judgment. You might find it interesting to turn to Table 1 and answer the questions before reading the article.

PSYCHOLOGICAL SERVICES are being offered for sale in all parts of the United States. Some of these are bona fide services by competent, well-trained people. Others are marketing nothing but glittering generalities having no practical value.

In the field of engineering, chemistry, power sources, and raw materials supply, the average businessman has learned to think realistically and to demand quantitative evidence concerning the value of an item before buying it. In the novel field of psychological measurement, on the other hand, many executives are still amazingly gullible. They often purchase expensive "employee selection" programs with no scientific evidence that the service offered has any value whatever.

A common device of the high-pressure salesman who is dispensing a fake line of psychological "tests" runs something like this: "Statistics can be used to prove anything. Let me give you a real demonstration. You take this personality test yourself, and I'll give you the report based on your scores. If you don't agree that it is amazingly accurate, I won't even try to sell it to you." The gullible personnel manager takes the test, reads the report, is

Reprinted from Ross Stagner, "The Gullibility of Personnel Managers," *Personnel Psychology*, Vol. 11 (Cleveland: Personnel Psychology, 1958), pp. 347–352, by permission of the publisher and the author.

amazed by its accuracy, and spends a lot of his company's money for a device not worth the paper and printing.

Does this sound too extreme? Do you think the personnel manager is the best possible judge of a report on his own personality? Do you think this is the only sound basis for deciding about the validity of a test? Skeptics will be interested in the following report of a simple experiment conducted with a conference of personnel managers at the University of Illinois.

Method

The procedure involved giving the personnel managers a published personality inventory and collecting the blanks for scoring, assuring them that the reports would be returned within a few hours. The test was actually scored, according to the published key. However, *two* reports were prepared, one using a mimeographed profile sheet which showed each man exactly how he scored as compared with norm groups; this gave him a quantitative result which could be used practically. The other report was a "fake" personality analysis published by Forer (1949) with slight modifications to make it more plausible. The thirteen items shown in Table 1, which were collected by Forer from dream books and astrology charts, were interspersed with rather critical comments about the personality being tested. The person's name was written in red pencil at the top of the sheet, and the thirteen items listed were circled in red; thus, every man received an identical "personality analysis."

At the second meeting of the group, the fake report was distributed first. Everyone was asked to read only his own personality analysis, which was given by the items marked in red. Thus it appeared that each individual was getting a report designed for himself alone. (No such direct assertion was made by the speaker, but the illusion was effectively communicated.)

Each man was then asked to read over the items marked for him and decide how accurate he thought the description was. He was provided with a five-step scale, as follows: amazingly accurate; rather good; about half and half; more wrong than right; almost entirely wrong. He was asked to check this scale both for over-all impression and for each of the items marked in red.

After the "validity analysis" had been collected, the participants were asked to compare their personality reports. Upon discovering that all were identical, they set up a terrific noise, apparently compounded of resentment at being duped and amusement at themselves for being tricked.

After brief discussion, the genuine profile sheets were distributed and the difference between glittering generalities and a quantitative set of scores emphasized. The importance of statistical data on reliability and validity was also discussed at this point.

Table 1

Evaluations of Items by 68 Personnel Managers When
Presented as a "Personality Analysis"

Item	Judgment as to accuracy of item Per cent * choosing				
	a†	b	c	d	e
1. You have a great need for other people to like and admire you.	39	46	13	1	1
4. You have a tendency to be critical of yourself.	46	36	15	3	0
5. You have a great deal of unused capacity which you have not turned to your advantage.	37	36	18	4	1
7. While you have some personality weaknesses, you are generally able to compensate for them.	34	55	9	0	0
9. Your sexual adjustment has presented problems for you.	15	16	16	33	19
10. Disciplined and self-controlled outside, you tend to be worrisome and insecure inside.	40	21	22	10	4
12. At times you have serious doubts as to whether you have made the right decision or done the right thing.	27	31	19	18	4
15. You prefer a certain amount of change and variety and become dissatisfied when hemmed in by restrictions and limitations.	63	28	7	1	1
16. You pride yourself as an independent thinker and do not accept others' statements without satisfactory proof.	49	31	12	4	4
18. You have found it unwise to be too frank in revealing yourself to others.	31	37	22	6	4
20. At times you are extroverted, affable, sociable, while at other times you are introverted, wary, reserved.	43	25	18	9	5
21. Some of your aspirations tend to be pretty unrealistic.	12	16	22	43	7
23. Security is one of your major goals in life.	40	31	15	9	5

* Not all percentages add to 100% because of omissions by an occasional subject.
† Definitions of scale steps as follows: a. amazingly accurate. b. rather good. c. about half and half. d. more wrong than right. e. almost entirely wrong.

Results

Perhaps the most important results were to be found in the insights reported by the participants, who quickly grasped the significance of the demonstration. However, numerical findings will be of some interest.

In terms of over-all evaluation of the "fake analysis," 50 per cent of a group of 68 personnel managers marked the description as amazingly accurate. Other judgments divided between "rather good" (40 per cent) and "about half and half" (10 per cent).

For comparison, we may cite results of two other groups. In a group of college students, 25 per cent considered this same "personality analysis" to be "amazingly accurate" and another 37 per cent judged it "rather good." In a class of industrial supervisors studying "human relations," the same personality analysis was considered "amazingly accurate" by 37 per cent, with 44 per cent rating it "rather good." Thus 62 per cent of the students and 81 per cent of the supervisors, as compared with 90 per cent of the personnel men, chose the first two steps on the validity scale defined in Table 1. The two industrial groups are not significantly different; the *greater skepticism of the students* * may have been due to their greater familiarity with test forms, and perhaps to some skepticism about the intent of the instructor.

The results for a group of 68 personnel managers on the eleven specific items are given in Table 1. It is clear from this table that any report using sentences such as those making up items 15, 16, 4, 20, 23, and 10 *will be popular with the recipient.** Even items 1, 5, 7, and 18 will get a good reception. Only items 9, 12, and 21 failed to get an enthusiastic approval from at least 30 per cent of the population.

Similar results were obtained from the group of supervisors, as well as from several classes of college students. It thus appears that the present finding need not be limited to personnel managers alone, although they merit special consideration because of their role in deciding upon employee selection devices.

Discussion

Industrial psychologists have some valuable wares to sell. But quacks and charlatans are always quick to move in on a new field and replace solid utility with glittering generalizations. The astonishing aspect of this demonstration to a professional psychologist is the credulity of the industrialist.

The sweeping character of the statements utilized in the fake personality analysis should be readily recognized. These propositions are so general that they can apply to anyone; as we note, 30 per cent to 50 per cent of a group of practicing personnel men accept most of them as "amazingly accurate" in an imputed self-description. Thus the shrewd salesman can easily dupe the personnel man *by appealing to his belief that his own judgment is better than statistics.** (Dozens of such demonstrations will be required to shake

* Editor's italics.

this belief in some industrialists' minds.) Seeing that the "test" elicits such remarkable insights into his own personality, the personnel manager concludes that it will do equally well with the applicants he wishes to analyze. It will, of course, do exactly as well; that is, it will spew out *glittering generalizations which apply to everyone and are distinctive for no one.** It will have no differential value for selection, placement, training, or any other personnel function.

It should be noted that these fake "personality reports" need not be phrased identically. The salesman need not use all thirteen of the items given in Table 1 for a given person, nor is he limited to these; there are many others, equally acceptable, some more flattering (these go to the higher executives). Thus the salesman can "test" several men in one organization without running out of nice generalizations. By judicious combinations of such items he can continue for quite a while without saying anything.

The present findings are not unique. Forer (1949) found that typical college students were easily taken in by his items. Sundberg (1955) reports that few people choose their own personality diagnosis, based on the Minnesota Multiphasic Personality Inventory, when it is matched with a set of vague generalizations like these. Dunnette (1957) comments, "It is an unfortunate fact that many otherwise hardheaded businessmen are today behaving in a rather gullible fashion" in regard to tests, and he credits Dr. Paul E. Meehl with coining the phrase, "the Barnum effect," to refer to the deceptive effect of these glittering generalities incorporated in testing reports.

These observations will not, it is hoped, decrease the interest of personnel men in professionally sound, scientifically evaluated personality measures. While most psychologists are cautious in recommending such devices, it seems certain that they can be utilized in certain industrial situations. Especial importance should be attached to the presence of quantitative data on reliability, on group norms, and on validation. Curiously enough, it seems that the third of these is least important. Validation needs to be repeated inside the establishment, with reference to criteria of performance appropriate to the position under study. But a test which does not elicit reliable individual differences, and a satisfactory spread of scores when applied to populations comparable to that in the establishment, cannot function as a personnel device. At best, it may make the employees think management is interested in them; at worst, it may result in erroneous placements, waste, and personnel disturbance.

The old Roman saying runs, *Caveat emptor*—let the buyer beware. This holds for personnel testing devices, especially as regards "personality tests." The personnel manager should avoid being seduced by the flattering report

* Editor's italics.

on his own fine qualities into purchasing a test which is worthless when evaluated scientifically.

IMPLICATIONS

You may find it interesting to discuss with other students the implications of your own answers to the thirteen items in Table 1. How did your responses compare with those of the personnel managers'? How do you explain the results? How would you proceed to convince business and personnel men of the superiority of reliable and valid measures produced by psychologists?

Another procedure would be to try to duplicate this experiment with a group of people who are planning to enter personnel work.

REFERENCES

Consult the Bibliography for references cited in the article.

33

USING THE APPLICATION BLANK TO REDUCE OFFICE TURNOVER

Edwin A. Fleishman and Joseph Berniger

Almost everyone has at one time or another filled out an application blank—for entrance to school or camp, for a job, or for some other appointment. The application asked for specific biographical data, and it may have seemed routine. If constructed well and completed by the applicant conscientiously, the application blank is a partial summary of his history. Depending upon how it is used, it should have predictive value. Fleishman and Berniger describe how the ordinary application blank becomes a psychological instrument.

Other commonly used personnel procedures may be refined. The interview and the rating scale, if tested, revised, and employed by

Reprinted from Edwin A. Fleishman and Joseph Berniger, "One Way to Reduce Office Turnover," *Personnel Psychology*, Vol. 37 (Cleveland: Personnel Psychology, 1960), pp. 63–69, by permission of the publisher and the senior author.

persons trained in their use, can be quite effective in personnel selection or other placement.

The following article is an example of how to use a simple application blank together with accumulated research on company records.

THOUGH THE APPLICATION BLANK, in one form or another, is omnipresent in business and industry, all too often it is used in a superficial and unsystematic manner. In many employmet situations, for example, the personnel interviewer either merely scans the blank for items he considers pertinent or uses the information only as a point of departure for the employment interview. As a result, much of the wealth of information in the application blank is going to waste, or worse, is often improperly used. In actual fact, however, there is sufficient evidence to indicate that, properly validated and used, the application blank can markedly increase the efficiency of the company's selection procedures.

The rationale for using the application blank (though this is seldom verbalized explicitly) is that the applicant's personal history, such as his previous experience and interests, is predictive of his future success on the job. And, indeed, it does seem reasonable to assume that such data as previous employment history, specific skills, education, financial status, marital record, and so forth, reflect a person's motives, abilities, skills, level of aspiration, and adjustment to working situations.

A number of assumptions can be made from such information. For example, the fact that an applicant has held a similar job indicates the likelihood of his transferring some of his training to the new job. Similarly, what he has done successfully before is likely to reflect his basic abilities in that area, as well as his interest in and satisfaction derived from these activities. Such personal history items as age, number of dependents, years of education, previous earnings, and amount of insurance have also been found to correlate with later proficiency on the job, earnings, length of tenure, or other criteria of job success. It should be emphasized however, that the items found to be predictive of success in one job may not be the same for another, similar job—even in the same company. Furthermore, even for the same job, some items on the application blank may be more predictive of one particular aspect of job performance than of other aspects (for example, turnover, accidents, or earnings).

Hand in hand with this consideration is the fact that, in personnel selection, the application blank is usually reviewed as a whole by an employment interviewer, a procedure that obviously involves a great deal of subjective judgment on his part. Consequently, the success of the form in predicting job performance depends not only upon the accuracy of the job description used as a reference, but also upon the skill of the interviewer and, most importantly, on his knowledge of the validity of individual items in relation to certain jobs and criteria. Unfortunately, however, it is this last critical point that most organizations fail to check out with empirical data. In this article we shall endeavor to point out that such data are not difficult to obtain and may materially help the employment interviewer in arriving at better hiring decisions.

Design of the Study

The study outlined here describes the way in which the potential value of the routine application blank used at Yale University was enhanced through appropriate research methods. The purpose of the study was to develop a way of scoring the application blank to select clerical and secretarial employees who were most likely to remain on the job. In other words, it was designed to explore the possibility of using the blank as part of a selection program aimed at reducing turnover.

The first step in the study was to find out which items in the application blank actually differentiated between short-tenure and long-tenure employees who had been hired at about the same time. For this purpose, 120 women office employees, all of whom had been hired between 1954 and 1956, were studied. Half of these, designated the "long-tenure" group, were women whose tenure was from two to four years and who were still on the job. The other 60 employees had terminated within two years and accordingly were designated the short-tenure group. Of this group, 20 per cent had terminated within six months and 67 per cent within the first year. The sample excluded known "temporaries" and summer employees. The women studied had all been hired as "permanent" employees, and all who had left had done so voluntarily.

The application blank in question is similar to those used in most organizations. It takes up four pages and includes approximately forty items—personal data, work history, education, interests, office skills, and the like. The original application blanks of the employees in both the short- and long-tenure groups were examined and the responses to the individual items were then compared to determine which, if any, differentiated the employees who terminated from those who stayed and, if so, which items were the best predictors of tenure.

A preliminary review suggested the ways in which to classify the answers to the various items. The next step was to tally the responses for each group and then convert them to percentages to facilitate comparisons. Some examples of items that did and did not differentiate between the two groups are shown in Table 1. As the table shows, local address, for instance, was a good differentiator, but previous salary was not. Certain responses to the question of age also distinguished between the two groups, as did "reason for leaving last employment," "occupation of husband," and "number of children."

Table 1

How Item Responses by Long- and Short-Tenure Office Employees Compared

Application Blank Items	Percentage of:		Weight Assigned to Response
	Short-tenure group	Long-tenure group	
Local address			
Within city	39	62	+2
Outlying suburbs	50	36	−2
Age			
Under 20	35	8	−3
21–25	38	32	−1
26–30	8	2	−1
31–35	7	10	0
35 and over	11	48	+3
Previous salary			
Under $2,000	31	30	0
$2,000–$3,000	41	38	0
$3,000–$4,000	13	12	0
Over $4,000	4	4	0
Age of children			
Preschool	12	4	−3
Public school	53	33	−3
High school or older	35	63	+3

Weighting the Items

Since some items were found to be better predictors of tenure than others, it seemed reasonable to assign them more weight in the actual hiring procedure—the next step in our study. Thus, items that did not discriminate were weighted zero (*i.e.*, they were not counted). Others were weighted negatively (they counted against the applicant), and still others, positively (in favor of the applicant). For example, an address in the suburbs was more characteristic of short-tenure employees, and so this response was scored negatively. An address in the city, on the other hand, was scored positively. Similarly, "age over 35" received a positive weight, but "under 30" received a negative weight.

Next, the size of the weight was determined. Items that showed a bigger percentage difference between the long- and short-tenure groups were given a higher weight. For example, "age under 20" was weighted −3, whereas "age 26–30" was weighted only −1. (Though there are more precise methods for assigning weights [Stead and Shartle, 1940], we found that the simple but systematic procedure described above yielded comparable results.)

An applicant's total score is, of course, obtained by adding or subtracting the weights scored on each item on the application blank. In our first sample, we found that total scores ranged from −17 to 27, the average score for the short-tenure group being −2.3, while that for the long-tenure group was 8.9—a difference of 11.2, which is highly significant statistically. The correlation between the total scores made by these employees and their subsequent tenure was .77.

This correlation was, of course, misleading and spuriously high since we had calculated it from the very sample from which we had determined the weights for the individual items in the first place. To obtain an unbiased estimate of the validity of our scoring procedure, we had to try it out, therefore, on an independent sample of employees.

The Cross-validation Study

Accordingly, the application blanks of a second random sample of short- and long-tenure girls, hired during the same period, were drawn from the files. Again, the short-tenure group consisted of girls who had left within two years and the long-tenure group was composed of those who were still on the job after two years or more. The scoring system developed on the first sample was then applied to the application blanks of this second group (85 clerical and secretarial employees).

The range of scores for this sample was −10 to 21, and the correlation with subsequent tenure was .57. This confirmed that the weighted blank did possess a high degree of validity for predicting tenure. The average score for the short-tenure group was −0.7, while that of the long-tenure group was 6.3. Again, this was a statistically significant difference. A recheck was also made on the individual items, which showed, in general, that those items which differentiated in the first sample did so in the second sample as well.

We had, then, a selection instrument that indicated the probability of an applicant's staying with the organization or not, but the question of how to use it in reaching the actual hiring decision still remained. Of course, such factors as the relative importance of turnover in the organization, the number of available applicants during a hiring period, and other selection procedures in use have to be taken into account here. It is desirable, nonetheless, to set a score on the application blank that does the best job of differentiating between "long-" and "short-"tenure risks at the time of employment. In other words, what is needed is a cut-off score that will maximize correct hiring decisions; or—to put it another way—a score that will minimize both the number of people hired who will turn out to be short-tenure employees and the number rejected who would have actually remained on the job.

To establish our cut-off score, we used the method of "maximum differentiation." In other words, we tabulated the percentage of employees reaching or exceeding each score point in the range, −10 to 21. We then calculated the differences between the percentages obtained in the two groups at each score point to find the point of greatest differentiation.

The result is shown in Table 2, from which it will be seen that in our case the difference between the two groups reached its maximum at a score of +4. This told us that applicants scoring 4 points or more were most likely to stay on the job two years or more, whereas those scoring less than 4 could be considered potential short-tenure employees.

Figure 1 shows the degree of success that would have been achieved if this cutting score of +4 had been used on our second sample of 85 em-

Table 2

Obtaining a Cutting Score by Using "Maximum Differentiation"

| | | Percentage of Subjects at or above a Given Score | | |
| | | A | B | |
	Total Score	Percentage of long-tenure employees	Percentage of short-tenure employees	Index of Differentiation (A Minus B)
	21	4	0	4
	20	4	0	4
	19	4	0	4
	18	12	0	12
	17	16	0	16
	16	20	0	20
	15	20	0	20
	14	24	0	24
	13	24	3	21
	12	28	3	25
	11	32	5	27
	10	36	8	28
	9	40	10	30
	8	40	14	26
	7	44	15	29
	6	48	17	31
	5	60	20	40
Cutting Score	4	68	22	46
	3	72	27	45
	2	72	32	40
	1	72	39	13
	0	80	42	18
	−1	80	46	14
	−2	80	54	16
	−3	84	66	18
	−4	92	68	24
	−5	92	76	16
	−6	92	85	7
	−7	96	90	6
	−8	96	94	2
	−9	100	98	2
	−10	100	100	0

Point of Greatest Differentiation (noted beside scores 5 and 4)

ployees. The shaded areas represent the percentage of correct hiring decisions, and the unshaded areas, the percentage of incorrect hiring decisions. As may be seen, the personnel interviewer would have hired two out of three of the employees who stayed more than two years, and rejected approximately four out of five of those who had left before that time.

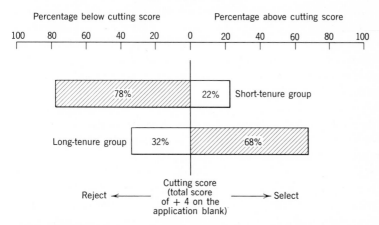

Figure 1. Percentage of correct hiring decisions that would have been obtained through using cutting score.

Finally, to facilitate routine scoring, we constructed a cardboard template for each page of the application blank (Wood, 1947). In the template are windows, which expose only the responses to be scored. The weights for each response are printed on the template next to the appropriate window.

An interesting offshoot of our study was the picture it yielded of the woman office worker most likely to be the best long-tenure risk at Yale University. We arrived at it by using the application blank items that differentiated between long- and short-tenure employees in both our original and our cross-validation samples. Here is a profile of the typical long-tenure woman office employee at Yale:

She is 30 years old or over, has a local address rather than a suburban one, is married (but not to a student), or is a widow. Her husband is most likely to be an executive or a professional man. She may have one or two children, but if she does, they are of high-school age or over. At least one member of her family has been employed at Yale. She herself is not employed at the time of application. She has had a business, secretarial school, or college education, and can often speak more than one language. If she can type, she does so at a speed of 50–60 words per minute. Usually, she cannot take shorthand—but if she does, it is at a relatively high rate of speed. She does not list more than one outside interest aside from work, and that one indicates that she is most interested in organizations and people. Finally, she spent at least two years at her last job.

The findings of our study bear out those obtained in previous studies at the Prudential Life Insurance Company (Kreidt and Gadel, 1953) and the Minnesota Mining and Manufacturing Company (Kirchner and Dunnette, 1957), both of which showed that a high degree of predictability of turnover among female office employees was achieved from a weighted application blank. Our study extends the generality of these findings from two diverse companies to a university organization. However, an examination of all three studies underscores the fact that the specific biographical items contributing to prediction of turnover vary from one organizational setting to the next. Thus, while the validity of the general technique for predicting turnover has been established for clerical employees, the weighted application blank that will work best for a particular company must be tailor-made for that organization.

Another consideration worth mentioning, perhaps, is that though the biographical data used here have been found to be most useful in predicting turnover, other studies have indicated that such data are also of value in predicting accidents and proficiency. (They have been found especially useful in predicting proficiency in the sales field [The AI-4-48, 1951].) Of course, turnover and proficiency are not unrelated—it is well known that many girls leave because of low proficiency. However, the company that uses other selection instruments to predict proficiency can combine them with the weighted application blank scores and thereby select employees who will be the best risks in terms of both proficiency *and* tenure.

One final point: the research described in this article is relatively inexpensive. Indeed, most companies have file drawers literally bulging with application blank data that are well suited to the kind of analysis described here.

IMPLICATIONS

How did the use of the application blank in the selection differ from its use in most situations? Can you think of other ways to use personal information that has been carefully collected and buttressed by research? What personal history items in addition to those used here would you suggest for use in classifying both successful and ineffective salesmen? Research workers?

REFERENCES

Consult the Bibliography for reference cited in the article.

34

THE INDIVIDUAL AS A MEMBER OF MULTIPLE GROUPS

Anne Anastasi

The term *organization man,* the title of a popular book of a few years ago, has become part of our vocabulary. William H. Whyte, an editor of *Fortune* Magazine, wrote about life under the protection of the big organization that promises security and a high standard of living. As a result of this organization life, Whyte maintains, the American is turning from *ideals of hard work, thrift, and competitive struggle* to an ethic that emphasizes the *group* as a source of creativity, belief in *belonging* as the ultimate need, and use of science to achieve these ends. Further, he sees an inhibiting of individual initiative and imagination, an emphasis on techniques over content, stress upon the skills of attaining a goal isolated from the ultimate goal. Whyte, along with David Riesman (1950) and others, emphasizes the strength of conformity to external forces rather than to individual values.

To look into the question of the effect of groups on individuals, we might turn to a summary statement by Anne Anastasi in *Differential Psychology,* an impressive volume on individual differences. She analyzes the nature of a variety of psychological groups and then succinctly discusses individuality in terms of group influences.

The Individual as a Member of Multiple Groups

PSYCHOLOGICALLY the individual belongs to every group with which he shares behavior.[1] From this point of view, group membership is to be defined in terms of behavioral rather than biological categories. The effective grouping is not based upon the individual's race or sex or body build, but upon his experiential background. Thus if the individual is reared as a member of a certain national group with its own traditions and cultural background and its own peculiar complex of stimulating conditions, he will display the behavioral characteristics of that group regardless of his racial origin. It should be understood, of course, that mere physical presence does not constitute group membership in a psychological sense. If a Negro child were brought up in a community composed exclusively of whites, he would not necessarily receive the same social stimulation as a white child. Similarly, a boy who is brought up exclusively by female relatives will not

[1] This criterion of a psychological group is essentially that formulated by Kantor (1929), who seems to have been the first to discuss social behavior in terms of *shared responses* to objects having common stimulus functions.

313

develop the personality traits of a girl. A psychological group is based solely upon shared behavior and not upon geographical proximity or biological resemblance.

It follows from such a concept of group that any one individual is effectively a member of a large and varied set of groups. A *multiplicity of behavioral groups*, large and small, cut across each other in the individual's background. . . . The individual is born into a broad cultural division such as, for example, "Western civilization," with its characteristic sources of stimulation. He will develop certain aptitudes, emotional traits, attitudes, and beliefs as a result of his affiliation with this group. He is also a member of a given national group with its more specific traditional ways of acting.

If the individual displays certain physical characteristics, such as a particular skin color, facial conformation, and body build, he may be classified as a member of a given "racial" group which occupies a distinct position within the broader national division. Insofar as his racial background leads to certain social distinctions and culturally imposed differentiations of behavior, it will operate as an effective grouping. The same may be said of sex. If, within a given society, traditional beliefs in regard to sex differences exist so that the sexes are exposed to dissimilar psychological stimulation, then the individual's sex will in part determine his behavioral characteristics.

There are a number of other behavioral groupings which, although less frequently recognized and less clearly defined, may be equally influential in the individual's development. Thus it will be recalled that important psychological differences are usually found between the city-bred and country-bred child, as well as between different social classes. Similarly, the particular state, province, or other major division of a nation in which the individual is reared, and even the specific town and neighborhood in which he lives, will exert significant influences upon his intellectual and emotional development.

Other groups with which an individual identifies himself behaviorally include his occupational class, his religion, his political party, his club, his educational institution. That such groupings represent clear-cut cultural distinctions is readily illustrated by the stereotypes which have become attached to many of these groups. To people within our society, a distinct picture will be suggested by the mention of such designations as country doctor, businessman, Roman Catholic, Orthodox Jew, Republican, Rotarian, Harvard man. These groups influence the individual's behavior in two ways. First, they directly stimulate and foster certain ways of acting. Secondly, the reactions of other people to the individual are influenced by their knowledge of his group affiliation. The social attitudes and "social expectancy" which the individual encounters will in turn affect his behavior.

Family groupings, with their characteristic activities and traditions, constitute another important part of the individual's psychological environment. The degenerate Jukes and Kallikaks, eminent families such as the

Huxleys and the Darwins, and many other striking examples testify to the cultural influence of family membership. Cutting across such family groupings are age distinctions. "Stages" are socially imposed upon the continuous life activities of the individual and he is treated more or less differently at each period. The individual may also look upon himself as belonging to a particular generation—he may be a member of the "older generation," the "young married set," the "teen-agers," and so forth. Even such apparently minor factors as one's hobbies and recreations will, in turn, affect the individual's subsequent behavior. Psychological membership in many new groups may result from a newly developed interest in bowling, stamp collecting, or early American pressed glass. The number of behavioral groupings could easily be multiplied. These examples will suffice to illustrate the nature of such groupings and their effect upon behavior development.

The individual may be regarded partly as a resultant of his multiple group memberships. To be sure, each individual also undergoes experiences that are absolutely unique to himself. Such experiences are probably less significant, however, in shaping the more basic aspects of his personality than is his shared behavior. The experiences that are common to a group of individuals have a certain degree of permanence in the sense that they will tend to be repeated more often and to be corroborated or re-enforced by other similar experiences. In general, the more highly organized the group, the more consistent and systematic will be the experiences its members undergo. This will tend to make the shared experiences on the whole more effective than the purely individual. Moreover, even the individual's idiosyncratic experiences will generally have certain cultural features which differentiate them from the idiosyncratic experiences of persons in other cultures. Thus an individual may compose a poem which is unique in its totality and to this extent unlike any poem ever written by any other person; but the fact that the poem is a political satire, that it is composed in the English language and in iambic pentameter, and that it is written with a ball-point pen are among the many distinctly cultural features of such an activity.

In view of the pronounced effect of such shared or common behavior upon the individual's development, it may appear surprising that individuals are no more alike in their behavior repertoire than we ordinarily find them to be. The extent of individual differences within any one group is extremely large. In fact, the variations among·individuals have always proved to be more marked than the differences from one group to another. How can the "individuality" of each person be explained in terms of his shared experiential background?

The key to this problem seems to lie in the *multiplicity* of overlapping groups with which the individual may be behaviorally identified. The number of such groups is so great that the *specific combination* is unique for each individual. Not only does this furnish a stimulational basis for the existence of wide individual differences, but it also suggests a mechanism whereby the individual may "rise above" his group. There are many examples of individuals who have broken away from the customs and traditional ways of acting of their group. Through such situations, modifications of the group itself may also be effected.

In these cases the individual is not reacting contrary to his past experience, as might at first appear. This would be psychologically impossible. His behavior is the result of psychological membership in various *conflicting* groups. Many group memberships can exist side by side in a composite behavioral adjustment. But in certain cases two or more groups may foster different ways of reacting to the same situation. This enables the individual to become aware of the arbitrariness of the restrictions and tradition of each group, to evaluate them critically, and to regard them more "objectively." Membership in many diverse groups frees the individual from the intellectual and other limitations of each group and makes possible the fullest development of "individuality."

IMPLICATIONS

Does Anastasi hold the same views as Whyte? If not, can you express the difference between their views? From Anastasi's analysis, how do you evaluate the force of individuality in a democracy like ours? To what extent do you think membership in multiple groups will free the individual from the *conformity forces* of the centralized mass media—advertising, television, radio, and magazines? To what overlapping cultural groups do you belong?

REFERENCES

Whyte's book (1956) is stimulating reading, and Riesman's (1950) has become a classic.

CHAPTER VIII

HUMAN RELATIONS, INDUSTRY, AND LAW

35 COMMUNICATION: BARRIERS AND GATEWAYS

Carl R. Rogers

Has it occurred to you that many of our contemporary human problems are in part a breakdown in communication? Marriages heading toward divorce, labor-management disagreements leading to *strikes, international conflicts* escalating toward major wars, and parent-child misunderstandings reflected in *youth crises* are a few examples of situations in which adversaries lack a clear understanding of each other's views. We find in these cases accusations and counteraccusations, aggressive and defensive statements, but little attempt to understand each other's views and to deal with them in an effective, mutually satisfying way. Probably today, more than at any other time in man's recorded history, there is greater effort toward accommodation of differing viewpoints—a realization that in order to live, we must let live.

Rogers, a pioneer in the use of counseling and psychotherapy for adjustment to human problems, is qualified to suggest an attitude of mind as well as a *modus operandi* for dealing with human conflict. You probably will find a new use of the term *communication*—namely, communication with ourselves, within our personality—referring to understanding those aspects of our experience which we deny to awareness and which are not available to the managing part of ourselves but influence our behavior nonetheless.

IT MAY SEEM CURIOUS that a person like myself, whose whole professional effort is devoted to psychotherapy, should be interested in problems of communication. What relationship is there between obstacles to communication and providing therapeutic help to individuals with emotional maladjustments?

Actually the relationship is very close indeed. The whole task of psychotherapy is the task of dealing with a failure in communication. The emotionally maladjusted person, the "neurotic," is in difficulty, first, because communication within himself has broken down and, secondly, because as a result of this his communication with others has been damaged. To put it another way, in the "neurotic" individual parts of himself which have been termed unconscious, or repressed, or denied to awareness, become blocked off so that they no longer communicate themselves to the con-

Reprinted from Carl R. Rogers, "Barriers and Gateways to Communication," *Harvard Business Review,* Vol. 30 (Boston: Harvard University, 1952), pp. 46–52, by permission of the publisher and the author.

scious or managing part of himself; as long as this is true, there are distortions in the way he communicates himself to others, and so he suffers both within himself and in his interpersonal relations.

The task of psychotherapy is to help the person achieve, through a special relationship with a therapist, good communication within himself. Once this is achieved, he can communicate more freely and more effectively with others. We may say then that psychotherapy is good communication, within and between men. We may also turn that statement around and it will still be true. Good communication, free communication, within or between men, is always therapeutic.

It is, then, from a background of experience with communication in counseling and psychotherapy that I want to present two ideas: (1) I wish to state what I believe is one of the major factors in blocking or impeding communication, and then (2) I wish to present what in our experience has proved to be a very important way of improving or facilitating communication.

Barrier: The Tendency to Evaluate

I should like to propose, as a hypothesis for consideration, that the major barrier to mutual interpersonal communication is our very natural tendency to judge, to evaluate, to approve (or disapprove) the statement of the other person or the other group. Let me illustrate my meaning with some very simple examples. Suppose someone, commenting on this discussion, makes the statement, "I didn't like what that man said." What will you respond? Almost invariably your reply will be either approval or disapproval of the attitude expressed. Either you respond, "I didn't either; I thought it was terrible," or else you tend to reply, "Oh, I thought it was really good." In other words, your primary reaction is to evaluate it from *your* point of view, your own frame of reference.

Or take another example. Suppose I say with some feeling, "I think the Republicans are behaving in ways that show a lot of good, sound sense these days." What is the response that arises in your mind? The overwhelming likelihood is that it will be evaluative. In other words, you will find yourself agreeing, or disagreeing, or making some judgment about me such as "He must be a conservative," or "He seems solid in his thinking." Or let us take an illustration from the international scene. Russia says vehemently, "The treaty with Japan is a war plot on the part of the United States." We rise as one person to say, "That's a lie!"

This last illustration brings in another element connected with my hypothesis. Although the tendency to make evaluations is common in almost all interchange of language, it is very much heightened in those situations where feelings and emotions are deeply involved. So the stronger our feelings, the more likely it is that there will be no mutual element in the communication. There will be just two ideas, two feelings, two judgments, missing each other in psychological space.

I am sure you recognize this from your own experience. When you have not been emotionally involved yourself and have listened to a heated discussion, you often go away thinking, "Well, they actually weren't talking about the same thing." And they were not. Each was making a judgment, an evaluation, from his own frame of reference. There was really nothing which could be called communication in any genuine sense. This tendency to react to any emotionally meaningful statement by forming an evaluation of it from our own point of view is, I repeat, the major barrier to interpersonal communication.

Gateway: Listening With Understanding

Is there any way of solving this problem, of avoiding this barrier? I feel that we are making exciting progress toward this goal, and I should like to present it as simply as I can. Real communication occurs, and this evaluative tendency is avoided, when we listen with understanding. What does that mean? It means to see the expressed idea and attitude from the other person's point of view, to sense how it feels to him, to achieve his frame of reference in regard to the thing he is talking about.

Stated so briefly, this may sound absurdly simple, but it is not. It is an approach which we have found extremely potent in the field of psychotherapy. It is the most effective agent we know for altering the basic personality structure of an individual and for improving his relationships and his communications with others. If I can listen to what he can tell me, if I can understand how it seems to him, if I can see its personal meaning for him, if I can sense the emotional flavor which it has for him, then I will be releasing potent forces or change in him.

Again, if I can really understand how he hates his father, or hates the company, or hates Communists—if I can catch the flavor of his fear of insanity, or his fear of atom bombs, or of Russia—it will be of the greatest help to him in altering those hatreds and fears and in establishing realistic and harmonious relationships with the very people and situations toward which he has felt hatred and fear. We know from our research that such empathic understanding—understanding *with* a person, not *about* him—is such an effective approach that it can bring about major changes in personality.

Some of you may be feeling that you listen well to people and yet you have never seen such results. The chances are great indeed that your listening has not been of the type I have described. Fortunately, I can suggest a little laboratory experiment which you can try to test the quality of your understanding. The next time you get into an argument with your wife, or your friend, or with a small group of friends, just stop the discussion for a moment and, for an experiment, institute this rule: "Each person can speak up for himself only *after* he has first restated the ideas and feelings of the previous speaker accurately and to that speaker's satisfaction."

You see what this would mean. It would simply mean that before presenting your own point of view, it would be necessary for you to achieve the other speaker's frame of reference—to understand his thoughts and feelings so well that you could summarize them for him. Sounds simple, doesn't it? But if you try it, you will discover that it is one of the most difficult things you have ever tried to do. However, once you have been able to see the other's point of view, your own comments will have to be drastically revised. You will also find the emotion going out of the discussion, the differences being reduced, and those differences which remain being of a rational and understandable sort. . . .

If, then, this way of approach is an effective avenue to good communication and good relationships, as I am quite sure you will agree if you try the experiment I have mentioned, why is it not more widely tried and used? I will try to list the difficulties which keep it from being utilized.

Need for Courage

In the first place it takes courage, a quality which is not too widespread. I am indebted to Dr. S.I. Hayakawa, the semanticist, for pointing out that to carry on psychotherapy in this fashion is to take a very real risk, and that courage is required. If you really understand another person in this way, if you are willing to enter his private world and see the way life appears to him, without any attempt to make evaluative judgments, you run the risk of being changed yourself. You might see it his way; you might find yourself influenced in your attitudes or your personality.

This risk of being changed is one of the most frightening prospects many of us can face. If I enter, as fully as I am able, into the private world of a neurotic or psychotic individual, isn't there a risk that I might become lost in that world? Most of us are afraid to take that risk. Or if we were listening to a Russian Communist . . . how many of us would dare to try to see the world from his point of view? The great majority of us could not *listen*; we would find ourselves compelled to *evaluate*, because listening would seem too dangerous. So the first requirement is courage, and we do not always have it.

Heightened Emotions

But there is a second obstacle. It is just when emotions are strongest that it is most difficult to achieve the frame of reference of the other person or group. Yet it is then that the attitude is most needed if communication is to be established. We have not found this to be an insuperable obstacle in our experience in psychotherapy. A third party, who is able to lay aside his own feelings and evaluations, can assist greatly by listening with understanding to each person or group and clarifying the views and attitudes each holds.

We have found this effective in small groups in which contradictory or antagonistic attitudes exist. When the parties to a dispute realize that they are being understood, that someone sees how the situation seems to them, the statements grow less exaggerated and less defensive, and it is no longer necessary to maintain the attitude, "I am 100 per cent right and you are 100 per cent wrong." The influence of such an understanding catalyst in the group permits the members to come closer and closer to the objective truth involved in the relationship. In this way mutual communication is established, and some type of agreement becomes much more possible.

So we may say that though heightened emotions make it much more difficult to understand *with* an opponent, our experience makes it clear that a neutral, understanding, catalyst type of leader or therapist can overcome this obstacle in a small group.

Size of Group

That last phrase, however, suggests another obstacle to utilizing the approach I have described. Thus far all our experience has been with small face-to-face groups—groups exhibiting industrial tensions, religious tensions, racial tensions, and therapy groups in which many personal tensions are present. In these small groups our experience, confirmed by a limited amount of research, shows that this basic approach leads to improved communication, to greater acceptance of others and by others, and to attitudes which are more positive and more problem-solving in nature. There is a decrease in defensiveness, in exaggerated statements, in evaluative and critical behavior.

But these findings are from small groups. What about trying to achieve understanding between larger groups that are geographically remote, or between face-to-face groups that are not speaking for themselves but simply as representatives of others, like the delegates at Kaesong? Frankly we do not know the answers to these questions. I believe the situation might be put this way: As social scientists we have a tentative test-tube solution of the problem of breakdown in communication. But to confirm the validity of this test-tube solution and to adapt it to the enormous problems of communication breakdown between classes, groups, and nations would involve additional funds, much more research, and creative thinking of a high order.

Yet with our present limited knowledge we can see some steps which might be taken even in large groups to increase the amount of listening *with* and decrease the amount of evaluation *about*. To be imaginative for a moment, let us suppose that a therapeutically oriented international group went to the Russian leaders and said, "We want to achieve a genuine understanding of your views and, even more important, of your attitudes and feelings toward the United States. We will summarize and resummarize these views and feelings if necessary, until you agree that our description represents the situation as it seems to you."

Then suppose they did the same thing with the leaders in our own country. If they then gave the widest possible distribution to these two views, with the feelings clearly described but not expressed in name-calling, might not the effect be very great? It would not guarantee the type of understanding I have been describing, but it would make it much more possible. We can understand the feelings of a person who hates us much more readily when his attitudes are accurately described to us by a neutral third party than we can when he is shaking his fist at us. . . .

Summary

In closing, I should like to summarize this small-scale solution to the problem of barriers in communication, and to point out certain of its characteristics.

I have said that our research and experience to date would make it appear that breakdowns in communication, and the evaluative tendency which is the major barrier to communication, can be avoided. The solution is provided by creating a situation in which each of the different parties comes to understand the other from the *other's* point of view. This has been achieved, in practice, even when feelings run high, by the influence of a person who is willing to understand each point of view empathically, and who thus acts as a catalyst to precipitate further understanding.

This procedure has important characteristics. It can be initiated by one party, without waiting for the other to be ready. It can even be initiated by a neutral third person, provided he can gain a minimum of cooperation from one of the parties.

This procedure can deal with the insincerities, the defensive exaggerations, the lies, the "false fronts" which characterize almost every failure in communication. These defensive distortions drop away with astonishing speed as people find that the only intent is to understand, not to judge.

This approach leads steadily and rapidly toward the discovery of the truth, toward a realistic appraisal of the objective barriers to communication. The dropping of some defensiveness by one party leads to further dropping of defensiveness by the other party, and truth is thus approached.

This procedure gradually achieves mutual communication. Mutual communication tends to be pointed toward solving a problem rather than toward attacking a person or group. It leads to a situation in which I see how the problem appears to you as well as to me, and you see how it appears to me as well as to you. Thus accurately and realistically defined, the problem is almost certain to yield to intelligent attack; or if it is in part insoluble, it will be comfortably accepted as such.

This then appears to be a test-tube solution to the breakdown of communication as it occurs in small groups. Can we take this small-scale answer, investigate it further, refine it, develop it, and apply it to the tragic and well-nigh fatal failures of communication which threaten the very existence of our modern world? It seems to me that this is a possibility and a challenge which we should explore.

IMPLICATIONS

Can you recall some examples of Rogers' statement that the stronger our feelings, the more likely it is that there will be no mutual element in the communication, that individuals will be expressing two different ideas of feelings and missing each other in psychological space? There is the suggestion here that *we cannot communicate effectively with others in critical areas if we cannot communicate within ourselves.* See to what extent you regard these suggestions as practicable for more effective communication with others.

You and other students should find it interesting to stage a demonstration in small groups in which two individuals who are poles apart on an issue first debate the issue, then after a time put into practice the suggestion Rogers made in the article. In the latter case, *each individual can speak for himself only after he has restated the ideas and feelings of the previous speaker accurately and to that speaker's satisfaction.* In doing this, note whether there is a decrease in defensive and exaggerated statements and in evaluation and critical behavior, and, on the other hand, an increase in positive and problem-solving activity.

REFERENCES

You doubtless have noted that Rogers has related the issues of communications to psychotherapy. Rogers' view on psychotherapy is mentioned briefly in Selection 43. One of his basic books is *Counseling and Psychotherapy* (1951).

36 ACHIEVEMENT DRIVE AND ECONOMIC GROWTH

David C. McClelland

Do you realize that as an American youth you in all probability have strong achievement needs?

Here we have a selection by a psychologist who has developed methods for assessing differences in achievement motivation and has related this factor to effective business management and to the broader problems of achieving cultures or achieving societies. How does he assess individual achievement? What is the pattern of behavior found in the achieving personality?

WHAT ACCOUNTS for the rise in civilization? Not external resources (*i.e.*, markets, minerals, trade routes, or factories), but the entrepreneurial spirit which exploits those resources—a spirit found most often among businessmen.

Who is ultimately responsible for the pace of economic growth in poor countries today? Not the economic planners or the politicians, but the executives whose drive (or lack of it) will determine whether the goals of the planners are fulfilled.

Why is Russia developing so rapidly that—if it continues its present rate of growth—it will catch up economically with the most advanced country in the world, the United States, in 25 or 30 years? Not, as the U.S.S.R. claims, because of the superiority of its Communist system, but because—by hook or by crook—it has managed to develop a strong spirit of entrepreneurship among its executives.

How can foreign aid be most efficiently used to help poor countries develop rapidly? Not by simply handing money over to their politicians or budget makers, but by using it in ways that will select, encourage, and develop those of their business executives who have a vigorous entrepreneurial spirit or a strong drive for achievement. In other words: *invest in a man, not just in a plan.*

What may be astonishing about some of these remarks is that they come from a college professor, and not from the National Association of Manufacturers. They are not the defensive drum rattlings of an embattled capitalist, but are my conclusions, based on nearly fifteen years of research, as a strictly academic psychologist, into the human motive that appears to be

Reprinted from David C. McClelland, "Business Drive and National Achievement," *Harvard Business Review,* July–August (Boston: Harvard University, 1962), pp. 99–112, by permission of the publisher and the author.

largely responsible for economic growth—research which has recently been summarized in my book, entitled *The Achieving Society* (McClelland, 1961).

Since I am an egghead from way back, nothing surprises me more than finding myself rescuing the businessman from the academic trash heap, dusting him off, and trying to give him the intellectual respectability that he has had a hard time maintaining for the last fifty years or so. For the fact is that the businessman has taken a beating, not just from the Marxists, who pictured him as a greedy capitalist, and the social critics, who held him responsible for the Great Depression of the 1930's, but even from himself, deep in his heart.

One of the queerest ironies of history, as John Kenneth Galbraith points out in *The Affluent Society*, is that in a sense Marx won his case with his sworn enemies, the capitalists. Marx loudly asserted that they were selfish and interested only in profits. In the end many agreed. They accepted the Marxist materialistic view of history. The modern businessman, says Galbraith, "suspects that the moral crusade of reformers, do-gooders, liberal politicians, and public servants, all their noble protestations notwithstanding, are based ultimately on self-interest. 'What,' he inquires, 'is their gimmick?' " (Galbraith, 1958).

If not only the Marxist, but Western economists, and even businessmen themselves, end up assuming that their main motive is self-interest and a quest for profit, it is small wonder that they have had a hard time holding their heads high in recent years.

But now the research I have done has come to the businessman's rescue by showing that everyone has been wrong, that it is *not* profit per se that makes the businessman tick but a strong desire for achievement, for doing a good job. Profit is simply one measure among several of how well the job has been done, but it is not necessarily the goal itself.

The Achievement Goal

But what exactly does the psychologist mean by the "desire for achievement"? How does he measure it in individuals or in nations? How does he know that it is so important for economic growth? Is it more important for businessmen to have this desire than it is for politicians, bishops, or generals? These are the kinds of questions which are answered at great length and with as much scientific precision as possible in my book. Here we must be content with the general outline of the argument, and develop it particularly as it applies to businessmen.

To begin with, psychologists try to find out what a man spends his time thinking and daydreaming about when he is not under pressure to think about anything in particular. What do his thoughts turn to when he is by himself or not engaged in a special job? Does he think about his family and friends, about relaxing and watching TV, about getting his superior off his back? Or does he spend his time thinking and planning how he can "sell" a particular customer, cut production costs, or invent a better steam trap or toothpaste tube?

If a man spends his time thinking about doing things better, the psychologist says he has a concern for achievement. In other words, he cares about achievement or he would not spend so much time thinking about it. If he spends his time thinking about family and friends, he has a concern for affiliation; if he speculates about who is boss, he has a concern for power, and so on. What differs in my approach from the one used by many psychologists is that my colleagues and I have not found it too helpful simply to *ask* a person about his motives, interests, and attitudes. Often he himself does not know very clearly what his basic concerns are—even more often he may be ashamed and cover some of them up. So what we do is to try and get a sample of his normal waking thoughts by asking him just to tell a few stories about some pictures.

Stories Within Stories

Let us take a look at some typical stories written by U.S. business executives. These men were asked to look briefly at a picture—in this case, a man at a worktable with a small family photograph at one side—and to spend about five minutes writing out a story suggested by the picture. Here is a very characteristic story:

The engineer is at work on Saturday when it is quiet and he has taken time to do a little daydreaming. He is the father of the two children in the picture —the husband of the woman shown. He has a happy home life and is dreaming about some pleasant outing they have had. He is also looking forward to a repeat of the incident which is now giving him pleasure to think about. He plans on the following day, Sunday, to use the afternoon to take his family for a short trip.

Obviously, no achievement-related thoughts have come to the author's mind as he thinks about the scene in the picture. Instead, it suggests spending time pleasantly with his family. His thoughts run along *affiliative* lines. He thinks readily about interpersonal relationship and having fun with other people. This, as a matter of fact, is the most characteristic reaction to this particular picture. But now consider another story:

A successful industrial designer is at his "work bench" toying with a new idea. He is "talking it out" with his family in the picture. Someone in the family dropped a comment about a shortcoming in a household gadget, and the designer has just "seen" a commercial use of the idea. He has picked up ideas from his family before—he is "telling" his family what a good idea it is, and "confidentially" he is going to take them on a big vacation because "their" idea was so good. The idea will be successful, and family pride and mutual admiration will be strengthened.

The author of this story maintains a strong interest in the family and in affiliative relationships, but has added an achievement theme. The family actually has helped him innovate—get a new idea that will be successful and obviously help him get ahead. Stories which contain references to good new ideas, such as a new product, an invention, or a unique accomplishment of any sort, are scored as reflecting a concern for achievement in the person who writes them. In sum, this man's mind tends to run most easily along the lines of accomplishing something or other. Finally, consider a third story:

The man is an engineer at a drafting board. The picture is of his family. He has a problem and is concentrating on it. It is merely an everyday occurrence —a problem which requires thought. How can he get that bridge to take the stress of possible high winds? He wants to arrive at a good solution of the problem by himself. He will discuss the problem with a few other engineers and make a decision which will be a correct one—he has the earmarks of competence.

The man who wrote this story—an assistant to a vice president, as a matter of fact—notices the family photograph, but that is all. His thoughts tend to focus on the problem that the engineer has to solve. In the scant five minutes allowed, he even thinks of a precise problem—how to build a bridge that will take the stress of possible high winds. He notes that the engineer wants to find a good solution by himself, that he goes and gets help from other experts and finally makes a correct decision. These all represent different aspects of a complete achievement sequence—defining the problem, wanting to solve it, thinking of means of solving it, thinking of difficulties that get in the way of solving it (either in one's self or in the environment), thinking of people who might help in solving it, and anticipating what would happen if one succeeded or failed.

Each of these different ideas about achievement gets a score of $+1$ in our scoring system so that the man in the last incident gets a score of $+4$ on the scale of concern or need for achievement (conventionally abbreviated to n Achievement). Similarly, the first man gets a score of -1 for his story since it is completely unrelated to achievement, and the second man a score of $+2$ because there are two ideas in it which are scorable as related to achievement.

Each man usually writes six such stories and gets a score for the whole test. The coding of the stories for "achievement imagery" is so objective that two expert scorers working independently rarely disagree. In fact, it has recently been programed for a high-speed computer that does the scoring rapidly, with complete objectivity, and fairly high accuracy. What the score for an individual represents is the frequency with which he tends to think spontaneously in achievement terms when that is not clearly expected of him (since the instructions for the test urge him to relax and to think freely and rapidly).

Thinking Makes It So

What are people good for who think like this all the time? It doesn't take much imagination to guess that they might make particularly good business executives. People who spend a lot of their time thinking about getting ahead, inventing new gadgets, defining problems that need to be solved, considering alternative means of solving them, and calling in experts for help should also be people who in real life *do* a lot of these things or at the very best are readier to do them when the occasion arises.

I recognize, of course, that this is an assumption that requires proof. But, as matters turned out, our research produced strong factual support. Look, for instance, at Exhibit I. It shows that in three countries representing different levels and types of economic development, managers or executives scored considerably higher on the average in achievement thinking than did professionals or specialists of comparable education and background. Take the two democratic countries shown there:

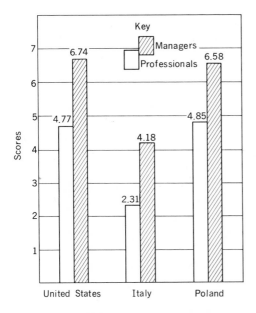

Exhibit I. Average *n* Achievement scores of managers and professionals in three countries.

In the United States the comparison was between matched pairs of unit managers and specialists of the same position level, age, educational background, and length of service in an electric appliance company. The managers spent more of their time in the test writing about achievement than the specialists did.

The same was true of middle-level executives from various companies in Italy when contrasted with students of law, medicine, and theology who were roughly of the same intelligence level and social background.

In other words it takes a concern for achievement to be a manager in a foreign country like Italy, for instance, just as it does in the United States. It is worth noting in passing, however, that the level of achievement thinking among Italian managers is significantly lower than it is among American managers—which, as will be shown later, quite probably has something to do with the lower level and rate of economic development in Italy.

What about a Communist country? The figures for Poland are interesting because (1) the level of concern for achievement is about what it is in the United States, and (2) even in businesses owned and operated by the state, as in Poland, managers tend to have a higher concern for achievement than do other professionals.

Another even more striking result, not shown in Exhibit I, is the fact that there is *no real difference* between the average *n* Achievement score of managers working for the U.S. government (9.3) and those in U.S. private business generally (8.90). Apparently, a manager working for the Bureau of Ships in the Department of the Navy spends as much time thinking about achievement as his counterpart in Ford or Sears, Roebuck; government service does not weaken his entrepreneurial spirit. Whether he is able to be as effective as he might be in private business is another matter, not touched on here.

Careful quantitative studies of the prevalence of achievement concern among various types of executives also yield results in line with what one would expect. Thus, sales managers score higher than other types of managers do.

In general, more successful managers tend to score higher than do less successful managers (except in government service where promotion depends more on seniority). The picture is clear in small companies, where the president tends to score higher than his associates. In large companies, the picture is a little more complicated. Men in the lowest salary brackets (earning less than $20,000 a year) definitely have the lowest average *n* Achievement scores, while those in the next bracket up ($20,000 to $25,000 a year) have the highest average *n* Achievement level. Apparently an achievement concern helps one get out of the ranks of the lowest paid into a higher income bracket. But from there on, the trend fades. Men in the highest income brackets have a somewhat lower average concern for achievement, and apparently turn their thoughts to less achievement-oriented concerns. Possibly, these men are doing well enough to relax a little.

Businessmen and Achievement

Businessmen usually raise either one of two questions at this point:

(1) "Where can I get this test for *n* Achievement? It sounds like a good way of picking young executives!"

(2) "Why is this concern for achievement specific to being a success as a business manager? What about other types of achievement? Why isn't the

entrepreneurial spirit necessary for success as an opera star, a preacher, a great teacher, or a great scientist?"

The answer to the first question, unfortunately, is simple: no practicable, marketable test for assessing achievement concern exists as yet. The method of measurement we have been using is too sensitive, too easily influenced by the social atmosphere surrounding the people who take the test, to give reliable individual results. Under carefully controlled conditions, it works adequately to distinguish large groups of people like managers versus professionals, but it is not yet useful for individual selection. What we have here is a theoretical, scientific "breakthrough," not a practicable working device.

The second question is harder to answer but it takes us further in the direction of understanding exactly what kind of a person it is who spends a lot of his time thinking about achievement. To begin with, the facts are clear: many important types of professionals (doctors, lawyers, priests, or research scientists) fail to score on the average as high as business executives, yet, clearly their work is in every sense as much of an achievement as the businessman's. How come?

Let us consider a particular case for a moment—that of the research scientist. Certainly his work represents an important achievement, for he is the one who often makes the breakthrough on which new technological and economic advances depend. Shouldn't he be thinking about defining a problem, doing a good job of solving it, getting help from experts, etc.?

Yet, when we tested a number of such scientists—including several outstanding Nobel prize winners—we found, somewhat to our surprise, that they were not unusually high in n Achievement but rather tended to be average. Then it occurred to us that having a very high concern for achievement might make a person unsuitable for being a research scientist. Why? Simply because in research a man must often work for what may become very long periods of time without any knowledge of how well he is doing. He may not even know if he is on the right track for as much as five or ten years. But a man with a high need for achievement likes to know quickly whether he is accomplishing anything and quite possibly would become frustrated by the lack of feedback in basic science as to whether he is getting anywhere. He would then more likely move into an area such as management where results are more tangible. On the other hand, the research scientist obviously needs *some* achievement concern, or he is not likely to want to engage in his occupation at all.

Characteristics of Achievers

Considerations like these focus attention on what there is about the job of being a business entrepreneur or executive that should make such a job peculiarly appropriate for a man with a high concern for achievement. Or, to put it the other way around, a person with high n Achievement has certain characteristics which enable him to work best in certain types of situations that are to his liking. An entrepreneurial job simply provides him with more opportunities for making use of his talents than do other jobs. Through careful empirical research, we know a great deal by now about the man with high *n* Achievement, and his characteristics do seem to fit him unusually well for being a business executive. Specifically:

1. *To begin with, he likes situations in which he takes personal responsibility for finding solutions to problems.* The reason is obvious. Otherwise, he could get little personal achievement satisfaction from the successful outcome. No gambler, he does not relish situations where the outcome depends not on his abilities and efforts but on chance or other factors beyond his control. For example:

Some business-school students in one study played a game in which they had to choose between two options, in each of which they had only one chance in three of succeeding. For one option they rolled a die and if it came up, say, a 1 or a 3 (out of six possibilities), they won. For the other option they had to work on a difficult business problem which they knew only one out of three people had been able to solve in the time allotted.

Under these conditions, the men with high *n* Achievement regularly chose to work on the business problem, even though they knew the odds of success were statistically the same as for rolling the die.

To men strong in achievement concern, the idea of winning by chance simply does not produce the same achievement satisfaction as winning by their own personal efforts. Obviously, such a concern for taking personal responsibility is useful in a business executive. He may not be faced very often with the alternative of rolling dice to determine the outcome of a decision, but there are many other ways open to avoid personal responsibility, such as passing the buck, or trying to get someone else (or a committee) to take the responsibility for getting something done.

The famed self-confidence of a good executive (which actually is related to high achievement motivation) is also involved here. He thinks it can be done if *he* takes responsibility, and very often he is right because he has spent so much time thinking about how to do it that he does it better.

2. *Another characteristic of a man with a strong achievement concern is his tendency to set moderate achievement goals and to take "calculated risks."* Again his strategy is well suited to his needs, for only by taking on moderately difficult tasks is he likely to get the achievement satisfaction he wants. If he takes on an easy or routine problem, he will succeed but get very little satisfaction out of his success. If he takes on an extremely difficult problem, he is unlikely to get any satisfaction because he will not succeed. In between these two extremes, he stands the best chance of maximizing his sense of personal achievement.

The point can be made with the children's game of ring toss, some variant of which we have tried out at all ages to see how a person with high *n* Achievement approaches it. To illustrate:

The child is told that he scores when he succeeds in throwing a ring over a peg on the floor, but that he can stand anywhere he pleases. Obviously, if he stands next to the peg, he can score a ringer every time; but if he stands a long distance away, he will hardly ever get a ringer.

The curious fact is that the children with high concern for achievement quite consistently stand at moderate distances from the peg where they are most apt to get achievement satisfaction (or, to be more precise, where the decreasing probability-of-success curve crosses the increasing satisfaction-from-success curve). The ones with low n Achievement, on the other hand, distribute their choices of where to stand quite randomly over the entire distance. In other words, people with high n Achievement prefer a situation were there is a challenge, where there is some real risk of not succeeding, but not so great a risk that they might not overcome it by their own efforts.

Again, such a characteristic would seem to suit men unusually well for the role of business entrepreneur. The businessman is always in a position of taking calculated risks, of deciding how difficult a given decision will be to carry out. If he is too safe and conservative, and refuses to innovate, to invest enough in research or product development or advertising, he is likely to lose out to a more aggressive competitor. On the other hand, if he invests too much or overextends himself, he is also likely to lose out. Clearly, then, the business executive should be a man with a high concern for achievement who is used to setting moderate goals for himself and calculating carefully how much he can do successfully.

Therefore, we waste our time feeling sorry for the entrepreneur whose constant complaints are that he is overworking, that he has more problems than he knows how to deal with, that he is doomed to ulcers because of overwork, and so on. The bald truth is that if he has high n Achievement, he loves all those challenges he complains about. In fact, a careful study might well show that he creates most of them for himself. He may talk about quitting business and living on his investments, but if he did, he might then *really* get ulcers. The state of mind of being a little overextended is precisely the one he seeks, since overcoming difficulties gives him achievement satisfaction. His real problem is that of keeping the difficulties from getting *too* big for him, which explains in part why he talks so much about them because it is a nagging problem for him to keep them at a level he can handle.

3. *The man who has a strong concern for achievement also wants concrete feedback as to how well he is doing.* Otherwise, how could he get any satisfaction out of what he had done? And business is almost unique in the amount of feedback it provides in the forms of sales, cost, production, and profit figures. It is really no accident that the symbol of the businessman in popular cartoons is a wall chart with a line on it going up or down. The businessman sooner or later knows how well he is doing; salesmen will often know their success from day to day. Furthermore, there is a concreteness in

the knowledge of results which is missing from the kind of feedback professionals get.

Take, for example, the teacher as a representative professional. His job is to transmit certain attitudes and certain kinds of information to his students. He does get some degree of feedback as to how well he has done his job, but results are fairly imprecise and hardly concrete. His students, colleagues, and even his college's administration may indicate that they like his teaching, but he still has no real evidence that his students have *learned* anything from him. Many of his students do well on examinations, but he knows from past experience that they will forget most of that in a year or two. If he has high *n* Achievement and is really concerned about whether he has done his job well, he must be satisfied with sketchy, occasional evidence that his former pupils did absorb some of his ideas and attitudes. More likely, however, he is not a person with high *n* Achievement and is quite satisfied with the affection and recognition that he gets for his work which gratify other needs that he has.

The case of the true entrepreneur is different. Suppose he is a book publisher. He gets a manuscript and together with his editors decides that it is worth publication. At time of issuance, everyone is satisfied that he is launching a worth-while product. But then something devastatingly concrete happens—something far more definite than ever happens to a teacher —namely, those monthly sales figures.

Obviously not everyone likes to work in situations where the feedback is so concrete. It can prove him right, but it also can prove him wrong. Oddly enough, the person with high *n* Achievement has a compelling interest to know whether he was right or wrong. He thrives and is happier in this type of situation than he is in the professional situation.

Two further examples from our research may make the point clearer. Boys with high *n* Achievement tend to be good with their hands, to like working in a shop or with mechanical or electrical gadgets. What characterizes such play again is the concrete feedback it provides as to how well a person is doing. If he wires up an electric circuit and then throws the switch, the light either goes on or it does not. Knowledge of results is direct, immediate, and concrete. Boys with high *n* Achievement like this kind of situation, and while some may go on to become engineers, others often go into business where they can continue getting this kind of concrete feedback.

IMPLICATIONS

How strong do you estimate your motivations toward achievement to be, judging from the descriptions in this selection? Do you find achievement motivation lessening in your peer group, as compared with that of your parents? What is your estimation of the strength of your motivation toward affiliation, your motivation toward some creative venture? In what respect is this selection like and unlike Selection 29, on the business executive?

REFERENCES

More studies of the achievement need and of other needs will be found in Atkinson (1958). For a somewhat detailed summary of the findings on achievement motivation, up to the date of publication, see Byrne (1966).

37 ACCIDENTS: CONTEMPORARY THEORIES OF SAFETY PSYCHOLOGY

Willard Kerr

You may have heard the phrase "accident proneness," a tendency for an individual to have repeated accidents in a given area of activity. How valid do you think this concept is? What are other psychological explanations of accidents? To what extent are unusual and distracting environmental stress associated with accident frequencies? Will the frequency of accidents be reduced by the kind of environment that allows the worker freedom to set attainable goals and rewards him for being alert?

The following selection considers various explanations of accidents and summarizes interesting facts on accidents and their correlates.

Background

PROBABLY THE MOST universally ignored area of safety psychology is that pertaining to the psychological climate of the workplace. A devotion to safety gadgets on the one hand and concern for the alleged proneness factors within the accident repeater on the other hand has led to the almost total neglect of the situational factors which help shape work

Reprinted· from Willard Kerr, "Contemporary Theories of Safety Psychology," *Journal of Social Psychology*, 45 (Provincetown: The Journal Press, 1957), pp. 3–9, with permission of the publisher and the author.

personality and help manufacture accident-free or accident-liable employees.

Many investigators (Van Zelst, 1954) have shown that becoming a safe worker is a typical learning function. The decline in accidents from date of employment in the typical job is a representative learning curve. But like other learning curves, the decline in error performance can be obstructed by a multitude of other factors. It now appears that *a chief obstruction to the rapid decline in error performance is defective psychological climate.** This conclusion, to be supported in this paper, stands in sharp contrast to past emphasis upon the accident proneness theory.

The Accident Proneness Theory

Before presenting the crucial evidence on this theory, the term "accident proneness" should be defined. *Accident proneness* is a constitutional (*i.e.,* permanent) tendency within the organism to engage in unsafe behavior within some stated field of vocational activity. A temporary tendency to have accidents is not proneness; it is liability. And proneness is not general; that is, its referrent to an activity field must be limited to be meaningful, for, obviously, *everyone* is "accident prone" in a general sense because there are potential tasks that no human being can perform without accident (*e.g.,* climb the outside walls of the Empire State Building to the top with one's bare hands).

Professors Mintz and Blum (1949) and Maritz (1950) have shown that the *accident proneness theory has been explaining entirely too much of the industrial accident rate.** The research of Cobb (1938–39), Johnson (1946) Whitlock and Crannell (1949), Forbes (1939), Farmer and Chambers (1929), and Harris (1949) point toward the same conclusion. Mintz and Blum showed that the frequency of "repeater" accidents approximates a pure chance (Poisson) distribution. Maritz then suggested that the final crucial test of variance in the industrial accident rate accounted for by proneness is the correlation between one's accidents experienced over two different periods of accident exposure—such as the last two years and the next two years. Ghiselli and Brown (1948) have collated eighteen such coefficients from the literature, and the present author has computed their median; it is .38. This typical value suggests that only about 15 per cent of the variance in individual accidents is accounted for by variance in individual accident proneness; furthermore, this even may be spuriously high because such coefficients are contaminated by the correlation of the worker's position hazard with the consistency of his accidents over split time periods. In fact, it is almost certain that much, if not most, of this 15 per cent of potential variance due to accident proneness actually is due to environ-

* Editor's italics.

mental factors (temperature differences, fumes, congestion-space-threat differences, etc.) left uncontrolled and hence correlated with each other in the eighteen coefficients cited.

Even allowing the unreasonable assumption that these eighteen coefficients were not influenced by fatigue and stress differences in different job locations, the 15 per cent of variance in accidents "accounted for" by proneness still leaves 85 per cent of the variance in accident rates unaccounted for.

It is interesting that an earlier study of automobile drivers by Forbes (1939) arrived independently at the similar conclusion that the accident *repeater contributes not more than three or four per cent to the accident problem.** Both Johnson (1946) and Thorndike (1951) who later surveyed the entire research literature on automobile safety likewise found that such constitutional factors as basic aptitudes yielded negligible relationships with accident records. Relevant, also, is the fact that Hunt, Wittson, and Burton (1950) computed the psychiatric discharge rate at Naval induction stations and subsequently during World War II to vary between 4 and 9 per cent (such dischargees were, of course, those individuals regarded as "prone" to behavior unsafe to themselves and/or their country).

Two situational or climatic theories may explain the remaining non-chance variance.

The Goals-Freedom-Alertness Theory

Plainly, both management and union training activities, policies, and leaderships are responsible for some interference with the normal decline of error performance.

In stating this theory now, we hold that *great freedom to set reasonably attainable goals is accompanied typically by high quality work performance.* This theory regards an accident merely as a low-quality work behavior—a "scrappage" that happens to a person instead of to a thing. Raising the level of quality involves raising the level of alertness; such high alertness cannot be sustained except within a rewarding psychological climate. The more rich, therefore, the climate in diverse (economic and noneconomic) reward opportunities, the higher the level of alertness—and the higher the level of work quality. Obviously, the rewards system must be geared to support high-quality work behavior.

In business practice some training interferes by too much "telling what to do and what not to do" and too little encouragement to the new worker to do his own thinking and "stand on his own feet." Union leadership likewise often is guilty of too much propagandizing and not enough "asking" in relations with new workers. Such initial climate for the new worker is

* Editor's italics.

less conducive to alertness than to a relatively unmotivated, resigned, passive conformity to the apparently already structured total situation.

Accidents, of course, show that the total situation is *not* firmly structured and from them the worker gradually accepts more self responsibility in order to survive. But an accident is an expensive teaching device. Furthermore, if it occurs in a climate in which the employee is expected to supply his energy but not his opinions or ideas, the accident is misunderstood as a foreign intruder which does not belong in the scheme of events. In such circumstances, it rarely occurs to management, union, or worker that an accident is made necessary and inevitable in order to teach the employee his own individuality and essential personal dignity.

Even the teaching efficiency of the accident itself is interfered with, however, if most aspects of the total psychological climate in effect deny that the individual's own mental content is important.

If the climate encourages the individual to set up long-term and short-term goals with reasonable probability of attainment, the *Gestalt* of the work situation seems less fixed and the worker feels himself to be a significant participant. Significant participation makes for habits of alertness, problem-raising, and problem-solving. The psychological work environment must *reward the worker emotionally for being alert,** for seeking to contribute constructive suggestions, for passing a tip to a co-worker on how best to do something or how not to get hurt, and for achievement out of the ordinary. The worker must feel free to exercise influence over his environment.

Considerable evidence supports this theory. Factory departments with more movement of personnel among departments, that is, intra-company transfer mobility, have fewer accidents (Kerr, 1950b), the same is true of departments with greater promotion probability for the typical employee (r is $-.40$). Departments with the best suggestion records (rewarded) tend to have fewer accidents. Additional evidence of the influence of the stimulating individual climate on safety is found in the tendency toward fewer accidents in individual-type than in crew-type jobs at the International Harvester Works (Keenan, *et al.*, 1951). In individual-type work, the employee rarely is uncertain about his responsibility for consequences; he better knows his immediate work goals. Another interesting bit of evidence is that in two different studies (Keenan, *et al.*, 1951; Kerr, 1950b) the factory departments with incentive pay systems, although problem departments in regards to monotony, lower job prestige, and lower promotion probability, still have no more accidents than departments without incentive pay systems. This seems in such defiance of expectations as to suggest that incentive pay systems restrict accidents by encouraging greater individual initiative and alertness.

* Editor's italics.

Accidents are more frequent in jobs of lower-rated prestige (Keenan, *et al.*, 1951; Kerr, 1950b); one interpretation of this finding is that climatically the job must seem worthy enough to the worker to sustain his euphoria level. This interpretation is supported by the finding of Hersey (1936) that out of 400 accidents which were studied clinically, more than half took place when the worker was in a worried, apprehensive, or some other low emotional state.

This individual goals-freedom-alertness theory suggests the climatic need for providing emotional reward opportunities for alertness—such as special economic incentives, prestige-building honors, extra privileges, machine and work space decoration contest participation, and representation on special committees and councils. These rewards held as attainable goals by workers in relatively "dead end" jobs should operate to raise the average level of alertness, not just to hazards but to everything.

The Adjustment Stress Theory

The individual goals-opportunity-alertness theory of safety seems to cover much of the variance not covered by the proneness theory, but some variance still remains and it appears necessary to verbalize a third theory. Probably almost all of the remaining variance can be explained by a third theory—*an adjustment stress theory. It holds that unusual, negative, distracting stress upon the organism increases its liability to accident or to other low-quality behavior.* This too is a climatic theory, because environment is internal as well as external, and this theory refers to distractive negative stresses imposed upon the individual organism either by internal environment (such as disease organisms, alcohol, or toxic items) or by external environment (such as temperature excesses, poor illumination, excessive noise level, excessive physical work strain). Its stresses are different from those experienced by the accident prone; their stresses result from a *constitutional* inadequacy. Ordinary adjustment stress is *not* the result of constitutional inadequacy but of temporary conditions.

What often appears at first to be constitutional accident proneness may be shown very clearly upon more careful examination to be the operation of *temporary* stress factors. The most sobering example of this is found in the curve of accident rates of successive age groups of industrial workers (Kerr, 1950b). This curve shows high rates in the first ten years of the worklife and a secondary increase in rates between the ages of forty and fifty-five. These age periods also are the great stress periods in the typical worklife; this is suggested by the fact that the accident-rate curve and the turnover-rate curve superimpose almost perfectly upon each other when plotted through successive age groups of the industrial population. The alleged proneness within the young accident repeater is largely dissipated when one considers that most of the stress is environmental—and associated with adjustment to work discipline, attaining self-sufficiency away from parental ties, courtship, marriage, assumption of family economic responsibilities, and the struggle for a foothold on a vocational ladder that seems to lead somewhere worthwhile. Another set of obvious stress explanations comes to mind to account for the "middle-age boom" in accident rate.

Temporary stress factors which already have been found significantly correlated with accident rates include employee age (Kerr, 1950b), workplace temperature (Griffith, 1950), illumination (Vernon, et al., 1931), mean rated comfort of the shop (r is $-.70$), degree of operational congestion, obvious danger factor threateningly present, manual effort involved in job (r is .47), weight of parts handled, frequency of parts handled (Keenan, et al., 1951), alcohol consumption (Vernon, 1937), and influence of disease organisms (Newbold, 1919).

Complementary Limitations and Interpretations

It seems wise to emphasize that both of these new theories of safety complement each other as well as existing proneness theory. In the goals-freedom-alertness theory it must be recognized that (a) even under an optimal opportunity climate, individuals who lack the characteristics necessary for the work probably will continue to have accidents; (b) excessive physical stresses can cause accidents in any psychological climate; and (c) psychological stresses relative to adjustment to changing life aspirations, family and marital affairs, etc., still will carry over into the workplace psychological climate and cause accidents.

In the adjustment stress theory it must be admitted that individual differences do exist in ability to withstand what ordinarily would be stress-inducing situations. Yet, such individual differences account for less than one fifth of the variance in individual accident rates; therefore, the limitations on the accident proneness theory appear to be much more severe than those on the adjustment stress theory. The fact is that both employer judgment and job applicant judgment operate to prevent the operation of any great amount of accident proneness. While all of us are accident prone for one task or another, we don't ordinarily apply for or allow ourselves to be engaged in such tasks—and we probably couldn't get hired for such tasks if we tried.

On the basis of the evidence summarized and the author's own estimates, the variance in accident rates among industrial personnel probably distributes in terms of theoretical causation according to the following pattern:

Accident proneness	1% to 15%
Individual goals-opportunity-alertness	30% to 40%
Adjustment stress	45% to 60%
Total Variance	100%

Constructive thinking about the individual goals-opportunity-climate and about adjustment stresses should assist industry to escape the defeatism of the overly emphasized proneness theory and better understand and control accidents.

IMPLICATIONS

How many accidents—even minor ones that have caused slight injury or little destruction of property—have you had in your life? Have they occurred under similar conditions? If so, describe these conditions. Do your accidents seem to be due to a constitutional proneness, an *accident liability* (a temporary tendency), or can you relate them to the psychological climate at the time of the accident?

What do the theories supported by the data presented in this article suggest to you regarding the prevention of accidents in your daily life? Can you suggest specific conditions that should prevail to lower accident frequency or prevent accidents?

REFERENCES

Consult the Bibliography for references cited in the article. See also Greenwood and Woods (1919), Kitson (1922), and McGuire (1955). See Fleishman (1967) and Maier (1965), two industrial psychology textbooks, to learn of other problems in industry and commerce that have been attacked by psychologists.

38 THE USE OF PSYCHOLOGISTS IN LEGAL PRACTICE

Robert S. Redmount

What specific contributions can the contemporary practicing or academic psychologist make to the legal profession? Psychologist Redmount is a member of the Connecticut Bar and is well acquainted with the scientific activities and professional background of a clinical and

Reproduced with the permission of the author and *The Practical Lawyer*, 101 North 33rd Street, Philadelphia, Pa. 19104. Subscription Rates: $10 a year, $2.00 a single issue. "The Use of Psychologists in Legal Practice" appeared in the February 1965 issue, Vol. 11, No. 2, pp. 23–38.

consultant psychologist. He has written the following article in a popular vein for his fellow lawyers, and in it he brings up the kinds of cases that they frequently encounter. He suggests how lawyers may use the resources of a psychologist to add to their cases reliable facts about individual behavior. Redmount is probably more enthusiastic about the value of psychological knowledge and techniques than some psychologists are; but he is intimately acquainted with the support that the expert's data and opinions lend to a lawyer and his client. He cites precedents for the use of certain procedures, and he presents the controversy and the court's decision on whether psychologists are independent experts in the area of mental disorder.

THE CREATIVE PRACTICE of law is a sensitive and resourceful blend that combines prudence in its reliance upon tested and established rules and procedures, and enterprise in its use of newer views and procedures that may prove attractive and highly effective. In the practice of law, one gauges the promise of newer methods and techniques in terms of their probable or proven ability to protect and conserve the interests of clients, to create advantage for a client because of the appeal of their added skill and reliability, and to clarify and afford more reliability on matters of notable uncertainty. They may demonstrate their value to the attorney in counseling with his client in the law office or to the court in its consideration of some litigable issue.

The increasing range of systematic skills, techniques, and information about human behavior held by the psychologist, some well established and recognized and others experimental in character, affords a fertile resource to be tapped by the creative attorney in his practice of law. Following are some possibilities, both tried and untried, that may benefit an attorney in his office practice and in the conduct of litigation.

Drafting Wills

Mr. Elder Crotchety, a client of strong passion and conviction, wishes to draft a will containing substantial devises and legacies that are highly partisan and unexpected. He knows that his designing sons will not approve and can be expected to contest the will on grounds of mental incompetence or undue influence. He wants his attorney to make the will, and the issue of competency or capacity, as ironclad as possible against destruction in court. He advises his attorney to leave no stone unturned in the exercise of effective preventive law procedures.

Attorney Sharp knows that mental incompetence and undue influence are legal concepts but that they assume some factual basis in judgments of human conduct. An attack on competency and capacity seeks to show poor operative intelligence and judgment, perhaps a lack of emotional stability verging on the abnormal, and possibly some distorted thinking and ideas.

Certification of Mental Competency

Gauged by professional standards and practices, among the most widely recognized and accepted individual psychological measures of intelligence (including within it denominators of alertness, comprehension, mental control, and social judgment) is the Wechsler Adult Intelligence Scale. The Rorschach Technique is a measure widely used to gauge emotional stability, and this, as well as the Thematic Apperception Test, is broadly used to assess distortion in, and the character of, thinking and ideas.

These assessment techniques have a history of decades of use in measuring mental and emotional capacities and dispositions in educational, military, medical, and other settings. Thousands of persons have been evaluated by these assessment techniques, which may be highly skillful and informative when they are utilized by competent and experienced psychologists.

Attorney Sharp might suggest to his client that, by taking a standard psychological examination in conjunction with the execution of his will, he may seek to certify his competency. Expert opinion may be offered and supported by measured facts and standards. The competence, relevancy, and probity of this timely expert certification may be strongly argued on the facts in a progressive court, albeit there is as yet a dearth of legal precedent and litigation on the procedure.

This evidence should be viewed as more probative than the later reconstruction and retroactive judgments of competency that are now utilized. The cost in time and expense is negligible where an estate has any substantial value.

Damages in Accident Cases

Mrs. Fairly Hirt was recently involved in an automobile accident involving the negligence of another driver. Mrs. Hirt claims that her head was injured in the accident, that she had headaches that have now subsided, but that she has suffered permanent brain injury affecting her capacity to work. She has memory lapses and has confusion and difficulty with mental control (e.g., in arithmetic problems) such as did not previously exist. She also claims that she wrenched her back and now has severe, intermittent low back pains and, as a consequence of the accident and injury, she suffers a perpetual nervous condition.

The defendant claims and seeks to prove that Mrs. Hirt was always an emotionally unstable person and given to passing aches and pains of minor intensity. Defendant also claims Mrs. Hirt simply has a poor memory and is poor in arithmetic. The defendant's position is that there is no brain injury.

Attorney Tortle, for the plaintiff, seeks to prove not only brain damage and resultant consequences because of the accident and injury, but also an increase in anxiety and emotional disturbance. He also wishes to establish a degree of pain such as would indicate the need for very substantial compensation on the matter of pain, as well as upon the issues of mental and emotional injury.

Examinations for Brain Injury

Attorney Tortle observed, during a period of military hospitalization when on wartime duty, that psychologists were used to assess whether cortical functions had been impaired in a manner that had come to be recognized as characteristic of brain-injured persons. Psychological examinations, consisting of standardized and clinical tests of intellectual functioning, memory, perceptual-motor skills, and the like, were utilized as supportive evidence. The same or similar psychological examinations were used—and now, with the benefit of extensive clinical experience, continue to be used regularly —to suggest whether there might be evidence indicative of brain injury and to verify or anticipate the findings of neurologists on this issue.

Examinations for Emotional Disorder

It is also well-established practice for psychologists to conduct standard psychological examinations of emotional disturbance and disorder, either as a part of, or independently from, psychiatric examinations on the matter. The Rorschach and Thematic Apperception Test techniques, along with other techniques and measures, are widely used to give evidence of emotional instability and of the patterns of conduct that may result, and evidence of changes in emotional status and the like.

Measurement of Pain

The measurement of pain is a somewhat more uncertain, and consequently not a standard, psychological procedure. However, techniques that have been subjected to experimental verification have been developed and have been used by psychologists for this purpose. Generally, the psychologist's clinical examinations of a person require perhaps the greater part of a day, and then some additional hours are needed to evaluate the data and to prepare a report.

Competence of Psychologist to Testify

Attorney Tortle also has the benefit of favorable legal precedent to use the qualified psychologist and his proper examinations, not yet so much to assess pain, but more particularly to assess mental and emotional disturbance and abnormality. Psychologists in increasing numbers of cases have testified on such matters. The issue of the psychologist's competence to do so has been litigated in recent years consistently in the psychologist's favor.

The issue of the psychologist's competence and qualification to render expert testimony in the field of mental disturbances and disorders was thoroughly litigated in *Jenkins* v. *United States*, 307 F.2d 637 (D.C. Cir. 1962). The court sat en banc to consider the issue raised by virtue of the fact that the psychologist's professional opinions were excluded in the case by the trial court on grounds that the psychologist was incompetent to testify as an expert in the matter.

A brief as amicus curiae was submitted by the American Psychological Association. It argued that psychology, a learned profession with a considerable history and tradition, provides systematic training and occupational experience in the assessment of behavior and behavior disorders, that the profession of psychology is controlled and guided by ethical standards and certification practices, and that properly qualified psychologists are, indeed, expert in the field of mental disorder.

A brief as amicus curiae was also submitted by the American Psychiatric Association in opposition to this argument. This brief argued that mental disturbances and disorders are exclusively within the medical province, that psychiatrists are the only established medical experts on the matter, that psychological examinations and results are a part of the psychiatric examination to be evaluated by psychiatrists, but that they do not have independent standing and psychologists are not independent experts on the matter of mental disorder.

The court, in a 7–2 opinion, upheld the view that psychologists are independent experts in matters relating to the existence and effects of mental disorder and that the failure to allow the opinion of qualified psychologists on this issue is reversible error.

This holding is in line with the strong preponderance of decisions on the matter. See *Hidden* v. *Mutual Life Ins. Co.*, 217 F.2d 818, 821 (4th Cir. 1954); *Watson* v. *State*, 273 S.W.2d 879 (Tex. Crim. 1954); *Carter* v. *Oklahoma*, 376 P.2d 351 (Okla. Crim. 1962); *People* v. *Hawthorne*, 293 Mich. 15, 291 N.W. 205 (1940) (dictum); *State* v. *Padilla*, 66 N.M. 289, 347 P.2d 312 (1959) (dictum).

While these holdings have mostly to do with criminal matters, where mental disturbance or disorder comes up in connection with the issue of insanity, the psychological issues and evaluations in mental disturbance or disorder in tort matters are very similar and sometimes identical.

Testimonial Reliability

Attorney H.E. Wonders is interviewing a prospective witness in his office, on behalf of a client. The witness, Pete Soshur, asserts unequivocally that he saw Mr. Panicki, and no other, behind the wheel of the car that brushed the plaintiff, knocked him down, and then sped off. If true, then Attorney Wonders feels he has an airtight case against Mr. Panicki on the matter of accident liability.

But, what if Mr. Soshur is not accurate in his identification and ultimately is proved to be lacking in credibility? Attorney Wonders' interview with Mr. Soshur is not entirely reassuring on this matter. He feels, too, that, since the matter of liability may well rest on Mr. Soshur's credibility, the judge, as the only trier in the case, is going to be strongly influenced by impressions and evidence relating to Soshur's ability to make accurate identification.

Testing Ability to Identify or Estimate

The ability to make correct identifications and estimations of physical reality (as in gauging distance, speed, color, and size) is measurable by psychologists using precise scientific procedures. While there are few widely used, standardized tests for these purposes, a psychologist can use brief, objective laboratory procedures to judge the reliability or consistency of a person's identification or estimation abilities, and he may compare one person's performance to that of others so as to get some judgment of relative capability.

Admittedly, at this point, this would require some creative interest and skill on the part of a psychologist, but these procedures can be developed for forensic purposes. The value of this kind of evidence is likely to be in the objective, scientific judgment procedure, with probative value in the findings.

There is little or no tradition for the legal use of such evidence, but it may well appeal to an attorney or a court as having value, at least as a check upon impressionistic judgments of credibility. It may appeal as an addition to courtroom examination techniques and findings that determine credibility mostly by inference from logical inconsistencies or from approximately related observational oversight.

The laboratory procedures involved, particularly once they are developed, can be brief and inexpensive. In such circumstances, Attorney Wonders might feel the expenditure involved would be well worth-while if he had some greater assurance about witness Soshur's capabilities to make identification and, in addition, could present some objective evidence on this matter in court. The psychologist, being well-trained in precise experimental methods and in the assessment of behavior, would be quite competent to develop examining procedures and to make such appraisals.

Trademark Cases

The Pepsicoke Bottling Company has fixed itself in public consciousness with its famous trademark "Pepsicoke 8" and the distinctive sign "P" enveloped by an 8.

A new competitor, the Pepticole Bottlers, Inc., has recently entered the market with its product. "Pepticole ∞" and the distinctive sign "P" enveloped by the sideways 8.

Pepsicoke, fearing the damage to its markets and public name, claims a trademark infringement and brings action against Pepticole Bottlers. The attorney for Pepsicoke seeks to establish, as an important element in his case, that the trademarks "Pepsicoke 8" and "Pepticole ∞" are confused by the public, and that the public assumes that "Pepticole ∞" is really "Pepsicoke 8."

Measurement of Associations

The psychologist, as a trained experimenter on matters of human conduct, can develop brief, simple, timed-exposure association experiments and carefully designed inquiries to compare reactions to "Pepsicoke 8" and "Pepticole ∞." This scientific evidence, based on a substantial and representative consumer sample, is likely to be of considerable probative value and may create a strong impression.

Such scientific experimentation, though brief for individual subjects, may involve some time and cost because of the desirability of having a good sample of consumer reactions. However, sampling may vary in scope, depending upon how virtually conclusive one requires or desires the experimental evidence to be. If the damages sought and the prospect of winning (with good evidence) are substantial, the time and expenditure for carefully conducted experiments relating to trademark infringements may be well spent.

Precedent has existed for the use of psychologists and their skills in trademark litigation since the case of *Coca-Cola Co.* v. *Chero-Cola Co.*, 273 Fed. 755 (D.C. Cir. 1921). In this case, psychological tests and experiments were used and testimony regarding these was received, but the testimony was not placed in issue or commented upon.

Domestic Relations Problems

Cyrus D. Kingman, an old friend and client of Attorney Foster Corplaw, is involved in a domestic dispute with his wife, and they have decided to seek a divorce. Attorney Corplaw, who has been asked to handle the matter, feels rather uncomfortable about it. His law firm does not handle divorce cases as a general rule, but he would like to help his old friend, Cyrus Kingman. He has known Cyrus and Beth Kingman for a long time and would like to see them stay together.

He wonders if divorce is necessary and if there are possibilities for reconciliation. On the other hand, he does not want to advise the Kingmans to seek reconciliation if this is likely to prove a rather involved and fruitless process. He wonders, too, how to advise them concerning custody of their two children if they should seek a divorce. He does not want to be unjust or insensitive to either spouse or to the needs of the children. He has some ideas of his own about the problems but knows that he does not have the degree of expert skill and knowledge that would be most penetrating in assessing the situation.

Advice on Marital Problems

Problems of family relations and child development have long been a familiar area of study for psychologists. In recent years, an increasing number of clinically trained psychologists have provided services as family relations and child development specialists. Some psychologists provide services as marriage counselors. Their functions are diagnostic, providing assessments and recommendations. They are also corrective, providing counseling and therapeutic services.

Attorney Corplaw might enlist the brief consultation of a psychologist who has special skills and sensitivities for marital problems. Such a person might meet with the Kingmans and, in the process of interview and examination, develop reliable judgment about the problems of the marriage, the prospects for conciliation, and desirable adjustments in the event of divorce. The Kingmans' involvement with a psychologist for this purpose would be brief and comparatively inexpensive. Attorney Corplaw would have a firmer basis from which to make further recommendations and to take further action with the Kingmans.

Family Affairs

Jeremiah Harwork and his wife Jenny are thinking of retiring. Through industry and frugality over thirty-five years, they have built up a prosperous business and a tidy nest egg. Jeremiah would like to perpetuate the Harwork Company in the Harwork family, but he is not sure how to go about it.

He would like to turn the business over to his son, Buzzy, but he doubts that Buzzy has the stability and the wisdom to oversee the business properly. He also has a daughter, Dolores, who appears to be rather unstable. He is not sure whether he should make provision for her care and guardianship in any disposition he makes, or whether he can count on her to be self-sustaining and a source of strength in protecting and preserving the Harwork interests.

Mr. and Mrs. Harwork differ in their view of the problem. Mr. Harwork feels some sort of a trust arrangement is desirable or that the interests should be assigned to other reliable management within the Harwork family. Mrs. Harwork wishes to make an outright assignment of the interests to the children, since she is confident they are perfectly capable of managing their affairs prudently. The Harworks have never agreed in their assessment of their children.

Furthermore, Mrs. Harwork is fearful that her husband really intends to convey the Harwork Company to a favorite brother of his, with the brother to offer assurances of a place for Buzzy and Dolores in the organization. Mrs. Harwork does not have confidence that her husband's brother would, as a practical matter, abide by any such understanding.

The Harworks have decided to place the matter in the hands of their trusted advisor, Attorney Solomon Pater, and they seek his advice as to the best course of action.

Attorney Pater, from his familiarity with the Harworks, is convinced that neither will be satisfied unless each can feel that the attorney is on his side and will be partial to his point of view. They both seek vindication, notably concerning their disparate views of the children, as much as they seek a solution. Neither is inclined toward a compromise or an experimental approach, since each is adamant in his need for full approval of his viewpoint.

Advice on Family Relationships

Attorney Pater is faced with a delicate situation involving many psychological factors. There is obviously hostility and suspicion between the Harworks where their children are concerned. It is perhaps desirable or necessary that the Harworks deal, at least briefly, with the psychological problem of their mutual feelings and their individual relationship with their children as a basis for better understanding and agreement.

From an astute professional point of view, it would also be important to know how deep-seated and sustaining are Buzzy's limitations. How unstable and perhaps mentally ill is the daughter, Dolores? In fact, a clinically trained and experienced psychologist can be called upon to deal with such problems, to offer tactful assistance and clarification through conferences with the Harworks and evaluation of their children.

This becomes an instrument for the clarification of problems as an adjunct to effective legal consultation and services. The discharge of tensions and uncertainties of a psychological nature might well be worthwhile to the Harworks. Attorney Pater would be in a position to develop a legal solution to the Harworks' family-business problems that would be acceptable.

Standards of Conduct

In a suit against T-Am Airlines and Jason Service, Mrs. Dora Fright alleges that she was assaulted in flight by Mr. Service, acting in his capacity as a steward for the airline, and that T-Am was negligent in hiring Service for a position as steward. She claims that she suffered physical and mental anguish when she was assaulted by Mr. Service, that she is now permanently fearful of flying and this seriously handicaps her because of the travel requirements in her business, and that she suffers, in consequence of the assault, a permanent nervous condition.

The stipulated facts are that Mrs. Fright was enplaned along with other passengers on a T-Am flight from Chicago to San Francisco. At a certain point in the flight, passengers were cautioned that they were about to experience a good deal of bumpiness and discomfort.

During this period of fairly severe bumpiness, Mrs. Fright became hysterical. She began to cry and to moan. Then she became more upset and started to shriek and threatened to run up the aisle. She panicked, shouted that the plane was going to crash and that she was going to die, and she threatened to jump out of the plane.

Mr. Service, the steward, observing Mrs. Fright was hysterical and in a state of panic, and that, on this account, other passengers were becoming more upset and fearful, slapped Mrs. Fright in the face and told her very sternly to be quiet. Mrs. Fright, who was on the edge of her seat at the time, fell back into her seat sharply but without apparent injury, and her panic subsided. Shortly thereafter, the plane emerged from the area of turbulence, and the flight was continued and completed without further event.

Mr. Service and T-Am claim that Mr. Service's conduct was reasonable and proper under the circumstances, that he was rendering first aid, and that no assault is involved. Mrs. Fright argues that it was unnecessary for Mr. Service to strike her and this constituted a wanton act, that, had she been left alone, her momentary fears would have subsided, and that it was known and announced that the period of air turbulence would be brief.

A principal point in the litigation is whether Mr. Service did, in fact, act in the manner of a reasonable man and properly as a steward under the circumstances. The defendants risk considerable loss, in reputation and in monetary damages, should Mrs. Fright win her case or should there be a substantial settlement in her favor.

Attitude and Behavior Sampling

In view of the circumstances, Attorney Dilgent, for the defendants, desires to make the reasonable-man issue as airtight in his clients' favor as he possibly can. The services of a psychologist would be helpful in properly framing the issue and in conducting a brief systematic survey of opinion of a comparatively small, select sample of psychologists and psychiatrists familiar with hysterical conduct, of lay or random or average persons, and of stewards of T-Am and other airlines.

Courts and jury are still free to infer as they will about the proper expectation of a reasonable man, but carefully developed, systematic information on the matter, scientifically acquired by experts such as psychologists, is at least strong evidence.

The problem of legal admissibility of survey evidence would appear to rest more on the issue of proper and careful sample selection and sampling techniques (probity) than on the objection that evidence of this kind is hearsay (competency). It does not appear that survey techniques and information have been used as evidence relating to conduct of the reasonable man. They have been offered in evidence, however, on matters relating to trade practices. Some of the issues regarding the admissibility of survey evidence have been raised and litigated in *United States v. Aluminum Co. of America*, 35 F. Supp. 820 (S.D. N.Y. 1940) and *United States v. E.I. duPont de Nemours & Co.*, 177 F. Supp. 1 (N.D. Ill. 1959).

Since this assessment is brief in scope and does not entail large or broad sample surveying, the expense in the acquisition of this information is not likely to be excessive or prohibitive for use in litigation. The positions of T-Am and Mr. Service may be substantially supported by such evidence.

Competency Hearings and Insanity Pleas

The parents of Johnnie Malhom have retained Attorney David Goliath to defend their son against a charge of homicide. Johnnie, an excitable and sometimes morose young man, has killed his girl friend's father in a fit of rage.

Clinical Examination of Mental Status

Attorney Goliath has decided upon insanity as his best line of defense. He already has a psychiatric expert witness who will testify to the insanity of his client. He may well be able to fortify his case if he also utilizes a clinical psychologist and the specialized examination conducted by this expert as further, independent evidence.

Clinical psychologists conduct standard psychological examinations, consisting of the Rorschach, Thematic Apperception Test, and other techniques to determine the nature and extent of mental and emotional disorders in individuals. Substantial precedent exists for the acceptance and use of such testimony where the issue of insanity arises in criminal litigation. The psychologist's role as an expert witness on this matter has been upheld against challenge. See *Jenkins v. United States*, 307 F.2d 637 (D.C. Cir. 1962); *Carter v. Oklahoma*, 376 P.2d 351 (Okla. Crim. 1962); *Watson v. State*, 273 S.W.2d 879 (Tex. Crim. 1954); *People v. Hawthorne*, 293 Mich. 15, 291 N.W. 205 (1940) (dictum); *State v. Padilla*, 66 N.M. 289, 347 P.2d 312 (1959) (dictum).

Attorney Goliath might create a stronger impression in behalf of his client if he were to utilize a range of expert opinion, perhaps consisting of the testimony of a psychiatrist, or two psychiatrists, and a clinical psychologist.

Behavior Tendencies

Mrs. Ruth Iluck has brought suit against the Double Stamp Department Store, claiming serious injury as a result of the defendant's negligence in permitting obstructions in passageways. Mrs. Iluck's attorney, Louis Dessein, expects the defendant to make a strong argument of the facts that Mrs. Iluck had a slight accident in the same store a year before, that she had an automobile accident three years previously, and that she had had other occasional accidental injuries. Defendants seek to avoid liability in part by establishing that Mrs. Iluck is accident prone.

The existence or clear nonexistence of specific behavior tendencies and character dispositions are difficult matters to measure. At best, they are inferred, usually from a heuristic combination of prior acts and behavior that seem to be encompassed by a certain kind of notion or judgment, e.g., that John Doe has the character disposition to be dishonest.

Assessment of Accident Proneness

Psychologists, in their research use of a variety of personality measures, have sought to establish by psychological criteria the syndrome of accident proneness. Though findings are not conclusive as to the existence or measurement of such a syndrome, there is psychological evidence and opinion on the matter.

Attorney Dessein may effectively counter the Department Store's line of defense by presenting a psychologist as an expert witness to give evidence as to the scientific status, or lack of status, of the concept of accident proneness. He may have his client take a pertinent psychological examination of personality and, from expert testimony as to the results, perhaps establish that his client is not accident prone according to the best criteria available from scientific studies of the matter.

This evidence may be admissible, if only because it is based on systematic study of the issue and, to state the matter conservatively, is at least as valuable as the highly impressionistic data and judgments about behavior tendencies that are now permitted in testimony.

Personality Injury in Personal Rights and Custody Cases

Mrs. Adolph Prusse seeks to protect her daughter, eight-year-old Penny, from the influence of her ex-husband. She alleges his conduct is detrimental to the welfare of the child. She has petitioned to have visitation rights denied Penny's father on the ground that his sustained efforts to provide the child with sex education are immoral, unhealthy, and can cause permanent damage to her personality.

Mr. Prusse has made it a practice during Penny's authorized visits to him to show her pictures of nudes and to explain sexual relations to her. He has encouraged her nudity and has made it a point to have her see him nude when they arise in the morning and when he is in the bathroom. Mr. Prusse is adamant in his belief that such conduct is desirable and necessary so that Penny will have a full and accurate understanding of sex early in life. He argues that, as a result, she will benefit in that she will not be confused, hurt, or offended by sexual contact and experience when she becomes older.

Studies of Personality Development

Attorney Wright, counsel for Mrs. Prusse, is aware of a considerable body of psychological findings, knowledge, and opinion resulting from clinical and experimental investigations of child development. To support his client's position, he may call upon a qualified psychologist to provide expert testimony on professional information and opinion about the effects of different sex information practices, rendered at different ages, upon the personality development of a child.

Attorney Justin, representing Mr. Prusse in opposition to the petition, seeks to probe another factual issue in the case. To offset the effects of expert testimony, however limited, in favor of Mrs. Prusse, he might introduce psychological expert testimony of another sort. From a knowledgeable analysis of the existing body of psychological findings and opinion, he can present evidence showing the effect upon personality development when a child loses or is denied contact with a male parent.

Expert knowledge and testimony is unlikely to be conclusive. However, it may be sought and valued by the trial court as another and substantial course of information to aid in arriving at a difficult decision on a complicated and not altogether familiar matter.

Business Organization and Management

Mr. J. Small Tycoon, a man in his early sixties, has decided to retire from active management of his corporate business. At the same time, he wishes to retain substantial control and to be assured that the enterprise will continue to be well managed and profitable. His stock holdings in the corporation represent a very substantial part of his wealth and he does not wish to see their value jeopardized. Mr. Tycoon meets with his attorney, Learned Wise, to seek his advice on some workable arrangements for the transfer of management and the granting of some minority control in the corporation to others who would carry on an active interest.

One possibility that has occurred to Mr. Tycoon is that he could vest some interest in, and give over managerial control to, some of his trusted long-time lieutenants. Mr. J.T. Figures, the comptroller, has an excellent grasp of the financial end of the business. He, perhaps, could be the new president, but he is a mild-mannered person who may have difficulty in being strong enough in the position to assert effective authority. Mr. Jonas Kitteridge is a whiz at technical development and knows how to get new products into production, but he lacks the breadth of knowledge or interest for over-all company direction. Swifton Rockett, the marketing manager, is a dynamo at marketing, but he is likely to run a loose, one-man show.

Mr. Tycoon has kept a firm hand on the corporate wheel, enabling these and other rather different personalities to jell as a unit. He is afraid that if he transferred to each of the aforenamed managers a 10-per-cent interest in the corporation and gave each top managerial responsibility, with one as the over-all leader, much bickering, rivalry, and inefficiency would develop.

He wonders if there is some way to organize management so as to capitalize on the strengths of his men and, at the same time, contain their liabilities. Mr. Tycoon feels that, since Attorney Wise is not only corporate counsel but also secretary to the corporation, he might have some valuable suggestions as to how to combine the legal and business solutions to his client's retirement problem.

Mr. Tycoon has also been informally negotiating for the purchase of a successful smaller company in the same line of business. This company is run by a very capable energetic younger man, Sylvester Bright, who appears to have the talent for making a success of corporate ventures. Mr. Tycoon is also considering Mr. Bright as the new president of the Tycoon Corporation, and this enters into his mind as he negotiates with Mr. Bright. However, he wonders if Mr. Bright would work well with Tycoon's trusted top lieutenants, whom he would like to retain. The question also arises of the kind of stock split that would be most desirable under such a management arrangement.

It is also possible that Mr. Bright's company could be merged with Mr. Tycoon's organization, or it could be retained as a wholly owned but independently managed subsidiary. Which arrangement would be most feasible would depend in part on the kind of personnel organization and working relationships that could be developed between the key personnel of the two companies.

Personnel Appraisal

A function that is well established and widely recognized for some psychologists is the psychological assessment of personnel and the resolution of management organization problems using professional evaluation techniques and insights. Mr. Wise might be particularly helpful to his client, Mr. Tycoon, if he were to suggest personnel appraisal and consultation with a competent psychologist on the complex human relations problems presented in Mr. Tycoon's alternatives for arranging his personal retirement. The expert information and assessment is an adjunct to the legal consultation. It can be both helpful and reassuring to client Tycoon and attorney Wise as a basis for designing and executing the specific legal arrangements that would best carry out Mr. Tycoon's intent.

Statistical Probabilities in Behavior

Mr. Frank Devoir, a defendant in a serious automobile accident involving large damage claims, is accused of wantonly reckless driving, which appears as the initial cause of the accident. It is alleged that this defendant, traveling at a high rate of speed, flagrantly and with wanton disregard ignored a stop sign and improperly entered a highway intersection. In consequence, the plaintiff, who had the right-of-way but was a short distance from the intersection, applied his brakes quickly, came to a sudden halt, and was severely damaged and permanently injured by another car that did not or could not stop and hit him from the rear.

Mr. Devoir seeks to mitigate, if not completely to avoid liability, by proving that it was virtually impossible for him to see the stop sign under the circumstances. Firstly, there was a black car some distance ahead consistently traveling in his lane and directly toward him, and this occupied his attention. Secondly, his attention was also drawn to the cars, including the plaintiff's, coming up quickly from the left, and he assumed they would slow down for him. Thirdly, he was traveling into a setting sun with a yellowish glow and could not readily see the yellow stop sign with this background and other distractions. Fourthly, he was initially traveling fast, but not an improper rate of speed, and this gave him less than five seconds in which to see all the relevant elements, including the stop sign, and come to a stop.

Perceptual Capability. The defendant's argument here rests on a number of psychological assumptions and on the probabilities of certain behavior occurrences given certain circumstances. For instance, if a large background (sun and horizon) and a small object in front of it (stop sign) are of nearly the same (yellow) color, how many seconds will it take to see the small object from some distance away, with or without distractions? If a large moving object is directly in front, at what distance and in what length of time can an observer note a small stationary object (stop sign) in front of him? If a person is given five seconds to notice several objects varying in movement, color, and position, and perhaps importance, which will he observe and which will he omit? Since there is some variation among the reactions of different persons, the answers to each of these questions, pertinent to the defendant's case, may be expressed in terms of the statistical probability that a person would or would not perceive or act in a certain way.

The defendant's attorney might help his cause if he called a qualified psychologist to advise, and perhaps testify, as to the relevant scientific information in psychology that would throw light upon or answer the questions concerning the statistical probabilities or possibilities in personal conduct. Perception and perceptual capability is, and has been, a major area of experimentation for psychologists for many years. Many findings have been accumulated, and some may be relevant to the problems and issues presented in the defendant's case.

The Professional Qualifications and Choice of a Psychologist

Psychology, though an older science, is an emergent profession. There are over 20,000 members of the American Psychological Association, an organization founded in 1892 and the only national organization representing the discipline of psychology.

Today, every state has a state psychological organization affiliated with the American Psychological Association. Fifty-three per cent of the states have certification or licensing laws relating to the practice of psychology before the public. Thirty-nine per cent of the states have nonstatutory regulatory bodies, usually associated with the state psychological organization.

Qualified psychologists may be distinguished not only by certification but also by their specialized interests and competences. The national organization has some twenty different divisions. Among professional practitioners there are, notably, clinical psychologists, industrial psychologists, experimental psychologists, marriage counselors and child development specialists, educational and school psychologists, counseling psychologists, and social psychologists. Some psychologists can develop and are proficient in varying combination of skills and problems and are equipped to deal with a variety of the problems with which an attorney is concerned.

Conclusion

Psychologists, for the most part, have little practical experience with attorneys and with the legal context. Some have served as expert witnesses, and others may have been approached or consulted more informally by attorneys. There are differences in training, interest, attitude, and temperament among psychologists, as there are among attorneys. Likely, factors of personal adjustment, involving matters of attitude and temperament, between a particular attorney and psychologist will determine whether natural professional barriers and biases can be overcome, and whether the psychologist, his skills and his knowledge, can be successfully utilized by the attorney.

IMPLICATIONS

What bodies of psychological knowledge and techniques mentioned by lawyer-psychologist Redmount are unknown to you? Did any ideas of how other psychological facts and methods might be used occur to you as you read this article? The psychologist who has a scientific orientation is likely to be extremely cautious about generalizations and is reluctant to indulge in dogmatic statements. Do you anticipate that his orientation may vary somewhat from that of the attorney who usually feels that he must have an airtight case and looks for clear-cut distinctions, such as sane or insane, competent or incompetent, innocent or guilty, rather than for the continuous gradations and indistinct lines between various increments of human behavior?

REFERENCES

For a modern, thorough review of suggestions concerning the psychologist and the law, see Anastasi (1964). The interest of psychologists in this area of conduct is longstanding. In 1908, Munsterberg published a book entitled *On the Witness Stand*. In the 1930s, there appeared volumes by Burtt (1931) and Robinson (1935); currently, there are entire books devoted to psychological aspects of the law: Dudycha (1955) and Toch (1961). In addition, there are journal articles by Schofield (1956), McCary (1960), and Hoch and Darley (1962).

39 BRAINWASHING—SOCIAL PSYCHOLOGICAL FACTORS

Edgar H. Schein

Can we explain why some Americans during the Korean conflict collaborated with the enemy? Schein, a psychiatrist who extensively interviewed repatriates returning to the United States, presents in this selection the *social psychological factors* in brainwashing. He discusses its social aspects, since the Chinese seemed to emphasize control over groups rather than individuals.

IN THIS PAPER I will outline some of the constellations of stress which prisoners of war faced during the Korean conflict, and describe some of the reaction patterns to these stresses. Rather than presenting a complete catalogue of their experiences (Schein, 1956), I

Reprinted from Edgar H. Schein, "Reaction Patterns to Severe, Chronic Stress in American Army Prisoners of War of the Chinese," *Journal of Social Issues*, Vol. 13 (Washington, D.C.: The Society for the Study of Social Issues, 1957), pp. 21–30, by permission of the publisher and the author.

have selected those aspects which seem to me to throw some light on the problem of collaboration with the enemy. I will give particular emphasis to the *social* psychological factors, because the Chinese approach to treatment of prisoners seemed to emphasize control over groups, rather than individuals.

My material is based on a variety of sources. I was in Korea during the repatriation, and had the opportunity to interview extensively twenty unselected repatriates. This basic material was supplemented by the information gathered by three psychiatrists, Drs. Harvey Strassman, Patrick Israel, and Clinton Tempereau, who together had seen some 300 men. On board ship returning to the United States, I also had the opportunity to sit in on bull sessions among repatriates in which many of the prison experiences were discussed. Additional details were obtained from the army dossiers on the men.

The typical experience of the prisoner of war must be divided into two broad phases. The first phase lasted anywhere from one to six months, beginning with capture, followed by exhausting marches to the north of Korea and severe privation in inadequately equipped temporary camps, terminating in assignment to a permanent prisoner of war camp.

The second phase, lasting two or more years, was marked by chronic pressures to collaborate and to give up existing group loyalties in favor of new ones. Thus, while physical stresses had been outstanding in the first six months, psychological stresses were outstanding in this second period.

The reactions of the men toward capture were influenced by their *over-all attitude toward the Korean situation.** Many of them felt inadequately prepared, both physically and psychologically. The physical training, equipment, and rotation system all came in for retrospective criticism, though this response might have been merely a rationalization for being captured. When the Chinese entered the war, they penetrated into rear areas, where they captured many men who were taken completely by surprise. The men felt that when positions were overrun, *their leadership was often less than adequate.** Thus, many men were disposed to blame the UN command for the unfortunate event of being captured.

On the psychological side, the men were not clearly aware of what they were fighting for or what kind of enemy they were opposing. In addition, the reports of the atrocities committed by the North Koreans led most men to expect death, torture, or nonrepatriation if captured.

It was in such a context that the soldier found his Chinese captor extending his hand in a friendly gesture and saying "Welcome" or "Congratulations, you've been *liberated*." This Chinese tactic was part of their "lenient policy" which was explained to groups of prisoners shortly after

* Editor's italics.

capture in these terms: because the UN had entered the war illegally and was an aggressor, all UN military personnel were in fact war criminals, and *could* be shot summarily. But the average soldier was, after all, only carrying out orders for his leaders who were the real criminals. Therefore, the Chinese soldier would consider the POW a "student," and would teach him the "truth" about the war. Anyone who did not cooperate by going to school and by learning voluntarily could be reverted to his "war criminal" status and shot, particularly if a confession of "criminal" deeds could be obtained from him.

In the weeks following capture, the men were collected in large groups and marched north. From a physical point of view, *the stresses during these marches were very severe:* * there was no medicine for the wounded, the food was unpalatable and insufficient, especially by our standards, clothing was scarce in the face of severe winter weather, and shelter was inadequate and overcrowded. The Chinese set a severe pace and showed little consideration for weariness that was the product of wounds, diarrhea, and frostbite. Men who were not able to keep up were abandoned unless they were helped by their fellows. The men marched only at night and were kept under cover during the day, ostensibly as protection against strafing by our own planes.

From a psychological point of view, this situation is best described as *a recurring cycle of fear, relief, and new fear.* * The men were afraid that they might die, that they might never be repatriated, that they might never again have a chance to communicate with the outside, and that no one even knew they were alive. The Chinese, on the other hand, were reassuring and promised that the men would be repatriated soon, that conditions would improve, and that they would soon be permitted to communicate with the outside.

One of the chief problems for the men was the *disorganization within the group itself.* * It was difficult to maintain close group ties if one was competing with others for the essentials of life, and if one spent one's resting time in overcrowded huts among others who had severe diarrhea and were occasionally incontinent. Lines of authority often broke down, and with this, group cohesion and morale suffered. A few men attempted to escape, but they were usually recaptured in a short time and returned to the group. The Chinese also fostered low morale and the feeling of being abandoned by systematically reporting false news about United Nations defeats and losses.

In this situation, goals became increasingly short-run. As long as the men were marching, they had something to do and could look forward to relief from the harsh conditions of the march. However, arrival at a temporary camp was usually a severe disappointment. Not only were physical condi-

* Editor's italics.

tions as bad as ever, but the sedentary life in overcrowded quarters produced more disease and still lower morale.

What happened to the men under these conditions? During the one- to two-week marches, they became increasingly apathetic.[1] They developed a slow, plodding gait, called by one man a "prisoners' shuffle." Uppermost in their minds were fantasies of food: men remembered all the good meals they had ever had, or planned detailed menus for years into the future. To a lesser extent, they thought of loved ones at home, and about cars which seemed to them to symbolize freedom and the return home.

In the temporary camps, disease and exposure took a heavy toll in lives. But it was the feeling of many men, including some of the doctors who survived the experience, that some of these deaths were not warranted by a man's physical condition. Instead, what appeared to happen was that some *men became so apathetic that they ceased to care about their bodily needs.* * They retreated further into themselves, refused to eat even what little food was available, refused to get any exercise, and eventually lay down as if waiting to die. The reports were emphatic concerning the lucidity and sanity of these men. They seemed willing to accept the prospect of death rather than to continue fighting a severely frustrating and depriving environment.

Two things seemed to save a man who was close to such "apathy" death: *getting him on his feet and doing something,** no matter how trivial, or getting him angry or concerned about some present or future problem. Usually it was the effort of a friend who maternally and insistently motivated the individual toward realistic goals which snapped him out of such a state of resignation. In one case such "therapy" consisted of kicking the man until he was mad enough to get up and fight.

Throughout this time, *the Chinese played the role of the benevolent but handicapped captor.** Prisoners were always reminded that it was their own air force bombing which was responsible for the inadequate supplies. Furthermore, they were reminded that they were getting treatment which was just as good as that which the average Chinese was getting. One important effect of this was that a man could never give *full* vent to his hostility toward the Chinese, even in fantasy. In their *manner* and *words* they were usually solicitous and sympathetic. The Chinese also implied that conditions could be better for a prisoner if he would take a more "cooperative" attitude, if he would support their propaganda for peace. Thus a man was made to feel that he was himself responsible for his traumatic circumstances.

Arrival at a permanent camp usually brought relief from many of these physical hardships. Food, shelter, and medicine, while not plentiful,

---

* Editor's italics.

[1] A more detailed discussion of the apathy reaction may be found in Strassman, Thaler, and Schein (1956).

appeared to be sufficient for the maintenance of life and some degree of health. However, the Chinese now increased sharply their efforts to *involve prisoners in their own propaganda program, and to undermine loyalties to their country.** This marks the beginning of the second phase of the imprisonment experience.

The Chinese program of subversion and indoctrination was thoroughly integrated into the entire camp routine and involved the manipulation of the entire social milieu of the prison camp. Its aims appeared to be to manage a large group of prisoners with a minimum staff of guards, to indoctrinate them with the Communist political ideology, to interrogate them to obtain intelligence information and confessions for propaganda purposes, and to develop a corps of collaborators within the prisoner group. What success the Chinese had stemmed from their *total* control of the environment, not from the application of any one technique.

The most significant feature of Chinese prisoner camp control was the systematic *destruction of the prisoners' formal and informal group structure.** Soon after arrival at a camp, the men were segregated by race, nationality, and rank. The Chinese put their own men in charge of the platoons and companies, and made arbitrary selections of POW squad leaders to remind the prisoners that their old rank system no longer had any validity. In addition, the Chinese attempted to undermine *informal* group structure by prohibiting any kind of group meeting, and by systematically fomenting mutual distrust by playing men off against one another. The most effective device to this end was the practice of obtaining from informers or Chinese spies detailed information about someone's activities, no matter how trivial, then calling him in to interrogate him about it. Such detailed surveillance of the men's activities made them feel that *their own ranks were so infiltrated by spies and informers that it was not safe to trust anyone.**

A similar device was used to obtain information during interrogation. After a man had resisted giving information for hours or days, he would be shown a signed statement by one of his fellow prisoners giving that same information. Still another device was to make prisoners who had not collaborated look like collaborators, by bestowing special favors upon them.

A particularly successful Chinese technique was their use of testimonials from other prisoners, such as the false germ-warfare confessions, and appeals based on familiar contexts, such as peace appeals. Confessions by prisoners or propaganda lectures given by collaborators had a particularly demoralizing effect, because only if resistance had been *unanimous* could a man solidly believe that his values were correct, even if he could not defend them logically.

* Editor's italics.

If the men, in spite of their state of social disorganization, did manage to organize any kind of group activity, the Chinese would quickly break up the group by removing its leaders or key members and assigning them to another camp.

Loyalties to home and country were undermined by the systematic manipulation of mail. Usually only mail which carried bad news was delivered. If a man received no mail at all, the Chinese suggested that his loved ones had abandoned him.

Feelings of *social isolation* * were increased by the complete *information control* * maintained in the camps. Only the Communist press, radio, magazines, and movies were allowed.

The weakening of the prisoner group's social structure is particularly significant because we depend to such an extent on consensual validation in judging ourselves and others. The prisoners lost their most important sources of information and support concerning standards of behavior and beliefs. Often men who attempted to resist the Chinese by means other than *outright* obstruction or aggression failed to obtain the active support of others, often earning their suspicion instead.

At the same time, the Chinese did create a situation in which meaningful social relationships could be had through common political activity, such as the "peace" committees which served as propaganda organs. The Chinese interrogators or instructors sometimes lived with prisoners for long periods of time in order to establish close personal relationships with them.

The Communist doctrines were presented through compulsory lectures followed by compulsory group discussions, for the purpose of justifying the conclusions given at the end of the lectures. On the whole, this phase of indoctrination was ineffective because of the crudeness of the propaganda material used in the lectures. However, its constant repetition seemed eventually to influence those men who did not have well-formed political opinions to start with, particularly because no counterarguments could be heard. The group discussions were effective only if their monitor was someone who could keep control over the group and keep it on the topic of discussion. Attempts by the Chinese to use "progressive" POW's in the role of monitors were seldom successful because they aroused too much hostility in the men.

The Chinese also attempted to get prisoners to use mutual criticism and self-criticism in the fashion in which it is used within China.[2] Whenever a POW was caught breaking one of the innumerable camp rules, he was required to give an elaborate confession and *self-criticism,* * no matter how trivial the offense. In general, the POW's were able to use this opportunity to ridicule the Chinese by taking advantage of their lack of understanding

---

* Editor's italics.
[2] See the paper by Robert J. Lifton (1957).

of slang and American idiom. They would emphasize the wrong parts of sentences or insert words and phrases which made it apparent to other prisoners that the joke was on the Chinese. Often men were required to make these confessions in front of large groups of other prisoners. If the man could successfully *communicate by a linguistic device his lack of sincerity, this ritual could backfire* * on the Chinese by giving the men an opportunity to express their solidarity (by sharing a communication which could not be understood by the Chinese). However, in other instances, prisoners who viewed such public confessions felt contempt for the confessor and felt their own group was being undermined still further by such public humiliation.

Various tales of how prisoners resisted the pressures put on them have been widely circulated in the press. For example, a number of prisoners ridiculed the Chinese by playing baseball with a basketball, yet telling the Chinese this was the correct way to play the game. Such stories suggest that morale and group solidarity was actually quite high in the camps. Our interviews with the men suggest that morale climbed sharply during the last *six to nine months* of imprisonment when the armistice talks were underway, when the compulsory indoctrination program had been put on a voluntary basis; and when the Chinese were improving camp conditions in anticipation of the repatriation. However, we heard practically no stories of successful group resistance or high morale from the first year or so in the camps when the indoctrination program was seriously pursued by the Chinese. (At that time the men had neither the time nor the opportunity to play any kind of games because all their time was spent on indoctrination activities or exhausting labor.)

Throughout, the Chinese created an environment in which *rewards* * such as extra food, medicine, special privileges, and status were given for cooperation and collaboration, while *threats* * of death, nonrepatriation, reprisal against family, torture, decreases in food and medicine, and imprisonment served to keep men from offering much resistance. Only imprisonment was consistently used as an actual punishment. *Chronic* resistance was usually handled by transferring the prisoner to a so-called "reactionary" camp.

Whatever behavior the Chinese attempted to elicit, they always *paced* their demands very carefully, they always required some level of *participation* from the prisoner, no matter how trivial, and they *repeated* endlessly.

To what extent did these pressures produce either changes in beliefs and attitudes, or collaboration? Close observation of the repatriates and the reports of the men themselves suggest that the Chinese did not have much success in changing beliefs and attitudes. Doubt and confusion were created in many prisoners as a result of having to examine so closely their own way

* Editor's italics.

of thinking, but very few changes, if any, occurred that resembled actual *conversion* to Communism. The type of prisoner who was most likely to become *sympathetic* toward Communism was the one who had chronically occupied a low status position in this society, and for whom the democratic principles were not very salient or meaningful.

*In producing collaboration, however, the Chinese were far more effective.** By collaboration I mean such activities as giving lectures for the Communists, writing and broadcasting propaganda, giving false confessions, writing and signing petitions, informing on fellow POW's, and so on; none of these activities required a personal change of belief. Some 10 to 15 per cent of the men chronically collaborated, but the dynamics of this response are very complex. By far the greatest determinant was the amount of pressure the Chinese put on a particular prisoner. Beyond this, the reports of the men permit one to isolate several sets of motives that operated, though it is impossible to tell how many cases of each type there may have been.

1. Some men collaborated for outright opportunistic reasons; these men lacked any kind of stable group identification, and exploited the situation for its material benefits without any regard for the consequences to themselves, their fellow prisoners, or their country.

2. Some men collaborated because their egos were too weak to withstand the physical and psychological rigors; these men were primarily motivated by fear, though they often rationalized their behavior; they were unable to resist any kind of authority figure, and could be blackmailed by the Chinese once they had begun to collaborate.

3. Some men collaborated with the firm conviction that they were infiltrating the Chinese ranks and obtaining intelligence information which would be useful to the UN forces. This was a convenient rationalization for anyone who could not withstand the pressures. Many of these men were initially tricked into collaboration or were motivated by a desire to communicate with the outside world. None of these men became ideologically confused; what Communist beliefs they might have professed were for the benefit of the Chinese only.

4. The prisoner who was vulnerable to the ideological appeal because of his low status in this society often collaborated with the conviction that he was doing the right thing in supporting the Communist peace movement. This group included the younger and less intelligent men from backward or rural areas, the malcontents, and members of various minority groups. These men often viewed themselves as failures in our society, and felt that society had never given them a chance. They were positively attracted by the immediate status and privileges which went with being a "progressive," and by the promise of important roles which they could presumably play in the peace movement of the future.

* Editor's italics.

Perhaps the most important thing to note about collaboration is the manner in which the social disorganization contributed to it. A man might make a slanted radio broadcast in order to communicate with the outside, he might start reading Communist literature out of sheer boredom, he might give information which he knew the Chinese already had, and so on. Once this happened, however, the Chinese rewarded him, increased pressure on him to collaborate, and blackmailed him by threatening exposure. At the same time, in most cases, his fellow prisoners forced him into further collaboration by mistrusting him and ostracizing him. Thus a man had to stand entirely on his own judgment and strength, and both of these often failed. One of the most common failures was a man's lack of awareness concerning the effects of his own actions on the other prisoners, and the value of these actions for the Chinese propaganda effort. The man who confessed to germ warfare, thinking he could repudiate such a confession later, did not realize its immediate propaganda value to the Communists.

A certain percentage of men, though the exact number is difficult to estimate, exhibited chronic resistance and obstructionism toward Chinese indoctrination efforts. Many of these men were *well integrated with secure, stable group identifications who could withstand the social isolation and still exercise good judgment.** Others were chronic obstructionists whose histories showed recurring resistance to any form of authority. Still others were idealists or martyrs to religious and ethical principles, and still others were anxious, guilt-ridden individuals who could only cope with their own strong impulses to collaborate by denying them and over-reacting in the other direction.

By far the largest group of prisoners, however, established a complex compromise between the demands of the Chinese and their own value system. This adjustment, called by the men "playing it cool," consisted primarily of a physical and emotional withdrawal from the whole environment. These men learned to suspend their feelings and to adopt an attitude of watching and waiting, rather than hoping and planning. This reaction, though passive, was not as severe as the apathy described earlier. It was a difficult adjustment to maintain because some concessions had to be made to the Chinese in the form of trivial or well-timed collaborative acts, and in the form of a feigned interest in the indoctrination program. At the same time, each man had to be prepared to deal with the hostility of his buddies if he made an error in judgment.

Discussion

This paper has placed particular emphasis on the social psychological factors involved in "brainwashing" because it is my opinion that the process

* Editor's italics.

is primarily concerned with social forces, not with the strengths and weaknesses of individual minds. It has often been asserted that drugs, hypnotic techniques, refined "mental tortures" and, more recently, implanted electrodes can make the task of the "brainwasher" much easier by rendering the human mind submissive with a minimum of effort. There is little question that such techniques can be used to elicit confessions or signatures on documents prepared by the captor; but so can withdrawal of food, water, or air produce the same results. The point is that the Chinese Communists do not appear to be interested in obtaining merely a confession or *transient* submission. Instead, they appear to be interested in producing changes in men which will be lasting and self-sustaining. A germ-warfare confession alone was not enough—the POW had to "testify" before an international commission explaining in detail how the bombs had been dropped, and had to tell his story in other prison camps to his fellow POW's.

There is little evidence that drugs, post-hypnotic suggestion, or implanted electrodes can now or ever will be able to produce the kind of behavior exhibited by many prisoners who collaborated and made false confessions. On the other hand, there is increasing evidence (Hinkle and Wolff, 1956; Lifton, 1956) that Russian and Chinese interrogation and indoctrination techniques *involve the destruction of the person's social ties and identifications, and the partial destruction of his ego.** If this is successfully accomplished, the person is *offered a new identity for himself and given the opportunity to identify with new groups.** What physical torture and deprivation are involved in this process may be either a calculated attempt to degrade and humiliate a man to destroy his image of himself as a dignified human being, or the product of fortuitous circumstances, *i.e.*, failure of supply lines to the prison, loss of temper on the part of the interrogator, an attempt to inspire fear in other prisoners by torturing one of them, and so on. We do not have sufficient evidence to determine which of these alternatives represents Communist intentions; possibly all of them are involved in the actual prison situation.

Ultimately that which sustains humans is their *personality integration born out of secure and stable group identifications.** One may be able to produce temporary submission by direct intervention in cortical processes, but only by destroying a man's self-image and his group supports can one produce any lasting changes in his beliefs and attitudes. By concerning ourselves with the problem of artificially creating submission in man, we run the real risk of overlooking the fact that we are in a genuine struggle of ideas with other portions of the world and that man often submits himself directly to ideas and principles.

To understand and combat "brainwashing," we must look at those social

* Editor's italics.

conditions which make people ready to accept new ideas from anyone who states them clearly and forcefully, and those social conditions which give people the sense of integrity which will sustain them when their immediate social and emotional supports are stripped away.

IMPLICATIONS

Of all the various techniques used by the Chinese in the Korean conflict, which are most understandable to you? Do you find it difficult to understand why certain techniques were effective? Which techniques? Why do you think the emphasis here is on social forces and not on the strengths and weaknesses of the individual persons? A group of psychologists—Farber, Harlow, and West (1957)—point out three aspects of the usual kind of brainwashing: *debility, dependency,* and *dread,* or *DDD*. They point out that resistance to suggestions given by the enemy can be broken down by intense and simultaneous application of these conditions. Are these three conditions the primary factors in Schein's article? In discussing (1) loss of customary social supports, (2) disturbance of the individual's identity with, and roles in, his social system, and (3) the substitution of new group identity, does Schein add any new factors to debility, dependency, and dread? How is the identification with a new group accomplished when it occurs?

REFERENCES

Consult the Bibliography for references cited in the article.

IX

ABNORMALITY AND MENTAL HEALTH

40

AN AUTOBIOGRAPHY OF A SCHIZOPHRENIC EXPERIENCE

Anonymous

You probably know of *psychosis* as a form of serious mental illness and have heard of *schizophrenia,* a functional psychosis and the most common disorder among hospitalized mental patients. Few college students, however, have had any direct contact with a person with schizophrenia, often described as a lack of harmony or a "split" in personality functioning—particularly between emotions and conduct.

There are several forms of schizophrenia, with different kinds of symptoms. The woman who writes about her experience in the following selection is afflicted with catatonic schizophrenia, characterized by symptoms of unusual postures, repetitive movements, and speech. This patient was not completely in contact with the real world but, rather, had withdrawn into a world of her own. She reported awareness of some of the events in her environment, but she had no desire to communicate with reality. She talked extensively with imaginary companions and reported visions and delusions. Although we lack an observer's description of this patient, the patient herself gives us an indication of her behavior as others might see it as well as a vivid description of her own thoughts and feelings.

MOST OF WHAT FOLLOWS is based on an unpublished autobiography written in the spring of 1951, shortly after I had returned home from the second of the three episodes of my schizophrenic experience. My disorder was diagnosed as catatonic schizophrenia.[1] The three episodes occurred over a four-year period. I am concentrating here chiefly on a description of the first episode. This occurred after I had received a year and a half of psychotherapy consisting of weekly contacts with a psychiatric social worker at a child guidance clinic. I had gone for this help when I

[1] The writer was confined at Sheppard Pratt Hospital from November 1948 through April 1949. The diagnosis was catatonic schizophrenia. Remission occurred after three weeks under sodium amytal. The second confinement was at the same hospital from November 1949 through January 1950. Remission was spontaneous. The third confinement was at St. Elizabeths Hospital, and again the diagnosis was catatonic schizophrenia. It lasted from July 1951 through September 1952. Remission occurred after a series of seven electric shock treatments which were administered in July of 1952.

Reprinted from an anonymous article, "Case Report: An Autobiography of a Schizophrenic Experience," *Journal of Abnormal and Social Psychology,* Vol. 51, 1953, pp. 677–689. Copyright 1953 by the American Psychological Association, and reproduced by permission.

had come to feel unable to deal with the problems that had arisen in my relations with my children. The disorder was coincidental with processes of personality change which had started some time before I went to the child guidance clinic for help and which continued after recovery from the acute illness.

Background

Social Position

When I first went to the child guidance clinic, I was, in terms of our social structure, the wife of a professional man and I had come from a professional, middle-class background. I had myself been trained as a social caseworker after I completed college.

I was married when I was twenty-one years old. During the following ten years, I had three children. At the time I experienced the first schizophrenic episode, I was thirty-six years old.

Ever since my college days, I had been an active member in groups interested in political and social reform and world peace. I had done organizational work and publicity for the C.I.O. union, to which I belonged, and later for the women's auxiliary. I became active for a time in a cooperative nursery school which my youngest child attended, and during the year before my illness had served as president of the organization. I had also been a collector for the Community Chest in my neighborhood. As a family we lived in our own home and were stable and settled in a particular locality.

In my personal relations I had always had an adequate number of friends and had never had any difficulty in making close friends. I had, however, been under the strain of steadily increasing anxiety at the time I consulted the clinic, and had also reached an impasse in which I felt incompetent as a mother. One of the chief problems I presented was my feeling that I lacked sufficient warmth in my relations to my two oldest children. My relation to my youngest child was secure and satisfying.

Marital and Sexual Adjustment

I was faced during the period of psychotherapy with a crisis in my marital relationship and just before illness had decided upon divorce, which I finally obtained several years later after recovery from the schizophrenic disorder. Most of the clinical work was focused at first on the difficulties I had about asserting myself in personal relationships, and as I obtained emotional support from the therapist I began to be more self-confident. I began to use a greater amount of independent initiative and judgment in my daily life, and my relations to the children began to improve. The need for greater decisiveness and assertiveness in my relation with my children made it impossible for me to continue long-established relations of overdependency and overidentification which I had maintained in relation to my mother and my husband. There was a simultaneous break with both identifications. My long-suppressed negative reactions to certain aspects of my husband's personality finally came to the forefront. I had previously related to my husband both in a semimaternal and managerial as well as a submissive way. Hostility had been breaking through openly in dreams before I went for help, but generally I had been able to keep hostility and derogatory feelings out of consciousness so that I was able to maintain an adequate amount of warmth and tenderness in the relationship. The final break with my husband therefore constituted a severe emotional deprivation for me. It deprived me of physical and emotional closeness to which I had been accustomed for many years.

I sought compensations for this increasing isolation. I became involved in an intense love affair which aroused a feeling of semicompulsive dependency on this relationship. I seemed to be torn from my moorings and alienated from my former self because I had temporarily lost my normal investment in other interests. Intense feelings about childhood frustrations and disappointments in relation to my father were stirred up at this time and I seemed to feel these early deprivations more keenly in retrospect than I had during my childhood.

My dependency needs were acute at this time but an overinvestment in the extramarital relationship was causing me to lose powers of moral control and to disregard the interests of my children. I made desperate efforts to break the overattachment, and thought finally that I had succeeded. I found the best corrective was writing poetry and intellectual work which enabled me to fight off feelings of incipient depression. Creative activity was intensified but finally became compulsive and overabsorbing. I was not able to maintain a normal extraverted relation to my children, or to switch my attention at will to practical details of living. I experienced a sudden feeling of creative release before my illness, was convinced that I was rapidly attaining the height of my intellectual powers, and that for the first time in my life, I would be able to function up to the level of my ability in this direction.

During my entire married life I had been semifrigid, *i.e.*, I had been unable to attain orgasm except occasionally during sleep. I had, however, enjoyed sexual relationships, found them relaxing and emotionally renewing, and had seldom been bothered by residual tension. Capacity for sexual response increased gradually during the years of marriage but I remained semifrigid even in the extramarital relation described above. Divorce was finally necessary because I no longer felt attracted to my husband sexually after the emotional break was made.

I attained adequate capacity for vaginal orgasm during the recovery phase after the third episode of illness. The increase in sexuality that was associated with loss of inhibition had a terrifying impact during the early phases of psychosis and was expressed symbolically in the experience of "hell-fire" described below and in other ways. During the recovery phases, increased sexuality posed severe problems of control. The situation was aggravated at times by my isolation and by intense religious emotions which stimulated the entire body and increased the need for sex. For a while, casual relations with men were both intensely pleasurable and emotionally satisfying, since they were associated with a mystical and religious type of nonpersonal love and acceptance of other people. This phase wore off gradually and I returned to my usual needs for personal intimacy and personal love, lack of which increased my frustration and unhappiness in casual relations.

Changes in Self-perception

The new self-confidence I was obtaining from the relation with my therapist enabled me to see more clearly certain aspects of myself which I had seen before only dimly, outside of full awareness. To these aspects of my personality I had a strong negative reaction. My new perceptions disturbed the picture I had long held of myself as being primarily a highly social person, interested in community problems, and in the welfare of others. Later, during some periods of illness, I saw myself also as cold, indifferent to others, withdrawn, and at times as impulsively cruel. I became aware of the strength of my competitive ambitious feelings which had, however, largely been kept in check by my actual preoccupation with more highly social interests. I had expressed feelings of social distance and status by maintaining subdued but occasionally conscious attitudes of impatience and contempt for other people who did not seem to be as quick or competent as myself.

I also felt just before illness that I had failed to give an adequate amount of love to my two older children, and that I had not had full interest in their development as individuals after they had outgrown the stage of early childhood. The extramarital affair intensified insight and self-rejection because I felt that there were limiting and egotistical elements in my love, that I was giving no more than I was receiving, and that I still had an insufficient degree of love for my children.

Loss of Ego Support

Throughout most of the period of therapy I had a desire to impress my therapist and to win her approval. I went out of my way to take pains with my dress and personal appearance when I saw her. Later on, I began to feel that my point of view was changing, that my values were different from hers, and that there was no longer as much common ground for discussion. I also felt I knew myself better than she knew me. I was failing to communicate a good many of my half-formed thoughts about myself, partly because of limitations of time, and partly because these thoughts were not fully clear even to myself. At this point I was no longer able to obtain emotional support from the transference relationship.

In addition to increased loneliness caused by my marital problem, I was also conscious of an increasing intellectual isolation. I was losing a previously established sense of close group identification with organizations to which I had formerly belonged as I became aware that my views were beginning to differ from those of others which I had once accepted. I had previously had a sense of "we-ness" both in regard to family and other group associations. This was being replaced by a sense of personal separateness.

The Illness

The Onset Stage

A few weeks before my illness I began to regress into success daydreams somewhat similar to, though not quite as naive and grandiose, as those I had had during early adolescence. I was puzzled by this tendency, though not greatly alarmed because it hardly seemed that my daydreaming self was a part of my adult ethical self. At the onset of panic, I was suddenly confronted with an overwhelming conviction that I had discovered the secrets of the universe, which were being rapidly made plain with incredible lucidity. The truths discovered seemed to be known immediately and directly, with absolute certainty. I had no sense of doubt or awareness of the possibility of doubt. In spite of former atheism and strong antireligious sentiments, I was suddenly convinced that it was possible to prove rationally the existence of God. I remember at the time trying to write an essay on cognition. I began to write compulsively and at the same time was aware that I was developing schizophrenia. I found later among the disorganized notes which I had carefully hidden away a number of passages that were quite lucid as well as others that were incoherent and full of symbolic sexual content. I also felt that I was embarking on a great Promethean adventure. I was filled with an audacious and unconquerable spirit. As panic mounted, I grew afraid of being alone, had an intense desire to communicate. I had for a short time a sense of exclusive mission but was able to struggle consciously against messianic delusions. These tendencies were replaced by a sense of burdensome and exclusive responsibility, which continued throughout the entire several years of illness.

Some Special Characteristics of the First Episode

During the first episode I was hyperactive and extremely tense. Feelings of guilt and self-rejection which I had started to have before onset were in evidence during the acute phase of illness only to a very minor degree and were expressed symbolically and nonrationally. It was only later on, during more rational and integrated periods of disturbance, that I developed an intense guilt consciousness and conscious self-repudiation. These guilt feelings were finally resolved and dissipated during periods of comparative rationality. I shall not discuss here the emotional functions of the guilt experience.

I did not feel especially isolated or actively lonely during the projective, fear-ridden first episode. I had little or no desire to communicate with real people, although I talked extensively with an imaginary companion. I felt painfully lonely during later phases of disturbance when I was more rational and in relatively normal contact with other people.

The World Disaster Experience

Shortly after I was taken to the hospital for the first time in a rigid catatonic condition, I was plunged into the horror of a world catastrophe. I was being caught up in a cataclysm and totally dislocated. I myself had been responsible for setting the destructive forces into motion, although I had acted with no intent to harm, and defended myself with healthy indignation against the accusations of others. If I had done something wrong, I certainly was suffering the consequences along with everyone else. Part of the time I was exploring a new planet (a marvelous and breath-taking adventure) but it was too lonely, I could persuade no one to settle there, and I had to get back to the earth somehow. The earth, however, had been devastated by atomic bombs and most of its inhabitants killed. Only a few people—myself and the dimly perceived nursing staff—had escaped. At other times, I felt totally alone on the new planet.

The issue of world salvation was of predominant importance and I was trying to tell people how to go back to the abandoned earth. All personal matters relating to my family were forgotten. At times when the universe was collapsing, I was not sure that things would turn out all right. I thought I might have to stay in the endless hell-fire of atomic destruction. The chief horror consisted in the fact that I would never be able to die. I thought I would either have to figure out some form of suicide or else get a lobotomy.

During some of the time that I was dislocated in interplanetary space, I was also having vivid fantasies in connection with water, and these afforded me considerable relief. Water represented conservation of life, in contrast to its destruction by fire.

Water fantasies had started one or two days after admission to the hospital. I suddenly felt I had been plunged into a sea, was drowning and struggling for breath. At that point I realized that I was in a sedative tub. I saw that I was strapped in such a way that I was in no danger of drowning. I knew that as long as I was awake I would not need the straps because I would be careful not to drown, but I continued to feel terrified.

Water fantasies returned at times when I was given wet-pack treatments. I clearly remember reciting to myself some lines of Swinburne. I recalled only the first stanza of the poem and falsely interpolated at the end a line belonging to the second, thus skipping all parts in which the poet expressed a longing for death:

> I will go back to the great sweet mother
> Mother and lover of men, the sea.
> I will go down to her, I and none other,
> Close with her, kiss her, and mix her with me;
> Cling to her, strive with her, hold her fast;
> O fair white mother, in days long past
> Born without sister, born without brother,
> Wrought without hand in a world without stain.

It was not I who wanted to go back to the sea, because I myself was the sea, or maternal principle. The haunting recollection of this poem was followed by a vivid pleasurable hallucination of rape, by which I became pregnant. The entire illness after that was emotionally identified with childbirth, that is, with productive suffering. The baby had been too difficult to deliver, there had been a Caesarian operation, but vaguely in some way, the symbolic child could be saved though there was no actual child.

It was only at times when I was plunged directly into hell-fire that I felt there was no effort I could make except in the direction of death. At other times, though I seemed to be almost pulled apart in a disintegrating universe, I felt there must be some way I could hold things together. I was somehow an indispensable link in preventing total collapse. I was unable to think coherently or plan any action, but I had to use my poetic imagination instead, for poetry could be counted on not to lead me astray. As soon as I struggled into a little more coherence, I tried to think of other things I must do. What about "know thyself"? This did not seem to be helpful. Then I hit upon Polonius' lines:

> This above all: to thine own self be true,
> And it must follow as the night the day,
> Thou canst not then be false to any man.

After I remembered this, I was also able to feel that I was involved in the struggle for world peace and progress. The universe stopped whirling about so drastically and I felt more like my old self.

Quite frequently, during the following months, I kept coming back to Shakespeare's advice, which gave me some reassurance. I had, however, seen Laurence Olivier's *Hamlet* a few weeks before becoming sick, and had thought at the time that the statement would only apply to persons who had trustworthy social selves to begin with. This was my problem in a nutshell. There was a part of myself that had not been trustworthy, attributes which I had not liked, and which had to be eradicated. I was by no means rejecting myself completely, for incorporated into that self were all the values I cherished most. My feeling for nature, art, and science, any my general love of life seemed to be entirely in harmony with my value system and inseparable from it. I became aware during my first illness of the tremendous debt which I owed to the past.

During the first three weeks of hospitalization, I saw visions at various times. The capacity to see visions did not return after this period. These visions could be divided into two categories. The first type had no relation to and was not suggested by surrounding objects in the material environment, but were entirely projections of inner states of consciousness and appeared before my eyes in the same way that a motion picture is presented to the eye of the observer. The second type did not constitute true visions, but could rather be called visual hallucinations and distortions, sometimes suggested by the play of light and shadow, etc., acting upon an overwrought imagination. The true visions had definite but rather complex content and my attention was focused on grasping their meaning.

Occasionally during subsequent periods of disturbance, there was some distortion of vision and some degree of hallucination. On several occasions my eyes became markedly oversensitive to light. Ordinary colors appeared to be much too bright, and sunlight seemed dazzling in intensity. When this happened, ordinary reading was impossible, and print seemed excessively black.

The Formation of the Delusional System

After the first few weeks of extreme disorganization, I began to acquire some relatively stable paranoid delusions. These delusions were accompanied by fear, and were based in part on erroneous perceptions and hallucinations, as well as on erroneous inferences from accurate perception. I also had a sense of discovery, creative excitement, and intense, at times mystical, inspiration in intervals when there was relief from fear.

During the paranoid period I thought I was being persecuted for my beliefs, that my enemies were actively trying to interfere with my activities, were trying to harm me, and at times even to kill me. I was primarily a citizen of the larger community. I was trying to persuade people who did not agree with me, but whom I felt could be won over, of the correctness of my beliefs. The only trouble was that it was difficult to get people to listen to me.

The picture of myself which I had at this time was much the same as that which I had always carried around with me during most of my adult life before I had become ethically self-conscious. I was a worthy citizen and was not afflicted with a sense of failure as a mother. I had regained a sense of inner control. I was once more a mature competent adult with great reserves of strength, and this was how I had almost always felt. I did, however, feel different from normal to the extent that I was in the midst of a bewildering and terrifying situation unlike anything I had ever encountered before. I was being compelled to focus attention on a new set of facts. Because of the continuously unpredictable nature of the delusional occurrences in the ward, the sense of routine and habit was almost entirely absent, I was dealing with novelty, consciousness was much more narrowly and sharply focused than normally, and a large mass of my previous memories and life reactions were inaccessible to me.

At no time during the first episode did I entirely lose feelings of personal guilt, and I retained some capacity for ethical awareness. In this situation, however, too great a preoccupation with problems of self-valuation would have impeded the fulfillment of my social mission. For the most part, my attention was directed toward problems in external reality, as it appeared to me. I was extraverted, not introverted, in spite of what might have been appearances to the contrary.

In order to carry through the task which had been imposed upon me, and to defend myself against the terrifying and bewildering dangers of my external situation, I was endowed in my imagination with truly cosmic powers. The sense of power was not always purely defensive but was also connected with a strong sense of valid inspiration. I felt that I had power to determine the weather which responded to my inner moods, and even to control the movement of the sun in relation to other astronomical bodies. None of these powers gave me feelings of competence or satisfaction. They had been given to me to cope with an emergency. I did not know how I obtained them and I derived no feeling of special importance from them. Whatever "magical" powers I did have were directed solely to the control of nonhuman forces, and I did not feel that I had any control over people. I was, on the contrary, acutely aware that in relation to the nursing staff, doctors, etc., I was singularly helpless and unable to make my wants known. Sometimes I did feel that I was able to acquire added power or psychic forces which I was able to use in a defensive way to keep other people from getting control of me. I was also afraid that other people had power to read my mind, and thought I must develop ways of blocking my thoughts from other people.

I was carrying through a predominantly maternal role when I was not preoccupied with the more neutral role of world citizen. I was the one who must protect other people, and I was doing so to the best of my ability. I had never been more conscious of being a woman and a mother. Every once in a while an "inner voice" would say to me "Think of the children first and you will be all right." I clung desperately to this advice, even though it was far from sufficient to ward off fear.

I actually thought very little about my own children. I was convinced that my two older children were safe and well taken care of by relatives and had no wish to see them, but from time to time I did have a strong desire to take my youngest child in my arms. I was also convinced, most of the time, that he was dead. . . . Occasionally I had an intense longing for another baby, a longing so great that it amounted to a physical ache in the breasts. . . .[2]

---

[2] In an omitted section, Anonymous goes on to describe intense and overwhelming feelings of anger, aggression, fear, and sympathy directed toward individuals (fellow patients, nurses, her children, etc.) in her environment. She also reports on a set of religious confusions.

Conflict About Life Sacrifice

I felt serious anxiety about my capacity to surrender my life voluntarily in any and all circumstances when required in the interests of another individual. Included in the notes which I had written during the initial phase of panic, I found the following statement:

> The instinct of the individual to survive is the strongest instinct of all, and we know very well that this is so. Our first impulse is to save ourselves. Any other reaction to a personal danger situation is routed through devious channels. The race can survive only through the individual. Thus though we appear to be working against our own interests, we are not. This is the basic riddle of the universe on a feeling level. Inability to solve it has created a racial neurosis on the subject.

It would have been more correct to say that I had a long-standing personal neurosis on the subject. When I was about twelve or thirteen years old, I had heard that persons (both men and women) were sometimes decorated for bravery because of heroic actions in which the life of another person was saved. I wondered at the time whether I would have the courage to act in this way. I was afraid I would be paralyzed by fear, that I would stop too long to calculate risks, and that I would not act to help the other person if there were a serious chance that I might lose my own life. I pictured myself as totally alone and unobserved with the unknown person who was in danger. I shoved aside the question and forgot about it during adult life, although I think it did cross my mind occasionally when I read about heroic rescues in the newspaper.

It was this long-buried fear of failure in such a type of "cold" isolated situation that was for me one of the sources of greatest anxiety in the early catatonic state of disorganization. This fear was not conscious during acute disturbance. I was, however, being accused of treachery by the entire social group. For a brief time (just before the world catastrophe described above) I felt I was being ostracized by all my friends and relatives. No such person as myself had ever existed. I alone knew that I existed, but could convince no one of this fact.

The fear about my own cowardice and my excessively strong self-protective impulses did not become conscious until a good while after recovery from the second episode, when self-confidence about other types of performance had been restored, and I felt myself to be a normally adequate mother. I had a great resistance to bringing the matter into full awareness, but when I was finally able to do so I realized that I would never dare to say that I would not have failed in a situation of this type. If there had been real danger, perhaps I would have thought, "Why lose two lives rather than one?" while actually there might have been some chance of successful action. Perhaps, on the other hand, I would have become so immediately identified with the person who needed help that I would have been able to act impulsively. There was also the not too pleasant thought that I might have acted differently if under observation by others than if I had been alone. I would never know what I would have done.

In finally thinking through the issue, I recognized that I would never feel justified in risking my life in this way as long as I had children dependent on me, but that if I no longer had such responsibilities, the rule would apply. I also felt that a man who failed to act in this way toward a neighbor or member of his fraternal in-group would be considered a weakling by others, and would consider himself a weakling provided he accepted the standard as morally valid or socially necessary. A childless woman might not have been so strongly condemned in the past in this respect, but new mores are being evolved because of the emancipation of women. Girls are taught first-aid and life-saving techniques along with boys. Just before the second period of hospitalization I planned to join a volunteer rescue and fire-fighting squad in my local community and was upset when I learned that women were not eligible for membership.

Rules regarding life sacrifice are enforced by group opinion as well as by individual acquiescence in their validity. The penalty for violation is loss of "social face" if caught by others, and loss of self-respect if caught by the self. I certainly had not been born with an instinct to act in this way, yet bravery of this type was a vital component of my ego ideal. . . .

Chief Personality Changes

The chief personality changes which I consider took place in myself during the period of six or seven years which included the psychosis can be summarized as follows: (1) I lost a chronic, diffused anxiety which I had long carried around in adult life; (2) I grew more capable of self-assertion without anxiety; I acquired a more secure sense of adult authority in my relation with my children. These changes also included a shift from the masochistic to a nonmasochistic emotional orientation; (3) I lost a sense of excessive dependency on other adults; a sense of personal separateness and isolation replaced a former capacity for identification with other individuals and with groups; (4) My relations with people generally became easier and more relaxed; I acquired a greater capacity for warmth and outgoing interest in all sorts of people; (5) I acquired a deeper sense of human equality and of the potential dignity of every human being; (6) My interest in competitive evaluations of myself and others was decreased to a marked degree; (7) There were changes in psychosexual adjustment, including a change from a chronic state of semifrigidity to a state of sexual adequacy; (8) My intellectual capacities functioned more freely and more efficiently than before; (9) I changed from a nonreligious to a religious type of orientation, acquiring a sense of religious dependency and capacity for religious communication.

IMPLICATIONS

To what extent do you see here an apparently normal, active person with a family, who develops a psychosis in adulthood? In what manner do you see better the link between normality and abnormality? What normal activities persisted during the psychotic break? In what ways does this woman's description of the most distressing aspects of her psychotic episode remind you of the "bad" dream of a normal individual? Give some of the specific examples of the *hallucinations* (false perceptions), *delusions* (false thinking), and *motor disturbances* she experienced. What do you think helped her to recover?

REFERENCES

See Jackson (1960) and Arieti (1955) for discussions of two general groups of patients who develop schizophrenia: the *process group* with slow onset, no obvious precipitative factors, and chronically poor achievement in school and work; the *reactive group* in which onset is acute, symptoms floridly psychotic, and identifiable events common. See also Herron (1962) and Garmezy and Rodnick (1959).

The NIMH operates the Center for Studies of Schizophrenia and issues periodic reports on its work. One example is *Special Report: Schizophrenia.* National Institute of Mental Health, 5600 Fishers Lane, Rockville, Maryland 20852.

41

MURDER AS AGGRESSIVE BEHAVIOR

Leonard Berkowitz

How does the psychologist regard murder after examining the data collected by behavioral scientists? Does murder fit into the formula *frustration leads to aggression?* Destruction of human life is the ultimate in aggressive behavior. Note how Berkowitz organizes and summarizes the findings about killers, and what factors besides strong aggressiveness lead some frustrated personalities to commit homicide.

Murder

$\mathbf{D}$ESPITE THE ATTENTION given to homicides in fiction and the popular press, such crimes constitute only a tiny fraction of the illegal actions committed in this country. One tenth of 1 per cent of the arrests reported by the police of some 1,500 American cities in 1958 were for homicide, and most of these probably were due to negligence rather than deliberate intent (Sutherland and Cressey, 1960). Too many lives are taken violently, but murder is a relatively rare phenomenon in our complex society. It apparently is a fairly unusual response to unusual circumstances.

Most of the people displaying these extreme reactions, furthermore, probably would never commit murder again if released from jail. With the exception of hired killers, they typically are not hardened criminals. One study of ninety-six convicted murderers found only about half of the men had even been arrested before. Two thirds of the sex offenders and over 90 per cent of the property offenders surveyed, in comparison, had such prior records.[1] Murderers, by and large, are not habitual lawbreakers and once released from prison are relatively good parole risks (Clinard, 1957). They have taken a life, in most cases at least, not because of a persistent urge to kill, but because their emotions flared up out of control in response to an extreme thwarting. "Most murders," says one authority (cited in Clinard, 1957), "are crimes of passion—explosive reactions to a difficult situation."

Individual Characteristics

To say that the violence was provoked by frustrating circumstances is not to rule out the importance of personality characteristics. Experts generally are agreed that the killer's life history has made him susceptible to such "explosive reactions." Another person exposed to the same final instigating condition might have exerted better control over his emotions or may not have been as strongly aroused by the thwarting.

Not surprisingly, many murderers have had a history of frequent frustrations. Palmer (1960) interviewed the mothers of fifty-one male murderers in order to determine how the life experiences of these men had differed from those of their nearest-age nonhomicidal brothers. He found the murderers had apparently suffered many more physical and psychological frustrations, such as illnesses, accidents, and harsh treatments. Because of these relatively frequent thwartings (as I suggested earlier), they conceivably developed a fairly great readiness to perceive further frustrations in the world about them, tended to exhibit relatively intense anger in response

---

[1] According to at least one study (Berg and Fox, 1947), Negro murderers are more likely than white murderers to have prior convictions for assaultive crimes.

to these thwartings, and did not learn strong restraints against socially dis-approved actions. Any one frustration, then, was likely to provoke an extreme reaction, and so Palmer also reported the murderers had shown more frequent socially unacceptable aggression than their brothers as they matured. The nonhomicidal siblings probably had stronger inhibitions against antisocial behavior, and what aggression they exhibited tended to be of the controlled, socially acceptable variety.

Homicides may be more common in lower socioeconomic groups than in the higher social strata (Henry and Short, 1954; Falk, 1959) partly be-cause of the greater number of deprivations to which the lower-class individual is typically subjected throughout his lifetime. Lower-class exist-ence is relatively frustrating. Research . . . has indicated some of the areas in which the lower-class person is often seriously thwarted. For example, he is frequently prevented from satisfying his economic and status wishes, and his parents probably were also somewhat more punitive toward him in childhood than would have been the case if his had been an average middle-class family. Living in such an environment, he is all too likely to show the consequences of these deprivations: a tendency to intense emotional out-bursts as well as to psychoses.

Berg and Fox (1947) have made use of the frustration-aggression hy-pothesis in explaining the relationship between intelligence and homicides. Consistent with other researchers, they observed that a sample of two hundred murderers had reliably lower school achievement and intelligence than did a control group of other prison inmates and suggested that the former's low intelligence level had led to their being frustrated relatively severely by their victims. But if the killers had been thwarted on this one occasion (presumably in an argument with the victim), they probably had also experienced a good many frustrations in other situations throughout their lifetimes. These recurrent frustrations could have led to the final violent outburst when the murder was committed.

Another reason for such an extreme emotional flare-up can be found in the murderers' occasionally weak inhibitions against socially disapproved behavior. Murderers generally violate criminal laws less frequently than do most property offenders or people guilty of nonhomicidal assaults. They can restrain their antisocial inclinations in most situations. These inner con-trols, however, may not be too strongly rooted and can give way under periods of severe emotional stress. Wood (1961) has published evidence in accord with this analysis in his previously mentioned study of crime in Ceylon. In contrast to robbers and burglars, the murderers in his sample tended not to be regular gamblers or rowdies. They also were less likely to have a police record. But, attesting to their tenuous controls, almost as many murderers as robbers and burglars used alcohol. Their religion and village customs frowned on intoxicating beverages, but they tended to drink more often than most of the noncriminals around them.

Sociological Determinants

Social conditions producing frequent severe frustrations together with comparatively weak inhibitions against socially disapproved behavior should give rise to a disproportionately high incidence of murders if the present reasoning is correct. Such seems to be the case. We already have seen, for example, that there are high homicide rates in poor and deteriorating city areas. The people living in these urban areas usually experience a good many serious thwartings and in many instances, as was pointed out earlier, have not learned strong inhibitions against unlawful behavior. Frustrations and weak inhibitions are particularly characteristic of lower-class Negroes and may explain why the Negro homicide rate is much higher than that of whites (Sutherland and Cressey, 1960; Falk, 1959).

Much the same argument can also account for regional differences in the incidence of homicides. Thus, there were only 1.5 homicides per 100,000 population known to the police in New England in 1958, while this rate rose to 9.5 in the South Atlantic states (Sutherland and Cressey, 1960). Many Southerners, of course, have been seriously thwarted throughout their lives because of the poverty of their part of the country. But in addition, the lower-class Southerner is more likely than his New England counterpart to feel that he must seek personal retribution for any "wrongs" done to him. His social code often justifies striking out on his own against the people harming him.[2]

We must remember, however, that recurrent frustrations and weak inner controls only create a predisposition to extreme aggression. They do not actually impel such behavior. The frequently thwarted person is easily aroused, and not constantly angry. He does not attack just anyone for the sake of releasing some supposed pent-up "hostile energy." But he can become enraged fairly easily in the course of his daily life. This is why killers and their victims generally come from the same groups, why, for example, whites usually kill whites, Negroes kill primarily other Negroes, and the victims often are relatives or acquaintances of their murderers (Clinard, 1957; Falk, 1959). The murder victim probably had frustrated his slayer in some argument or fight, thereby precipitating the violent, uncontrolled emotional reaction leading to his death.

Frustrations also account for changes in homicide rates as business conditions alter. Henry and Short (1954) have demonstrated that murders committed by whites tend to be most frequent when business conditions are bad. Negro homicides, on the other hand, decrease in such times of depression and are most common when the country is relatively prosperous.

---

[2] Several authorities have suggested that homicide rates are high in the South because "cultural definitions call for personal violence in some situations" (Clinard, 1957, p. 214). Along similar lines, Wolfgang (1958) has contended after an analysis of almost 600 cases of criminal homicide in Philadelphia, that many murders take place in a "subculture of violence" which gives social approval to "quick resort to physical aggression."

Along with Henry and Short, I would say the variation in homicide rates stems primarily from differences in frustrations. But contrary to these writers, it seems to me the thwartings arise, at least in part, from comparisons the individual makes with others in his own group.[3] When a low-status white person loses his job in a depression, he finds himself deprived of status and economic goods relative to those of his friends and acquaintances who still have jobs. However, since Negroes are generally the first to be fired in hard times, poor business conditions act as a leveler in this group. Nearly all lower-class Negroes suffer from economic privations in a depression, and they do not see themselves as being much worse off than their peers. Prosperous times, however, permit some Negroes to get economically well ahead of their peers. Those not doing too well conceivably feel greatly deprived in comparison with wealthier Negroes; they are frustrated, and anger results.

Effects of Death Penalties

Restraints against socially disapproved behavior are most effective . . . when they are based upon relatively stable moral attitudes rather than on the fear of punishment. The person who believes criminal actions are morally wrong will refrain from engaging in such behavior in most situations, whether he anticipates punishment for the criminal activity or not. However . . . inhibitions based primarily upon fear of punishment are likely to be operative only when the individual expects to be caught and punished for carrying out the disapproved activity.[4]

This reasoning explains why the threat of a death penalty does not reduce the incidence of murders (Cressey and Sutherland, 1960). When a person commits a murder, he usually has done so in a fit of violent rage. He certainly does not think of being apprehended by the police at such times. There are few if any cues in the situation to remind him of the police. The only thing that could have restrained his violence in the absence of such external danger stimuli would have been strong internal prohibitions against antisocial aggression. *Stable and strong internal controls are more likely to prevent murders than are death penalties; the latter often are out of sight and out of mind.*

---

[3] Henry and Short have contended that the individual is most likely to compare his own status with that of people in other social strata. If he is in a high stratum, he supposedly wants to be better off than the low-status group, while the low-status individual presumably wants to be closer to the higher social levels. The present book argues, on the other hand, that such comparisons tend to be primarily with others in one's own social level. The same objection was raised earlier against A.K. Cohen's (1955) conception of the status deprivations presumably felt by lower-class boys.

[4] People undoubtedly differ in the extent to which they expect to succeed in a risky undertaking. One person may characteristically expect not to get caught if he carried out a crime, while another, more pessimistic, individual may anticipate only the worst and thus would be less likely to commit a crime.

IMPLICATIONS

What do you see as the major conditions leading to homicide besides recurrent frustrations? Are there certain implications about the death penalty in this discussion? What is an effective preventive, if not drastic punishment? To what extent is it possible to lessen some of the frustrations the individual experiences? What are some feasible programs to bring about stronger and stabler internal controls in the potential murderer? What other ideas came to you as you read the Berkowitz discussion of murder?

REFERENCES

For a vivid, human-interest description of the lives of several individual murderers, see Truman Capote's *In Cold Blood* (1965). A good, simply written, psychological discussion of aggression is by Aronson (1972). Consult the Bibliography for further references cited in the article.

42   SUICIDE: SELF-DIRECTED HOSTILITY

Leonard Berkowitz

A person takes his own life and shocks us all. Why? What do the data and interviews to date show us about the suicidal personality? Does it fit the hypothesis that frustration leads to aggression? If so, aggression toward whom? Toward the source of frustration—even if oneself? Study Berkowitz's discussion of the individual with self-blame.

Suicide

FEW HUMAN ACTIONS seem to be as difficult to understand as suicide. A fifty-year-old industrialist committed suicide supposedly (according to the newspapers) because he recently had sold his firm and was despondent at no longer controlling its destiny. He left an estate of over two million dollars. Did he feel there was nothing left in life for him?

Such an explanation probably is much too simple to be true. Suicide is a highly complex phenomenon, and there is relatively little agreement among authorities as to its cause or even how the potential self-killer should be treated.

Some of the confusion in the study of suicidal behavior arises from the multiplicity of reasons for self-destruction. The eminent French sociologist Emile Durkheim (1951) listed three types of suicides: *altruistic, egoistic,* and *anomic.* In the first of these, the person takes his own life in order to benefit other people. A good example of this is seen in the World War II Japanese kamikaze pilots who dived their planes into American warships. The egoistic suicide, on the other hand, is concerned primarily with himself rather than with others. Not bound to other people by close personal ties, he is wrapped up in his own personal problems and kills himself when he cannot attain his individualistic goals. Finally, the anomic type of suicide presumably occurs when social values disintegrate in a crisis situation and the individual feels "lost." The disruption of the collective order stimulates men's appetites, making them "less disciplined precisely when they need more disciplining." Some people are "declassified" as they are thrown into lower social levels by the cultural turmoil. They must restrain their needs, but they cannot do so. The new social conditions forced on them may be regarded as intolerable, and feeling all is hopeless and meaningless in a world bereft of values, they may take their own lives.

Other writers also insist it is wrong to account for suicides in terms of a single type of motivation. Thus, one authority (Jackson in Shneidman and Farberow, 1957) established a continuum ranging from "irrational" suicides—such as the psychotic who kills himself because he believes the world is coming to an end—to "rational" self-destruction as in the case of the cancer victim suffering from extreme pain. An analysis of over seven hundred notes written by white, native-born suicides also points to the desirability of distinguishing among suicide types. Shneidman and Farberow (1957) found a much higher incidence of direct aggression references (either against the self or others) in the notes written by the younger self-killers, while the "wish to die," characterized by hopelessness, fear, and despair, was predominant in the majority of notes written by suicides over sixty years of age. The younger victims apparently were angrier than the older group and probably did not commit suicides for the same reasons.

Individual Considerations

. . . One possible explanation for suicides: the inhibition of outward-directed aggression. Following a line of thought essentially similar to the orthodox Freudian conception . . . , Dollard et al. (1939) suggested that aggression against the self was a consequence of the blocking of all other aggressive reactions to frustration. Just as "aggressive energy" supposedly turned inward if not discharged in attacks upon other people (cf. Hartmann et al., 1949), aggressive responses to the frustrater, the Yale psychologists contended, presumably heightened the instigation to self-aggression. Suicide, then, could conceivably be regarded as an extreme manifestation of inhibited aggression.

There is some evidence that suicide victims do have stronger internal controls against unlawful behavior than do murderers. Wood (1961) reported, for example, that Ceylonese who had taken their own lives were less likely to use alcohol, have a police record, or a reputation as a neighborhood bully than the people charged with killing someone else. But whether such strong restraints were primarily responsible for the self-destruction is, of course, open to question. Other factors are also involved in suicides. According to several psychiatrists (cf. Chs. 2 and 3 in Shneidman and Farberow, 1957), suicidal actions often stem from several complex motives, such as:

1. A *wish to punish some frustrater.* Many victims apparently delighted in the belief that a particular person, someone who supposedly had hurt or tormented them, would feel sorry and—more important—guilty when learning of the suicide.

2. *Yearning for self-punishment and rebirth.* Self-destruction often is self-punishment for crimes the suicide victims thought they had committed. (In some cases the "crime" supposedly arose from "death wishes.") Fenichel (1945) has maintained that self-destruction during fits of melancholia is typically instigated by desires for forgiveness. This self-punishment could then lead to a new start by alleviating guilt. Children and schizophrenics are said to feel that if they can kill the "bad me" they could then achieve a rebirth as a less wicked person.

3. Paradoxically, suicide victims may believe their self-destruction will not really mean the end of their existence. Potential suicide victims sometimes develop grandiose fantasies in compensation for the frustrations they have suffered, and according to psychiatric observations, such fantasies often include ideas of immortality and omnipotence (Shneidman and Farberow, 1957). They will punish themselves, and perhaps other people as well, by taking their lives, but they will still exist to enjoy the after-effects of their action. Consistent with this, Shneidman and Farberow (1957) have reported that suicide notes frequently contain admonitions and instructions perhaps "indicative of unrealistic feelings of omnipotence and omnipresence." The victims presumably "cannot successfully imagine [their] own death and . . . complete cessation."

We cannot say how often such beliefs and desires occur in the incipient suicide or, for that matter, how important these feelings are in the instigation of the self-murder. But it is clear that many suicides are extreme attacks upon the self arising from guilt and self-blame. Inhibitions against attacks upon others may be present and may have had an important role in the sequence of events leading to suicide. Self-killers evidently are frequently angry with other people; their strong inhibitions could have interfered with earlier, milder angry outbursts. Nevertheless, they are extremely angry with themselves as well, and this is important. *Hostility is directed toward the self, at least in part, because the self is regarded as a frustrater.*

Sociological Considerations

Henry and Short (1954) have employed the frustration-aggression hypothesis in explaining social-status differences in suicide rates, assigning the notion of self as frustrater a prominent place in their theorizing. In almost every status hierarchy, and regardless of the basis for the stratification, members of high-status groups tend to kill themselves at a greater rate than do lower-status people. Thus, while suicides are relatively common at both ends of the economic scale, they occur most often among the well-to-do. Similarly, more whites than nonwhites kill themselves, commissioned officers are more prone to take their own lives than are enlisted men of the same race, and men are greater suicide risks than women. (In this last regard it is assumed men have a higher status than women because of their positions in the economic system of our society.)

To account for these differences in self-destruction, the sociologists made use of two sets of empirical findings. First, the inverse correlation between business conditions and suicide rates is generally highest for the higher-status groups. Depressions lead to more suicides in the upper than the lower social strata. The people in the upper strata probably suffer greater deprivations than their lower-status peers as a result of harsh business conditions; there is a greater discrepancy between their predepression and depression conditions, and consequently they are frustrated more severely. But in addition to such greater frustrations in higher-status levels, social relationships also affect the likelihood of committing suicide, as Durkheim stressed (1951). People having close ties with others are a lesser suicide risk than people living in emotional isolation. Married people, for example, are not as prone to kill themselves as single, widowed, or divorced individuals of the same age, and city dwellers, often having only relatively anonymous and impersonal contacts with others, have a higher suicide rate than people living in the more tightly knit rural communities.

Henry and Short used the concept of "external restraints" to integrate these data. The lower-status person typically does not have the freedom possessed by the members of the higher social groups. He has to accede to the demands of his supervisor and/or employer, and he lacks the financial wherewithal even to think of becoming his own master. In general, his actions are subject to relatively great restraints by his social superiors. Similarly, the individual enmeshed in close relationships with other people also experiences restraints. He has obligations to his family and friends. He must conform to their expectations. He often has to comply with their wishes.

These external restraints, as hampering as they might be, serve an important function in times of stress, according to Henry and Short. They "provide immunity from suicide" presumably because they permit the individual to blame others for his troubles. The individual cannot attack himself for the frustrations he suffers if other people must share in the responsibility for his actions.

The Henry and Short argument is an intriguing one. Their reliance on the concept of "external restraints" might appear forced but actually is in complete accord with scientific tradition. Scientists must seek to develop unifying principles capable of showing that apparently diverse phenomena (e.g., the suicidal deaths of a wealthy person and of a lonely city dweller) are special cases of a more general phenomenon (self-blame for a frustration). The present writer does not reject the Henry-Short emphasis upon external restraints altogether but would prefer to add to this argument. High social status in our society produces more than a relative freedom from restraints. (Indeed, in many cases, well-to-do families feel they have a good deal of responsibility and obligations to others. Witness the Rockefellers.) What may be more important is the greater emphasis upon self-reliance and self-accomplishment in the upper social levels. Middle-class parents frequently teach their children that a person is primarily responsible for whatever happens to him (cf. Kohn, 1959). The lower-class individual, on the other hand, tends to see himself as the hapless victim of forces beyond his control. Thus, *since the people from the upper social levels generally regard themselves as masters of their own fate, they also must blame themselves for their social and economic failures.* In extreme cases, such self-blame can lead to suicide.

IMPLICATIONS

You might find in a newspaper a report of a suicide in which certain facts of the individual's life and circumstances are given. How would you classify the suicide—as *altruistic, egoistic,* or *anomic?* Do you have enough information on the suicide victim to know whether his act gives credence to the concept of *external restraints?* To the concept of a *self-punishing personality trend?*

REFERENCES

Consult the Bibliography for references cited in the article.

CHAPTER X

COUNSELING AND PSYCHOTHERAPY

43

IDEAS OF PSYCHOTHERAPY

Norman D. Sundberg and Leona E. Tyler

Every individual suffers disturbing emotional and mental difficulties. When they become acute, the individual or members of his family seek professional assistance. The patient enters into a counseling or psychotherapy relationship. What does the psychotherapist expect to happen? The client shows change in some way; what is the nature of this change?

Before we look at Selections 44 and 46, dealing with two very different kinds of psychotherapy, let us review, with the help of Sundberg and Tyler, the various *goals* of psychotherapy and examine their *common features.*

Iᴛ ᴍᴀʏ ʙᴇ that a slightly frivolous historian in a time to come will look back on our twentieth century and label it *The Age of Psychotherapy.* Hundreds of thousands of men, women, and children are seeking help from thousands of "therapists" of one kind or another: psychiatrists, psychologists, marriage counselors, school counselors, social workers, and clergymen—ministers, rabbis, and priests. Dozens of books are written each year presenting the theory and practice of psychotherapy to technical specialists, students, and the general public. Psychotherapy figures prominently in novels, plays, movies, and television programs. What is it that all these participants are attempting to accomplish? In this chapter we will analyze their purposes and some of the ideas about how they are to be achieved, as they have been set forth by the psychotherapists who have written about their profession.

Ways in Which Goals of Therapy Have Been Formulated

In this field even more than elsewhere in clinical psychology, complex and elaborate theories have arisen. Undoubtedly, Freudian psychoanalysis is the most influential, but the impact of the views of Adler and Jung, Horney and Sullivan, Rogers, Mowrer, and many others has been strongly felt. Instead of discussing these theories one at a time, however, we shall attempt a different kind of classification.

In the theories as they stand, there is considerable confusion, arising from various sources. One source of confusion is that the ideas of every theorist undergo continual modification as he lives and works. The concepts Freud stressed in 1910 are not identical with those upon which he rested his theoretical structure in 1935. Rogers' second book on psychotherapy differs markedly from his first. Thus, it is difficult to write for the beginning student of clinical psychology an account of one of these comprehensive theories that includes *all* the concepts, early and late, actually incorporated in the thinking of some of its adherents.

Another reason for confusion in the theories therapists have produced about therapy is that they overlap. If such theories are taken up one by one, the student is confronted with the task of judging for himself how great this overlapping is. This is especially difficult for an inexperienced person because much of the common ground is found in practice rather than in conceptualization. Psychologists and psychiatrists, when *writing* about their work, are most likely to stress the aspects they consider to be unique or original, while they slight the aspects that fit in with many other theoretical orientations. Thus, the student trying to find a way of approaching his own professional tasks is likely to assume that the differences between theories are sharper than they actually are, and he may conclude that he is required to identify himself with one and only one of the theorists and to repudiate the others. The richness of his own theoretical formulation and the range of his helpfulness to others may be diminished by such a decision.

Therefore, instead of outlining the different complex approaches to therapy connected with the names of Freud, Rogers, Sullivan, and the other founders of systems or schools, we shall discuss first the principal purposes therapy has been thought to accomplish by some influential thinker at some stage of his development. We shall then look for common threads and basic issues and attempt to put the separate pieces together in a new way.

The first of these major purposes basic to some kinds of therapy might be labeled *strengthening the patient's motivation to do the right things*. It is the oldest of the aims we shall discuss. Suggestion in all its forms, ranging from gentle advice to the use of hypnosis to produce tendencies to act in specified ways, is one kind of procedure through which this purpose is carried out. Encouragement and inspiration, whether administered through informal praise and appreciation or through books and sermons, are intended to serve this purpose. Long before there were any professional specialties like psychology, this kind of treatment was constantly attempted. In our own time, therapeutic organizations like Alcoholics Anonymous attribute most of their success to this kind of influence.

A second purpose of therapy that has often been stated is *to reduce emotional pressure by facilitating the expression of feeling*, the process called *catharsis.* When the average layman thinks about therapy, it is probably this meaning he is most likely to connect with it. Dozens of motion pictures have given dramatic portrayals of a sudden relief from neurotic symptoms and anxiety following a flood of emotional expression touched off when contact is made with some repressed memory. Like suggestion and inspiration, the use of this process of emotional expression covers a wide range of depth and intensity, from the common "blowing off steam" at work or at home to the use of drugs or hypnosis to enable a patient to relive a traumatic experience.

A third way of formulating the purpose of therapy makes use of concepts from the psychology of development. Therapy aims to *release the potential for growth.* A basic growth tendency in every person is postulated, a tendency toward maturity and integration. Unfortunate circumstances or adverse influences can block or temporarily reverse this process, but cannot destroy it completely. What therapy aims to do is to remove these obstacles, whatever they are, and allow the person to start growing again along the lines of his own unique pattern. The psychotherapist should not be thought of as a mechanic, locating and repairing defects in a piece of equipment, but rather as more like a gardener, removing weeds, providing light, nutrients, and moisture to stimulate a plant intrinsically disposed to grow. Two aspects of developmental theory may be distinguished. One calls for *the analysis of each life stage* in childhood to ascertain what kinds of neurotic symptoms and faulty character structures may have arisen from failure to negotiate it successfully. The discussions by psychoanalysts of symptoms arising through arrested development at the oral, anal, phallic, or latency period have this focus. The emphasis psychoanalysts place on the necessity for *transference,* a term signifying the process of projecting childish attitudes onto the therapist, comes from the conviction that early periods must in some sense be relived emotionally if personality reorganization is to occur. The other aspect of developmental theory, expressed more clearly by Jung and by Rogers than by Freud, places the emphasis on *development as a process that continues throughout life,* whatever the early handicaps have been. A person is so complex that many avenues of growth and creativity are open to him if they can only be recognized and encouraged. Whether the emphasis is on unraveling the tangled strands of childhood or on opening up new vistas for the future, developmental theories have in common the assumption that therapy means discovering ways of facilitating a natural process rather than undertaking the construction of something new.

A fourth way of stating the purpose of therapy is *habit change.* Neurosis or maladjustment are viewed as the end result of a learning process in which undesirable or ineffective habits have been formed. For many reasons these may be difficult to get rid of, once the person is saddled with them. The task of the therapist, then, is to arrange learning situations in which the patient can modify such undesirable habits or replace them by others. There was real excitement among psychologists when J.B. Watson reported in 1920 that an irrational fear for furry animals had been experimentally produced in a child using conditioned response methods, and when M.C. Jones reported a few years later that conditioning could also be used to remove such fears from children's experience. These experiments seemed to point the way to a rational, scientific kind of therapy free from mystery and uncertainty. The years since the 1920's have sobered hopes for simple methods of "emotional reeducation," as many irrational fears have proved to be impervious to such treatment. But straightforward conditioned response methods are still used quite widely in the treatment of behavior patterns such as enuresis and alcoholism, and the modification of social habits such as shyness and tactlessness is often attempted through planned learning situations. Probably more important, however, than these specific applications of the psychology of learning to particular kinds of cases is the task some theorists have undertaken of reformulating *all* the principles of psychotherapy in terms of learning. A thriving partnership between psychoanalysis and learning theory has resulted in an attack on some interesting research problems. Most psychologists engaged in therapy would agree in principle that therapy *is* learning. They would agree much less well about just what the faulty habits are that need to be changed, and what sort of learning process it is that therapy sets in motion.

A fifth purpose of therapy, in some ways related to the two preceding ones, is *the modification of the cognitive structure of the person,* by which is meant the interrelated set of concepts and fixed ideas that determine his perceptions of the world around him, of other persons, and of himself. Theorists who approach the problems of therapy from this direction have surmised that the roots of a person's difficulties lie in his basic misconceptions about the nature of things, mistaken ideas he acquired at some former period of his life. He is likely to be quite unaware of these cognitive structures. The conclusions to which they lead him are axioms, taken for granted. A generation ago, Alfred Adler discussed the effects of this phenomenon under the graphic term *life style.* More recently, George Kelly in his *Psychology of Personal Constructs* (1955) has presented not only a coherent theoretical statement of this point of view, but also a number of ingenious methods for identifying the basic cognitive structures in an individual and for helping him to modify them if they need changing. The theoretical formulations of Carl Rogers have emphasized the importance of clear, finely differentiated perceptions of self and the world as a basis for effective living. As many clinical psychologists see their task today, the aim of therapeutic activity is to make a client aware of his basic cognitive structures and enable him to produce some change in the pattern. Change will often come automatically once the person becomes aware that one of his "personal constructs" is inconsistent with other aspects of his personality. Lecky's oft-quoted little book, *Self-Consistency* (1945), stimulated much thinking along these lines.

A sixth stated purpose of therapy is *self-knowledge*, broadly defined. This, like habit change, can be an extremely inclusive concept. It is basic to most counseling and rehabilitation activities. The client is given aptitude and interest tests and helped to examine his own capacities, attitudes, needs, background, and opportunities. Self-knowledge is also prominent among the goals of psychoanalysis. The attempt to bring unconscious material into consciousness where the ego of the person can cope with it is so basic in therapeutic procedure that for many theorists this growth in self-knowledge *is* therapy. The word that has been much used as a label for the process of attaining self-knowledge is *insight*. As a theoretical concept, insight is not being stressed as much at present as it was in previous periods. There has come the recognition that an intellectual awareness of all the recesses of one's personality does not necessarily make for psychological health. There must be some emotional quality to such insight if it is to be effective, and it has proved to be very difficult to state how the word is to be defined in these emotional terms. Furthermore, striking improvements occurring in the absence of any manifestation of insight whatever have seriously challenged those who would use self-knowledge as a central therapeutic concept. In short, it seems that insight is neither a necessary nor a sufficient factor in therapy. Nevertheless, it still has its place as an important organizing concept, and the procedures most commonly used in therapy perhaps serve this purpose better than any other.

The last type of theory to be considered here emphasizes *interpersonal relationships*. According to such a theory, we must look for the sources of all psychological ills in the person's relationships to the "significant others" in his life. Here, too, some therapists place the emphasis on the very earliest periods of life as the time when the patterns for future relationships are laid down. They hope, by understanding what occurred then, to find ways of modifying these patterns so that they will no longer exert unhealthy influences on present relationships. Other workers pay more attention to their client's current relationships to spouse, children, friends, and colleagues. They hope to find relationships which may be changed for better rather than to identify the remote childhood origins of the difficulties. One major resource inherent in all types of therapy for producing change in interpersonal relationships is the fact that the client is at the time experiencing a new relationship, without the defects of those previously formed—his relationship to the therapist. A strong emphasis on *communication* distinguishes the interpersonal theories of therapy. Isolation and estrangement are involved in much psychological disturbance. One way to combat them is to improve communication.

Furthermore, the possibilities for therapeutic intervention are not limited to the things that can happen between just two individuals. The unique advantage of *group therapy* is that it allows the participants to establish new relationships, observe and study them, and modify them in constructive ways. Patients can make emotional contact with others as individuals; they can also practice the different *roles* they must play in dealing with other people—whether children, bosses, co-workers, or strangers. Clinical psychologists join sociologists in the interest they take in the mental health effects of *social systems*. As a natural extension from the interpersonal approach, some psychotherapists have been asking: Should we be attempting to treat this individual at all? Would it not be a sounder procedure to try to improve some particular social system of which he is a part, and thus increase the level of health and soundness of all the persons who are caught in it? Thinking of this sort has stimulated careful scrutiny of the social situation to be found in a mental hospital—the whole institution and the individual ward—in a search for ways to change the relationships of physicians, nurses, aides, and patients to one another. The work that marriage and family counselors do often rests on a consideration of the kind of a complex system the wife, husband, and children together constitute rather than on the psychological characteristics of one member of the family. The therapist sees the importance of understanding, and perhaps changing, the dynamics of the small groups encountered in the course of living—work groups, recreation groups, and classroom, for example. The implications of this therapeutic approach are very far-ranging. It has even been said that our whole modern society is a kind of neurotic organism needing therapeutic reorganization.

In many situations, psychologists join in collaborative efforts with physicians providing *somatic treatment*, such as the use of drugs, shock therapy, physiotherapy, or other forms of medical treatment. Physiological changes can have direct effects on behavior, or they may make a person more amenable to ordinary psychotherapy. Even nonpsychiatric patients, such as persons who must undergo surgery and are anxious and distraught, can be helped by brief psychotherapy or counseling. In all somatic cases, psychological treatment must be coordinated with medical treatment. The psychological goal in such cases will fall under one or more of the purposes of therapy we have discussed.

Common Features

It is not possible to distinguish very sharply between the leading schools of psychotherapy on the basis of such aims as we have been outlining. Most writers put stress on more than one of these purposes, selecting different combinations, weighting them differently, and finding different kinds of links between them. Rogers, for instance, stresses the ideas of catharsis, self-knowledge, perceptual shifts, and creative growth. His publications over the years show that he has emphasized catharsis less and creative growth more as time has passed. Freud's early formulations centered on catharsis and self-knowledge, but he later shifted the focal point to development and interpersonal relationships in infancy and childhood. Adlerian therapists devote a good deal of attention to perceptual and cognitive structures and social relationships, but use suggestion and advice to promote self-knowledge and habit change. One of the reasons for the many controversies in the field of psychotherapy may be that there are so many ways in which complex theories can be contrasted with one another!

The procedures actually used show much common ground. In the first place, all methods of personal therapy must concentrate on bringing about *a sufficient lowering of the patient's level of anxiety so that he will be able to permit himself to explore the painful areas of his experience.* An interview where the person is guaranteed privacy, freedom from interruptions, and complete confidentiality has the effect of making him feel at least a little safer than he does at other times in other places. Special group situations may also produce this relaxed attitude. More important is the whole attitude of the therapist and the feeling he communicates to the patient in many subtle ways that he is no longer alone with his troubles. The strength of another person has been added to his own.

Dealing with anxiety is one of the basic skills that a psychotherapist must acquire, and it can never be learned from books or lectures. It is not accomplished by simple kinds of verbal reassurance, no matter how earnest. Furthermore, the goal can never be to eliminate anxiety completely, because anxiety constitutes the principal motivation for undertaking therapy as well as the chief reason for resisting it. Some therapists approach the problem of reducing anxiety by combining tranquilizing drugs with psychotherapy in the treatment of severely disturbed cases. To calm a person enough so that he can face all kinds of potentially threatening inner feelings and outer situations and cope with them may be a valuable treatment maneuver. But to carry this so far that he no longer cares what happens to him or no longer sees the sharp outlines of unyielding facts is not therapy. One of the reasons alcoholics have responded less well to psychotherapy than many other types of neurotic patient is that drinking has become a habitual way of reducing their anxieties—too much.

The second thing that all varieties of therapy attempt to do is to create *a strong personal relationship that can be used as a vehicle for constructive change.* In individual therapy this is a relationship between patient and therapist; in group methods the ties between group members may be the important ones. Research by Fiedler (1950a, 1950b) has suggested that the nature of this relationship may be very similar for kinds of therapy that are differently labeled. It is a significant fact that many theoretical writers, as their experience increases, come to place much more emphasis on this variable. At first, Freud insisted most on the necessity of achieving *insight*; as time passed, *transference* took its place as his central concept, and he turned his attention to the way in which the patient relates himself to his doctor during the different stages of treatment. More recently in psychoanalytic writings there has been a strong emphasis on *counter-transference*, or the way in which the doctor relates himself to the patient. Other theorists also talk about the therapeutic *interaction*—what the situation means to the therapist as well as to the client.

The important idea arising from all of this discussion is one that beginning students sometimes miss—that it is necessary for the therapist himself to participate on a deep emotional level in the psychological process that constitutes therapy. Verbal techniques and skills are no substitute for this emotional participation. There are hazards for the doctor as well as for the patient in launching out upon the deep waters the two of them must traverse together. Learning to deal with such hazards is a far more difficult thing than learning to say something appropriate in response to a client's remark. We shall have more to say of this later.

Another common feature in many diverse systems of thinking about psychotherapy is an emphasis on *communication as a way of enabling the patient to establish connections with his own inner and outer worlds.* Obviously, any talking involves communication to some degree. It might be maintained with some plausibility that all psychological disorders *are* essentially communication problems and that treatment consists in repairing or installing lines of communication so that they will connect the patient with the complex human world in which he must function and assist him in articulating his own thoughts and feelings, thus making them more accessible. At any rate, some of the most essential of the therapist's skills are the ways he has of facilitating free expression in the client with whom he is working. This, like the emotional participation discussed above, is not just a matter of knowing what to say. It consists rather in a sensitive awareness of the way the other person feels, a general perceptiveness that makes it possible for him to pick up faint clues and to grasp meanings in confused and halting attempts to say something—or even in silence, for that matter. A sense of being understood acts as a powerful motivating force for a troubled client, encouraging him to try to communicate more of his experience. To provide this understanding requires great effort as well as extreme sensitivity. One must listen to the other person with a kind of concentrated yet relaxed attention that one seldom brings to the other situations of life. It may even be that it is this *interested attention* rather than the understanding itself that promotes further effort on the part of the client, since occasional failure to grasp some particular meaning seems not to impede therapeutic progress. However, needless to say, if the therapist, well-meaning though he may be, never quite understands what the client is trying to say, the therapeutic process is hardly likely to continue for long.

One of the limitations of psychotherapy as commonly practiced today is that it is almost impossible to make it available to troubled persons whose verbal skills are limited. Most of the patients who receive this form of treatment from private practitioners or public clinics are middle- or upper-class persons of above-average intelligence and with better-than-average education. Even in these privileged parts of the population (Hollingshead and Redlich, 1958) many individuals are unable to express themselves very well verbally. It has occurred to many psychologists who are impressed with the enormous need for therapy that greater use must be made of *nonverbal forms of communication.* In clinics for children, the use of toys, finger paints, clay, and many other kinds of equipment and materials as media in which they can express themselves has become standard procedure. Even very young children are able to express in such ways thoughts and feelings which they are quite incapable of putting into words. Child therapists must learn to receive communications coming to them in these forms. Some attention has been given in recent years to ways of encouraging nonverbal kinds of expression in adults also. One method, Moreno's psychodrama, has been in use for a considerable period of time and a fairly large body of literature concerning it has accumulated. Therapy using music, painting, or the dance has been tried. Group therapy using activities is not uncommon. There have been nonverbal attempts to condition regressed patients in hospitals. All these new ways of dealing with patients remind us that when we say that communication is essential to therapy we must be sure that we do not define communication too narrowly.

One additional feature characterizes all forms of psychotherapy: *some degree of commitment on the part of the patient, his decision to participate, to try.* This, like the other aspects we have been discussing, is not a simple matter and cannot be brought about by the therapist's use of some particular technique. It is often said, for example, that therapy can occur only if the client takes the initiative by seeking out the therapist, if only by calling the clinic for an appointment. Most professional workers try to arrange things so that this will be the way in which therapy begins. If a college teacher is concerned about the state of mind of a student in his class, the counseling psychologist who is consulted will suggest that the student—not the instructor—call the Counseling Center for an appointment. But the principle involved here is far broader and more fundamental than policies with regard to appointment procedures. Even a person who makes his own arrangements for interviews may feel passive and ambivalent about the whole procedure. On the other hand, rebellious clients forced into therapy by relatives, employers, courts, or school administrative officers may shift their attitudes and make the sort of commitment we are talking about. Especially in early interviews, the therapist's skill can contribute to this end. It requires that one carefully avoid any contest of wills, any obvious or subtle attempt to control the client. But one must also avoid what looks like indifference, an attitude that what the client decides to do is immaterial to the therapist. What the therapist's whole attitude (it cannot be communicated by words alone) must say is: "I really want to help you. I hope you'll give this a trial. But I'm not going to force you or trick you into compliance. The decision really does rest with you." The therapist must be able to communicate hope to the client but without promising anything except sincere effort. What he is asking the person to do is to invest something of himself—a great deal, really—in an enterprise for which a successful outcome cannot be assured.

Once this commitment has occurred, therapy becomes a sort of *partnership*. Menninger (1958) has called the arrangement a *contract* in which each participant agrees to do something in exchange for something from the other person, and both agree to follow certain implicit rules. This, too, is something that characterizes all forms, all schools. There are differences in the way the work to be done is distributed—differences from case to case as well as from one theoretical school to another. But therapy is work, and hard work, for both participants. Both will go through periods of elation as well as periods of extreme discouragement. Progress will often be followed by relapses. Therapy is one of the most fascinating and rewarding of human undertakings, but it is never simple, never easy.

It is generally agreed that patients and clients, even children (Allen, 1942), must be willing to accept changes in themselves if therapy is eventually to succeed. However, this does not mean that psychologists should refuse to work with poorly motivated clients such as chronic schizophrenics, resentful juvenile delinquents, and patients with character disorders. Even though the attitudes of such persons make formal psychotherapy impossible, desirable changes can sometimes be produced by means of direct suggestion, environmental influences, or group activities. There is always room for innovation and research in understanding and modifying behavior.

IMPLICATIONS

Try to express specific examples of the seven purposes of psychotherapy, which we have summarized as (1) to do the right things, (2) to get expression of feelings, (3) to release potentials for growth, (4) to bring about habit change, (5) to modify the cognitive structure, (6) to increase self-knowledge, and (7) to effect health-producing interpersonal relationships. Then you can better understand the common features in these various aims. Can you recall some instances in which someone aided you at a time of crisis by *reducing your anxiety?* How was this brought about? What are some examples of the kind of communication between people that help to establish connection with a client's inner and outer world?

REFERENCES

For further reading on the viewpoints expressed by Sundberg and Tyler (1962), see Hall and Lindzey (1957). In their book, they discuss the views of Freud, Adler, Jung, Horney, Sullivan, and Rogers. A summary of the views of the followers of Freud is found in Selection 47. Some of Jung's views are presented in Selection 51. See also Mowrer (1954) and Patterson (1966).

A somewhat different attempt to acquaint the lay reader with various forms of psychotherapy is by Bry (1972). She is a psychotherapist and has interviewed nine therapists who approach therapy differently. She asked them what they were trying to do and how they worked. They represent psychoanalytic, Jungian, Frommian, Gestalt, behavioral, family group, encounter group, and nude marathon therapy.

44

THE CONDITIONING THERAPIES

Joseph Wolpe, Andrew Salter, and L.F. Reyna

One approach to emotional disturbances, particularly the neuroses, is to regard them as learned, persistent, and nonadaptive habits that merely have to be unlearned by reconditioning. The following selection is a simple discussion of a movement in psychology and psychiatry to do just this.

Anxiety is a feeling of dread, an objectless "fear," a concern over impending doom or a possible unacceptable consequence of events. Phobia, another fear response mentioned by Wolpe, may be defined as excessive fear in the absence of real danger. How are the conditioning techniques that are developed in the animal laboratory applied in the clinical situation? You will note that the clinician uses behavior and its instigation to treat what some psychologists regard as subjective experience. The conditioning therapist uses a kind of therapy known

From *The Conditioning Therapies: The Challenge in Psychotherapy*, edited by Joseph Wolpe, Andrew Salter, and L.J. Reyna. Copyright © 1964 by Holt, Rinehart and Winston, Inc. Reprinted by permission of Holt, Rinehart and Winston, Inc. and the senior author.

as reciprocal inhibition, in which symptoms or complaints of the patient are decreased when the stimuli are presented under conditions in which the response is inhibited.

NOW LET US CONSIDER the conditioning therapies. These methods stem from the conception that neuroses are persistent unadaptive habits that have been conditioned (that is, learned). If this conception is correct, the fundamental overcoming of a neurosis *can* consist of nothing but deconditioning—or undoing the relevant habit patterns.

The most characteristic and common feature of neurotic habits is anxiety. There is persuasive evidence, both experimental and clinical, that the great majority of neuroses are fundamentally conditioned autonomic responses (Wolpe, 1958). The individual has persistent habits of reacting with anxiety to situations that, objectively, are not dangerous. Typical stimuli to which the response of anxiety may be regarded as neurotic are the sight of a bird, the interior of an elevator, asking a favor, or receiving a compliment. Experimentally it is possible to condition an animal to respond with anxiety to any stimulus one pleases merely by arranging for that stimulus, on a number of occasions, to appear in an appropriate time relation to the evocation of anxiety; and by manipulating various factors one can obtain an emotional habit that is utterly refractory to extinction in the ordinary way (Wolpe, 1948, 1958). In human neuroses one can usually elicit a history of similar kinds of conditioning. Human neuroses, too, are characterized by the same remarkable resistance to extinction. Since neurotic reactions are, as a rule, autonomic reactions first and foremost, this resistance is in keeping with Gantt's observations of the great refractoriness of cardiovascular conditioned responses to extinction.

It is implicit in conditioning theory that recovery from neurosis should be achieved by applying the learning process in a reverse direction: whatever undesirable behavior has been learned may be unlearned. In experiments performed about fourteen years ago, I demonstrated in cats that had been made neurotic experimentally how this unlearning can be brought about (Wolpe, 1948, 1958). Anxiety reactions had been strongly conditioned to a small confining cage and to other stimuli, and could not be made to extinguish despite repeated exposure to the stimuli. The anxiety response habits could, however, be overcome in piecemeal fashion by counterposing feeding to weak anxiety responses. At first, stimuli distantly similar to the conditioned stimuli were used, until anxiety decreased to zero, and then, step by step, stimuli closer in resemblance to the original conditioned stimuli were introduced, until even the strongest eventually lost its power to evoke anxiety. These findings led to the framing of the reciprocal inhibition principle of psychotherapy, which is that *if a response inhibitory of anxiety can be made to occur in the presence of anxiety-evoking stimuli, it will weaken the bond between these stimuli and the anxiety.*

Experience with human neuroses indicates that the principle has quite general validity; in addition to feeding, a good many other kinds of responses,[1] each of which, empirically, appears to inhibit anxiety, have been successfully used to weaken neurotic anxiety-response habits and related neurotic habits. The reciprocal inhibition principle also affords an explanation for the therapeutic effects of interviewing as such (which is seemingly the main basis of the successes of the traditional therapies) and for so-called spontaneous recoveries.

I have described elsewhere (1958) the deliberate therapeutic use of a considerable range of anxiety-inhibiting responses. I shall briefly review those most widely employed—assertive, relaxation, and sexual responses.

Assertive responses are used where there is a need to overcome neurotic anxieties that arise irrationally in the course of interpersonal relationships —such anxieties as prevent a person from expressing his opinions to his friends lest they disagree, or from reprimanding inefficient underlings. The essence of the therapist's role is to encourage appropriate assertiveness, the outward expression, wherever it is reasonable and right to do so, of the feelings and action tendencies that anxiety has in the past inhibited. In other words, the therapist instigates "acting out." Each act of assertion to some extent reciprocally inhibits the anxiety, and in consequence somewhat weakens the anxiety response habit. The assertion required is not necessarily aggressive, and behavior in accordance with affectionate and other feelings may need to be instigated. The maneuvers involved are largely similar to those described by Salter (1949), though the rationale upon which he bases them is different.

Relaxation responses were first used on a scientific basis by Jacobson (1939), who demonstrated that they have autonomic accompaniments opposite to those of anxiety. His method of intensive training in relaxation for use in the life situation, though of great value, is rather cumbersome. More economical and clearly directed use of relaxation is made in the technique known as *systematic desensitization* (Wolpe, 1958, 1961).

Lang reports its use in the context of snake phobias, but its range of application is very wide indeed.[2] The therapist has to identify the categories of stimuli to which the patient reacts with anxiety, and then rank the

---

[1] Gellhorn and Loofbourrow (1963) present a number of modern instances of reciprocally inhibitory relationships between reactions in both the somatic and the autonomic nervous systems. (See also Gellhorn, 1961.)

[2] Some people are erroneously under the impression that this method is effective only for classical phobias. The word "phobia" refers to clearly defined stimulus sources of neurotic anxiety. The conditioning therapist differs from his colleagues in that he *seeks out* the precise stimuli to anxiety, and finds himself able to break down almost every neurosis into what are essentially *phobic systems*. Their subject matter extends far beyond the classical phobias, and includes such contents as neurotic fears of incurring obligations, of being watched, or of receiving praise. (See Wolpe, 1964.)

stimuli of each category in order of intensity of evoked anxiety. In the course of about six interviews, the patient is given training in relaxation in parallel with this. When the preliminaries have been completed, the patient is made to relax as deeply as possible (in some cases under hypnosis), and then instructed to imagine the weakest of the anxiety-evoking stimuli for a few seconds. The instruction is repeated at short intervals, and if the response to the stimulus has been weak initially, it declines, on repetition, to zero. Under these circumstances, what apparently happens is that on each occasion the relaxation inhibits the anxiety, to some extent, and somewhat weakens the anxiety-evoking potential of the stimulus concerned. With repetition this potential is brought down to zero.

Recent studies have demonstrated:

that the effects of desensitization are due to the procedure itself and not to suggestion or transference (Wolpe, 1962; Lang, pp. 47–48);

that after one or two sessions it can be predicted with virtual certainty whether a patient will respond to this treatment or not; and

that in phobias with independently measurable parameters, such as acrophobia, the numbers of therapeutic operations involved show consistent mathematical relationships to the stages of decrement of the phobia (Wolpe, 1963) that are suggestively similar to the psychophysical law proposed by Stevens (1962).

Sexual responses are used to inhibit anxiety responses conditioned to sexual situations. By manipulating the conditions of sexual approaches so that anxiety is never permitted to be strong, reciprocal inhibition of anxiety by sexual arousal is effected, and the anxiety response habit is progressively weakened. It is usually possible to overcome impotence or premature ejaculation in a few weeks.

The question is, how effective are these and related techniques in procuring the recovery of neurotic patients in terms of Knight's criteria? *

Using the whole range of available methods according to their indications, I have reported between 1952 and 1958 three series of results embracing 210 neurotic patients. Every patient in whom the reciprocal inhibition techniques had been given a fair trial was included in the series. Nearly 90 per cent of these patients were rated on Knight's criteria as either apparently cured or much improved after an average of about thirty therapeutic interviews. The cases were unselected in the sense that no case diagnosed as neurotic was ever refused treatment. Psychotics and psychopaths were not accepted for treatment unless by error of diagnosis.

Until recently, there were no other studies involving considerable numbers of patients, although numerous accounts had been published describ-

---

* Briefly, these are: symptomatic improvement, increased productiveness, improved adjustment to and pleasure in sex, improved interpersonal relationships, and ability to handle ordinary psychological and reality stresses. See Knight (1941).—Ed.

ing the successful treatment of individuals or small groups. Hussain reports 95 per cent of 105 patients whom he treated by a direct approach involving hypnosis apparently recovered or much improved. Recently, I received from the Hospital for Mental and Nervous Diseases at St. John's, Newfoundland, a report by Drs. Alastair Burnett and Edmond Ryan of the treatment of one hundred neurotic patients on learning theory principles. The usual treatment period was five weeks. The evaluation of outcome was on Knight's criteria. Substantial improvement occurred in almost every case (Burnett, 1962). Twenty-five of the patients were followed up over a year or more, and fifteen of these (60 per cent) were then either apparently cured or much improved. Another 32 per cent were rated "moderately improved." As the outcome of five weeks of therapy this is quite noteworthy. Burnett and Ryan express the view that these methods make effective psychotherapy available for the first time to "fairly large numbers of rural, unsophisticated patients who have limited formal education."

In Table 1, the results of characteristic behavior therapy series are compared with those of the two major psychoanalytic series discussed above.

A critical question is, of course, the durability of the results obtained

Table 1

Comparative Results

Series	No. of cases	Apparently cured or much improved (recoveries)	Percentage recoveries
Psychoanalytic Therapy			
Collected series of psychoneuroses			
Knight (1941)			
a. Over 6 months' therapy	383		63.2
		242	
b. Total cases	534		45.3
Psychoanalytic Fact-Gathering			
Committee Brody (1962)	210	126	60
a. Completely analyzed cases	210	126	60
b. Total cases	595	(184)	(31)[a]
Behavior Therapy			
Wolpe (1958)	210	188	89.5

[a] This percentage is calculated from data of the Fact-Gathering Committee of the American Psychoanalytic Association, as follows. It is granted that the whole "completely analyzed" group of 306 would have shown the 60 per cent recovery rate found in the 210 who were followed up, giving 184 recoveries for 306 patients. These would appear to be the sum total of patients claimed as apparently cured or much improved out of the whole group of 595, which includes 289 who discontinued analysis (Brody, 1962; Masserman, 1963).

by conditioning methods. The answer appears to be that they are practically always long-lasting. In 1958, I was able to report only one relapse among forty-five patients who had been followed up for periods ranging from two to seven years. Published communication from other conditioning therapists indicates that their experience is essentially the same. Furthermore, whenever resurgence of symptoms has occurred, and could be investigated, it has always been found to be related to specific events that could clearly have reconditioned the neurotic emotional habit. Learning theory predicts that *unless* there are intervening events that directly recondition neurotic reactions, recovery from neurosis that is radical in the sense defined earlier in this paper will be lasting, no matter by what maneuvers it has been obtained. There are facts that bear out this prediction. I elsewhere reported (Wolpe, 1961) a survey of follow-up studies on neurotic patients who, with various therapies, other than psychoanalysis, had either recovered or improved markedly. Of 249 patients followed up from two to fifteen years only four had relapsed. This finding is not only in line with conditioning theory, but also directly contrary to the expectations of the psychoanalytic theory of neurosis.

Conclusions

The comparison I have presented is, of course, not based on data emanating from a controlled study on matched patients. Such a study, which should include an untreated group of patients similarly matched, is obviously desirable. Nevertheless, I submit that the evidence justifies now substituting behavior therapy for psychoanalysis in the training of therapists, and not temporizing until absolute proof has been provided. There are some who favor waiting for a study on matched groups of patients on the ground that the inferior results of psychoanalysis may be attributable to the psychoanalysts having to treat more difficult cases. There are several reasons for thinking this unlikely. In the first place, while conditioning therapists as a rule undertake treatment of all cases of neurosis, psychoanalysts are often very selective, and surely do not refuse those whom they believe they could *easily* help. Second, conditioning therapists frequently overcome neuroses that have been unsuccessfully treated by psychoanalysis, and often for many years. Third, in private practice, the individual medical practitioner tends to send *all* his neurotic cases to a favored psychotherapist, whether analyst or not. Fourth, it is at least tangentially relevant that, as already noted, psychoanalysts often profess a disinterest in symptomatic recovery, claiming that they aim at something "deeper," such as radical personality change. It may, however, be noted parenthetically that the analysts often represent this alleged deep kind of change as being *prerequisite* to durable freedom from symptoms, a proposition that evidence I have quoted flatly contradicts.

The present position is clear. As far as the evidence goes, conditioning therapies appear to produce a higher proportion of lasting recoveries from the distress and disability of neurosis than does psychoanalysis. Even if a controlled study were to show an equal, or even higher, percentage of recovery for psychoanalysis, the time it requires would remain incomparably greater, and conditioning therapy would therefore still deserve preference. The possible public health implications are great. A psychotherapist who uses behavioristic techniques can handle over ten times as many patients per year as the therapist who employs psychoanalysis, and with greater hope of success for each patient. Effective treatment has thus become possible for many more victims of neurotic disturbance—and at much less expense than psychoanalysis requires.

IMPLICATIONS

Can you visualize, by the patient suffering from a psychological illness, what the therapist does? How is this curative? What everyday behavior might be changed by this procedure? How does this kind of therapy differ basically from family therapy, discussed in Selection 46, sexual inadequacy discussed in Selection 8, or any of the other therapies discussed in Selection 43?

REFERENCES

Consult the Bibliography for references cited in the article.

45 UNDERSTANDING THE ALCOHOLIC
Ronald J. Catanzaro

For a long time, the nondrinker and the moderate drinker viewed the chronic inebriate as a person of defective character; alcoholism was not regarded as a health or psychological problem. Today, most professional workers, including the educated clergyman, know that the individual with poor control over alcoholic drinking is in some way allergic to the effects of alcohol as a beverage.

Reprinted from Ronald J. Catanzaro, publication of Conference on Alcoholism (Lake Windermere Lodge, Roach, Missouri, 1964), by permission of the author.

Alcoholism has been called a disease, and some biologists hypothesize that the drinker has a metabolic pattern that results in nutritional deficiencies that predispose him to addiction to alcohol. The studies in the following selection show characteristics commonly found among alcoholics. In the United States the excessive use of alcohol is a serious health problem, with personal and social dangers, and it is not decreasing in magnitude. Its control will require the intelligence of all professions concerned with the welfare of the human being. Psychological conditions predisposing the individual to addiction are significant; thus rehabilitation of the alcoholic requires psychological as well as medical, clerical, and psychiatric resources.

The following selection is a portion of an address given at one of the many conferences on alcoholism sponsored by the National Institute of Mental Health, U.S. Public Health Service. The author gives special attention to the religious resources because, as he points out, it has been discovered that 42 per cent of the people interviewed in a survey on alcoholism went first to the clergy for help with their problem.

One of the organizations that has been most helpful in keeping the alcoholic sober is Alcoholics Anonymous. It has a nonsectarian religious orientation. The psychologist, with his objective orientation, may regard this whole-person commitment on the part of the alcoholic as both a social and psychological force that can affect behavior. We have included that portion of the address which describes seven of the twelve steps of Alcoholics Anonymous—the heart of the organization's creed and program and a good example of the lay therapeutic approach. Catanzaro is medical director of the Alcoholic Rehabilitation Program at Avon Park, Florida.

Understanding the Alcoholic

IN THE INTEREST of understanding the alcoholic, let us explore together: (1) factors which appear to be important in causing a person to become an alcoholic and (2) factors which prevent him from having his disease arrested.

Factors Causing a Person to Become an Alcoholic

No one knows all the factors involved in causing a person to become an alcoholic. In light of the current literature on alcoholism and my own experience in the field, most theories of etiology of alcoholism fall into three categories: biological, psychological, and sociocultural.

Biologic Theories. Inherited peculiarities of body biology have been indicted as the cause of alcoholism by many. Dr. E.M. Jellinek (1960), one of the most distinguished workers in the field of alcoholism, compiled a number of studies dealing with rates of alcoholism in families. He found an over-all average of 52 per cent of alcoholics had at least one alcoholic parent. Conversely, the expectancy rate of alcoholism in the children of families where at least one parent is an alcoholic is between 20 and 30 per cent. In contrast, the expectancy rate of alcoholism in the general population is only between 2 and 3 per cent. Two additional personal observations have always struck me as very interesting. Firstly, many of my alcoholic patients have stated that they literally lost control of the use of alcohol with their first experience with alcohol as a teenager. As one alcoholic told me: "The first time I remember drinking was when I was fourteen down in my Daddy's wine cellar. I drank until I got so drunk and sick I vomited." Many never touched a drink again until years later, and when they did, they again drank to the point of drunkenness and have continued to do so since. One might postulate that these people have a high degree of genetic biologic determinancy for addiction to alcohol.

The second interesting observation is that some of my patients are overly dependent, immature, emotionally unstable, come from broken or unhappy homes, and in general have most of the characteristics frequently thought to be the basis of alcoholism by those who adhere to psychologic factors as the cause. Several of these people have told me how they actually set out to become alcoholics during a very unhappy period in their lives. They hoped that once they became an alcoholic, they wouldn't care about anything anymore, including their troubles. They reported drinking heavily over many months and finally decided the whole experiment was a failure; they didn't get much of a lift out of drinking and were tired of the hangover effects of alcohol so they quit without any trouble. Some of them stated they take occasional social drinks now and have no desire to drink heavily. One might postulate that these people have a very low degree of genetic biologic determinancy to become addicted to alcohol—"they just don't have what it takes."

Exactly how would such a genetic biologic factor work? R.J. Williams (1949) postulates that alcoholism may be caused by an inherited metabolic pattern which results in nutritional deficiencies and consequently gives rise to a craving for the specific nutrient called alcohol. No such metabolic deficiency has ever been proven. Does the alcoholic suffer from some other type of metabolic abnormality such as an endocrine imbalance which biologically predisposes him to become addicted to alcohol as J.J. Smith postulates? Again, no conclusive evidence of this has yet come to light. Could the alcoholic genetically inherit an emotional make-up which predisposes to alcoholism (Diethelm, 1955)? A fascinating idea, but no convincing evidence has ever been uncovered. Others that hold to biologic etiology of alcoholism state that if the biologic factor was not inherited, it may well be acquired. Through repeated bouts of heavy drinking, a person may develop an unusual sensitivity to alcohol, that is, he may actually become allergic to alcohol as many members of Alcoholics Anonymous believe. Again, no such allergy has ever been demonstrated.

Psychologic Theories.   Other workers in the field of alcoholism feel that since no biologic peculiarities of alcoholics have been discovered, in spite of extensive investigation, the most likely cause of alcoholism lies in the psychologic area. Howard Clinebell, a doctor of theology and a Methodist minister, carefully interviewed 77 alcoholics regarding their home life as a child. He found that 57 per cent of the alcoholics came from severely inadequate homes (Clinebell, 1956). The four outstanding parental characteristics of these homes were authoritarianism, success worship, moralism, and overt rejection. The first three of these characteristics are in part subtle forms of rejection also. The growing child needs generous portions of parental love and harmony. He must feel wanted because of what he is, not because of what he can give to the parents. He must be taught self-control, but a control which is flexible and adjustable to life demands. He must be allowed to mature emotionally so that he can release strong emotions in an efficient and harmless way and thus allow his temperament to remain on a relatively even plateau during his life. His parents must enable him to change the focus of his life from a typically self-centered childish pattern to an extroverted pattern. Finally, his parents must instill in him a reason for living, a spiritual sense of values.

In the best of homes, parents fall short of accomplishing this. It has been observed though that children from severely inadequate homes, as were the people in Dr. Clinebell's study, are correspondingly severely stunted in their psychological growth in many of the above areas. It has also been observed that emotionally immature adults meet their problems as would a child. One of the outstanding characteristics of children is their vivid imagination, i.e., their ability to shut out reality. Consider children's fairy tales which invariably end on the theme "And they lived happily ever after." Real life certainly does not always end in happiness. Consider now an adult with the emotional make-up of a child. Is it unreasonable to postulate that this emotionally immature adult, finding that he is unable to meet life's everyday problems because he is emotionally stunted, attempts to solve his problems in a make-believe childish manner, say by drinking a magic potion (alcohol) which will make his problems disappear temporarily? And when the magic potion begins wearing off and he again begins to feel his problems, he simply drinks more potion. Eventually life is unbearable without the potion.

In psychologic tests of alcoholics, the following are the most commonly found characteristics (Clinebell, 1956): (1) high level of anxiety in interpersonal relations; (2) emotional immaturity; (3) ambivalence toward authority; (4) low frustration tolerance; (5) grandiosity; (6) low self-esteem; (7) feelings of isolation; (8) perfectionism; (9) guilt; (10) compulsiveness.

Alcohol's ability to reduce a high level of anxiety in interpersonal relations has caused Dr. Jellinek to dub alcohol "a social lubricant." Many alcoholics early in their disease use alcohol as a drug for calming anxious and insecure feelings which arise at a social gathering. As their disease progresses, they seem to become even less able to relate to people and therefore become even more dependent on alcohol to "get in the mood to relax and have fun." Thus, as their inability to deal with people effectively becomes more pronounced, they need increasing amounts of alcohol to blot out this increasingly unpleasant reality. It has been my personal experience in a follow-up study of alcoholics treated in a military hospital that the ones who have attained the longest period of sobriety are usually the ones who have noted most improvement in ability to get along with their friends. Conversely, the ones who have been able to maintain little sobriety also note little improvement in ability to get along with their friends.

Emotional immaturity includes being excessively moody, demanding that one's desires be met promptly, having a violent temper, expressing one's emotions through acts rather than words, and being self-centered. Certainly many alcoholics can be described thus. It is not certain, though, whether these alcoholics had always been this way or became this way only after their disease of alcoholism had become established.

Ambivalence toward authority as emphasized by Giorgio Lolli is an extremely prevalent symptom of alcoholics. A constant struggle goes on in many alcoholics between the need to be dependent and subservient and the need to be dominant and mighty. The common example is the alcoholic who married a domineering wife because of his need to be dependent on someone, and upon getting drunk beats her up to prove he is really the dominant one.

Low frustration tolerance is part of emotional immaturity and is a common attribute of children as well as alcoholics. It is this limited ability to stand frustration that often causes the alcoholic to resume drinking.

Grandiosity is present in the alcoholic when he is sober as well as drinking. Everyone knows of the alcoholic sitting in a bar who boasts to his drinking chums of the fantastic business deal he is about to close tomorrow. And when the alcoholic sobers up the next morning, he manifests the opposite side of the same coin. He states to his wife: "I'm the worst person in the world, I've failed in everything I've ever done." To be all that bad is no small accomplishment either.

Low self-esteem is one of the important traits that helps alcoholics continue to drink. "When I drink I feel like a champ, a king, and the next morning I realize what a crumb I am," as one alcoholic expressed it to me. This being the case, what a great temptation it is to have "just one more drink" to feel good again.

Feelings of isolation are the natural outgrowth of his inability to get along with people. As the alcoholic continues drinking, his behavior and conversation become less acceptable to those about him, and consequently his family and friends begin isolating him from their social circle.

Perfectionism and compulsiveness are components of grandiosity. All three of these symptoms are largely an outgrowth of intense feelings of guilt, feelings of being unloved and unlovable. The alcoholic must prove that he is better than his fellow man so that he will not have to feel so guilty about his failures whenever he is sober. For the alcoholic, to be successful is to be loved, to fail is to be unloved.

In order to avoid feeling the guilt which facing unpleasant reality would cause, the alcoholic builds up defenses which are founded in unreality. Tiebout calls these defenses an "alcoholic shell," thus indicating the brittle barrier one must traverse before getting the alcoholic to face his problem realistically. The alcoholic in order to feel worthwhile must maintain a self-image which is identical to his ideal self. As his disease progresses his real self becomes farther and farther removed from this ideal self. In order to feel secure, he must therefore blot out his real self, which he does partly with alcohol and partly with his alcoholic shell of excuses. This unrealistic feeling of being secure in one's own make-believe world is quite comparable to the brand of philosophy expounded by Charles M. Schulz's cartoon character, "Peanuts," when he says, "Security is a thumb and a blanket."

Consequently, we must understand that asking a man to admit he is an alcoholic is asking him to surrender his meticulously constructed shell of unreality, to realize his life has become confused and chaotic and to acknowledge that he has fallen miserably short of the ideal itself which he so desperately needs to be. One must note here the parallel between the phenomenon of truly accepting one's self as an alcoholic who must now try to refrain from drinking in order to be at peace with himself and the phenomenon of religious conversion where one truly accepts one's self as a sinner and must now try to refrain from sinning in order to be at peace with himself.

Of all the psychological characteristics involved in making a person addicted to alcohol, it appears that the two most important characteristics are a chronic high-anxiety level and a chronic inability to face unpleasant reality. These two factors combine to make one not only an alcoholic, but also an addictive personality. It is well known by those who work extensively with alcoholics that someone addicted to alcohol can easily become addicted to other drugs, including barbiturates, certain tranquilizers, chloralhydrate, paralydehyde, etc. Thus, other addicting drugs which also reduce anxiety and blot out reality may be readily substituted for alcohol.

A classical experiment helping to elucidate the mechanism of addiction to alcohol was made by Masserman and Yum (1946). They produced a neurosis in cats by creating an internal conflict in them between fear of pain and desire for food. They taught the cats to push a lever which released a pellet of food to them. Then they placed an electric charge on the lever which shocked the cats whenever they touched the lever. The cats thus were torn between a desire for food and a fear of being shocked.

They began behaving in a characteristically neurotic way, losing all interest in activities which previously occupied them. When the cats were given an injection of alcohol, their anxiety was alleviated, their neurotic conflict was numbed and they resumed pressing the lever, eating and behaving normally. Alcohol, which is classified by physiologists as an anesthetic, had made the shock they received painless, that is, as long as they had alcohol in their body. Soon they had become addicted to spiked milk which they had previously ignored. In this particular experiment with cats, the addiction was broken only after the original neurosis was extinguished. In human beings it appears that even after successful psychoanalytic treatment of underlying neurosis the addictive tendency does not disappear.

Sociocultural Theories. Since the importance of sociocultural factors in the causation of alcoholism is the particular area of interest of Dr. Pittman (1962), I will point out only one observation. Alcoholism tends to be extremely common among certain ethnic groups such as the Irish and French. This fact does not appear to be explained simply by observing that most Irishmen and Frenchmen have tasted of spirits at some time in their life. In a recent study of the Jewish culture, it was reported that 91 per cent of the group had first tasted alcoholic beverages while they were between the ages of five and seven years old. Yet alcoholism is very rare among the Jews. Thus, some other factor besides exposure to alcohol must determine whether the person becomes an alcoholic or not.

Factors Which Prevent Him from Breaking His Addiction

What are the key factors which prevent the alcoholic from successfully breaking his addiction? First of all one must understand the point that Dr. E.M. Jellinek (1960) emphasized so often, that alcoholism is a *progressive disease*, i.e., the alcoholic progressively deteriorates. Initially, then, such personality traits as marked anxiety in interpersonal relations, emotional immaturity, feelings of inadequacy, etc., may be important in causing a person to begin drinking heavily. As he passes from heavy social drinking to early alcoholism, deterioration begins. Thus, personality traits which were originally defective become even more defective and new character defects are added. In addition, realities of life become progressively more grim as the alcoholic begins neglecting his problems rather than solving them.

The nonprofessional community around him regards these events simply as signs of moral weakness and lack of will power. Upon sobering up each morning the alcoholic, who himself holds similar moral convictions as does the community about him, also begins regarding himself condescendingly. The only way he can relieve these agonizing feelings is to drink some more. Even the professional members of the community, including doctors, nurses, clergymen, social workers, etc., often hold the same erroneous views as does the rest of the community. Thus the trap is complete. Everywhere he turns for help—to his own resources, to his family and friends, to his minister and doctor—he meets a condescending stare. How then can this vicious cycle be broken?

Treatment Resources

The problem of getting the alcoholic under treatment and keeping him there is certainly one of the major problems in the field of alcoholism today. Often, the alcoholic initially has to be coerced into treatment, partly because of his agonizing memories of being repeatedly rejected and partly because of his fear of squarely facing reality. At other times, the alcoholic himself initiates the plea for help but does not succeed in finding it. Although there is no pat answer for successfully treating the alcoholic, there are available community resources which are of great aid in achieving this goal. Brief mention will now be given of each of these resources.

1. Well-informed and interested clergymen are essential. A study recently published in a booklet entitled *Americans View Their Mental Health* (Gurin, *et al.*, 1960) revealed that 42 per cent of the people interviewed went first to the clergy for help with their personal problems. If the alcoholic or his family who first turns to the clergy for help meets with misinformation or lack of understanding, it may be many years before another try is made at arresting this dreadful disease.

2. Local physicians who understand the problem of alcoholism are invaluable in helping the alcoholic to "dry out" successfully and then in helping him to continue his sobriety (Catanzaro, 1964). Most communities have at least a few such understanding physicians and the clergyman should make it his business to become acquainted with them before their help is needed in treating an alcoholic parishioner.

3. Almost every sizable community has its active chapter of Alcoholics Anonymous. The clergyman should acquaint himself with at least one male and one female member of this group so that he can enlist their aid when a parishioner seeks help. The minister and several members of the parish should attend at least a few meetings of Alcoholics Anonymous so they can better understand and counsel the alcoholic when he comes for help.

4. The alcoholic is often involved with the traffic court and the probate court (Anon., 1963). A judge who has become interested in rehabilitating alcoholics rather than avoiding or punishing them is an invaluable ally for any professional person trying to help the alcoholic.

5. The clergyman should acquaint himself with and support his local Council on Alcoholism. These councils have as their chief goal to replace the community's erroneous and harmful concepts of alcoholism with accurate and constructive information. This makes it much easier for the alcoholic and his family to begin breaking the vicious cycle of addiction.

6. A long list of good books on alcoholism, which will greatly aid the minister in his pastoral counseling of the alcoholic and his family, is available from the National Council on Alcoholism, New York Academy of Medicine Building, 2 East 103rd Street, New York, N.Y. 10029. Outstanding in this regard are the books by Howard Clinebell and Thomas Shippe, both of whom are ministers, by Marty Mann who is the founder of the National Council on Alcoholism, and by Dr. David Pittman, Director of the Alcoholic Treatment and Research Center in St. Louis.

As soon as an alcoholic has dried out and has begun building up defenses against drinking, he must find a new way of life if he is going to remain sober. True rehabilitation of the alcoholic implies not only abstinence from the use of alcohol, but also a real change in the patient's personality. If an alcoholic stops drinking and remains functioning in a grossly inadequate manner, little has been accomplished. Alcoholics Anonymous epitomizes in one word the personality change which must accompany successful sobriety; they call it "Serenity." What does "Serenity" involve? It involves an inner feeling of being at peace with one's self, one's fellow man, and one's God. The Twelve Steps of Alcoholics Anonymous are specifically pointed at these three areas of one's personality.

If you are now asking "How can the clergy best use its special talents to help the alcoholic?" the answer lies in this word "Serenity." To repeat the definition, Serenity: "an inner feeling of being at peace with one's self, one's fellow man, and one's God." Yes, one's God! Here is where the clergyman must be of help. No other member of the rehabilitation team can so effectively help a man be at peace with God as can a minister. To emphasize the alcoholic's need to be at peace with God, I will quote the second through the seventh steps of the Twelve Steps of Alcoholics Anonymous (Anon., 1955):

Step 2. Came to believe that a power greater than ourselves could restore us to sanity.

Step 3. Made a decision to turn our will and our lives over to the care of God as we understand Him.

Step 4. Made a searching and fearless moral inventory of ourselves.

Step 5. Admitted to God, to ourselves, and to another human being the exact nature of our wrongs.

Step 6. Were entirely ready to have God remove all these defects of character.

Step 7. Humbly asked Him to remove our shortcomings.

Through continued pastoral counseling, the alcoholic can be once more made aware of the Gospel, whereas for years he had thought of God, like one alcoholic put it, as "The Ten Commandments carrying a big stick."

Whether or not it is true that a loss of spiritual values is important in the development of alcoholism, it is felt by many of those who treat alcoholics successfully that a vital part of recovery from alcoholism is finding a new meaning to life, having a spiritual reawakening of one's life. And who can be more effective in this area than a minister? An alcoholic whom I treated, who did not maintain any semblance of sobriety, told me once, "What's there to stay sober for? Life has no meaning for me; there's really nothing to live for. The only time I can forget about how empty my life is, is when my brain is full of alcohol." One wonders what effect a spiritual reawakening would have had on the course of this man's illness.

Finally, where does the psychiatrist fit into the alcoholic rehabilitation team? The psychiatrist due to his specialized training first as a physician and second as one interested in the psychological aspects of illness can help in three principal ways:

1. As an understanding physician, the psychiatrist can help the alcoholic dry out, acquaint him with the various modalities of help in the community and give him supportive psychiatric help while he is trying to firmly establish his sobriety.

2. As a professional member of the community, the psychiatrist can aid the community in understanding the alcoholic and promote the community, to set up adequate treatment facilities for him (Jones, 1962).

3. After the alcoholic has maintained his sobriety for six months or more and has explored at least a few of the community resources available to help him, he may still find himself debilitated by neurotic conflicts. The psychiatrist can at this time employ more classical techniques of psychotherapy to aid him in resolving these residual internal conflicts. Before the alcoholic has been sober for at least six months, his ego structure is not sufficiently stable to withstand the frequently upsetting experience of the usual psychoanalytic techniques used in treatment of neurosis.

In summary, the more we understand about the alcoholic, what causes him to get ill, what prevents him from getting well, and how we in our own special fields can be of particular help to him, the more effective will be our efforts to answer his cry for help.

IMPLICATIONS

After reviewing the biological, psychological, and sociocultural themes, you may want to take a position as to what you think are the most essential conditions leading to alcoholism. You may find it interesting to discuss your position with someone who differs from you, utilizing from this article the data that support your conclusions as well as the significance of these data. Possibly you have concluded that, whereas individuals with an alcoholic problem have many factors in common, each individual is complex and unique, and the means of getting him to face the reality of his condition and to accept assistance and treatment will vary among individuals. You may have a specific person in mind, and you might speculate as to which of the resources mentioned in this selection might be most effective.

REFERENCES

Under "Treatment Resources," in the preceding article, Catanzaro calls your attention to books that are helpful in counseling the alcoholic and his family, available from the National Council on Alcoholism.

An example of this kind of assistance is found in a recent publication by Whitney (1965), who has had long experience in getting the alcoholic into the hands of the proper person for treatment. She presents three interesting cases of male alcoholics and a fourth case of a female. A textbook treatment of the problems of alcoholism will be found in Coleman (1972).

46   FAMILY THERAPY: UNDERSTANDING AND CHANGING BEHAVIOR

Richard G. Murney and Robert N. Schneider

Can it be that what is "wrong" with the mentally ill person does not reside in him alone? Is he better understood in the context of his significant social relationships—his family? How does this viewpoint alter traditional therapy? How does the therapist proceed to study communications among members of the family?

Murney and Schneider, who have been using the family-therapy approach with their mentally ill patients and their families over a period of time, clearly and interestingly describe their professional activities.

CONSIDER WHAT HAPPENS to a family when one of its members has a psychiatric breakdown and must be hospitalized. In therapy with such a family in which the identified patient was a twenty-one-year-old only son in his first hospitalization, for "schizophrenic reaction, paranoid type," it became clear that his breakdown had a profound effect on his parents. Even after one year of hospitalization and marked improve-

Reprinted by permission of the authors.

ment in their son, the parents were suffering in such a way that it had many of the qualities of grieving or mourning. The son's psychiatrist was sufficiently concerned about the father's depressive tendencies that he recommended private psychiatric treatment. These parents had practically stopped socializing with their friends after their son was hospitalized. In family therapy their inability to live their own lives became especially poignant and obvious when the prospect of the father's vacation arose. The parents wanted their son to be given a leave from the hospital to go with them on a trip. Although this was highly possible, they were asked by the therapist about their vacation plans should their son not be granted a leave. Their response was that, of course, they would go nowhere. As they expressed it, they couldn't go away on a vacation, knowing that their son would have to stay at the hospital. (It should be noted that they were considering a week's trip, to a place within 200 miles of the hospital; as mentioned, their son was showing progressive improvement and was going home every weekend so that the longest the family would be separated would have been one week.) The obvious overinvolvement of these parents in their son's difficulties comprised one of many considerations that resulted in therapeutic intervention with the whole family. Before going into other such considerations, it might be well to discuss what family therapy is and how it arose.

What Is Family Therapy?

Family therapy can be defined as a *kind of therapy that focuses on the family as a unit*, even though only one of its members is obviously disturbed and is identified in and by the family as "sick, bad, stupid, or crazy" and therefore in need of help. Implied in this definition are a great many ideas, attitudes, and approaches that are relatively new among people who work in the applied areas of the behavioral sciences. In essence, a discussion of family therapy in terms of these newer emphases is the purpose of this paper. It might be well to outline these newer orientations and to briefly describe how they arose, particularly as they relate to the appearance and development of family therapy.

The above definition has three important aspects: (1) an emphasis on the family as a whole, *i.e.*, a focus on family interactions; (2) a new way of looking at the person in the family who is considered to be disturbed, the "identified patient"; and (3) a new way of considering the kinds of human behaviors that people find problematic, for which the term *dysfunctional* will be used. Let us consider each of these aspects.

Family Interactions

Most simply, it can be supposed that family therapy arose as a practice because it offers some advantages that are not provided by other approaches to solving behavior problems. Since it has long been recognized that family relations play an important role in the development and maintenance of behavior problems, it is somewhat paradoxical that until quite recently families were not seen as units in the therapy situation. It became gradually apparent to therapists who were trying to effect changes in individual behavior that working with the individual alone was not enough—either for an understanding of the problems or to bring about lasting improvements. Seeing families in interaction promised to such therapists a better way to understand problems as well as to find solutions.

The Identified Patient

Experiences in observing family interactions have also altered the ways in which the identified patient is understood. Families who come to the attention of a therapist almost always have one member whom they think of as the "sick one," or the "bad one." However, although one person has been identified as a "patient" by the family, the therapist prefers to deemphasize the focus on this one member and to shift the focus to family interactions. He prefers this approach because current considerations are bringing into question the traditional concepts of mental illness, delinquency, and so on, as reflecting something wrong with the person. The newer view considers that what is wrong does not entirely reside *in* the person, and it can be better understood in the context of the person's significant interpersonal relationships.

Dysfunction

The term *dysfunction* will be used to designate the "what is wrong" mentioned above. Most students of human behavior agree that the family as a social unit has a number of functions to perform and maintain. Briefly these functions usually include meeting the emotional needs of each family member, transmitting various culturally prescribed values and behaviors to the offspring, and providing an atmosphere for growth and development. The term *dysfunction* refers to the breakdown or distortion of any of these necessary functions. In actuality, the disruption of any one of these functions usually affects the others so that the entire system is disrupted. It is in this sense that a family system can be dysfunctional.

If family interactions are important, and if the identified patient is not the sole locus of difficulty, then it is reasonable to consider the idea that not only *persons* but also *families* can be dysfunctional. Family therapy focuses on family dysfunction, and some of the best clues to dysfunction can be found in the patterns of communications that a family demonstrates. More about communication will be said later.

To *summarize*, family therapy arose as a method of dealing with dysfunctional behavior because (1) traditional viewpoints about individual dysfunction began to appear inadequate in the understanding they provided and (2) traditional therapies began to appear limited with regard to producing changes in dysfunctioning.

Why Family Therapy?

With some idea of what family therapy is and how it arose, a series of questions reasonably follows: Under what circumstances is family therapy indicated? What kinds of problems are reasonably and profitably approached via family therapy? Should family therapy be offered rather than any other form of therapy? Should it be offered in combination with other approaches? Each of these questions emphasizes a slightly different aspect of the problem, but the basic question that can be asked is, Why family therapy? To answer this question requires that a number of factors be considered. For convenience, two classes of considerations can be distinguished: (1) theoretical considerations and (2) practical considerations.

Theoretical Considerations
Certain guidelines about therapeutic intervention can be derived from the existing body of theory and knowledge concerning human behavior and behavior change. When family therapy is specifically under consideration, answers to such questions as, What do we know about family structure and function? and What do we know about behavior disorder? can be helpful. Along these lines there are at least two major theoretical considerations that would recommend family therapy as a suitable approach.

The *first* of these comes from evidence which indicates that *whatever is happening with one family member is related to, and has its impact on, the whole family group.* Family interrelationships can be thought of as a system: change in one part of the system depends, to some extent, on what is going on in the total system and has its effects, in some ways, on the whole system. In this sense, dysfunctional behavior on the part of one family member can be understood, at least in part, to be related to the total family system, and it can be expected, to a significant degree, to have its effects on the system. Family therapy would be indicated, then, when it is recognized that the entire family's functioning is involved, even though dysfunctioning is most apparent in one family member.

This consideration is illustrated by the case that opened this discussion. The quality of the feelings expressed by the parents in the case had two aspects—first, out of a sense of duty they would have felt neglectful to "go off and leave" their son "stuck at the hospital for a week"; second, they expressed their genuine belief that they couldn't possibly enjoy themselves under those circumstances. Without going into further detail, this incident can be used to exemplify what was happening in this family system as a result of a disruption imposed by psychiatric hospitalization. In the first place, the meaning of the "grieving" observed in the family organization and its implications about this family and its "sick" member were considered. One of the things that has been observed about the families who have a schizophrenic member is the lack of differentiation, or "separateness," of the members of these families. It is as if the family system is a tightly organized whole and that each member relinquishes his own individuality to that whole.

This lack of separateness implies many things about such a family; but the special point being made here is that, when the son in this family had a breakdown, it *directly* and *overwhelmingly* affected the lives of his mother and father—they *had to* suffer as he suffered. They had to grieve, or mourn, his loss from the family unit, almost as if he had been lost to death. The individual functioning of each of the parents, as well as their cooperative functioning as a married couple, was markedly affected by the breakdown in functioning of the son (and these alterations in the parents' functioning, in turn, had their effects on the son). One of the goals of therapy with this family was to help the parents recover their individuality, to help the son develop his own sense of separateness, and to help the family as a unit to participate in the whole, without the necessity of totally subjugating the identity of each to that whole. A great deal could be said about lack of family and individual differentiation and the development of schizophrenia, but it is beyond the scope of this discussion.

To *summarize* the point being made here, family therapy seemed indicated for this family because it was considered that the son's progress could only be continued and maintained, and the mother's and father's equilibrium re-established, if the family relationships were the focus of therapeutic intervention.

A *second* kind of theoretical consideration concerns the *meaning and nature of dysfunctional behaviors.* Traditionally, these behaviors have been considered to be symptoms of mental illness, with the locus of the difficulty seen as within the person. Currently, a new look is being taken at these problems, and there is evidence to support an approach that attempts to understand such difficulties not simply as reflecting deficits of character or personality, but also as reflecting difficulties in important, ongoing, interpersonal relationships. Thus, the focus is shifting from attention to the personality functioning of the "sick" one to the meanings of his "sick" behaviors in the context of his relationships to others, especially his family.

Although the sick member's personality function is by no means ignored in this approach, emphasis shifts from the study of the "intrapsychic" to a more intensive attempt to understand the person's significant relationships as well as the *other* persons in these relationships. Perhaps another way of characterizing this shift in emphasis is to describe it as a move from considering only a dysfunctional *person* to the possibility of considering dysfunctional *relationships.* This places the meaning of "symptoms" in an entirely new context (which will receive further discussion in the next section). But to return to our main point, family therapy would seem indicated when it appears that the identified patient's symptoms are indirect manifestations of problematic family relationships. A general kind of example, without going into specific details, can be cited. It is not uncommon, in child-guidance work, to have a child brought in by his parents for treatment because he is a "behavior problem." In therapy with these families, it has been found that in order to understand the meaning of the child's dysfunctional behavior, it is necessary to explore conflicts between the parents; frequently it has been found that parents who are not able to recognize or deal directly with their own conflicts become focused on the child, who mediates their difficulties. When these marital conflicts become recognized and new ways of coping with them are learned, the behavior problem of the child discontinues. In these situations it is common that the particular nature of the child's problem is directly related to the hidden conflict between the parents. It goes without saying that in therapy all of these details must be explored in order to understand why the parents cannot deal with their conflicts more directly, why they have focused on this particular child (if there are other children), why the child displays his problem. The important point here is that the symptoms of the child are directly related to, and have their meaning in, dysfunctional family relations, and do not simply "reside in" the child.

To *summarize* the theoretical considerations that recommend family therapy, evidence (research and clinical) indicates (1) that families of an identified patient are more often than not intimately involved in the beginnings and maintenance of his difficulty, and (2) that his difficulty is therefore as much reflection of dysfunctional family relationships as it is an expression of dysfunction on his part alone. To try to reach an enduring resolution of dysfunction, then, requires that families of identified patients cannot be excluded from therapeutic intervention.

Practical Considerations

So-called practical considerations are closely related to the theoretical and proceed from them.

One practical consideration concerns the "closeness" in the family of the identified patient. The more involved the family is with the identified patient, the greater is the likelihood that family therapy is indicated. This is most often true when the identified patient is a child, but it is also true in other instances, as with some identified patients who are hospitalized with psychiatric difficulties. In these instances, in which the family is very involved, the therapist might find himself doing family therapy inadvertently and informally, e.g., on the telephone in response to frequent inquiries about the identified patient and his progress. Even excluding the theoretical considerations which would point to family therapy as the *best* approach, a therapist might find it more productive of his time and energies to formalize his interactions with family members by setting up a definite time to meet and talk with them.

A second practical consideration concerns the progress (or lack of it) with a given identified patient. When there is a reasonable expectation that a patient should be improving and he is not, a search for the reasons behind this failure might lead to the exploration of family relations. With hospitalized psychiatric patients, this possibility can be reflected in a variety of ways: (1) the patient readily improves in the hospital but has a setback every time he goes home; (2) the patient is judged to have gained as much as possible from hospitalization, is ready to return to his family, but the family is, quite honestly, not ready to receive him; and (3) the patient does not or cannot use other therapeutic approaches because he tends to minimize his difficulties and thereby avoid confronting them. The immediacy of dealing with his own family members who usually are very aware of problems makes it more difficult for him to avoid, evade, or minimize difficulties that require his attention.

A final set of practical considerations that can only be touched on here involve the role of the therapist. In the first place, therapists whose previous therapeutic endeavors excluded contacts with their patients' families have characterized their subsequent experiences with family therapy as "eye-opening." In general, they feel that their understanding of the patient (not to mention the family interactions) becomes a gread deal more comprehensive than was ever possible in individual therapy. In addition, therapists typically observe that family therapy offers a much wider range of possible kinds of intervention than can be planned in advance. In short a common observation made by therapists is that family therapy provides new and increasingly varied kinds of participation in psychotherapy both for the patients and for the therapists. From this point of view, family therapy becomes practical when the therapist becomes dissatisfied with the limitations of understanding and therapeutic progress imposed by other forms of therapy.

These, then, are the general kinds of considerations—theoretical and practical—that might indicate family therapy. Having discussed to this point the what and why of family therapy, let us turn now to the how.

How Does Family Therapy Proceed?

There are many different ways to approach therapy with families, and there is a large and growing literature on the subject. In this discussion, one such approach will be described, the *communications* approach. The presentation is divided into two main sections: first, a discussion of what is meant by communication, why it is a point of focus in therapy, and how it is used in therapy; and second, a discussion of communications theory as it underlies the practice of family therapy.

A *Focus on Communications*

In this context the word *communications* refers to the interactions or transactions, both *verbal* and *nonverbal*, that take place necessarily when any two (or more) people get together. In the next section, more will be said about an assumption underlying human relationships, namely, that people cannot *not* communicate. Granting this assumption provides a very helpful focus of procedure in family therapy: since people unavoidably communicate, their communications *in the therapy* session provide a method both for understanding the people and for attempting to alter their relationships. With this focus, the process of therapy, in large part, consists of gaining an understanding of how the family members communicate with each other.

How does each person express his thoughts, feelings, and actions? Are his expressions clear, direct, and relatively consistent? In turn, how are they "received" by the other family members? Are his "messages" *understood* as the "sender" means for them to be? If not, what are the sources of communication breakdown? With these and many other similar questions in mind, the therapist begins to formulate a picture of how the members of a given family communicate. But even more importantly, he tries to make clear to the family the patterns of communication that he observes in order to help the family members reach a better understanding of themselves, each other, and the nature of their interactions. The process of communication, then, serves the dual purpose of helping the therapist to understand and to intervene in the functioning of the family. Additionally, to the extent that he can express himself clearly, directly, and explicitly, his communication can serve as a model for understanding and improving family relationships. Thus the communication process comprises a method of inquiry as well as a vehicle for intervention, and it is primarily to serve these purposes that it provides the basic focus in family therapy.

Another useful purpose served by focusing on communications in therapy resides in the emphasis that is placed on *interaction*. Most typically it is the current, ongoing, here-and-now interactions of the family that receive attention, and this is of value for at least two reasons: (1) there is a reality about immediacy that has an impact on people which is often lacking in more abstract discussions of thoughts, feelings, and actions; (2) focusing on interaction de-emphasizes the placing of "blame" on any particular family member. In connection with the latter, it has been observed that in searching for an understanding of the sources of family difficulties, people often tend to distort this search into a placing of blame. In part this stems from the tendency to consider dysfunctioning as a personal trait, residing *in* a person; in part it stems from attempts to seek out cause-and-effect relationships. In any event, the tendency to find someone to blame —even when it is oneself—almost always impedes progress, and in family therapy this tendency can be dealt with by focusing on family interactions: since interaction must involve participation by at least two people, blaming any particular person becomes less meaningful.

It is important to note at this point that the process of family therapy is not only an analysis and explication of the communication process. Typically, a great deal of time is devoted to *specific and concrete family problems*—problems that have a long history in the family, such as how the "rules" are made, and problems that arise from crises that occur. At these times the communications processes are in the background, perhaps always under the watchful eye of the therapist but not providing the content of the discussion. In this way there is a going back and forth between the content of problems and the *process* of understanding and resolving them (*i.e.*, the communication process).

Communications Theory

It has been relatively recently that human communication has become the subject of scientific observation and study. Defining human communication broadly as any behavior occurring in a social context, the students of this approach focus upon the ways in which people affect each other by the "message character" of their behavior. The message character of behavior refers to the fact that all behavior contains messages from one person (the sender) to another (the receiver). Current ideas about the nature of these messages will be presented below. The important point to be made here is that within the framework of the communications approach, relationships and interactions between people rather than internal intrapsychic processes in a single person are the focus of investigation. In communication *theory* there have developed three basic premises about the message character of behavior, which are directly and productively applicable to an understanding of the processes of family function and dysfunction. Although these premises can be stated quite simply, their implications can throw light upon a complex array of phenomena which are observed in the arena of family interactions.

Premise 1. One cannot *not* communicate. This follows with logical inevitability from the definition of human communication as any behavior in a social context. People often believe that they are not communicating unless they are intentionally directing a spoken or written message to someone. Yet, silence or the failure to act in a manner appropriate to a given situation are only two of many nonverbal ways of communicating. In most instances these responses are indirect ways of commenting upon the communication of another. As a tactic in human interactions, their indirectness has both a positive and negative value. On the positive side it lends itself to tactful disagreement as preliminary and preparatory to more direct communication. Where open disagreement can not yet be tolerated, it is potentially possible that this tactic may open the way to mutual understanding. More frequently, however, such indirectness is used to disqualify the communication of another. Disqualification here refers to a kind of communication by which one can disagree with or negate another and yet evade responsibility for taking a stand. For example, your ignoring the greeting of another by silence may disqualify his implication of a friendly relationship. Should he, however, interpret your silence as a snub and call it to your attention, you can easily plead that you didn't hear him, were preoccupied, and so on. This denial is possible because of the ambiguity of the explicit behavior—silence—which may or may not be a means of conveying an implicit disqualification.

Premise 2. The message that the sender intends to convey is not necessarily the message that is received. This premise is obviously closely related to the first premise. In the foregoing example, the silence perceived as a snub may not have been intended as such. Each of us tends to consider his own view of reality as the only possible one and to expect that others share this view. When it becomes obvious that another does not share this view, the disagreement is frequently attributed to deliberate distortion, stupidity, or craziness on the part of the others. Badness, stupidity, and sickness then are the angry accusations frequently heard when two people interpret each other's messages differently or differ in their understanding of the context of the situation in which they are communicating. "Hello, how are you today?" intended by the speaker as a conventional, casual greeting may be responded to by a hypochondriac as a message of deep interest in his physical well-being and an invitation to describe in morbid detail his myriad symptomatology. Suffice it to say, the ensuing interaction may result in either or both parties angrily resenting the stupidity of the other. "Did you like that play the other night?" a question which may be intended as conversation opener in a social gathering may easily be interpreted as a simple request for information. Such an interpretation, made in such a context and followed by a simple yes or no response, may in turn be received as a snub.

Premise 3. "Every communication has not only a content or an information message but also contains within it another message which is *about* this information message." This second message "frames" the content message in that it tells (1) how the sender intends for the information to be received and (2) how the sender conceives of his relationship to the receiver. One aspect of this framing of the content is provided by both general and specific aspects of the context in which the communication occurs. A quiet "Please come over here and sit down" spoken by a mother to her young child may have quite a different meaning when spoken in a formal social gathering with many adults present than when said in a gathering of young children. It is easily seen, further, that many other nonverbal aspects of this communication, such as tone of voice, gestures and facial expression, will serve further to frame the literal words of the information message so that the receiver may understand "what it is about" and how the sender is construing their relationship at this point. The manifold opportunities for conflict between these levels of message, *i.e.*, the level of literal information content and the contextual messages which frame it, are apparent. This conflict may, in the instance cited, lead the child to act other than in accord with the message content, and thus in a "disobedient" way. Conflict then can occur because of incongruity between levels of message within a communication. Conflict in communication may also occur because of discrepancies and incongruities between the message content of two communications separated in time. For example, the parent who first asks a child whether he "would like" to carry out some task, thus implying a free choice, and who later berates the child for not doing as he "was told," conveying that he was *not* free to choose, sets up this type of conflict for the child.

Approaching the treatment of family dysfunction with these three premises in mind, the therapist has an immediate focus upon the ways in which family members undercut and disqualify each other, form coalitions, and develop rules of interaction and relationships. These rules establish role expectancies and functions and maintain without the awareness of the family members the dysfunction of the family system. For example, the wife who makes the apparently justifiable complaint that her husband is too passive and tells him that she wants him to be dominating and assertive, is not usually aware of the implications of her communication. The therapist, however, should see the trap which she has built for herself and her husband. No matter what he does now, the husband cannot please his wife. If he continues to act as he has, she can still complain of his passivity. If he attempts to be assertive and dominating, she will see his efforts as only another example of his passive following of what she tells him and thus as not genuine. As a consequence, the rules of their interaction which require his passivity and her dominance continue in effect. This peculiar situation results from the paradoxical attempt to demand behavior which by its nature can only be spontaneous. "Don't be so obedient" poses the same dilemma for the child. If he continues to do as he is told, he is wrong. If he now refuses to do so, he still is obeying and so is still wrong. Such paradoxical communications occur in all families and appear to be an unavoidable part of human interactions. Their effects appear to be serious, in terms of individual and family dysfunction, only when several conditions exist: (1) there is frequent repetition of the same type of communication conflict; (2) the relationship is such that the freedom to comment upon the resulting dilemma is not allowed; (3) there are an insufficient number of conflict-free areas of interaction.

In the course of family therapy, it is frequently possible to identify, explicate, and alter these conditions. For example, one mother of an adult, male schizophrenic patient protested with great frequency her utter devotion to her son saying, "Everything I do is for you." The son's effort then to object to any of her behavior was automatically a display of ingratitude. Efforts on the patient's part to point up this dilemma were nullified by the mother's development of symptoms of physical illness (most often angina pectoris) which eloquently conveyed to her son the message that his ingratitude was killing her. Without attempting a full description of the therapeutic efforts to alter the pattern of dysfunctional communication, it will be simply pointed out that the therapist was able through his genuine interest to encourage the mother both to do things for her husband, without reference to the son, and to begin to allow herself the satisfaction of legitimate personal indulgence.

To *summarize*, then, three basic premises of communication theory contribute significantly to the understanding of family interaction and provide a basis for therapeutic interventions that can alter dysfunctional family processes. The communication styles and patterns of the individual and of the family can be understood and used for change when the therapist bases his approach upon these premises. Other aspects of communication theory, not considered in this brief paper, are also of value to the family-oriented psychotherapist.

Having viewed what family therapy is, why it has developed, and how it uses communications theory, we ask, "What can be said of its *future prospects?*" Most needed is the development of terms and concepts adequate to the description and communication of the complex phenomena being observed. Much current research effort is being devoted to this problem. As more family therapists are trained, a more widespread use of this approach is inevitable. Further, as a body of common knowledge about the varying characteristics of different types of family systems is developed, variations in technique and method appropriate to these different types can be expected. At this time, family therapy provides both a hope and a promise for more effective ways of dealing with problems of human behavior through attention to their significance in the context of family interrelations.

IMPLICATIONS

Can you see applications here to *any* individual with emotional or adjustment problems? What are the implications of this article for the improvement of such an adjustment? Can you illustrate the various *blocks to effective communication* in everyday experiences?

You and your classmates may find it interesting to illustrate poor and good communication by staging a dialogue. Arrange a conversation on any subject of interest with emotional ramifications—such as the problem of getting a date or trying to make a good impression on a hard-boiled prospective employer. Two students play the roles of the communicating individuals. Set the stage as to where they are talking and what led up to the interaction. Then let the two interact naturally. They may attempt to communicate as much information as possible; or one may try to cut the other party off by giving as little verbally or nonverbally as possible. The class can then take notes on what takes place under two degrees of communication.

REFERENCES

The following are suggested for further reading: Ackerman (1958), Bell (1963), Bowen (1960), Haley (1962), Jackson and Satir (1961), Morris and Wynne (1965), Satir (1964), and Watzlawick (1964).

47   FREUD: THEME AND VARIATIONS

Staff of Time *Magazine*

Most students have read a few introductory paragraphs on Sigmund Freud, his psychoanalysis, and some of the variations from Freud's original systems. Some may have read parts of books by Freud, Jung, Adler, Horney, or Fromm. It is rare to find a simply written, brief presentation of Freud's major concepts and the main variations by some of his followers.

The following selection is a tight, highly simplified presentation. It represents a good review of the major ideas and resembles a set of introductory lecture notes on Freud and some other outstanding psychoanalysts. How much it will mean to you will depend on previous knowledge, supplementary lectures, or further reading in the books that review *psychoanalytic theory*. The editors of *Time* Magazine thought this article was of sufficient interest to present it to their average readers. It is being used here as a sample of the better popular scientific writing that you may want to read during and after your college years.

> *If self-analysis made Freud a relatively adjusted man, it never blunted the sharpness of his search for under-*

standing. He was too restless an explorer to remain content with his theories, worked until his death on amendments and additions. He was far less tolerant toward others' discontent with his theories, bitterly opposed some followers' deviations, but might well have accepted others that have developed since. Some rudiments of the Freudian main theme and principal variations:

SIGMUND FREUD held that the nature of man is essentially biological; man is born with certain instinctual drives. Most notable: the drive toward self-gratification. Basic mental energy, or *libido*, is equated with sexual energy by making the word "sex" stand for all pleasure.

Infant's first search for gratification is limited to release of hunger tension—*oral* phase. If there is no nipple handy, he puts thumb in mouth. Next comes satisfaction from defecation—*anal* phase. Third, pleasure from sensation in sexual parts—*phallic* phase. (Association of sexual gratification with reproduction—*genital* phase—does not come until sexual maturity.) Beginning about age two, the child's emotional attachment to mother leads to wishes to displace father—*Oedipal feelings* (the older, more rigid concept of an Oedipus complex is now frowned upon).

The psyche is divided horizontally into *conscious* and *unconscious*, vertically into *id*, *ego* and *superego*. Gradually the child's unconscious fills more or less deliberately with things forgotten (*suppressed*) because they are unpleasant, and, more importantly, with emotions and drives which are too painful ever to be tolerated in consciousness (*repressed*).

The *id*, entirely unconscious, most primitive part of the mind, is concerned only with gratification of drives. The *ego*, almost entirely conscious, develops from experience and reason, deals with perception of the environment, tries to go about governing id. *Superego*, largely unconscious, sits as judge, decides whether or not ego may permit id the gratification it seeks; it is conscience, made up of attitudes absorbed unwittingly in childhood and (to a much less extent) of attitudes consciously learned or adopted later.

Neurosis, to Freud, results from unsuccessful attempt by the personality to achieve harmony among id, ego, and superego, and this failure in turn results from arrest of development at an *immature* stage. Commonest cause of emotional disharmony: failure to resolve *Oedipal feelings*. Example: many girls who profess to seek marriage actually avoid it because the prospect activates the threat of unacceptable emotions which are *fixated* to their fathers.

Among the *mechanisms* used to deal with conflicts: *projection* involves denial of an unacceptable element in the self and projecting it onto others, e.g., man who bangs desk and shouts: "Who's excited? You're excited, not me!" *Reaction formation* covers conversion of unacceptable hostility into cloying solicitousness, seen in many do-gooders and some overprotective mothers who unconsciously *reject* their children.

Another way of using libidinal energy: *sublimation* into constructive and creative work or play.

To *resolve* neuroses, patient on couch tells in *free association* all that comes into his mind, especially about early *trauma* (shock). Since infancy and much of childhood are consciously "forgotten," these experiences must be recaptured with the help of the language of dreams—perhaps the most important single tool of analysis. There is no absolute symbolism (snakes may be phallic to one dreamer but to another merely reminiscent of a trip to the zoo), hence no universal key to the meaning of dreams. Analysis is complete when the patient has developed social responsibility, having dredged up all pertinent childhood traumas, recognized his unconscious Oedipal and other socially unacceptable impulses, and learned at a deep emotional level rather than a superficial intellectual level to live with such id-bits.

Alfred Adler (1870–1937) developed "individual psychology," which denies the overriding importance of infantile sexuality, argues that sexual maladjustments are a symptom, not a cause of neurosis. Adler gave *inferiority complex* to the language, said infants have *inferiority feelings* because they are small, helpless. Lack of parental tenderness, neglect or ridicule may make these feelings neurotic. Natural tendency is to seek *compensation* by becoming superior, hence open struggle for naked power. *Power drives* are often neurotic because directed to impractical goals. Emphasized ego over id.

Carl Gustav Jung of Zurich holds that primal *libido*, or *life force*, is composed of both sexual and nonsexual energy, accepts an individual unconscious similar to Freud's but sees also a *collective unconscious* containing man's "racial memories." Within this are emotional stereotypes (*archetypes*) common to all races of man, e.g., the Jovian figure of the "old, wise man," the earth-mother. In Jungian "analytical psychology," the analyst participates more actively than in Freudian analysis. Jung aims especially at people over forty, largely because he believes they most feel the need of a religious outlook, which he encourages.

Otto Rank (1884–1939) went Freud one better, held that Oedipal feelings came too late to be decisive. Real trouble, said he, was *birth trauma*— the shock of having to leave the warm security of the womb for the harsh reality of separate life. Anxiety caused by this experience formed sort of reservoir which should seep away gradually during maturation. If it persisted, then neurosis set in. Rank hoped to shorten analysis by going back to birth trauma, ignoring most of childhood.

Karen Horney (1885–1952) applied the thinking of anthropologists and sociologists to psychoanalysis, gave great weight to cultural factors in neurosis. Rejected Freud's biological orientation, emphasized importance of *present life situation*. Modified Adler's concept of neurotic goals, adding that these contain their own sources of anxiety. Thus in coping with one difficulty, patient may set up neurotic defenses which bring on new difficulties, ad so on. Widely remembered for her unfortunately titled book, *Self-Analysis* (1942), which is no do-it-yourself kit for cracks in the psyche.

Harry Stack Sullivan (1892–1949) held that the human individual is the product of *interpersonal relations*, based an entire analytic theory on this concept. Pattern of child's earliest nonsexual relationships with significant figures largely (but not rigidly) determines the pattern of all later *interpersonal integration*. Man's aims are seen as pursuit of satisfaction (biological) and pursuit of security (cultural). If society denies satisfaction in sexual sphere, neurosis may result, but according to Sullivanians (a numerically small but influential school in the United States), it comes far more often from frustration, for whatever reason, in cultural sphere.

Erich Fromm of Manhattan and Mexico City denies that satisfaction of instinctual drives is focal problem, points out that man has fewer inherited behavior patterns than any other creature. In feudal times, he argues, the stratified, crystallized society wherein every individual knew his place gave security. Renaissance and mercantilism brought *freedom from* antilike existence but conferred (except on a privileged few) no *freedom to* work toward individual self-fulfillment. Thus neurosis today results mainly from frustrations which present trend of society threatens to intensify.

IMPLICATIONS

Try to define in your own words the human processes called id, super-ego, and ego by Freud. Can you think of someone you know whose behavior Freud would say results from unsuccessful attempts at harmony among ego, superego, and id? * Speculate on some examples of Jung's archetypes or the emotional stereotypes common to all races of men. To what extent does an accurate description of human behavior consist of the insights of all psychoanalysts? You might find it valuable and interesting to list these insights as you have found them important in your observations of other people.

* Think but don't act. We are not trying to encourage amateur and untrained psychoanalysts in all of the suggested projects in this book. Use this caution—may your psychological insights help you in your adjustment rather than serve as a means of offending others.

REFERENCES

All of the ideas presented are basic to psychoanalytic theory, and you may want to read or question further sources on those ideas that are not clear in this summary. Other psychoanalysts referred to in the article are outstanding contributors to the movement. Selection 51 presents some of Jung's ideas. Adler, Horney, Sullivan, and Fromm have all impressed students of personality as well as the better-informed reading public. Rank's writings have influenced two outstanding American personality theorists—Rogers and Murray.

Hall and Lindzey (1957) present an informative discussion of the views of these theorists in a chapter on social psychological theories. Another standard reference on *theories of personality* is by Bischof (1970). In it you will find further references to primary sources by Freud and the other psychoanalysts. Hall (1954) has written a book on Freudian psychology. Fromm's books (1947, 1955) have had wide circulation in the United States. The Ansbachers (1956) have edited a book on Adler's ideas. Also, see Maddi (1972).

You will doubtlessly recognize many of the concepts, such as "ego defense mechanisms," "ego," "unconscious," "free association," as standard in most introductions to personality; they can be reviewed in any standard text.

CHAPTER XI

RELIGION, DREAMS, HYPNOSIS, ESP

48

RELIGION:
A PSYCHOLOGIST VIEWS IT

Gordon W. Allport

Traditionally, college students have seemed to favor religion as a good topic for bull sessions. Empirically oriented psychologists, however, have not concerned themselves greatly with the topic of religion. Allport is an exception. Beginning with facts from studies, he and an associate conducted a questionnaire investigation on the religious attitudes and practices of the college student, the results of which are summarized in the following article.

Later, Allport explored the role of religion in the adult personality. In considering the criteria of a *mature personality*, he names "a unifying philosophy of life" as highly important. He then inferentially asks if personal religion or the religious sentiment is always a unifying philosophy of life. What is his answer?

Included here are excerpts from two of Allport's books, *The Individual and His Religion* and *Pattern and Growth in Personality*, to show how some psychologists interested in the total personality relate religion to individual behavior and experience.

The Religion of Youth

MAY WE SUM UP by saying that (1) most students feel the need of including a religious sentiment somewhere within their maturing personalities; (2) for the most part they *believe in a God*,* though their view is not usually of the traditional theistic variety; (3) a bare quarter are in *essential matters orthodox* * and historically faithful to theological dogma; (4) the majority maintain some of the forms of traditional religious practices including prayer; (5) but the majority are clearly dissatisfied with institutional religion as it exists, so much so that 40 per cent of those who feel a religious need yet repudiate the church in which they were reared. If we take the entire student population who have had a religious upbringing, including those who feel no religious need and those who do, we find that 56 per cent reject the church in which they were trained.

It would be wrong to imply that these findings are peculiar to the present college generation. We know that for years the trends here described have been under way. A study (Katz and Allport, 1931) conducted at the Uni-

* Editor's italics.

versity of Syracuse in 1926, for example, revealed that half the students at that time felt that, while they needed religion in their own lives, the current practices of the church were unsatisfactory. Only about one third felt that on the whole these practices were satisfactory—an estimate much like that obtained in the present study. Further, in respect to attitudes toward the deity, actually fewer of the Syracuse students in 1926 endorsed the extreme theistic position, although at the same time a smaller percentage endorsed agnosticism or atheism. Whereas at Syracuse only about 10 per cent abstained altogether from church attendance and devotional practices, our figure is nearer to one third. We must, of course, remember that not only a difference of time is here involved but also a different type of college population.

One additional comparison in time is of interest. A certain question included in our survey was identical with a question asked of 3,000 students at the University of Wisconsin in 1930. It had to do with attitudes toward the church. Very few in either institution subscribed to the position that the "Church is one sure and infallible foundation of civilized life"—6 per cent at Cambridge and 4 per cent at Wisconsin. But the second most favorable answer showed a significant difference. "On the whole," the statement reads, "the Church stands for the best in human life, although certain minor shortcomings and errors are necessarily apparent in it, as in all human institutions." To this proposition, 37 per cent of Harvard and Radcliffe students in 1946 gave assent, but only 24 per cent of Wisconsin students of both sexes in 1930. Correspondingly, statements markedly unfavourable to the church received much more endorsement sixteen years ago than today (Sheldon, 1942).

Such trend studies as are available, therefore, show that the disaffection of modern youth is probably no greater today than it was fifteen or twenty years ago. The problem is perennial, probably has been so for the last hundred years, perhaps longer.

The Religious Sentiment *

When we speak of a person's "unifying philosophy of life" we are likely to think first of his religion. (Spranger, we saw, regarded it as the most comprehensive and integrative of all value orientations.)

But here an immediate distinction must be drawn. The religious sentiments of many people—perhaps of most people—are decidedly immature. Often they are holdovers from childhood. They are self-centered constructions in which a deity is adopted who favors the immediate interests of the individual, like a Santa Claus or an overindulgent father. Or the senti-

* Reprinted from G.W. Allport, *Pattern and Growth in Personality* (New York: Holt, Rinehart and Winston, 1961), pp. 300–303, by permission of the publisher and the author.

ment may be of a tribal sort: "My church is better than your church. God prefers my people to your people." In cases of this sort, religion merely serves self-esteem. It is utilitarian and incidental in the life. It is a defense mechanism (often an escape mechanism) and does not embrace and guide the life as a whole. It is an "extrinsic" value in the sense that the person finds it "useful" in serving his immediate ends.

Studies show that ethnic prejudice is more common among churchgoers than among nonchurchgoers (Allport, 1954). This fact alone shows that religion is often divisive rather than unifying. Extrinsic religion lends support to exclusions, prejudices, hatreds that negate all our criteria of maturity. The self is not extended; there is no warm relating of self to others, no emotional security, no realistic perception, no self-insight or humor.

In short, we certainly cannot say that the religious sentiment is always a unifying philosophy of life.

At the same time, the religious sentiment may be of such an order that it does provide an inclusive solution to life's puzzles in the light of an intelligible theory. *It can do so if the religious quest is regarded as an end in itself,** as the value underlying all things and desirable for its own sake. By surrendering himself to this purpose (not by "using" it), religion becomes an "intrinsic" value for the individual, and as such is comprehensive and integrative and motivational (Allport, 1950).

It may help to understand the religious sentiment thus defined if we *compare it with humor.** In one respect only are they alike. Both set a worrisome event in a new frame of reference, smashing, as it were, the context of literal-mindedness. Both humor and religion shed new light on life's troubles by taking them out of the routine frame. To view our problems humorously is to see them as of little consequence; to view them religiously is to see them in a serious scheme of changed meaning. In either case a new perspective results.

In all other respects they are different. Humor depends on seeing incongruity in events; religion sees an ultimate congruity. Since experiences cannot possibly be regarded at any one time as of great moment and as trivial, it follows that we cannot be simultaneously both reverent and jesting. We may joke and pray about the same disturbing events in life, but never at the same time.

What keeps the religious person from becoming a cynic—as thoroughgoing humorists must be—is the conviction that at bottom something is more important than laughter, namely, the fact that he, the laugher, as well as the laughter itself, has a place in the shceme of things. When this important issue is decided, there is still plenty of room for jesting. In fact, a case might be made for the superior sense of humor of the religious person

* Editor's italics.

who has settled once and for all what things are sacred and of ultimate value, for nothing else in the world then needs to be taken seriously. He can see that hosts of happenings are ludicrous, that men and women, including himself, are given to amusing vanities, actors upon a stage. To him nothing in their coming and going is of consequence unless it happens to touch the matter of their ultimate value in the scheme of things.

It is only the core and aim of a religious outlook that are beyond the reach of humor. Human foibles related to the religious intention are possible sources of amusement, examples being incongruous episodes that occur in church. But such incongruity does not affect the priority of the "ultimate concern."

Religion always involves more than a man's cognitive processes; nevertheless, being a response of the total self, rational thought is not excluded. All faith—whether religious or not—is an affirmation where knowledge, though made use of, is not the decisive factor. It is a truism that all men live by faith, for no one has knowledge that his values are worth-while; he only has faith that they are. Religious faith differs from other faith chiefly in its comprehensive character. It holds that, if knowledge were present, one would find that the universe as a whole, the facts of existence, the puzzling clash of good and evil, all make coherent sense. As for the content of one's religious faith, one takes what to him is the best and most rational "fit." *Mature (intrinsic) religion* * is a completely embracing theory of life but it is not a theory that can be proved in all detail.

Here we must reject the view that all religious impulses in a life are infantile, regressive, or escapist. That such "extrinsic" religion exists there is no doubt. Nor can we accept the view that institutional and orthodox religion is always a childish submission to authority and therefore immature. Plenty of thoughtful people find historic and traditional forms of religion the "best fit" to their own groping in terms of meaning and comprehensiveness. And so even orthodox religion may reflect more than childish awe and habit; it may reflect a carefully chosen, mature, and productive philosophy of life.

But we must not make the reciprocal error and assume that religion is the only unifying sentiment. Logically perhaps, since it aims to encompass all that lies within experience and all that lies beyond, it is ideally designed to confer unity. But the fact remains that many people find a high degree of unification in other directions.

W.H. Clark obtained judgments from approximately three hundred well-educated persons, nearly half of whom were listed in *Who's Who*. When they were asked to rate the constructive factors leading to creativity in their lives, the chief factor turned out to be "interest and satisfaction in work for its own sake," followed by a "desire to know and understand." Third came the desire

* Editor's italics.

to aid society. On the average, "religious motivation" came lower on the list, about equal to the "desire to create beauty." But an important fact is that people differ greatly in their ratings of the importance of religion. They tend to give it a high place or a very low place. The fairly low average ranking is due to the fact that the majority of cases studied did not consider it as their chief source of motivation (Clark, 1955).

Thus we cannot say for certain how common is the comprehensive religious sentiment as a unifying philosophy of life. There is evidence, however, that college alumni, when they are a decade or two out of college, are more religious than they were in college (Nelson, 1956; Kelly, 1955; Bender, 1958). The search for religious meaning seems to grow with advancing years.

[We can best conclude this discussion with the following excerpt, the final paragraphs in Allport's *The Individual and His Religion* in which he summarizes his theme.]

The Solitary Way *

My theme has been the diversity of form that subjective religion assumes. Many different desires may initiate the religious quest, desires as contrasting as fear and curiosity, gratitude and conformity. Men show a varying capacity to outgrow their childhood religion, and to evolve a well-differentiated mature religious sentiment. There are many degrees in the comprehensiveness of this sentiment and in its power to integrate the life. There are different styles of doubting, different appreperceptions of symbols, contrasting types of content that vary both with the culture and with the temperament and capacity of the believer. There are innumerable types of specific religious intentions. How the individual justifies his faith is a variable matter, and the certitude he achieves is his alone.

From its early beginnings to the end of the road, the religious quest of the individual is solitary. Though he is socially interdependent with others in a thousand ways, yet no one else is able to provide him with the faith he evolves, nor prescribe for him his pact with the cosmos.

Often the religious sentiment is merely rudimentary in the personality, but often, too, it is a pervasive structure marked by the deepest sincerity. It is the portion of personality that arises at the core of the life and is directed toward the infinite. It is the region of mental life that has the longest-range intentions, and for this reason is capable of conferring marked integration upon personality, engendering meaning and peace in the face of the tragedy and confusion of life.

A man's religion is the audacious bid he makes to bind himself to creation and to the Creator. It is his ultimate attempt to enlarge and to complete his own personality by finding the supreme context in which he rightly belongs.

* Reprinted with permission of The Macmillan Company from *The Individual and His Religion* by Gordon W. Allport. Copyright 1950 by The Macmillan Company.

IMPLICATIONS

How do you find the attitudes of students today—alike or different from those of 1946? Do you agree with the author that a religious sentiment or some other unifying philosophy of life is essential to the well-integrated personality? In your experience, how many people did you encounter who have a *mature religious sentiment,* as described by Allport? How would you test a religious orientation to determine whether it is a mature one or a holdover from childhood? Evaluate the paragraphs under "The Solitary Way" both objectively, as a critical student of psychology, and subjectively, as a person with a certain attitude toward religion.

Later, Allport (1968) conducted a study that showed empirically a correlation between *extrinsic* religion (which serves the individuals by providing comfort, security, and social status) and prejudice. He found that people with extrinsic religious orientations tend to be more prejudiced than those with intrinsic orientations.

REFERENCES

Early in the history of psychology, James (1902) wrote a book on religious experiences. Consult also the Bibliography for references cited in the article.

Another approach to the experience of self-centeredness in human beings is found in Bakan (1966), *The Duality of Human Experience.* Bakan used the term *agency* for our tendency to be self-assertive, self-protective, and self-expansive, the term *communion* for our tendency to be at one with another organism.

Agency emphasizes the existence of an organism as an individual—the "I"; communion refers to the participation of the individual in some larger organism of which he is a part—the "we." Agency manifests itself in alienation, aloneness, and isolation. It also is seen in the tendency to repress thought, feelings, and impulses. Communion expresses itself in contact, openness, and union. It is found in the lack of and removal of repression.

Bakan's basic idea points to the importance of the integration of agency and communion or the mitigation by communion of the strong agentic tendencies in man. Without such mitigation, agentic tendencies become destructive.

This book will be highly stimulating to the student who is interested in such basic phenomena.

49

WHAT PEOPLE DREAM ABOUT

Calvin S. Hall

People differ in the attitude they take toward dreams, ranging from a dread of dreaming to an eager interest in what sleep will bring. One intelligent, well-traveled, middle-aged man stated that he looked forward each night to a new dream. He usually read each evening before going to sleep, either travel books or fiction, and consequently his dreams were often an extension of his readings or of the characters in the stories. He stated that he has dreamed of places he has never seen. Sometimes these places are a combination of fragments of previous experiences. Once he made the statement that his most creative moments are in his dream life. He said, "I don't paint, play a musical instrument, or write well, yet my dreams are highly original. Parts of them are as good as some of the motion pictures I have seen."

The psychologist Gardner Murphy (1947) has said, "Probably no sphere of personality expression is richer with individuality than dreaming. . . . Most dreams have a lush or lavish quality which unambiguously bespeak greater psychic freedom and creativeness" (pp. 431–432).

Dreams were very important to Freud and Jung in understanding personality. However, few investigators have studied the content of the dream as extensively as has Hall, and he presents in the following article an analysis of thousands of dreams. He includes a discussion of what the dream does and can mean to the individual. To Hall it is a means of solving problems, and it expresses the person's views of himself and the world about him.

MAN'S DREAMS have always interested and perplexed him. From ancient times and from every civilization and culture, we have evidence of man's concern about the meaning of dreams. They have been interpreted variously as divine messages, as the experiences of disembodied souls roaming heaven and earth during sleep, as visitations from the dead, as prophecies of the future, as the sleeping person's perceptions of external stimuli or bodily disturbances (what Thomas Hobbes called "the distemper of inward parts"), as fulfillments or attempted fulfillments of wishes (Freud), as attempts by the dreamer to discern his psychic development in order to plan for the future (Jung), as expressions of one's style of life (Adler), as attempted resolutions of conflicts (Stekel).

Probably all of these theories, however ancient their origin and however nebulous their validity, have their votaries today. Dream books based on the theory that dreams foretell the future are undoubtedly as widely consulted today as they were during the Renaissance, when the dream book compiled by the second-century soothsayer Artemidorus was republished in many languages and editions, and was plagiarized and elaborated by numerous opportunists, who in that day as in this knew a good thing when they saw it.

Even in modern times, speculations about dreams have been long on theory and short on observation. What do people dream about? What is the content and character of their dreams? As far as I know, no one has made an extensive and systematic study of these questions. To be sure, psychoanalysts have given much careful analysis to the dreams of deranged and disturbed persons, but even for this unrepresentative segment of mankind there are no large-scale surveys of the content of their dreams.

The writer has undertaken to make such a survey, for the purpose of obtaining some empirical facts as a foundation for theorizing. He has collected more than 10,000 dreams thus far, not from mental patients but from essentially normal people. They were asked to record their recollection of each dream on a printed form which included questions requesting certain specific information, such as the setting of the dream, the age and sex of the characters appearing in it, the dreamer's emotions and whether the dream was in color. Obviously we cannot know how faithfully the subjects' recollections mirrored their actual dreams, so, strictly speaking, we should call our project a study of what people *say* they dream about. This has ever been the case and probably always will be, for no one has discovered a means of transcribing a dream while it is being dreamed.

We *classified* * the dream material so that it could be studied statistically. From the many possible methods of classification we chose, as a beginning, a simple breakdown into five fundamental categories: (1) the dream setting, (2) its cast of characters, (3) its plot, in terms of actions and interactions, (4) the dreamer's emotions, and (5) color.

What are the most common settings in people's dreams? An analysis of 1,000 dreams reported by a group of educated adults provided 1,328 different settings. These could be classified into ten general categories. The most frequent scene was a part of a dwelling or other building; this accounted for 24 per cent of all dreams. The other settings, in order of frequency, were: a conveyance of some kind, most commonly an automobile, 13 per cent; an entire building, 11 per cent; a place of recreation, 10 per cent; a street or road, 9 per cent; a rural or other outdoor area, 9 per cent; a store or shop, 4 per cent; a classroom, 4 per cent; an office or factory, 1 per cent; miscellaneous (including restaurants, bars, battlefields, hospitals, churches,

* Editor's italics.

and so on), 14 per cent. In dreams occurring in part of a dwelling, the most popular room is the living room, with the bedroom, kitchen, stairway, and basement following in order.

The outstanding feature of these dream settings is their commonplaceness. The typical dream occurs in prosaic surroundings—a living room, an automobile, a street, a classroom, a grocery store, a field. The dreamer may not always recognize the details of the place, but usually it is a type of scene with which he is familiar; seldom does he dream of a bizarre or exotic environment. Yet, dream settings apparently are not entirely representative of waking life, as far as frequency is concerned. Considering the amount of time that people spend in places of work, such as offices, factories, and classrooms, these places appear with disproportionately low frequency in dreams. On the other hand, conveyances and recreational places occupy a larger share in dreams than they do in waking life experiences. In other words, in our dreams we tend to show an aversion toward work, study, and commercial transactions and an affinity for recreation, riding, and residences.

For a study of *characters appearing* * in dreams, we divided our subjects into two groups according to age, since it seemed likely that older people might differ from younger ones in the persons they dreamed about. The younger group was aged eighteen to twenty-eight, the older thirty to eighty. Let us consider the younger group first. They furnished a total of 1,819 dreams. In 15 per cent of these, the only character was the dreamer. In the remaining 85 per cent, in which two or more characters appeared, the average number was two persons besides the dreamer.

Who are these characters? Of the persons other than the dreamer, 43 per cent appeared to be strangers, 37 per cent were identified as friends or acquaintances of the dreamer, 19 per cent were family members, relatives, or in-laws, 1 per cent were famous or prominent public figures. The relatively infrequent appearance of prominent persons in dreams supports other evidence possessed by the writer that dreams rarely concern themselves with current events. Among the members of the family, the character that appears in dreams most often is mother (34 per cent); then come father (27 per cent), brother (14 per cent), and sister (12 per cent).

We also classified the characters in dreams by sex and age. It turns out that men dream about males twice as often as they do about females, whereas women dream almost equally about both sexes. In the dreams of both men and women, 21 per cent of the characters are not identified as to sex.

The analysis showed, as is not surprising, that people dream most often about other people of their own age. In the sample of dreams from the subjects in the eighteen-to-twenty-eight age group, 42 per cent of the dream

---

* Editor's italics.

characters were the dreamers' peers in age, 20 per cent were older, 3 per cent were younger, and 35 per cent were of unspecified age.

We found that in general there were no very pronounced differences between the characters in the dreams of the young and older groups. Older people dream more about family and relatives and less about friends and acquaintances, which is not very surprising, since the younger dreamers were for the most part unmarried. Older people also dream more about younger characters and less about older characters and peers than do younger dreamers. We may generalize our findings by saying that while children are dreaming about their parents, their parents are dreaming about them, and while husbands are dreaming about their wives, their wives are dreaming about them.

We come now to *actions or behavior:** What do people do in their dreams? We classified 2,668 actions in 1,000 dreams. By far the largest proportion (34 per cent) fall into the category of movement—walking, running, riding, or some other gross change in bodily position. We found that contrary to popular belief, falling or floating in dreams is not very common. After movement, the next most common activities were talking (11 per cent), sitting (7 per cent), watching (7 per cent), socializing (6 per cent), playing (5 per cent), manual work (4 per cent), thinking (4 per cent), striving (4 per cent), quarreling or fighting (3 per cent), and acquiring (3 per cent). From this it can be seen that passive or quiet activities occupy a large part of dreams, while manual activities are surprisingly infrequent. Such common waking occupations as typing, sewing, ironing, and fixing things are not represented in these thousand dreams at all; cooking, cleaning house, making beds, and washing dishes occur only once each. But strenuous recreational activities, such as swimming, diving, playing a game, and dancing are fairly frequent. In short, dreamers go places more than they do things; they play more than they work; their activities are more passive than active.

What of the relations between the dreamer and the other characters in his dream? We classified the interactions in a sample of 1,320 dreams in various categories according to degrees of friendliness or hostility. In general, hostile acts (by or against the dreamer) outnumber friendly ones 448 to 188. In the hostile sphere, the acts of aggression ranged from murder (2 per cent) and physical attack (28 per cent) to denunciation (27 per cent) and mere feelings of hostility (8 per cent). The friendly acts ranged from an expressed feeling of friendliness to the giving of an expensive gift.

The *emotions felt* * by dreamers during their dreams were recorded in five classes: (1) apprehension, including fear, anxiety, and perplexity; (2) anger, including frustration; (3) sadness; (4) happiness; and (5) excitement, including surprise. Apprehension predominated, accounting for 40

* Editor's italics.

per cent of all dream emotions; anger, happiness, and excitement were tied with 18 per cent each, and sadness was the least frequent, 6 per cent. Thus 64 per cent of all dream emotions were negative or unpleasant (apprehension, anger, sadness) and only 18 per cent (happiness) were positively pleasant.

Yet, paradoxically in the judgment of the dreamers themselves, the dreams as a whole were rated pleasant much more often than unpleasant. They found 41 per cent of the dreams pleasant, 25 per cent unpleasant, 11 per cent mixed, and 23 per cent without feeling tone. Older dreamers reported more unpleasant dreams than younger ones, but the difference was not great.

A question that has puzzled many students of dreams is why some of them are seen wholly or partly in natural *colors* * ("technicolor"). I am afraid I have little to contribute to the solution of this puzzle beyond a few figures and a few negative conclusions. In a survey of over 3,000 dreams, 29 per cent were colored or had some color in them and the rest were completely colorless. Women report color in dreams more often (31 per cent) than do men (24 per cent). There is a slight tendency for people over fifty to have fewer colored dreams than those under that age. Many people never experience color in dreams; on the other hand, a few have all their dreams in color.

What is the psychological significance of technicolored dreams? We have compared the dreams of people who dream entirely in color with those of people who never dream in color and have found no difference in any aspect of their dreams. We have compared the colored with the colorless dreams of the same person without discovering any way in which they differed. Nor can we find any single specific symbolic meaning in a particular color. We are forced to conclude on the basis of our present evidence that color in dreams is merely an embellishment, signifying nothing in itself.

What do all these facts on the content of dreams mean? I shall present my *general theory of dreams* * and show how some of the foregoing findings fit into this theory.

Dreaming is thinking that occurs during sleep. It is a peculiar form of thinking in which the conceptions or ideas are expressed not in the form of words or drawings, as in waking life, but in the form of images, usually visual images. In other words, the abstract and invisible ideas are converted into concrete and visible images. By an odd process which we do not understand, the sleeping person can see his own thoughts embodied in the form of pictures. When he communicates his dream to another person, he is communicating his thoughts, whether he knows it or not.

During sleep we think about our problems and predicaments, our fears

* Editor's italics.

and hopes. The dreamer thinks about himself: what kind of person he is and how well fitted he is to deal with his conflicts and anxieties. He thinks about other people who touch his life intimately. His conceptions are purely egocentric; there appears to be no place in dreams for impersonal, detached thoughts. Accordingly the interpretation of dreams—the translation of the dreamer's images into his ideas—gives us an inner view of him, as though we were looking out and seeing the world as he sees it. We see how he looks to himself, how others look to him, and how he conceives of life. This is the heart of the matter, and the reason why dreams are important data for the psychologist.

How a person sees himself is expressed in dreams by the parts the dreamer plays. He may play the part of a victim or an aggressor or both; he may conceive of himself as winning in spite of adverse circumstances, or losing because of these same adversities. He may assume the role of a saint or a sinner, a dependent person or an independent one, a miser or a philanthropist. As Emerson said, "A skillful man reads his dreams for his self-knowledge."

Although the characters in his dreams are many and varied, they probably all have one thing in common—they are all emotionally involved in the dreamer's life. If this is so, one may well ask, why do we dream so often about strangers? The answer is that they are not really strangers but personifications of our conceptions of people we know. A person who conceives of his father as stern and autocratic, for example, may in his dreams turn his father into an army officer or a policeman or a school-teacher or some other symbol of strict discipline. Very likely he will also have other conceptions of his father, and for each conception he finds an appropriate older figure who personifies the particular father conception uppermost in his mind at the time of the dream. Many of these father figures will be strangers to the dreamer, although the qualities expressed will be familiar enough to him.

Similarly, the dream setting may portray *the ways in which the dreamer looks at the world.** If he feels that the world is closing in on him, he dreams of cramped places; if the world appears bleak, the dream setting is bleak. Tumultuous and tempestuous scenery—raging seas, milling crowds, exploding bombs, thunderstorms—betokens an outlook of insecurity and chaos. In one series of dreams studied by the writer, there was a plethora of dirty, dank, and dismal settings—a visible projection of the dreamer's conception of a world decaying.

Dreams are filled with the *gratification* * or attempted gratification of impulses, particularly sexual and aggressive impulses. They tell us how the dreamer regards these impulses. If he thinks of sex or aggression as wicked,

* Editor's italics.

the expression of these impulses in his dreams will be followed by some form of punishment or misfortune. If he conceives of sex as a mechanical matter, he may have a dream like that of one young man who reported a nocturnal emission dream in which a lady plumber turned on a faucet for the dreamer. We study dreams, therefore, not to discover the wish motivating the dream, as Freud did, but rather to determine how the dreamer conceives of his wishes.

Dreams also provide a vista of the *dreamer's conceptions of his conflicts.** The dramatic quality of a dream—its plot, tensions, and resolutions—is derived from an underlying conflict in whose grip the dreamer feels himself to be. In a series of dreams from the same individual, we can see his conflict running like Ariadne's thread through the labyrinth of his dreams. The conflict may hang on with surprising tenacity over a period of years. Apparently, the conflicts that motivate dreams are basic ones which rarely become resolved. We suspect that these internal wars have their origins early in life and are not easily, if ever, brought to a satisfactory conclusion.

In our studies of many dream series, a few conflicts stand out as being shared by many people. One such inner tug-of-war is that between the progressive pull of maturity, growth, and independence and the regressive pull of infantile security, passivity, and dependence. This conflict is particularly acute during adolescence and the late teens and early twenties, but in a large proportion of people it persists through later ages and returns to prominence in old age.

Another ubiquitous inner conflict is that between conceptions of good and evil—the moral conflict. The opposing forces are those of impulse and conscience. The dreamer impulsively kills a dream character and is then punished for his crime. Or he is driven to express sexuality for which he suffers some misfortune.

A third conflict arises out of the tug between the opposing tendencies toward integration and disintegration. By integration is meant all of the life-maintaining and love-encompassing aims of man; by disintegration, the forces of death, hate, fear, and anxiety which produce disunity and dissolution. One pole affirms life and love, the other affirms death and hate. Anxiety dreams and nightmares express the conception of personal disintegration.

We study dreams in order to enlarge our understanding of man. They yield information that is not readily obtained from other sources. This information consists of man's most personal and intimate conceptions, conceptions of which not even the person himself is aware. It is important to know these conceptions, for they are the foundation of man's conduct. How we view ourselves and the world around us determines in large measure how we will behave.

* Editor's italics.

IMPLICATIONS

What impressed you most about Hall's findings? How do your dreams duplicate or vary from the kinds of dream content and processes related here? Have you gained any ideas as to what your dreams can mean to you? Possibly, you may find it interesting to discuss the implications of these findings with your fellow students. Include a discussion of the conflicts, shared by many people, that are dramatized in dreams.

REFERENCES

See Rapaport (1951), Hall and Van de Castle (1966), Hall and Norby (1972) and Van de Castle (1971).

50 A PREFACE TO THE THEORY OF HYPNOTISM

Robert W. White

Most people have heard of hypnosis, and some have even seen an individual hypnotized. Hypnosis has almost universal human interest because the trancelike state seems so abnormal and rare to common experience. Hypnosis has had a long association with the magical, mystical, theatrical, and sensational. It also has had a history of association with medicine and science, beginning in the eighteenth century with the Viennese physician Mesmer. In addition, it has some status at present in psychological research and training.

How do we know *what hypnosis is, how it is brought about,* and *who can be hypnotized?* Hypnosis is a temporary state, trancelike in nature, induced by a hypnotic operator. It is a condition of altered attention. The subject appears to have for the time relinquished his normal self-management to the hypnotist. He is hypersuggestible and seems to be compelled to obey the instructions of the hypnotist if he is motivated to cooperate with the hypnotist.

Hypnosis is usually *produced* by having the subject relax and fix his gaze on some point or object while the operator monotonously verbalizes suggestions of relaxation and drowsiness. In a short time the sub-

From Robert W. White, "A Preface to the Theory of Hypnosis," *Journal of Abnormal and Social Psychology*, Vol. 4, No. 36, 1941, pp. 479–484. Copyright 1941 by the American Psychological Association, and reproduced by permission of the publisher and the author.

ject will appear to go to sleep and will pass into a sleeplike, lethargic condition. If the procedure is successful, he will exhibit the behavior commanded by the hypnotist. Some of the events that may occur during hypnosis are described in the following excerpt. The events can range widely, including alterations in memory and perceptions, paralysis, changes in vasomotor activity, and muscular rigidity.

The question of who can be hypnotized cannot be answered briefly. People vary from complete nonsusceptibility to hypnosis to high susceptibility. The factor of depth of hypnosis from light to deep also must be considered. In a situation of security and confidence, it has been stated, willing subjects can undergo some degree of hypnosis by a responsible hypnotist. The best method of determining susceptibility is the actual attempt at hypnosis.

Psychologists, being primarily investigators and scientists, are interested mainly in the facts and theories of hypnosis—the *what* and the *why*. In the excerpt, White also discusses some facts of hypnosis, many of which are found under laboratory conditions. He advances the theory that hypnosis is *goal-directed striving,* a concept found useful in psychology. We see how a psychologist marshals the data about a process and then builds a theory to explain it.

Facts Which Require Explanation

To begin with, we shall review briefly the facts that any theory of hypnosis is called upon to explain. What are the characteristics which make hypnosis a perennial object of wonder and amazement? Three things appear to create surprise. One of these is that the hypnotized person can effectuate suggestions lying outside the realm of ordinary volitional control; he can do things that he could not possibly do in the normal state. No less surprising, however, is the way a hypnotized person carries out those suggestions lying within the realm of volition. Stiffening the arm or clasping the hands are actions that anyone could perform volitionally, but in hypnosis they occur without benefit of volition, unaccompanied by the experience of intention, yet at times so strongly that the subject seems unable to arrest them when he tries. Furthermore, hypnotic actions are carried out with a curious lack of humor and self-consciousness, often with an air of abstraction and drowsiness, and they do not seem to have the claim over subsequent memory to which their recency and importance entitle them. Finally, it is a constant source of amazement that these rather drastic effects can be brought about simply by talking. If a person suffered a head injury, took a drug, or was worked into a state of violent emotion, radical changes in the control of behavior would be expected as a matter of course, but no one can believe that mere words entering the ears of a relaxed and drowsy subject can be sufficient cause for the changes which actually take place. It will repay us to consider each of these items in a little more detail.

1. *Hypnotic transcendence of voluntary capacity* is strikingly illustrated by insensitivity to pain. One of the most dramatic chapters in the history of hypnotism is its use by James Esdaile about 1845 as an anaesthetic in major surgical operations. There is still no more convincing way to persuade a skeptic that hypnosis is "real" than by showing that ordinarily painful stimuli can be endured without signs of pain. Carefully controlled experiments designed to exclude every possibility of error have reaffirmed the reality of this phenomenon and have shown that the inhibition extends to such nonvoluntary processes as pulse rate and the galvanic skin reaction (Dynes, 1932; Sears, 1932). Along somewhat different lines, recent experiments show that muscular strength and resistance to fatigue are at least somewhat increased (Williams, 1929) and that recall is substantially improved in consequence of hypnotic suggestions (Stalnaker and Riddle, 1932; White, Fox, and Harris, 1940). There is still some reason to believe that older claims concerning the production of blisters, cold sores, and digestive reactions are not without foundation, although the investigation of these topics has suffered from a lack of control experiments (Frick, Scantlebury, and Patterson, 1935; Hull, 1933; Pattie, 1941). Whatever the ultimate decision upon one or another of the latter claims, there is no danger of concluding that hypnotic suggestion can produce a number of effects beyond the realm of volition, and that among these effects is an increased control over autonomic functions. The implication of these facts for a theory of hypnotism will be considered in a later section.

2. It is not necessary, however, to depend upon these facts of transcendence in order to demonstrate that hypnotic behavior differs from voluntary. If we confine ourselves to actions which could perfectly well be performed intentionally, there is still a *distinct difference in the way they are performed* in response to hypnotic suggestion. When retrospection is possible, as often happens after relatively light hypnosis, a crucial difference in the accompanying experience can be recognized. Janet (1925) reports that a patient, ordinarily suggestible, one day declared that the suggestion "did not take." "I am quite ready to obey you," she said, "and I will do it if you choose: only I tell you beforehand that the thing did not take." This patient clearly recognized the difference between obedience, when one intentionally carries out another person's command, and suggestion, when the action executes itself without the experience of intention, even in defiance of it.

Bleuler, describing his experiences when hypnotized, said, "I felt my biceps contracting against my will as soon as I attempted to move my arm by means of the extensor muscles; once, on making a stronger effort to carry out my intention, the contraction of the flexors became so energetic that the arm, instead of moving outward as I had intended, moved backward on the upper arm." "At other times," he said again, "I felt that the movement was made without any active taking part by my ego, this being especially marked with unimportant commands" (Forel, 1907).

One of the writer's subjects reported himself as "quite marveling at the way my arm stayed up, apparently without volition on my part. I was still aware of myself off in a corner looking on." Observations such as these could be multiplied indefinitely, but further emphasis is scarcely necessary. It is sufficient to remember that subjects after light trances can almost always give evidence concerning their susceptibility, and that their own spontaneous criterion is whether or not they had the feeling of collaborating in the production of the suggested actions. Though there is a hazy borderland between intentional and automatic acts, in the majority of cases, subjects can readily discriminate between the two. Hypnotic suggestion not only transcends the limits of volitional control but also dispenses with volition when bringing about actions which normally lie within those limits.

Subsequent report is frequently impossible because of post-hypnotic amnesia. Even so there is an appreciable difference between hypnotic behavior and the everyday intentional performance of like actions. For one thing, the subject's manner differs from the ordinary: he seems literal and humorless, he shows no surprise and makes no apology for bizarre behavior, he appears entirely unself-conscious, and very often he acts abstracted, inattentive, almost as if he were insulated against his surroundings. Braid's notion of monoideism serves very well to describe the impression a hypnotized person makes on an outside observer. For another thing, hypnotic behavior does not seem to occupy a proper place in the subject's memory. He disclaims recollection of recent and often very complicated actions which in the ordinary way he seems to have every reason to remember. Thus, whether we choose an introspective criterion or whether we prefer external observation, we are entitled to be surprised at the difference between hypnotically suggested actions and similar actions intentionally performed.

3. *The procedure by which hypnosis is made to occur does not seem adequate to produce such an effect.* So great is this discrepancy that for many years it was customary to assume a magnetic force, an invisible fluid, or some similar powerful agent, passing from the operator into the subject. With the decline of such theories, there has been a tendency to argue that the phenomena of hypnosis are after all not unique, that under suitable conditions they can all be duplicated without resort to a hypnotic procedure. It is known, for example, that under stress of excitement and violent emotion, people surpass by a wide margin their usual levels of muscular strength and endurance. In like circumstances there is often a considerable degree of anesthesia for the pain of fairly serious injuries. Hyperamnesia occurs during free association, in drowsy states, and in dreams. Many actions which cannot be initiated by themselves without the experience of intention take place quite involuntarily when embedded in a context of other actions, as in playing a game. Perhaps these claims are justified; perhaps there is no phenomenon in the repertory of hypnotic suggestion which cannot be pro-

duced in some other way. But, even if this be true, we are not exempt from explaining why the hypnotic procedure, which does not create excitement and violent emotion, which does not put one to sleep, which makes no use of free association, which virtually excludes a context of other actions, and which especially with practice requires very little time, brings about so momentous an effect. It is legitimate to be surprised at the power of hypnotic suggestion.

The task which confronts a theory of hypnosis is roughly defined by the three foregoing peculiarities. Any such theory must explain how (1) the hypnotic procedure brings about (2) the nonvolitional performance of acts that ordinarily require volitional assistance and (3) the performance of acts outside the normal range of volition.

Hypnotic Behavior as Goal-Directed Striving

When Charcot discovered that it was possible to reproduce the symptoms of hysteria by means of hypnosis, he surmised that the two phenomena were closely related, indeed, that they were aspects of the same underlying condition. This dubious bond, however, was not sufficient to keep hypnosis and hysteria long on an equal footing of medical interest. Thus it happened that the theory of hypnotism lingered at the Salpêtrière stage, while the theory of hysteria advanced steadily from Charcot's time to the present, becoming at last the basis for a new understanding of all neurotic conditions and the starting point for modern dynamic psychology. The central insight which transformed the theory of hysteria was the idea that symptoms spring from strivings, that neurosis is an outcome of conflict among fundamental impulses rather than a damaged state of the nervous system. Such a view would have been impossible without the still more basic insight that large parts of a person's striving may take place unconsciously, forming no part of his organized picture of himself and his intentions. In psychopathology these once radical notions have gradually worked their way to acceptance.

The benefits of this progress have been largely withheld from the theory of hypnotism. Two concepts, *automatism* and *dissociation*, once useful in understanding hysteria but long since modified, reshaped, and animated with dynamic ideas, have persisted in a peculiarly literal and lifeless form in hypnotic theory. Automatism, invoked to explain the nonvolitional character of hypnotic behavior, implies that hypnotized persons are helpless executants of the operator's will as this is expressed in verbal suggestion. Dissociation, called upon to account for amnesia, post-hypnotic phenomena, and those instances when impressions seem to be excluded from awareness or when intentions fail to govern motor processes, implies the subject to be in a state of temporary fragmentation such that different parts of his behavior take place independently without their usual communication.

These ideas deserve the respect which is due to first approximations, but their prolonged survival keeps the theory of hypnotism in swaddling clothes when it should be grown to adult stature.

The concept of striving, so useful in other parts of psychology, needs to be applied in thorough-going fashion to the behavior of the hypnotized person. This application may be embodied in the following statement: *hypnotic behavior is meaningful, goal-directed striving, its most general goal being to behave like a hypnotized person as this is continuously defined by the operator and understood by the subject.* This point of view is not original with the present writer, having been previously maintained by Rosenow (1928), Lundholm (1928), Pattie (1935, 1937), and Dorcus (1937), who have found it more satisfactory in explaining the facts subsumed under both automatism and dissociation. The hypnotized person is seen not as an almost inanimate object, upon which strange effects can be wrought by touching the right levers or tapping the right lines of cleavage, but as a human being who hears and understands and who tries to behave in the different ways which are proposed to him. The adoption of such a hypothesis should not, of course, depend upon one's general preferences in psychological theory. It is the argument of the present paper that hypnotic behavior, on the face of it, can be adequately described and adequately understood in no other way than as goal-directed striving.

IMPLICATIONS

To what extent are you able now, after reading these facts and the theory proposed, to see hypnosis as compatible with waking behavior? What other behavior, less rare than the hypnotic trance, can you recall that is somewhat related to hypnosis? What about its relationship to somnambulistic behavior or *sleepwalking, absent-mindedness,* or behavior while being intently absorbed in another activity such as an athletic game? Can you think of any other phenomena related to hypnosis?

REFERENCES

In an interestingly written book, Moss (1965) points out that in thirty-one years ending in 1959, 971 entries dealt with hypnosis in the *Psychological Abstracts,* a journal of abstracts of the articles and books of a psychological nature. There is currently a reawakened interest among psychologists, but this was preceded by a period of skepticism and negativism. Moss, in addition to a history of the phenomenon, discusses the power of hypnosis, theories about it, and its current status.

Hilgard (1965) has published a volume consisting of studies on hypnosis and discussing issues such as the nature of hypnosis, representative hypnotic phenomena, and factors in hypnotic suggestibility.

51 MAN'S UNCONSCIOUS PROCESSES

Carl G. Jung

Man is rational, but he also has an *irrational* side of which he is unconscious or only vaguely conscious. We are indebted first to Sigmund Freud for systematizing this idea that has appeared again and again in literature. Freud emphasized the dynamic nature of these unconscious processes. Unacceptable urges and wishes that cannot be reviewed consciously are repressed but retain their drive nature, appearing in dreams, slips of speech, unconscious mannerisms, and creative ventures of the individual. He maintained that much of man's conflictory and contradictory nature can be understood in terms of the operation of unconscious processes.

Jung saw the unconscious aspects of man as involving *more than repressed sexual and aggressive impulses*. Unconscious processes also contain complements of our conscious strivings: the predominantly extroverted individual has introverted unconscious tendencies; the male has a hidden feminine side; the idealistic, well-behaved person has baser, more hostile repressed impulses. Jung went further, prompted by his interests in many different cultures widely separated by space and even by time—mythology, ancient symbols, and rituals in primitive cultures. He saw all men as possessing *common racial origins* in their personalities. The civilized individual has predispositions that are a heritage from his very distant ancestors. Jung hypothesizes that these predispositions influence man's behavior.

Here we will look at a selection from Jung's writings as he discusses unconscious influences in the extroverted person. He illustrates these influences with a case and discusses generally what can happen when infantile and primitive dispositions are ruthlessly suppressed rather than understood and guided. Then we shall deviate from our usual format and in an Editor's Comment summarize some of Jung's ideas that would require many pages from Jung's books to cover.

From *Psychological Types*, by C.G. Jung, trans. H.G. Baynes (London: Routledge & Kegan Paul, 1923), pp. 422–426. Reprinted by permission of Routledge & Kegan Paul and Princeton University Press.

I⟋т мау регнарѕ seem odd that I should speak of an "attitude of the unconscious." . . . I regard the relation of the unconscious to the conscious as compensatory. The unconscious, according to this view, has as good a claim to an "attitude" as the conscious. . . .

The attitude of the unconscious as an effective complement to the conscious extraverted attitude has a definitely introverting character. It focusses libido upon the subject factor, *i.e.*, all those needs and claims which are stifled or repressed by a too extraverted conscious attitude. . . . A purely objective orientation does violence to a multitude of subjective emotions, intensions, needs, and desires, since it robs them of the energy which is their natural right. Man is not a machine that one can reconstruct, as occasion demands, upon other lines and for quite other ends, in the hope that it will then proceed to function, in a totally different way, just as normally as before. Man bears his age-long history with him; in his very structure is written the history of mankind.

The historical factor represents a vital need, to which a wise economy must respond. Somehow the past must become vocal, and participate in the present. Complete assimilation to the object, therefore, encounters the protest of the suppressed minority, elements belonging to the past and existing from the beginning. From this quite general consideration it may be understood why it is that the unconscious claims of the extraverted type have an essentially primitive, infantile, and egoistical character. . . .

I remember the case of a printer who, starting as a mere employee, worked his way up through two decades of hard struggle, till at last he was the independent possessor of a very extensive business. The more the business extended, the more it increased its hold upon him, until gradually every other interest was allowed to become merged in it. At length he was completely enmeshed in its toils, and, as we shall soon see, this surrender eventually proved his ruin. As a sort of compensation to his exclusive interest in the business, certain memories of his childhood came to life. As a child he had taken great delight in painting and drawing. But, instead of renewing this capacity for its own sake as a balancing side interest, he canalized it into his business and began to conceive "artistic" elaborations of his products. His phantasies unfortunately materialized: he actually began to produce after his own primitive and infantile taste, with the result that after a very few years his business went to pieces. He acted in obedience to one of our "civilized ideals," which enjoins the energetic man to concentrate everything upon the one end in view. But he went too far, and merely fell a victim to the power of his subjective infantile claims.

But the catastrophic solution may also be subjective, *i.e.*, in the form of a nervous collapse. Such a solution always comes about as a result of the unconscious counterinfluence, which can ultimately paralyze conscious action. In which case the claims of the unconscious force themselves categorically upon consciousness, thus creating a calamitous cleavage which generally reveals itself in two ways: either the subject no longer knows what he really wants and nothing any longer interests him, or he wants too much at once and has too keen an interest—but in impossible things. The suppression of infantile and primitive claims, which is often necessary on "civilized" grounds, easily leads to neurosis, or to the misuse of narcotics such as alcohol, morphine, cocaine, etc. In more extreme cases the cleavage ends in suicide.

It is a salient peculiarity of unconscious tendencies that, just insofar as they are deprived of their energy by a *lack of conscious recognition*, they assume a correspondingly destructive character, and as soon as this happens their compensatory function ceases. They cease to have a compensatory effect as soon as they reach a depth or stratum that corresponds with a level of culture absolutely incompatible with our own. From this moment the unconscious tendencies form a block, which is opposed to the conscious attitude in every respect; such a block inevitably leads to open conflict.

EDITOR'S COMMENT

The preceding excerpt is from one of Jung's early books in which he introduces introversion and extroversion—the tendency to withdraw into oneself and be concerned with inner experience on the one hand and the tendency to be preoccupied with social life and the external world on the other hand. In these few paragraphs he shows the human need for *balance* between conscious materialistic goals and less conscious impulses from earlier life, serving *creative* needs.

Jung suggests that ignoring unconscious and nonrational forces in oneself may be in part the cause of extreme behavior, neuroses, loss of zest for life, the use of drugs, and even suicide. Contrariwise, he has told his patients that when their conscious minds no longer see any possible road ahead and are blocked, their unconscious processes react to the unbearable standstill. He is telling his patients in therapy to explore the latent possibilities in themselves, their *deep creative tendencies*, to find out what kind of persons they are, and to live accordingly. His supportive relationship with his patients bolsters the patients' courage to do this.

Here are summarized a few more of Jung's observations from his psychoanalytic practice and his study of man's present and past—his dreams, myths, rituals, and neurotic and psychotic symptoms. Jung regards the *realization of selfhood* and the development of unique potentialities as life's goal, which tends to be reached as the person is able to *unite the many conflicting tendencies* within himself, especially conscious and unconscious processes, into an integrated, whole, balanced personality.

The middle age of man is crucial. It is a time when the individual becomes more introverted and less impulsive; physical and mental vigor are supplanted by social, religious, civic, and philosophic interests. Coping with the environment and with sexual and aggressive urges becomes less predominant; conversely, a search for *personal meaning, wholeness, and self-identity* in a universal context are in the forefront. Religion at this time of life becomes more important. Jung is frank in stating that man possesses a natural religious function and that his mental health and stability depend on the proper expression of this function in addition to the satisfaction of his basic physical drives. Jung defines religion broadly, referring to all attitudes of mind that give careful consideration to the dynamic factors man has always conceived as powers, spirits, demons, gods, laws, or ideals.

IMPLICATIONS

Which of Jung's ideas given here have the greatest meaning to you? Attempt to state them in your own words. What were the unconscious processes in the case of the printer? What are the unique potentials in your life that may be developed? How do you react to Jung's idea that man possesses natural religious functions? Try to state some example of unconscious processes in some individual you know.

REFERENCES

Some scholars regard Jung as one of the greatest thinkers of this century, since his writings have stimulated scholars in so many areas and his many ideas are so provocative. Whereas the intellectual world has great respect for him, psychologists for a long time regarded him critically despite the influence of his broader concepts. His findings were grounded on clinical and less easily verified findings rather than on experimental studies. His writings, say Hall and Lindzey (1957), who devote an excellent chapter to his ideas and influence, "stand as one of the most remarkable achievements in modern thought." They attribute this to his original and audacious thinking, which has few parallels.

Jung is sometimes difficult to read and at other times very expressive. Two of his many works often cited are *Modern Man in Search of a Soul* (1933) and *Psychology and Religion* (1960). Fordham (1961) has written a readable book on Jung's works. William Douglass (1959) has contributed an excellent review of several of Jung's volumes.

The most recent book by Jung (1964) and his students—readable and beautifully illustrated—is entitled *Man and His Symbols*. Here is illustrated the appearance of man's symbols (an expression of his unconscious) throughout his history. There are chapters on ancient myths and visual arts, among other important symbols.

52 ESP AND MENTAL TELEPATHY: AN EVALUATION

Ernest R. Hilgard

In almost every introductory class, students raise questions about the validity of *mental telepathy, clairvoyance, supernaturalism, mediums,* and other occult effects. These phenomena are sometimes called parapsychology. Certain of these effects have been studied under laboratory conditions, and psychologists do have definite opinions about the possible existence of the basic phenomenon known as ESP (extrasensory perception). We are referring here to perception that requires no sense organ stimulation. Psychologists vary in opinion about ESP, from the majority who say "an unlikely possibility" to other less frequently voiced opinions of "an impossibility" or "an unknown." You will note in the selection that Hilgard thinks we should reserve judgment as to its validity.

Ever so often a student will relate the experience of having a catastrophic dream "at the very same time" that a good friend or relative is in a serious accident. He may indicate belief that the dream communicated the accident to him and that this communication was a direct one between the "mind" of the victim and himself at the time of the disaster. Invariably, upon questioning, the student does not have data on the exact time of the dream or the accident, nor does he have any other validating evidence. When further questioned, the student will admit that he has dreamed of accidents when no accidents have occurred.

The discussion of extrasensory perception by Hilgard is one of the most thorough, clear, and concise presentations of this phenomenon from the standpoint of contemporary psychology.

Most of the experiments that have been done on extrasensory perception have used a deck of twenty-five cards, containing five different kinds of cards with these simple symbols on them: a square, a plus sign, parallel wavy lines, a star, and a circle (see Figure 1). The cards are shuffled, and one subject acts as a sender. The sender remains in one room, picks up a card and studies it carefully while the other subject, the receiver, tries at the same time "to read the mind" of the sender. He does this by calling out either "star," "square," "circle," "plus," or "parallel lines." His judgment can then be recorded as a hit or a miss.

With this brief introduction you are ready to read the description of extrasensory perception experiments and those on psychokinesis. You will observe that Hilgard's critical discussion of these phenomena

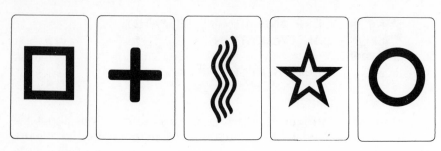

Figure 1. ESP cards, 25 in a pack.

offers us an understanding of why psychologists are dubious about the existence of these and similar "supernatural" phenomena.

Extrasensory Perception

IF THERE ARE so many influences upon perception other than those coming from the presented stimuli, are there perhaps perceptions that require no sense-organ stimulation whatsoever? The answer to this question is the source of a major controversy within contemporary psychology over the status of *extrasensory perception* (ESP). A minority of psychologists believe that the evidence for the existence of certain forms of ESP is now incontrovertible (*e.g.*, Murphy, 1949; Rhine and Pratt, 1957; Soal and Bateman, 1954; Thouless, 1950). Despite these contentions, most psychologists remain unconvinced.

The phenomena under discussion are of four main kinds:

I. Extrasensory perception (ESP)
   1. Telepathy, or thought transference from one person to another.
   2. Clairvoyance, or the perception of objects or events not influencing the senses.
   3. Precognition, or the perception of a future event.
II. Psychokinesis (PK), whereby a mental operation affects a material body or an energy system (*e.g.*, wishing for a number affects what number comes up in the throw of dice).

The experimenters go at their work in accordance with the usual rules of science and generally disavow the connection between this work and spiritualism, supernaturalism, mediumistic phenomena, and other occult effects. Yet the phenomena with which they deal are so extraordinary, and so similar to the superstitious beliefs of nonliterate people, that many scientists disavow even the legitimacy of their inquiries. Such *a priori* judgments are out of place in science, however, and the real question is whether or not the empirical evidence is acceptable by ordinary scientific standards. Many psychologists who are not convinced would find it congenial to accept evidence that they found satisfactory. For example, the possibility of some sort of influence from one brain to another, other than by way of the sense organs, would not be inconceivable within the present framework of science were the facts of telepathy to be established in some orderly fashion. Some of the other phenomena are more difficult to find believable (precognition, for example), but if the evidence were firm, previous thought patterns would have to yield to the facts.

The case for ESP is based largely on experiments in card-guessing, in which, under various conditions, the subject attempts to guess the symbols on cards randomly arranged in packs. The usual pack consists of 25 cards with five symbols, so that a chance performance would be 5 hits per pack. Even very successful subjects seldom reach as high a level as 7 hits, but they may score above 5 often enough to meet acceptable standards of statistical significance. If the experimenter or "sender" thinks of the symbol at the time the subject makes his record, the experiment is one on telepathy; if the experimenter does not perceive the card at all (it may be face down on the table before him or sealed in an envelope), then the experiment is one on clairvoyance. The kind of evidence used in support of the nonchance nature of the findings can be illustrated by the successive runs of one "sensitive" subject, Mrs. Gloria Stewart, studied in England over a long period (Table 1). If the evidence is viewed in the same spirit as that from any other experiment, it is clear that Mrs. Stewart responded above chance on the telepathy trials, but not on the clairvoyance ones. This fact also meets certain objections about card arrangements sometimes used against such experiments, for her chance performance on the clairvoyance trials shows that above-chance scores are not an inevitable result of something having to do with the shuffling of the cards. The telepathy results are above the expected level in 11 of the 13 runs of 200, and the average scoring level of 6.8 hits (instead of 5) per pack of 25 is well above chance.

The complaint has been voiced that ESP results are not subject to systematic variation through ordinary experimental control. This also is not entirely fair to the findings. For example, there are some order effects reported, in which early trials are more successful than later ones (Rhine and Humphrey, 1944; McConnell, Snowdon, and Powell, 1955), and there is reported evidence that an attitude favorable to ESP, noted in advance, leads to positive results, while an unfavorable attitude leads to scoring below chance levels (Schmeidler and McConnell, 1958).

Thus, empirical findings are offered in support of ESP and PK, which meet ordinary statistical standards. Why, then, do not the results become a part of established psychological science? Many arguments have been used against the work, but they usually boil down to a few such as the following: (1) the fact that many claims of extraordinary phenomena in the past have turned out to be false when investigated; (2) certain problems in statistical inference that arise when very large numbers of trials are used to establish the significance of small differences; (3) the failure of improved methods to yield better results than crude methods; and (4) general lack of orderli-

Table 1

Results of Interspersed Telepathy and Clairvoyance
Trials with One Subject *

Chronological order of successive groups of 200 trials	Hits per 200 trials (Expected = 40)	
	Telepathy Trials	Clairvoyance Trials
1945	65	51
	58	42
	62	29
	58	47
	60	38
1947	54	35
	55	36
	65	31
1948	39	38
	56	43
1949	49	40
	51	37
	33	42
Total hits	707	509
Expected hits	520	520
Difference	+187	−11
Hits per 25 trials	6.8	4.9

Source: Soal and Bateman (1945), p. 352.
* Each group of 200 trials consisted of alternating blocks
of 50 telepathy and 50 clairvoyance trials.

ness in the phenomena, without which rational theorizing cannot replace
the highly irrational theories now used to account for what occurs.

These arguments are not, in fact, decisive, and it is desirable to keep an
open mind about issues that permit empirical demonstration, as the ESP
phenomena do. At the same time it should be clear that the reservations of
the majority of psychologists are based on more than stubborn prejudice.

The following critical discussion is provided for those who might care to
look a little further into these issues.

Critical Discussion

Why Many Psychologists Find ESP
Experiments Unconvincing

We may expand a little upon the objections that psychologists have to the
ESP and PK experiments and to *psi*, the special ability attributed to the
"sensitive" subject.

1. *General scepticism about extraordinary phenomena.* Throughout history there have always been reports of strange happenings, of ghosts, little men, poltergeists (noisy spirits who engage in throwing things about), dreams foretelling the future. The continuing appearance of these stories does not make them true, any more than reported flying saucers establish the visits of men from Mars. Painstaking investigation by the U.S. Air Force yields no "flying saucers"; nobody ever traps the Loch Ness monster. A famous mediumistic case (still mentioned favorably by Soal and Bateman, 1954) is a case in point. Eusapia Palladino was a medium who was able to make a table move and produce other effects, such as tapping sounds, by the aid of a "spirit" called John King. Investigated repeatedly between 1893 and 1910, she convinced many distinguished scientists of her powers, including the distinguished Italian criminologist Lombroso and the British physicist Sir Oliver Lodge. She was caught in deceptive trickery as early as 1895, and the results were published. Yet believers continued to support her genuineness, as some do today, even though in an American investigation in 1910, her trickery was abundantly exposed (Jastrow, 1935; Rawcliffe, 1959). Two investigators, dressed in black, crawled under the table unobserved and were able to see exactly how she used her foot to create the "supernatural" phenomena. When, therefore, those most convinced about ESP are also convinced about already disproven phenomena, their testimony carries less weight than if they were more critical. A similar case in point is Rhine's belief in an ESP interpretation of "water-witching" or "dowsing," in which water is discovered by means of a divining rod (Rhine and Pratt, 1957). Careful study of this bit of primitive magic shows that success in water-witching requires no such explanation (Vogt and Hyman, 1959).[1] While attacking ESP experiments on the basis of the belief systems of the investigators is a kind of *argumentum ad hominem,* and hence somewhat unfair, it is understandable that one is less likely to trust the observations of a person known to be gullible than one known to be critical.

2. *Problems of statistical inference with large numbers and small effects.* One of the major contributions of ESP research to scientific psychology may turn out to be the attention it has drawn to the circumstances that make a scientific finding believable. It is commonly supposed that tests of statistical significance are sufficient guarantees of objectivity, and hence a satisfactory statistical outcome should lead to acceptance of a hypothesis as plausible. This turns out not to be the case in ESP experiments, and it is probably not the case in other experiments either. Statistical tests merely tell us how well measurement seems to establish something that is already plausible; if it is not plausible, we search for some source of error that has produced the non-chance result. For example, in a major attempt to produce random digits by an electronic roulette wheel (The RAND Corporation, 1955), it proved very difficult to eliminate bias; in fact, a sample of 125,000 digits tested after the machine had been running a month departed from a random distribution by an amount that was statistically significant. One does not argue that some devilish scientists was using PK to

---

[1] It may come as something of a surprise that there are estimated to be some 25,000 waterwitchers in America—more than all the psychologists who are members of the American Psychological Association (Vogt and Hyman, 1959).

foul the machine; one assumes that the machine somehow ran down with continuous use.

Let us compare this example with an experiment performed in Rhine's Duke University laboratory (Rhine, 1942). He was trying to detect whether or not a subject might, through some combination of ESP and PK, influence the positions of cards in a mechanical shuffler. In all, 51 persons wrote down their predictions of the orders in which cards would come out of a mechanical shuffler two to ten days later, the order of cards emerging from the shuffler being further complicated by having the cards cut by hand at a random trial. The experiment was carefully performed, and in a total of 57,550 trials the results were at chance level—just 11 hits in excess of expectation. But was this plausible result accepted? No; further statistical analyses were made. Two more of these, based on the division of the trials into segments, failed to yield non-chance results. Finally, a fourth analysis, based on a complex effect called a "covariance of salience ratio," gave a non-chance effect, with odds of 625 to 1 in its favor. When belief in bizarre effects is carried this far, it is no wonder that the unconvinced begins to suspect the statistics, even though the rules are followed and all computations are accurate.

There is a scientific problem here. A phenomenon may be rare and still important; hence large numbers of subjects or experiments may be needed if its existence is to be established. But the "good" or "sensitive" ESP subjects are rare. Soal and Bateman (1945), state that no such subject has turned up in America since 1938, despite the continuing research in the field, and in England they have but three who maintained the ESP ability for a considerable time. These unusually sensitive subjects tend to reach a level of about 7 of 25 hits, instead of the 5 expected; such an ability is not very significant from a social point of view, no matter how established it may be statistically. The possibility of some undetected bias, as was found in the electronic roulette wheel, is real enough to temper belief.

3. *Failure of improved methods to increase the yield.* In most scientific fields, the assay from the ore becomes richer as the methods become more refined. But the reverse trend is found in ESP experiments; it is almost a truism in research in the field of telepathy and clairvoyance that the poorer the conditions the better the results. In the early days of the Duke experiments, subjects yielding high ESP scores were rather common, one virtuoso averaging, in the course of 650 trials, 10.7 hits in 25 instead of the 5 expected. As the experiments have become better controlled, however, these high-scoring subjects have disappeared.

4. *Lack of systematic consistency in the phenomena.* Sensitive subjects in the Rhine laboratory appear to be about equally successful at clairvoyance and telepathy; but the English subjects appear to be good at telepathy and not at clairvoyance. Other peculiarities emerge. In a famous series of experiments in England, Mr. Basil Shackleton (one of the three good subjects mentioned above) gave no evidence of either telepathy or clairvoyance when scored in the usual way against the target card. Instead, he was shown to be successful in *precognition telepathy*, that is, in guessing what was *going to be* on the experimenter's mind in the next trial. He was unsuccessful in clairvoyance, no matter how scored (Soal and Bateman, 1954). Why, the skeptic asks, does the direct

telepathy fail with Mr. Shackleton in favor of something far more mysterious than the telepathic success of Mrs. Stewart? [2]

Because the *psi* ability does not follow the ordinary rules, explanations of its operation can be produced with the greatest of freedom. It need not be affected in any ordinary way by space or time, so that success over great distances is accepted as a sign of its extraordinary power rather than something to cause a search for artifacts. Similarly, the precognition experiments are merely evidence that it is as easy to read what is *about* to be on someone else's mind as what is on it now. The PK effects, which require the sorting of cards or the rolling of dice by mental effort ("mind over matter"), are nevertheless said to occur without any transfer of physical energy, thus presumably violating the usual belief in the conservation of energy. But in any experimental work *some* aspects of time and space have to be respected, such as spatial form and color and order of suuccession in time. Unless some restraint is shown, one might invent such hypotheses as that the subject was sometimes perceiving the cards in reverse order, sometimes in a place-skipping order, and so on; any significance test that depends upon coincidences requires some respect for order.

The believer in *psi* is impatient with this kind of criticism. He says that we ask more of him than we do of other experimenters. In fact, we do ask more. To demonstrate something highly implausible requires better evidence than to demonstrate something plausible. The reason is that supporting evidence for the plausible finding comes from many directions, while the implausible one must hang upon the slender thread of nonrandomness until certain systematic relationships are found that tie it firmly to what is known.

IMPLICATIONS

To what extent are you convinced, as are many psychologists, that extrasensory perception, psychokinesis, and similar "supernatural" phenomena are an improbability? If not, are you able to state arguments and supply data that will withstand the general skepticism of the scientist? One way to test your understanding of the scientist's criticism of these phenomena is to review them, preparatory to a critical discussion with someone who is a staunch believer in ESP and related occult effects. You might find an interesting means of integrating the criticism of ESP offered by psychologists. Why do you think so many people want to believe in ESP? Is it the same motivation found in those who patronize fortune tellers, or is there a different motivation in their case?

---

[2] Mrs. Stewart, who failed in clairvoyance also, was above chance in hits on the target card, but *also* on the preceding card and the following card.

REFERENCES

Consult the Bibliography for references cited in the article.

A volume by Rhine *et al.* (1965) presents some of the research in the parapsychological field.

BIBLIOGRAPHY

Ackerman, N.W. *The Psychodynamics of Family Life.* New York: Basic Books, 1958.

Adrian, E.D. *The Physical Background of Perception.* Chapter 5. Oxford: Clarendon, 1947.

"The Al-4-48 in Use: A Selection Study." Hartford, Conn.: Life Insurance Agency Management Association, 1951.

Allen, F.H. *Psychotherapy with Children.* New York: Norton, 1942.

Allen, R.M. *Personality Assessment Procedures.* New York: Harper, 1958.

Allport, G.W. *Becoming: Basic Considerations for the Psychology of Personality.* New Haven: Yale University, 1955.

———. *The Individual and His Religion.* New York: Macmillan, 1950.

———. *The Nature of Prejudice.* Cambridge, Mass.: Addison-Wesley, 1954.

———. *Pattern and Growth in Personality.* New York: Holt, Rinehart & Winston, 1961.

———. *The Person in Psychology.* Boston: Beacon Press, 1968.

———. *Personality: A Psychological Interpretation.* New York: Holt, 1937.

———. "Religion and Prejudice," in Gordon W. Allport (ed.), *Personality and the Social Encounter.* Cambridge, Mass.: Addison-Wesley, 1954, Chapter 16.

Anastasi, A. *Fields of Applied Psychology.* New York: Macmillan, 1964.

Andrews, T.G. A factorial analysis of responses to the comic as a study in personality. *J. Gen. Psychol.*, 28:209–224. 1943.

Anon. *Alcoholics Anonymous.* New York: Alcoholics Anonymous, 1955, p. 59.

Ansbacher, H.L., and Ansbacher, R.R. (eds.). *The Individual Psychology of Alfred Adler.* New York: Basic Books, 1956.

Anson, B.J. *Atlas of Human Anatomy.* Philadelphia: Saunders, 1951.

Arieti, S. *Interpretation of Schizophrenia.* New York: Brunner, 1955.

Aronson, E. *The Social Animal.* San Francisco: Freeman & Co., 1972.

Asch, S.E. Studies of independence and conformity: I. A minority of one against a unanimous majority. *Psychol. Monogr.*, 70 (416), 1956.

Atkinson, J.W. (ed.). *Motives in Fantasy, Action and Society.* New York: Van Nostrand, 1958.

Atkinson, R.C., and Wilson, H.A. (eds.). *Computer-Assisted Instruction.* New York: Academic Press, 1969.

Axline, V. *Play Therapy.* Boston: Houghton Mifflin, 1947.

Bain, R. Sociology and psychoanalysis. *Amer. Sociol. Rev.*, I. 2:203–216. 1936.

Bakan, D. *The Duality of Human Existence.* Chicago: Rand McNally, 1966.

Baldwin, J. Letter from a region in my mind. *New Yorker*, 38 (65). 1962.

———. *The Fire Next Time.* New York: Dial, 1963.

Bandura, A. *Principles of Behavior Modification.* New York: Holt, Rinehart & Winston, 1969.

Bandura, A., and Kupers, C.J. Transmission of patterns self-reinforcement through modeling. *J. Abnorm. Soc. Psychol.*, 69:1–9. 1964.

——, and Menlove, F.L. Factors determining vicarious extinction of avoidance behavior through symbolic modeling. *J. Person. Soc. Psychol.*, 8:99–108. 1968.

——, and Mischel, W. The influence of models in modifying delay of gratification patterns. *J. Person. Soc. Psychol.*, 2:698–705. 1965.

Barber, T.Y., DiCara, L.V., Kamiya, J., Miller, N.E., Shapiro, D., and Stoyva, J. *Bio-Feedback and Self Control, Reader.* Chicago: Aldine-Atherton. 1970.

——. *Bio-Feedback and Self Control, Annual.* Chicago: Aldine-Atherton. 1970.

——. *Bio-Feedback and Self Control, Annual.* Chicago: Aldine-Atherton. 1971.

Barron, F. The disposition toward originality. *J. Abnorm. Soc. Psychol.*, 51:478–485. 1955.

Bass, B.M. *Organizational Psychology.* Boston: Allyn & Bacon, 1965.

Battle, Esther S., and Rotter, J.B. Children's feelings of personal control as related to social class and ethnic group. *J. Pers.*, 31:482–490. 1963.

Bavelas, A. Role-playing and management training. *Sociatry*, 1:183–191. 1947.

Bay, C. Political and apolitical students: fact in search of a theory. *J. Soc. Issues*, 23(3):76–92. 1967.

Bayton, J.A., Austin, J.A., and Burke, K.R. Negro perception of Negro and white personality traits. *J. Pers. Soc. Psychol.*, 1:250–253. 1965.

Beadle, G. W., and Tatum, E.L. *Proc. Natl. Acad. Sci.*, 27:499–506. 1941.

Bell, J.E. "Recent Advances in Family Group Therapy," in M. Rosenbaum and M. Berger (eds.), *Group Psychotherapy and Group Function.* New York: Basic Books, 1963.

Bender, J.E. Changing patterns of religious interest. *The Humanist*, 18:139–144. 1958.

——. "Continuities and Discontinuities in Cultural Condition," in C. Kluckhohn and H. Murray (eds.), *Personality in Nature, Society and Culture.* New York: Knopf, 1955.

Bennett, C.C., and Rogers, C.R. Predicting the outcomes of treatment. *Amer. J. Orthopsychiat.*, 11:210–221. 1941.

——. The clinical significance of problem syndromes. *Amer. J. Orthopsychiat.*, 11:222–229. 1941.

Berelson, B., and Steiner, G.A. *Human Behavior: An Inventory of Scientific Findings.* New York: Harcourt, Brace. 1964.

Berg, I., and Fox, V. Factors in homicides committed by 200 males. *J. Soc. Psychol.*, 26:109–119. 1947.

Bernard, J. Parties and issues in conflict. *Conflict Resol.*, 1:111–121. 1957.

Berne, E. *Games People Play—The Psychology of Human Relations.* New York: Grove Press, 1964.

Bernstein, R.E. *J. Lab. Clin. Med.* 40: 707–717, 1952.

Bills, R.E. "Manual for the Index of Adjustment and Values." Unpublished manuscript. University of Alabama, College of Education. 1961.

——, Vance, E.L., and McLean, O.S. An index of adjustment and values. *J. Consult. Psychol.*, 15:257–261. 1951.

Bischof, L.J. *Interpreting Personality Theories.* New York: Harper, 1970.

Blakeslee, A.F. *J. Heredity*, 23:106. 1932.

——. *Proc. Natl. Acad. Sci.*, 48:298–299. 1918.

Bledsoe, J.C. Self-concepts of children and their intelligence, achievement, interests, and anxiety. *J. Individ. Psychol.*, 20:55–58. 1964.

Block, Jeanne H., Haan, Norma, and Smith, M. Brewster. "Activism and apathy in contemporary adolescents," in J.F. Adams (ed.), *Contributions to the Understanding of Adolescence*. New York: Allyn & Bacon, 1967.

Blum, R.H., et al. *Drugs*, Vol. I; *Society and Drugs*, Vol. II. *Students and Drugs*. San Francisco: Jossey-Bass, 1969.

Bowen, M. "A Family Concept of Schizophrenia," in D.D. Jackson (ed.), *The Etiology of Schizophrenia*. New York: Basic Books, 1960.

Bowlby, J. The nature of the child's tie to his mother. *International J. Psychoanalysis*, 39:1–24. 1958.

Boyd, G.F. The levels of aspiration of white and Negro children in a nonsegregated elementary school. *J. Soc. Psychol.*, 36:191–196. 1952.

Bradford, L.P., and Lippitt, R. Building a democratic work group. *Personnel*, 22:2–13. 1945.

Breyer, J.L., and May, J.G. The effects of race and socioeconomic status on imitative behavior in children using white male and female models. Presented at Southeastern Psychological Association, 1968.

Brody, E.B. Social conflict and schizophrenic behavior in young adult Negro males. *Psychiat.*, 24:337–346. 1961.

———. Color and identity conflict in young boys. *Psychiat.*, 26:188–201. 1963.

Brody, M.W. "Prognosis and Results of Psychoanalysis," in J.H. Nodine and J.H. Moyer (eds.), *Psychosomatic Medicine*. Philadelphia: Lea & Febiger, 1962.

Bronfenbrenner, U. The changing American child: a speculative analysis. *Merrill-Palmer O. Beh. Develop.* 7:73–84. 1963.

———. The mirror image in Soviet-American relations. *J. Soc. Issues*, 17:45–46. 1961.

Bronz, S.H. *Roots of Negro Racial Consciousness*. New York: Libra Oybkusgers, 1964.

Brown, C. *Manchild in the Promised Land*. New York: Macmillan, 1965.

Browne, R.S. The case for black separation. *Ramparts*, September 1967.

Brunswik, E. "The Conceptual Framework of Modern Psychology," in *International Encyclopedia of United Science*. Chicago: University of Chicago, 1952.

Bry, A. *Inside Psychotherapy*. New York: Basic Books, 1972.

Burgess, E.W., and L.S. Cottrell. *Predicting Success and Failure in Marriage*. Englewood Cliffs, N.J.: Prentice-Hall, 1939.

———, and Wallin, P. *Engagement and Marriage*. New York: Lippincott, 1953.

Burnett, A., and Ryan, E. "The Outpatient Treatment of Neurosis by Reciprocal Inhibition Methods," in mimeograph. Newfoundland: St. John's Hospital, 1962.

Burt, C. (review). Critical notice: *Creativity and Intelligence* by J.W. Getzels and P.W. Jackson. *Brit. J. Educ. Psychol.*, 32:292–298. 1962.

Burtt, H.E. *Legal Psychology*. Englewood Cliffs, N.J.: Prentice-Hall, 1931.

Byrne, D. *An Introduction to Personality—A Research Approach*. Englewood Cliffs, N.J.: Prentice-Hall, 1966.

Caldwell, J.S., Richardson, D., Waage, R., and Dean, J. Semantic differential responses to "black," "white," and related verbal stimuli. Paper presented at the Western Psychological Association, Vancouver, B.C., June 1969.

Cameron, H. A review of research and an investigation of emotional dependency among Negro youth. *J. Negro Educ.*, 36:111–120. 1967.

Capote, T. *In Cold Blood*. New York: Random House, 1966.

Carlson, R.O. How can the social sciences meet the needs of advertisers? *Printer's Ink*, 242:44–56. 1931.

Cashdan, S. Sensitivity groups, problems and promise. *Profess. Psychol.*, 1:221–223. 1970.

Catanzaro, R.J. Treatment of the alcoholic. *Southwestern Med.*, 45:115–117. 1964.

Chapanis, A. *Research Techniques in Human Engineering*. Baltimore: Johns Hopkins University, 1959.

Clark, K.B. *Dark Ghetto: Dilemmas of Social Power*. New York: Harper & Row, 1965.

———, and Clark, M.K. "Racial identification and preference in Negro children," in T.M. Newcomb and E.L. Hartley (eds.), *Readings in Social Psychology*. New York: Holt, Rinehart & Winston, 1947.

Clark, W.H. A study of some of the factors leading to achievement and creativity, with special reference to religious skepticism and belief. *J. Soc. Psychol.*, 41:57–69. 1955.

Cleaver, E. *Soul on Ice*. New York: Dell, 1968.

Clinard, M.B. *Sociology of Deviant Behavior*. New York: Holt, Rinehart & Winston, 1957.

Clinebell, H.R., Jr. *Understanding and Counseling the Alcoholic*. Nashville, Tenn.: Abingdon, 1956.

Cobb, P.W. Unpublished reports to Highway Research Board, Washington, D.C. 1938–39. Summarized in H.M. Johnson, "The Detection and Treatment of Accident-Prone Drivers." *Psychol. Bull.*, 43:489–532. 1946.

Coch, L., and French, J.R.P., Jr. Overcoming resistance to change. *Hum. Relations*, 1:512–532. 1948.

Cohen, A.K. *Delinquent Boys: The Culture of the Gang*. New York: Free Press, 1955.

Coleman, J.C., *Abnormal Psychology and Modern Life*. Glenview, Ill.: Scott, Foresman, 1972.

Coleman, J.S., et al. *Equality of Educational Opportunity*. United States Department of Health, Education, and Welfare. Washington, D.C.: Government Printing Office, 1966.

Combs, A.W. Intelligence from a perceptual point of view. *J. Abn. Soc. Psychol.*, 47:662–673. 1952.

Comer, J.P. The social power of the Negro. *Scientific American*, 216:21–27. 1967.

Coopersmith, S. *The Antecedents of Self-Esteem*. San Francisco: Freeman, 1967.

Cory, D.W. *The Homosexual in America*. New York: Greenberg, 1960.

Cox, C.M. *Genetic Studies of Genius. II: The Early Mental Traits of Three Hundred Geniuses*. Stanford: Stanford University, 1926.

Craise, J.L., and Trent, J.W. Commitment and conformity in the American college. *J. Soc. Issues*, 23 (3):34–51. 1967.

David, P.R., and Snyder, L.H. *Social Psychology at the Crossroads*. New York: Harper, 1951.

Derbyshire, R.L. United States Negro in conflict. *Sociol. and Soc. Res.*, 51:63–77. 1966.

———, and Brody, E.B. Marginality, identity, and behavior in the Negro: a functional analysis. *International J. Soc. Psychiat.*, 10:7–13. 1964a.

———. Identity and ethnocentrism in American Negro college students. *Mental Hygiene*, 48:202–208. 1964b.

———. Social distance and identity conflict in Negro college students. *Sociol. and Soc. Res.*, 48:301–314. 1964c.

———, and Schliefer, C.B. Family structure of young adult Negro male mental patients: preliminary observations from urban Baltimore. *J. Nerv. Ment. Dis.*, 136:245–251. 1963.

Deutsch, M. The effect of motivational orientation upon trust and suspicion. *Hum. Relations*, 13:123–140. 1960a.

———. The face of bargaining. *Operation Res.*, 9:866–897. 1961.

———. A theory of cooperation and competition. *Hum. Relations*, 2:129–152. 1949.

———. Trust and suspicion. *Conflict Resol.*, 2:265–279. 1958.

———. Trust, trustworthiness, and the F scale. *J. Abnorm. Soc. Psychol.*, 61:138–140. 1960b.

———, and Kraus, R.M. The effect of threat upon interpersonal bargaining. *J. Abnorm. Soc. Psychol.*, 61:181–189. 1960.

Diethelm, O. *Etiology of Chronic Alcoholism.* Springfield, Ill.: Thomas, 1955, Chapter 3.

Diggory, J.C. *Self-Evaluation: Concepts and Studies.* New York: Wiley, 1966.

Doane, B.K., Mahatoo, W., Heron, W., and Scott, T.H. Changes in perceptual function after solution. *Canad. J. Psych.*, 13:210–219. 1959.

Dollard, J. Hostility and fear in social life. *Soc. Forces*, 17:15–25. 1939.

———, et al. *Frustration and Aggression.* New Haven, Conn.: Yale University Press, 1939.

Dorcus, R.M. Modification by suggestion of some vestibular and visual responses. *Amer. J. Psychol.*, 49:82–87. 1937.

Douglass, W. A wise man and a young science. *Contemp. Psychol.*, 4:72–75. 1959.

Downey, J. *Creative Imagination.* London: Routledge & Kegan Paul, 1929.

Dreger, R.M., and Miller, K.S. Comparative psychological studies of Negroes and whites in the United States. *Psychol. Bull.*, 57:361–402. 1960.

———. Comparative psychological studies of Negroes and whites in the United States: 1959–1965. *Psychol. Bull.* In press.

Dudycha, G.J. et al. *Psychology for Law Enforcement Officers.* Springfield, Ill.: Thomas, 1955.

Dunnette, M.D. Use of the sugar pill by industrial psychologists. *Amer. Psychologist*, 12:223–225. 1957.

———, and Kirchner, W.K. "The Role of the Psychologist," in *Psychology Applied to Industry.* New York: Appleton-Century-Crofts, 1965.

Durkheim, E. *Suicide.* New York: Free Press, 1951.

Dynes, J.B. An experimental study in hypnotic anesthesia. *J. Abnorm. Soc. Psychol.*, 27:79–88. 1932.

Easton, R.H., Carr, R.J., and Whiteley, J.M. Issues in the encounter group movement. *Counseling Psychologist*, 3:89–120. 1972.

Ellison, R. *Invisible Man.* New York: Random House, 1952.

Erikson, E.H. *Childhood and Society.* New York: Norton, 1950.

———. *Childhood and Society.* 2nd ed. New York: Norton, 1963.

———. "Identity and the Life Cycle," in G.S. Klein (ed.), *Psychological Issues.* New York: International Universities, 1959.

———. Memorandum on identity and Negro youth. *J. Soc. Issues*, 20(4):29–42. 1964.

———. "The Concept of Identity in Race Relations: Notes and Queries," in T. Parsons and K.B. Clark (eds.), *The Negro American.* Boston: Houghton Mifflin, 1966.

Etzioni, A. "International Prestige, Competition and Coexistence," in Q. Wright, W.M. Evan, and M. Deutsch (eds.), *Preventing World War III: Some Proposals.* New York: Simon & Schuster, 1962.

Eysenck, H.J. *Behaviour Therapy and the Neuroses*. Oxford: Pergamon, 1960.

Fairbanks, G., and Guttman, N. *J. Speech and Hearing Research*, 1:12. 1958.

Falk, G.J. Status differences and the frustration-aggression hypothesis. *Int. J. Soc. Psychiat.*, 5:214–222. 1959.

Farber, I.S., Harlow, H.G., and West, L.J. Brainwashing, conditioning, and DDD. *Sociometry*, 20:271–285. 1957.

Farmer, E., and Chambers, E.G. A study of personal qualities in accident proneness and proficiency. *Ind. Health Res. Bd. Reports*, 55. 1929.

Fenichel, O. *The Psychoanalytic Theory of Neurosis*. New York: Norton, 1945.

Ferster, C.B., and Perrott, M.C. *Behavior Principle*. New York: Appleton-Century-Croft, 1968.

Feshbach, S. Dynamics and morality of violence and aggression: some psychological consideration. *Amer. Psychologist*, 26:281–292. 1971.

Fiedler, F.E. The concept of an ideal therapeutic relationship in psychoanalytic, nondirective, and Adlerian therapy. *J. Consult. Psychol.*, 14:436–445. 1950a.

———. The concept of an ideal therapeutic relationship. *J. Consult. Psychol.*, 14:239–245. 1950b.

Fishel, L.H., and Quarles, B. *The Negro American: A Documented History*. Glenview, Ill.: Scott, Foresman, 1967.

Fishman, J.R., and Solomon, F. Youth and social action. *J. Soc. Issues*, 20(40):1–28. 1964.

Flacks, R.E. The liberated generation: an exploration of the roots of student protest. *J. Soc. Issues*, 23(3):52–76. 1967.

———. Student activists: result, not revolt. *Psychol. Today*, 1(6):18–25. 1967.

Flaherty, B.E. (ed.). *Psychophysiological Aspects of a Space Flight*. New York: Columbia University, 1961.

Fleishman, E.A. *Studies in Personnel and Industrial Psychology*. Rev. ed. Homewood, Ill.: Dorsey, 1967.

Forbes, T.W. The normal automobile driver as a traffic problem. *J. Gen. Psychol.*, 20:471–474. 1939.

Fordham, F. *An Introduction to Jung's Psychology*. Baltimore: Penguin, 1961.

Forel, A. *Hypnotism and Psychotherapy*. New York: Rebman, 1907.

Forer, B.R. The fallacy of personal validations: a classroom demonstration of gullibility. *J. Abnorm. Soc. Psychol.*, 44:118–123. 1949.

Frank, J. "The Motivational Basis of a World Without War," in Q. Wright, W.M. Evan, and M. Deutsch (eds.), *Preventing World War III: Some Proposals*. New York: Simon & Schuster, 1962.

Frankl, V.E. *Man's Search for Meaning*. Boston: Beacon, 1963.

Frazier, E.F. *Black Bourgeoisie*. New York: Free Press, 1957.

Freud, S. *Collected Papers, IV*. The relation of the poet to daydreaming. Encyclopedia article on psychoanalysis written in 1922. London: Hogarth, 1922.

Frick, H.L., Scantlebury, R.E., and Patterson, T.L. The control of gastric hunger contractions in men by hypnotic suggestion. *Amer. J. Physiol.*, 113:471. 1935.

Fromm, E. The case for unilateral disarmament. *Daedalus*, 89:1015–1028. 1960.

———. *Escape from Freedom*. New York: Rinehart, 1941.

———. *Man for Himself*. New York: Rinehart, 1947.

———. *The Sane Society*. New York: Holt, Rinehart & Winston, 1955.

Galbraith, J.K. *The Affluent Society*. Boston: Houghton Mifflin, 1958.

Garmerzy, N., and Rodnick, E. Premorbid adjustment and performance in schizophrenia: implication for interpreting heterogeneity in schizophrenia. *J. Nerv. Ment. Dis.*, 129:450–466. 1959.

Gebhard, P.H., Gagnon, J.H., Pomeroy, W.B., and Christenson, C.V. *Sex Offenders*. New York: Harper & Row, 1965.

Gellhorn, E. Prolegomena to a theory of emotions. *Perspec. Biol. Med.*, 4:403–436. 1961.

——, and Loofbourrow, G.N. *Emotions and Emotional Disorders*. New York: Harper, 1963.

Gerson, W.M. Mass Media socialization behavior: Negro-white differences. *Social Forces*, 45:40–50. 1966.

Getzels, J.W., and Jackson, P.W. *Creativity and Intelligence*. New York: Wiley, 1962.

Ghiselli, E.E., and Brown, C.W. *Personnel and Industrial Psychology*. New York: McGraw-Hill, 1948.

Gibby, R.G., Sr., and Gabler, R. The self-concept of Negro and white children. *J. Clin. Psychol.*, 23:144–148. 1967.

Glueck, S. (ed.). *The Problem of Delinquency*. Boston: Houghton Mifflin, 1959.

Golann, S.W. Psychological study of creativity. *Psychol. Bull.*, 60:548–565. 1963.

Goldzieher, M.A. *The Endocrine Glands*. New York: Appleton-Century, 1939.

Gollob, H.F., and Levine, J., Distraction as a factor in the enjoyment of aggressive humor. *J. Person. Soc. Psychol.*, 5:368–372. 1967.

Goodall, J. My life among wild chimpanzees. *National Geographic*, 124:272–303. 1963.

Goode, E. *Marijuana*. New York: Atherton Press. 1969.

Greening, T.C. Sensitivity training: cult or contribution. *Personnel*, May–June, 18–25. 1964.

Greenwood, M., and Woods, H.M. *Report No. 4. Indust. Fatigue Res. Rep.* London: Her Majesty's Stationery Office, 1919.

Gregor, A.J., and McPherson, D.A. Racial attitudes among white and Negro children in a deep-South standard metropolitan area. *J. Soc. Psychol.*, 68:95–106. 1966a.

——. Racial preference and ego-identity among white and Bantu children in the Republic of South Africa. *Genet. Psychol. Monogr.*, 73:217–253. 1966b.

Griffith, J.W. "The Time Factor in a Psychological Analysis of Accidents." Master's thesis, Illinois Institute of Technology, 1950.

Grollman, A. *Essentials of Endocrinology*, 2nd ed. Philadelphia: Lippincott, 1947.

Grziwok, R., and Scodel, A. Some psychological correlates of humor preferences. *J. Consult. Psychol.*, 20:42. 1956.

Guilford, J.P. *Personality*. New York: McGraw-Hill, 1959.

——. Structure of human intellect. *Science*, 122:875. 1955.

——, et al. *University of Southern California Psychology Laboratory Reports*: 4, 1951; 8, 1952; 11, 1954; 16, 1956.

Gurin, G., Veroff, J., and Feld, S. *Americans View Their Mental Health*. New York: Basic Books, 1960.

Haggstrom, W.C. Self-esteem and other characteristics of residentially desegregated Negroes. *Diss. Abstracts*, 23:3007–3008. 1963.

Haley, J. Whither family therapy? *Fam. Proc.*, 1:69–100. 1962.

Hall, C.S. *A Primer of Freudian Psychology*. Cleveland: World, 1954.

——, and Lindzey, G. *Theories of Personality*. New York: Wiley, 1957.

Hall, C.S., and Norby, V.J. *The Individual and His Dreams*. New York: New American Library (Signet), 1972.

———, and Van de Castle, R.L. *The Content Analysis of Dreams*. New York: Appleton-Century-Crofts, 1966.

Hall, W.B. Creativity: a selective annotated bibliography. *Professional Psychol.*, 2:307–312. 1971.

Hammer, E.F. (ed.). *The Clinical Application of Projective Drawing*. Springfield, Ill.: Thomas, 1958.

Haring, N.G., and Phillips, E.L. *Analysis and Modification of Classroom Behavior*. Englewood Cliffs, N.J.: Prentice-Hall, 1972.

Harlow, H.F. The heterosexual affectional system in monkeys. *Amer. Psychologist*, 19:1–9. 1962.

———. Learning to love. *Amer. Scientist*, 54:244–272. 1966.

———, and Hansen, E.W. "The maternal affectional system of rhesus monkeys," in H.L. Rheingold (ed.), *Maternal Behavior in Mammals*. New York: Wiley, 1963.

———, and Harlow, M.K. "The affectional systems," in A.M. Schrier, H.F. Harlow, and F. Stollnitz (eds.), *Behavior of Nonhuman Primates*, 2:287–334. New York: Academic Press, 1965.

———, and Woolsey, C.N. (eds.). *Biological and Biochemical Bases of Behavior*. Madison: University of Wisconsin, 1958.

Harris, F.J. A comparison of the personality characteristics of accident and non-accident industrial populations. *Amer. Psychologist*, 4:279. 1949.

Hartmann, H., Kris, E., and Lowenstein, R.M. Notes on the theory of aggression. *Psychoanalytic Study of the Child*, v. 3–4. New York: International Universities, 1949.

Havemann, E., and West, P.S. *They Went to College*. New York: Harcourt, Brace, 1952.

Heath, C.W., et al. *What People Are*. Cambridge, Mass.: Harvard University, 1945.

Henry, A.F., and Short, J.F., Jr. *Suicide and Homicide*. New York: Free Press, 1954.

Henton, C.L., and Johnson, E.E. *Relationship between self-concepts of Negro elementary school children and their academic achievement, intelligence, interests, and manifest anxiety*. Office of Education, Washington, D.C., 1964.

Herron, W.G. The process-reactive classification of schizophrenia. *Psychol. Bull.*, 59:329–343. 1962.

Hersey, R.B. Emotional factors in accidents. *Person. J.*, 15:59–65. 1936.

Hicks, D.J. Imitation and retention of film-mediated aggressive peer and adult models. *J. Person. Soc. Psychol.*, 2:97–100. 1965.

Hilgard, E.R. *Introduction to Psychology*, 3rd ed. New York: Harcourt, Brace & World, 1962.

———. *Hypnotic Suggestibility*. New York: Harcourt, Brace & World, 1965.

Hinkle, L.E., and Wolff, H.C. Communist interrogation and indoctrination of "enemies of the State." *Arch. Neurol. Psychiat.*, 76:115–174. 1956.

Hoch, E.L., and Darley, J.G. A case at law. *Amer. Psychologist*, 17:623. 1962.

Hollingshead, A.B., and Redlich, F.C. *Social Class and Mental Illness*. New York: Wiley, 1958.

Hull, C.L. *Hypnosis and Suggestibility*. New York: Appleton-Century-Crofts, 1933.

Hunt, W.A., Wittson, C.L., and Burton, H.W. Further validation of naval neuropsychiatric screening. *J. Consult. Psychol.*, 14:485–488. 1950.

Icheiser, G. Misunderstandings in human relations. *Amer. J. Sociol.*, 55 (Part 2):1–70. 1949.

Imanishi, K. "Social Behavior in Japanese Monkeys, *Macaca fuscata*," in C.H. Southwick (ed.), *Primate Social Behavior*. New York: Van Nostrand, 1963.

Institute for Applied Experimental Psychology. *Handbook of Human Engineering Data*. Medford, Mass.: Tufts College, 1952.

Jackson, D.D. *The Etiology of Schizophrenia*. New York: Basic Books, 1960.

———, and Satir, V.M. "Historical Antecedents of Family Therapy," in N.W. Ackerman, F.L. Beatman, and S.N. Sherman (eds.), *Exploring the Base for Family Therapy*. New York: Family Service Association of America, 1961.

———, and Weakland, J.H. Conjoint family therapy. *Psychiat.*, 24:30–45. 1961.

Jacobson, E. *Progressive Relaxation*. Chicago: University of Chicago, 1939.

Jacobson, E.H., and Schachter, S. (eds.). Cross-national research: a case study. *J. Soc. Issues*, 10 (4). 1954.

Jahoda, M. *Current Concepts of Positive Mental Health*. New York: Basic Books, 1958.

———. "Toward a social psychology of mental health," in M.J.E. Senn (ed.), *Symposium on Healthy Personality*. New York: Josiah Macey Jr. Foundation, 1950.

James, W. *Varieties of Religious Experience*. New York: Longmans, Green, 1902.

———. *Memories and Studies*. "The Moral Equivalent of War." New York: Longmans, Green, 1911.

Janet, P. *Psychological Healing*. 2 vols., trans. E. & C. Paul. London: Allen & Unwin, 1925.

Janis, I.L., and Katz, D. The reduction of intergroup hostility: Research problems and hypotheses. *J. Conflict Resolut.*, 3:85–100. 1959.

Jastrow, J. *Wish and Wisdom*. New York: Appleton-Century, 1935.

Javik, M.E. The psychopharmacological revolution. *Psychol. Today*, 1:51–59. 1967.

Jellinek, E.M. *Disease Concept of Alcoholism*. New Haven: United Printing Service, 1960.

Jessor, R., and Hammon, K. "Construct Validity and the Taylor Anxiety Scale," in M.T. Mednick and S.A. Mednick (eds.), *Research in Personality*. New York: Holt, Rinehart & Winston, 1963.

Johnson, D.M. Psychology versus literature. *Harper Books and Authors*, 12:1–4. 1961.

Johnson, H.M. The detection and treatment of accident-prone drivers. *Psychol. Bull.*, 43:489–532. 1946.

Jones, M. *Social Psychiatry*. Springfield, Ill.: Thomas, 1962. Chapter I: "Social Psychiatry and the Changing Community."

Jung, C.G. *Man and His Symbols*. New York: Doubleday, 1964.

———. *Modern Man in Search of a Soul*. New York: Harcourt, Brace, 1933.

———. *Psychology and Religion*. New Haven: Yale University, 1960.

Kalmus, H., Denes, P., and Fry, D.B. Effect of delayed acoustic feedback on some nonvocal activities. *Nature*, 175:1078. 1955.

Kantor, J.R. *An Outline of Social Psychology*. Chicago: Follett, 1929.

Kaplan, B., Reed, R.B., and Richardson, N. A comparison of the incidence of hospitalized cases of psychoses in two communities. *Amer. Sociol. Rev.*, 21:572–579. 1956.

Kardiner, A., and Ovesey, L. *The Mark of Oppression: A Psychosocial Study of the American Negro*. New York: Norton, 1951.

Katz, D. (ed.). Attitude change. *Pub. Opin. Quart.*, 24:163–365. 1960.

——. Current and needed psychological research in international relations. *J. Soc. Issues*, 17:69–78. 1961.

——, and Allport, F.H. *Students' Attitudes*. Syracuse: Craftsmen, 1931.

Keenan, V., Kerr, W.A., and Sherman, W.E. Psychological climate and accidents in an automotive plant. *J. Appl. Psychol.*, 35:108–111. 1951.

Kell, B.L. "The Predictive Possibilities of the Component-Factor Method of Diagnosis as Applied to Children with Behavior Problems." Master's thesis, Ohio State, 1942.

Keller, S. The social world of the urban slum child: some early findings. *Amer. J. Orthopsychiat.*, 33:823–831. 1963.

Kelley, H.A. Moral evaluation. *Amer. Psychologist*, 26:293–300. 1971.

Kelly, E.L. Concerning the validity of Terman's weights for predicting marital happiness. *Psychol. Bull.*, 306:202–203. 1939.

——. Consistency of the adult personality. *Amer. Psychologist*, 10:659–681. 1955.

Kelly, G.A. *The Psychology of Personal Constructs*, v. 1. New York: Norton, 1955.

Kelly, J. T., and Ansbacher, R.R. (eds.). *The Individual Psychology of Alfred Adler*. New York: Basic Books, 1956.

Kelman, H.C. "A Proposal for Internationalizing Military Force," in Q. Wright, W.M. Evan, and M. Deutsch (eds.), *Preventing World War III: Some Proposals*. New York: Simon & Schuster, 1962.

Keniston, K. The sources of student dissent. *J. Soc. Issues*, 23(3):108–138. 1967.

——. *The Uncommitted: Alienated Youth in American Society*. New York: Harcourt, Brace and World, 1965.

Kerr, W.A. "Psychological Climate and Safety." Address, Midwest Safety Show, National Safety Council, Chicago, May 4, 1950a.

——. Accident proneness of factory departments. *J. Appl. Psychol.*, 34:167–170. 1950b.

Keys, A. *Biology of Mental Health and Disease*. New York: Hoeber, 1952. "Experimental Induction of Neuropsychoses by Starvation."

Killian, L.M. *The Impossible Revolution?* New York: Random House, 1968.

——, and Grigg, C.M. *Racial Crisis in America*. Englewood Cliffs, N.J.: Prentice-Hall, 1964.

Kimber, J.A.M. An introduction to the marriage counselor and his work. *Psychol. Rep.*, 8:71–75. 1961.

King, C.C., et al. *J. Applied Physio.*, 5:99–110, 1952.

Kinsey, A.C., Pomeroy, W.B., and Martin, C.E. *Sexual Behavior in the Human Male*. Philadelphia: Saunders, 1948.

——, and Gebhard, P.H. *Sexual Behavior in the Human Female*. Philadelphia: Saunders, 1953.

Kirchner, W.K., and Dunnette, M.D. Applying the weighted application blank technique to a variety of office jobs. *J. Appl. Psychol.*, 41:206–208. 1957.

Kirk, R.L., and Stenhouse, N.S. Ability to smell solutions of potassium cyanide. *Nature*, 171:400–409. 1953.

Kitson, H.D. A critical age as a factor in labor turnover. *J. Indust. Hygiene*, 4:199–203. 1922.

Klebanoff, S.G. "Psychologists in Institutions," in W.B. Webb (ed.), *The Profession of Psychology*. New York: Holt, Rinehart & Winston, 1962.

Knight, R.P. Evaluation of the results of psychoanalytic therapy. *Amer. J. Psychiat.*, 98:434–446. 1941.

Koford, C.B. "Population dynamics of rhesus monkeys on Cayo Santiago," in I. DeVore (ed.), *Primate Behavior*. New York: Holt, Rinehart & Winston, 1965.

Kohn, M.L. Social class and the exercise of parental authority. *Amer. Sociol. Rev.*, 24:352–366. 1959.

Kreidt, P.H., and Gadel, M.S. Prediction of turnover among clerical workers. *J. Appl. Psychol.*, 37:338–340. 1953.

Landis, C., and Ross, J.W.H. Humor and its relation to other personality traits. *J. Soc. Psychol.*, 4:156–175. 1933.

Larson, S. "The Role of Law in Building Peace," in Q. Wright, W.M. Evan, and M. Deutsch (eds.), *Preventing World War III: Some Proposals*. New York: Simon & Schuster, 1962.

Lashley, K.S. *Psychol. Rev.*, 54:333–334. 1947.

Lazarus, A.A. The elimination of children's phobias by deconditioning. *Med. Proc.*, 5:261–265. 1959.

———. The results of therapy in 126 cases of severe neurosis. *Behav. Res. Ther.*, 1:69–80. 1963a.

———. The treatment of chronic frigidity by systematic desensitization. *J. Nerv. Ment. Dis.*, 136:272–278. 1963b.

Lazarus, R.S. *Patterns of Adjustment and Human Effectiveness*. New York: McGraw-Hill, 1969.

Lecky, P. *Self-Consistency: A Theory of Personality*. New York: Island, 1945.

Leuba, C. Laughter: two genetic studies. *J. Genet. Psychol.*, 58:201–209. 1941.

Levitas, G.B. *The World of Psychology*, v. I & II. New York: Braziller, 1963.

Lewin, K. "Group Decision and Social Change," in T.M. Newcomb and E.L. Hartley (eds.), *Readings in Social Psychology*. New York: Holt, 1947.

———. *Principles of Topological Psychology*. New York: McGraw-Hill, 1936.

———, Lippitt, R., and White, R.K. Patterns of aggressive behavior in experimentally created social climates. *J. Soc. Psychol.*, 11:271–299. 1939.

Lifton, R.L. "Thought reform" of western civilians in Chinese communist prisons. *Psychiatry*, 19:173–198. 1957.

Likert, R. *New Patterns of Management*. New York: McGraw-Hill, 1961.

Lippitt, R., Bradford, L.P., and Benne, K.D. Socio-dramatic clarification of leader and group roles. *Sociatry*, 1:82–91. 1947.

Lomax, L.E. The Negro revolt against "the Negro leaders." *Harper's Magazine*, 220:41–48. 1960.

Lundholm, H. An experimental study of functional anesthesias as induced by suggestion in hypnosis. *J. Anal. Psychol.*, 23:337–355. 1928.

Machover, K. *Personality Projection in the Drawing of the Human Figure*. Springfield, Ill.: Thomas, 1962.

MacKinnon, D.W. Personality and the realization of creative potential. *Amer. Psychologist*, 20:273–281. 1965.

———. (ed.). *The Creative Personality*. Berkeley, California: University of California. General Extension. 1962.

Maddi, S.R. *Personality Theories—A Comparative Analysis*. Homewood, Ill.: The Dorsey Press, 1972.

Maier, N.R.F. A human relations program for supervision. *Indust. and Lab. Relat. Rev.*, 1:443–464. 1948.

———. "Improving Supervision Through Training," in A. Kornhauser (ed.), *Psychology of Labor Management Relations*. Champaign, Ill.: Industrial Relations Research Assn. 1949.

———. *Psychology in Industry*. 3rd ed., Boston: Houghton Mifflin, 1965.

Malcolm X, with the assistance of A. Haley. *The Autobiography of Malcolm X.* New York: Grove, 1965.

Maritz, J.S. On the validity of inferences drawn from the fitting of Poisson and negative binomial distributions to observed accident data. *Psychol. Bull.,* 471:434–443. 1950.

Maslow, A.H. "Self Actualizing People: A Study of Psychological Health," in W. Wolff (ed.), *Values in Personality Research.* New York: Grune & Stratton, 1950.

———. *Toward a Psychology of Being.* New York: Van Nostrand, 1962.

Masserman, J.H. "Ethology, Comparative Biodynamics, and Psychoanalytic Research," in J. Scher (ed.), *Theories of the Mind.* New York: Free Press, 1963.

———, and Yum, K.S. An analysis of the influence of alcohol on experimental neurosis in cats. *Psychosom. Med.,* 6:36–52. 1946.

Masters, W.H., and Johnson, V.E. *Human Sexual Response.* Boston: Little, Brown, 1966.

Mauriac, F. *Thérèse.* Trans. Gerard Hopkins. London: Eyre & Spottiswoode, 1951.

May, R. *Existential Psychology.* New York: Random House, 1961.

———. *Psychology and the Human Dilemma.* New York: Van Nostrand, 1967.

McCary, J.L. A psychologist testifies in court. *Amer. Psychologist,* 15:53–57. 1960.

McClelland, D.C. *The Achieving Society.* New York: Van Nostrand, 1961.

McConnell, R.A., Snowdon, R.J., and Powell, K.F. Wishing with dice. *J. Exp. Psychol.,* 50:269–275. 1955.

McDonald, R.L., and Gynther, M.D. Relationship of self and ideal-self descriptions with sex, race, and class in Southern adolescents. *J. Pers. and Soc. Psychol.,* 1:85–88. 1965.

McGhee, P.E., and Crandall, V.C. Beliefs in internal-external control of reinforcements and academic performance. *Child Devel.,* 91–102. 1968.

McGill, W.J. *Behavior Genetics and Differential Psychology.* Symposium. American Psychological Association: New York, 1957.

McGuire, F.L. A psychological comparison of accident-violation-free and accident-incurring automobile drivers. *Camp Lejeune Naval Medical Field Research Lab.,* February 1955.

McKinney, F. *Psychology of Personal Adjustment.* New York: Wiley, 1960.

———. *Understanding Personality: Cases in Counseling.* Boston: Houghton Mifflin, 1965.

McNeil, H. "Factors Significantly Related to the Later Adjustment of Children Presenting Problem and Delinquent Behavior." Master's thesis, Ohio State, 1944.

McNemar, Q. Lost: our intelligence. *Amer. Psychologist,* 19:871–882. 1964.

Mednick, M., and Mednick, S.A. *Research in Personality.* New York: Holt, Rinehart & Winston, 1963.

Megargee, E.I. A comparison of the scores of white and Negro male juvenile delinquents on three projective tests. *J. Proj. Tech. and Pers. Assessment,* 30:530–535. 1966.

Melzack, R., and Scott, T.H. The effects of early experience on the response to pain. *J. Comp. Physiol. Psychol.,* 50:155–161. 1957.

Menninger, K. *Theory of Psychoanalytic Technique.* New York: Basic Books, 1958.

———. What the girls told. *Saturday Rev.,* 36. 1953.

Merton, R.K. *Social Theory and Social Structure: The Self-Fulfilling Prophecy.* Rev. ed. New York: Free Press, 1957.

Middleton, R. Alienation, race, and education. *Amer. Sociol. Rev.*, 2:120–127. 1963.

Miller, N.E., and Dollard, J. *Social Learning and Imitation.* New Haven: Yale University, 1941.

Mintz, A., and Blum, M.L. A re-examination of the accident proneness concept. *J. Appl. Psychol.*, 33:195–211. 1949.

Morland, J.K. The development of racial bias in young children. *Theory Into Practice*, 2:120–127. 1963.

Morris, G.O., and Wynne, L.C. Schizophrenic offspring and parental style of communication. *Psychiatry*, 28:19–44. 1965.

Moss, C.S. "Brief Crisis-Oriented Hypnotherapy," in J. Gordon (ed.), *Handbook of Hypnotherapy.* New York: McGraw-Hill, 1953.

———. *Hypnosis in Perspective.* New York: Macmillan, 1965.

Mowbray, J.B., and Cadell, T.E. Early behavior patterns in rhesus monkeys. *J. Comp. and Phys. Psych.*, 55:350–357. 1962.

Mowrer, O.H. *Psychotherapy: Theory and Research.* New York: Ronald, 1953.

———. "What Is Normal Behavior?" in L.A. Pennington and I.A. Berg (eds.), *An Introduction to Clinical Psychology.* 2nd ed. New York: Ronald, 1954.

Moynihan, D.P. "Employment, Income, and the Ordeal of the Negro Family," in T. Parsons and K.B. Clark (eds.), *The Negro American.* Boston: Houghton Mifflin, 1966.

Munroe, R. *Schools of Psychoanalytic Thought.* New York: Holt, Rinehart & Winston, 1955.

Munsterberg, H. *On the Witness Stand.* New York: McClure, 1908.

Murphy, G. *Human Nature and Enduring Peace.* Boston: Houghton Mifflin, 1945.

———. *In the Minds of Men.* New York: Basic Books, 1953.

———. *Personality: A Biosocial Approach to Origin and Structure.* New York: Harper, 1947.

———. The place of parapsychology among the sciences. *J. Parapsychol.*, 13:62–71. 1949.

Murstein, B. *Handbook of Projective Techniques.* New York: Basic Books, 1965.

National Planning Association. *Causes of Industrial Peace.* Washington, D.C., 1953.

Nelson, E.N.P. Patterns of religious attitude from college to fourteen years later. *Psychol. Monogr.* (424). 1956.

Newbold, E.M. A contribution to the study of the human factor in the causation of accidents. *Indust. Fatigue Res. Bd. Rep. 34.* London: Her Majesty's Stationery Office, 1919.

Newcomb, T.M. Autistic hostility and social reality. *Hum. Relations*, 1:69–86. 1947.

Nielson, G.S. *Psychology and International Affairs: Can We Contribute?* Copenhagen: Munksgard, 1962.

Nissen, A.W., Chow, K.L., and Semmes, J. Effects of restricted opportunity for tactile kinesthetic and manipulative experience on the behavior of a chimpanzee. *Amer. J. Psychol.*, 64:485–507. 1951.

Noger, J. The diplomacy of disarmament. *Internat. Conciliation.* 526. Carnegie Endowment for International Peace, 1960.

Ortega y Gasset, J. *The Modern Theme.* New York: Norton, 1933.

Osgood, C.E. An analysis of the cold war mentality. *J. Soc. Issues*, 17:12–19. 1961.

————, Suci, G. J., and Tannenbaum, P.H. *The Measurement of Meaning*. Urbana, Ill.: University of Illinois Press, 1957.

Osterberg, A.E., Vanzant, F.R., Alvarez, W.C., and Rivers, A.B. Studies of pepsin in human gastric juice. III. Physiological aspects. *Am. J. Digestive Dis.*, 35:35–41. 1936.

Palmer, S. Frustration, aggression, and murder. *J. Abnorm. Soc. Psychol.*, 60:430–432. 1960.

Patterson, C.H. *Theories of Counseling and Psychotherapy*. New York: Harper and Row, 1966.

Pattie, F.A. The genuineness of hypnotically produced anesthesia of the skin. *Amer. J. Psychol.*, 49:435–443. 1937.

————. The production of blisters by hypnotic suggestion. *J. Abnorm. Soc. Psychol.*, 36:62–72. 1941.

————. A report of attempts to produce uniocular blindness by hypnotic suggestion. *Brit. J. Psychol.*, 25:230–241. 1935.

Pavlov, I.P. *Conditioned Reflexes and Psychiatry*, trans. W.H. Gantt. New York: International, 1941.

Peterson, R.E. The student left in American higher education. *Daedalus*, 71(1):293–317. 1968.

Pettigrew, T.F. *A Profile of the Negro American*. New York: Van Nostrand, 1964a.

————. Negro American personality: why isn't more known. *J. Soc. Issues*, 20:4–23. 1964b.

————, and Thompson, D.C. (eds.). Negro American personality. *J. Soc. Issues*, 20(2). 1964

Phillips, J.D. Report on discussion 66. *Adult Educ. J.*, 7:181–182. 1948.

Pincus, G., and Thimann, K.V. *The Hormones*. New York: Academic Press, 1948.

Pittman, D.J., and Snyder, C.R. *Society, Culture, and Drinking Patterns*. New York: Wiley, 1962.

Premack, D. Toward empirical behavior laws. I: Positive reinforcement. *Psychol. Rev.*, 66. 219–233. 1959.

————. *Reinforcement Theory*. Nebraska Symposium on Motivation. Lincoln: University of Nebraska Press, 1965.

————, and Schwartz, A. "Preparations for Discussing Behaviorism with Chimpanzees," in F. Smith and C.A. Miller (eds.), *The Genesis of Language in Children and Other Animals*. Cambridge, Mass.: M.I.T., 1966.

Proshansky, H., and Newton, P. "The Nature and Meaning of Negro Self-Identity," in M. Deutsch, I. Katz, and A.R. Jensen (eds.), *Social Class, Race, and Psychological Development*. New York: Holt, Rinehart & Winston, 1968.

Pyle, N.E. *The Psychology of Learning*. Baltimore: Warwick & York, 1921.

Rabin, A.I. *Projective Techniques in Personality Assessment*. New York: Springer, 1968.

Raimy, V.E. *Training in Clinical Psychology*. Englewood Cliffs, N.J.: Prentice-Hall, 1950.

Rainwater, L. Crucible of identity: the Negro lower-class family. *Daedalus*, 95:172–216. 1966.

RAND Corporation. *A Million Random Digits*. New York: Free Press, 1955.

Rank, O. Psychology and social change. *Newsletter of Amer. Assn. of Psych. Soc. Workers*, 4:3. 1935.

Rapaport, D. *Organization and Pathology of Thought.* New York: Columbia University, 1951.

Rapoport, A. "Aggressiveness, Gamesmanship and Persuasion," in Q. Wright, W.M. Evan, and M. Deutsch (eds.), *Preventing World War III: Some Proposals.* New York: Simon & Schuster, 1962.

Rasmussen, A.T. The morphology of pars intermedia of the human hypophysis. *Endocrinology,* 12:129–150. 1928.

——. A quantitative study of the human hypophysis cerebri, or pituitary body. *Endocrinology,* 8:509–524. 1924.

——. The weight of the principal components of the normal male adult human hypophysis cerebri. *Am. J. Anat.,* 42:27. 1928.

Rawcliffe, D.H. *Illusions and Delusions of the Supernatural and Occult.* New York: Dover, 1959.

Rees, E.W., and Copeland, N.K. Discrimination of differences in mass of weightless objects. *USAF WADD Tech. Rep.,* 60:601. 1960.

Rhine, J.B. Evidence of precognition in the covariation of salience ratios. *J. Parapsychol.,* 6:111–143. 1942.

——, and Humphrey, B.M. The PK effect: special evidence from hit patterns. I. Quarter distributions of the page. *J. Parapsychol.,* 8:18–60. 1944.

——, and Pratt, J.G. *Parapsychology, Frontier Science of the Mind.* Springfield, Ill.: Thomas, 1957.

——, et al. *Parapsychology from Dubre to FRNM.* Durham, N.C.: Parapsychology Press, 1965.

Richardson, S.A., and Royce, J. Race and physical handicap in children's preference for other children. *Child Devel.,* 39:467–480. 1968.

Riesman, D. *The Lonely Crowd.* New Haven: Yale University, 1950.

Ring, G.C., et al. Estimation of heart output from electrokymographic measurements in human subjects. *J. Appl. Physiol.,* 5:99–110. 1952.

Robinson, E.S. *Law and Lawyers.* New York: Macmillan, 1935.

Roe, A. *The Making of a Scientist.* New York: Dodd, Mead, 1952.

——. *The Psychology of Occupation.* New York: Wiley, 1956.

——, Gustad, J.W., Moore, B.W., Ross, S., and Skodak, M. *Graduate Education in Psychology.* Washington, D.C.: American Psychological Association, 1959.

Rosen, S.R. Personality and Negro-white intelligence. *J. Abnorm. Soc. Psych.,* 61:148–150. 1960.

Rogers, C.R. *The Clinical Treatment of the Problem Child.* Boston: Houghton Mifflin, 1939.

——. *Counseling and Psychotherapy.* Boston: Houghton Mifflin, 1951.

——. Some observations on the organization of personality. *Amer. Psychologist,* 2:358–368. 1947.

Rosenow, C. Meaningful behavior in hypnosis. *Amer. J. Psychol.,* 40:204–235. 1928.

Russell, B. "Psychology and East-West Tension," in Q. Wright, W.M. Evan, and M. Deutsch (eds.), *Preventing World War III: Some Proposals.* New York: Simon & Schuster, 1962.

Russell, R.W. Roles of psychologists in the "maintenance of peace." *Amer. Psychologist,* 15:95–109. 1960.

Rustad, W.H. *J. Clin. Endocrinol. Metabolism,* 14:87–96. 1954.

Ryan, T.A. *Work and Effort.* New York: Ronald, 1947.

Salter, A. *Conditioned Reflex Therapy.* New York: Farrar, Straus, 1949; Putnam, 1961.

Sampson, E.E. Student activism and the decade of protest. *J. Soc. Issues*, 23(3):1–34. 1967.

Sanford, N. (ed.). *College and Character*. New York: Wiley, 1964.

———. Personality development during the college years. *J. Soc. Issues*, 12. 1956.

Satir, V.M. *Conjoint Family Therapy*. Palo Alto, Calif.: Science and Behavior, 1964.

Schaller, G.B. *The Mountain Gorilla: Ecology and Behavior*. Chicago: University of Chicago Press, 1963.

Schattenbrand, G., and Bailey, P. *Introduction to Sterotaxis, with an Atlas of the Human Brain*. 3 v. New York: Grune & Stratton, 1959.

Schein, E.H. The Chinese indoctrination program for prisoners of war. *Psychiatry*, 19:149–172. 1956.

Schmeidler, G.R., and McConnell, R.A. *ESP and Personality Patterns*. New Haven: Yale University Press, 1958.

Schofield, W. Psychology, law, and the object witness. *Amer. Psychologist*, 11:1–7. 1956.

Scott, E.M. Personality and movie preference. *Psychol. Rep.*, 3:17–18. 1957.

Sears, R.R. An experimental study of hypnotic anesthesia. *J. Exp. Psychol.*, 15:1–22. 1932.

Sechrest, L., and Wallace, J. *Psychology and Human Problems*. Columbus, Ohio: C.E. Merrill Books, Inc., 1967.

Seeman, M. Status and identity: the problem of inauthenticity. *Pacific Sociol. Rev.*, 9:67–73. 1966.

Selvin, H.C., and Hagstrom, W.O. "Determinants of support for civil liberties," in S.M. Lipset and S.S. Wolin (eds.), *The Berkeley Student Revolt*. New York: Anchor, 1967.

Sheldon, W.H. *Varieties of Human Temperament*. New York: Harper, 1942.

Sheperd, C.R. *Small Groups: Some Sociological Perspectives*. San Francisco: Chandler, 1964.

Shneidman, E.S., and Farberow, N.L. *Clues to Suicide*. New York: McGraw-Hill, 1957.

Shoben, E.J. Toward a concept of the normal personality. *Amer. Psychologist*, 12:183–189. 1957.

Shurcliff, A. Judged humor, arousal and the relief theory. *Person. Soc. Psychol.*, 8:360–363. 1968.

Skinner, B.F. *The Behavior of Organisms*. New York: Appleton-Century-Crofts, 1938.

———. The experimental analysis of behavior. *Am. Scientist*, 45:4. 1957.

———. The science of learning and the art of teaching. *Harvard Educ. Rev.*, 24:86–97. 1954.

Smith, G.H. *Motivation Research in Advertising and Marketing*. New York: McGraw-Hill, 1954.

Soal, S.G., and Bateman, F. *Modern Experiments in Telepathy*. New Haven: Yale University Press, 1954.

Sohn, L.B. "Neo-neutralism and the Neutralization of the United Nations," in Q. Wright, W.M. Evan, and M. Deutsch (eds.), *Preventing World War III: Some Proposals*. New York: Simon & Schuster, 1962.

Somers, R.H. "The Mainsprings of the Rebellion: A survey of Berkeley Students in November, 1964," in S.M. Lipset and S.S. Wolin (eds.), *The Berkeley Student Revolt*. New York: Anchor, 1967.

Spock, B. *Baby and Child Care*. New York: Pocket Books, 1946.

Stagner, R. *Psychology of Personality*. 3rd ed. New York: Holt, Rinehart & Winston, 1961.

Stalnaker, J.M., and Riddle, E.L. The effects of hypnosis on long-delayed recall. *J. Gen. Psychol.*, 6:429–440. 1932.

Stead, W.H., and Shartle, C.L. *Occupational Counseling Techniques*. New York: American, 1940.

Stein, M., Vidich, A., and White, D. *Identity and Anxiety*. New York: Free Press, 1960.

Stern, P.J. *The Abnormal Person and His World*. New York: Van Nostrand, 1965.

Stevens, S.S. The surprising simplicity of sensory metrics. *Amer. Psychologist*, 17:29–39. 1962.

Strassman, H.D., Thaler, M., and Schein, E.H. A prisoner of war syndrome apathy as a reaction to severe stress. *Amer. J. Psychiat.*, 112:998–1003. 1956.

Sultan, E.E. A factorial study in the domain of creative thinking. *Brit. J. Educ. Psychol.*, 32:78–82. 1962.

Sundberg, N.D. The acceptability of "fake" versus "bona fide" personality test interpretations. *J. Abnorm. Soc. Psychol.*, 50:145–147. 1955.

————, and Tyler, L.E. *Clinical Psychology*. New York: Appleton-Century-Crofts, 1962.

Suppes, P.D., and Morningstar, M. Computer assisted instructors. *Science*, 166:343–350. 1969.

Sutherland, E.H., and Creasey, D.R. *Principles of Criminology*. 6th ed. Philadelphia: Lippincott, 1960.

Symonds, P.M. *The Ego and the Self*. New York: Appleton-Century-Crofts, 1951.

Taylor, C.W., and Holland, J.L. Development and application of tests of creativity. *Rev. Educ. Res.*, 32:91–102. 1962.

Terman, L.M. Kinsey's "Sexual Behavior in the Human Male": Some comments and criticisms. *Psychol. Bull.*, 45:443–454. 1948.

————. *Psychological Factors in Marital Happiness*. New York: McGraw-Hill, 1938.

————, and Oden, M. *Genetic Studies of Genius. IV: The Gifted Child Grows Up*. Stanford: Stanford University Press, 1947.

Thelen, M.H. Long term retention of verbal imitation. *Devel. Psychol.*, 3:29–31. 1970.

————. The effect of subject race, model race, and vicarious praise on vicarious learning. *Child Devel.*, 42:972–977. 1971.

————, and Fryrear, J.L. Imitation of standards of self-reward and the influence of race. *Devel. Psychol.*, 5:133–135. 1971a.

————. Imitation of self-reward standards by black and white female delinquents. *Psychol. Reports*, 29:667–671. 1971b.

————, and Soltz, W. The effect of vicarious reinforcement on imitation in two social-racial groups. *Child Devel.*, 40:879–887. 1969.

Thorndike, E.L. *The Psychology of Learning*; v. 2 of *Educational Psychology*. New York: New York Bureau of Publications. Teachers College, Columbia University, 1913.

Thorndike, R.L., Some methodological issues in the study of creativity. *Proceedings of the Invitational Conference on Testing Problems*. Princeton: Educational Testing Service, 1962.

————. The human factor in accidents. *USAF School of Aviat. Med. Rep.*, Randolph Field, Tex., 1951.

Thouless, R.H. Thought transference and related phenomena. *Proc. Royal Inst. of Great Britain,* 1950.

Thurstone, L.L. *Scales for the Measurement of Social Attitudes.* Chicago: University of Chicago Press, 1931.

Tillich, P. *The Courage to Be.* New Haven: Yale University Press, 1952.

Tindall, G.T., and Kunkle, E.C. Pain-spots densities in human skin. An experimental study. *A.M.A. Arch. Neurol. Psychiat.,* 77:605–610. 1957.

Toch, H. *Legal and Criminal Psychology.* New York: Holt, Rinehart & Winston, 1961.

Torrance, E.P. Measurement and development of the creative thinking abilities. *Yearbook of Education: The Gifted Child.* London. 1962.

Toussieng, P.W. Hangloose identity, or living death, the agonizing choice of growing up today. *Adolescence,* 3(1):307–318. 1968.

Ulrich, R., Stachnik, R., and Mabry, J. *Control of Human Behavior from Cure to Preparation,* vol. 2. Glenview, Ill.: Scott, Foresman, 1970.

Van de Castle, R.L. *The Psychology of Dreaming.* New York: General Learning Press, 1971.

Van Zelst, R.H. The effect of age and experience on accident rate. *J. Appl. Psychol.,* 38:313–317. 1954.

Vernon, H.M. *Accidents and Their Prevention.* New York: Macmillan, 1937.
———, Bedford, T., and Warner, C.G. A study of absenteeism in certain Scottish collieries. *Indust. Health Res. Bd. Rep.* 62. London: Her Majesty's Stationery Office, 1931.

Vogt, E.Z., and Hyman, R. *Water Witching U.S.A.* Chicago: University of Chicago Press, 1959.

Wallace, R.K., and Benson, H. "The Physiology of Meditation," in *Altered States of Awareness.* San Francisco: Freeman, 1972.

Watzlawick, P. *An Anthology of Human Communication.* Text and 2-hour tape. Palo Alto, Calif.: Science and Behavior, 1964.

Weitz, J. Selecting supervisors with peer ratings. *Pers. Psychol.,* 11:25–35. 1958.

Whaley, D.L., and Malott, R.W. *Elementary Principles of Behavior.* New York: Appleton-Century-Crofts, 1971.

Wheelis, A. *The Quest for Identity.* New York: Norton, 1958.

White, R.W. Motivation reconsidered: The concept of competence. *Psychol. Rev.,* 66:297–333. 1959.
———. *Lives in Progress.* New York: Dryden, 1952.
———, Fox, G.F., and Harris, W.W. Hypnotic hypermnesia for recently learned material. *J. Abnorm. Psychol.,* 35:88–103. 1940.

Whitlock, J.B., and Crannell, C.W. An analysis of certain factors in serious accidents in a large steel plant. *J. Appl. Psychol.,* 33:404–408. 1949.

Whitney, E.D. *The Lonely Sickness.* Boston: Beacon, 1965.

Whyte, W.H. *The Organization Man.* New York: Simon & Schuster, 1956.

Wilcox, R.C. (ed.). *The Psychological Consequences of Being a Black American.* New York: Wiley, 1971.

Wilder, J. Facts and figures on psychotherapy. *J. Clin. Psychopath.,* 7:311–347. 1945.

Wilder, R.M. "Experimental Induction of Psychoneuroses through Restriction of Intake of Thiamine," in *Biology of Mental Health and Diseases.* New York: Hoeber, 1952.

Williams, R.J. *Biochemical Individuality.* New York: Wiley, 1956.
———. The effect of hypnosis on muscular fatigue. *J. Abnorm. Psychol.,* 24:318–324. 1929.

————. A medical approach to the problem drinker. *Quart. J. Stud. Alcohol.,* 4. 1949.

————. *J. Heredity,* 51:91–98. 1960.

Wish, H. *The Negro Since Emancipation.* Englewood Cliffs, N.J.: Prentice-Hall, 1964.

Wolfgang, M.E. *Patterns in Criminal Homicide.* Philadelphia: University of Pennsylvania, 1958.

Wolpe, J. "An Approach to the Problem of Neurosis Based on the Conditioned Response." M.D. thesis, University of Witwatersrand, Union of South Africa, 1948.

————. Isolation of a conditioning procedure as the crucial psychotherapeutic factor. *J. Nerv. Ment. Dis.,* 134:316–329. 1962.

————. The prognosis in unpsychoanalyzed recovery from neurosis. *Amer. J. Psychiat.,* 117:35–39. 1961.

————. *Psychotherapy by Reciprocal Inhibition.* Stanford: Stanford University, 1958.

————. Quantitative relation in the systematic desensitization treatment of phobias. *Amer. J. Psychiat.,* 119:1062–1068. 1963.

————. The systematic desensitization treatment of neurosis. *J. Nerv. Ment. Dis.,* 132:189–203. 1961.

————. Behavior therapy in complex neurotic states. *Brit. J. Psychiat.,* 110:28–34. 1964.

Wood, A.L. A socio-structural analysis of murder, suicide, and economic crime in Ceylon. *Amer. Sociol. Rev.,* 26:744–753. 1961.

Wood, W.F. A new method of reading the employment questionnaire. *J. Appl. Psychol.,* 31:9–15. 1947.

Woodworth, R.S. *Dynamics of Behavior.* New York: Holt, Rinehart & Winston, 1958.

Works, E. Residence in integrated and segregated housing and improvement in self-concepts of Negroes. *Sociol. and Soc. Res.,* 46:294–301. 1962.

Wylie, R.C. *The Self-Concept.* Lincoln, Neb.: University of Nebraska Press, 1961.

Young, P.T. Laughing and weeping, cheerfulness and depression: A study of moods among college students. *J. Soc. Psychol.,* 8:311–334. 1937.

USE OF THE SELECTIONS

TOO OFTEN, anthologies for introductory psychology have been collections of readings that are meaningful mainly for the instructor. Such readings are intended to be routinely assigned to the student for later testing by objective examination, and the student reads to pass the examination rather than *to react and think through the ideas presented*. This book is designed to offset the routine aspects and to attain the goal concerned with reacting to ideas.

The instructor may want to use the material as a stimulus to develop his own approach. He may want to add to the "Implications" given after each article. He may perceive other implications in terms of a critique of methodology or theory.

This common reading core will enable students to compare their comprehension of and reactions to the selections by forming groups within the large lecture room. (For example, three or four students in the first row may form a group with three or four students immediately behind them, and so on throughout the room.) Twenty minutes or so of free or preguided discussion can produce valuable ideational interaction and possibly some pertinent insights. One student may act as a recorder for each group, and the remainder of the hour can be used to raise the puzzling questions discussed by the group or to report significant reactions.

Some articles can be used as a basis for a brief critical written reaction. The reports can be read by a grader or by a member of the class assigned by the instructor to evaluate his peers' critiques. Alternately, several articles, together with appended bibliographies, can be the basis of longer papers to be read by the instructor or a grader. The instructor might find it expedient to schedule either an oral (group) or a written report integrating several selections.

Greater meaningfulness to the ideas and concepts presented in the articles can be fostered by having the students divide into small peer groups to discuss class projects, such as those suggested in the "Implications" sections. (For example, see Selection 24 on human relations, Selection 13 on alternatives to war, Selection 35 on communication, and Selection 46 on family therapy.)

The following list contains the topics usually covered in an introductory course, with the corresponding number and title of each selection in this book. This list will enable the instructors to assign readings relevant to text material.

DEVELOPMENT
 6. Modern Approach to Values: Maturity
 16. Growth and Crises of the Healthy Personality
 17. The Child's Inner Life: Interpretation of Projective Devices
 18. Personality: Its Biological Foundations
DRIVES AND MOTIVATION
 1. Man's Search for Meaning
 7. Sexual Behavior: Reviews of the Kinsey Reports
 8. Sexual Inadequacy: Masters and Johnson Explained
 36. Achievement Drive and Economic Growth
FEELING AND EMOTION
 2. Laughter: Its Functions
 3. A Sense of Humor
 9. Homosexuality—Why?
 15. The Nature of Love
FRUSTRATION AND RESOLUTION
 10. The Student Activist
 11. Psychology of Women
 12. Black Identity and Personality
 37. Accidents: Contemporary Theories of Safety Psychology
MENTAL HEALTH AND PSYCHOTHERAPY
 40. An Autobiography of a Schizophrenic Experience
 41. Murder As Aggressive Behavior
 42. Suicide: Self-Directed Hostility
 43. Ideas of Psychotherapy
 46. Family Therapy: Understanding and Changing Behavior
HUMAN LEARNING AND FORGETTING
 21. Controlling Behavior: Premack Principle
 23. Teaching Machines
 39. Brainwashing—Social Psychological Factors
 44. The Conditioning Therapies
LANGUAGE AND THINKING
 22. Imitation, Modeling, and Self-Reward
 24. Human Relations: A Technique for Training Supervisors
 35. Communication: Barriers and Gateways
 49. What People Dream About
PERCEPTION AND ATTENTION
 26. Seeing in the Dark
 31. Sensitivity Training

INDEX